The Enchanting World of Food

Katie Barney

Conduit Press

Easton, Maryland

Front Cover Design: Jean Harper Baer, Baltimore, Maryland

Photograph: Katie Barney

Copyright © 2019   Conduit Press

Published by Conduit Press, 307 Goldsborough Street, Easton, MD 21601

Library of Congress Cataloging-in-Publication Data

Printed and Bound by Country Press, Lakeville, Massachusetts

ISBN: 978-0-9666610-1-9

Introduction

"It is useful to know something of the manners of different nations, so that we may be enabled to form a more correct judgment regarding our own, and be prevented from thinking that everything contrary to our customs is ridiculous and irrational – a conclusion usually come to by those whose experience has been limited to their own country." Rene Descartes

My love of international food dates back many years to the time when we had neighbors and friends who had come from different parts of the world. Early memories are of the Hadnagys on Long Island who were such close friends of my parents. Judy's recipes are included in this book. At Briarcliff College I belonged to the International Club, and for two years had a roommate from Florence, Italy, and my senior year from Tehran, Iran. I was able to do the "Grand Tour" of Europe after my sophomore year and spent part of the summer in Florence and Viareggio. Who could learn to love Italian cuisine! I then went off to graduate school at the University of Pennsylvania involving myself with the International Center. The University of Pennsylvania Museum of Archeology and Anthropology is one of the finest in the world, and includes extensive collections of early drinking vessels, food utensils, and remains of food and drink.

But it was several years later marrying into the Holmes family I was truly exposed to good food and wines. My late father-in-law Allen Holmes was President of the International Wine and Food Society. Through him and my mother-in-law I came to appreciate pairing wine and foods, and it was a challenge to cook for them and their four sons! I subscribed to Gourmet, Wine & Food, Bon Appetit, and collected the Time/Life series on food. I loved this life, moving from Philadelphia to New York, San Francisco, Washington and Cleveland. I involved myself with the International Visitor Centers (and the National Council for International Visitors) and Council on World Affairs, hosting guests from all over the world. In Cleveland I served as President of the International Visitor Center. Later moving to Newport, Rhode Island I took on that role again. Living in Greenwich, Connecticut I worked with United Nations staff, and moving back to Washington with THIS for Diplomats at Meridian House. To all these groups and the special people I have known over these many years I dedicate this book. I also wish to thank the many embassies, consulates, other organizations, and friends who allowed me to publish this book.

One of the things I most heartily believe in is preserving the customs and traditions that each nation has. You must have respect for other people's customs, even if you do not agree with them. If you are the guest of honor, and a sheep or fish's eye is presented to you, take a deep breath and eat it. Otherwise you will offend your host. Countries are so diverse this book cannot even begin to highlight all of their different regions and cuisines. Whole books could be written on each of these countries. The book is not only filled with wonderful recipes from every country around the world, plus a few others, but the history of the countries and their cuisines, the dining etiquette, and some interesting Did You Know. The olive branch is a symbol of peace, hope, and understanding.

And last but not least I would like to thank Jean Baer who has been my most ardent supporter in getting my books published. I met her 20 years ago through Women Entrepreneurs of Baltimore (WEB) when we were both unemployed and needed to get on with our lives. We both found our ways and since that time she has produced all the covers of my books, and done the printing for brochures and business cards.

Afghanistan

Afghanistan is located in southern Asia, north and west of Pakistan, and east of Iran. Archeological work in Afghanistan suggests that humans inhabited this area over 50,000 years. Civilization dates back to c3000 BC and after 2000 BC semi-nomadic tribes moved into the area. The Zoroastrianism religion was thought to have started in Afghanistan between 1800-800 BC. C 6th BCE the Achaemenid Persian Empire took over the area and later Alexander the Great later captured the country. The Seleucid Empire controlled the area until 305 BCE when it became part of the Indian Maurya Empire. Many other empires arose, and from the Middle Ages to the 19th c the region was part of Khorasan. Arabs brought the Muslim religion in the 7th c. In 1219 Genghis Khan destroyed much of the land. During 19th c Anglo-Afghan war much of the country was under Great Britain's rule. Today Afghanistan contains many tribes and ethnicities, but an independent country. In 1776 the capital was changed from Kandahar to Kabul. Pashtu and Dari are the national languages.

Dining Etiquette

Families often live together (several generations) in a walled compound known as a kala. The family is very important in the Afghan culture. This is a patriarchal society and one does not ask about women in the family. Many women cannot attend school or earn a living. In some areas widows cannot remarry. Elders and ancestors are very much respected.

It is an honor to be a guest in a home. Men shake hands greeting and departing, and may also embrace each other. Women and men do not shake hands or have eye contact. Men should not initiate a conversation with women, and vice versa, unless it is family. Honor is important. Women must dress properly covering the whole body from the neck down, and it is best to wear a scarf also. Women will greet each other, kissing each other several times on both cheeks.

If invited to a home please bring a gift – fruit, sweets, or pastries in a box. Be discreet and place the gift unnoticed by the host. Gifts are not opened in front of guests. Green wrapping is used for weddings. Please remove your shoes before entering a home. For a meal you will usually be seated on the floor on cushions or carpets. A cloth is spread over the rug or dining table and is known as the dastarkhan or sofrah. Sitting is according to status, so wait till you are asked to be seated. Sit with your legs crossed, not stretched out with your toes pointed outward. A child will most likely present a "aftabah wa lagan", a copper bowl to wash one's hands. Soap and a towel are provided. The dastarkhan is spread with breads, side dishes, relishes, appetizers, salads, rice, and fruit. The food is arranged very tastefully. Food is eaten and passed with the right hand. Do not eat with your left hand. Food will be eaten with the right hand making your food into a ball at your fingertips. Utensils may also be provided. Leave some food on your plate, or it will be replenished. Consumption of alcohol is forbidden.

When invited for tea, food and tea will be served. Please do not refuse. When you have had enough cover your glass with your hand and say "bus".

Kaddo Bowrani (Baby Pumpkin with Yogurt Sauce)

Serves 4-6

1 small pumpkin (baby or spookies work best)
¾ cup sugar

¼ cup vegetable oil
Cinnamon

Preheat oven to 350
Slice the pumpkin and remove the seeds. Peel the outer skin. Slice into 2-inch pieces lengthwise. Heat the oil in a skillet and add the pumpkin. Cook covered on medium heat for approximately 10 minutes, turning once. Remove from the skillet and place in a small roasting or baking pan. Sprinkle the pumpkin with the sugar and cinnamon. Cover tightly.
Bake for 30 minutes or until soft. Time may differ according to the hardness of the pumpkin.
Serve warm with yogurt sauce

Yogurt Sauce

1 cup plain yogurt
1 teaspoon fresh cut diced garlic

Dash of salt

Stir ingredients together until smooth
Recipe courtesy of the Helmand Restaurant, Baltimore, Maryland USA

Cuisine

The food is a blend of the different ethnic groups - Pashtuns, Tajiks and Uzbeks, and Indian cuisine and derives from the crops grown in the country. These include wheat, maize, barley, rice, grapes, pomegranates, apricots, berries, plums, oranges, melons, nuts (walnuts, pistachios, almonds and pine nuts), vegetables and dairy products such as yogurt and whey. Dishes will include garlic, onions, tomatoes, spring onions, potatoes and fruit. Both fresh and dried fruit are used in cooking. Nangarhar province is known for its "Malta" oranges and olive oil. Apples and apricots are grown in Wardak province, and pomegranates in Kandahar province. Mint, saffron, coriander, cilantro, cardamom, and black pepper are widely used spices. Lamb and chicken are the main meats used in cooking. Rice may be served at all meals.

Afghan Specialties

Palao – national dish – chalow with meat and stock, and then sprinkled with fried raisins, slivered carrots and pistachios
Chalow – white rice baked in an oven with oil, butter and salt. This is served with qormas
Yakhni Palao - chalow rice to which is added meat and stock

Zamarod palao – spinach gorma and chalow
Serkah palao – rice with meat and stock, vinegar and spices
Shebet palao – rice with fresh dill and raisins
Narenj palao – rice with saffron, orange peel, pistachios, almonds and chicken

Mash palao – rice with mung beans, apricots, bulgur

Alou balou palao – rice with cherries and chicken

Bata – sticky rice

Qormas - stew or casserole made of fried onions, meat, fruit, vegetables and spices. Yogurt, chicken, lamb or beef, spinach or other greens can be added to the stew.

Qorma Alou-Bkhara wa Dalnakhod – qorma with sour plums, lentils, cardamom, veal or chicken

Khameerbob – pasta style dough in the shape of a dumpling. Fillings may include onions, ground beef, topped with tomato sauces, yogurt, sour cream

Goroot sauce – goat cheese and garlic, or yogurt and mint

Askak – dumplings with leeks, topped with ground meat and goroot sauce

Mantu – steamed dumplings with onion and ground meat

Kabab – mainly uses lamb, chicken, ground beef and served with naan

Kuftah – meatballs

Shorma - soups

Torshi – pickled fruits and vegetables

Kadu bouranee – sweet pumpkins

Aush – noodles

Bichak – turnover with potato or ground meat filling

Shorwa – beet soup

Dolma – stuffed grape leaves

Badenjan – eggplant with potatoes and tomatoes

Chatney – pepper sauces

Quroot – dried yogurt

Salata – tomato, onion, and cucumber salad

Naan – thin bread made out of white and whole wheat flour

ObiNon – white flour bread

Lavash – thin bread

Sheer berinj – rice pudding

Baklava – honey pastry

Gosh feel – fried pastries with powdered sugar and pistachios

Kulcha – cookies baked with char-wood

Holidays and Special Occasions

Nau Roz – New Year Festival – picnics
Apple Blossom Festival – held in Wardak to celebrate spring
Ramadan – month of fasting
Eid al Fitr – breaking of Ramadan fast
Eid al Adha – in honor of the Prophet Abraham's willingness to sacrifice his son. Lamb and goat are given to the poor.
Weddings – much dancing takes place before dinner which is usually a buffet. Palao, Chalow, kababs, and breads will be served, followed by desserts and fruit. The bride and groom then walk to the wedding cake and the musicians will sing "Baada Baada Elahee Mubarak Baada - Man dil ba tu dada am Tawakol ba khoda," which means "congratulations, I gave you my heart now I leave it to God". The couple cut the cake and a family member will cut the cake into small pieces and serve the guests. Later the Attan, the national dance of Afghanistan will be performed as it was at the beginning of the wedding.

Beverages

Bottled water, soft drinks and juices, coffee and tea (chai) are drunk in this Muslim country. Nuristan province has produced wine since ancient times. Wine making was reintroduced by Hounzas in 1969.

Albania

The Republic of Albania is in southeastern Europe bordered by Montenegro to the northwest, Kosovo to the northeast, Macedonia to the east and Greece to the south and southeast. The Illyrians were the first inhabitants followed by the Greeks in the 8th c BC. In 395 AD Albania became part of the Byzantine Empire, and remained part of the Ottoman Empire until it declared its independence in 1912. Italy invaded Albania in 1939. It later became allied with the Communists, but today is a democratic country under its 1998 constitution. The capital Tirana, was part of the Ottoman Empire beginning in 1614 under Sulejman Bargini, although its origins date back to ancient times. Tirana became the capital in 1920. Albanian is the official language.

"Our house belongs to God and the guest" from the Kanum of Leke Dukagjini

Dining Etiquette

Please shake hands greeting and departing. Men and women may kiss if they know each other well. Gift giving is very important, and if you are given something, please return with your own gift. Never give money as it could be misconstrued as a bribe! Flowers are not usually presented. Instead take a small painting, book, or something from your own country. If there are children present, please bring something for them. Drinks will be served, often raki, the national drink. The hostess will seat the guests at the table. Dishes will probably be served by the host. There may be an abundance of food, even though the family may not have much. Please do not start eating until the hostess does. Guests of honor may be presented with a baked sheep's head. Smoking is allowed in public places, and many Albanians still smoke. The toast is "Gzuat" – "all good things to you".

Cuisine and Beverages

The cuisine has been influenced by the Ottomans and Italians. Wheat, corn, okra, eggplant, artichokes, figs, tomatoes, olive oil, olives, peppers, feta, rice, mint, cabbage, grapes, grape leaves, cornmeal (maize); and dairy products, especially yogurt, sour cream (smetana) and sour milk are part of the diet. During the warmer months raw vegetables are served with yogurt and coarse salt. Mint is used in meat dishes, salads, and drinks. Meats include lamb, mutton and chicken. The main meal is lunch with salad, vegetables and meat, plus yogurt or curd cheese. Fish would be served along the coastal areas. This would include sea-bream, bass, eels, koran (trout from Lake Ohrid, and Shkodra carp. Noodles are served with many meals. Dessert is usually fruit or crème caramel. At breakfast you might be served pilaf (rice) or paca (soup made out of innards). Albanian vineyards produce wine, grapes such as Kallmet (red) and Shesh (red and white). The Korce produces merlot and Tokay wines. Grapes are also used to make *raki,* an alcoholic grape juice, the country's national drink. When offered raki, please drink it, or you will insult your host. Much coffee is drunk, usually cappuccino, espresso or kake turke with sugar and the grounds brewed together. When having coffee, take time. There is no such thing as a quick cup! Albania also produces its own cognac and beer.

Gjellë me Arra të Ellit (Elli's Veal or Chicken with Walnuts)

Serves 4

A particular Albanian dish that my wife, Jane, and I enjoyed at the home of Bardhyl Pollo and his wife, Elli, in Tirana instantly became my favorite of all favorites. The attractive and charming Elli, knowing of my propensity for unique Albanian food, had invited us to their home for dinner where we were served one of the most delectable meals it has been our privilege to eat. That evening, I cast all good manners aside as I requested a <u>second</u> helping! Clearly, Elli has a gourmet-chef's touch, so I implored her to give me the recipe in order to share it with others. She graciously agreed, and the dish that I have named *"Elli's Veal or Chicken with Walnuts"* appears below for all to enjoy!
Recipe and comments courtesy of Van Christo, Frosnia Information Network

2 tbls. flour
15 finely crushed shelled walnuts
2 beaten egg yokes
1 minced garlic clove

½ cup butter
2-3 lbs of veal or chicken meat, cut up in 1" cubes

Place the meat or chicken in a saucepan and cook over medium heat until tender. Then remove the meat setting it aside in a dish while leaving the remaining juices in the saucepan.
In another saucepan, add the flour and stir over heat until it becomes light brown in color (do not overcook!) and add the half a stick of butter. Then, add the finely crushed walnuts, minced garlic clove, and the two egg yolks, stirring constantly.
Add the juices from the other saucepan and stir until all the ingredients thicken. Immediately remove from the heat to avoid solidifying the egg yolks.
Then fold in either the meat or chicken.
Pan fry the remaining half stick of butter until brown and pour over the four servings.

Tirana Fergese with Peppers (pepper appetizer)

Serves 4

½ lb. green or red peppers
1 lb. red tomatoes
½ lb. salted cottage cheese or Greek feta cheese

1 tbls. flour
½ cup butter
3 tbls. virgin olive oil
Salt, pepper and chili pepper to taste

Peel the skin off the tomatoes and peppers. Saute them in a saucepan for 5-7 minutes only in the olive oil and then set them aside to cool down for 15 minutes. Dice them the way you like. In another saucepan, melt the butter. Add flour, cottage or Feta cheese, and black pepper, salt and chili pepper to taste. Mix all the ingredients together and place them in saucepan. Put saucepan in a preheated 350 oven for 15 minutes. Take out and serve immediately.
Recipe courtesy of Chef Hasan Dajti and Frosnia Information Network

Albanian Specialties

Kos – yogurt
Dhallia – yogurt cocktail
Soup fidhe - egg lemon soup
Pace koke - sheep's head soup
Kukurec - stuffed sheep's innards
Fërgesë tirane, - fried dish of meat, liver, eggs and tomatoes
Pule medrop – roast stuffed chicken
Gjelle me zarzavata – vegetable casserole
Shish kebab – meat and vegetables roasted on a skewer
Tavë kosi or tavë elbasani - mutton and yogurt dish

Tanabour – yogurt soup
Tarator - a cold yogurt and cucumber soup
Oshaf - fig and sheep's milk pudding (dessert)
Cakes soaked in honey
Burek – phyllo dough with various cheeses and herbs; onions and tomatoes, or other fillings
Ismir simit – sesame biscuits
Qofte – fried meat cylinders, served with a tomato or mint, garlic, yogurt sauce
Candied fruit
Emator – almond puff pastry

Holidays and Special Occasions

*Karnavale*t – Carnival begins the Sunday before Lent in the villages, with men wearing costumes and going to homes to entertain.

Qumështor, a custard dish made of flour, eggs, and milk, is served before the beginning of *Lent*.

During *Dita a Veres*, the spring festival on March 14th, a sweet cake, ballakum Elbasani is baked.

The *Islamic Bektashi* sect mark the end of the ten-day fasting period of matem with ashura, a pudding made of cracked wheat, sugar, dried fruit, crushed nuts, and cinnamon.

Easter is celebrated in the Orthodox Church. Roast lamb represents Jesus Christ, the Lamb of God. The whole week is a celebration with fasting before, and the breaking of the fast on Easter Eve. Afterwards Resurrection services are held with people greeting each other saying "Krishti Ungjall" "Christ is Risen". The custom is to break red Easter eggs. This dates back to after the Ascension when Mary Magdalene presented the Emperor of Rome with a red egg, and said "Christ is Risen". The egg is the symbol of Jesus' tomb, and renewal of life by breaking out of it. The red symbolizes the blood of Christ and the egg, the new life within.

Rusicat – Mid-Pentecost- the Wednesday halfway between Easter and Pentecost women go from house to house to get ingredients to make Holy Bread for use in the Liturgy to prepare for the Ascension. Women make the bread and other goodies and again dye eggs red.

Grure – memorial service for the dead. Grure is place in the center of the church on a table with a candle. Grure is boiled wheat with sugar, nuts, and raisins.

Kolendrat – is celebrated the week before Christmas when women bring out kolendra, rolls in various shapes representing the gifts brought for the baby Jesus.

Christmas – stuffed turkey or lamb, baklava and rice pudding

New Year's Eve – women bake lakror, a pie with a coin placed under it. The pie is twirled, then cut. The person receiving the coin is brought good luck for the coming year.

Weddings are very elaborate occasions and often the whole village will be invited and may last for several days.

Algeria

Algeria, located on the Mediterranean coast of north Africa is bordered by Tunisia in the northeast, Libya in the east, Niger in the southeast, Mali and Morocco in the west and northwest, Its almost 2.4 million square km are made up of a hilly region along the coast with a few harbors. Inland are steppe, the Atlas and Ahaggar Mountains, and then the Sahara desert. The Berbers were known to have lived in the region since 10,000 BC. Rome took over in 200 BC, then it was part of the Byzantine Empire, followed by the Arabs, Spanish, Ottomans, French, and becoming an independent country in 1962. The capital, Algiers, was founded in 944 by Bologhine ibn Ziri, the founder of the Berber Zirid–Sanhaja dynasty. Arabic is the official language. French is spoken along the coast, and there are various dialects of Berber.

Dining Etiquette

Family, honor, and personal relations are very important. Please shake hands greeting and departing. Use honorific titles – Dr., professor, etc. Always greet elders first. Women extend their hand first, otherwise do not shake your hand with them. There is, no prolonged eye contact. Women must dress very discreetly. When invited to a home please remove your shoes before entering. Remember it is an honor to be a guest. Please bring pastries, flowers, or fruit. Give your gift with the right or both hands. Gifts are not opened when received. Men and women will be seated separately. Always accept refreshments. Dining may be on couches around a table, cushions around a low table, or mats on the floor. You will wash your hands before and after the meal. Most food is eaten with your hands, using your right hand only. If bread is served it can be used to eat, or to soak up liquid. Couscous is eaten with a spoon, stews with a fork. Leave a little on your plate or you be served more. Do not criticize or put a person down. Remember this is a Muslim country and alcohol may not be served. The month of Ramadan is observed by fasting from sunrise to sunset.

Cuisine

Algeria produces grains, wheat, barley, oats, vegetables, fruit – citrus, figs, dates, grapes, and apricots. Wheat and dates have been cultivated for millennia. Semolina wheat was introduced by the Carthaginians, couscous the Berbers, and the Romans grains. The Arabs brought saffron, nutmeg, ginger, cloves and cinnamon. The Spanish introduced oranges, plums and peaches, olives and olive oil; the Turks sweet pastries and the English tea. Later the French influenced much of the life in the country bringing "French" bread. Tomatoes, potatoes, zucchini, and chilies came from the Americas. Also used are coriander, cumin, parsley, and mint.

Couscous

Couscous, the national dish, is usually served with lamb, chicken or fish, or stews. Couscous is also used to make sweets.

Serves 6-8

4 cups chicken stock
½ stick butter
2 cups couscous
¼ cup fresh mint

1 cup currants
½ cup pine nuts
2 scallions, sliced

Bring the stock and butter to a boil in a sauce pan. Remove from the heat. Stir in the couscous slowly. Cover. After five minutes fluff the couscous.
Add the remaining ingredients.
Serve hot or cold.
Long grain, basmati, or wild rice can be substituted for the couscous.
Cranberries can be substituted for the currants and walnuts for the pine nuts.

Harira (lamb, bean and spice dish)

Harira is served during Ramadan to break the fast.

Serves 4

2 tbls. butter
1 lb. lamb, cubed
1 onion, chopped
2 tomatoes, chopped
1 stalk celery and leaves, chopped
¼ cup parsley, chopped
2 tbls. fresh coriander
½ tsp. ground ginger
½ tsp. ground turmeric
1 ½ tsp. cinnamon
Borek

½ tsp. fresh ground pepper
7 cups water
½ cup green lentils
1 cup chickpeas
4 oz. vermicelli
Juice of ½ lemon
Fresh coriander
Lemon slices
Dates

Melt the butter and saute the lamb and onion until just browned. Add the tomatoes, celery, parsley, coriander, ginger, turmeric, cinnamon, pepper, water, lentils, and chickpeas. Bring to a boil for 10 minutes. Reduce heat and simmer for two hours.
Add vermicelli, and cook 5 minutes. More water can be added if it is too thick. Stir in the lemon juice.
Serve hot with lemon slices, coriander, dates, and borek.

Algerian Specialties

Smen - aged, cooked butter
Maghreb Tajine – stew of lamb or chicken with fresh vegetables and dried fruits
Makrout – pastry with fruit
Samsa – fried pastry
Chorbo – soup
Marqa – vegetable and meat stew in tomato sauce
Vegetables – carrots, chickpeas, tomatoes
Mechoui – whole lamb cooked on a spit, seasoned with herb butter, accompanied with dried fruits, dates, vegetables and bread

Mint tea – offered to guests
Sharbat – fruit or nut milk drink
Sahlab – milk drink
Basbousa – semolina cake
Tamina – roasted semolina with butter and honey
Banadura Salata B'Kizbara - Tomato and Coriander Salad
Brochettes – kebabs
Shakshuka – stew with vegetables
Meloui – layered bread, often served at Ramadan

Holidays and Special Occasions

Being mainly a Muslim nation the holy day dates vary from year to year.
Ramadan - Muslims do not eat or drink from sunrise to sunset
Idul- Fitr – three day feast at the end of Ramadan
Sacrifice Feast – held after the holy pilgrimage to Makkah (Mecca)
Prophet Mohammed's birthday – usually September or October

Beverages

Wines have been made in Algeria since the time of the Phoenicians and later the Romans. Beginning in the 7th c wine making was prohibited by the Muslim rulers. The vineyards are replanted after the French took over in 1830. Later in the century when the phylloxera epidemic destroyed the vineyards in France, Algeria exported wine to France. Today there are over 70 wineries. Most of the vines are planted near the Moroccan border, and mainly produce red wines.

Andorra

The Principality of Andorra is a small country in southwestern Europe, located in the eastern Pyrenees Mountains and bordered by Spain and France. The Principality was formed in 1278. The role of monarch is exercised jointly by the two co-princes, the President of France and the Bishop of Urgell, Catalonia, Spain. Its capital, Andorra la Vella, is one of the highest capital cities in Europe, being at an elevation of 1023 meters. The official language is Catalan, although Spanish, French, and Portuguese are also commonly spoken.

Dining Etiquette

When entertained please bring a small gift and please be punctual. Please shake hands greeting and departing. Good friends may embrace. Drinks will be served before a meal. Guests will be seated at the table by the hostess, with the male guest of honor to her right. Please wait for your hostess to begin eating. Please eat continental style with the fork in the left hand and knife in the right. Food may be served, passed, or as a buffet. When finished please place your knife and fork together.

Cuisine and Beverages

The food is mainly Catalan in the south with French and Italian influences in the north - pasta, meat, bread, fish and vegetables. Pasta, potatoes, fish, vegetables, cheese, sausages, pork and ham are used in cooking. Only 2% of Andorra is cultivable, so foodstuffs are mainly what is available – hare, goat and sheep cheeses, snails, wild boar, venison, duck, trout, wild mushrooms, beans, nuts, berries, honey, cabbage, spinach, onions and garlic. Meats and fish are cured and dried.

Wines are imported from neighboring Spain and France. Spanish sangria is served during the summer. Sidra is Spanish cider. Natural springs in the Pyrenees provide bottled water. Aigua d'Andorra was once bottled in the country but the plant is now closed. Con gas is fizzy water; sin gas is still water. Coffee is served not only in the morning, but as a way to get together with others.

Andorran Specialties

Coques   flavored flat cakes
Truites de carreroles -mushroom omelette
Cargols – oven roasted snails served with olive oil and salty, or aioli
Truncha – trout wrapped in ham
Coca massegada – sweet snacks

Courgette (zucchini) charlotte with Andorran veal sweetbreads and ceps (mushrooms)
Escudella – chicken, butifarra sausage, veal, meatballs, pig snout and trotters, potatoes, cabbage, beans and pasta shells
Cunillo – rabbit stewed in tomato sauce

Trinxat (potatoes and cabbage)

Serves 6

1 cabbage, cut into quarters	12 slices bacon
6 medium red potatoes	1 tbsp. olive oil
1 tsp. sea salt	4 cloves garlic, chopped
1 tsp. fresh ground pepper	

In a pot cover the potatoes and cabbages with water. Bring to a boil, and cook until vegetables are tender. Drain. Mash cabbage and potatoes, and season with salt and pepper.
Fry bacon in a skillet until crispy. Drain off some of fat. Place bacon on paper towels. Break into pieces.
In skillet with bacon fat and olive oil cook garlic until just tender.
Add bacon and garlic to mashed cabbage and potatoes.
Using same skillet and oil make the mixture into cakes and fry on both sides until browned.
Can be served with salted herring or sardines.

Cannelloni Andorrana (cannelloni with meat served with a béchamel sauce)

Makes about 24

Cannelloni

Filling

2 tbls. olive oil	½ lb. ground beef
2 tbls. butter	½ cup grated parmesan cheese
1 small onion, chopped	¼ cup white wine
1 clove garlic, minced	1 egg, beaten
½ lb. ground veal	Pinch of nutmeg

Heat the olive oil and butter in a skillet and saute the onion. Add the garlic, veal and beef until meat is just slightly browned. Stir in the parmesan cheese, wine, egg and nutmeg.
Cook the cannelloni until just al dente. Lay the cannelloni on a sheet of wax paper. Put the meat mixture in a pastry bag and along the short edge of the cannelloni put about 2 inches of the meat. Roll up to form a tube. Bake on a sheet with olive oil and covered with aluminum foil at 350º for 15 minutes. Serve hot with the béchamel sauce.

Bechamel Sauce

4 tbls. butter	1 cup cream
¼ cup flour	½ cup dry white wine or vermouth.

Melt the butter in a sauce pan. Stir in the flour, then cream until thickened. Add wine.

Angola

Angola is a country in south-central Africa bordered by Namibia on the south, the Democratic Republic of the Congo on the north, Zambia on the east; and the Atlantic Ocean on the west. The country is rich in petroleum and diamonds. The settlers were Bantu tribes of the Bakongo kingdoms who established trading routes and cities along the west coast of Africa. Trade was with Great Zimbabwe for copper and iron for salt, food and raffia textiles. Beginning in the 16th c Angola was a Portuguese overseas territory, receiving its independence in 1975. The capital, Luanda, was founded by the Portuguese explorer Paulo Dias de Novais in 1576 as "São Paulo da Assumpção de Loanda". Portuguese is the official language.

Dining Etiquette

The Angolans are hospitable people and enjoy entertaining. Dinner is usually around 8 o'clock. Please bring a small gift of fruit, flowers, chocolates, or a gift for the home. Please shake hands greeting and departing. Close friends may embrace, kiss, or offer a back slap. Elders are always greeted first and one should bow when introduced. Women do not usually look the other person in the eye. Kola nuts are given to an entering guest as a symbol of hospitality and friendship. When seated, food may be served in a communal bowl. The oldest person is served first and places food in an individual bowl. If meat is served the men and elders receive the largest portions. When served please eat all that is offered as a sign of respect.

Cuisine and Beverages

The cuisine has been influenced by the Portuguese and the use of spices, and the Congo. In the province of Huila (Buchiman tribes) the people have cooked traditional dishes for hundreds of year. In Central Angola dishes are made with milk, curds, and whey. Four ethnic groups reside in Angola, each with its own cuisine. The Ovimbundu of the central highlands and southeast are farmers harvesting cassava, maize and massambala (cereal). The Kimbundu live near Luanda and to the east, and their cuisine has been influenced by the Portuguese. The Bakongo live in the northwest and near the Congo. Their main dishes are doro wat (chicken stew) and nitter kibeh (a sauce). The Lunda and Chokwe reside in the northeastern part. Their traditional dishes are muamba nsusu and mkiba. Much of the food is grown on plantations (shambas). Dishes often include steamed or boiled vegetables, peas, beans, grains. Seafood, meat, chicken cassava, yams, black-eyed peas, cabbage, sweet potatoes, onions, peanuts, plantains, and chili pepper are used in spicy stews. Fruits available are grapes, mangoes, bananas, plantains, papaya, and avocado. Wild animals such as crocodile, monkey, warthog, and others are consumed. The food is prepared by roasting, boiling, or baking. Meals will include rice, yams or porridge. Spices used are garlic, melegueta pepper, cloves, black peppercorns, cardamom, nutmeg, turmeric, and curry powder. Beer is produced from honey and grains, often maize or millet. Wine is made from the sap of palm trees, or imported from South Africa.

Cocada Amerela (Yellow Coconut Pudding with Cloves)

Serves 8

2 cups of sugar
6 cups water
4 whole cloves

4 cups finely grated coconut
12 egg yolks
Ground cinnamon

Combine the sugar, water and cloves in a saucepan. Stirring, bring to a boil. Boil until the temperature reached 230° on a candy thermometer.
Reduce the heat to low, and with a slotted spoon remove the cloves.
Add the coconut, 1 cup at a time, stirring after each addition. Continue to cook for 10 minutes, or until the coconut is translucent. Remove from heat.
In a bowl beat the egg yolks for about 1 minute. Continue beating until they start to thicken. Stir in one cup of the coconut mixture. Then add to the coconut syrup in the pan. Stirring constantly, cook over moderate heat for about 10 minutes or until mixture thickens to pull away from sides and bottom of pan in a solid mass.
Pour the pudding into a heatproof dish or 8 individual dessert dishes.
Serve at room temperature or refrigerate for 2 hours to cool completely.
Serve with a dusting of ground cinnamon.

Angolan Specialties

Kakusso – from Bengo province
Crabs and mussels – Naimbe province
Cocada amarela – dessert made of sugar, coconut, egg yolks and cinnamon.
Fish calulu – dried fish with onions, tomatoes, palm oil, garlic, sweet potato leaves or spinach
Biltong – salting and drying meat
Dried meat calulu – use dried meat instead of fish
Funge – manioc flour pudding
Mufete de cacuso – tilapia with tomato sauce

Chicken muamba – chicken, onion, palm hash, garlic, okra
Cabidela – chicken, chicken blood with rice and cassava dough
Egusi – leaf vegetable soup with ground seeds
Farofa – cooked manioc
Palm oil beans
Caakiri – fonio, millet, or maize dessert
Kanyah – rice, groundnut, sugar dessert
Ngalakh – karew, peanut butter, and bouye dessert

Holidays and Special Occasions

Carnival – February/March
Mukanda- a tribal initiation for Chokwe boys, held in November
Caldeirada de cabrito is a goat meat stew served with rice, a traditional dish for Angolan Independence Day, November 11.
Christmas is celebrated at midnight on December 24th with cozido de bacalhau, cooked cold fish, with vegetables, turkey with rice and wine. Gifts of cakes and fruit are exchanged. On December 25th people go to church.

Antigua and Barbuda

Antigua was first settled by the Siboney or "stone people" who arrived c1775 BC. The Arawak arrived about the time of Christ from South America, introducing agriculture and crops such as pineapples, corn, sweet potatoes, peppers, guava, tobacco and cotton. Later settlers were the Caribs. Christopher Columbus named the island Antigua in 1493. Cattle were introduced. English settlers arrived from St. Kitts in 1632, and produced tobacco, ginger, indigo and sugar. Sugar became the main crop c1674. Later slaves from Africa brought eddos, okra, yams, eggplant, and sweet potatoes. Mangoes and breadfruit were introduced by the English. Food customs were also influenced by the Portuguese and Lebanese. St. John's is the capital. English is the official language.

Dining Etiquette

When invited to a home please bring a small gift – flowers, wine, or something for the home. Please shake hands greeting and departing. Drinks and hors d'oeuvres will be served before a meal. The hostess will seat the guests with the male guest of honor to her right. Food may be served, or served buffet style. Please wait till the hostess starts. Eat continental style with the fork in the left hand and knife in the right. When finished place the knife and fork together. The toast is "Cheers".

Cuisine

The cuisine is a mix of Creole, English and international flavors. Fresh fruit include black pineapple, breadfruit, christophene, mangoes, papayas, melons, oranges, grapefruit, banana, coconuts, kiwi, limes, and soursop. Popular vegetables and starches are sweet potatoes, pumpkin, corn, rice, eggplant, and macaroni. Spices are used for seasoning.

Beverages

The West Indies have produced rum for hundreds of years when the sugar plantations were prominent beginning in the 17th c. Beginning in the 1950s Cavalier produced Muscovado Rum, and in the 1960s Antigua Rum. There is also English Harbor Rum. Happy Jack is rum punch. The Antigua Brewery makes Wadadli beer. Other drinks are Mauby, Seamoss, tamarind, raspberry, mango, hibiscus, passion fruit, guava, coconut water, soursop juices, lemonade, and ginger beer.

Cornmeal Cou Cou (Fungi)

Fungi is considered the national dish of Antigua. Serve it with vegetables, salted cod-fish, tomatoes, garlic and onions, or pepperpot.

2 cups cornmeal
4 cups water
1 tsp. salt
4 okra, sliced

1 small onion, chopped
1 tbls. fresh cilantro, chopped
1 tbls. fresh parsley, chopped
2 tbls. butter

In a bowl combine the cornmeal and 2 cups water.
In a sauce pan combine the salt, okra, onion and herbs with other 2 cups of water. Bring to a boil and simmer 10 minutes. Strain and save liquid.
In another saucepan bring the cornmeal and ½ okra mixture to a boil, stirring constantly. Gradually add the remaining liquid. Continue until cornmeal is thoroughly cooked. Add the okra and herb mixture. Stir in butter.
Serve warm.

Antigua and Barbuda Specialties

Barbecue chicken
Cured and smoked hams
Roast suckling pig
Curried meats, fish or beef
Salted codfish with tomato sauce
Blackened fish, cockles, shrimp, spiny lobster, snapper, mahi mahi, shark, conch, octopus, oyster, flying fish, kingfish dishes
Pancakes with curried beef, chicken or potatoes
Ducana - grated sweet potato, coconut, sugar, and spices steamed in a banana leaf. This is served with salt fish stew.
Pepperpot stew - salted meat, yams, squash, okra, aubergine, spinach, pumpkin, dasheen leaves, plantain, and fried cornmeal dumplings
Fungi – cornmeal and okra pudding
Souse - pork marinated in lime juice, onions, hot and sweet peppers, and spices
Potato dumplings
Callaloo - spinach soup with cloves or crab
Goat water – hot peppers, cinnamon, cloves
Seasoned rice
Sugarcake – sugar and coconut cake
Bambula – cassava bread
Key lime mousse
Coconut tarts
Tamarind stew
Rice pudding

Holidays and Special Occasions

Saturdays – barbecues are set up selling rice and chicken, dumplings, soup and other island specialties
Holy Thursday and Good Friday – no meat consumed
Easter – church, but many head to the beaches with picnics
Day of Independence (November 1) – family dinners
Christmas – ham, turkey, vinadarlush – garlic pork or stewed pork; rice, pigeon peas, yams, green figs

Argentina

Argentina, located in South America, borders Paraguay and Bolivia to the north, Brazil and Uruguay to the northeast, and Chile to the west and south. Humans are known to have inhabited the area since 11,000 BC in Patagonia. The early indigenous peoples were the Diaguitas, Huarpes, and Sanavirones. The Inca Empire, under Sapa-Inca Pachacutec, conquered the northwestern part of Argentina in 1480. The Guaraní raised yucca, sweet potato, and yerba mate. Spanish explorers arrived in 1516 and in 1542 the Viceroyalty of Peru included all of South America. Buenos Aires became the capital of the Viceroyalty of the Río de la Plata in 1776. A national unity government was established in 1861. Spanish is the official language.

Dining Etiquette

Please be slightly late when invited for a meal. Men should wear a jacket and tie. Dinner is served late, usually around 10 PM or later. Please shake hands greeting and departing using good eye contact. Women will kiss friends on the cheek. The oldest or guest of honor will be introduced first. Please bring a gift for the hostess such as something for the home, flowers, candy, or liquor which has high import taxes. Gifts are opened immediately. Drinks and hors d'oeuvres will be served. The hostess will seat the guests. Do not begin eating until the hostess picks up her fork. Food is eaten continental style with the fork in the left hand and knife in the right. Keep your hands at table level, and no elbows on the table. If passing a dish do so to your left. Never cut your lettuce. Instead use your knife and fork to pick it up. Please wait for a toast before drinking your wine or beverage. The host will pour the wine. The toast is "Salud". Please leave a small portion of food on your plate when you are finished. When finished place your knife and fork face down with the handles to the right, or crossed. The fork and spoon at the top of your place setting are for dessert. Brandy and coffee may be served at the end of a meal. Please call or write a thank you note to your hostess to thank her for the meal.

Chimichurri (parsley sauce)

½ cup olive oil	¼ cup parsley, finely chopped
¼ cup red wine vinegar	1 tsp. oregano
1 onion, finely chopped	½ tsp. cayenne
2 cloves garlic, minced	Salt and pepper

Combine the ingredients in a bowl. Let stand for 2-3 hours. Serve with grilled meats.

Cuisine

The cuisine is a blend of Spanish, Italian, French, German, Welsh, and Andean. Beef, lamb, goats, chickens, wheat, corn, grapes and raisins, milk, beans, soybeans, tomatoes, onions, lettuce, eggplant, squash, potatoes, olives, nuts, garlic, pumpkins, quinoa, chile peppers, chayote, cassava, kiwicha, zucchini, apples, pears, peaches, avocados, kiwi, and plums are grown. In warmer regions lemons, sugar cane, plantains grapefruit, bananas, watermelons, tangerines, pineapples, palm trees (hearts of palm) and oranges are harvested. Along the coast and lakes fish and shellfish – spider crab, squid, octopus, pollock, salmon, trout, and oysters are used in cooking. Argentina is famous for both its beef and wines. The cattle were brought by the Spaniards to the pampas. The gauchos lived in the pampas eating the wild cattle which they caught with a bola – three stone balls held together with leather straps or lassos. The meat was eaten by the gauchos and the hides sold. Each region has its own specialties and may depend on those who settled in the region whether it be influenced by the Italians, Germans, Welsh (Patagonia) or others. On the 29th day of a month the Italians cook noqui de papa or potato gnocchi to symbolize the end of the month and that your kitchen might only have potatoes, flour and eggs left in it. When eating the gnocchi in a restaurant place money under your plate for good luck and prosperity. The northeast has a large abundance of freshwater fish. Beef and other meats are usually broiled or roasted, or cooked using a grill called a parrilla.

Argentinian Specialties

Asado – barbecued (grilled) beef, lamb, chicken, sausages, livers and kidneys

Emapanadas – pastries with meat, cheese, corn, or other stuffing

Sausages – morcilla (blood sausage), chorizo,

Mollejas – sweetbreads

Milanesa – breaded meats

Estafado, guisos, pucheros - stews

Matambre "kill hunger" – marinated flank steak covered with spinach, hard-boiled eggs, carrots and onions, rolled up and tied with a string, then poached or roasted

Pastel de Cambraye – sweet beef pie with peaches and meringue served at weddings in Cambraye

Pisa- pizza

Squash can be made into soup, fritters, puddings, stews

Jamones serronas - ham

Pastas – tallarines, ravioles, gnocchi, canelones

Faina – thin chickpea flour bread; faina and pizza are often eaten together

Humitas – corn cakes

Humitas en chala – humitas wrapped in cornhusks, and then steamed or boiled

Fish - bacalao (dried cod), calamari, octopus,

Chimichurri - sauce with garlic, parsley and served with beef

Fideos – pasta dish

Churcut – sauerkraut

El locro – stew with corn

Corderito (lamb) and ciervo (deer) roasts are popular in Patagonia

Tamales – steamed meat in cornhusks or banana leaves

Sorrentinos – pasta stuffed with mozzarella, ham or ricotta

Polenta is with a sauce and cheese

Medialunas- croissants

Pane casero – wheat bread

Queso – cheese

Salsa golf – mix of ketchup and mayonnaise

Dulce de leche – milk, sugar, and vanilla that is boiled and made into a paste to use in cakes, pancakes, or on toast

Alfajores – shortbread cookies

Churro – fried pastry with dulce de leche

Arroz con leche – rice pudding
Marzipan – almond paste
Helado – ice cream or sorbets (which date to
the early 19th c when snow was used in
desserts in Mendoz)

Pastelitos de mil hojas –quince pastries
Llao llao – candy from the south

Carbonada Criolla (Baked Pumpkin with Beef, Vegetables and Fruit)

Serves 6

1 large pumpkin
1 stick butter
¼ - ½ cup sugar
2 tbls. olive oil
2 lbs. beef, cut into cubes
1 medium onion, chopped
1 green pepper, chopped
2 cloves garlic, grated
4 cups beef stock

3 medium tomatoes, finely chopped
1 tsp. dried oregano
1 bay leaf
2 medium sweet potatoes, peeled and cut into cubes
2 medium potatoes, peeled and cut into cubes
1 small zucchini, sliced
3 ears corn, sliced in rounds
4 peaches, peeled, pitted and sliced

Preheat oven to 375°
Using a sharp knife cut a lid from the top of the pumpkin, leaving the stem. With a spoon, scrape out the seeds and fibers. Save the seeds and bake with a little salt and olive oil as a snack.
Brush the inside of the pumpkin with the butter. Sprinkle the cavity with the sugar, rotating the pumpkin to coat all of inside.
Place the pumpkin in a baking dish and bake 45 minutes or until tender, but not falling apart.
Heat the olive oil in a large pan and brown the beef. Transfer to a platter. Add the onions, and green pepper to the pan and sauté until the vegetables are soft. Add the garlic. Pour in the beef stock and bring to a boil. Scrape sides so nothing sticks.
Add the meat to the pan and stir in tomatoes, oregano, bay leaf, salt and pepper to taste. Cover and simmer for 15 minutes.
Add the sweet and white potatoes. Cover and cook 15 minutes. Add the zucchini and cook 10 minutes. Add corn and peaches. Cook 5 minutes.
Pour all the ingredients into the pumpkin and put on its lid. Bake in oven 15 minutes.
Serve on plates. Can be transferred to platter, but is rather cumbersome and may fall apart!

Holidays and Special Occasions

Semana Santa (week before Easter) - fish, empanadas de vigilia – vegetables or tuna, and guisados with bacalao (cod). No meat is eaten.
Easter - Families attend mass. An asado (barbecue) usually with lamb is prepared. Dessert may be huevos de Pascua – chocolate eggs and Rosca de Pascua – cake with custard and cherries in the shape of a ring to symbolize eternal life.

Christmas Eve and into Christmas (Navidad) – migas (finger sandwiches); lengua a la vinagreta – cow tongue; matambre relleno – rolled flank steak; vitel tone – veal in tuna sauce; salads especially potato and Waldorf; tomato rellenos; huevos rellenos de pate; canapes navidenos – empanada with ham, cheese, olives, tomatoes, and herbs; pionono – spong cake with chicken or tuna, cheese, tomatoes, artichokes, and mayonnaise; fiambre alemain – crepes with ham, cheese, tomatoes, lettuce, olives and mayonnaise; roast pork; turrons; pan dulce. Some families do cook a suckling pig or do asado - barbecue as this time of year it is very warm.

Beverages

Mate is a drink made from the dried leaves and branches of the yerbe mate plant. It has a bitter flavor so sugar, herbs, or orange peel may be added. In the northeast it may be mixed with fruit juices or alcohol. Hot water is poured into the cup. The drink is served in cups made from gourds, bone or horns, also called mate and sipped with a straw. Sometimes the cup is served communally. *Mate cocido* is also made from the yerbe mate leaf, boiled and served with sugar or milk. Yerbiao is mate mixed with gin. Most of the yerbe mate is produced in Corrientes and Misiones. In the northeast mate may be mixed with juices or alcoholic beverages. Another popular drink is cider often drunk at Christmas and New Year's. Aguardiente (firewater) is made from sugar cane. Liqueurs are also flavored with egg, anise, orange, coffee, cherry and dulce de leche. Hesperidina is a liqueur made from orange peels and dates c 1890. Boldo is a digestive tea. Drinks made from chocolate are also popular.

Wine has been made in Argentina since 1556 when grapes were planted in the Cuyo region. The earliest wines were produced by the Spaniards for communion during the Catholic Mass, especially by the Jesuits in Alta Garcia. The wines have been influenced by the Italian, Spanish, French and German immigrants. Since the 1880s the province of Mendoza has produced outstanding wines, including Malbec which has gained international acclaim. Malbec is mainly grown around Mendoza at the base of the Andes. The region is sunny, dry, and cool, so that the grapes are not exposed to rot or insects, and have a long growing season. The San Juan vineyards produce sweeter wines, more for dessert consumption, Vermouth, and raisins. Rio Negro is noted for sparkling and white wines. Fruit wines are made using apples, pears, peaches, and grapes. An artificially sweetened wine is known as abocados. Torrontes is a white wine produced in the Calchaquies Valleys. Distilled wines made from grapes are also produced.

Every type of grape is produced in Argentina. The country is divided into three wine producing regions:
North-West – provinces of Salta, Catamarca and La Rioja – dry white wines, Malbec and Cabernet
Central-West – provinces of San Juan and Mendoza – white, cabernet, merlot, Malbec, dessert wines, vermouth
South – Cabernet and Semillon

Beer (cervasa) has also been produced since the 1860s by colonists from Alsace, followed by Poles. Towns brewing beer are San Carlos, Rio Segundo, Cordoba, Quilmes, Lavallol, San Miguel de Tucuman, Mendoza and Salta. The carob tree bark is used to make aloja beer and patay bread.

Armenia

Armenia is bordered by Turkey to the west, Georgia to the north, Nagorno-Karabakh Republic and Azerbaijan to the east, and Iran and the Azerbaijani exclave of Nakhchivan to the south. Civilization here dates back to the Bronze Age including the Hittite Empire (established 18th c BC), the Mitanni (1500-1300 BC), and Hayas-Azzi ((1500-1200 BC). The Nairi (1200-900 BC) and the Kingdom of Uratu (1000-600 BC) reigned over the highlands. In 301 AD the empire stretched from the Caspian to the Mediterranean Sea. Yerevan, the capital, was founded in 782 BC by King Argishti and is located near Mt. Ararat, thought to be where Noah of The Bible arrived after the Great Flood. The official language is Armenian, which dates back to c 405 and first spoken by Mesrop Mashotz, an Orthodox priest.

Dining Etiquette

Please be prompt, or just a few minutes late, when invited for a meal. Please bring a wrapped gift, which will not be opened in front of the presenter. Please shake hands greeting and departing, Men will embrace for familiar friends and kiss on the cheek. Women friends will greet each other with a hug and kiss on the cheek. People will stand close to each other when speaking and may touch each other. Try to maintain good eye contact. Beverages will be served. The hostess will seat the guests. Food is eaten continental style with the fork in the left hand and knife in the right hand. Keep your hands at table level. Often many toasts may last for a while. The toasts are made by the tamada (tastemaker) and will be good wishes and may go on for long periods of time with toasts being reciprocated. Vodka or wine is used for the toasts. All men are expected to drink to the toasts.

Harissa (wheat porridge with chicken)

Harissa is one of the oldest dishes of Armenia.

1 cup whole wheat kernels	Salt and pepper to taste
2 cups shredded cooked chicken or turkey	4 cups chicken broth
½ cup butter	4 cups boiling water
1 tsp. paprika	

Wash the whole wheat kernels and soak overnight in hot water. Keep in a warm place, preferably covered. Pour off water.
Add the shredded meat to the chicken broth and boiling water and cook slowly until all the liquid is absorbed. Then add the salt and pepper and beat the mixture until it becomes smooth like a well cooked mush. Add more water if necessary to make the mixture smooth. Melt the butter with the paprika and pour over each serving.
Recipe courtesy of Armella Shakaryan, Embassy of the Republic of Armenia, Washington, DC

Cuisine

The Armenian cuisine has been around for thousands of years and uses aromatic spices, fresh vegetables, fruits and meats. The Armenians domesticated cattle in the highlands using them for meat and dairy products, and bred poultry. In the valleys grains, rice and beans were cultivated. Fruit prospered such as apricots, peaches, apples, pears, quince, cherries, mulberry, figs, pomegranates, strawberries, cantaloupe, and water melons. Fruits can be raw, dried, pickled or marinated. Alexander the Great brought apricot trees from Armenia to Greece in the 4th c. Early cooking was done in a clay furnace known as a tomir, and can still be seen in rural areas. Chopped meat and filled pastries or vegetables are part of the cuisine. Meats are grilled, roasted, boiled or stewed. Spices and herbs have always been used and include salt, pepper, coriander, fenugreek, mint, tarragon, basil, thyme, red pepper or paprika, mint, dill, parsley, tarragon, cumin, garlic, onion, cinnamon, cardamom, cloves, saffron, and vanilla. Lamb, eggplant, yogurt and sour cream, burghul (cracked wheat), eggplants, Swiss chard, zucchini, squash, tomatoes, peppers, onions, fruits, nuts (walnuts, almonds, pistachios, and pine nuts are mainly used in cooking. Food is cooked in butter or olive oil. Vegetables may be served raw, cooked, or pickled. Different sauces might be tomato, pepper, yogurt, or tahini. Fish comes from the rivers or the Caspian Sea. Dinner will include appetizers (mezze) – almonds, olives, sausages, stuffed vine leaves, hummus; soup; salads; an entrée; and dessert, then coffee. Bread is eaten with meals. Salads are made with olive oil, salt, vinegar and lemon juice.

Armenian Specialties

Chechil – braided string cheese
Bozzbash –lamb or mutton soup
Khoravats – grilled or barbecued meats
Gharsi khoravats – khorovats in lavash
Khashlama – boiled meat and potatoes
Khash – cow's feet, herb and broth soup, served with garlic and lavash (flat bread) – eaten early morning during the winter
Shashlyk – skewered lamb, from shashka – sword
Kchuch - meat or fish dish with vegetables, cooked in a clay pot
Basturma – dried raw beef
T'ghit – fruit leather, plum puree and boiled, topped with fried onions and eaten with lavash
Matnakash – wheat leavened bread
Lahmajoun – thin crusted dish with meat, herbs and spices
Tjvjik – fried liver and kidneys with onions
Spas – egg, flour, and yogurt soup
Arganak – chicken soup

Blghourapour – wheat soup cooked with grape juice
Brndzapour – rice and potato soup
Dzavarapour – wheat, potato, tomato puree soup
Flol – beef soup with dumplings
Krchik – sauerkraut, wheat, potato and tomao puree soup
Snkapur – mushroom soup
Kiufta – meatballs
Karshm – walnut, bean, chickpea and spice soup served with red pepper and garlic
Ghapama – pumpkin stew with rice, raisins, apples, sugar and apples
Labneh - yogurt
Pilav – rice
Eetch – cracked wheat salad
Byorek – phyllo pastry with meat, onion and pepper filling
Alani – peaches stuffed with walnuts and sugar
Kadaif – dough with cheese or walnut filling and sugar syrup

Holidays and Special Occasions

7 is considered a lucky number on New Year's Day

The Armenian *Christmas* is celebrated on January 6th. The week before families fast and eat no animal foods. Instead they will eat – cheoreg (braided bread), pilaf, vegetables, rice pudding, figs, paklava, and anoush abour (a pudding of wheat, berries, apricots, nuts, cinnamon and pomegranate seeds), dried and fresh fruits, nuts, cheese, topig, cheoreg, boereg, and kurabia.

On *Christmas Eve* the meal might include fried fish or other seafood, lettuce, and spinach, and anoush abour with a star of slivered almonds and is eaten after the Christmas Eve service in churches.

January 6th (*Christmas*) – lamb and a feast to break the fast

Lent - Topig – chickpea and wheat dough filled with onions, walnuts, currants, tahini and spices; byorek made with spinach and tahini sauce.

Easter Eve - Jajukh – cucumber, yogurt, garlic dip

Easter – Harissa, cheoreg

Hisnag (Advent) – soup given to the poor

New Year's Eve – anoush abour. On New Year's pomegranate seeds (symbolizing "plenty") are broken on doorsteps

Nshkhar is a bread used for Holy Communion and Mas "piece" is a piece of leftover bread from the Nshkhar, given to worshippers after a church service

Beverages

"If you drink wine a lot, it is too bad. If you don't drink wine, it is much worse. But if you do take it moderately, it is excellent." Old Armenian proverb

Wines have been produced in Armenia for thousands of years. Even in the bible Noah planted the first vineyards on Mt. Ararat. Areni, a red wine, is made with grapes from vineyards that date back to c 1000 BC. Pomegranate wines are also drunk, as is Ilevan which can be a dry white from Tavush, semi-sweet from the Kahket grape in Tavush, or dry red from Areni grapes. Yerevan Brandy is produced in Yerevan. The brandy was Winston Churchill's favorite. At the 1900 Paris International Exhibition the brandy won the Grand Prix in the City of Light and could be called a` Cognac. Today the company is owned by Pernod Ricard. In January 2011 archeologists announced that the oldest wine making vat, along with crushed grapes, leaves and seeds had been discovered in an Areni cave dating back 6000 years. During the Soviet occupation of Armenia vineyards were destroyed to curb the drinking of alcohol.

Leban is a yogurt drink. Popular brands of beer are Kotayk, Erebuni, Kilikia, and Gyumri. Kvas is a drink made from sweet, fermented bread. Artsakh is a vodka made from fruit, such as mulberry, grown in the highlands and Artsakh. Sharots is a drink with grape juice and doshab syrup, spices and a walnut on a string. Jermuk and Hayk, Sari are bottled mineral waters. Coffee is drunk very strong Kefir is a fermented milk drink and Tarkhun soda, a tarragon flavored drink.

Did You Know?

The pomegranate is a symbol of fertility, abundance and marriage.

Aruba

Aruba is an island of the Netherland Antilles in the southern Caribbean Sea, located 27 km north of the coast of Venezuela. The first inhabitants of the island were Caquetios Amerinds of the Arawak tribe who migrated from Venezuela c 850 BCE. The earliest settlements date back to c 1000 AD. The first Europeans to settle on the island were Spaniards in the 1499. Since 1636 Aruba has been part of the Kingdom of the Netherlands. During World War II, together with Curaçao, Aruba became a British protectorate from 1940 to 1942 and a US protectorate from 1942 to 1945. Aruba received its independence in 1996. The capital Oranjestad, was built around Fort Zoutman in 1796. The official languages are Dutch and Papiamento.

Pastechis (Traditional Aruban breakfast, also served as a snack)

Pastry

4 cups of flour 1 tbs. of baking powder	2 tbs. margarine
1 tsp. salt	1 egg beaten
1 tbs. sugar	1 cup of water
2 tbs. vegetable shortening	

Put all ingredients into a large bowl except water. Mix well. Add water, a little bit at a time to form dough. When the dough is pliable, knead it well.

Meat Filling

1 lb. finely chopped beef without fat	2 tbs. raisins
1 tbs. margarine	1 tbs. piccalilli Hot red pepper, finely
1 medium onion, finely chopped	chopped, to taste; preferably Madame
1 small green sweet pepper, finely chopped	Jeanette Soy sauce, freshly ground black
1 celery stalk, finely chopped	pepper, cumin, nutmeg, to taste

In large frying pan combine all ingredients except beef. Cook over medium heat, stirring till well combined and onion and celery are soft. Add beef and cook till well combined while stirring. Roll the dough into a very thick sheet, then cut out circles about three inches in diameter. Place one tablespoon filling in the center of one pastry circle. Top it with a second circle. Lightly moisten edges and press the circles together. Fold or roll the edges over slightly and flute them as pie crust. Fry the pastechis in deep, hot vegetable oil until golden brown. They may be prepared in advance and heated in the oven just before serving.
Recipe courtesy of VisitAruba.com

Dining Etiquette

Please be prompt when invited for a meal. Please bring a gift for the home, wine, or flowers. Shake hands greeting and departing. You will be served beverages. The hostess will seat you with the male guest of honor to her right. Eating is continental style fork in the left hand, knife in the right. Please do not start until the hostess does. Food will be served at the table or buffet style. When finished place your knife and fork together. The toast is "Proost".

Cuisine and Beverages

The early settlers realized that Aruba did not produce abundant agricultural products. Instead they raised horses and cattle, mango, millet, coconut and aloe. Today most are imported, although aloe is still harvested. Rice, chicken, lamb, beef, and fish are the mainstay. Fish include conch which is made into stew, fried, or fritters; kingfish, tuna, shrimp, turtle, snapper, mahi mahi, barracuda, and grouper. Peas and rice are served with many meals. Stews and soups are made with vegetables, fish, chicken, and meat. Fruit include plantains, pineapple and coconut.

Balashi Beer is produced on the island and is similar to a Dutch Pilsner. Fruit drinks and alcoholic beverages mixed with fruit juices are popular.

Aruba Specialties

Keshi yena – Gouda cheese, spices, meat or seafood dish with a sauce
Webo yena – deviled eggs
Salada di batata - potato salad
Johnny cakes – made from cornmeal
Satee – marinated meat on skewers
Pan bati - beaten flat bread
Sopi di mariscos – seafood soup
Kreeft stoba – lobster stew
Promenton yena – stuffed peppers
Pinchos di cabaron – shrimp kebab

Bolo ponche crema – eggnog cake
Bolo borracho – rum cake
Pan dushi – sweet rolls
Pudin di coco – coconut pudding
Soenchi – meringue kisses
Cocada – coconut candy
Kesio – flan
Pan lefi – sponge cookies
Bolo di banana – plantain pudding
Tert di prium – prune tart
Banana den forno – baked bananas
Pan bollo – bread pudding with rum sauce

Holidays and Special Occasions

15, 50, 75th birthdays are considered important events and call for a major party.
At children's parties piñatas with filled sweets are hung from the ceiling. The children are blindfolded and try to hit the piñata with a stick to break it.
Bolo pretu is a dark fruit cake served on special occasions and is the traditional wedding cake.
On December 5th the birthday of Sinterklaas (St. Nicholas) is celebrated with gifts for the children.
In June the Dia di San Juan was celebrated with the song "Dera Gai", the burying of the rooster. It occurred on the Feast of St. John the Baptist to give thanks for the harvest. Today a calbas (gourd) is used instead of the rooster.
Christmas – ayaka is prepared from banana leaves, ground meat, olives, prunes, and a dough that is shaped into a square and held with a string.

Australia

Australia, located in the Southern Hemisphere, is comprised of the Australian continent, the island of Tasmania and other smaller islands in the Indian and Pacific Oceans. Australia has been inhabited for over 40,000 years, and perhaps 70,000 years ago. According to Australian Aboriginal mythology and the animist framework developed in Aboriginal Australia, the Dreaming is a sacred era in which ancestral totemic spirit beings formed The Creation. The Dreaming established the laws and structures of society and the ceremonies performed to ensure continuity of life and land. Some 10–12,000 years ago, Tasmania became isolated from the mainland, and some stone technologies failed to reach the Tasmanian people (such as the hafting of stone tools and the use of the Boomerang). In southeastern Australia, near present-day Lake Condah, semi-permanent villages of beehive shaped shelters of stone developed, near bountiful food supplies. By 1788, the population existed as 250 individual nations, many of which were in alliance with one another, and within each nation there existed several clans, from as few as five or six to as many as 30 or 40. Each nation had its own language and a few had multiple, thus over 250 languages existed, around 200 of which are now extinct. Dutch explorers arrived in 1606, but it was not until 1770 it was claimed by Britain. Permanent European settlers arrived at Sydney in 1788 and came to control most of the continent by end of the 19th century. Bastions of largely unaltered Aboriginal societies survived, particularly in Northern and Western Australia into the 20th century, until finally, a group of Pintupi people of the Gibson Desert became the last people to be contacted by outsider ways in 1984. In 1901 Australia became a federation known as the Commonwealth of Australia. Canberra, the capital, was founded as a planned city in 1908. English is the official language, along with the Aboriginal languages.

Dining Etiquette

When entertained please be prompt. Please bring a gift – flowers (gladioli are for remembrance only), a bottle of wine, or something for the home. Shake hands meeting and greeting and say "Good Day". The Aussies have a great sense of humor, use first names, and can be quite informal. You might even offer to bring a dish for the meal. Drinks and appetizers will be served. The hostess will seat the guests at the table with the male guest of honor to her right. Please eat continental style with the fork in the left hand and the knife in the right. Food is usually served platted, but may also be a buffet. Barbeques are very popular. Please do not start until the hostess raises her fork. Elbows are kept at table level. Soup is eaten by moving the spoon toward the back of the bowl. When finished place your knife and fork together with the handles facing right. The toast is "Cheers" or "cherio". Please clink glasses when toasting. Australia has very strict drunk driving and seatbelt laws!

Lamb Skewers with Lemon &Garlic

Serves 4

500g lamb leg steak, diced
1 red capsicum, cut into 2cm pieces
2 garlic cloves, crushed
1 lemon, juiced
½ teaspoon dried mint

½ cup low-fat Greek-style yoghurt
4 large coliban potatoes
olive oil cooking spray
80g mixed salad leaves
1 Lebanese cucumber, thinly sliced

Thread lamb and capsicum alternately onto (pre-soaked) skewers.
Combine half the garlic, ¼ cup lemon juice and mint in a ceramic dish.
Add skewers and turn to coat in garlic mixture. Season with salt and pepper. Cover and refrigerate for 30 minutes, if time permits.
Combine remaining garlic and yoghurt in a small bowl. Season with salt and pepper. Refrigerate until ready to serve.
Pierce each potato with a fork and place on a microwave-safe plate. Microwave, uncovered, on high (100%) for 8 to 10 minutes or until just cooked through. Allow to cool slightly. Cut potatoes into 1cm-thick slices.
Preheat barbecue grill and plate on medium-high heat. Spray skewers with oil. Grill for 3 to 4 minutes each side for medium or until cooked to your liking.
Spray potato slices with oil. Cook on barbecue plate for 2 minutes each side or until golden. Remove potato to a plate.
Divide salad leaves and cucumber between plates. Top with skewers. Serve with potato and yoghurt.
Recipe courtesy of Andrew McGowan, Medowie, NSW, Australia

Cuisine

The indigenous Australians lived as hunter gatherers, using whatever food was available to them including kangaroo, wallaby, emu, berries, fruit, and fish along the coast. With the arrival of the British and Irish, cattle, sheep, sugar cane, and wheat were introduced. Today with many diverse immigrants the food has been influenced by Asian, Korean, Middle Eastern and other cuisines. Many types of vegetables are grown - artichoke, asparagus, beanshoots, beetroot, broccoli, cabbage, cauliflower, cucumber, leek, lettuce, mushrooms, peas, pumpkins, and spinach, capsicum, cucumber, eggplant, squash, tomato, and zucchini. Seafood is bountiful and includes rock lobsters, tuna, crayfish, crab, prawn, salmon, oysters, mussels, whiting, gemfish, redfish, snapper, bream, flathead, morong, leatherjacket, John Dory, mullet, pigfish, squid, and abalone, to name a few. In fact over 1000 species of fish live in the Australian waters! Flake is often used in fish and chips. Trout are found in fresh water. Fruit include rhubarb, pineapples, plums, mangoes, currants, strawberries, blackberries, apples, raspberries, and peaches.

Because of the size of the country there are regional specialties. In Victoria and South Australia the food has been influenced by the Germans and Italians. Fresh fruit, vegetables, grapes for wine and nuts are produced. Meats are smoked, sausage made, and fruits and vegetables pickled and preserved. In Queensland barramundi (fish), bug (similar to a crab or crayfish), mud crabs, and macadamia nuts are used in cooking. In Sydney oysters are prevalent. Western Australia is noted for apples, crayfish, figs, lobster, prawns, scallops, tropical fruits, and salt from Cape Cuvier. Tasmania grows hops, apples, raspberries, strawberries, honey, vineyards; has fresh water trout, and along the coast crayfish, abalone, oysters.

Australian Specialties

Vegemitc – yeast paste to spread on toast

Pavlova – dessert made with meringue, whipped cream and fruit, named after ballerina Anna Pavlova

Barbie (barbecues) – beef, sausage, prawns, kangaroo, lamb, vegetables, fruits

Carpetbagger steak – beef stuffed with oysters

Anzac biscuits – oat and coconut biscuits that became popular during World War I

Australian Jack – oatmeal bread

Violet crumble – chocolate candy

Jaffas – chocolate in an orange shell

Meat pies

Snag - sausage

Damper – wheat soda bread

Fish and chips

Pasties – turnover with meat

Bugs – clawless crustacean

Lamingtons – day old sponge cake filled with raspberry and chocolate and dipped in coconut

Chiko Roll- similar to Chinese spring roll

Bangers and mash – sausage and mashed potatoes

Chook – chicken

Bush tucker – native food in the outback

Cut lunch – sandwich

Dead horse – tomato sauce

Lollies- candies

Entrée – appetizer

Coffee Basted Lamb Roast – Outback Australia Style

1 lamb roast - either leg or shoulder
Several cloves of garlic
1 tbls. salt
1 tbls. dry mustard powder
1 cup milk

1 tbls. instant coffee powder
(Or one cup of very strong milky coffee)
1 cup stock - beef, veal or vegetable
2 tbls. raspberry or strawberry jam, or cranberry sauce

Heat oven   (350° F depends on oven)
Cut garlic into slivers and insert into meat. Mix salt and mustard together, rub over lamb. Place in suitable greased roasting pan and roast for 1 hour.
Dissolve coffee in boiling water, add milk, then pour over lamb. Return to oven. Continue cooking meat, basting with coffee liquid at regular intervals until lamb is cooked to personal preference. Remove lamb roast to rest, wrap in foil. Scrape pan to loosen coffee and lamb juices and add stock and jam. Stir well to blend. Simmer to reduce and thicken gravy, adding any juices from resting lamb. Season gravy with salt and pepper to taste, pour into serving jug. Thinly slice lamb and serve generous portions.
Best served with traditional vegetables (potato, carrot pumpkin, parsnip) roasted in a separate pan. And also steamed green peas, beans. May also be served with Couscous.
Sit back and enjoy appreciative sighs from contented guests.
Recipe courtesy of Norman and Barbara Crossley, Clifton Springs, Victoria, Australia

Holidays and Special Occasions

January 26 (*Australia Day*) – picnics
Shrove Tuesday – pancakes
Lent – hot cross buns
Easter – chocolate eggs, lamb or chicken, vegetables
Christmas – since Christmas falls during the summer, warm weather foods are served. They will include roast turkey, cold meats, ham, seafood, salads, Pavlova, Christmas puddings, and plum pudding.

Beverages

Wines have been produced in Australia since the British colonized the country in 1788. Most of those died out quickly, but Royal Navy Captain Arthur Phillip, John Macarthur, Gregory Blaxland planted vineyards near Sydney Cove that seemed to thrive. Medical doctors promoted the benefits of wine, including Dr. Lindeman and Dr. Christopher Penfold, for which two wineries are named. Wine was first exported to England in 1854. The "father of Australian wines" was an emigrant from Scotland James Busby who traveled to France before leaving for Australia. He wrote "A Treatise on the Culture of the Vine and the Art of Making Wine". In the 1830s John Reynell established the first commercial winery in New South Wales with cuttings from the Cape of Good Hope. This became Thomas Hardy and Sons, and is now part of Constellation Wines Australia. Most of the wine is grown in New South Wales, South Australia, Victoria and Western Australia. The Hunter and Barossa Valleys are noted wine producing regions. Today there are over 60 regions producing over 100 varieties of grapes. Australia is now the world's fourth largest exporter of wine. The bag-in-the –box wines were first introduced in Australia in the 1970s.

Billy tea is made by boiling water over an open fire and adding a gum leaf. The swagman in Waltzing Matilda was brewing the tea and eating a stolen sheep when he committed suicide. The lyrics were composed in 1887.

Beer is also produced in Australia. James Squires founded the first commercial brewery in 1798. The Cascade Brewery in Hobart, Tasmania has operated since the 19th c. Fosters and Victoria Bitter are the better known brews.

Did You Know?

Gin and whiskey distilleries were begun after World War I.
The early military guards had rum privileges and were known as the "Rum Corps".
The Beer Can Regatta is held in Darwin in June. The boats are constructed out of beer cans!
Australians first introduced bag-in-the-box wines in the 1970s.
Peach Melba was concocted at the Savoy Hotel, London, but is named for the Australian soprano Nellie Melba.
Worms in the rain forest of Australia can grow to lengths of 11 feet!

Austria

Austria is a landlocked European country flanked by Switzerland, Germany, the Czech and Slovak Republics, Hungary, Slovenia, Italy, and Liechtenstein. Its 32,369 square miles are made up of the Alps, valleys, and the Danube River in the east. The capital, Vienna, was an ancient Roman city (Vindobona) founded on the Danube River c 1st c AD. Austria was settled in about 800 BC by the Celts, later the Romans, the Habsburg Empire, and in 1529 the Turks invaded. During World War II Austria became part of Germany. Today Austria is a parliamentary democracy made up of 9 leander (provinces). German is the official language.

Dining Etiquette

Always be punctual. When being entertained please bring flowers, or a small gift. Red flowers are given to display affection, and an even number is considered unlucky. Gifts are usually opened when received. Please shake hands greeting and departing. Women extend their hand first. Some men may kiss the hand of the lady. Titles are important when people are first introduced. Men stand when introduced to a woman and hold chairs and doors for her. When speaking, it is impolite to have one's hands in your pockets. Cocktails will be served before the dinner. Please remain standing until asked to be seated. The male guest of honor is seated to the right of the hostess. Napkins should be placed in your lap when seated. Please wait for the hostess to start. Hands should be kept above the table, not in the lap. Food is eaten continental style, fork in the left hand, knife in the right. A knife can be used to push with the fork. Fish and potatoes should only be cut with a fork. Rolls are broken before eating. Toasting is initiated by the host with everyone looking him in the eye, saying "Prost", "Zum Wohl", "to your health", glasses are clinked, and all may drink. When finished place the knife and fork together with the handles facing to the right. The honored guest will offer a toast to the host to say "Thank you".

For the opening of the opera and New Year's Eve black or white tie is de riguer. Afternoon tea "jause" will include tea and/or coffee, pastries and sandwiches.

Cuisine

Austrian food is world renowned – a blend of German, Middle Eastern and continental European. Vienna has its own specialties – liver dumpling soup, strudels, Sacher Torte, and fabulous pastries. Linzer has its famous torte made with raspberry or currant jam and dates back to the 17th c. Styria is noted for game, fish, pork, capons, and wine. Burgenland has been influenced by Hungary – pike, carp, bean soup, roast goose, and pastries. Carintha is known for game and fish. Favorite dishes use sour cream, liver pates, veal, mushrooms, game, chicken, goose, smoked or fresh trout, and watercress.

Wiener Schnitzel (veal dipped in eggs and bread crumbs, then sautéed)

2 pounds boneless leg of veal
cut into ¼ inch-thick slices, pounded thin
1 cup lemon juice
1 tsp. salt
¼ teaspoon freshly ground pepper
3 eggs
3 tbls. milk

½ cup all-purpose flour
1 cup dry bread crumbs
1 ½ cups lard or clarified butter
lemon slices
parsley sprigs

Arrange the veal in a single layer in a large baking dish. Pour the lemon juice over veal; let stand 1 hour, turning the veal twice. Drain veal; pat dry. Sprinkle veal with salt and pepper. Beat eggs and milk in pie plate. Coat veal with flour; dip in egg mixture; coat with crumbs; shake off excess. Refrigerate at least 20 minutes. Heat lard in large heavy skillet until it begins to smoke (about 300°). Fry 1 cutlet at a time in lard until golden brown, about 2 minutes each side; drain on paper toweling; keep warm until all cutlets are cooked. Garnish with lemon slices and parsley springs.
Recipe courtesy of the Embassy of Austria, Washington, DC

Austrian Specialties

Backhendl – breaded fried chicken
Paprika huhner – chicken paprika
Liptauer – farmers cheese with paprika and caraway seeds
Knodel – potato dumplings
Kasnudln – filled noodle squares from Carintha
Kraut fleckerl – noodles and cabbage
Nockerl - dumplings
Semmeln – breakfast rolls
Maronicremesuppe – cream of chestnut soup
Brennsuppe – brown soup
Steirische suppe – sour cream soup
Tafelspitz – boiled beef dish

Rindsuppe – beef broth
Mélange – coffee with milk; mélange mit schlag – coffee with whipped cream; mokka – black coffee
Marzipan – almond paste candies
Salzburger nockerl – dessert soufflé from Salzburg
Speckknodel – Tyrolian dumplings
Tortes – layered cakes using ground nuts or crumbs with cream and jam were invented in Vienna
Linzertotorte – cake with nuts and chocolate, and jam filling
Apfelstrudel – apple strudel
Palatschinken – pancakes

Roter Rubenkren (beets with horseradish and apples)

4 large beets, cooked and sliced
1 large apple, sliced thinly
2 tsp. or more horseradish
1 tbls. sugar

1 tsp. caraway seeds
½ cup vinegar

Place the beets, apple, horseradish and caraway seeds in a salad bowl.
Heat the vinegar and sugar. Pour over the beets. Refrigerate and serve cold.

Sachertorte (Sacher Gateau)

Sachertorte is a famous chocolate torte served with whipped cream from the Hotel Sacher, Vienna. The tort was concocted by Franz Sacher in 1832 in honor of Prince von Metternich. During the Allied Occupation of Vienna, the Sacher Hotel was used as the British Senior officers Club.

5 oz. butter	8 egg whites and 2 oz. sugar
5 oz. baker's chocolate	5 oz. flour
3 ½ oz. castor sugar	pinch of salt
8 egg yolks	

Beat the butter, chocolate and sugar until fluffy, stirring in the egg yolks one by one. Whisk the egg white, add the sugar and fold carefully into the butter mixture adding the flour as you go along. Butter a cake tin, sprinkle with flour, put in the cake mixture and bake slowly for 1 ½ hours. Turn out on to a cake rack and allow to cool. Glaze the top of the cake with hot apricot jam and cover with chocolate icing.

Icing

7 oz. sugar	3 oz. bittersweet chocolate
7 oz. water	

Bring sugar and water to boil and boil until the mixture candies, then add the chocolate and boil until the mixture is thick, but fluid. Spread this with wet knife over the cake.
Recipe courtesy of the Embassy of Austria, Washington, DC

Holidays and Special Occasions

Carnival – faschingskrapfen – jelly donuts
Easter – Osterprinze (sweet bread), cold meats, lamb, colored eggs; Osterlamm (sponge cake in the shape of a lamb)
December 6th – St. Nicholas' Day – gifts for children
Christmas Eve – break of the fast during Advent
Christmas – fired carp, goose, ham, kekse (small cakes); fried carp; Sacher torte; cookies – Muskatnockerln (nutmeg macaroons); Rumkugeln (Rum and Walnut Balls); Vanillekipferl (vanilla crescents); Zimtsterne (cinnamon stars); lebkuchen, and sterne; chocolates; Gluhwein (mulled wine) and Rumpunsch (rum punch) Potivica is a traditional Christmas bread.

Beverages

Wines have been produced in Austria since Roman times. At Lenz Moser the cellars are over one thousand years old, with the Mosers making wine since 1124. Dr. Lenz Moser invented mechanization in the vineyards. Rust became a free town in 1681 by providing 500 jugs of wine to the Emperor annually. During the 18th c the Emperor declared wine and food could be sold on the premise of the vineyard, thus the many heuriger selling wine and food throughout the country. Heurig means "this year's" wine and when the inns have the newest harvest, fir branches are placed over the entrances. The wine is drunk in the taverns and may never be bottled. Weinkosten "wine festivals" are held during the summer and fall tastings. The main wine regions are Lower Austria, Styria, Burgenland "The Land of Castles" and once part of Hungary, and Vienna. Vineyards are called rieds. Krems is noted for its viticulture school and museum and as an area that also made mustard and gunpowder. Popular liqueurs are Kirshwasser (cherry), Himbeerbrandy (raspberry), and Slibovitz (plum).

Riesling comes from a vintner named Ritzling who in 1301 planted a small vineyard along the Ritzlingbach which flows into the Danube west of Durnstain. Riesling was later grown in Germany and then brought back to Austria.

The oldest breweries are the Grosser in Goss, with beer made in the monastery since 1020 and the Braurerei Hirt in Friesach, a brewery since 1270. The beers are full-bodied, malty with a purity code from the Habsburgs. If drinking beer one can order "vom Fass" – on tap from the keg; a Krugel – ½ liter glass; or Seidel – 1/3 liter glass. Birnenmost is an amber colored cider with a fruity flavor.

Did You Know?

The Hoher Market in Vienna is on the site of a Roman settlement or "castellum" that dates to c 100 BC. The Romans named it Vindobona and planted vineyards that survive to this day.
At the time of the Crusades soldiers arrived in Vienna with Eastern spices that included pepper, ginger, cinnamon, and cloves.
During the Baroque era lavish banquets were given that would include at least eight courses, usually with multiple dishes.
During the invasion of 1683 the Turks introduced coffee and the crescent roll, later known as the croissant (kifelin) which was made in the shape of the sign of Turkey with the slogan "We will eat you!' The first coffee house was the Blue Bottle. Today there are still many coffee shops including Café Sperl which opened in 1880.
The Salzkammergut "Salt Estates" have been an important salt mining region since c800BC. Salt was used for preserving meat, and was highly prized.
Many famous Austrians have dishes named for them:
Beef Tegetthoff – named for Admiral Tegetthof – beef with mussels, oysters, shrimp, mushrooms, and truffles
Cabbage Metternich- cabbage with potatoes
Emperor Franz Josef I – Kaiserschmarrn – pancake with sugar and raisins
Beef ribs Margarethe Maultasch – ribs dished named for Margarethe, daughter of King Henry of Tyrol

Azerbaijan

Azerbaijan is a country in the Caucasus region of Eurasia bounded by the Caspian Sea to the east, Russia to the north, Georgia to the northwest, Armenia to the west, and Iran to the south. Civilization in Azerbaijan dates back at least 10,000 years. The Scythians in the 9th C BC and the Medes 900 -700 BC were known to occupy the region which was conquered by the Achemnids c 550 BC and Zoroastrianism became the religion. Later it was part of Alexander the Great's empire and in 252 C.E. under the Sassanids, it became a vassal state. In the 4th c King Umayr officially adopted Christianity. Later the Byzantines and the Caliphate brought Islamic practices, followed by Iranian dynasties. Azerbaijan became a democratic republic in May 1918 and was the first Muslim country to grant women equal rights. Russians invade for oil in 1920 and in 1991 Azerbaijan became an independent nation. Baku capital, dates back to the 1st c AD, and became the capital in 1501. The official language is Azerbaijani

Dining Etiquette

The people are a very family oriented society. They are warm people, and enjoy entertaining. When invited for a meal, please arrive promptly, or only up to 30 minutes late. Please remove your shoes before entering a home. Pita bread, salt and sherbet are given as a sign of hospitality. Please bring a small wrapped gift of flowers (odd number), pastries or something from your country. The gift will be refused twice and then accepted. Gifts are not opened in front of the presenter. Men shake hands greeting and departing, and if known to each other a kiss on the cheek. Women will hug and kiss on the left cheek, or will shake hands whom they are first meeting. A woman will extend her hand first to a male. Beverages will be served. The hostess will lead the guests into the dining room and will show you your seat. Please wait to sit. The hostess will serve the food with the eldest first, then the guests. Keep your hands above the table when eating. Food is eaten and passed with the right hand.

If invited into the countryside do enjoy the pleasure of a samovar tea party with tea made in a samovar.

"For the dining room, it is necessary to arrange a comfortable, clean place with some decorations and fragrant odors. While eating, maintain an atmosphere of calmness, rest and satisfaction. Don't digress from eating; think only about the food you eat. Take food in small portions or sips, so it can be slowly digested. Avoid negative emotions like anger, irritation and dissatisfaction."
Muhammad Azam Khan (18th century)

Shorgoghal (Spice-Filled Flaky Bread)

"Along with scrumptious multi-layered *pakhlava* (baklava) and tender nut-filled *shekerbura*, spice-infused flaky bread *shorgoghal* (alternative spelling: *shor goghali*) is another irresistible edible attribute of Novruz. In fact, the three are a must on a festive goodie-filled tray, *khoncha,* a centerpiece of Novruz table. For its shape, the golden crust and the yellowish spice filling it encases, shorgoghal is regarded as the symbol of the sun. There can be as many as 9-12 layers of thinly opened dough in the *shorghogal*. This recipe yields 9 layers, but you can go as high as 12 if you roll your dough into smaller circles. A common wisdom holds that the more layers in the dough, the flakier the baked breads will be. Usually, *shorgoghal* is enjoyed with sweetened black tea, the authentic Azerbaijani way. Happy Spring, Happy Novruz to all of you!"

Makes 16 to 18 breads

Dough

1 package (¼ ounce /2 ¼ teaspoons) active dry yeast	2 tsp. salt
1 cup warm water	1 cup milk, at room temperature
6 cups all-purpose flour, plus extra for kneading	1 egg
	7 ounces unsalted butter, melted and cooled

In a small bowl, dissolve the yeast in the warm water and let stand until frothy, about 10 minutes. Sift the flour into a large mixing bowl. Add the salt and mix well. Make a well in the center and add the yeast mixture, milk, egg and butter. Stir with your hands to incorporate the ingredients. Scrape the dough onto a lightly floured surface and knead until smooth and elastic, and not tight, about 10 minutes. If the dough is still sticky, add more flour and knead but do not overdo with the flour. Put the dough back in the large mixing bowl, cover with a kitchen towel or a plastic wrap and let rise in a warm spot, until it doubles in bulk, about 1 ½ hours. The dough will be puffy and soft when poked with a finger.

Spice Filling

2 tbls. fennel seeds	¼ tsp. ground black pepper
2 tbls. anise seeds	2 cups all-purpose flour
½ tsp. turmeric powder	4 ounces (1 stick) unsalted butter, melted and cooled
1 tsp. salt	

Roast the fennel seeds and anise seeds on a hot skillet for about 2 minutes, until their aroma rises. (Roasting will raise their aroma and enhance their flavor, but it is optional. You can also use them as is).
Grind the spices in a spice grinder or using a mortar and pestle. In a medium mixing bowl, combine all the ingredients for the filling except the butter. Stir to mix. Gradually add the melted butter and rub with your fingers, until you obtain fine crumbs. Set aside.

Butter Spread

17 oz. unsalted butter
½ tsp. salt

When the dough has risen, prepare the butter spread. Melt the butter. Season with salt and set aside.

Have 2 large baking sheets ready.

You will need a large working area divided into two, to roll and assemble the layers. Shape the risen dough into a log and divide the log into 9 equal pieces. Shape each piece into a ball. Work with one ball at a time, and cover the rest with a kitchen towel.

Sprinkle some flour onto your working area. Using a thin rolling pin, roll out one ball, into a 20-inch circle, 1/16 inches thick. When you roll the dough, from time to time, sprinkle it with flour and spread all over the circle, to prevent the dough from sticking to the rolling pin and for easier rolling. Wrap the rolled out circle around the rolling pin and unwrap on another side of the working area.

Drizzle 4 tablespoons of the butter spread onto the circle and spread over the circle with your hand. Continue rolling up the remaining dough balls in the same fashion, placing them on top of each other and brushing with butter, except for the last circle, which should not be buttered (You can roll out the subsequent dough ball into smaller circles and place on top of the previous, then stretch in all directions to fit the larger circle). Now, gently pull the sides of the layered circle to stretch, until it is about 24 inches in diameter or as far as it can go (this will thin the rolled out layers yielding flakier breads).

Next, using a sharp knife, cut the circle into 2-inch wide strips, and cut the strips into rectangles, about 12 inches long, leaving the short sides of the circle as is, not cutting them. Beginning from one narrow side of one rectangle, gently roll it into a tight roll-up. Next, proceed with either methods (method 2 yields a flakier pastry) below to stuff the pastry:

Method 1: Take the roll-up in your hand, and bring the edges of one of its ends together to seal. Holding the roll-up with its sealed end down, with your fingers press in the middle of the unsealed end of the roll-up to hollow it up, all the way to the bottom, until you obtain a hollowed cone. Fill the cone as directed in the next step.

Method 2: (for a flakier pastry): Take the roll-up in your hand and holding both ends of it, twist it three times. Press the twisted log between your hand to flatten it slightly. Now, using your fingers push the middle of the disk to the sides to hollow it out (it should look like a mushroom cap). Fill the cone as directed in the next step.

Fill the hole with 1 ½ to 2 tablespoons of the filling, packing it gently. Bring the edges of the open end of the pastry together and seal to close. You will obtain a stuffed pastry.

Place the pastry on a flat surface and press gently with your hand to flatten it into a 4-inch disk, about 3/8-inches thick.

Continue with the remaining roll-ups in the same manner and place them on the baking sheets, spacing them at least 1 inch apart.

Place the pastry onto the baking sheets.

For the Top

2 egg yolks, to glaze
1 tbls. poppy seeds

Preheat the oven to 360F.
With your index finger, gently press in the center of the pastry to make a shallow indentation. Place a pinch of the spice filling in the indentation. Brush the tops of the pastries with the eggs yolks and sprinkle with poppy seeds. Bake for 40 minutes, or until golden on top, rotating the pans half way through. Remove from the oven. Allow to cool completely before serving. Keep the pastries in a large saucepan covered with lid, or in any other covered container.
Recipe and quote courtesy of Feride Buyuran: www.azcookbook.com. Food from Azerbaijan and Beyond

Cuisine

The Azerbaijan cuisine uses fresh vegetables and greens, yogurt; herbs - mint, cilantro (coriander), dill, basil, parsley, tarragon, leeks, chives, thyme, marjoram, green onion, and watercress, black pepper, sumac, saffron, nuts, dried fruits; fish from the Caspian Sea - salmon, kutum, sardines, grey mullet; black caviar from sturgeon; meat -mainly mutton and beef. Saffron-rice plov is the national dish and black tea the national drink which is drunk after food is eaten and may be accompanied by fruit preserves. Side dishes may include goy (green leaves), bread, white cheese or qatik (yogurt). Dessert is usually seasonal fruit rather than sweets

Azerbaijani Specialties

Plov - rice is served in its own dish with Gara – meat, dried fruit, eggs, fish, and herbs. Saffron rice plov is the national dish
Piti – mutton soup with vegetables
Kufta bozbash - pea soup with lamb and potatoes
Kebabs and Shashliks – lamb, beef, chicken, fish, especially sturgeon usually marinated first
Narsharab – pomegranate sauce
Chorek – bread
Choban – tomato and cucumber salad
Qovurma – stewed mutton or lamb with onions, tomatoes, and saffron
Gutab – thin dough cooked on a griddle stuffed with ground lamb, butternut squash, cheese, or spinach
Dolma – stuffed vine or cabbage leaves
Ghormeh sabzi – herb stew

Ghabli – rice, lentil, meat, potato, groat dish
Dushbara – dumplings stuffed with lamb and herbs and served in a broth
Lavangi – chicken stuffed with walnuts and herbs
Baliq – grilled fish with plum sauce
Toyuq – chicken soup
Aash – thick soup made from various ingredients
Sulu khingal – lamb soup with noodles
Dovga – yogurt soup with sorrel, spinach, rice, peas and mutton
Surhullu – pasta with dried meat
Salyan çörəyi –bread baked in a clay oven
Halva – malted wheat candy
Paklava – baklava
Peshmak – rice, flour and sugar candy
Girmapadam – pastry with chopped nuts
Shakarbura – crescent shaped pastry with nuts

Holidays and Special Occasions

Sweet pastries such as paklava and shakabura (pie with nuts and sugar), plov, shyra (nonalcoholic beverages) are usually eaten for weddings and funerals, and other special occasions.

Weddings (toy) are held on separate occasions, one for the girl when she can wear any color dress and invite family and friends; the other is the boy when the bride can wear a white dress with a red sash. At this time the bride and groom sit together. Tables are laden with pov, nuts, meats, kebabs, chestnuts, raisins, dricd apricots, salads, and drinks.

Novruz (New Year) – celebration on four Wednesdays before the vernal equinox in the spring – samani (millet porridge) represents fertility and is concocted on the last Wednesday for females only. Twelve days before seven things - salt, bread, a painted egg, rue, a piece of coal and a mirror are placed on a copper tray and left for 12 days. Plov, cookies and fruit are eaten. On the eve of Novruz the family gathers and the head of the family will be the first to taste of the holiday food. Doors to homes are opened and food is offered – sweets, paklava, nogul, pistachios, fruit, raisins, nuts. Guests' hands are sprinkled with rose water and then served tea made with cardamom, canella (bark similar to cinnamon) and ginger.

During celebrations plov is garnished with raisins and apricots, is served with meat, fried chestnuts and onions. During Novruz wheat is fried with raisins and nuts.

Beverages

Wine has been produced in Azerbaijan dating back to the 2nd millennium BC in Kültəpə, Qarabağlar, and Galajig. Wine making in the region was known to the Greeks as far back as the 7th c BC. During the Arab empire wine was made near Ganja and Barda. Today vineyards are found in the foothills of the Caucasus Mountains, Kur-Araz lowlands, with Ganja, Nagorno-Karabakh and Nakhchivan the wine producing centers. Seventeen types of vine are grown and sixteen table grapes varieties. Wine and cognac are produced in the Tovuz region.

Beer is also brewed, especially light lagers. The best known is Xirdalan, produced by Baki-Castel in Baku. Vodka is also produced and Azerbaijan has fine mineral waters. Sherbets are cold drinks made fruit juice which is boiled with sugar and rosewater usually added. They can be made from pomegranate, lemons, strawberries, cherries, apricots or mint.

Did You Know?

In 2009 Azerbaijani bakers produced the largest baklava in the CIS book of records, using seven thousand eggs, 360 kg nuts, 20 kg almonds, 350 kg sugar and flour.

The Bahamas

The Commonwealth of the Bahamas lies fifty miles off the Florida coast in the Atlantic Ocean, and are a string of about 700 coral islands and 2000 cays. It includes Andros, New Providence, Grand Bahama, Eleuthera, Bimini, Harbour Island, San Salvador, The Abacos, Berry Islands, Cat Island, Long island, Spanish Wells and the Exuma chain. The islands were settled by the Arawak Indians from South America in the 9th c AD. During Christopher Columbus' first voyage in 1492 he landed on an island called Guananhani by the Arawak and renamed it San Salvador "Holy Savior". The word Bahamas comes from the Spanish meaning "Bajamar" "Shallow Waters". King Charles I of England granted proprietary rights to Sir Robert Heath in 1629, and it remains a member of the British Commonwealth. The capital, Nassau, was originally named Charles Town, and in 1695 renamed Nassau in honor of the English king William II, formerly William of Orange-Nassau.

Dining Etiquette

Please be punctual when invited for a meal, even though everyone may be "on island time". Please take flowers or wine. Shake hands greeting and departing. Men stand when ladies enter a room, hold chairs and doors for them. Drinks will be served before dinner. The hostess will seat the guests with the male guest of honor to her right. Food may be served on the table or buffet style. Wait for the hostess to begin. After dessert coffee or liqueurs may be served. The host initiates the toast by raising his glass and saying "Cheers". Do write a thank-you note after being entertained.

Cuisine

Bahamian food make use of local products such seafood- conch, grouper, yellow tail, red snapper, lobster, crab, flying fish; fresh fruits – limes, seagrape, bananas, mango, coconut, sour sop, tamarind, papaya, hog plum; vegetables- spinach, peas, yucca, cassava, and beans. Conch is a main staple served as a salad, chowder, fried as fritters, or "cracked" in a flour batter. Stews and curries are made with chicken, mutton, lamb, or souse, pig's feet. Favorite desserts are guava duff, sour sop ice cream, benne (sesame seed) cake, and coconut tarts. Boiled fish and grits are often eaten for breakfast. Most food is imported and expensive.

Bahamian Specialties

Fish chowder

Conch fritters

Roast chicken

Peas and rice

Banana pudding

Guava Duff

Serves 8

4 cups flour	1 tsp. salt
1 cup sugar	½ cup vegetable oil
1½ tsp. baking powder	2 cups finely sliced guava

Combine all the ingredients and mix together. Add the oil. Knead approximately 10 minutes until smooth and pliable. Place on a flat surface and roll out ¼ in. thick. Spread sliced guava over the dough. Wrap in foil. Cook in a double boiler for 1 hour.
Cut dough into slices. Pour sauce over the dough.

Sauce

1 lb. butter	1 cup finely sliced guava
½ cup sugar	¼ cup brandy
2 8 oz. tins sweetened condensed milk	

Blend butter and sugar together approximately 15 minutes. Add the condensed milk and guava and blend 2 minutes. Add brandy and blend 1 minute.
Vanilla can be substituted for the brandy.
Recipe courtesy of the Embassy of the Bahamas, Washington, DC

Rum Cake

1 cup butter	2 tsp. baking powder
1 cup sugar	1 tsp. vanilla
1 cup brown sugar	½ cup dark rum
4 eggs	1 cup walnuts, walnuts, almonds, or macadamia nuts
1 cup milk	
3 cups flour	

Preheat oven to 350º
Cream the butter and sugars. Add the eggs, milk, flour, baking powder and vanilla. Stir in the rum and nuts.
Pour into two greased bread pans or cake pans.
Bake for 35 minutes, or until a toothpick comes clean. Remove from pans.
To keep moist pour a little more rum over the cakes.
Dried fruit or raisins can be also be used in the recipe.

Holidays and Special Occasions

Christmas - baked ham and turkey with stuffing, green peas and rice, yam or sweet potatoes, baked macaroni and cheese, potato salad, coleslaw and vegetables.
Boxing Day – Junkanoo (named after John Canoe, an African chieftain) Parade starts at 4AM, ending at 9AM with boiled fish and johnnycakes. Other foods are black cake, ginger beer, apples, grapes, garlic pork, pepper pot, pickled onions and ham
New Year's Eve – is called Watch Night. Everyone parties and goes to church.

Bahama Mama

1 oz. coconut rum	2 oz. pineapple juice
1¼ oz. gold rum	Dash of Angostura Bitters (optional)
1½ oz. Nassau Royale Liqueur	1/6 oz. grenadine
2 oz. orange juice	1 cherry and/or slice of orange or lemon

Mix all liquid ingredients together. Pour into a glass and garnish with cherry or lemon or orange slice.
Recipe courtesy of the Embassy of the Bahamas

Beverages

Sugar Cane was brought by Christopher Columbus from the Canary Islands on his second voyage. Rum is made from the fermented juice of sugar cane which is then boiled to make a syrup, and allowed to crystallize or form molasses. The island rums are white or light colored, 80%. In 1959 the Bacardi Distillery moved some of its operations to New Providence from Cuba. A pineapple rum is also available. A Nassau Royale is a sugar cane liqueur, very sweet and served after dinner. Favorite drinks are Goombay Smash (pineapple juice, rum and apricot brandy), Bahama Delight (grapefruit juice and campari), or a Bahama Mama. Switcha is a lemon, sugar and water mixture. Beer is also produced on the islands. Campari is made from the cascarilla shrub.

Did You Know?

The Arawak drank maize beer and cultivated cassava, guava and yucca.
Bananas were imported to islands from the Canary Islands in the 16th c.
In 1795 all revenue from liquor licenses was turned over to the Church of England.
Andros, the "bonefishing capital of the world" was named in the 16th c "La Isla del Espiritu Santo" "Island of the Holy Spirit".

Bahrain

The Kingdom of Bahrain is an archipelago of thirty-three islands (707 sq. km) in the Persian Gulf. The country has been inhabited since ancient times, and was once part of the Persian Empire. Arab tribes and clans eventually settled here. In 1797 the Al Khalifa moved to Bahrain and became the ruling family. Oil was discovered in 1932 providing a vast income for the kingdom, and before that pearls were retrieved from the coastal waters. The capital is Manama. The official language is Arabic. English, Farsi and Urdu are also spoken. The name Bahrain comes from the Arabic "Two Seas".

Dining Etiquette

The Bahrainis are very hospitable people and you will always be made to feel welcome in a home. If entertained please be prompt. If your host(ess) has removes his/her shoes please remove yours. Please shake hands greeting and departing. Women do not shake hands unless they extend them first. Please accept the tea or coffee offered. When served coffee take the finjan (cup) with your thumb and index finger using your hand. The social hour may be long. Please leave almost after the meal has been served. If you are seated on the floor, cross your legs (no bottom of soles showing), or kneel on one knee. Eat with your right hand, using your hand as a scoop. If you are an honored guest you may be served a sheep's head. Leave some food on your plate to show that you have had an abundant meal. Please reciprocate the hospitality. Families and loyalty to them are very important.

Cuisine

Bahrain has almost no agriculture, though dates, bananas, citrus fruit, mangoes, pomegranates, tomatoes, onions, melons, and cucumber are grown here. Goat, cattle and sheep are raised on the arid land. Fish – hamour (grouper), crayfish, lobster, tuna, safi (rabbit fish), chanad (mackerel), sobaity (sea bream) and shrimp are caught in the coastal waters. Chicken lamb, shrimp or fish are usually served with rice. Fish is grilled, fried or steamed. Spices are used in cooking, especially cinnamon, cardamom, and turmeric.

Bahraini Chickpea Kabab- Kabab Alnikhi

1 tsp. ground coriander seeds
1 tsp. cumin seeds
½ inch fresh ginger
2 cloves garlic
1 cup chickpea flour
1 tsp. ground mixed spices (cinnamon,
cumin, cardamom, cloves).
1 tsp. baking powder

2 grated magi cubes
2 medium onion, chopped
1 tbls. tomato paste
2 medium tomato, grated
½ bunch finely chopped cilantro leaves
2 eggs
½ cup water oil for frying

Roast coriander seeds and cumin seeds until fragrant. Grind after it cools down. And mix it with ½ inch fresh ginger and 2 cloves garlic and beat in the mortar.
Place the chickpea flour, ground mixed spices, and (roasted ground coriander, cumin seeds with ginger and garlic), baking powder into a medium bowl.
Combine all ingredients, except oil and mix well. You could add the water gradually as you mix. Cover and leave aside for an hour.
Place oil in a saucepan, about 1 ½ inches deep, then heat.
Add eggs to the mixture while heating oil and mix well.
Spoon dough, 1 heaping tablespoon of dough at a time, into the oil and fry until light brown, turning kababs over once
Continue until all the dough is finished. Drain on paper towels; then serve warm.
Recipe courtesy of Aysha Murad, Cultural Counselor, Embassy of the Kingdom of Bahrain, Washington, DC

Bahrain Specialties

Harees – wheat dish with meat eaten during amadan
Machboos – spiced fish or meat with rice
Kharoof mahshi – stuffed leg of lamb
Mahamer – sweet rice with dates or sugar
Momowash – rice with small shrimp
Mbezar – rice with dried turmeric and chile powder
Mbasal – rice with sauteed onions
Muaddas – rice and lentil dish
Mattaai – chickpea flour, spices, peanuts, and mung beans served at weddings and holidays
Maghlaq – oatmeal date bread
Sambosa "samosa" – fried pastry with filling
Falafel – deep fried chickpea balls
Shawarma – lamb or chicken cut from a rotating spit, served in pita bread
Samboussas – pastries with spiced meat

Qoozi – lamb stuffed with rice, hard boiled eggs, spices and onions
Khubz – flatbread baked in a special oven
Mahyawa sauce – a fish sauce usually served with khubz
Halwa – sugar dessert with corn flour, rose water, saffron served at weddings
Halwa showaiter – jelly dessert with cornstarch, saffron and nuts
Assidah – whole wheat flour porridge
Legaimaat – deep fried balls with date syrup
Mahala – wheat flour pancake served at weddings and Ramadan
Sago – sago, sugar, and water served at Ramadan

Bahraini Shrimp and Mung Beans Machboos

3 cups water
2 cups basmati rice
½ cup mung beans
2 tomatoes, small cubes
½ kg shrimp (shelled)
3 onions, finely chopped
4 cloves garlic
½ inch ginger, cut into small pieces
¼ cup cilantro leaves, chopped
1 green hot pepper, as desired
2 teaspoons curry powder

1 ½ teaspoons turmeric powder
1 teaspoon cumin powder
2 cinnamon sticks
1 teaspoon cardamom powder
1 whole cardamom
2 tbls. butter
¼ cup dried black lemon powder
4 tbls. oil
Salt according to taste
1 tablespoon tomato paste
1 tbls. lemon juice

Wash and soak rice just 15 minutes before cooking it.
Wash the shrimp. Fry shrimp and garlic in a pan .Cook until the shrimp become opaque in color.
Fry onion and ginger, green hot pepper in butter and oil until golden brown in the cooking pot.
Add the fried shrimp and garlic, tomato cubes, curry powder, cinnamon, bay leaves, cardamom, cilantro, black lemon, cumin, tomato paste, curry powder, turmeric, lemon juice. Stir over heat for 5 minutes until well fried.
Add water. Bring to a boil then simmer for 3-5 minutes.
Drain rice and stir into sauce with Magi cubes or salt.
Add the boiled mung beans.
Bring it to the boil and simmer for 10 minutes.
Cover tightly with aluminum foil.
Simmer over low heat for 25-30 minutes or until rice is cooked.
Serve rice on a large platter.
Recipe courtesy of Aysha Murad, Cultural Counselor, Embassy of the Kingdom of Bahrain. Washington, DC

Holidays and Special Occasions

During Ramadan no food or drink is consumed during the day.
Eid el-Fitr – biryani (rice with meat and spices), sweet pastries and sweetmeats

Beverages

Gahwa – Arabic coffee served in a small handleless glass cup known as a finjan. Drink only three cups and then shake the cup to show you are finished.

Did You Know?

Gahwa was originally used for wine "wine if Islam", until later it was used for the unroasted coffee beans that were ground to keep one awake during ceremonies.

Bangladesh

Bangladesh is bordered by India, Burma (Myanmar) to the southeast and the Bay of Bengal to the south. The borders of Bangladesh were established with the partition of Bengal and India in 1947, when the region became the eastern part of the newly formed Pakistan. The country became independent in 1971. The Bengal region dates back four thousand years, when the region was settled by Dravidian, Tibeto-Burman, and Austro-Asiatic peoples. Bangladesh lies in the fertile Ganges Delta, but is so low lying that monsoons, cyclones, and other natural disasters yearly besiege the country. Dhaka, the capital, under Mughal rule in the 17th century, was known as Jahangir Nagar and was a provincial capital and trading center. It developed into a large city under the British in the 19th century. The official language is Bangla. The country is 90% Muslim.

Dining Etiquette

Please arrive promptly when invited for a meal. Shake hands greeting and departing. Women only shake hands if they extend theirs. Women will greet with the nod of their head. Men when speaking usually stand close together. Gifts are usually given by family members during Ramadan and the Hajj. However if you are visiting a home please bring sweets, flowers (not white), or chocolates. Gifts are presented with both hands, and are not opened until later. Meals are usually divided by sex. You will most likely be seated on an asan, a small carpet on the floor. The meal will be served on a large platter (thala) with the rice in the center, salt, chilies and limes on the upper right side, and bowls (batis) of food along the top. Please wash your hands before eating and eat with your right hand. Do not start until the oldest person does. If you pass something do so with the right hand. Dishes are eaten with a small amount of rice starting with ghee poured over the rice; then shukto – bitter herbs or vegetables, dals with roasted or fried vegetables. The vegetable dishes follow, then mutton or chicken, and dessert. Paan (betel leaves) are given to help digestion. In other homes there may be a dining table with chairs and utensils, but the food is still served on the thala.

Cuisine

The Bangladesh (Bengali) cuisine has been influenced by the Darvidians, Aryans, Muslims and later the British, then the Chinese. Dhaka was part of the early trade route with Delhi. Tea was introduced by the British.

The dishes use ginger, instead of garlic and onions in curries; saffron, mace; ghee; fish from the rivers, often fried in a spicy paste; pears, tomatoes, cucumbers, mangos, bananas, lychee, watermelon, bamboo, palm, jackfruit, red lentils, mung beans, mustard oil (shorsher tel) and paste, and coconut. Dishes also include garlic, ginger, coriander, cumin, mustard seed, poppy seed, turmeric, green chili peppers, limes, cardamom, cinnamon and yogurt. Rice is cooked puffed, fried, boiled, beaten, or left to ferment, and served at the meal. The major crops are jute, sugar cane, tea, tobacco, oil seed and pulse (which is used mainly as dal).

The south is close to the sea, so fish, fried and dried fish are used mainly in cooking. Around the central region, including Dhaka fried rice and meat dishes are popular. In the north and northwest curries, spices, and fish are used; and in the northeast lake fish, fruit and pickles. Seafood include, hilsa, rohu, koi, magur, shing, pangas, prawn, lobster, shrimp, pomfret, carp and catfish.

Chicken Biryani

Serves 6

3 – 3 ½ lb. chicken, but into pieces	3 tsp. red chili powder
2 cups uncooked basmati rice	1 tbls. coriander powder
4 tsp. whole garam masala	5 tbls. oil
4 tsp. ground garam masala	2 tsp. turmeric
3 cups water	2 cups yogurt
2 tbls. butter, softened	1 medium tomato, chopped
4 cloves garlic, chopped	4 bay leaves
1 medium onion, chopped	½ tsp. saffron
4 tsp. fresh grated ginger	2 tbls. rose water

Put 2 tsp. ground garam masala, bay leaf, rice and water in a saucepan. Bring to boil. Simmer until water is gone and rice is tender.
Heat oil in a pan. Add whole garam masala and onions and cook until onions are golden brown and tender. Add garlic, ginger, chili powder, coriander, turmeric, yogurt, and tomato. Cook for 5 minutes. Add chicken. Cook until chicken is tender, about 20-25 minutes.
Preheat oven to 350°
In a baking dish layer the rice, then chicken, butter, rest of garam masala. Top with rice layer. Sprinkle over it saffron and rose water. Cover and bake 10 minutes.

Marinade

1½ tsp. red chili powder	1 cup yogurt
1 tbls. fresh ginger, grated	Salt to taste
2 cloves garlic, minced	
1 tsp. Garam Masala	
1 tsp. turmeric	

In a bowl combine the marinade ingredients.
Add chicken. Cover for 1 hour.

Bangladeshi Specialties

Biryani – meat or vegetables, spices, rice and yogurt

Bhorta – mashed vegetables and mustard oil, often mixed with fish or shrimp

Pulao – rice with bay leaf, cinnamon sticks, and fried onion

Singara –spicy potato and vegetables, fired in a dough

Roti kalai – lentil flat bread

Korma – curried lamb

Bhuna – spicy pastes (red chili, ginger, cinnamon, onion, and garlic) are used to cook with meat, vegetables or fish

Bhendi bhaji – fried okra

Begun bhaja – fried eggplant

Dal – lentils sautéed with spices, onions, and garlic

Shorche ilish – fried ilish with mustard onion sauce

Makher Taukari - fish curry with red chili powder, turmeric, garlic, onion, green chilies, and cilantro

Saak-er Ghanto – made from various vegetables such as eggplant, pumpkin, potato and spinach.

Shami kebab – curried meatballs

Chicken tikka (grilled chicken)

Shish kebab – skewered lamb, beef or chicken

Masala –mixed spices, including hot chilies or turmeric (hot), used to coat food

Chana chaat – chickpeas with onions, tomatoes, spices, popped rice and fried vegetables

Samosas – fried dough with meat, vegetables, cheese, and potatoes

Achar – pickles - lemon, ginger, onion, garlic, etc. Often mixed pickle with several vegetables or fruit indredients is also made.

Luchi – deep fried flat bread

Paratha – deep fried bread that is often stuffed

Lassi – yogurt drink, often with fruit or tomatoes added

Sabzi – mixed vegetables with ground ginger, garlic, onion, cumin, and chili pepper pastes

Naan – flatbread

Pitha – fried rice flour snack with different fillings

Mishti doi – sweet yogurt

Ras malai – dessert made from paneer (cottage cheese) balls and served with clotted cream and ground nuts and spices

Rosogolla – chhana (cottage cheese) balls with semolina flour in a sugar syrup

Pantua – cottage cheese fried in ghee or oil and served with syrup

Chomchom – sweet of paneer, water, milk, sugar, flour, saffron and cardamom

Khir – rice pudding

Muri – puffed rice

Jhal muri – spicy puffed rice

Panch phoran – spice mixture of carum roxburghianum seeds, cumin, black cumin, fenugreek, and anise

Beverages

Tea gardens rise on the hill slopes of Sylhet and Chittagong districts. Tea (cha), fruit drinks, water, Borhani (a spiced drink made from yoghurt with spices drunk with biryani, or soft drinks are served. Alcoholic beverages are forbidden, though Mod or Bangla are homemade liquors and choo, a rice beer. Hunter Beer is now legally produced in the country, as is Siraji brand whiskey, produced by the Jamuna Group, part of Crown Beverage Ltd.

Vegetable Samosas

Phyllo pastry, thawed and wrapped in a damp towel.

Filling

3 large potatoes, boiled and mashed	¼ tsp. turmeric
2 tbls. vegetable oil	2 green chilies, seeded and chopped
½ tsp. black mustard seeds	1 cup fresh peas
1 onion, chopped	1 tbls. water
1 tsp. ground coriander	2 tbls. coriander
1 tsp. ground cumin	2 tbls. mint
1 tbls. fresh ginger, grated	oil

Heat the oil in a skillet. Add the mustard seeds, then onions and ginger, cooking until onions are tender. Stir in the coriander, cumin, ginger, and turmeric. Add the potatoes, chilies, peas, and water. Cook for 5 minutes. Stir in coriander and mint. Cool to room temperature.
Cut phyllo into strips about 3x3 inch squares.
Place a spoonful of the mixture along the diagonal of each square. Fold over to match other side. Seal with oil or a little water.
To deep fry the samosas heat 2-3 inches of oil in a skillet. Deep fry the samosas for 2-3 minutes. Place in the oven to keep warm.
To bake the samosas preheat the oven to 375°. Bake in the oven 10-15 minutes or until golden brown. Serve hot.
Lamb can be substituted for the potatoes and peas.

Holidays and Special Occasions

Winter Harvest Festival – pitha (rice flour sweets)
Ramadan – fasting from sunrise to sunset
Id-ul-Fitr (breaking of fast after Ramadan) – vermicelli in milk, korma curries of chicken, beef or lamb, dals, pollaus, shawi – dessert with rice noodles fried in butter, and boiled in milk and sugar
Id-uz-Zaha (from the Koran and Bible the sacrifice of Isaac by Abraham) – sacrifice lambs, goats, rams, cows, or camels. Three days of feasting – pollaus, curries, raytas, curries, barbequed meats
Shab e Baraat – fireworks and feasting to celebrate God's riches
Muharram – celebrates the saint Hussain who fell in battle against Yazid over 1400 years ago. – zarda (rice with saffron) and kheer (milk and rice pudding with cashews and raisins)
At feasts, weddings, and other rituals, paan, chewing betel leaves with areca nut; spicy beef dishes, kheer, biryani.
Weddings and births - Laddu (chickpea flour, sugar, cooked in ghee and shaped into a ball); Rosogolla, Sandesh, Pantua and Mishti Doi
Biryani is part of ceremonies like weddings, and sometimes puffed rice (muri) is used.

Barbados

Barbados, the easternmost island of the Caribbean covers 166 square miles made up of coralline limestone with rocky coastlines, rolling hills and beaches. The country was nicknamed "Little England" and English manor houses surrounded by sugar cane fields and rows of trees dot the countryside. Bridgetown, the capital took its name from Chamberlain Bridge, formerly in the heart of the city. Once an Amerindian island with Arawak and Caribs as original settlers, the island received its name from Portuguese explorers "Isla de los Barbados". The ficus trees appeared to have beards! Later, the English settled the island developing the sugar cane plantations which made Barbados part of the Triangular Trade chain. English is the official language.

Pepperpot Stew

Serves 6

1 quart water
2 lbs. beef stew meat
½ lb. salt pork, or bacon
1 large onion, chopped
1 red pepper, chopped
1 green pepper, chopped
2 large cloves garlic, minced
1 large leek, chopped, or 4 scallions, chopped
1 tsp. thyme

¼ tsp. cloves
½ tsp. marjoram
½ tsp. or more cayenne, or hot pepper sauce
1 carrot, sliced
4 okra, sliced
1 large yam, peeled and diced
1 ½ cups coconut milk
¼ cup dark rum

In a Dutch oven or large pan combine the ingredients, except coconut milk and rum. Bring to a boil. Cover and simmer for at least one hour, until meat and vegetables are tender. Add more water, if needed. Stir in coconut milk and rum.
This can also be baked in the oven at 350° for 1 hour, or longer.

Cuisine

Eating in Barbados is a true island experience with a mix of European, African and island influences. These include a variety of fruits and vegetables, fish, rice, spices and rum. Plentiful fish are lobster, shrimp, flying fish, dorado, red snapper, turtle, tuna, kingfish, and Crane Chubb. Fruit and vegetables include mangoes, papayas, bananas, cucumbers, guava, avocados, coconuts, squash, tomatoes, breadfruit, and eggplant; and meat – goat, black-bellied sheep, and cows.

Dining Etiquette

Please be prompt when invited for a meal. Bajans are very warm and friendly, and very hospitable. Shake hands and smile greeting and departing. Good friends will embrace. If entertained at home please bring flowers or a gift for the house. Drinks will usually be served. Please wait for your hostess to seat you. Food is eaten continental style, fork in the left hand and knife in the right hand. Tables are set with utensils for all courses, and several courses might be served. The extended family is still very important, and several generations may be included in meals. Hands are often used when conversing. Do not place your hands on your hips as this is a sign of defiance. As in many English households tea may be served in the afternoon.

Barbadian Specialties

Conkies – rolled banana leaves with cornmeal, raisins, sweet potatoes, pumpkin and coconut
Pickled cucumber
Creamy yam pie
Boiled breadfruit with Creole sauce
Fried and steamed flying fish (The fried flying fish were the best I ever ate. Of course, they were prepared by the cook in the home we were staying!)
Pigeon peas and rice
Cou-cou- cornmeal and okra
Jug-jug – Guinea corn and green peas

Roti – curried meat in a a dough
Christophenes – a squash-like vegetable
Buljol – cold salad of codfish, tomatoes, onions, pepper and celery
Callaloo soup – okra, crabmeat, coconut, and pumpkin
Sea moss jelly
Pudding and souse – sausage made from pig's blood and head cheese
Green turtle
Do try the thick molasses and brown (less refined) sugar

Holidays and Special Occasions

Easter – ham, hot cross buns,
Oistins Fish Festival – Easter weekend
Crop Over Festival – mid July to early August – to celebrate the end of the sugar cane harvest
Christmas – jug-jug (beef stew), peas and rice, macaroni pie, turkey, ham, black cakes, guava duff, pudding and eggnog
Boxing Day – visiting family and friends
Weddings are held in churches, followed by receptions in a local hall, restaurant or hotel with much drinking and feasting, and elaborate wedding cakes.
Sunday and holiday picnics

Beverages

Barbados has been making rum for over 350 years! It is noted for dark or heavy brown rum. The drink is made from crushed sugar cane that is extracted from molasses, then fermented. Dunder (residue from previous distillations) or yeast is added and the mixture aged in charred oaken casks. Sugar caramel is added for the very dark color. Rum was once known as "Kill Devil"!

Belarus

Belarus is bordered by Russia to the north and east, Ukraine to the south, Poland to the west, and Lithuania and Latvia to the north. Belarus was once inhabited by Slavic tribes and then the Varangians. The Kievan Rus' state was founded about 862, and then the region was part of the Duchy of Polatsk, the Grand Duchy of Lithuania, and the Polish-Lithuanian Commonwealth. Belarus first declared independence on March 25, 1918, forming the Belarusian People's Republic but the Bolsheviks and the Red Army took over and it became the Byelorussian Soviet Socialist Republic in 1919. During World War II the country was occupied by the Germans. Belarus became a republic in 1991. The capital Minsk, dates back to at least the 11th c. Belarusian is the official language.

Fried Black Radish with Honey

2 large black radishes
2 tbls. olive oil or butter

2 tbls. honey

Peel the radishes and soak in cold water for at least 15 minutes. Cut into very thin slices.
Heat the olive oil or butter in a skillet. Add the radish slices and cook until crispy. Drain on a paper towel.
Pu radishes on a plate and drizzle with honey.

Draniki (Grated Potato Pancakes)

Serves 6

6 potatoes, peeled and grated
1 medium onion, peeled and grated
Vegetable oil

Salt
Sour cream

Combine the potatoes, onions, and a small amount of salt in a bowl.
Heat some oil in a skillet. Drop a spoonful of the potatoes mixture in the oil. Turn when browned and crispy, about 2-3 minutes per side.
Serve with sour cream.

Dining Etiquette

Men shake hands greeting and departing, keeping good eye contact. If they know each other well, they will hug. Women will kiss friends three times on alternating cheeks starting with the left. Women should initiate a handshake with a man. Older people in Belarus will introduce themselves using their first name and the name from their father and you should use this when addressing them. To show hospitality, a host traditionally presents an offering of bread and salt when greeting a guest or visitor. Beverages will be served. The hostess will seat the guests for a meal. Food is eaten continental style with the fork in the left and knife in the right. The toast is "na zdo ro vie" "to your health". The Belarusans eat a light breakfast and heavier meals at lunch and dinner

Many Belarusians own dachas (country houses) where they have gardens, and might bring visitors on weekends. Banya (steam baths) are popular, where you can jump into snow, cold water or lake afterwards, and then are hit with damp birch twigs. Personal relationships are very important. Whistling inside a building is considered bad luck!

Cuisine

The Belarus cuisine has been influenced by the agricultural products produced there, and the cuisines of Russia, Ukraine, Lithuania, and Poland. Traditional Belarus dishes developed over a period of time such as goose with green peppers; pork and salted pork fat, potato, noodle, and pasta dishes. Potatoes have been an important part of the diet since the 18th century. Meat was usually eaten on special occasions. To preserve meat it was salted or dried. Dishes will include vegetables such as carrots, potatoes, sorrel, pumpkins, cabbage, turnips, black radish, sorrel, nettles, lentils, kidney beans, beans, peas, mushrooms, tomatoes, cucumbers, beetroot, and onions; grains – rye, barley, oats, and wheat; herbs – garlic, fennel, parsley, linseed, horseradish, calamus, mustard, juniper, caraway, coriander, basil; meats that are cured or smoked – hams, chicken, goose, turkey, pork, mutton, beef, duck, sausages, salami; fish from the rivers – trout, perch, carp, sturgeon, eel, bream, pike, tench, and herring; fruit – wild strawberries, plums, cherries, ashberries, canker berries, bilberries, cranberries, red whortlberry, raspberries, pears, and apples; dairy products – cheese, butter, sour cream, curd cheese, siyr (fermented cheese), cream, and ice cream. Game such as elk, deer, boar and beaver were consumed. Rye bread is served at meals. Mushrooms can be pickled, dried or powdered. Breads are mainly made from rye, are heavy, and use a special leavening. Caraway, linseed, sunflower, or rye seeds can be incorporated into the bread.

Specialties

Borshch, a soup made with beetroot, and served hot with sour cream.
Perepecha – flat cakes
Polivka – soup of cereals and vegetables
Zatirika – red beet soup served with dumplings
Pike Perch a la Radiziwill
Dracheny - potato dish with mushrooms
Machanka – pork stew

Kelecki – potatoes stuffed with meat
Machanka z blinami - meat with pancakes and special white sauce
Okroshka – kvass and vegetable soup
Eggs stuffed with mushrooms
Pirozhki – meat or cabbage pasties
Harbuz – pumpkin pudding with noodles
Shchy – cabbage soup
Morkva- carrot

Gryzhanka – turnip soup
Garbuzok – pumpkin soup
Pirazhki – potato patties
Karavaj - honey, eggs, raisins, sour cream, butter
Kanun, Babina Kasa - porridge
Kulaha - berry pancake with rye flour and honey
Yushka, galki, bream, and tench – types of fish, baked or boiled

Zatrika- dough boiled in water, then milk and salt pork added
Potatoes with beetroot salad
Cucumbers with honey
Mushrooms – can be salted, dried, pickled, or served fresh
Paparac kvietka – fern flower salad
Piernik – cake with halvah (a paste made of nuts, sugar and oil) and jam
Solodukha – malt dough

Holidays and Special Occasions

During Lent it was forbidden to eat meat and dairy products, a lot of fish and mushrooms. Zhur, a soup of meat or milk and oat water, is made prior to Lent.

For Christmas Eve bread is not cut, but broken with one's hands.

On Christmas hay is put on a table, covered with a cloth and then the table set. Twelve dishes are served to symbolize the twelve apostles of Christ with him at the Last Supper. Dishes are made with mushrooms, fish

Kuccia - barley porridge for Christmas served with butter or fat

Christmas to New Year's – fortune telling games, including one that uses a rooster and corn. Young maidens sit and when the rooster choses to eat corn from one of them, she will be the next to marry.

Weddings – round loaf of bread

Birthday parties – kasha (boiled wheat pudding with raisins, sugar, eggs and baked)

Matchmaking – a matchmaker would arrive at a potential bride's home and offer food and drinks. If the suitor was acceptable, the matchmaker and he would appear at the bride-to-be's home with vodka and the bride's parents would provide the food. This might be repeated several times.

Funerals – after the service a meal is held for family and friends

Pyachysta is a traditional holiday dish, a boiled, stewed or roasted sucking pig, fowl or pork or beef.

Beverages

Vodka (harelka) is the main alcoholic beverage, though beer and wine are also drunk. Vodka was first produced here in the 15th c. Kvas is made from fermenting bread of wheat, rye or barley. Black tea, coffee, soft and fruit drinks and mineral water are also served. Kompot is a juice, mainly from red berries with which sugar and water are added. Maducha is a honey drink. Beloveszhskaya is a bitter liquor are made from over 100 different herbs. Kulaga is a thick beverage made from berries, flour, sugar, and honey.

Belgium

The Kingdom of Belgium lies centrally in Europe bordered by the Netherlands, the North Sea, Germany, Luxembourg, and France. The country is comprised of a maritime plain in the north, hills and valleys to the south, and the Ardennes Forest in the east. Brussels, the capital was founded in the 10th c by the Bishop of Cambrai. The earliest known inhabitants were the Belgae tribes. Julius Caesar invaded in 57BC, making the region part of the Roman Empire. Later invaders were the Franks (3rd c AD), the Celts, part of the Holy Roman Empire, The Austrian Habsburgs, and Napoleon annexed it in 1794. It became independent in 1830. Three languages – Flemish, French, and German are spoken.

Asparagus, Flemish Style

Servings: 4-6

3 lbs. white asparagus
8 tbls. (1 stick) unsalted butter
3 hard-cooked and peeled large eggs
1½ tsp. fresh lemon juice

¼ cup fresh chopped parsley
Salt and ground black pepper
Pinch of grated nutmeg

Trim the white asparagus with a vegetable peeler, from just under tip to stem end, to remove woody skin.
Bring a large pot of salted water to boil.
Bundle asparagus up and tie with kitchen twine. Trim ends evenly. Gently place in boiling water and immediately lower heat to simmer. Cover pot. Simmer for approximately 15-30 minutes, depending on thickness of stems. When tender, remove bundle and carefully drain on kitchen towel, being careful of tender tips.
Melt the butter over low heat in a small saucepan. If the hard-cooked eggs are completely cold, plunge into hot asparagus water for 1 minute. Remove, dry and peel.
In a small bowl, mash the complete egg with a fork. Add the melted butter, lemon juice, parsley, nutmeg and salt and pepper. Mix thoroughly.
Arrange the asparagus on individual plates. Pour Flemish sauce to cover the middle of the asparagus. Serve immediately while everything is still warm.
Recipe courtesy of Dr. Michelle Loewinger, U.S. Embassy, Brussels

Dining Etiquette

Be punctual for a meal. Please shake hands greeting and departing. Ladies precede men through doors, and offer their hands first. When greeting someone you know please kiss three times, alternating checks. Men or younger people should stand when a lady or older people enter the room. Please bring a gift – flowers (not chrysanthemums which are a sign of death), or something special from your country. Drinks or an aperitif will be served. The hostess will seat the guests. Please sit after she has been seated. The male guest of honor will be to her right. Do not start until the hostess begins. When eating do so continental style – fork in the left, knife in the right hand. Fish is served with an additional knife and fork. Wrists should be kept on the table, no elbows. Please do not talk with food in your mouth. When finished place your knife and fork across the middle of the plate with the fork tines down and the cutting edge of the knife towards you. Tea and/or coffee are served after the meal. Toasts are made by raising the glass, catching the eye of the person being toasted, and then saying "A votre santé" – French; "Gzeonheid" – Flemish; or "to your health".

Mussels with Herbs

Serves 4

24 mussels in shells	½ cup fresh bread crumbs
2 cloves garlic, minced	2 tbls. butter, melted
2 tbls. parsley, finely chopped	Juice of ½ lemon
1 tsp. tarragon	Lemon slices

Preheat the oven to 350°
Scrub the mussels and place on a cookie sheet. Place in oven for just a couple of minutes until shells open. Remove from oven and let cool for a couple of minutes. Remove one shell and leave the mussel in the remaining shell.
In a bowl combine the garlic, parsley, tarragon, bread crumbs and butter. Sprinkle with the lemon juice.
Top the mussels with the bread crumb mixture.
Bake for 5-10 minutes until just warmed.
Serve hot with lemon slices.
Clams or oysters can be substituted for the mussels.

Cuisine

Belgian food is a wonderful blend of fresh vegetables – endive and asparagus; fruits – plums, cherries, strawberries, and grapes; Ardennes ham; sausages; game – hare, roebuck, wild boar, quail, partridge and pheasant; fish – eel, lobster, oysters, mussels, sole, herring, shrimp, crayfish and fresh water fish. Chocolate was introduced via Spain from the Americas in the 17th c and has been world renowned ever since. French fries are often served with mayonnaise, not ketchup Breakfast is usually coffee or tea, bread or rolls, jams and butter. Dinner is served at 7 or 8 PM.

Belgian Specialties

Waterzooi – chicken or fish soup
Bouef a la flamanade – beef and beer
Carbonnade – beef and beer stew
Belgian frites – fried potatoes
Moules frites – mussels and fried potatoes

Waffles (gaufres) – served with whipped cream and strawberries, butter and sugar, and other combinations.
Hochepot – meat, vegetable and herb stew
Tarte liegeoise – fruit tarte
Speculoos – sweet cookies

Holidays and Special Occasions

Carnival – parades, fancy costumes, parties and lots of food
Easter – colored Easter eggs and chocolates in the shape of rabbits and eggs; lamb
December 6 – Sinterklaas visits children bringing presents and food which is placed in shoes left out for him.
Weddings – wedding receptions are very elaborate occasions with much feasting and dancing.

Beverages

The Belgians are known for their beers which are drunk with meals rather than as cocktails. Beer making goes back over 1000 years, mainly in the monasteries, six of which are still producing beer. Traditional beers made in abbeys are known as quadruple with dried fruit flavors. Beers are of several types, the best known being Gueuze which is made by spontaneous fermentation with wheat, malted barley, and three year old hops; and Lambic also made by spontaneous fermentation though no yeast is added. It is stored in barrels for several years, then bottled with a cork and wire and allowed further fermentation. Kriek – Lambic is a cherry flavored beer. De Struise Brouwewrs, Picobrouwerji Alvinne, De Leite, and de la Sienne are among the newer brewers.St. Louis Framboise, produced by Brouwerij Van Honsebrouck, is fruit lambic, made partially with raspberry juice. Anheuser-Busch InBev is the world's largest brewer. Wine, beer or mineral water is served with meals.

Did You Know?

A Pot van Olen is a 3 handled beer mug from Olen that was used by horse riders, so they could drink while riding with their servants!
A drink call Mort Subite got its name "sudden death" from dice players in Kobbegem who played games and might have to be called back suddenly to the office, and played "sudden death" to end the game!
St. Feuillien Paskeol Beer (Easter beer) is made at the Brasserie St.-Feuillien in Roeulx.
Belgian chocolates are world famous. Cacao was first grown in South America, but Spaniards brought it to Europe, and to Belgian in the 17th c when Belgium was ruled by Spain. When the Congo became part of Belgium cacao was also exported to Belgium. Today there are over 300 companies that produce chocolate candies.

Belize

The small country of Belize lies between Mexico to the north and west, Guatemala to the south and west, and the Caribbean Sea to the east. The coastline consists of the second longest barrier reef in the world, cays, and is flat and swampy. Inland are the Maya Mountains. The history of Belize dates from Mezo-American cultures that go back to 6000 BC. Starting c 1000 BC the Olmec, predecessors of the Mayans appeared. Spanish explorers appeared in the 16th c and built trading posts and missions. The first British settlement was in 1631, and the country was later called British Honduras. During the 19th c sugar cane was introduced and mainly exported to England. Belize is still a member of the British Commonwealth, but became independent in 1981. Belmopan is the capital.

Etiquette

Please be punctual when invited for a meal. Shake hands greeting and departing. Women don't usually shake hands, but if good friends will hug with one arm, and pat on the back when meeting. The hostess will introduce the guests. Please bring a gift – wine, whiskey, Scotch, candy, or something for the home. Drinks – beer or rum- will be served before dinner. Guests are served first and may eat first. Do accept all food offered. Take a small amount if you are not sure you will like it. When finished, push your plate forward with the silverware together. Dessert and coffee are not usually taken after the meal. The toast is "Cheers" or "To your health".

Beans and Rice

Serves 4

1 can red kidney beans, drained, or fresh red kidney beans; dried kidney beans need to be soaked overnight
2 tbls. vegetable oil
1 small onion, peeled and chopped

½ cup green pepper, chopped
1 tsp. chili powder
1 cup rice
¾ cup water
¾ cup coconut milk

In a pan heat the oil and sauté onions and pepper until tender. Add beans and chili and cook until beans are very soft.
In another pan bring the water and rice to a boil. Turn to simmer until rice is tender. Stir in the coconut milk and the beans.
The beans can also be served over the rice.

Cuisine

The cuisine of Belize is a mix of Mesoamerican, British, Scottish, African, East Indian, Mexican, and Caribbean influences. For thousands of years the Mayans raised corn, beans, squash, sweet potatoes, and vanilla, which are still used in cooking. The Mayan made offerings to the gods in plantings, and knew that the fields should lie fallow for two seasons after planting. The habanero pepper is only grown on the Yucatan Peninsula. Mesoamerican products include tomatoes, peppers, squash, pumpkin, avocado, papaya, corn, sweet potatoes, cotton, tobacco, turkeys, and vanilla. Sugar cane is a major crop and exported. Stann Creek is the center of the citrus industry, where the main crops are oranges, bananas, mangoes, and grapefruit. Cacao is also grown. Maize is used to make tortillas, stews, drinks, and flour. Found in some dishes will be gibnut (a rodent), armadillo, iguana, conch, and sea turtle.

Breakfast is eaten 6:30-7 am and may consist of eggs, tortillas, oatmeal, breads, coffee or tea. Lunch is between 12-2 pm and is the heaviest meal of the day with rice and beans, meat, fish, or chicken, soup, tortillas and salad. Dinner is served 6-9 pm and is similar to lunch.

Belize Specialties

Red kidney beans and rice; rice and beans with coconut milk; or stewed rice and beans served with chicken, meat, or fish.

A boil up consists of yams, plantains, cabbage, pickled pig tails, steamed fish with a sauce of onions, tomatoes and coconut oil.

Local hot sauce made from Habanera peppers (very spicy)

Curried dishes

Cochinita Pibil is slow roasted pork with annatto seed paste and wrapped in plantain leaves

Popular Creole dishes are – cowfoot soup; conch soup with okra; coconut milk bread; stewed or fried chicken; fried fish; iguana; and for dessert bread, rice or sweet potato puddings.

Cashew nuts are widely grown, and their fruit is used to make jellies and wines.

Fish include squid; conch – fried, fritters, soup or ceviche; rock or spiny lobster; shark; turtle; shrimp; barracuda; snapper; sea bass; halibut; sailfish; marlin; grouper; tuna; and abalone.

Plantains are baked or fried.

Gacho – flour tortilla with cheese, beans, and a tomato sauce

Chimole – stew of chicken, pork or beef with eggs or corn

Escabeche is a chicken soup seasoned with oregano and thyme, lightly broiled, then roasted and served in a light and clear chicken soup seasoned with onions, black pepper, allspice, and Jalapeno pepper.

Panadas – corn dough with fish or refried bean filling and a sauce

Garnaches – tortillas with refried beans, onions and cheese

Fried plantains

Johnny cakes with coconut milk

Soursoup ice cream

Cassava pudding

Fruit Cake

Dukunu (stuffed corn husks)

Corn husks

4 cups corn fresh from cob, about 4-6 ears

3 tbls. butter

½ cup coconut milk

Salt

1 tbls. sugar

2 tsp. baking powder

Preheat oven to 400°

Place the corn in a baking dish and coat with the butter. Bake in the oven for 20 minutes, or until tender. Remove from oven and coconut milk, a little salt, sugar and baking powder. Place in a food processor until smooth.

Spoon 2 tbls. mixture into a corn husk. Fold one side to other and then seal ends.

Steam in a steamer for about 30 minutes.

Holidays and Special Occasions

March 9 – Baron Bliss Day – fishing and sailing regattas

Holy Saturday, Easter Sunday, Easter Monday

Battle of St. George's Caye Day – September 10th – in 1798 British buccaneers fought with the Spanish over the territory of Belize and won. Today the event is celebrated with parades, local foods, drink and music.

Independence Day – September 21st – carnivals, local arts and crafts, music, and local dishes

Garifuna Day – November 19th – this commemorates the arrival of the Garinagus (Black Caribs) in the south in 1823. There is a reenactment of the arrival and Garinagu dishes prepared with local vegetables and seafood.

Christmas – ham, turkey, rice and beans, potato salad, black fruitcake, white relleno (soup with pork-stuffed chicken and raisins), pebre (roasted pork and gravy), tamales with ground meat or chicken are served in plantain leaves at Christmas, and rumpopo (eggnog)

Beverages

Belize produces beer and rum. Two popular drinks are rum popo - rum, condensed milk, and eggs; and seaweed – agar, milk, sugar and alcohol. Belikin Beer is named for the ancient Mayan name for Belize and means "Road to the Sea". Craboo and blackberry wine are also produced.

Cashew wine is made from fermented cashew nut.

Did You Know?

The largest mango plantation in the world is located north of Dangriga.

The Mayans used cacao for currency.

The Mennonites in Blue Creek and Shipyard engage in agriculture, have their own style of dress and language, and originally came from Pennsylvania.

Friday is considered an unlucky day; Saturday and Monday lucky days.

Coca Cola gave a large tract of land to the Nature Conservancy for the enlargement of the Rio Bravo Conservation Area.

Benin

The Republic of Benin, is a country in West Africa, bordering Togo to the west, Nigeria to the east and Burkina Faso and Niger to the north. Abomey, the capital was the former capital of the Dahomey Empire which ruled much of West Africa from the 1600s until about 1900. The 17th c royal palace was once the largest structure (3 miles in circumference) in West Africa, as each king added on to it. Much of it was torched in 1892 by King Behazin, so it would not be captured by the French. Until 1960 Benin was a French colony. The country was called Dahomey until 1975, and has been a Democratic government since 1991. The capital is Porto-Novo but the seat of government is Cotonou. The official language is French, with Fon, Yoruba, and approximately 50 others spoken. The people are known as Beninois.

Dining Etiquette

Please be prompt, and hopefully speak French. Shake hands with those present. Friends may kiss on the cheek. Your host will pour you a drink and take a sip before handing it to you. You then take a sip, and spit a little on the floor before drinking. This shows the drink is safe, and you are remembering the dead. Hospitality offering food and drink is part of the culture. Eating may be done sitting on the floor or at a table. Food is eaten with the right hand fingers. Never eat or present something to someone with the left hand. The food is served communally with a starch and sauce.

Cuisine

Benin is mainly a wooded savannah and semiarid plateaus in the north, and in the south a coastal plain with many agricultural products. In the south the main crop is corn served with beef or pork, or seafood such as prawns, crabs, and lobsters. In the north yams or millet couscous are served with peanut or tomato sauces. Most of the food is very spicy. The hot sauce is called "pillipilli. Rice, couscous, beans, and fruit are used in cooking. It makes use of vegetables, corn, yams, cassava, millet, fish and chicken, rice, and porridge. There is little meat. Different flours are WO (corn flour), amala (yam flour), and gari (ground cassava). Oranges, bananas, mandarin oranges, pineapples, kiwi, tomatoes, avocado, cheese, and peanuts are also used in the dishes. Okra is used as a vegetable and to thicken stews. Fish are smoked, dried, or fresh when served in the south. Most cooking is still done outdoors, and most homes do not have refrigerators.

Kuli Kuli (fried peanut balls)

1 cup roasted salted peanuts
1 tsp. ground ginger
¼ tsp. cayenne

1 tbls. water
Peanut oil

Place the ingredients in a food processor until a paste forms. Place in a towel and wring out any excess oil.
In a bowl combine the peanuts, ginger, cayenne and water. Form into small balls.
Heat the oil in a skillet. Fry the balls until golden brown.

Benin Specialties

Ago Glain – shellfish or crabs in a tomato and onion sauce with peanut butter, palm oil and chilies.
Akassa - cornmeal porridge or pap, served as the base for a stew
Aloko – deep-fried plantain slices.
Akpan - fried corn dumplings served with a dipping sauce
Smoked fish - fish smoked over an open fire.
Fufu and garri - paste from yam or cassava tubers
Moyo - sauce served with fried fish, made from tomatoes, onions and peppers.
Peanut soup - peanut, tomato, and carrot soup served with chicken.
Yovo doko - doughnuts, also called beignet.

Akkara - fritters made from skinned black-eyed peas.
Calalu- stew of meat and greens in a tomato, palm oil and hot chili sauce with okra and dried prawns
Sauce d'Arachide - peanut sauce of onion, peanut butter and tomato paste with ground chilies served with meat on a bed of rice
Wagasi in Sauce - Wagasi cheese served in a tomato-based sauce with chilies, garlic and onions.
Pate – pounded cassava dish that is dipped into spicy sauces
Lamounou dessi is a sauce made with fish, smoked shrimp, vegetables and chilies.

Holidays and Special Occasions

August 15 – pilgrimages and yam festivals
Voodoo, the national holiday - ago glan is made from shellfish, tomatoes, onions, and hot sauce.

Beverages

The national beer is La Beninoise, a pale lager. Tchouk (Choukachou) is the millet beer which is brewed locally in Benin. Palm wine is also produced.

Did You Know?

Ganvie is said to be the largest stilt village in Africa. Over 20,000 people live in this fishing village. After each military exercise, 40 captives were sacrificed, their blood mixed with palm oil and alcohol, then poured into the temple's ground in Abomey to provide nourishment for ancestors.

Bermuda

Bermuda is a 20.6 square mile archipelago, comprised of seven main islands, about 600 miles off the U.S. east coast. Hamilton, the capital, was founded in 1815. The history of the island dates from 1503 when Juan de Bermudez, a Spanish explorer, discovered the islands. The first English settlers arrived in 1609. Bermuda is a self-governing British colony.

Dining Etiquette

Please be prompt when invited out. Appropriate gifts are flowers, wine, or something for the hostess. Lilies are for funerals and Easter. Please shake hands greeting and departing. Men stand when introduced to ladies, and hold chairs and doors for them. Drinks and hors d'ouevres will be served. The hostess will escort guests to the table with the guest of honor to her right. Food may be passed or served. Food is eaten with the fork in the left hand, knife in the right. When finished place the knife and fork together. Dessert and coffee are then served. Thank the hostess departing, and please write a thank you note. Some restaurants and clubs may require jackets after 6PM. For garden parties, ladies wear light colored dresses and hats. The Governor is introduced as "His Excellency". The toast is "Cheers", or "to your health".

Fish Chowder

Serves 8

8 red potatoes, diced	½ stick butter
½ lb. smoked bacon	1 tsp. sea salt
1 large onion, chopped	1 tsp. fresh ground pepper
1 red pepper, chopped	½ tsp. thyme
2 cloves garlic, minced	2 bay leaves
1 large tomato, chopped	1 tsp. peppercorns
2 stalks celery, chopped	¼ tsp. cloves
3 lbs. codfish filets, cut into pieces	Sherry peppers
2 quarts half and half	Rum

Brown the bacon in a skillet. Remove and saute onions, celery, red pepper, and tomato until tender. Stir in garlic.
In a pot bring the potatoes to a boil, and cook until tender. Drain potatoes and put back in to pot. Add bacon, onions, fish, half and half, salt, pepper, thyme, bay, peppercorns and cloves. Bring to a boil. Simmer for a few minutes until fish is flaky.
Serve in bowls with sherry peppers and a dash of rum, or Worcestershire sauce or Tabasco.

Cuisine

Since early times Bermudians have enjoyed local fish, once dried and salted for preservation. Fish include rockfish, spiny lobsters with no claws, snapper, tuna, shrimp, codfish, mussels and pompano. Prickly pear and bay grape are native to the island. The palmetto berries were eaten as bread and to the early Virginia colony. The leaves were used to thatch roofs. The cedar tree, known for its beautiful wood, died out in the 1940s, but its berries were used in a beverage and the dried sap eaten like candy. English settlers brought pumpkins, corn, onions, arrowroot and herbs. Bermuda onions were introduced about 1616 from England. Cassava, sugar cane, avocados, pineapples, plantains, and pawpaw were imported from the West Indies. Loquats were brought by Governor Reid in 1850. Hog money, the currency dating from 1615, received its name from the hogs that arrived on an early ship! In April a peppercorn ceremony is held by the Masonic Lodge which pays rent for its headquarters, the Old State House, with one peppercorn!

Bermuda enjoys a variety of cooking influenced by the English, Americans, and other islands. Almost all foodstuffs are imported and subject to heavy duties. Tea is served at some of the finer hotels in the afternoon. Sherry peppers are used in many dishes and a dish of sherry peppers (red bird peppers soaked in sherry) and rum are always added to a fish chowder. Bermuda onions (sweet) and cassava are used in cooking.

Bermudian Specialties

Popular dishes are West Indian Pepper Pot; fish and chips; Hoppin' John (black-eyed peas and rice; steak and kidney pie; conch fritters; onion and mussel pies; codfish and potatoes; syllabub (made of guava, wine and cream); fried bananas; and fish chowder.

Holidays and Special Occasions

New Year's Day – "Hoppin John"
Good Friday –hot cross buns, codfish cakes and family picnics
Guy Fowlkes Day – sweet potato pudding
Christmas – turkey, ham, Christmas pudding, fruitcake, and cassava pie
Weddings – two cakes are always baked - pound cake with gold leaf for the groom and a tiered fruit cake with silver leaf and small cedars for the bride.

Beverages

Special run concoctions are indigenous to Bermuda and almost every person arrives home talking about a "Dark and Stormy", Gosling's Black Seal Rum (named for refilling champagne bottles claimed from the British Officer's Mess and corked with black seal), served with ginger beer and a lime! Goslings was founded in 1806. Other drinks are rum swizzles, shrubs, or milk punch. Biby, a colonial alcoholic drink made from crushed palmetto and fermented, was later banned!

Bhutan

Bhutan is located in the eastern Himalayas, bordered to the north by the People's Republic of China (Tibet), India to the south, east and west. Subtropical plains are located in the south and the high Himalayans to the north. The country was believed to be inhabited as early as 2000BC. Most of the records were destroyed during the great fire in 1827 in Punakha, which was the original capital and seat of government. Thimphu became the capital in 1961. Dzongkha is the National Language of Bhutan. The country is referred to as "Druk-yul "Land of the Thunder Dragon". The name Bhutan was given to it by the British. The country is made up of several ethnic groups – the Sharchops in the east; Ngalops in the west; and the Lhotshampas.

Dining Etiquette

Etiquette in Bhutan follows "driglam namzha", which is respect for authority, marriage and family, and pride in civic duty and dates back to a royal decree in 1989. People's behavior is governed by this, as is gift giving, speaking to those in authority, how to eat and be served, and dress, All of this has been influenced by Buddhist traditions and one should show respect for this. The monarchy has promoted "Gross National Happiness" as a goal for the country. Men wear a *gho,* a long robe, with a belt called a *kera;* and carry a small knife. Women wear a *kira,* a long dress, over a silk blouse wonju and with a short jacket *toego.*

When invited for a meal please arrive promptly. Please bring a small gift, and if in a container, the container will be returned with sweets or candy. Please use your right hand or both hands to receive a gift. Gifts are not opened in front of the presenter. Gifts are refused three times before being accepted. Please greet people with a slight nod of the head, or when meeting older people, bow slightly. People will also bow with their hands open and the palms open. When an older person enters a room everyone present is expected to stand, and not be seated until the older person has done so. Using the word "la" at the end of a sentence is a sign of respect. Please wait to eat until everyone has been served, and the host will invite you to eat. Guests are always served first.

Cuisine

The different ethnic groups have influenced the cooking of Bhutan. Much of the country is mountainous, but in the valleys mushrooms, apricots, apples, asparagus, spinach, pumpkins, turnips, radishes, tomatoes, river weed, onions, green peas, strawberries and other fruits, chilies, and spices are grown. Grains in the diet include rice, buckwheat, and barley. These are cooked with beef, chicken, pork and dried yak; and meals will include rice and tea. Rice is served in a bangchung (woven bamboo bowl).

Bhutan Specialties

Yak – all parts are used, milk is dried and made into cheese and milk, and the skin fried as a snack

Phaksha Paa - Pork cooked with spicy red chilies, and may include radishes or spinach

Hoentoe - buckwheat dumplings stuffed with turnip greens, datshi (cheese), spinach and other vegetables

Jasha Maru - Spicy minced chicken, tomatoes and other vegetables served with rice.

Red Rice: pale pink, sticky rice

Zhasonpa – curry with chicken

Pumpkins, white radishes, potatoes, cabbage, cauliflower, beans, rice

Pa - curry –with chili, meat, vegetables, and rice

Rice – two varieties - white and red

Desi – white rice, butter, sugar, raisins, and saffron

Zow – fried rice with sugar, butter, and oilseeds

Puta – wheat noodles, grown in eastern Bhutan

Kharang – corn kernels dried in bamboo shoots and then coarsely ground. These are added to curry to make thukpa (breakfast porridge)

Momos – dumplings stuffed with beef, pork, or cabbage and cheese

Shel roti – rice flour, salt, sugar and made into a paste and fried

Goep - Tripe with spicy chilies and chili powder.

Ema Datshi

Ema Datshi is the national dish of Bhutan. It is made from Datshi, a local cheese and spicy peppers. Vegetables such as green beans, potatoes, and mushrooms can be used also. The peppers are the capsicum annum, a red, hot and spicy pepper grown in Bhutan. Ema means "chili" and Datshi "cheese". The cheese is made from the curds of cows or yak.

½ lb. chilies (green or fiery hot red), remove seeds from chilies and chop
1 medium onion, peeled and chopped
½ cup water
2 tomatoes, chopped
4 cloves garlic, minced

½ lb. cheese – use a hard cheese such as Gruyere or Parmesan, or a softer cheese like cheddar. Some people even use blue cheese
Cooked red or brown rice

Place the onions, water, and oil in a pan. Bring to a boil. Simmer for 10 minutes. Add the tomatoes and garlic and simmer for 5 minutes.
Add the cheese for 2 more minutes. Do not let it melt.
Serve with rice.

Jasha Maroo (Maru) (chicken with garlic)

Serves 4

2 tbls. oil	1 leek, chopped
6 cloves garlic, chopped	2 lbs. boned chicken breasts, cubed
4 green chilies, seeded and chopped	1 cup water
2 tbls. fresh grated ginger	Coriander
2 onions, chopped	Red or white rice
2 tomatoes, chopped	

Heat the oil in a skillet and add garlic. Cook until just browned. Add the ginger and chilies. Cook for 1 minute.

Add the onions, leeks, tomatoes, and chicken. Cook for 5 minutes. Add water and cook for 10 more minutes, or until chicken is tender.

Serve over rice and garnished with coriander leaves.

Holidays and Special Occasions

Losar, the New Year, is celebrated for three days. On the first day changkol is made from chang (beer).

National Day on December 17th commemorates the monarchy and the king serves food and joins in games and dances.

Religious festivals are held throughout the year with picnics.

When a new baby is born the mother receives no visitors other than family. She is then presented with eggs, rice or maize, and the baby given money for good luck. The mother drinks arra, a hot drink with butter and eggs to stimulate her milk.

At the time of death one visits the bereaved family bringing a white scarf, an uneven amount of money and food, including whiskey for the deceased.

When moving into a new home, gifts of eggs, apples, potatoes, or presents from a garden will be presented.

Beverages

The Bhutanese drink tea, suja (butter tea), and ara (locally made wine).

Did You Know?

By law the Bhutanese cannot kill wild animals, and cannot prevent them from eating their crops. A 1995 law preserves at least 60% of the land as forested

Bolivia

The South American country of Bolivia is landlocked, wedged between Brazil to the east and north, Paraguay and Argentina to the south, Chile and Peru to the west. Bolivia's history dates back more than 7000 years with the Amarya. The Incas conquered the area c1200 AD. Diego de Almargo, a Spanish conquistador founded a site near Oruro in 1535, and Spain claimed the region in 1538, and was known as Upper Peru. It gained its independence in 1825 and was named after its liberator, Simon Bolivar. La Paz, the capital, was founded in 1548 by the Spanish conquistadors and named Nuestra Senora de la Paz (Our Lady of Peace). Spanish is the official language, with Quechua and Aymara also spoken.

Dining Etiquette

Family (several generations may live together) and old boy networks are still very important in the country. If invited for a meal please be punctual. Ask before arriving if dress is informal or formal. As a house present take wine, liquor, candies, leather goods, flowers (yellow means contempt for a person, purple is for funerals), gifts for children, books or pictures of one's country, but not food, which is considered an insult to the hostess. Gifts are not opened in front of the presenter. Please shake hands meeting and departing. Close friends may greet each other with a hug, a handshake, two or three pats on the shoulder and another handshake Women will often embrace, kiss each other on the cheek, and may walk arm in arm. People may stand close to each other when conversing. Drinks – wine or beer will be served. Glasses are refilled when empty. The hostess will announce the meal and lead the guests into the dining room. The host and hostess will be seated at each end with the guest of honor to the right of the hostess. Grace is almost always said. The guest of honor is always served food first. Food is eaten continental style with the fork in the left hand knife in the right, soup and dessert spoons above the plate. A knife and fork are used to eat fruit. Never eat with your hands, and please don't put your hands in your lap. Always eat everything on your plate. If it's not to your liking, take a very small serving. Bottled water should be drunk. Vegetables and fruit should be thoroughly washed and peeled. At the end of your meal, thank your hostess and the host will reply "Provech" –"I hope the meal will be useful to you". Toasting is initiated by the host, who raises his glass and others follow. The toast is "Salud".

The women of Bolivia wear colorful skirts (la pollera), and in rural areas la pollera with a shawl (manta). Different hats distinguish where they are from. Many women still wear their hair in braids.

Pollo Rebozado (Chicken in Tomato Sauce)

Serves 6

3-3 ½ lb. chicken, cut into pieces
3 eggs
¾ cup milk
¼ cup cornmeal
Fresh ground pepper
½ cup vegetable oil
1 medium onion, peeled and chopped

6 tomatoes, peeled and chopped
½ cup white wine
¼ cup fresh parsley, chopped
3 bay leaves
1 tbls. marjoram
Salt and pepper to taste

In a bowl beat the eggs, milk and cornmeal. Dip the chicken pieces into the batter.
Heat ¼ cup of oil in a skillet. Add the chicken, a couple of pieces at a time until browned. Place on a plate with a paper towel.
In a large pan heat ¼ cup oil and add the onions. Cook until tender 4-5 minutes. Stir in the tomatoes, wine, and herbs. Cook for 5 minutes. Add the chicken.
Cover and cook for 30-35 minutes until chicken is tender. Add salt and pepper ofr flavor. Remove bay leaves.
Serve with rice.

Cuisine

Bolivian food is a mix of international cuisine and national dishes. For thousands of years the Amarya have subsisted on corn, cereals, beans, squash and peppers. Coca is used to treat soroche, dulls the senses for cold and exhaustion, women chew it at childbirth to ease pain, the grooms gives it to the father of the bride, and at death mate de coca is drunk at the wake and the leaves placed in the coffin. Coca was once restricted to royalty, priests, and others of high rank. Its leaves were used for bartering. The Spanish chewed it and the Catholic Church attempted to ban its use. When the Church found people needed it, the Church thrived on a new business! A wine was even made in Paris of coca during the 1880s by Angelo Mariani and named Vin Mariani. The llama was domesticated, used for meat and clothing. Cattle raising is very important in this landlocked country. Beef, quinoa, barley, potatoes, sugar, soy beans, cacao, almonds, tropical fruits – avocados, bananas, chermoyas, and pineapples are raised. The people enjoy spicy food – picante.

Today the main meal of the day is taken at lunch which usually consists of a soup, salad, meat and vegetables, a second dish or dessert. Dinner is usually the same with coffee served afterwards. Wine, soft drinks, or water are served with meals. A favorite place to meet is in the market places. And people still take siestas in the afternoon!

Bolivian Specialties

Sajta de Pollo – chicken in a spicy sauce with "tunta" (dehydrated potatoes)
Saltenas – meat or cheese stuffed pastries
Empanadas – pastries with meat

Locro – chicken, rice and banana soup
Chicharron de pacu – fish, rice and yucca
Majao – rice with eggs, beef and fried bananas

Silpancho - meat with rice and potatoes
Pacumulu – rice with grilled beef, fried yucca and cheese
Aji de carne – pepper meat, usually beef or pork
Sopa de mani – peanut soup
Valdiviano con huevos – soup with eggs

Parilladas – meat roasted over an open fire
Chuno – frozen potatoes that are used as a starch in stews, with eggs or fish
Fish from Lake Titicaca
Alfajores de almendras – almond cookies
Pastelitos de coco – coconut tarts

Holidays and Special Occasions

Carnival – dancing, elaborate costumes and pouring water on people. Food will include confite (candy stuffed with nuts or fruit).
Lent – time of fasting
Good Friday - fish
Easter Vigil (Saturday before Easter) – people go to church and purchase wax candles with a cross etched in them. Five grains of wheat are put into the melted wax to symbolize the wounds of Christ. In August the Aymara women make a beer offering to Pachamama, Mother Earth, giving thanks for farms and good health.
All Soul's Day –food is prepared for the deceased
Christmas – picana de pollo (chicken stew) eaten at midnight on Christmas Eve; pan dulce (sweet Christmas bread);
*Wedding*s – usually in a church, followed by a dance and reception. Wedding rings are worn on the right hand.

Beverages

Since all alcoholic beverages must be imported they are very expensive, and one should learn to drink the local beers, wines, pisco or chichi. Chicha blanca is served at births, weddings, funerals and other occasions. Chicha, from fermented corn made by the Aymara for hundreds of years, is intoxicating and can burn one's mouth at first, and takes a little getting used to. Beer is also produced. Cruzena being the best known, is produced by German brewmasters in Santa Cruz. Remember at this high altitude alcoholic beverages will hit you hard. Drink mate instead. If you are asked to pour a drink, never do so with your left hand. Pour forward, as pouring backward means you hate the person! There is a story a former British ambassador was given a drink of chichi by Mariano Melgarejo, a former dictator, but would not accept it, which was considered an insult to the people. He was forced to drink a barrel of chocolate, and was led through the streets of La Paz on a donkey, sitting backwards! Wine is produced in the Cochabamba region.

Did You Know?

Salar de Uyuni is the world's largest salt flat, measuring over 4,000 square miles and 12,000 feet above sea level. There is a salt museum made entirely of salt!
Lake Titicaca is the highest navigable body of water in the world.
From midnight Maundy Thursday to midnight Good Friday no alcoholic beverages may be sold or served.

Bosnia and Herzegovina

Bosnia and Herzegovina is located in southeastern Europe, on the Balkan Peninsula, and is bordered by Croatia to the north, west and south, Serbia to the east, and Montenegro to the southeast. Bosnia has been inhabited since at least the Neolithic age by the Illyrians. The Celts migrated into the region in the fourth century BC. The region was then populated by a number of different peoples speaking distinct languages. Conflict between the Illyrians and Romans started in 229 BC, but it was not until 9AD that Rome annexed the region. Later the Slavs, Franks, and Hungarians invaded followed by the Ottomans who destroyed every castle and fort. Beginning in 1878 the Austro-Hungarian Empire remained dominant until 1918. Following World War I Bosnia and Herzegovina joined the South Slav kingdom of Serbs, Croats and Slovenes which became Yugoslavia. Yugoslavia was invaded by Germany in 1941. From 1945 it was a socialist state, until war broke out in 1992. Today Bosnia-Herzegovina is a parliamentary republic. The capital, Sarajevo, dates back to prehistoric times, and was an Ottoman stronghold for years. The official languages are Bosnian, Croatian and Serbian.

Dining Etiquette

The Bosnian-Herzegovina people are known for their hospitality. Some may be Muslim and do not eat pork or drink alcohol.

Please arrive punctually when invited for a meal. You may be asked to remove your shoes on arrival. Please bring a small gift – sweets, a gift for children, or something for the home. Please shake hands greeting and departing. Women will kiss three times on alternating cheeks. You will be served beverages and perhaps some finger food. The hostess will seat you at the dining table. Food is eaten continental style with the fork in the left hand and knife in the right. Cold meats, cheese and small appetizers will be served, followed by the main course, then dessert, coffee and tea. If you would like more please ask the hostess, if not finish what is on your plate. If beverages are served let someone else fill your glass, and you will do the same for that person. Toasts are initiated by the host and the toast is "zivjeli".

Cuisine

The cuisine has been influenced by the foods of the Turks, Mediterranean, Austro-Hungarians, and other Central European countries. The dishes use spices especially paprika, vegetables - tomatoes, potatoes, onions, garlic, peppers, cucumbers, carrots, cabbage, mushrooms, spinach, zucchini, beans, fruit – plums, grapes, apricots, apples, quince, cherries, figs, pears; horseradish; dairy products – cheeses, yogurt, sour cream, pavlaka (soured cream, and various cheeses; pickled vegetables as a side dish; fish; meats – lamb, beef, pork, and chicken, which are mainly grilled.

Cevapcici (beef and ground lamb on skewers)

The National dish of Bosnia-Herzegovina

Serves 6

1 tbls. butter	1 lb. ground beef
1 small onion, peeled and finely chopped	1 egg white, beaten
2 cloves garlic, minced	Salt and pepper, to taste
1lb. ground lamb	1 tbls. sweet paprika

Heat the butter in a skillet and add the onion until translucent. Add garlic. Place in a mixing bowl.
Add the lamb, beef, egg white, salt, pepper and paprika. Mix well.
Shape the meat mixture into small cylinders about 2 inches long, packed firmly. Cover and refrigerate for 1 hour.
Arrange the cylinders on skewers, several to a skewer. Cook on a grill until desired pinkness.
They also can be cooked in the oven or under a broiler.
Remove from skewers. Serve with warm pita bread, chopped onions, or rice.
Ground pork can also be used.

Bosnian-Herzegovin Specialties

Sirneka – similar to burek, but made with farmer's cheese
Sarma or japrak – vine leaves, or pickled or fresh cabbage leaves stuffed with meat and rice
Sogan dolma – stuffed onions
Bosanski lonac – Bosnian hot-pot – beef or mutton with vegetables cooked in an earthenware pot
Janjetinu – roasted lamb for special occasions
Kebabs – lamb, beef, or chicken with vegetables, sauces, pita bread
Kajmak - cheese spread
Ajvar – red pepper puree
Musaka – meat and potato layered dish
Grah – bean stew with meat
Pilav – rice or grain cooked in broth
Chorba – meat and vegetable soup
Tarhana – soup with pasta
Cufte – meatballs
Bosanski lonac – meat stew cooked over an open fire

Sudzuk – beef sausage
Bamija – veal and okra stew
Kacamak – cornmeal and potato dish
Kljukusa – baked grated potato dish
Pljeskavica
Filovane paprika – fried peppers with meat sauce
Dolma – stuffed grape leaves
Duvec – vegetable stew
Grasak – pea stew
Popara – bread soaked in hot milk and served with kajmak
Zeljanica – spinach pie
Tursija – pickled vegetables
Tufahije – baked apples with raisins and walnuts
Baklava – phyllo with nuts and sugar syrup
Ruzica – similar to baklava, but with raisins
Sutlijas – rice pudding
Jabkovaca – phyllo with apples
Tulumbe – dried dough with syrup
Hurmasice – pastry with syrup

Burek Phyllo with Ground Meat

Serves 4-6

¼ cup oil
1 large onion, chopped
1½ lb. ground lamb
½ lb. ground beef
½ cup parsley, chopped

Salt and pepper
4 eggs, beaten
1 lb. phyllo
Yogurt

Heat the 1 tbls. of the oil in a skillet and add the onions. Add the ground meats. Cook until meat is slightly browned. Drain off any excess fat. Add parsley and salt and pepper to taste. Remove from heat and let cool.
Grease a 13x9 inch baking dish.
Divide the phyllo in half. Place 2 sheets in baking dish brush with oil. Repeat using ½ of phyllo. Spoon the meat onto the phyllo.
Repeat with 2 sheets and oil until all phyllo has been used. Brush top with remaining oil. (extra oil may be needed). Cut through phyllo so at least 12 squares or triangles are formed.
Pour the eggs over the phyllo. Cover and refrigerate for 2 hours.
Preheat oven to 350°. Bake 45 minutes or until golden brown.
Serve with yogurt.
Burek can also be made with fillings such as cheese, potato, spinach or pumpkin, and is often eaten with kiselo mljeko (yogurt)

Holidays and Special Occasions

The Christian holidays are observed by the Eastern Orthodox and Roman Catholics. Muslims celebrate Ramadan and the other holidays.
Lent – fasting
Holy Saturday – women take baskets of food to the churches to be blessed
Easter – elaborately painted Easter eggs, mainly painted with green and red; cold dishes such as ham, sausage, cheese, breads
Christmas – pojaca (pastry with cheese), sarma, breads

Beverages

Wines are produced in Bosnia-Herzegovina and include Zilavka, a white wine and Blatina, a red wine, both made in Herzegovina. The wine regions are Mostar, Citluk, Ljubski, Stolac, Domanovici, and Medugorje. Rakia is an alcoholic drink made from fermented fruit, especially made from grapes or plums, while Prepecenica is rakia that is double distilled. Other rakia may be made with apricots, apples, pears, quince, cherries, and figs. Sljovovica is plum brandy. Beer is also brewed. Very strong coffee influenced by the Turks is drunk. Fruit juices and mineral water are also available.

Botswana

Botswana is located in southern Africa, bordered by South Africa to the south and southeast, Namibia to the west and north, and Zimbabwe to the northeast, and Zambia. Botswana has been inhabited by the Tswana tribe. The earliest inhabitants of the country were the Bush people. Remains of the Iron Age have been found in the Limpopo Valley and Tswapong hills. During the 19thc tensions existed between the tribes, the Ndebele from the northeast and the Boer settlers in the Transvaal. In 1885 the British put Bechuanaland under its protection. The northern part became what is known today as Botswana and the southern part of the Cape Colony. Independence from Britain was achieved in 1966 with Gaborone as the capital. English and Swetswana are the official languages, plus other tribal languages. Much of the Kalahari Desert is located in Botswana where the people have been hunter gatherers for centuries.

Dining Etiquette

Please shake hands greeting and departing. The people are very polite, so please use your "thank-you", "please", or "hello ma'am or sir". Elders are much respected, and always enter a door or be seated after they are. Please bring a gift, preferably something from your country. Please present and accept a gift with both hands. Signs of hospitality are a gift of a chicken, or to be invited for a meal or tea. Before a meal a basin with warm water and a towel is brought in by the wife or a child. Kneeling the person presents the water to the father, elders and visitors. Serving cold water means you are not welcome. Plates with stew, bogobe and vegetables will be brought out. The father or head of the family is served first, but the visitor is to take the first bite.

Cuisine

The cuisine is influenced by the different regions in Botswana. Rice is the staple starch. Beef, lamb, mutton, chicken, goat, river fish, wild game and birds are used in various dishes and stews. All of the animal is used including the intestines and tongue. Pork is considered unclean and not eaten in most parts of the country. Sorghum and maize are the main crops. Beans include cow peas, ditloo, letlhodi, dried bean leaves, and peanuts. Vegetables grown in the country are cabbage, spinach, carrots, onions, potatoes, tomatoes, sweet potatoes, lettuce, and okra. Many vegetables are dried or salted to be used at a later date. Fruits grown are marula, sour plums, watermelons, lerotse or lekatane. Spices are added to stews and other dishes and include curry, chilies, and chakalaka. Most meals are one pot stews. Much of the foodstuff is imported from South Africa. Around the delta near Maun one finds tigerfish, pike, and bream. The word Tilapia (a popular fish in the United States) comes from "thlapi" in the Tswana language.

Seswaa (Shredded Beef)

Seswaa or Chotlho – men cook meat with salt and water in a three-legged iron pot usually for special occasions. This is the national dish of Botswana and is served with morogo, a leafy green and cornmeal mush

Serves 6

2 lbs. beef, cut into small chunks
2 tbls. oil

1 large onion, peeled and chopped
Salt and pepper to taste

Preheat oven to 325°
Heat the oil in a skillet. Brown meat on all sides.
Place the beef, onion, salt and pepper, and enough water to cover the beef in the oven. Cook for 1 hour, or until most of water has been absorbed and meat is tender.
Shred meat and serve as stated above.

Specialties

Serobe – intestines and innards of goat, sheep or cow
Oxtail – spicy meat dish
Bogobe (porridge) is made with sorghum, maize or millet flour, stirred into boiling water to form a paste.
Ting - sorghum or maize can be fermented, served with milk and sugar. Ting can be eaten as part of a meal with meat and vegetables, and without the milk and sugar.
Tophi – bogobe with sour milk and lerotse
Matemekwane – dumplings
Diphaphatha – a flat cake
Magwinya – fat cakes

Morama – edible tuber
Mopane –grub that is cooked in ashes, boiled, fried or dried
Kalahari truffle – truffles grown in Botswana
Bamia-bamia – okra lamb stew
Maschi – tomato and beef dish
Meat pies – (from British influence)
Pap – porridge from maize
Samp – dried corn kernels
Vetkoek – Afrikaner pastry
Maere - butter
Mabowa – wild mushrooms and truffles

Holidays and Special Occasions

Christmas – roasted meats
Beef is served at weddings and funerals.
Chickens are cooked to honor a guest and show hospitality, usually in a three-legged iron pot

Drinks

Local soft drinks are Fanta, Coca Cola, and ginger beer. Local beer is also brewed and will be either clear or opaque. Sorghum beer is a local specialty. Castle and Lion are two lagers produced. Madila is fermented milk. Palm wine and Kjadi (made from honey and Grewia berries) are produced. Rooibos (Bush tea) is a red tea and free of caffeine.

Brazil

The Republic of Brazil is the fifth largest country in the world and occupies 47.7% of South America. It 3,290,000 square miles are made up of five regions – the north, the Amazon Basin, and the second longest river in the world; the northeast "the bulge" into the Atlantic Ocean; the southeast; south; and central west – the Central Plateau or Planalto Central. The earliest inhabitants were Indians that settled on Marajo Island and built shell mounds known as sambquis. The Tupi lived on the eastern coast when the Portuguese arrived. Pedro Cabral was the first European to set foot in Brazil in 1500, landing at Puerto Seguro and calling the land "Terra de Vera Cruz" or "Land of the True Cross". The brasil tree which produces a red dye was traded for Portuguese axes and knives. Brazil declared its independence from Portugal in 1822. Rio de Janeiro was founded in 1567 as the fortified port of Morro. Brasilia, the capital, was planned and developed in 1955. The official language is Portuguese.

Dining Etiquette

Dinner is a social occasion. When invited you may be slightly late. Dinner is served after 9PM. Please shake hands greeting and departing. Men are introduced first, but in shaking hands ladies extend theirs first. Men or women who know each other well will embrace, and women will kiss on each cheek. The people are very warm and friendly. Friendships, family and business ties are very important. Brazilians when speaking may stand very close to each other. Don't back away and keep good eye contact. Appropriate gifts when invited to a home are liquor, chocolates, flowers or something for the home. Cocktails will be served. The hostess will seat the guests with the guest of honor to her right. Meals are served in courses with wine. Please wait for the hostess to begin. Food is eaten continental style, fork in the left hand, knife in the right. If fish is served forks and knives are provided separately. When passing a salt shaker, pick up, then set it on the table before the person asking for it takes it. Otherwise this is considered bad luck. Dessert is eaten with a fork and spoon. When finished place your fork and knife together. Toasting is done for many occasions. A toast is made by raising the glass and saying "saude", or "chin-chin" "Cheers".

Soccer is a highly prized sport! Yawning in public is considered rude. Pulling your earlob means everything is OK. To beckon someone open and close your hand with the palm down. 13 is an unlucky number. Engagements may last for several years, and weddings very festive occasions. For a funeral cards and food are brought or sent to the immediate family. Black and purple are the colors of death.

Bobo de Camarao (shrimp in coconut milk)

3 lbs. fresh unpeeled large shrimp
2 medium chopped onions.
1½ lbs. of fresh manioc, chopped and boiled
8 garlic cloves chopped.
6 large tomatoes chopped.
1 cup of chopped cilantro
2 cups of coconut milk

1 cup of heavy cream.
3 soup spoon of dende oil
Salt and pepper
1 diced red sweet pepper.
1 diced green pepper.
1 cup extra virgin olive oil.

Peel and cut the manioc in small squares. Cook in salt water until very soft. Drain and reserve the liquid. Remove the manioc fiber. Mash the manioc using a fork or a potato masher, use a little of the reserved liquid. A food processor or blender can be use in this recipe.
Peel and devein the shrimp. Save the shell and make a broth to be used later.
In a medium wok saute the pepper, onions, garlic with the olive oil for 3 minutes, add the raw shrimps, cook 2 minutes, add the manioc puree, add the shrimps broth, the coconut milk, the heavy cream, half of the cilantro, stir well and cook for 5 minutes more. Add slowly the dende oil and stir well. Add salt and black pepper to your taste.
Add the remaining cilantro and serve with a Brazilian white rice.
Recipe Courtesy of Chef Gabriel Aubouin, Embassy of Brazil, Washington, DC

Cuisine

Brazil is a noted agricultural region, first growing sugar cane in the 16th c, then coffee and rubber. Chickens were brought to Brazil c1500 by the Portuguese. Santa Caterina was settled by Germans who produce fine chocolates and German food. Sugar cane was first grown by early Portuguese settlers. In 1637 Prince Maurice of Nassau (Dutch) further developed sugar cane plantations and the raising of cattle. Italian, Japanese, Portuguese, and Spanish immigrants came to work on coffee plantations circa turn of the 20th c.

Brazilian food uses many native ingredients - pumpkins, peppers, tapioca, potatoes, mate, vanilla, pineapple, avocados, papaya, beans, guarana, corn, bananas, palm oil and hearts of palm, coconut milk, cashew nuts, tomatoes, cacoa, and sugar. Others are arroz – white rice; feijao – black beans; farofel – manioc flour; carne – steaks; galinha – chicken; and reixe – fish. Feijoada, the national dish is made of black beans, sausage, beef, pork, and served with rice, kale, oranges and farofa – manioc flour fried with onions and egg, pupunha – palm fruit from the Amazon; churrascarias – Pequi – pungent fruit used to flavor rice; moqueca – fish and coconut milk stew; baru nut – similar to peanut flavor; mandioquinha – similar to a parsnip.

Regional Specialties

Parana - barreado, a meat and spice dish cooked in a clay pot for 24 hours.
Bahia – African influence, using coconut milk, ginger, peppers, coriander, shrimp, dende oil – palm oil, cashews, fish and fish stews, but also the Portuguese influence with eggs, meat, olive oil, and sugar. Food is often cooked slowly in clay pots. Bahia produces sugar cane and has a long coastline. Some specialties are vatapa – shrimp cooked with dende oil, coconut milk, bread and

served over rice. Sarapatel is a dish with the heart and liver of a goat or pig, its blood, tomatoes, peppers and onions. Caruru is a shrimp dish with red peppers and okra.

Pernanbuco- lobster, coconuts, shrimp, squid, peppers, cumin, crab; caldo de mocoto – cow's foot soup; carne de sol – salted beef served hot; and genpapo liqueur

Ceara – crab, lobster, shrimp, cashews, coconut, mangoes, sugar cane, palm oil, cacao, cattle, guava, coffee and bananas. Pacoca is sun-dried meat, mixed with manioc and roasted. Baiaode dois are sweet cakes made from sugar cane, rice, cheese, beans and butter.

Cachoeira – was founded in 1510 by Diego Alvares, who was saved by the Indians after being shipwrecked. He married the chief's daughter and founded the first sugar plantation.

Espirito Santo – was settled by the Germans and Italians in the 1800s and is noted for coffee plantations and fishing

Maranho – Sao Luis was once a sugar and cotton port

Maranguape – cachaca- sugar cane liquor

*Maranha*o – mussels, crab, shrimp and arroz con cuxa – rice, vinegar, vegetables and shrimp

Mato Grosso do Sul – meaning outback or savannah produces cattle, rice, cotton, soybeans, corn, and manioc.

Para (the Amazon region) – among the dishes are fish, cassava, manicoba – pork and cassava, and pato no tueupi – duck, cassava and a wild green herb; and tacaca, a yellow soup with shrimp and garlic. The region exports cacao, vanilla, cassia, and cinnamon.

Parana – received its wealth from gold, Madeira, coffee, and mate, which were shipped from Parangua. Today it exports corn, soy beans, cotton and vegetable oils.

Parnambuco was once a thriving region for sugar export.

Rio de Janeiro thrived as a port from the early 19th c exporting coffee. Penedo was settled by Finns in 1929 who planted citrus trees.

Rio Grande do Sul – home of the gauchos and cattle ranches, and churrrasco –grilled meats with a tomato and onion sauce; and chimarrao – mate tea. The region has two ports, Port Elegra and Pelotas which shipped dried beef, and today canned vegetables, fruits and sweets.

Manaus – fish and duck

Minas Gerais – is noted for dairy products, fruit, and cattle. Minas Gerais – is noted for dairy products, fruit, and cattle and among its dishes are roast pork with beans, manioc flour, eggs, kale, and tutu – refried beans

Porto Seguro – is noted for fishing, beans, sugar cane, manioc, and livestock.

Santa Caterina – was settled by Germans who produce fine chocolates and prepare good German foods.

Santarem – brazil nuts, black pepper, mangoes, fish, soybeans

Sao Paulo – founded in the 16th c by a Jesuit priest, was settled by many Jews, Italians, and Japanese who have influenced its cooking.

Rio de Janeiro– feijoada

Feijoada

This national dish of Brazil once used every part of the pig! Today I have streamlined the recipe to include beef and to make it as simple as possible. Not taking a day to prepare!

Serves 8

1 lb. black beans

3 lb. smoked beef tongue

1 lb. chorizo or linguica, sliced

½ lb. smoked bacon, cut into 3 in. pieces

1 lb. smoked lean and boneless pork chops

1 cup orange juice

1 cup red wine

Rice

Orange slices

Soak the beans overnight in water in a large pot. Heat the beans in the water to a boil. Simmer for 2-3 hours. Remove and mash 2 cups of beans and liquid.

Place the tongue in a pot of water. Cook for 3-4 hours, until tender.

Place the chorizo, pork chops and bacon in a pan Cover with water and bring to a boil. Cook ½ hour, or until tender. Drain. Add the beans, the orange juice and wine and cook 20 minutes more. Remove 1 ½ cups of the beans and puree.

Serve on a platter with the sliced tongue in the center, surrounded by the other meats. Serve with rice, remaining beans and sauce

Sauce

2 tbls. olive oil

1 large onion, chopped

4 garlic cloves, minced

2 tomatoes, chopped

4 jalapeno, seeded and chopped

Heat the olive oil in a skillet. Saute onion until tender. Add garlic, tomatoes and jalapeno. Stir in mashed beans. Simmer for 15 minutes.

Holidays and Special Occasions

Carnival – from caro vale (good-bye meat) – officially starts the Saturday before Ash Wednesday

Easter – bacalhau (salt cod), chocolates and chocolate eggs, Pacoca 9mixture of ground nuts and sugar to form a paste), Easter ring cake

Christmas - the dinner is served on December 24 with ham, roast pork, chicken or fish, salads, vegetables, often kale, nuts, fruits, Panettone, cakes or pies

Weddings – are followed by much feasting, dancing and toasting

Funerals – cards and food are brought to the immediate family

Caipirinha

For one drink

1 lime quartered	1 shot of cachaça
1 tbls. sugar	½ cup ice cubes with water

Place the lime and sugar in the bottom of a glass. Using a wooden spoon crush and mash the lime. Pour the cachaça and ice over. Stir well.

Beverages

Brazil produces wine, beer, and sugar cane based beverages such as rum. Most of the wine is grown in southern Brazil, around Bento Goncalves and Garibaldi. This area received much rainfall and the grapes are picked early, usually with low sugar levels. Near the Uruguayan border it is cooler and dryer.

The earliest known person to produce wine was Bras Cubas in the 16th c. During the 17th c Jesuit priests brought criolla vines to St. Nicholau in Rio Grande do Sul. In the 19th c Auguste de Saint-Hilaire studied Brazil's viniculture and concluded the best French vines could be grown near the Uruguayan border, where Almaden (founded here in 1932) has a winery. The Marques de Lisboa sent cuttings of Isabella from the U.S. east coast in 1832 and in 1840 other cuttings were brought by the American John Rudge. In 1875 Italian immigrants from Venice and Lombardy came with Trebbiano and Riesling. From 1960 on, the real growth in vineyards and producing exportable wines became a challenge. Martini and Rossi, Seagrams, Moet & Chandon and Remy Martin all invested in Brazil.

The main wine region is Rio Grande do Sul, followed by Sao Paula, Santa Caterina, Parana, Pernambuco, and Minas Gerais. Most wine was originally produced for local consumption, but now is exported.

Most beers are bottled and served in 300 and 600 liter bottles. Cachaca is clear, unrefined sugar cane that produces an 80 proof liquor. Caipirinha means "little country guy", the national drink is made of cachaca, lime, sugar and crushed ice. Other drinks are capirosca – vodka, lime, sugar and crushed ice; capirissima – rum, lime, sugar and crushed ice; and batidas – cachaca, sugar and fruit juice. Bahia produces a local liquor known as genipapo. Guarana is a soft drink made from a fruit of the Amazon region.

Coffee is grown here, and is drunk daily, especially with friends.

Did You Know?

The earliest colonists had to give 1/5 of their crops or profits to the Crown (Portugal).
The town of Lencois, meaning "Sheets" from the tents pitched for diamond seekers, provided the French with diamonds to drill the Panama Canal, Gothard Tunnel, and London Underground. Coffee, manioc and tourism make up the economy.

Brunei

Brunei is located on the north coast of Borneo in Southeast Asia. It is surrounded by the state of Sarawak, Malaysia and is separated into two parts by Limbang, Sarawak. Brunei dates back to the 7th c when it was part of the Srivijavan Empire of P'o-li, and later part of the Majapahit Empire. During the 15th c the people converted to Islam. Brunei became a British protectorate in 1888, and gained its independence in 1984. The capital, Bandar Seri Begawan, is located on the Brunei River, a region which has been inhabited since the 8th c. The official language is Bahasa Melayu

Dining Etiquette

Please arrive punctually, or up to twenty minutes late when invited for a meal. Please remove your shoes before entering a home. It is considered an honor to be invited. Please bring a gift of fruit or chocolates, though not wrapped in white paper which symbolizes death and mourning. Please give the gift with your right or both hands. Gifts are not opened when received. Men may shake hands greeting and departing. Only if a woman extends her hand should it be shaken. Please bow your head to an older person and shake hands with them first. Do not look at someone with direct eye contact. Please wait to be told where to sit. Beverages and food will be offered. Food will be served buffet style or on a tray in the center of the table. The guest of honor or eldest guest will be served first. Please eat and pass with your right hand. Some people may eat with their fingers, although you may be given a fork and spoon. If no utensils are present you will wash your hands before and after the meal with the bowl presented to you. When finished, place your fork down and the spoon crossed on top.

Brunei is a very strict Muslim country with no alcohol or pork served. The extended family still exists, and older members are shown great respect. The people are very polite and do no want to lose face or be embarrassed. Women should cover their arms and legs. Please do not wear yellow as it is the color of royalty.

Cuisine

The Brunei cuisine has been influenced by the food of Malaysia, Singapore, and China. The food is spicy and uses wheat, rice (grown in Brunei Muaca), noodles, chili, coconut milk, beef, water buffalo, chicken, seafood, and tropical fruits. The food is cooked according to Halal using the Muslim food rules.

Nasi Goreng

Serves 12

2 lbs. beef, very thinly sliced
¾ cup peanut oil
4 cloves garlic, minced
2 onions, peeled and minced
2 tsp. coriander
3 tbls. curry powder
½ tsp. cayenne
Salt and pepper
4 boneless chicken breasts, cut into thin slices
1 ½ lbs. cooked and deveined shrimp, cut into pieces
½ stick butter

6 green onions, chopped
3 cups uncooked rice
4 ½ cups water
Parsley, chopped
Cilantro, chopped
Chutney
Cucumber slices
Hard-boiled eggs, sliced
Raisins
Coconut
Chopped nuts

In a pan cook the rice and water to boiling. Simmer until tender. Fluff.

In a bowl combine ¼ cup peanut oil, 2 cloves minced garlic, the onion, 1 tsp. coriander, 1½ tbls. curry, and ¼ tsp. cayenne. Add salt and pepper for taste. Add the beef strips. Cover and let stand for 1 hour.

In another bowl combine ¼ cup peanut oil, the remaining garlic, coriander, cayenne, and 1 tbls. curry powder. Cover and let stand 1 hour.

Using two skillets cook the beef in one until just gently cooked; and in the other the chicken until just browned.

In another skillet heat the butter and ¼ cup peanut oil. Add the rice and 1 tbls. curry, stirring to coat the rice with the curry. Add the chicken and beef. Cook for about 20 minutes or until the rice is just browned.

Add the shrimp and half the green onions. Stir until warmed.

Pour onto a warm platter. Garnish with the remaining green onions.

Serve with separate dishes of the remaining ingredients.

This can also be served with broiled or boiled banana leaves.

Brunei Specialties

Ambuyat – sticky ball of sago starch dipped in a fruit sauce and served with grilled fish
Daging masak lada hitam – spicy beef with potatoes and beans
Serondeng pandag – garlic fried chicken wrapped in pandan leaves
Sasagun – rice, coconut and sugar dough served with bananas
Jit manis –rice, wheat, egg and sugar dough that is baked
Udang sambal serai bersantan – prawns with coconut milk

Satay – skewered grilled meats
Sambals – sauces, often spicy and made with coconut milk
Rendang – curried stews
Soto – soups
Nasi lemak- coconut rice
Sayur lodeh – curried vegetables
Roti – flat breads
Kurma – chicken with coconut and spices

Udang Sambal Serai Bersantan (prawns with coconut milk)

1 lb. shrimp, peeled and deveined
Salt and pepper
1 tbls. lime juice
1 large red chili pepper, seeded and chopped
2 cloves garlic, peeled and chopped

1 tbls. ginger root, grated
2 shallots, peeled and chopped
2 tbls. oil
½ cup coconut milk

Place the shrimp in a bowl with a little salt and pepper and lime juice. Add the pepper, garlic, ginger root, and shallots.
Heat a wok and add oil. Stir in the shrimp mixture. Pour in coconut milk and bring to a boil.
Reduce heat for 2 minutes.
Serve with rice and sliced limes.

Coconut Cake

1 cup butter
3 cups sugar
1 cup coconut milk
2 cups fresh grated coconut
2 tsp. vanilla

3 eggs
3 cups flour
2 tsp. baking powder
½ tsp. salt

Preheat the oven to 350°
In a bowl cream the butter and sugar. Beat in the eggs. Then add the coconut milk, grated coconut, and vanilla. Slowly add the flour, baking powder and salt, until all the ingredients are combined.
Pour the batter into 2 greased and floured cake pans, bundt pan or large baking dish.
Bake for ½ hour, or until a toothpick comes clean.
Remove from pans after cooling for at least 15 minutes.
Serve at room temperature with frosting, berries, or fruit.

Holidays and Special Occasions

Food served during festivals include satay, ketopat (lontong, rice cakes in banana and coconut leaves, rendang, serondeng padang, daging masak lada hitam
Weddings and funerals (forty days) – rice, coconut meat curries (santan)
Birth – a new born baby's mouth is sweetened with honey or dates. The placenta is placed in a palm leaf basket and hung in a tree or floated in a river.

Beverages

Coffee, tea, coconut milk, and fruit juices are served.

Bulgaria

Bulgaria is located in Eastern Europe with Romania and the Danube River to the north, Serbia and the Republic of Macedonia to the west, and Greece and Turkey to the south, and the Black Sea to the east. The earliest settlers were Thracians (Orpheus in Greek mythology), followed by the Romans who established Sofia and Plovidu. Most of the river ports had Roman names. The name comes from the Turkic people, the Bulgars, who settled with the Slavs in the 7th c. During the Middle Ages there were Bulgarian kingdoms. The Ottoman Turks ruled from 1396 until 1878, when it became an autonomous Turkish principality, and an independent kingdom in 1908. The capital, Sofia, dates from prehistoric times with ancient city walls going back to the 7th c BC, built by the Thracians. The original name was Serdica given by the Celtic tribe of Serdi dating back to the 1st c BC. The official language is Bulgarian. The Bulgarian alphabet was developed by the Greek monks, Cyril and Methodius in the 9th c.

Gyuvech

The national dish is a hearty stew. In Bulgaria this is cooked in an earthenware baking dish. Gyuvech is also the name of the earthenware pot it is cooked in. Pork or other meats can be used, and other vegetables. It is good made with pork and sauerkraut. Cheese dishes are also made in the gyuvech.

Serves 6-8

3 lbs. boneless lamb, cut into small pieces
¼ cup vegetable oil
2 onions, chopped
2 tomatoes, chopped
1 pepper, seeded and chopped
Salt and pepper
½ cup beef stock

8 oz. mushrooms, sliced
¼ cup olives
2 cups rice
3 cups water
½ cup red wine
Parsley, chopped

Preheat oven to 350°
Heat the oil in a skillet. Brown the meat in the oil. Add the tomatoes, pepper, salt and pepper. Add beef stock. Simmer for 10 minutes. Add mushrooms and olives. Pour into a casserole.
In a pan heat the rice and water to boiling. Reduce heat and cook until rice is tender. Fluff.
Add rice to the meat. Add the wine and a small amount of water.
Bake 10-15 minutes in oven, or until bubbling.
Serve with parsley

Cuisine and Beverages

The cuisine has been influenced by the Greeks, Turks, Thracians, Slavs, and proto-Bulgarians. Dishes might include eggplant, lamb, mutton, fish from the Black Sea, game – deer, wild boar, pheasant, duck, goat and bear, cheese, bread, dairy product, grains, beans, lentils, rice, wheat, lots of yogurt, vegetables, cheese, and nuts, especially walnuts, which are grown here.

Breakfast is a light meal, perhaps bread and butter or cheese, fruit and coffee. Lunch may consist of soup, meat or fish, potatoes, salad and a drink. Dinner is usually a hot dish and not as large as lunch. Salad is served before or with the meal. Bread can used for soaking up sauces and gravies. Cheese and crackers may be served before dessert. Turkish style coffee is served. Pastries also reflect the Turkish influence. The word "pectopaht", or restaurant picnic, means dining al fresco, or outside. A mekhana is a tavern.

Wine has been produced since the early Greeks inhabited Bulgaria, but was not produced during the Turkish invasion. Production picked up following World War II, and especially in the 1970s and 1980s. The three main regions are the Danube River in the north; Schoumen and the Black Sea in the east (white wines); and the Maritza Valley in central Bulgaria. Wines include chardonnay, sauvignon blanc, merlot, and cabernet sauvignon, pinot noir, and other varietals. Red grapes that have done well here areMavrud, Melnik, and Gamza. Other drinks produced in the country are from fruit; beers; Slivovitza – plum brandy; Pliska – brandy; rakia, grape and plum digestif; Mastika – aniseed based drink; Boza – fermented wheat or millet drink; and Ayran – chilled yogurt, salt and water drink for the summer.

Bulgarian Specialties

Sarmi – stuffed vine leaves
Kapama – meat and vegetable stew cooked in an earthenware dish
Rhodope chevenrme – lamb roasted on a spit
Meshana skara – mixed grill, often with skewered lamb and sausages
Shopska salata – vegetable salad
Iman bavalda – cold eggplant stuffed with vegetables
Kisselo mleko – yogurt dish
Cubrica – mixed spiced bread
Katmi – pancake
Loukana – flat sausage
Sirene po shopski – white cheese and vegetable dish

Kavarma kebapcheta – spicy beef or pork with a sauce
Ciorba – sour soup
Soupa sus topcheta – soup with meatballs
Shkembe chorba – tripe soup
Pile yahnia – chicken stew
Sirene – goat cheese
Kurban – meat stock soup
Kyopoolu – eggplant dip
Soupa – meat and vegetable stew
Shopska – tomato and cucumber salad
Snezhanka – yogurt and cucumber salad
Mekitsi – fried doughnuts
Garish – sponge cake

Tarator (yogurt and cucumber sauce)

1 cup yogurt
2 large cucumbers, sliced
2 cloves garlic, minced

2 tbls. vinegar
½ tsp. salt
½ cup walnuts, chopped

Combine the ingredients in a bowl.

Banitsa – (pastry with cheese)

Phyllo dough
1 lb. hard cheese
¼ cup parsley, chopped
2 eggs, beaten

¼ cup milk
1½ cups butter, melted
Vegetable oil

Preheat oven to 350°
Crumble the cheese in a bowl. Add the parsley, eggs and milk until a paste is formed.
Cut the phyllo into 4 rectangular strips. Brush each strip with butter.
Place a spoonful of the cheese at one end of the phyllo. Turn and make into a triangle. Cut from rest of strip. Repeat until all strips have been made into triangles with the cheese.
Bake in oven 15-20 minutes or until golden brown.

Holidays and Special Occasions

Sourvaki or St Basil's Day (New Year Tide) – gifts are brought to the elders by children who receive gifts of money. Once the custom to serve pork head, jellied pig's trotters, garlic, onions, walnuts, honey, wine and brandy, with the round loaf, pogacha with a silver coin, in the center of the table; and cheese pastry with luck tokens
Easter –eggs dyed red; Easter loaves of bread; kolak – ring shaped cake;
Andreevden (St. Andrew's Day), November 30 – people boiled wheat, millet, lentils, barley, beans and maize, so that the coming year would be fruitful. This day was also celebrated at Bear's Day when maize would be cooked in honor of bears, so they would not tramp down their fields.
St. Nicholas' Day – carp, ritual loaves, ribnik – fish baked in pastry
Christmas Eve – ritual bread was kneaded with "Silent Water" and molded into various shapes, and a large loaf, the bogovitsa, with a silver coin to bring good luck to the house. Tables were laden with beans, lentils, vine leaves with rice, dried fruit, garlic, walnuts, and wine
Christmas – goose served on sauerkraut; gifts come from Grandpa Koleda, the winter god
New Year's Eve – feast will include pig or turkey, rice, nuts, prune sauce, unleavened bread with a penny for good luck; ring for a wedding; and thimble for the old maid; champagne at midnight
On special occasions and holidays native costumes will be worn.
Name days are celebrated with a meal usually with lamb.
Festivals began hundreds of years ago to celebrate the beginning and end of the main seasons for agriculture and stock breeding, and are often centered around the winter and summer solstice, the vernal equinox, first full moon of spring, or other planetary events.

Burkina Faso

Burkina Faso is a landlocked country in West Africa bordered by Mali to the north, Niger to the east, Benin to the south east, Togo and Ghana to the south, and Côte d'Ivoire to the south west. The country was known to have been inhabited from 14,000 to 5,000 BC by hunter-gatherers in the northwestern region. These people used scrapers, chisels, and arrowheads. Between 3600 to 2600 BC farming settlements appeared. Later the people learned the use of iron, ceramics, and polished stone. The region was composed of Mossi kingdoms that in 1896 would become a protectorate of France. Independence came in 1960. Formerly called the Republic of Upper Volta it was renamed in 1984 Burkina Faso "country of the incorruptible people" "tough man" in More and Dioula, the native languages. Dioula is spoken in the west of Burkina Faso. The capital Ouagadougou dates back to the 15th c when the Ninsi tribes inhabited the region, and in 1441 the capital of the Mossi Empire. The official language is French. The people are called Burkinabe. There are over sixty ethnic and linguistic groups living in over 8000 villages.

Dining Etiquette

Please arrive punctually when invited to a home. Please bring a gift of flowers, chocolates, or something from your country, which is presented with both hands. Please shake hands greeting and departing. On special occasions the head may be tapped four times, two on each side. When greeting an older person shake hands supporting the right elbow with the left hand while shaking. Elders are treated with respect. Extended families may still reside together. Food is eaten with the right hand which dips into the fufu or rice to be made into a ball for the sauces.

Cuisine and Beverages

The eastern and central regions of the country are inhabited mainly by the Mossi, Gurmanche, Fulbe and Tuareg; the west and south by Bisa, Gurunsi, Lobi, Dagara, Bobo, Bwaba, and Samo each of which have their own cooking styles. Fufu, the main staple of the diet is made from millet or corn flour and eaten with a sauce. Sauces are made from baobab or sorrel leaves with shea butter or groundnut paste. In the south yams are eaten while in the north milk and dairy products are more important. The Bobo eat caterpillars. The Fulbe are still mainly semi-nomadic and follow their cattle for grazing. Very little meat is available, as most is kept for the bride price or sacrifice. Millet, corn, rice, sorghum, groundnuts (peanuts), yams, cattle, sugar cane (grown on plantations), manioc, okra, potatoes, maize, beans, chicken, guinea fowl, fresh water fish, and mangoes are the main products raised and used in cooking. Braised fish are fresh water fish cooked over a charcoal fire. Thursday in Gorom-Gorom on the edge of the Sahara a market highlights robed merchants on camels, Fula herders who sell livestock, and others who sell leather and jewelry.

Two brands of beer are produced – Sobra and Brakina. Dolo is a locally brewed millet beer. The beer is prepared by a woman known as the dolotiere. Dolo is brewed for three days in large jars and then served in a calabash. Bangui, palm wine, is made in the Banfora region. Other drinks are liquor, gappal (soured milk), Bissap (made from bissap flowers), Chapala (millet beer), yamoku (ginger drink), Zoomkoom (drink made with millet, ginger, lemon juice and tamarind), fruit juices, and tea.

Mango Chicken Curry

2 tbls. vegetable oil
½ cup chopped shallots
1 tbls. Thai red curry paste
1 tbls. minced peeled fresh ginger
1 lb. chicken tenders
2 14 oz. cans unsweetened coconut milk

½ cup dried mangoes, sliced
2 tbls. mango chutney
¾ cup chopped fresh cilantro
Salt and pepper
Fresh steamed rice

Heat the vegetable oil I n a heavy large skillet over medium heat. Add the chopped shallots and sauté until golden brown, about 5 minutes. Mix in the red curry paste and fresh ginger and cook for about a minute. Add the chicken tenders and sauté until cooked through, about 6 minutes. Using tongs, transfer the chicken to a bowl.

Add the unsweetened coconut milk and dried mangoes to the skillet and boil until mixture is reduced to 2 ¼ cups. Mix in the mango chutney and ½ cup cilantro. Return the cooked chicken to the skillet. Season to taste with salt and pepper. Stir to heat through. Sprinkle with remaining cilantro. Serve over rice.

Recipe courtesy of Sonny Kabore Blandine, Sonny Sechage, Ouagadougou, Burkina Faso

Burkanabe Specialties

Banfora – fried cakes with pineapple
Maan nezim nzedo – fish stew with okra, carrots, cabbage, beans, rice and tomato
To – dough made from millet, shorghum or corn which is dipped into sauces made with tomatoes, peppers, carrots, or other vegetables or meat if available.
Fufu – mashed yams that are formed into a ball to eat

Rice can be steamed with groundnut or spice sauces; browned in oil, or couscous with a sauce
Beef, mutton, goat, chicken, and fish are often cooked as kebabs (brochettes) over an open fire (barbecued)
Peanut stew
Munyu caf couscous – meat, onion, potato, cabbage, tomato, peanut butter stew served with couscous

Holidays and Special Occasions

Sacrifices – chicken, guinea fowl or cattle are used at shrines which may be no more than a rock or some other place chosen by the tribe
Birth of a child, weddings, and funerals – meat served
Festivals – special foods and local beer
Tabaski (Id al-Kabir) – Muslims sacrifice and eat a ram
Ramadan – Muslims fast from sunrise to sunset
In even numbered years in October the Salon des Artisanat de Ouagadougou takes place with Africa's largest crafts festival that includes music, food, fashion shows, dance, and theatre.

Burundi

Burundi, located in central Africa is bordered by Rwanda to the north, Tanzania to the east and south, and the Democratic Republic of the Congo to the west. The southwestern border is adjacent to Lake Tanganyika. In the north are the highlands that lead to the flood plain of the capital Bujumbura. The Twa, Tutsi, and Hutu have occupied Burundi for over 500 years, and as a kingdom by the Tutsi for over two hundred years. In the beginning of the 20th c Germany and Belgium occupied the region, and Burundi and Rwanda became a European colony known as Ruanda-Urundi. The country became independent in 1962. The capital, Bujumbura, lies in the Rift Valley, location of some of the oldest known human beings. French and Rundi are the official languages, with Swahili and other languages spoken.

Dining Etiquette

It is an honor to be invited for a meal. If you are invited for a meal please accept. Please arrive promptly. Shaking hands is part of the ritual of greeting and will be done in different ways. Please shake hands greeting and departing. Good friends may hug and kiss three times on alternating cheeks. In some parts of the country men do not shake hands with women. Gifts are not usually brought for a first visit, but after a friendship has been established. Gifts may be given to visitors. Then please bring food or a gift for the home. Allow more senior members to enter a room ahead of you. Hands are washed before and after a meal. If seated, the honored guest is next to the host. Do not point your feet at the food or the others eating. Honored guests are served first, then the oldest male, other men, women and children. Do not eat or drink until the oldest man has been served and begun eating. If a communal bowl is served use only the part of the bowl directly in front of you. Please try some or all of the food. Food is eaten with the fingers of the right hand. If you are offered utensils please eat with the fork or spoon in the right hand. If a bowl or plate is to be shared only eat from the part of the bowl directly in front of you

Extended family ties are very important, and families live in close proximity to each other. The Tutsi are divided into four clans – the Batare, Bezi, Bataga and Bambutsu. Respect for elders, chiefs, and ancestors is also very important.

Cuisine

The food has been influenced by the Tutsi and Hutu. Most people are still herders. Beans, corn, peas, millet, sorghum, cassava, sweet potatoes, bananas, plantains, maize, fruit, manioc, groundnuts (peanuts), cane sugar, carrots, cabbage, mustards seeds, and hot chilies are used in cooking. Coffee is also grown here. There is little meat except for some sheep, chickens, and goat, and fish from Lake Tanganyika. The main dish is made from cassava which is washed, pounded.

Sorghum is ground into flour for porridge which is made into a ball and then dipped into sauces or gravies. Food is cooked over an open fire outside the home and can be roasted, stewed or boiled.

Meali Meal

Meali Meal is the national dish and is served with stews, soups, or sauces

4 cups water   3 cups cornmeal
1 tsp. salt

Bring the water and salt to a boil in a pot. Stir in the cornmeal and simmer for about 10 minutes. Cover and let sit for 30-40 minutes.
Place on a platter and break off pieces of the meali meal.

Burundi Specialties

Brochette – meat on skewers, usually goat
Ibiharage –stewed red kidney beans
Bananas with beans - fried bananas, beans, onions
Boko Boko Harees – chicken, bulghur wheat, onions, and turmeric
Ndizi – plantains fried in palm oil

Ndagala –local fish dish
Nyana meat stew with tomatoes
Mukeko – steamed fish with tomatoes and onions
Renga renga – potato leaf and peanut stew
Ugali – maize flour and water paste

Holidays and Special Occasions

Unity Day on February 5th is celebrated with drinking.
Kubandwa – this festival celebrates the grain harvest and Kiranga, the spirit of dead ancestors.
Umuganuro – a drum is played and a virgin plants sorghum seeds for a good harvest.
The Christian holidays of Easter, Ascension Day, Assumption of the Virgin Mary, All Saints' Day and Christmas are observed.

Beverages

Urwarwa is a homemade banana wine, served on special occasions and drunk during a meal. The Primus Beer is brewed in Burundi. Impeke is a home brewed beer made from sorghum. Beer is drunk on special occasions such as marriage contracts. Beer is drunk with a straw.

Did You Know?

Cow milk cannot be warmed or drunk on the same day one eats peas or peanuts. At the death of a cow its meat is eaten and the horns stuck in the ground for good luck.

Cabo Verde

The Republic of Cape Verde is an archipelago of 15 rugged, volcanic islands located in the central Atlantic Ocean, 570 km off the coast of Western Africa. They are named for Cap Vert in Senegal. The Portuguese colonized the islands in the 15th c. They were uninhabited until 1462. During the 19th c Mindelo became a trading center. Cape Verde received its independence from Portugal in 1975. The capital Praia is located on the island of Santiago. Portuguese is the official language. Cape Verdean Creole (Kriolu and Kriole) are also spoken.

Cachupa Rica (typical Cape Verdean dish)

1 liter or 4 cups of beaten corn without bran
Liter of broad beans
¼ liter of kidney beans
¼ liter of wax beans
500gr of chicken
500gr of salted pork
2 meat sausages
3 small pork sausages
150 gr of bacon
200 gr of beef meat
3 cloves of garlic
2 onions
300 gr of pig trotter

2 big potatoes
2 yams;
200 gr of Savoy cabbage
500 gr cabbage
2 bay leaves
300 gr of sweet potato
300 gr of unripe bananas
200 gr of carrots
200 gr pumpkin
200 gr of fresh tomatoes
Oil
Salt and paprika and parsley at will

Put the dry beans and the corn in a pot with water the day before.
The next day put the dry beans and the corn with 2 laurel leaves in a bigger pot and let them boil.
Then make a stew with chopped onions, tomatoes, garlic, paprika, and salt and add to the corn and beans. Let boil for a while.
When the beans and corn are already cooked, add the meat chops, bacon, a pig trotter and sausages a pinch of salt and let cook. When these are almost cooked through, add potatoes, bananas, yams, cabbage, sweet potatoes, carrots, pumpkin, and parsley.
 Let the vegetables cook. Make sure you do not let the sauce dry, and check the salt.
When it is completely cooked, let it stand for a while and then it is ready to be served.
Serve the meat and the vegetables on a different plate and cachupa on a bowl.
Note: the dish can be made with white or yellow corn
Recipe courtesy of the Embassy of the Republic of Cape Verde, Washington, DC

Dining Etiquette

The Cape Verdeans are warm and hospitable people who enjoy entertaining. Please arrive punctually when invited to a home. Please shake hands greeting and departing. Close female friends will kiss on each cheek. People stand close to each other when speaking. Beverages will be served. Food is eaten continental style with the fork in the left hand and knife in the right. Several generations of a family may live together

Cuisine and Beverages

The Cape Verdean cuisine has been influenced by that of West Africa, Creole, and the Portuguese. The Africans brought crops grown in their countries, the Portuguese livestock, tomatoes, corn, peppers, pumpkins, cassava, bananas, mangoes, papaya and sugar cane. Goats were already being raised on the islands, and goat cheese is presently made here. Fish was in abundance being an island nation and included tuna, swordfish, moray eel, cuttlefish, mussels, lobsters, octopus and shrimp Salt was exported especially to Brazil. The most common spices are cinnamon, turmeric, cumin, ginger and paprika. Boiled maize, rice beans, cassava and sweet are served as side dishes. Potatoes, onions, tomatoes, manioc, cabbage, kale, beans, papaya, bananas, mangos, breadfruit, sugarcane, watermelons, guava, coconut, and avocados grow on the islands.

Grog(ue) made from sugar cane and wines are produced here. Caipiroska is made with vodka, sugar, ice and lime. Caipirinhia is made with grogue, sugar, ice and lime. Coffee is grown on terraced hillsides on the island of Fogo.

Cape Verdean Specialties

Cachupa – national dish – hominy (corn) and beans with meat or fish
Tscassina – salted goat eaten with cachupa
Bstilla – crisp pastry
Xerem – dried corn
Kuskus – very finely pounded dried corn and steamed in a binde (ceramic pot) served with butter and milk or molasses
Canja – chicken rice soup
Caldo de peixe – fish soup
Diable dentro – pastry with tuna, onions, tomatoes,

Fish are fried with onions or cooked with garlic
Vegetable soups
Feijao longo – stewed long beans
Brochette – grilled meats (kebabs)
Pudim de queijo – cheese pudding
Jag – beans and rice
Cuscus – steamed cornbread eaten with milk, honey or coffee
Xerem de festa – ground corn, salt pork, onion and pork dish

Holidays and Special Occasions

During celebrations cuscus and catchupa are served.
Saints' Days are observed with food, beverages, and dancing
Carnival – much partying

Christmas – much music, grog
Manchup - meat, beans, grains dish
Weddings - xerem de festa
July 5 – Independence Day

Cambodia

Cambodia is located in the southern part of the Indochina Peninsula in Southeast Asia and is bordered by Thailand to the northwest, Laos to the northeast, Vietnam to the east, and the Gulf of Thailand to the southwest. The word Kampuchea comes from the Kingdom of Kambuja, established by Indian settlers over 1800 years ago. The Khmer empire reigned from the 9th to 13th c. The French colonized the region in the 1860s until 1953, when Cambodia received its independence. Sihanouk was deposed in 1970 and 1975 the Khmer Rouge took over. The Vietnamese military ousted the Khymer Rouge in 1979 and 1991 the Paris Peace Agreement brought Sihanouk back from exile in France. The capital, Phnom Penh, on the banks of the Tonlé Sap, Mekong and Bassac rivers takes its name from the Wat Phnom ("Hill Temple"). The city dates back to at least 1372, and in 1866 became the permanent seat of government. The official language is Khmer.

Dining Etiquette

Please arrive promptly when invited for a meal. Please remove your shoes before entering a home (and also a pagoda). You may be presented with a bouquet of jasmine flowers, especially if you are a houseguest. Please place both hands together at chest level and bow your head in greeting. If you are holding something please bow only your head. Food is eaten with spoons or chopsticks, or with your fingers. Family and respect for elders is extremely important, as are ancestors. When seated do not point your feet toward another person or a Buddha. The head is considered sacred and one does not touch another person's head, even a child's. Do not stand higher than an older person, unless of course you are much taller. Do not raise your voice, or embarrass another person. Smile and make good eye contact.

Cuisine

The cuisine is a mix of Chinese, Vietnamese, Thai, Laotian, and the use of ingredients native to Cambodia. The French left their imprint with French bread and frog legs. Soup (samla) is eaten with other dishes. Food is cooked in a wok (chhang khtea). The staple food is rice. The main dish is rice and soup which may have fish, eggs, vegetables, or meat and a spicy broth. Different regions have their specialties of soup. Coconut milk is used in cooking. Peppercorns are grown on plantations near Kep. Fruit include bananas, oranges, and pineapples; vegetables beans, cassava, corn, soybeans and sweet potatoes. Along the coast crab is cooked with coconut milk and peppercorns. Fish is mainly freshwater from Tonle Saplake or the Mekong River. Salads are often mixed with beef and herbs.

Herbs and sauces are very much an important part of cooking. The most common herbs used are mint, basil, lemon grass, galangal, turmeric, garlic, shallots, and spring onions. Prahok trei sach (meaty prahok) goes with steaming or grilling vegetables; and bone prahok chhoeng for cooking soups. Tik trei, or fish sauce can be used in cooking or as a dipping sauce. Kapi (shrimp paste) is made from cleaned shrimp and salted, pounded, and then dried. Trei chha-ae is made from smoked fish to use in soups, salads, or with fresh vegetables. Bangkea kriem are dried fish used in making soups. Other ingredients in cooking are tamarind, limes, mangoes, rhizomes, and dried red chilies.

Cambodian Specialties

Num ompong – rice cookies with black sesame seeds
Samla kako "stirring soup" – made with fish, chicken, pork and kreoung
Samla cha pek – pork soup
Samla machou bangkanh – prawn soup
Samla kari sach moan – chicken curry
Samla kari saramann – beef curry
S'ngao chruok – sour soup made with fish, chicken, or herbs
Samla m'chou – also sour soups

Trey aing is a grilled fish wrapped in lettuce or spinach leaves and dipped in fish sauce (tuk trey)
Num-banh-chok samla kher – rice noodles with green curry
Charet bampong – fried crickets
Ph'lea – marinated fish
Kourng –fresh spring rolls
Chai ya – fried egg rolls
Bok 'l'hong – papaya salad
Trei aing – grilled fish

Amok (catfish with kreoung)

Amok is the national dish of Cambodia

Serves 4

2 lb. catfish or other type of fish, filleted
1 cup coconut milk
1 cup coconut cream

2 eggs
Kroeung (see below)
Banana leaves

In a bowl combine the coconut milk, coconut cream, and eggs. Stir in the Kroeung.
Place the fish in several banana leaves. Pour coconut mixture on top. Pin the leaves together.
Steam in a lan sin (Cambodian steamer) until fish is tender 20-30 minutes.
Serve with rice.

Kroeung

4 red chilies, soaked, drained and mashed into a paste
4 cloves garlic, minced
2 shallots, minced
2 tbls. lemon grass stalk
1 tsp. tumeric
1 tsp. galangal

10 kaffir lime leaves
1 tsp. salt
1 tbls. sugar
1 tsp. kapi (shrimp paste)
1 tbls. fish sauce
¼ cup baby spinach
Zest of 1 kefir lime

Combine the ingredients by pounding them in a bowl, or with mortar and pestle.

K'dam Samout Chha M'rech Kh'chei (crab with green peppercorns)

Serves 2

4 blue crabs	2 tbls. oyster sauce
¼ cup vegetable oil	¼ cup soy sauce
4 stems green peppercorn	1 tbls. sugar
3 oz. black peppercorns	2 scallions, chopped
4 cloves garlic, chopped	Cilantro
2 tsp. fish sauce	

Steam the crabs in steamer. Remove the shell and crab meat. Save shells.
Heat 1 tbls. oil and stir in green peppercorns until soft.
Heat remaining oil and add black peppercorns, garlic, fish sauce, oyster sauce, soy sauce and sugar, stirring for 2-3 minutes until it starts to thicken. Add scallions. Gently fold crab meat into mixture. Can be served in crab shells garnished with cilantro and green peppercorns.
½ lb. fresh crab meat can be substituted for the crabs.

Holidays and Special Occasions

The New Year is celebrated with family reunions, payment of debts, feasting, new clothes, flowers, fireworks, and forecasts for the New Year
Chrat Prea Ang Kal – the sowing season in May
Prachum Ben – offerings are made to ancestors in late September
In October or November the Festival of the Reversing Current (Water Festival) is celebrated with canoe races
Weddings - Ansam chruk – rice balls with banana; nom bat and nom kom – rice cakes; phleay – palm sugar and pastry in grated coconut
Sangksha Khnor – jackfruit pudding

Beverages

Rice beer has been produced in Cambodia since ancient times. Drawings in caves depict beer being drunk in coconut shells. Beer is still brewed here, although it is imported also. Soda Kroch chhmar is soda water with lemon.

Cameroon

Cameroon, located in west Central Africa is bordered by Nigeria to the west; Chad to the northeast; the Central African Republic to the east; and Equatorial Guinea, Gabon, and the Republic of the Congo to the south. Cameroon's coastline lies on the Bight of Bonny, part of the Gulf of Guinea and the Atlantic Ocean. The earliest inhabitants date from the Neolithic period. Later the Baka (Pygmies), followed by the Bantu about 2000 years ago settled in the region. The Sao culture centered around Lake Chad c 500 AD, but was destroyed by the Kotoko. The Portuguese arrived in 1472. The Germans established a settlement in 1884. After World War I Kamerun through a League of Nations mandate was split into French Cameroun and the British Cameroons in 1919. In 1960 French Cameroun became an independent country, and in 1961 with the British Southern Cameroons formed the Federal Republic of Cameroon. The capital, Yaounde, was founded by the Germans in 1881 for trading ivory. The official languages are English and French. Fula, Duala, Bassa, and almost 250 other dialects are spoken. The name comes from the Portuguese camareo "shrimp", as there so many shrimp found in the rivers.

Dining Etiquette

Please arrive punctually when invited to a Cameroon home. Please bring a gift, but not food as the hostess will provide enough of that for you. Shake hands greeting and departing. Moist towels will be given to wash hands before and after a meal. Food is eaten out of a communal bowl. Please use only your right hand dipping three fingers into the portion set in front of you. The dish will usually be fufu which you make into a ball and then dip it into the stews or sauces presented. Men are served first, followed by the women, and the children eat the remaining food. Please taste all of the food presented to you. The evening meal is the main meal for the day.

Cuisine and Beverages

Cameroon is divided in 10 regions each with its own ethnic groups. In the north corn, millet, and peanuts are grown and very much part of the diet. The Littoral region around Duoala grows cocoa, yams, cassava, beans, kalokaschis, grains, and nuts. In the south root vegetables – cassava and yams, and plantains prevail. In the Center and Southeastern regions plantain, maize and rice are part of the diet. In the Western, Southwestern and Northwestern regions fufu made from maize, yams, cocoyams, sweet potatoes, cassava and bananas is eaten. The Portuguese brought hot peppers, maize, cassava and tomatoes. The French introduced omelets and French bread. Cooking can be very time consuming and is mainly done over mud stoves, wood, kerosene, cow dung, crop remains, or charcoal fires in iron pots and long spoons and many homes have a smoker for fish or a biltong box for drying fish.

Beverages include locally made palm and banana wine, beer, corn beer (kwatcha) millet beer, and sodas. Muslims do not drink alcoholic beverages.

Ndole (the national dish - bitterleaf, peanuts, melon seeds, spices, fish, goat or beef)

Serves 4-6

1 cup peanuts	1 stalk celery
1 cup water	4 cloves garlic
1 lb. shrimp	1 lb. bitterleaf or spinach
1 lb. beef	2 tbls. Maggi bouillon
1 large onion, peeled and chopped	3 cups oil

In a pan cook the beef with the onions and celery, and Maggi. Cook until tender, or just browned.
Boil the peanuts in the water for 10 minutes. Drain. Cool. Put in blender until almost smooth. A little can be added. Add to meat.
In the blender add the onions and garlic until a paste forms. Add to meat.
Add the spinach and simmer for 5 minutes.
Heat some of the oil in a skillet and heat shrimp until they turn pink.
Stir into meat mixture.
Serve with Miondo Bobolo – fermented cassava and fried plantains.

Specialties

Cassava, yams, plantain, fruit – mangoes, oranges, papaya, bananas, pineapples, coconuts, grapefruit, limes; potatoes, rice, maize, okra, garden egg (eggplant), bitterleaf, beans, palm,
Fufu –pounded and boiled cassava, yams, rice or millet served with sauces, gravies, soup or stew. Can also be made from manioc, plantains and bananas
Bobolo – fermented cassava
Puff-puff- donuts
Brochettes – kebabs with chicken, beef or goat

Sangah – maize, cassava, and palmnut juice
Kwem – cassava leaves with palm nut juice
Nnam ngon – marrow with plantain leaves
Mbanga – palm nut soup with fish or meat
Ekoki – vigna beans and matabo seeds
Sauces – are made with cassava leaves, okra, tomatoes, salt, red pepper, Maggi seasoning
Food is eaten with spicy sauces
Bush meat – porcupine, giant rat, pangolin,
Fish – roasted or fried, sun-dried, smoked
Curries
Sauces served on fufu, mashed potatoes, and couscous

Holidays and Special Occasions

Like the cuisines of the country the different ethnic groups have their own traditions when food is served for births, weddings, funerals, planting season, harvest season and religious events. Chicken dishes, slaughtering and cooking sheep or goat are eaten on special occasions.
Muslims fast during Ramadan from sunrise to sunset and observe Eid-ul-Fitr, Eid-ul-Adha and Eid Miladun Nabi
Christians observe Good Friday (hot cross buns), Easter Sunday and Monday, and Christmas.
Ngondo Festival celebrated by Sawa in Douala during the dry season – dakere (steamed millet flour); brochette

Canada

Canada is the second largest country in the world. The history dates back to c 13,000 BC when Asians crossed the Bering Strait. The Vikings were known to have reached the east coast c 1000 AD. John Cabot claimed Newfoundland for England in 1497. The French sent many explorers, and from 1689-1763 the French and Indian wars were fought, culminating in the capture of Quebec City by the British. Through the Treaty of Paris in 1763 the French relinquished Canada to the British. Today Canada is a confederation with ten provinces and two territories. English and French are the official languages. Ottawa was founded in the 1800s as Bytown, and has been the capital since 1857. The official languages are English and French.

Dining Etiquette

Please shake hands greeting and departing. Men stand when introduced to ladies, hold doors and chairs for them. When invited to dinner please be punctual. Please bring a gift – wine, candies, whiskey or flowers. Cocktails and hors d'oeuvres will be served. The hostess will lead the guests to the dining room, with the male guest of honor seated to her right. The host and hostess will be seated at opposite ends of the table. Courses are served or all dishes will be passed at once. Please wait for the hostess to start. Please eat continental style with the fork in the left hand and knife in the right. Never put your elbows on the table. Please put your knife and fork together when you are finished. After the table is cleared dessert and coffee are served. The toast is "Cheers", "To your health", or in French "A Votre Sante".

Cuisine

Canadian food is defined by the influence of the Native Americans, British, French, and a melting pot of cultures, those that settled there from all over the world, and those resources available in the country. The Native Americans in the east knew about making maple syrup, hunted wild animals, foraged for berries, wild plants, and ate nuts. In the west salmon and marine animals were an important part of the diet. In the Arctic the Intuit lived on land and sea mammals, fish, and foraging for plants. Meat was consumed fresh but allowed to ferment into *igunaq* or *kiviak*. Snacks such as *muktuk* consist of whale skin and blubber and is eaten plain, or dipped in soy sauce. Chunks of muktuk are sliced with an *ulu* prior to or during consumption. Fish are eaten boiled, fried, and or dried. In the eastern part of Canada the British, French, Irish, Dutch and Scandinavian traditions were brought. In Canada's prairie provinces Ukrainian, German, and Polish cuisines are strong culinary influences. Also noteworthy in some areas of the British Columbia Interior and the Prairies is the cuisine of the Doukhobors, Russian-descended vegetarians. The Waterloo, Ontario, region and the southern portion of the Province of Manitoba have traditions of Mennonite and Germanic cookery. Jewish immigrants to Canada during the late 1800s introduced bagels, rye bread, and smoked meat. The Chinese mainly settled in western Canada and influenced the cuisine there. Canadian inventions include Pablum (baby's cereal) first made at Children's Hospital for Sick Children in Toronto. The chocolate bar was invented by A.D. Ganong; the banana split by Alfred J. Russell and Canada Dry Ginger Ale by J.J. McLaughlin.

Each province has its specialties, influenced by the people that settled and what is grown there.
Prince Edward Island – fish, oysters, lobsters, meat pies, and repure made from pork and potatoes
Newfoundland – a large meal here is called a "scoff". Favorite dishes are seafood, mainly cod; chowder; fish "n" brewis (salt fish and scrunchions); blueberries; figgy duff (steamed pudding); screech (a distilled beverage)
Nova Scotia – fish chowders; lobster; smoked fish; Lunenberg sausage; Solomon Grundy (herring); apple pie; Digby Chicko (smoked herring)
New Brunswick – fish; fiddlehead ferns; baked beans and brown bread; dulse (dried seaweed)
Ontario – the most diverse province in dining also offers very English traditions – beef, Yorkshire puddings, and meat pies
Quebec – cipaille (pie of game or beef and vegetables); temprette (bread with maple syrup and crème fraiche or whipped cream); tortiere (meat pie); cider; seafood; cheeses; sugar baked ham; pea soup; and maple syrup
Manitoba – goldye (smoked fish); wild rice; white fish caviar; beef; caribou (a drink made from part grain alcohol 40% and red wine)
Saksatchewan – beef, meat pies. Many Ukrainian Mennonites settled here and their influence is found in the food and customs.
British Columbia – trout, salmon, King crab, oysters, shrimp, cod; bannock bread; wild game. The Okanagan Valley is noted for fresh fruit – cherries, plums, grapes, and apples. Many Swiss and Germans settled here and influenced the cooking.
Northwest Territories – wild game – caribou and musk ox; fish – Arctic char, trout, grayling; muktuk (whale)
The Yukon – King crab; salmon; raspberries; wild game – moose and caribou

Beverages

Wine may have been produced as early as 1000 AD by the Vikings who called Newfoundland Vinland. Jacques Cartier found vines along the St. Lawrence River and Jesuit priests made sacramental wines beginning in 1636 in Quebec. The first real producer was Johann Schiller who started making wine about 1811 in Cooksville, Ontario. For a little over two hundred years Canada has mainly produced wine in the Niagara and St. Lawrence River regions. Further west wine is produced in the Okanagan Valley in British Columbia. During the Depression when apples rotted and could not be sold they were made into wine. Ice wine, ice beer, and ice cider are Canadian specialties. Other grape producing regions are near Lake Erie and the Annapolis Valley in Nova Scotia. Gin, Canadian "rye" whisky, Crown Royal, Canadian Club, Yukon Jack, Newfoundland Screech, fruit brandies, beer, liqueurs such as Maple Liqueur and Moose Milk and Calvados (apple brandy) are also made. The Bloody Caesar was invented in 1969 in Calgary, Alberta by Walter Chell. Caribou is a mix of red wine, maple syrup and Canadian whisky, consumed in Quebec during the winter.

Nanaimo Squares

This recipe is for a 9" X 12" brownie pan.

1ˢᵗ Layer

¼ cup granulated sugar
½ cup unsalted butter
5 tbls. cocoa powder
1 cup coconut, shredded

2 cups graham cracker crumbs
½ cup walnuts
1 egg

Line your brownie pan with parchment paper.
Melt the butter and set aside. Put sugar, cocoa powder, coconut, graham crackers and walnuts in a food processor. Blend until size and consistency of bread crumbs. Place into a bowl, add melted butter and egg and mix with hands. Put all in the brownie pan and spread evenly, press down to create a crust. Place in freezer, and freeze so that the 2ⁿᵈ layer can be spread more easily.

2ⁿᵈ Layer

½ cup unsalted butter, room temperature
4 cups powdered sugar

4 tbsp. milk
4 tbsp. instant vanilla pudding mix

Place all the ingredients in a food processor, and pulse until the consistency of an icing. Scrap sides with spatula in between pulses. With a warm stainless steel spatula, spread evenly over crust. Refrigerate until firm.

3ʳᵈ Layer

180 grams semi-sweet chocolate, sliced into shavings

150 ml heavy cream
75 grams unsalted butter, room temperature

In a sauce pot, bring cream to a boil. When cream comes to a boil, remove from heat and add chocolate shavings, stir until melted, then add butter and stir. Immediately pour over layers 1 and 2, and spread evenly with a spatula. Refrigerate
When portioning the squares, place a knife in very hot water, remove from water and dry with a towel, then cut. This will help to make clean cuts through the top layer of chocolate.
Recipe Courtesy of Chef Naylor, Canadian Embassy, Washington, DC

Chef Naylor's Maple Sugar Pie

Dough

3 cups flour	½ cup water
6 oz unsalted butter	1 egg yolk
1 tablespoon granulated sugar	

In a food processor, blend the flour, butter and sugar until small beads start to form. Mix egg yolk and water in separate bowl. Add egg yolk and water. Pulse until the mix starts to form a dough being careful not to over blend, it will become elastic. Remove and form a ball. Dust with flour and wrap in plastic. Place in refrigerator for 1 hour. Butter desired pie mold and sprinkle with flour. Spread flour evenly in mold, then shake off excess flour. Set aside.

Preheat oven to 350 F. Remove dough and roll on a floured surface until 1/8-1/4 inches thick. Place rolled dough in pie tray, lightly pressing against sides. Cut excess dough from edges and crimp with fingers or a fork. With a fork, poke holes in bottom of pie shell to avoid bubbling. Line the pie shell with tin foil and weigh down with dried beans. Place in preheated oven and blind bake for 30-40 minutes, or until edges start to show color. Remove from oven and remove foil with beans. Return to oven and bake for another 5-10 minutes or until golden brown. Remove and turn oven down to 300 F.

Filling

250 grams Maple sugar	4 eggs
½ cup flour	3 cups heavy cream
¼ cup 100% Maple syrup	

If the maple sugar is in a hard block or brick form, grate on a cheese grater before continuing. In a sauce pot, slowly heat cream over medium heat being careful not to boil. In a large bowl mix maple sugar and flour, then add the heated cream and whisk until smooth. Beat all the eggs in separate bowl and whisk into cream and maple mix a bit at a time. Now, add maple syrup and mix. Strain through a fine sieve.

Pour filling into pie shell and bake at 300 F. on middle rack of oven for 45-60 minutes, or until set. Avoid bubbling, this will cause the mixture to separate and lose its creamy consistency. Remove and place on cooling rack until set. Refrigerate until serving.

Recipe courtesy of Chef Naylor, Canadian Embassy, Washington, DC

Holidays and Special Occasions

Easter – Easter eggs, ham or lamb
Thanksgiving (2nd Monday in October) – turkey, stuffing, sweet, potatoes, and pumpkin pie
Christmas – beef, turkey, stuffing, potatoes, vegetables, pies, trifle
Boxing Day – parties and visiting with friends and family

Central African Republic (CAR)

The Central African Republic is landlocked country in Central Africa bordered by Chad in the north, Sudan in the northeast, South Sudan in the east, the Democratic Republic of the Congo and the Republic of the Congo in the south, and Cameroon in the west. Ancient cultures lived near the town of Bouar where megaliths stand in concentric circles. From c 1000 BC to 1000 AD Ubangian speaking, Bantu speaking, and Central Sudanic speaking groups settled in what is now Cameroon, Sudan and much of the CAR region. During the 19th c Muslim traders came into the area. In 1889 the French founded a town on the Ubangi River at Banqui, the future capital of Ubangi-Shari and later the CAR. In 1958 Ubangi-Shari took the name Central African Republic, receiving its independence from France in 1960. Most of the inhabitants speak Ubangian or Bantu languages. French and Sango are the official languages.

Dining Etiquette

It is an honor to be invited to a home. Men and older boys eat separately from the women and children. There are very strict rules about who dines with whom. Guests will eat separately as one does not look at another person while eating. Hands will be washed before and after eating. Food is eaten only with the right hand. The food is served communally on a platter. Guests will be seated or squatting on the floor in a circle around the food. Take a bit of the fufu or whatever is served with your right hand, form into a ball and dip it into the sauce. Water is drunk at the end of the meal. In restaurants in Banqui tables, chairs, forks and knives are used by diners.

Muamba de Galinha (chicken with palm oil and okra)

Serves 6

1 chicken, cut in pieces	2 chilies, seeded and chopped
Juice of 1 lemon	½ lb. okra, sliced
¼ cup palm oil	4 tomatoes, chopped
1 large onion, chopped	1 cup chicken stock
3 cloves garlic, minced	Salt and pepper to taste

Marinate the chicken in the lemon juice mixed with some salt for 1 hour.
Heat the palm oil in a skillet. Add the chicken and brown, cooking until just tender. Remove chicken
Add the onions to the skillet and cook until just translucent. Add more oil if necessary. Add garlic, chilies, okra, and tomatoes. Cook for 5 minutes. Add chicken and stock. Cook for 10 more minutes. Squash or othcr vegetables can be added to the dish.

Cuisine and Beverages

Located in Central Africa the CAR has its own style of cooking. Many of the dishes contain gombo (okra), rice, gozo (dried cassava), bananas, sorghum with a sauce made from vegetables, chicken, meat or fish. In more rural areas the people use cassava, bananas, plantains, palm nut oil, caterpillars and koko leaves. Native animals and fish are served with tomato or peanut sauces and hot chilies and greens. Meats are often marinated and deep fried, or dried. Banana leaves may be used for steaming or grilling. Manioc leaves are cooked and dried in the sun. Most food is cooked in a pot over an open fire away from the house. From 1930-40 cotton, tea and coffee became major exports. Being landlocked the people learned to breed sheep, goats, and cattle.

Local beer is brewed with sorghum and local liquors are produced from sorghum or cassava. Wines are made from palm or bananas.

Spinach Stew

Serves 4

1 tbls. oil	½ cup tomato paste
1 large onion, chopped	2 tbls. fresh grated ginger
4 cloves garlic, minced	1 tsp. paprika
1 red pepper, seeded and chopped	½ tsp. ground cumin
4 cups beef, chicken, or vegetable broth	½ lb. spinach
2 sweet potatoes, peeled and cubed	¾ cup peanut butter

In a pan heat the oil and add the onions until tender. Stir in garlic and red pepper. Add broth, sweet potatoes, tomato paste, ginger, paprika, cumin. Bring to a boil. Stir in spinach. Cook until sweet potatoes are tender. Stir in peanut butter until heated, and thickened.
Serve with sliced green onions or cilantro.

CAR Specialties

Fufu – fermented cassava root
Chicken and cumin stew
Palm butter soup
Bouille – porridges usually made from corn
or rice

Shrimp with yams
Makara – bread
Ngunza – manioc leaf salad

Holidays and Special Occasions

Many festivals occur during the year in which much food and drink is consumed. The festivals include birth, initiation, marriage, selection of tribal chiefs, death and ancestors. Many of the dishes are prepared with chicken. Chickens and goats are used for currency in marriages. August 13th is Independence Day and December 1 National Day.

Chad

Chad is a landlocked country in Central Africa bordered by Libya to the north, Sudan to the east, the Central African Republic to the south, Cameroon and Nigeria to the southwest, and Niger to the west. Archeological sites in Borkou-Ennedi-Bibesti date back to 2000 BC. The early people were known as the Sao, followed by Kanem Empire c 1000AD. This Empire controlled the Saharan trade routes. During the late 1800s the Sudan was in control of the region, followed by the French in 1900, and later became part of Ubangi-Shari, now the Central African Republic. Chad became an independent nation in 1960. The capital, Ndjamena, lies on the Chari River and was founded in 1900 by the French as Fort Lamy. The official languages are French and Arabic, Saro, Sango and at least 100 dialects are spoken.

Dining Etiquette

It is an honor to be invited for a meal in someone's home. Please arrive punctually. As a guest you may be given a present. Men greet each other with a handshake. Women usually nod a verbal greeting. You will be seated on a mat on the floor, and never point your feet towards the food or other guests. The host will tell the guests when to eat. Hands are washed before and after eating. Food is only eaten with the right hand. Men and women may eat separately. If there are children present do not give them eggs, as it might be a sign they will be thieves later in life.

Daraba (okra and sweet potatoes)

Serves 4-6

2 cups beef, chicken or vegetable stock
½ lb. fresh okra, chopped
3 tomatoes, chopped
1 large sweet potato, peeled and cubed
1 eggplant, peeled and cubed

1 cup spinach
2 chilies, seeded and chopped
¾ cup peanut butter
Salt and pepper to taste

Heat the stock in a large pan. Add the okra, tomatoes, sweet potato, eggplant, spinach and chilies. Bring to a boil. Simmer for about 30 minutes, or until vegetables are tender.
Remove 1 cup of liquid and mix with peanut butter. Add to vegetables. Stir until thickened.

Cuisine

In the north most people are Muslim living in the desert or semi-desert with fish such as tilapia, perch, eel, balbout, salanga, banda, and carp available. In the south more people are Christian, agricultural, with little fish, but use tubers, spices and fruit. Each region and ethnic group has its own food specialties. The staple foods are sorghum, millet, maize, manioc, potatoes, rice, peanuts and peanut butter, sesame, okra, cassava and cassava leaves, beans, fruit such as bananas, mangoes, guava, grapes, and dates. Mutton, chicken, mutton, goat, fish and beef may be available. Ndjamena serves as the regional market for livestock, dates, salt, and grains.

Squash Stew with Peanuts

Serves 4

2 tbls oil
1 celery stalk, chopped
1 carrot, chopped
1 onion, chopped
3 cups squash, peeled and cubed

2 potatoes, peeled and cubed
1 red pepper, seeded and chopped
4 cups chicken, beef, or vegetable stock
1 cup peanuts

Heat the oil in a pan. Stir in the celery, carrot, and onion until just tender. Add the squash, potatoes, pepper and stock. Bring to a boil. Simmer for 20 minutes, or until squash and potatoes are tender. Add the peanuts.
You can puree the soup or leave it with the chunky vegetables. Add peanuts after pureeing.
Peanut butter can be added instead of peanuts.

Chadian Specialties

Boule - porridge made from sorghum or millet served with sauces made from meat, dried fish, tomatoes, onions, and spices.
Aiysh ((north) or biya (south) - millet balls are dipped into sauces

Fangasou – millet breakfast dish
Fish is dried, salted, broiled, or smoked
Tan kul (south) – sauce for fish or meat
Nashif (north) – meat with spicy tomato sauce

Holidays and Special Occasions

Each of the ethnic groups and regions has its own celebrations. The Muslim fast during Ramadan. Christians celebrate Easter and Christmas. There are many festivals during the year which are celebrated with special foods. Independence Day is August 11th.

Beverages

Karcani or carcaje is a boiled hibiscus flower drink with ginger, cloves, cinnamon and sugar. Gala is a local beer. Fruit juices, and red and green tea are also served.

Chile

Chile, situated in the southwestern part of South America, occupies 302,778 miles, but at its widest point is only about 100 miles wide, but almost 2700 miles long. Chile's history dates to pre-Inca times and some of the oldest mummies, dating back over 8000 years have been found near Arica in the north. Stone Age hunters were known to settle Patagonia, and the Incas went as far south as the Maule River, south of which were the Araucanian Indians. The Spanish arrived in the 16th c, and Chile became part of the Viceroyalty of Peru. The far south in Patagonia was settled by the English, Welsh and Scots who founded large estancias "ranches" for raising sheep. The Lake region and towards Argentina was settled by Germans. In the 19th c Chinese arrived to work in the mines. Chile won independence from Spain in 1810. The capital, Santiago, was founded in 1541 by the Spanish explorer Pedro de Valdivia. Spanish is the official language.

Dining Etiquette

Family connections are still very important in Chile. Please be punctual when invited for a meal. Please send flowers ahead, bring chocolates, whiskey, or something for the home. Shake hands greeting and departing. People will often kiss and embrace (abrazo) even if they do not know each other well. Please show respect for elders and those of higher rank. Women keep their maiden name after marriage, and might add "de" and the husband's surname. Children take two last names, the first the father's, the second the mother's. Men stand when ladies are introduced, and hold doors and chairs for them. People may stand close to you, and use many hand gestures. Keep good eye contact. Drinks and hors d'oeuvres will be served. The hostess will invite the guests in for dinner, which is served in courses. The host and hostess will be seated at each of the table, with the guest of honor to the hostess' right. Please wait for the hostess to start. A meal is eaten continental style with the fork in the left hand, knife in the right. Fish and fruit fork and knives are used separately for those courses. Please keep your hands above the table, not in your lap. Bread is served before or with the meal. Wine is served with the right hand. The toast is "Salud" or "To your health". When leaving the abrazo is repeated for all those attending.

Cuisine

Chile is a long narrow country with very diverse regions. In the north the Atacama Desert where almost nothing grows to the central part which is almost Mediterranean to the south and Antarctica and the east with the Andes. Because of this the cuisine varies in each region.

Chile has an incredible amount of good seafood – salmon, trout, mussels, squid, corvine, congrio, swordfish, king crab, and scallops. The early Spaniards learned to cook with chilies, potatoes, corn, pumpkin, quinoa, and beans. Strawberries, grapes, apples, nectarines, peaches, blueberries, caricas (papaya) and other fruits are grown, and many exported. Olives grow well here and olive oil has become a major export.

Vegetables are not always served at meals. Instead potatoes, corn, beans, eggs, seafood and beef are the staples. Breakfast is a light meal, a morning break taken around 10, lunch about 1, tea late afternoon, and dinner often after 9:30. Lunch is served in several courses beginning with empanadas, soup, an entrée, fruit and dessert. Dinner is similar to lunch followed by tea or coffee.

Empanadas

4 cups flour
1 tbls. baking powder
Salt
1 egg yolk
1 egg, beaten
1 ½ cups warm milk
2 sticks butter
2 tbls. oil
1 tsp. paprika

1 large onion, finely chopped
½ tsp. chili powder
½ tsp. cumin
½ tsp. oregano
1 lb. ground beef
4 hard-boiled eggs, sliced
Black olives, sliced
Raisins

Dough

In a food processor combine the flour, baking powder, salt, egg yolk, egg, milk and butter until a ball forms. This can also be made in a bowl and kneaded.
Divide into 20 pieces and roll each thinly into a circle.

Meat Filling

Preheat oven to 400°
Heat the oil in a skillet with the paprika and onion and stir until softened. Add the chili, cumin, oregano. Add the meat and cook until browned.
Place a spoonful of the meat on the dough circle. Add a small amount of hard-boiled egg, olives, and raisins.
Fold the dough and seal edges with a small amount of milk.
Bake in oven, about 12 minutes, or until slightly browned. Serve hot.

Chilean Specialties

Merquen – spice blend
Humitas – corn paste wrapped in corn husks and boiled
Cazuela de ave – chicken and vegetable soup or stew
Carbonada – vegetable and meat soup or stew
Cazuela de Cordero – lamb and vegetable stew
Empanadas – meat pastries

Porotos Granados – cranberry beans with squash, corn, and other vegetables
Bife a lo pobre – steak with egg, fried potatoes, and onions -
Pastel de choclo
Curanto en hoyo – creole dish with meat and fish cooked in the ground
Locro – meat with vegetables and potatoes
Charquican – dried beef and vegetables

Caldillo de congrio – congrio fish stew
Caldillo de pascado – fish soup
Parrillada – grilled meats
Spoaipillas – fried pumpkin dough
Alfajores –round dessert cakes with manjar blanco

Empanaditas de crema – small cream pies
Calugas - fudge
Manjar blanco – sweet milk pudding
Color - garlic and paprika heated in oil

Pastel de Choclo (meat pie with corn crust)

Serves 4- 6

2 tbls. olive oil
2 onions, chopped
2 cloves garlic, chopped
½ cup raisins
1 chili, seeded and chopped
1 tsp. ground cumin
1 tsp. paprika
Salt and pepper

½ cup pitted black olives, sliced
½ lbs. ground beef or lamb
Kernels of 4 ears corn
1 cup milk
1 tbls. oil
1 cup cornmeal
2 cups cheddar cheese

Preheat oven to 350°
Heat the olive oil in a skillet and stir in the onions until translucent. Add garlic, chili, cumin, paprika, and some salt in pepper. Remove from pan. Add the ground beef to the pan and brown. Stir in the onion mixture.
Pour into a casserole. Sprinkle with the olives.
In a bowl beat the milk, oil, and cornmeal. Add the corn and cheese.
Pour over the casserole.
Chicken can be substituted for the beef, or use a combination of cooked chicken and beef.
Place in oven and cook 25-30 minutes or until golden.

Holidays and Special Occasions

Good Friday – only seafood is eaten
Easter - colored eggs, lamb or ham
Independence Day September 18 – empanadas, chichi, and dance the cueca (national dance)
Christmas –pan de Pascua (fruitcake)
A girl's 15th birthday is marked by a visit to her church, a gathering of family and friends, and much feasting to celebrate her coming of age.

Pisco Sour

For 1 drink

1 egg white, beaten	1 ½ tsp. lemon or lime juice
1 ½ tsp. sugar	3 ice cubes, or crushed ice
3 oz. Pisco	

In a mixing glass dissolve the sugar in the egg white. Add the Pisco, juice and ice. Shake vigorously. Pour into a cocktail glass.

Beverages

Chile has produced very fine wines for over four hundred years, originally for the sacrament at mass brought by Father Francisco de Carabantes to Copiapo in 1548. The earliest wineries were founded in the Maipo Valley, the central region adjacent to Santiago. The wine back then was stored in terra cotta amphorae. The grapes were Spanish pais, related to the Argentine criolla, Muscat, and California mission grapes. The soil contains lime, is at a good elevation, irrigated with a dry climate, perfect for vineyards. The growing season is about 5½ months, shorter than Europe. The vines proved resistant to phylloxera, and many vines are over a hundred years old. Los Vascos (in the Caneten Valley) dates back to 1750 when Miguel Echneique planted a vineyard. French grapes such as Cabernet Sauvignon, Sauvignon Blanc, Semillon and Merlot were brought by descendents in the 19th c. Concha y Toro, the largest vineyard, was founded in 1810 by Don Melchor. The oldest barrel dates to 1883, is from Bosnia, and stores up 22,000 liters of wine. In 1851 Silvestre Ochagavia brought over the first French vines. Cousino Macul is the only vineyard that grows 100% of its grapes on contiguous property.

Chincha is a fermented grape juice that can easily creep up on you. Pisco is distilled from grapes and is used in pisco sours made with egg white and lemon juice. Pichuncho is pisco and vermouth. Aguardiente "fire water" is a clear drink also distilled from grapes. Chile also produces beer, gin and vodka.

In 2010 a massive earthquake and many aftershocks produced extensive damage to Chile's wineries, destroying vineyards, irrigation systems, and millions of dollars of wine in barrels, tanks, and bottles. For a country whose wine sales and popularity had grown exponentially in the last twenty years this was devastating. However the wineries were up and running very quickly.

Did You Know?

The Jesuits imposed restrictions on the vineyards in the 17th c as alcoholism grew among the Indians. The land was used for other agricultural products.
In order to be resistant to earthquakes, especially wineries, many buildings in Chile are made of stone or brick and sealed with calicanto, a mixture of sand, egg whites, and wine!

China

The People's Republic of China is bounded to the north by Russia and Mongolia; to the east North and South Korea and the China Sea; to the south by Vietnam, Laos, Myanmar, and India; and to the west Pakistan and Afghanistan. China's history dates back over 600,000 years and is one of the world's oldest continuous civilizations. Most of the country was basically agrarian with nomads. During the Tang Dynasty (618-907 AD) land was given to eligible males to grow mulberries to produce silkworms, and wet rice was cultivated in the south. Trade in silk and porcelain with the Middle East grew (The Silk Road). During the 17th c European merchants sought trade, which was restricted to Canton. From 1958-61 China was hit hard with famines, when most people were forced to live in communes. Beijing was the first capital of the Yan Kingdom of the Spring and Autumn Period in the 8th c BC, and during the Yuan, Ming, and Qing Dynasties (1279-1911) to the present time.

Dining Etiquette

Friendship and connections are important. Please be prompt when invited for a meal. Please shake hands greeting and departing, letting the Chinese host extend his hand first, and with a nod and slight bow. Wives keep their maiden name. Children take the father's surname. The most senior or oldest person is introduced first. A glass of green tea is almost always served. If bringing a gift, make sure it is always wrapped, and when presented may be declined up to three times. White wrapping is used for funerals. 13 is bad luck, even numbers represent good luck. Gifts are not opened in front of the presenter. When invited to a home please bring a book, liquor, or pictures. Gifts are exchanged at banquets. Everyone should receive a gift, otherwise they will lose face. Never sign your name in red ink, as it means cutting off a friendship. Clocks are never given as the homonym for clock in Chinese means death. If people clap at you, please clap back.

The Chinese are noted for their elaborate banquets given to welcome guests. The guest of honor must reciprocate by giving one of equal stature. These should be planned well ahead are the menu and formalities are quite intricate. On the evening of the banquet the host arrives early to make sure the seating arrangements are correct. Guests, wearing coat and tie, or for ladies dresses or suits, will be met by the host and served tea. If you are applauded on arrival please applaud back. The guest of honor is seated facing the door and the host opposite. Up to twelve dishes will be served, usually from the center of the table. You are expected to try some of each. Take only one course at a time. The host may decide something on his plate is a true delicacy and may place it on the guest of honor. Consider it an honor, and do not return it. Always leave something on your plate, or it will be refilled. Never take too much, and never use your fingers. Bowls can be picked up for eating close to the mouth. The host will never take the last of something. This is a sign there is not enough. When finished place your chopsticks on the table, or chopstick holder. Never place them sticking out of a bowl, which means bad luck or death. Dropping chopsticks or upsetting a rice bowl is considered bad luck. Tea is not served with meals, but at the end and a moist towel will be given to each person. Soup is served last. Fruit might also end the meal. As soon as the banquet is finished the guest of honor must leave first. Other guests will follow.

Toasting is very much a banquet ritual. Three glasses will be set at each place for water, beer or a soft drink, and wine for toasting. The liquor used is mao-tai, made from sorghum and wheat yeast. The host toasts first, drinking to the health of each person, usually after the first course. Catch the eye of the person being toasted, raise the glass in both hands, drink, then overturn the glass to show it is emptied. Then the guest of honor toasts, and all others may follow. The toast is "Chin-Chin" or "Gan Bei". Do not clink glasses, but finish in one gulp. Women can join in the toasting.

Wonton Soup

Serves 4

1 lb. cooked shrimp, chicken, or sausage, or combination	2 tbls. grated fresh ginger
	2 tbls. soy sauce
2 tbls. sesame oil	1 package wonton wrappers
1 can sliced water chestnuts, drained	4 cups chicken stock
2 green onions, chopped	1 packed cup baby leaf spinach
2 tbls. dry Sherry	2 green onions, chopped
2 cloves garlic, minced	

In a food processor blend together the shrimp, sesame oil, water chestnuts, green onions, Sherry, garlic, ginger, and soy sauce.
Place the wonton wrappers on a cookie sheet. Spoon 1 teaspoon of the mixture into the middle of each wrapper. Bring two sides of wrapper together and then other two. Seal with water.
In a pot bring the stock to a boil. Add spinach and green onions. Drop in wonton. Cook for about 1-2 minutes, until wonton just softened.
Fried wonton can be made the same way. Except dropping them in soup, bring oil in a wok to a sizzle. Drop in wonton and cook until lightly browned. Serve with hot mustard.

Cuisine

The Chinese style of cooking has developed over thousands of years. Traditional medicine, which influenced the diet, can be traced back about 2000 years. During the Tang Dynasty (618-907 AD) the yin and yang of dining brought a balance in meals. Yin are the cool foods for calm; yang hot foods for stimulation. Flavors are complimented through the use of condiments and spices. The most commonly used are salt, ginger, soy sauce, coriander, star anise, hot peppers, sesame oil, salted black beans, and vinegar. Flavors are hot, sour, sweet, bitter and salty, which are also related to body parts. Herbs are an important part of the diet and maintaining a healthy body. Many of the staple dishes use rice or noodles with vegetables, a small amount of meat, and perhaps a sauce. Noodles are made from rice, buckwheat soba, udon, rice, cellophane or eggs. Fish is served along the coastline. Fruits have certain connotations – oranges (happiness); pomegranate (fertility); apples (peace); and a pear (prosperity). Fish is a symbol of abundance. Rice is a filler only. All the food is placed on the table at the same time, unless at an elaborate banquet. Hot foods are served in covered dishes.

Long-Life Noodles

Long-Life noodles are served on birthdays and the Chinese New Year to signify a long life. The longer the noodles, the longer the life!

Serves 4

8 large dried mushrooms
1 cup hot water
8 oz. noodles
4 tbls. vegetable oil
1 tbls. soy sauce

2 large cloves garlic, minced
3 tbls. shallots, minced
6 oz. mixed fresh mushrooms, sliced
3 tbls. oyster sauce
3 green onions or 6 chives, sliced

In a bowl soak the mushrooms for 20 minutes. Drain and reserve liquid. Slice the mushrooms.
Prepare the noodles according to the instructions on the package. Drain.
In a bowl combine 2 tbls. oil, soy sauce and noodles, until noodles are coated.
Heat the remaining oil in a wok. Stir in the garlic and shallots. Add all the mushrooms (dried and fresh). Add the mushroom liquid, oyster sauce, green onions, and the noodles. Serve warm.

Each region of China has unique dishes:

North – roasts, noodles, duck, mild sauces
Cantonese (south) – fresh seafood, dumplings, sweet and sour pork, dim sum "to touch the heart"
Shanghai (east) Fukien – crab rolls, pancakes
Szechwan (west) – spicy dishes
Beijing – dumplings, Mongolian hot pot, kebabs, oil, garlic, coriander, onion, vinegar
Fujien – fried foods, use of coconuts and pineapple
Xi'ia – mutton in dumplings or soup
Chaizhou – salty taste, dips, fried food, strong teas
Shechuan – hot, spicy, chili peppers, ginger, onions, garlic, poultry, pork, beans, beancurd, and eggplant
Hunan – herbs, flowers, pimento, hot bean curd; hot spicy food; chilies; garlic; ginger, vinegar, pork, ham, chicken, rice, sweet and sour dishes, glutinous rice cakes, rice candy. Desserts include Hunan steamed date buns and shredded radish pancakes
Hangzhou – famous for tea farming - Dragon Well or Longjing tea; fish, especially fried shrimp
Northern China – dumplings, buns, noodles, vegetables, bean sauces, white cabbage, duck, pork, chicken, seafood
Mongolian – barbeques, hot pots, wine, soy sauce, sesame oil, lamb – mainly grilled
Xinjang – mutton, pilau rice with apricots, noodle soup, grapes, and melons
Urumgi – a very Muslim area. Please eat with your right hand only. The eye of a sheep, a delicacy, is presented to the guest of honor, and must be ingested. The guest must also throw the head of the sheep through the hole in the roof of the yurt.
Shanghai – fried food, drunken chicken or shrimp (boiled and soaked in wine), scallions, ginger, garlic, hot peppers, noodles, vegetables, seafood. Meat is cooked in sugar, soy, ginger and sauces. The appearance of the food is important. It might be served in a melon or squash and vegetables

carved into various shapes. Xiao long bao are dumplings served for breakfast, not only in Shanghai, but elsewhere.

In the countryside the diet consists mainly of vegetables and cereal – in the north wheat and millet, and in the south rice.

Holidays and Special Occasions

Lunar New Year is a time for family feasts with ten courses or more. Foods include meats, noodles, mandarin oranges, and dumplings. In the north "bianshi" (flat food) dumplings made with vegetable and ground meat are served. Long, uncut noodles symbolize longevity; whole chickens and duck are served with the head and feet to symbolize family unity; clams, oysters, and dumplings represent wealth; roast pig purification and peace; oranges and tangerines represent happiness; a whole fish with head and tail is served to symbolize togetherness and good wishes; and jai purifies the body. The fish is served as the last course. Niangao are New Year's cakes. Families eat at round tables which are a symbol of unity. Give food as a gift which might be a ham, dried duck, or mandarin oranges. Children are given red envelopes with money and employees red envelopes with their bonuses.

Lantern Festival – yuanziao (sweet dumplings made from glutinous rice, rice flour and sugar fillings), symbolizing reunion.

Dragon Boat Festival is held on the fifth day of the fifth month of the lunar calendar to honor the departed soul of ch"u Yuan, a famous poet - jungzi (glutinous rice dumplings wrapped in bamboo or reed leaves and served with different savories);

The Moon Festival – mooncakes (pastries made with red bean paste, sesame seeds, dates, and egg yolks symbolizing harmony and perfection)

Hungry Ghost Festival – end of summer – The Chinese believe the gates of the spirit world open and ghosts look for paper and food offerings that are placed by families on altars outside

Eighth Day of 12th lunar month – labazhou – porridge of rice, millet, glutinous rice, sorghum, red beans, dates, walnuts and peanuts

Long noodles are served on birthdays to forecast a long life.

For the 79-80th birthday a special liqueur is served to encourage longevity.

Food offerings are also made at ancestral altars twice a month.

Weddings – longan (dried fruit), dates and nuts are served to symbolize a happy union and sons

Women in childbirth are given chicken soup, chicken and eggs. At the time of birth the newborn is given a chicken to feed the mother. Old people and the sick are also given chicken and eggs.

Beverages

China is known to have produced wine since the Hsia Dynasty (2183-1751 BC) when cereals were used, and later made from rice. This is 12-20 proof and made from fermented glutinous rice. Rice is cooked, yeast added for fermentation, all usually within eight days. Shaoxing (rice wine) is served warm in a small cup. Hejie Jiu (lizard wine) contains one dead lizard!

Chinese beer dates back nine thousand years, with recent archaeological findings showing that Chinese villagers were brewing beer type alcoholic drinks as far back as 7000 BC made with rice, honey, and grape and hawthorn fruits. Beer is brewed from rice, hops, and barley. The Chinese character for beer means "humble mouth liquor". Tsingtao beer was first brewed by Germans in China in 1903.

China is considered to be the first country to cultivate tea. Yunnan province, located in southwest China, produced the tea in old forests that are fertile from the Mekong River watershed. According to legend tea was invented by Emperor Shen Nung in 2737 BC when some tea leaves accidently fell into his boiling water. The first description of the tea ceremony dates to the 8th c "code of tea", described by the poet Lu Wu in "The Holy Scripture of Tea". Lantau Island grows "cloud and mist tea". Tea is drunk from small cups without handles.

Did You Know?

Rice is the symbol of fertility and purity. Rice was raised in the ShaTin Valley from 1644-1911 for the exclusive use of the emperors. Domesticated rice is thought to have been cultivated in the Yangtzu River Delta at Hemutu since c 5000 BC. Rice noodles are known to have dated back 6500 years in Huan province. Rice farming was brought from India about 2000 BC with artificial irrigation introduced c 5th-1st c BC. Winnowing, rotary winnowing fan, and the winnowing basket were developed by the Chinese. By the 11 c AD intensive rice cultivation existed with fertilizer from humans and animals. As in many parts of Southeast Asia the people, villages, and rice paddies were intertwined.
Wheat has been grown for over 5000 years in the Xinjiang Uygur autonomous region.
In China the pumpkin is the symbol of fruitfulness, health and gain, and is called the "emperor of the garden".
The Chinese were the first to make noodles, ketchup, cultivate peanuts, invented soy sauce about 500 BC and chopsticks c 4th c BC. Chow mein means fried noodles.
The first written word for cinnamon dates over 5000 years ago.
Chickens have been cultivated since c 2000 BC.
Citrus fruits are from south central China, especially kumquats, oranges and mandarin oranges.
The first reference to a lemon was made in 1175 AD by Fan Ch'en-ta.
Marco Polo learned about freezing sweet cream (ice cream) while visiting China.
Underground ice houses for preserving fish and food have been in use since at least 1100 BC.
Kumming, a city over 2,000 years old, was once a trading center for salt, silver, gold, silk and lumber.
Nanching has produced white porcelain since the 1st c AD. The word porcelain comes from the Portuguese "pourcellana" or "cowrie shells".
Harbin, which means "A place for drying fishing nets in the sun", linked China with Russia and Mongolia with the Trans Siberian Railroad, built in the 1890s.
Guangzhou and its port city Whampoa are situated on the historic trading routes dating back over 2000 years, and since 714 AD was the first official Chinese trading port. Starting in 1715 the British East India Company headquartered here.
Tai O is known for drying fish and 200 years ago had salt factories.
The wok was introduced using little fuel, great heat, food chopped in small pieces, and few utensils.
The pickling of cabbage with rice wine dates from the building of the Great Wall and the Tartars, later getting its name (sauerkraut) from the Austrians.
Ice House Street on Hong Kong was named for the ice shipped from the United States before the turn of the 20th c.

Colombia

Colombia is bordered to the east by Venezuela and Brazil; to the south by Ecuador and Peru; to the north by the Caribbean Sea; to the northwest by Panama; and to the west by the Pacific Ocean. Archeological sites at Monsú and Pubenza date from about 20,000 B. C. Hunter-gatherers were known to exist c 10,000 BC. They developed powerful political systems called cacicazgos. They farmed maize, potato, quinoa and cotton, had skilled goldsmiths; and traded emeralds, blankets, ceramic handicrafts, coca and salt. The Spanish arrived in 1499 creating the Viceroyalty of New Granada made up of what is now Colombia, Venezuela, Ecuador, the northern part of Brazil, and Panama with the capital Bogota. New Granada won its independence in 1833, but the Republic of Colombia did not occur until 1886. The capital Bogota, was first inhabited by the Muiscas, members of the Chibcha language family. The official language is Spanish.

Dining Etiquette

Please arrive slightly late when invited for a meal. Dinner may not be served until 10 PM or later. Please bring a gift – a plant, liquor, chocolates, or something from your country. If giving flowers please send in advance, but not lilies or marigolds which are for funerals. Gifts are not opened when received. Please shake hands greeting and departing. Close female friends may hug, and close male friends may give an abrazzo (hug). Drinks will be served. The hostess or host will seat the guests. The host will say "Buen provecho" "enjoy your meal" to start. Food is eaten continental style with the fork in the left hand and the knife in the right. Please keep your hands at table level, but no elbows on the table. Do try everything on your plate, but leave a small amount when you are finished. Family is important and elders treated with respect. Please stand when elders enter a room, and hold a chair for them when sitting. The toast is "Salud". Please wait for the host to make the first toast before you start drinking.

Cuisine

The dishes are a blend of foods native to Columbia with European influences. The main meal of the day is eaten at lunch. Arepa, rice, beans, potatoes, yams, corn, arracacha, cassava, avocado, fried plantains, chichorron (pork rind), fried eggs, ground steak, steak, trout, tripe soup, chicken, pork, fish, and coffee are part of the typical diet. Many tropical fruits grow in Colombia and include plantain, bananas, zapote, nispero, lulo, uchuva, passion fruit, borojo, curuba, mamoncillo, guanabana, guava, mango, apples, pears, blackberries, strawberries. The banana leaves are used in cooking and most of these fruits produce fruit juices. Bananas can be fried, boiled, or grilled. Coconut is used for oil, milk, stews, ice cream and desserts. Vegetables include onions, garlic, peppers, tomatoes, beans, and lentils.

The different regions of Colombia have their own dishes and varieties of foodstuffs grown as the country has mountainous regions, jungles, plains, valleys and plateaux. In Bogota and the Ande region ajiaco (chicken, corn, potato, avocado and guascas (Gallant Soldiers, an herb) soup is served with rice, avocado and tostadas. Cream and capers may also be served with this. At breakfast changua, a soup with milk, scallions and eggs may be served. The Colombian coastline lies along the Caribbean where dishes with fish, pork, coconut rice, and suero (similar to sour cream) are served. In the east grilled meats and fresh water fish are served. In the Amazon region beef and freshwater fish are common. Tumaco is known for its giant shrimp.

Bandeja Paisa

This is the national dish of Colombia and comes from the Antioquia region. Paisa is derived from Paisano, people from this part of the country. The Bandeja Paisa is made up of many different dishes. Put the rice on a platter. Serve the other dishes mounded around the rice, or in separate bowls, and top with the fried eggs, and sliced avocado.

2 cups cooked rice   Avocado, peeled and sliced
Fried eggs

Chorizo

4 chorizo   Oil

In a skillet sauté the chorizo until just browned.

Arepa (Cornmeal Bread)

2 ½ cups cornmeal   2 tbls. melted butter
1 tsp. salt   Vegetable oil
2 ½ cups hot water

Combine the flour and salt. Slowly pour in the hot water and melted butter, stirring with a wooden spoon until a dough is formed. Set aside for 15 minutes.
Divide the dough into 20 pieces, make into a ball, and then flatten.
Heat some oil in a skillet. Slowly put in dough and cook until browned on one side. Turn.
Serve hot.

Hogao (Tomato Sauce)

2 tbls. vegetable oil   2 cloves garlic, minced
3 scallions, chopped   1 tsp. cumin
2 tomatoes, chopped

Heat the oil in a sauce pan. Add the other ingredients. Cook until this has thickened into a sauce, about 15-20 minutes.

Frijoles Colombianos (Red Beans)

1 can red kidney beans, drained	1 tomato, chopped
1 tbls. oil	1 jalapeno, seeded and chopped
3 scallions, chopped	Cilantro
2 cloves garlic, minced	

Heat the oil in a sauce pan. Stir in the scallions and tomatoes until just softened. Add garlic and jalapeno. Stir in beans.
Serve warm garnished with cilantro.

Carne en Polvo (powdered beef)

1 lb. skirt or flank steak	½ tsp. cumin
2 cloves garlic, minced	Salt and pepper
1 onion, finely chopped	

In bowl combine the beef and other ingredients. Let marinate in refrigerator for at least 2 hours or overnight.
Place the meat in a skillet. Just cover with water. Cook 1 hour. Let cool.
In a food processor mince the meat.
Grilled meat can be substituted for the powdered.

Fried Plantains

4 plantains or bananas, peeled and sliced lengthwise	Vegetable oil

Heat some oil in a skillet and cook bananas 2-3 minutes per side. Drain on a paper towel. Serve warm.

Colombian Specialties

Arepas – corn cakes
Arepa de Queso - fried masa cakes with cheese
Tamales- corn cakes wrapped in bananas and steamed. They may be filled with chicken, potatoes, peas, carrots, rice
Tolimenses –tamales made from corn dough and filled with peas, carrots, rice, chicken, pork and spices and wrapped in plantain leaves
Lechona Tolimense – whole roast pig stuffed with rice, and vegetables. Pork is eaten on Sundays

Sancocho – fish, meat or chicken soup with corn, potatoes, yucca, plantain, and spices
Ajaico - chicken and potato soup or stew with galinsoga, a mountain herb usually native to Colombia
Cocido bogotano – beef and vegetable stew
Sopa de mondogo – tripe and vegetable soup
Bandeja paisa – bean, rice, fried eggs, chorizo, and pork rind served on a bandeja (platter)
Cazuela de mariscos – seafood stew
Mote de queso – chopped yam and cheese dish

Fritanga – grilled meats such as beef, chicken, pork feet, lamb, ribs and sausage with potatoes and arepas
Morcilla – blood sausage
Hogao – fried onion and tomato side dish
Chorizo – spicy sausage
Chunchillo – fried cow intestines
Empanadas – pastry with meat or other filling
Rice and beans
Cuchuco – wheat soup with fava beans, potatoes, ribs, peas
Arroz con pescado – fish and rice
Viudo de pescado – fish stew cooked in holes dug in the ground and covered with hot rocks
Piquette – chicken, pork, corn, white and sweet potatoes,

Aborrajado – deep fried plantains with cheese
Carimnolas – empanadas made with manioc
Pan de maiz – cornbread
Pandebono- corn flour, cheese and egg bread
Patacones – green plantains fried like pancakes
Quesillos – cream cheese wrapped in banana leaves
Pan de sagu – sago bread
Arequipe – boiled milk, sugar and vanilla that can be eaten by itself, with crackers, as a filling, or rolled into a ball with nuts (dulce de leche in other Latin American countries)
Arroz con leche – rice with milk
Arroz con coco – rice with coconut milk
Roscon – sweet bun with guava jelly

Holidays and Special Occasions

Semana Santa begins the Thursday before Palm Sunday with religious services
Easter – sopa de maiz (corn soup); cocido Bogotano (beef stew)
Christmas Eve – pork, ham, ajiaco Bogotano (chicken soup), roasted pig, or grilled meats, bunuelos, arepas, empanadas, hojuelas (fried dough with jam and sugar), natilla (Christmas flan with cinnamon, cornstarch and milk). Usually a toast with aguargiente, champagne or other drink is used.
A girl's 15th birthday is celebrated with an elaborate party, and gold is usually given as a present.

Beverages

Coffee (tinto) is grown on the cool mountain slopes on plantations, and exported all over the world. The ripe red berries are washed with the outer skin and pulp cleaned off; then soaked in tanks; a final washing, dried then roasted. Beer and wine are also produced in the country.

Other beverages are: Aguardiente- (fire water) an alcoholic beverage made from sugarcane that is the national drink; Chicha – alcoholic beverage made from corn; Aguapanela – dissolved panela (sugarloaf) in hot water which may be served with lime juice; Canelazo – alcoholic aguapanela with cinnamon and aguardiente served in glasses with the rims rubbed with sugar; Guarapo- fermented fruit, usually grapes and pineapple) kept in ceramic jars with panela added; Chirrinche – distilled guarapo; Refajo - made with kola, beer or rum; Champus – corn, pineapple and lulo drink; Salpicon – diced fruit and soda; and Lulada – made with lulo (a citrus fruit). Hot chocolate is made with hot water, milk, semi- sweet chocolate and cinnamon using a monillo for stirring.

Did You Know?

Colombia is one of the largest producers of orchids in the world. Vanilla beans come from the vanilla planifolia orchid.

The Comoros

Ngazidja (Grande Comore), Mwali (Moheli), Nzwani (Anjouan), and Mayotte comprise the archipelago Union of Comoros. The islands are located in the Indian Ocean between northwest Madagascar and northeast Mozambique off East Africa. The earliest settlers are believed to have arrived before the 6th c from Africa or Asia. Later Swahili settled here. Trade was mainly with Madagascar and the Middle East from the 11th to 15th c. The first Portuguese explorers arrived in 1506. The French established colonial rule in 1841. Comoros became independent from France in 1975, but Mayotte is a department of France. The capital, Moroni, is located on Grand Comore. The official languages are Comorian, Arabic and French.

Dining Etiquette

It is an honor to be invited to a Comorian home. Please remove your shoes before entering a home. Men shake hands greeting and departing. Women and children will eat in the kitchen or separately from the men who will eat in the dining or living room. Before a meal "bismillah" "thanks to Allah" is said. Food may be placed on a plate and eaten with a spoon, or your right hand only. Often you will be seated on a mat on the floor, not at a table. This is mainly a Muslim country so pork and alcohol are not served. Elders are treated with much respect. Families are matriarchal.

Cuisine

Trading stations were located on the spice route between India and Africa by Persian and Yemen merchants in the 15th and 16th c. The Swahili culture also influenced the cuisine. The Arabs introduced cooking with spices such as cloves, saffron, and cinnamon, pomegranate, and rice dishes. The Portuguese brought peppers, maize, chilies, tomatoes, bananas, pineapples, limes and oranges. Coconuts, cattle, vanilla, coffee, cocoa beans, cloves, basil, ylang-ylang, jackfruit, nutmeg, cardamom, palm, jasmine, cinnamon, copra, and sugar cane are raised on the islands. Being an island nation fish are readily available such as lobster, crab, shrimp, squid, and shark. Rice and meat or fish, spices, manioc and root vegetables, plantains and coconut milk are dietary staples. In most places the food is cooked outside the house.

Comorian Specialties

Langouste a la vanilla – lobster in vanilla sauce
Pilau mouton – mutton pilau
Le me tsolola – fried fish, meat, green bananas, onions and coconut milk

Poulet – chicken dishes with curry, coconut or other ingredients
Lentil dishes
Maharagwe – red bean and coconut stew
Supu – meat broth, usually eaten at breakfast

118

Laddu (ground rice, sugar, ghee and cardamom)

½ cups brown rice

1 cup sugar

1 tsp. ground cardamom

¼ cup water

¼ cup cashews and almonds, ground coarsely

2 tsp. ghee

½ cup fresh grated coconut

In a pan just slightly roast the rice until it puffs up. Let cool. Powder the rice. And transfer to a bowl.

Add almonds to the rice. Add coconut and cardamom.

In a pan heat the sugar and water until the sugar boils and froths. Add to rice. Add ghee.

Form into small balls.

Holidays and Special Occasions

Muslims celebrate the Birth of the Prophet, Ramadan with fasting, Eid al-Adha and Eid al-Fitr with fish, meat and other dishes.

The birthdays of local saints are celebrated at various times during the year.

Easter and Christmas are celebrated by Christians.

During festivals soups and salads with spicy sauces are served.

Dishes for special occasions will include beef, goat, white rice and curdled milk, cakes, porridge with the dried fruit of sago palm.

Weddings, births, circumcision and reburials mean much food such as chicken stews, salads and rice.

Beverages

Coffee is drunk very strong. Tea will often be spiced with lemongrass or ginger.

Democratic Republic of Congo

The Democratic Republic of the Congo borders the Central African Republic and Sudan to the north; Uganda, Rwanda, and Burundi to the east; Zambia and Angola to the south; the Atlantic Ocean to the west; and is separated from Tanzania by Lake Tanganyika in the east. This part of Africa has been inhabited for 80,000 years. The Semliki harpoon found at Katanda is one of the oldest harpoons ever found and dates from this period, and was used to harpoon large catfish. Beginning in the 2nd millennium BC people farmed millet, had domesticated livestock, and used palm oil. The Imbonga were known to have villages in Mbandaka and Lake Tumba and the Urewe in the east as far back as 650 BC, and the Ngovo 350 BC in Lower Congo. Iron smelting became important. In the 7th and 8th c. AD the Bantu arrived from western Africa to settle in the Congo basin and Bantu became the primary language. The Kingdom of Kongo was a powerful kingdom from the 14th to 19th c. European explorers arrived in the 1870s and in 1885 the Congo Free State was under Belgian rule. In 1908 it became the Belgian Congo; in 1960 achieving independence as the Republic of Congo; Zaire from 1971-97 (Zaire is the Portuguese name for the Congo River), and now the DR. Kinshasa, the capital, located on the Congo River, was once a fishing village, but became a trading post in 1881 under Henry Morton Stanley and named Leopoldville. Rubber was a leading crop under the Belgians. There are over two hundred ethnic groups and languages spoken in the DR and three large Bantu ethnic groups – Mongo, Luba, and Kongo, and the Hamitic - Mangbetu-Azande. Minority groups include Pygmy, Nilo-Saharian, and Afro-Asiatic. French and Swahili are the official languages.

Dining Etiquette

If you are invited for a meal please accept. Please arrive promptly when invited for a meal and remove your shoes. Please shake hands greeting and departing. Good friends may hug and kiss three times on alternating cheeks. In some parts of the country men do not shake hands with women. Gifts are not usually brought for a first visit, but after a friendship has been established. Then please bring food or a gift for the home. Allow more senior members to enter a room ahead of you.

Hands are washed before and after a meal. If seated, the honored guest is next to the host. Do not point your feet at the food or the others eating. Honored guests are served first, then the oldest male, other men, women and children. Do not eat or drink until the oldest man has been served and begun eating. If a communal bowl is served use only the part of the bowl directly in front of you. Please try some or all of the food. Food is eaten with the fingers of the right hand. If you are offered utensils please eat with the fork or spoon in the right hand. If a bowl or plate is to be shared only eat from the part of the bowl directly in front of you. There are no Bantu words for "please" or thank-you", so they may not be used.

Sharing what one has is very important in this culture. Gifts are given to visitors. Respect for elders, chiefs, and ancestors is very important. Family also is very important, and extended families live in close proximity. Western Congo families are matriarchal.

Fotoli (Corn and Chicken Soup)

Serves 6

1 3 lb. chicken, cut into pieces
3 cups corn dough
6 tomatoes
3 onions, chopped

1 small red or green pepper, chopped
Salt and pepper to taste
Palm oil
Water

Pour a small amount of the palm oil into a pot. Add the chicken and onions. Fry for 10 minutes. Add enough water to cover the chicken and add pepper and tomatoes. Cook till tender. Make the corn dough into small balls (dumplings) and add to the soup.
Serve warm.

Corndough

2 cups corn flour
1 cup grated cassava

Warm water to dampen flour and cassava

In a bowl combine the flour and cassava with just enough warm water to dampen. Shape into a ball. Cover with a clean cloth. Set in a warm place for 2-3 days allowing to ferment. This will have a slightly sour aroma.

Cuisine

The cuisine is influenced by the different regions of the DR. Cassava, peanuts and hot peppers arrived in the country in the 1500s. The cuisine has been influenced by native dishes, but also the French, Arabic and Asian.

The major agricultural products are cassava, okra, maize, corn, palm oil, bananas, mango, rice, coffee, manioc, potatoes, peanuts, chili pepper, sweet potatoes, yams, taro, plantain, tomatoes, pumpkins, peas, nuts, beans, onions, sugar cane, cabbage, and coffee. The most important crops are coffee and palm oil. Less than 2 percent of the land is cultivated. Dishes use locally grown products – fruits, grains, vegetables, dairy and meat such as, bushmeat, goats, beef and chicken, fish, oysters and shrimp from the coast, peanut butter and palm oil. Wild fruit, mushrooms especially used among the Luba, honey are collected in the rural areas. Green vegetables include cassava leaves, tshitekutaku, and okra. Fish are baked, boiled, fried, smoked or salted. Grasshoppers and caterpillars are also eaten. Sauces are made with tomatoes, onions, herbs, and hot chili or sweet green peppers.

Meals consist of a starch usually made from cassava or cornmeal (fufu or ugali) vegetables, meat, if available, usually goat, is made into a spicy stew. The fufu or ugali is rolled into a ball and dipped into the stew or sauce with an indentation made with the thumb. The cassava root is eaten as a vegetable or made into tapioca. Cassava leaves are edible.

DR Specialties

Mouambe - chicken in palm oil
Kwanga – fermented cassava bread, cooked and stored in banana leaves
Piri piri – chicken with chili pepper
Fufu – cassava dish
Sombe – boiled, mashed and cooked cassava leaves
Oto – yams, eggs, palm oil
Ndakala –dried fish
Pili pili – hot pepper
Saka saka – ground cassava leaves cooked in palm oil and peanut paste
Mabake – freshwater fish cooked in marantacee leaves
Fish baked in banana leaves

Lituma – baked mashed plantain balls
Mvambe – chicken with peanut sauce
Chikwanga – cassava pounded into a paste in banana leaves
Nataba grilled goat
Sweet potatoes with peanuts
Loso na madesu - rice mixed with beans
Mbembe – snails
Nkyekye – palm nut stew
Palm nut soup
Gari – roasted and ground cassava
Moin moin – hot pepper, onion and black-eyed pea paste

Holidays and Special Occasions

On Christmas Eve Christians attend church and take a present for the baby Jesus, usually food such as fruit. Since this is a warm climate Christmas is celebrated with tables set outside.
Special meals with spicy dishes are offered for initiation rites, births, puberty ceremonies, weddings, funerals, blessing of the spears, fisherman's prayer, and other occasions. Even if a family has only one chicken or animal they will be killed for holidays, funerals, weddings, and births. Families make their own beer and palm wine. Singing and dancing are very much a part of the ritual.

Beverages

Soft drinks are called sucre. Local beers are brewed from rice. Palm wine is made from the sap of the palm tree, which is then fermented with natural yeasts, and has an alcoholic content of 5-7 percent. Odae is fermented palm wine. Coffee is a major agricultural product.

Republic of Congo

The Republic of Congo is located in Central Africa, bordered by Gabon, Cameroon, the Central African Republic, the Democratic Republic of the Congo, the Angolan province of Cabinda and the Gulf of Guinea. The earliest inhabitants were the Pygmy who were later absorbed by the Bantu. The Bantu kingdoms of the Kongo, Loango and Take had trading routes in the Congo River basin. The Portuguese arrived in the 15th c. During the 1880s the region was part of France and in 1908 France formed French Equatorial Africa consisting of Middle Congo, Gabon, Chad and Oubangui-Chari (Central African Republic) with Brazzaville as the capital. In 1960 the middle Congo became the Republic of Congo. The capital, Brazzaville, located across the Congo River from Kinshasa, was founded in 1880 on the site of a Bateke village and named for Pierre Savorgnan de Brazza, a Franco-Italian explorer. French is the official language with 62 other languages spoken. The Kongo are the largest ethnic group.

Dining Etiquette

It is an honor to be invited to a Congo home. Please remove your shoes before entering. The guest of honor will be seated next to the host. Please wash your hand before and after eating. Please eat only with your right hand. A fork or spoon might be used, but only in the right hand. Food is eaten from a communal bowl with the guest of honor and elders first, followed by the men, then women and children. You will eat from the part of the bowl that is in front of you. Do not start eating until the oldest man has started.

Cuisine

The Congo has a fertile valley and rain forest and fish is available from the Congo River and along the coastline. The food has been influenced by the French, Asian and African cuisines. Much of the cooking takes place in front of the home, most of which are built of mud brick. Cassava, rice, palm oil, and peanuts are mainly used in cooking, along with the bread eaten. Fruits include bananas, citrus fruit, guava, mangoes, papaya, and pineapple. Vegetables include cabbage, carrots, green beans, onions, spinach, squash, potatoes, tomatoes, taro, and manioc. Oysters and shrimp are some of the seafood found here. Sugar cane, coffee, and cocoa are also harvested.

Mouambe (chicken in palm oil)

Serves 6

3 lb. chicken, cut into pieces
Juice of 1 lemon
1 jalapeno, seeded and minced
1 tsp. salt

2 tbls. palm oil
2 onions, chopped
3 tomatoes, chopped
1 cup palm butter

Combine the lemon juice, salt and jalapeno in a bowl. Add the chicken, turning to coat all sides. Set aside for ½ hour or more.
Heat the oil in a pot and add the onions and cook until just tender. Add the chicken and cook until it is browned on all sides. Stir in the tomatoes, and a small of amount of water, so pot does not burn. Add the palm butter. Cover and simmer 1 hour.
Serve with rice or fufu.
Peanut oil and butter can be substituted for the palm oil and butter for a dish called Muamba Nsusu.
Cayenne or other hot peppers can be substituted for the jalapeno
Beef, mutton, or fish can be substituted for the chicken.

Specialties

Piri piri – chicken with chili pepper
Saka saka – ground cassava leaves with palm oil and peanut paste

Makobe – fish cooked in marantacee leaves (member of arrowroot family)

Holidays and Special Occasions

During festivals chicken, plum wine and beer are consumed. Major holidays are New Year's when family and friends gather to celebrate the New Year with food and drink; Tree Day (March 6); Easter and Easter Monday; National Reconciliation Day (June 10); Independence Day (August 15); All Saints'; and Christmas. Christmas Eve families and friends eat rice, fufu, and stew or okra soup, meat and porridge. On Christmas families attend church services and are served rice, roast beef, mutton, chicken, or pork.

Beverages

Palm wine and beer are produced locally. Fruit juices such as pineapple, coconut, tamarind and mango are drunk. Other drinks are tea and coffee

Did You Know

Tribes and villages have totems representing animals. They cannot eat that animal as it is their protector.

Cook Islands

The Cook Islands were first settled in the 6th century by Polynesian people who migrated from Tahiti to the northeast. Spanish ships visited the islands in the 16th century; the first written record of contact with the islands came in 1595 with the sighting of Pukapuka by Spanish sailor Álvaro de Mendaña de Neira, who called it *San Bernardo* (Saint Bernard). Pedro Fernandes de Queirós, a Portuguese captain working for the Spanish crown, made the first recorded European landing in the islands when he set foot on Rakahanga in 1606, calling it *Gente Hermosa* (Beautiful People). British navigator Captain James Cook arrived in 1773 and 1777 and named the islands the *Hervey Islands*; the name "Cook Islands", in honor of Cook, appeared on a Russian naval chart published in the 1820s. In 1813 John Williams, a missionary on the *Endeavour* made the first recorded sighting of Rarotonga. The Cook Islands became a British protectorate in 1888, and in 1965 self-governing. Rarotonga is the capital. English is the official language, though Maori is still spoken, and used in the churches.

Dining Etiquette

Please arrive promptly if invited for a meal. Please shake hands greeting and departing. You may bring a gift from your own country, but here if a gift is given, a present or something else will be given in return. The people are very hospitable and enjoy entertaining. Guests will be seated at a table.

Family is very important and often extended families will live together. Society is still divided into clans. Flowers are given when people travel departing and returning.

Cuisine

The islands produce a number of tropical fruit and vegetables. Seafood – clams, octopus, lobster, crab, and fish and coconuts – coconut milk and coconut cream, grated coconuts and coconut hearts (heart of palm) are used in much of their cooking. Other ingredients are taro, arrowroot, ginger, lime, basil, garlic, bananas, pawpaw, papaya, cassava, breadfruit, coriander roots, and smoked sea salt. Banana leaves are used to wrap foods to cook them. Breadfruit can be boiled, roasted, fried, baked, or barbecued. Cassava is boiled. Seafood can be grilled or cooked underground in an umu or earth oven.

Ika (raw fish marinated in vinegar, oil, salt, onion, and coconut cream)

Serves 4-6

2 lbs. halibut, cod, or other white fish fillets, cut into bitesize pieces
1 cup fresh lemon or lime juice
1 medium onion, chopped
2 tsp. sea salt

2 scallions, chopped
½ bell pepper, finely chopped
1 tomato, chopped
1 cup coconut milk

Combine the juice, onion and salt in a bowl. Add the fish, cover and marinate for at least 3-4 hours in the refrigerator. Drain.
Combine the fish, scallions, pepper, tomato and coconut.
Serve immediately.

Cook Island Specialties

Rukau – mashed taro leaves with coconut sauce and onion
Rori – raw or cooked sea cucumber with butter and garlic
Lap lap - wrapped in banana leaves
Eke – octopus

Puaka – suckling pig
Soubise – white cream sauce containing onions.
Poke – dessert of banana and coconut milk or pawpaw

Holidays and Special Occasions

Observed holidays are New Year's Day, Anzac Day (April 25th), Queen's Birthday (first Monday in June), Constitution Day (August 4), Flag Raising Day (October 27), and Tiare (Floral) Festival Week in November.
Umukai "food from the oven" – is a feast held for special occasions. The food is cooked in an umu, earthen oven filled with firewood and basalt rocks with a banana wood grill placed over the hot rocks. Meat, ika and vegetables are wrapped in banana leaves, placed in a sack and put in the umu. The umu is covered and the food cooks for three hours or more. Other dishes are served with this such as potato salad and kava is served as a ceremonial drink.

Beverages

The most common fruit beverages are soursop, orange, mango, and coconut water. Kava is a drink made from the root of the pepper plant. The Matutu Brewing Company and Cooks Lager produce local beer in Rarotonga. Bush Beer is a beer brewed from oranges, bananas, or pawpaw, malt, yeast and sugar.

Costa Rica

Costa Rica, located in Central America, is bounded by Nicaragua on the north, the Caribbean Sea the east; Panama the south; and the Pacific Ocean to the west. The native people were of Mesoamerican and Andean stock. The Mesoamericans who built a structured society and raised corn, beans, and squash. Christopher Columbus discovered the country during his fourth voyage on September 8, 1502, naming it the Rich Coast of Veracruz. The region became part of the Viceroyalty of Spain. It became independent in 1821, and in 1823 part of the Federal Republic of Central America. In 1838 Costa Rica became a sovereign nation. San Jose was founded in 1737 as Villa de la Boca del Monte and became the capital in 1837. Spanish is the official language.

Dining Etiquette

When invited to a home be punctual, or a few minutes early. Please don't come uninvited. Tea, cocktail parties and dinners are very popular. Please bring a gift of flowers (not calla lilies which are for funerals), wine, chocolates, or something for the home. If the family has children bring a gift for them. People shake hands greeting and departing. Women extend hands first. Men if they know each other well will embrace. Women will usually touch the left forearm lightly or will kiss each other on the cheek. Wine or cocktails will be served. Please address people using titles or Mr., Mrs, or Miss. Beverages will be served. People may stand close to each other when speaking. The eldest son, father or hostess will escort guests into the dining room, where the male guest of honor is seated to the right of the hostess. Grace is usually said. Meals are served in courses, beginning with soup or appetizer, salad, entrée, and dessert. Wine, water, or juices are at each place. If you pass a dish do so to your left. Salad is eaten with a fork only or by pushing the the knife. The fork and spoon at the top of your dish are for dessert. When finished cross the knife and fork down, place parallel on the right side of the plate. Hands should be kept at table level. Coffee will be served after the meal is finished. Toasting is initiated by the host who raises his glass and says "Pura Vida" "pure life" or "Salud", then the others may drink.

Meals are social, not business occasions. They may last for several hours. Do call or write the hostess to thank her. Names are written with given name, father's last name, then the mother's maiden name. A woman keeps her surname after marriage and adds "de" to her husband's surname. The father's surname is the one used, but use all three in correspondence.

Cuisine

Records show that cacao beans, flour, pigs, lard, tobacco, chickens and liquor were used as barter in the 16 c. Livestock has been raised since the colonial period. The first exports were mules, and later cacao and tobacco, coffee, sugarcane, apples, grapes, melons, pineapples and cotton. Fruits were Costa Rica's major export after Minor C. Keith founded the United Fruit Company in 1872, and the British built most of the railroad system.

Costa Rican food is a combination of Spanish, continental and indigenous products. The Indians grew yucca, corn, pejibaye (orange fruit of palm), fished and used root vegetables. The different regions have their own produce and recipes. Vanilla; fruits – bananas, black raspberries, mamoes, guayabas (guavas), grapes, star fruit, granadillas (passion fruit), tamarindo, gunanabana, oranges, papaya, pineapple and melons; vegetables – tomatoes, corn, yucca, carrots, peppers, hearts of palm, (palmito), and greens; coconut; nuts; seafood- shrimp, scallops, clams, mahi-mahi, red snapper, pompano, oysters, lobsters; chicken; beef and pork, and machaca, a fresh water fish from the lakes are the main staples. Popular juices, batidos (milkshakes), refrescos (fruit shakes), preserves and candies are made from the fruit. Over a dozen varieties of lemons are available. A casado is a meal with beans, rice, fried plantains, salad, meat, corn on the cob, empanadas, and guizo de maize – corn stew.

Costa Rican Specialties

Tortillas, tamales, empanaditas and tacos
Chicharon – fried pork skins
Mondongo – tripe soup, usually served for Sunday dinner
Ceviche – fish marinated in lime and cilantro
Arroz con pollo – chicken with rice
Gallo pinto – rice and beans
Black beans

Pargo – red snapper
Spicy jerk chicken
Lobster with coconut curry
Masamorra – corn pudding
Cajeta de coo- white fudge made from coconut, sugar and citrus peel

Bacalos con Papas (Cod with Potatoes)

Serves 4

1 ½ lbs. cod
2 large tomatoes, chopped
2 green onion, chopped
1 cup corn
1 tsp. cumin
4 medium sized red potatoes, cubed

2 cloves garlic, chopped
1 jalapeno, seeded and chopped
½ tsp. sea salt
1 tsp. fresh ground pepper
½ cup cilantro (save ¼ c for garnish)

Preheat oven to 350°
Place the cod in a baking dish.
In a bowl combine the tomatoes, green onion, corn, cumin, potatoes, jalapeno, salt, pepper and cilantro.
Pour over the cod. Bake ½ hour, or until potatoes are tender. For a spicier dish add more jalapeno or cayenne.

Palmito Pie (heart of palm pie)

2 tbls. butter
1 onion, chopped
1 green pepper, chopped
1 cup rice
1 ½ cups water
2 tomatoes, pureed

½ tsp. oregano
½ tsp. thyme
Salt and pepper
4 cups cooked palmito
1 cup sour cream
½ cup grated cheddar or other cheese

Preheat oven to 350°
Melt the butter in a sauce pan and stir in the onion and pepper until tender. Add the rice and water. Bring to a boil. Simmer until rice is cooked. A little more water may need to be added.
In a bowl combine the tomatoes, oregano, thyme, and salt and pepper.
Place the rice in a buttered pie plate or casserole. Layer with the palmito, then sour cream, tomatoes, and grated cheese.
Bake for 20-30 minutes, or until top is just browned. Serve at once.

Holidays and Special Occasions

Lent – hearts of palm
Easter is celebrated with salted cod and potatoes (bacalos con papas); chiverres (similar to a pumpkin) is made into preserves called cabellito de angel (angel's hair); ceviche (marinated white fish in lime juice); Flor de Itabo (flowers stewed in butter with eggs and tomatoes).
At Christmas turkey and tamales are served.
New Year's Eve families and friends dress up and gather
The first birthday is important for a son. A girl celebrates her 15th birthday with a large party and presents. During an engagement teas and other parties are given for the bride-to-be. The evening preceding the wedding, a party is given at the bride's home with drinks, food and dancing. Weddings are held in churches, followed by receptions. Funerals are held within 24 hours of a person's death. Rosary is said at home for 9 days following. Mourners are given food, coffee, and liquor. A banquet is held on the 1st anniversary of a death.

Beverages

Costa Rica produces wine between Turrialba and Carago. Nance, a small yellow fruit, and palm nuts are used to make wine and brandy. Guaro is a sweet liquor distilled from sugar cane. Beer is brewed and coffee produced. Horchata is a sweet drink made from corn and cinnamon and Pinolillo a drink made with toasted corn

Did You Know?

Did you know that coffee beans were brought by the Europeans from Ethiopia and Arabia to Costa Rica? Here most of the coffee plantations (fincas) are located in the Central Valley and coffee grows best above 4,000 feet with temperatures between 59-82° F. Harvest is November to January when the berries are bright red.
Habanero chili peppers are grown here and many shipped to Louisiana to make hot sauce.

Cote D'Ivoire

The Cote D'Ivoire (Ivory Coast) is bordered on the west by Liberia and Guinea, Mali and Burkina Faso to the north, Ghana to the east, and the Atlantic Ocean to the south. The earliest known inhabitants may have resided here during the Upper Paleolithic Period (10,000 to 5,000 BC) as cooking and fishing implements have been found dating to that period. The Ehotilé (Aboisso), Kotrowou (Fresco), Zéhiri (Grand Lahou), Ega and Diès (Divo) later migrated south. There were two Anyi kingdoms, Indénié and Sanwi, which attempted to retain their separate identity through the French colonial period and after Côte d'Ivoire's independence. The region was part of the North African Berber trade routes around which the Sudanic empires developed. An 1843–1844 treaty made Côte d'Ivoire a protectorate of France and in 1893, it became a French colony, and received its independence in 1960. Yamoussoukro is the political capital and Abidjan the economic capital. The official language is French. There are over 60 indigenous ethnic groups and languages. The name comes from the large amount of ivory that was found in the country.

Dining Etiquette

It is an honor to be invited for a meal. Please arrive punctually. Men will shake hands greeting and departing. Female friends will each other three times on the cheeks, alternating sides. Men will eat with men, women and girls, and boys separately. The elders eat first. Food in large bowls is placed on a mat on the ground for all to share. Use only your right hand for eating. Rice is rolled into a ball and is used to eat meat and the sauces. Never reach across for food, but take only what is in front of you. Most people do not talk while eating, and if you need to cough or sneeze please excuse yourself. At the end of the meal a bowl will be passed to wash your hands. The toast is "Sante", "Good luck", or "to our friendship" and clink glasses.

Cuisine

The earliest settlers in the region lived on seeds, fruit, and hunted for animals. Later after the Portuguese arrived they set up trading centers, followed by the French who planted coffee, cocoa, bananas and palm oil. Today Cote d'Ivoire is the world's largest producer of cocoa, and the third largest producer of coffee.

The cuisine is diverse with the different ethnic groups having their own dishes. The Agni and Abron farm cocoa and coffee. The Senufo in the northern savannah grow rice, yams, peanuts, millet, and eat rice with a spicy peanut sauce. The Dioula in the northwest raise rice, millet and peanuts. The Kulango in the north grow yams, corn, peanuts, watermelons, and catch fish on the coast.

Grains are used in cooking with women pounding in bowls with wooden pestles. The food is cooked outdoors in pots. Many of the dishes are spicy. A maguis is an outdoor restaurant that sells braised food such as chicken or fish served with onions and tomatoes.

Among the common foodstuffs are cocoa, coffee, cassava, maize (corn), rice, millet, sorghum, yams, root vegetables, plantains, groundnuts (peanuts), bananas, peas, beans, eggplants and; fruit – mandarin, mango, passion, fruit, soursops, coconuts, pineapples, bananas, plantains; spicy chicken; seafood – tuna, sardines, shrimp, crabs (caught in baskets called flotor), bonito; palm and coconut oil; guinea fowl, goat, mutton, and chicken. Large snails are used in cooking soups, stews, dried and salted, grilled or eaten with a sauce.

Flank Steak with Coffee-Peppercorn Marinade

6 tbls. strong brewed coffee	1 tbls. fresh ginger, minced
2 tbls. balsamic vinegar	2 tbls. whole black peppercorns, crushed
2 tbls. extra virgin olive oil	1 tsp. sea salt
2 tbls. brown sugar	2 lb. flank steak, trimmed of fat
4 shallots or 4 cloves garlic, minced	

Whisk coffee, vinegar, oil, sugar, shallots, ginger, peppercorns, and salt in a glass dish large enough for the meat to lie flat. Add the steak and turn to coat. Cover and refrigerate for at least 1 hour and up to 8 hours.
Heat the grill to high.
Remove the steak from the marinade (discard the marinade). Lightly oil grill rack.
Place steak on the grill and cook for 4-5 minutes per side for medium rare.
Transfer the steak to a cutting board and let rest for 5 minutes. Slice thinly across the grain and place on a platter.
Recipe courtesy of Sarah Comerford, www.whatscookinginyourworld.com, and adapted from a recipe in www.eatingwell.com and Doha S.A., Bonqua, Cote D'Ivoire

Cote d'Ivoire Specialties

Fufu – national dish – is made with plantains, cassava or yams pounded into a dough and served with meat and a vegetable sauce
Mafe – meat in peanut sauce
Gari – ground cassava and water

Kedjenou – vegetable sauce made with peanuts, eggplant, okra or tomatoes
Attieke – steamed grated cassava
Aloko – deep fried plantain, with onions and chili, often eaten with grilled fish
Aitiu - corn paste

Beverages

Common beverages are Drogba – cold Solibra Bock beer; Bangui – local palm wine; and ginger beer. Fruit drinks are popular.

Holidays and Special Occasions

Yam Festival – the Akan celebrate with thanksgiving for the harvests; a memorial for the dead, to honor the yam, and keep away evil spirits. Mashed yams and soup are served.
Festival of Masks – in Man region in February
Carnival – in Bouake has a large amount of food involved
Ramadan - Muslim month of fasting from sunrise to sunset
Eid al-Fitr – Muslim day for prayer, food, and gift giving ending Ramadan, and can last longer. Dishes such as meats with sauces, rice, yams, eggplant, salads, stews, and soups will be served.
Eid al-Adha – the feast of the sacrifice – prayers followed by the sacrifice of a sheep, camel, or ox which is then eaten
Christians celebrate Good Friday, Easter, and Christmas. Reveillon is the Christmas Eve dinner served after midnight mass. Dessert is often a Yule log.
Coming-of-age, religious funeral and memorial ceremonies all involves food and drink
Funerals are very elaborate and occur forty days after the death. They can go on for days with drums, food, singing and dancing. Many people believe the soul lives on after death and must be given an elaborate funeral. Ancestors are consulted with food and drink.

Did You Know?

Ground cassava is better known as tapioca. In many parts of the world it used as a thickener.
The Ivory Coast is the largest exporter of cocoa in the world.

Croatia

Croatia is bordered on the north by Slovenia, the west the Adriatic Sea, east Hungary and south Bosnia-Herzegovina. The country has 1,185 islands! The history of the country dates back to prehistoric times and Neanderthal man. The Librunians and Illyrians came later, followed by the Greeks and in the 9th C AD the region was part of the Roman Empire. The Avars and Croats invaded during the 7th c. The Venetians controlled much of Dalmatia by 1428. Ottoman conquests began in 1493, and in 1524 was ruled by the House of Hapsburg. In 1918 the Croatian Sabor declared independence and the State of Slovenes, Croats and Serbs became the Kingdom of Serbs, Croats, and Slovenes. In 1931 the country was named Yugoslavia. In 1992 Croatia was recognized by the European Economic Community. The capital, Zagreb celebrated its 900th anniversary in 1994. The official language is Croatian.

Dining Etiquette

Please arrive punctually for a meal. Please bring a gift of flowers (odd numbers and not chrysanthemums which are for funerals), chocolates, wine, or a gift from your country. Please shake hands greeting and departing keeping good eye contact. Close friends will embrace and kiss on each cheek. You will be served drinks. The hostess will seat the guests at the table. Food will be served, or perhaps served buffet style. Please eat continental style with the fork in the left hand and knife in the right. Please wait for the host starts. Leave a small amount on your plate to show you are finished. The toast is "Zivjeli" "Cheers". When toasting everyone clinks their glasses and looks the person in the eye.

Cuisine

The different regions in Croatia have their own cuisine. Along the Dalmatian Coast fish is prevalent with Greek, Roman and Mediterranean influences. Inland is more Slavic in tradition, influenced by the Hungarians, Viennese and Turks. Ham, peppers, paprika, tomatoes, green salads, beans, and potatoes may be used in the cooking. Pastas and pizza have been influenced by the Italians. Grapes and olives are very much a part of the culture providing wine, olives and olive oil. Truffles - "black diamonds" - from the forest of Istria – black (3 varieties) and white, are mainly found around Motovun and Buzet. The largest truffle in the world was found by Giancarlo Zigante in 1999, weighing 3,000 pounds! Istria is known for its ham, fuzi (pasta), and boskarin (beef). Fish is mainly boiled or grilled, seasoned with herbs and olive oil, or served in stews, or cooked with potatoes. Lamb, beef, pork, veal, ham, sausage, blood sausages, salami are cured and smoked, cooked on the grill, roasted, or fried, boiled, or stuffed. Game and poultry include turkey, duck, chicken, and goose. Venison is also used in cooking in stews or goulash. Common seafood are lobster, mussels, oysters, octopus, shrimp, crab, white fish, tuna, cod, sardines, clams, dory, turbot, sea bass, and bream.

Calamari with Potatoes

500 g calamari
1.5 kg. potatoes
100 ml olive oil
2 cloves garlic

1 tbls. mixed spices
Parsley
Salt and pepper

Preheat oven to 220° C
Clean, wash and slice the calamari into 2 cm wide strips. Peel and thinly slice the potatoes
Chop the garlic and parsley
Pour half the olive oil into an oven proof casserole dish. Spread a layer of potato and sprinkle with salt.
Spread calamari over the potato and sprinkle with pepper, garlic, parsley and mixed herbs. Cover with the remaining potato. Sprinkle with more parsley and salt and pour remaining oil over top. Cover. Cook for 45 minutes.
Mixed herbs usually will include bay leaves and rosemary.
Recipe Courtesy of the Embassy of the Republic of Croatia to the United States, Washington, DC

Croatian Specialties

Cres - lamb
Tartufone – potato dumpling with chocolate filling and truffle
Cheese - made in Pag from ewe's milk and during maturation is covered with olive oil
Orahnjaca – dessert with flour, ground walnuts, yeast and sugar
Prsut – Dalmatian ham, often served as an appetizer
Hiladetina – head cheese
Salvonia – kule; fish fricassees; cakes
Lika – lamb, cabbage, potatoes, dairy products
Ispod peke – roasted under an earthenware dish
Gibanica – savory strudel
Kajmak – cream cheese
Fuzi – homemade pasta
Blitva – similar to spinach but bitter
Zagorje – Austrian, Swiss, Italian and Hungarian influences – dairy products
Turkey with mlinci (flat flour dumplings)
Strukli (boiled or baked dumplings with a cottage cheese filling, walnut rolls, squash rolls,

Janjetina – lamb with herbs
Odojak – roast pork
Escalope a la Baron Trenk – spicy schnitzel
Zogorska zlevka – corn flour cake
Zagrebackiodrezak – veal stuffed with ham and cheese
Kulen – spicy pork
Cesnovka – spicy sausage
Punjena paprika – peppers stuffed with meat
Sataras – roasted vegetables
Duvec – cooked vegetables
Soparnik – vegetable pie
Suibenek area – visovvacka begavica – dish made with lamb and sour ewe's milk
Mlinci – flatbread
Paskisir – sheep's milk cheese from Pag
Skripavac – famrers' cheese
Savijaca – apple or cheese strudel
Krafne – donut
Rozata - flan
Orehnjaca – nut roll
Palacinke – crepes with sweet fillings
Bucnica – courgette cake
Krostule – deep fried pastry

"Split" Cake

Pastry

5 oz. walnuts
5 oz. figs
5 oz. raisins

3-4 tbls. flour
9 egg whites, beaten to stiff peaks
9 tbls. sugar

Preheat oven to 350°
Chop the walnuts, figs, and raisins and mix with the flour. Fold in the beaten egg whites mixed with the sugar.
Pour into a buttered baking dish (14 x16 in). Bake for about 25 minutes. Cool
Cut the pastry lengthwise into three strips of equal width. Coat the first and second layers with the filling, arrange one on top of the other and cover with the third part.
Chill the cake well and decorate.

Filling

5 egg yolks
5 tbls. sugar

5 oz. butter
1 packet vanilla sugar

Cook the egg yolks and sugar in a pan, placed over simmering water stirring constantly until the cream thickens. Cool. Add beaten butter and sugar and blend evenly.
Recipe Courtesy of the Embassy of the Republic of Croatia to the United States, Washington, DC

Holidays and Special Occasions

During Lent meat and animal fat are not consumed by Catholics.
Catholics attend mass on Easter eve bringing baskets of bread, cheese, and eggs which are blessed by the priests and then eaten the next morning.
Easter – pinca (pastry); pisanica (decorated Easter egg)
Festival of Subotina (2nd Saturday in September) – beginning of the white truffle season
Christmas – fritule (fritters); purgerica –turkey with chestnuts, apples, bacon and lemons; bozicni kruh (bread); bozic pletenica (braided Christmas bread); kotonjata (quince candy); strudel; sarma (cabbage)

Beverages

Wine has been grown in Croatia since the early Greeks. Athenaeus of Alexandria wrote "at Issa… wine is made which is superior to every other wine whatever", this during the 2nd c BC about the island of Vis! The two main regions are Kontinetalna and Primorska. Both red and white wines are produced. Dessert wines include Malvazija, Muscat Ottone, and Prosek. There are also liqueurs and brandies – Marachino, Sljivovica (plum), Kruskovac (pear), Drenovac (cherry), Orahovac (walnut), Medovina (honey), and Lozovaca (grapes). Rakija is a grape drink known elsewhere as Grappa. Pivo (beer) is brewed, especially dark beers. Coffee is widely drunk, and there are many coffee houses. Mineral water is available with very high standards.

Cuba

Cuba is an island nation in the Caribbean consisting of the main island of Cuba, the Isla de la Juventud, and several archipelagos. The earliest inhabitants were the Taino or Arawak, and the Guanajatabey and Ciboney who hunted, fished, and were hunter-gatherers. Christopher Columbus landed on Cuba in 1492 and claimed it for Spain. Following the Spanish-American War Spain and the United States signed the Treaty of Paris in 1898 whereby Spain relinquished claim to Cuba. Cuba became independent from the United States in 1902 as the Republic of Cuba. The capital, Havana, was founded in 1515 as San Cristobal de la Habana. Spanish is the official language

Dining Etiquette

When invited for a meal please arrive promptly. Dinner is often at 9 or later. Please shake hands greeting and departing. Female friends will kiss; male friends may embrace. Men will rise when women enter a room and hold doors for them. Drinks will be served. The hostess will invite the guests into the dining room. The guest of honor will be seated to the right of the host. Start eating after the host says "Buen provecho". All dishes will be served at the same time. You will eat with your fork in the left hand and knife in the right. When finished please place your knife and fork parallel across the right side of the plate. Your hands should remain at table level and not in your lap. Knives and forks are used to cut fruit. When passing always pass dishes to your left. The toast is "Salud" "to your health".

Cuisine

Cuban cuisine is a blend of Spanish, African and Caribbean flavors. Being an island, fish, tropical fruits and vegetables are part of the diet. Meals may include rice and beans – congri (red beans and rice) or Moros Y Christianos (black beans and rice). Breakfast is usually Cuban bread and café con leche. The main meal will include meat, yucca, malanga or potato, plantains, and a salad. Chicken and pork are used in many dishes, and pork is always cooked for Christmas. The traditional cooking method for pork was smoked in an earthen pot covered with palm fronds. Many families have asados or barbeques.

The Cubans use yucca, malanga, black beans, coconuts, cassava, potatoes, plantains, corn, tomatoes, avocados, cucumbers, carrots, cabbages, radishes, limes and onions in their cooking. Cuban food is not spicy. Typical spices used are garlic, cumin, oregano and bay or laurel leaves. The bread is made with lard rather than oil.

Cuban Fried Eggs and Rice

Let me start with my favorite Cuban dish ever, fried eggs with rice. This is so plain that you'll never find it in any menus except that in Spain and Latin American they refer to it as Arroz a la Cubana (Cuban Rice). The rice is plain white rice (I follow the instructions on the package) and fried eggs, which in Cuba were deep fried. This makes the whites crisp up at the edges and more delicious, but other than that, there is no difference.

We like to serve it with fried ripe plantains; buy plantains that are not green, but yellow/black and wait for them to turn black (a couple of days), cut the ends and peel them with your hands as you would a banana, slice them on the bias about 1/2" thick and then fry in corn oil or any oil (not really deep fried but with a little more oil than usual), drain them in craft paper or paper towels. They should be very soft in texture and caramelized a bit. Or you can buy Goya frozen ripe plantains which you don't have to fry, just place in the oven and you are done. To serve arrange the rice in the center of a platter and surround it with the fried eggs. Serve the plantains separately. In Cuba this was usually served at lunch with some meat dish, either Picadillo or Bistek de Palomilla. I skip the meat because it is too much food. To eat, you serve yourself a couple of heaping serving spoonfuls of rice and place an egg (or two) on top, with your fork cut into the yolk and let it run onto the rice. Technically you shouldn't mix it much more but I like it totally mixed so I keep going until it is all cut up, whites included, and totally mixed. Place the plantains on the side and eat a fork full of rice/eggs and then cut into the plantain with the fork and follow with a piece of plantain. Oh, I forgot the eggs need salt so place the salt shaker on the table and let people pour their own. You won't believe how good this is. I must tell you that while I was in Peru I saw an interview of Gaston Acurio, the best Peruvian chef with over 30 restaurants worldwide including NY -- he was asked what his favorite dish was and without hesitation he answered: fried eggs and rice.
Recipe Courtesy of Esparanza Manas, New York City, New York

Cuban Specialties

Sofrito – sauce of onions or garlic, tomatoes, peppers, herbs, spices and ham fried in oil

Mojo – sauce with oil, garlic, oregano, orange juice, lime juice

Ropa vieja (old clothes) – shredded beef in a tomato sauce

Boliche – beef stuffed with chorizo and hard boiled eggs

Black bean soup – onion, garlic, bay leaf, salt and beans

Tamales- meat or other ingredients wrapped in corn husks and boiled

Guiso – corn soup

Caldosa – root vegetables and meat stew

Caldo gallego – white bean stew

Cocido de garbanzos – garbanzo stew

Sopa de frijol negro – black bean soup

Pescado asado – fish with almonds and onions

Boiled yucca

Tostones – fried green plantains

Alcaparrado – raisins, olives and caper mix used in cooking

Pastelilitos – pastry with fruit or meat

Croquetas – croquettes with meat cheese or fish and white sauce

Picadillo - ground beef with alcaparrado, rice, black beans and fried plantain; or ground beef with tomatoes, garlic, olives, onions, and raisins

Enchilada – fish in a sauce
Bacalao – salted cod
Fufu de platano – mashed plantains with meat, chicken or fish
Cuban sandwich – bread with pork, ham,
Elena Ruz sandwich – bread, cream cheese, strawberry jam, and turkey

Frita – grilled ground beef and chorizo patty on a bun with tomato, onion, lettuce
Coconut ice cream
Flan – sweet custard dessert
Pudin diplomatic – bread pudding
Bunuelos – fried dough with syrup and powdered sugar
Turrones – nougat candy

Moros y Cristianos (Black Beans and Rice)

Serves 6

½ lb. dried black beans
4 ½ cups water
½ large green pepper
3 thick bacon slices cut into small pieces
3 garlic cloves, chopped
½ green pepper, chopped
1½ cups long grain rice

½ large onion, chopped
1/3 cup olive oil
2 tsp. salt
Pepper
¼ tsp. oregano
1 bay leaf

Soak the beans in water with half green pepper for a few hours in a pan. Bring beans and water to a simmer and cook covered about 45 minutes or until almost done.
Cook bacon until crisp. Remove and set aside.
In bacon fat in skillet sauté onion, pepper, and garlic. Cook about 8 minutes. When done add to beans. Take out half pepper and add olive oil, salt, pepper, bay leaf oregano and bacon. Keep simmering and covered until beans are tender.
Add rice and simmer over low heat at least 1 hour or until all liquid has been absorbed. Taste to make sure rice is done. If not, keep cooking until rice is done. Fluff rice with a fork. Turn off heat and let it rest covered for 20 minutes.
Recipe of Courtesy of Angela Porta, Riverdale, New York

Holidays and Special Occasions

New Year's Eve – eat 12 grapes for wishes for New Year
During Lent many Christians fast, and some may not eat red meat
Semana Santa – Holy Week leads up to Easter and Good Friday is now a holiday in Cuba
Easter – there are processions and Easter services. Pork may or may not be served
Christmas Eve (Noche Buena) – cooking whole pig all day for roasted suckling pig, black beans and rice, yucca, cider, crème de vie (eggnog), mojitos, tropical fruits

Daiquiri

2 drinks

6 oz. light rum
2 tbls. fresh lime juice

2 tsp. sugar
Ice cubes or cracked ice

Combine the ingredients in a shaker and shake well. Stran into 2 chilled champagne glasses.
To make a banana, peach, pineapple, coconut, or other fruit daiquiri, add a small amoint of any of these. Best made in blender, rather than shaking!
A mojito is made the same way but adding mint leaves and club soda.

Beverages

Rum has been made from sugar cane that ferments as molasses and then is distilled since the 16th c. The rum is then aged in uncharred oak barrels. Clear rum is aged for three years; golden for five; and anejo for seven. Bacardi produced rum here until Fidel Castro came to power. Havana Club has been produced since 1878. Other rums are Matusalem Rum and Varadero Rum. The Cubre Libre (Rum and Coke, Angostura Bitters, lime, and perhaps gin added) may date from after the Spanish American War. The name comes from "Free Cuba" when Cuba received its independence. The daiquiri was named for a village outside Santiago de Cuba where a group of American engineers were helping to develop the Daiquiri iron mines. The men would gather at the Venus Hotel for a drink made with ice, rum, limes, and sugar. In 1900 Jennings Cox, the chief engineer, suggested the name. The drink was made famous in Ernest Hemingway's books. The mojito was drunk by the slaves on the island and concocted with white rum, lime, mint, sugar and sparkling water.

Cuba produces beer – Bucanero; Mayabe at Holguin's Mayabe Brewery; Cristal; and Hatuey, which has been bottled at Santiago de Cuba since 1927. Café con leche is strong coffee with scalding milk.

Did You Know?

In 1969 Fidel Castro removed Christmas from the calendar, so that the sugar cane could be harvested!

Curacao

Curaçao is an island in the southern Caribbean Sea off the Venezuelan coast. Curaçao is part of the ABC islands (Aruba, Bonaire, and Curaçao) of the Lesser Antilles or the Leeward Antilles. The original inhabitants were Arawak Amerindians. The Spanish arrived in 1499 and the Dutch in 1634. Willenstad, the capital, was founded by the Dutch West India Company, During the 18th and 19th centuries, the island changed hands among the British, the French, and the Dutch several times with Dutch rule returned in 1815, The country received its autonomy from the Dutch in 2010. The name may have come from a group of Portuguese sailors who landed here with scurvy which was treated with fresh fruit. The island became known as Ilha da Curação (Island of Healing or Indios Curacaos (healing Indians). The official languages are Papiamentu and Dutch.

Dining Etiquette

Please arrive punctually for a meal. Please shake hands greeting and departing. Drinks will be scrved. The hostess will seat the guests at the table. Please eat continental style fork in the left hand and knife in the right. Food may be served, passed or served buffet style. The toast is "Proost".

Cuisine and Beverages

The cuisine is a blend of Caribbean, Dutch, Indonesian, Spanish, and South American flavors. The food is called Kriyoyo (Creole). Promente (hot peppers) and pickled onions are eaten as a side dish. Red beans and rice are staples. Among the meat and fish are iguana, barracuda, goat, chicken, mahi mahi, and red snapper. Fish is fried or pickled. Curacao is a liqueur made from the dried peel of laraha oranges. The drink was first produced by the Senor family in the 19th c. Blue Curacao is made from Curacao with blue coloring added. Rum is also produced. The Amstel Brewery produces beer made from desalinated salt water. Fruit drinks are popular on the islands, as well as rum drinks.

Curacao Specialties

Kabritu stoba – stewed goat
Stoba – spicy stews made with papaya, beef or goat
Sopi – soups often are made with fruit such as bananas, pumpkins, cactus, or beef
Koko piska – fish and coconut soup
Piska hasa – red snapper

Erwten – pea soup with pork, ham and sausage
Yuana – stewed iguana
Keshi yena – stuffed cheese
Empana – cornmeal pastry with meat
Sult – pickled pig's ear and feet
Funchi – cornmeal dish
Yambo – okra

Lumpia – fried vegetable roll
Ayaka – meat tamales in banana leaves
Tutu – cornmeal, butter and beans
Pastechis - pastry with meat, cheese, tuna, or ham
Guiambo – okra and seafood soup
Konkomber – cucumber with papaya or cabbage and corned beef

Bami – long noodles with vegetables and meat
Sate – skewered meat with peanut sauce
Riisttafel - 20 course meal
Sunchi - meringue dessert
Panseiku – pralines with roasted peanuts
Zjozjoli – sesame seed candy
Bolo pretu – black fruit cake
Kokada - fresh grated coconut patties

Keshy Yena (Stuffed Cheese)

The Dutch brought Edam and Gouda cheese to Curacao and Aruba, and this has been a favorite dish.

Serves 6

3-4 lb. Edam or Gouda cheese
½ lb. ground beef, boneless chicken (cut into small piece), or shrimp (cut into small pieces) cooked
3 tbls. oil or butter
1 medium onion, finely chopped
1 green or red pepper, chopped
1 medium tomato, finely chopped

2 tbls. raisins
6 pimento stuffed olives
3 tbls. chopped sweet pickles or gherkin
¼ tsp. hot red pepper or Scotch bonnet peppers
Salt and pepper, to taste
¼ cup bread crumbs

Peel the wax casing off the cheese. Cut 1 in. slice off. Hollow out the cheese with a knife or spoon. Place cheese and 1 inch piece in water and soak for 1 hour. Grate the remaining hollowed out cheese. Remove the cheese and drain on a paper towel.
Heat the oil in a skillet and sauté onion and pepper for 5 minutes. Add the tomato, raisins, olives, pickles, hot pepper, and meat. Cook 5 minutes. Season with salt and pepper. Add the grated cheese and bread crumbs.
Preheat oven to 350°
Grease a baking dish big enough to hold cheese. Spoon the meat mixture into the hollowed out cheese. Top it with the 1 in. slice of cheese. Bake uncovered in the oven for 30 minutes, or until just browned. Serve immediately.

Holidays and Special Occasions

Carnival is a festive time with parades, costumes, and lots of eating
Easter – Easter eggs
December 6 - St. Nicholas Day – children leave a shoe with carrots and hay, and water for St. Nicholas' horse. If the children are good the carrots and hay will be replaced with gifts
Christmas – cured ham, smoked mackerel, pickled salmon; turkey, currant bread, fruitcake and poundcake

Cyprus

Cyprus is an island in the Mediterranean that since 1974 has been divided de facto into Greek and Turkish sectors, comprising 3,572 sq. miles. Civilization on the island dates to sometime between 7000-3000 BC when Neolithic settlements were established at Khirokitia and Sotira, copper was discovered, and ceramics produced. From 2300 BC on the Anatolians, Mycenean Greeks, Phoenicians, the Assyrians, Egyptians, Persians, Greeks, Romans, and Turks all occupied the island. Nicosia, once known as Lefkosia and Ledra, has been the capital since the 10th c. The "Green Line" divides the city.

Dining Etiquette

Please be punctual when invited for a meal. Please bring a gift for the home, chocolates, or flowers, .Shake hands greeting and departing. Good friends may embrace, and women kiss. Beverages will be served. The hostess will escort the guests to the table. The male guest of honor is seated to her right. Food will be served or buffet style. Please eat continental style with the fork in the left hand and knife in the right. Do not start until the hostess has lifted her fork. When finished please put your knife and fork together. The host initiates the toast, raising his glass, looking at his guests and says "Stin iya sou" "Health to you".

Pork Afelia

Serves 4

2 kg pork	Crushed coriander
Salt	Cumin seeds (optional)
Pepper	1 cup wine
	¾ cup oil

Cut the meat into cubes and marinate in wine, salt, pepper and coriander (cumin).
Heat the oil in a casserole, strain the meat, place in the casserole and cook until crisp and brown.
Remove the excess oil and add the marinade and the wine.
Cover the casserole and cook adding some water when necessary.
Serve with bulgur pilaf or potatoes.
Recipe Courtesy of the Cyprus Tourism Organization

Cuisine

The cuisine of Cyprus is a blend of Mediterranean, European and Middle Eastern. Since ancient times olives, herbs, almonds, dates, beans, chick peas, sunflower seeds, figs, grains, grapes, and lemons, peppers, courgettes, aubergines, avocados, okra, artichokes, tomatoes, lettuce and mint have been cultivated. Grains, wines, and oils were stored in pitharia, large earthenware pots. Cooking was done in communal ovens and open fires, using less olive oil than other nearby countries. Fruit grown on the island include oranges, grapefruit, strawberries, cherries, plums, nectarines, apricots, peaches, and watermelon. Karavas has lemon trees, some of which are almost one hundred years old and produce up to 5000 lemons each!

One of Cyprus' main exports is Halloumi, the national cheese. Other cheeses are feta, made from goat's milk and anari which is similar to ricotta. Kefalotiri and kaskavali are hard cheeses.

Cypriot Specialties

Meze – appetizers; mezedhes – little delicacies such as feta cheese, black and green olives, humus, sardines, sausage, taramosalata - smoked cod roe pate, tahini, skordalia, talattouri, melintzanosalata – aubergines with garlic and lemon, lountza – smoked pork, and cheese
Koupepia – grapes leaves with meat and rice
Souvla – lamb roasted on a spit
Ofto – roast meat and potatoes
Ofto kleftico – cooked outside in a sealed oven
Kelftis – means "robber" or stolen meat
Tavas – casseroles cooked in earthenware pots
Moussaka – ground lamb or beef with eggplant and custard-like topping
Stifado – rabbit or beef stew with wine, vinegar, onion and spices
Dolmas – stuffed grape leaves
Kebabs – grilled lamb or beef on skewers
Keftedes – meatballs
Hiromeri – leg of lamb marinated for 40 days in red wine and sea salt, then smoked

Pastitsio – macaroni with spiced meat and cream on top
Kolokasi – looks like a sweet potato
Melintzanes yiahni – baked aubergines, garlic and tomatoes
Pourgouri – cracked wheat steamed with fried onions and chicken stock to make a pilaf
Yemista – stuffed vegetables
Moukentra – lentils, rice and onions
Salata horiatiki – "village salad"
Louvia me lahana – greens with black-eyed peas served with olive oil and lemon juice
Spanakopitta – spinach with feta cheese, eggs in phyllo pastry
Avgolemono – egg and lemon soup
Loukanika – smoked sausage with coriander, and other herbs and spices
Pastourma – sausage with hot pepper and fenugreek
Lountza – fillet of pork
Fish – octopus, squid, red mullet, swordfish. These are usually grilled or served with tomato and garlic sauces.

Some favorite pastries and desserts are boureka (fresh curd cheese or meat filling and honey); kandaifi (pastry strands in the shape of a cigar and sipped in honey); mahelepi (pudding in rose water syrup); rizagalo (rice pudding); glygko (preserved fruits in syrup); daktyla ("ladies' fingers); pisides (in orange flower water syrup); and galatopoureko (phyllo pastry and cream filling).

Loukamades (donuts in honey syrup)

1 package dried yeast
1 tsp. sugar
1 ¼ cups warm water or milk
1 egg

3 cups flour
½ tsp. salt
Oil

Dissolve the yeast and sugar in ¼ cup of the water in a small bowl.
In a bowl combine the flour and salt and make a well. Pour in the yeast mixture and remaining cup of water. Add the egg and beat batter until it is smooth and elastic. Cover with a towel and let rise in a warm place for at least an hour, or until double in size.
Heat 3-4 inches oil in a pan and drop the batter by spoonfuls into the oil. Fry for about 2-3 minutes or until golden brown.

Honey Syrup

½ cup honey
½ cup sugar

½ cup water

Heat the ingredients in a pan until sugar is dissolved.
Pour over donuts. Honey only can be poured over the donuts.

Holidays and Special Occasions

New Year's or St. Basil's Day – people prepare a plate of boiled wheat (collifa) on which is placed a Vasipolitta cake. The cake is made of cream of wheat and the outside decorated with sesame seeds. Whoever finds the coin baked in the cake will have good luck in the coming year.
January 6 (Epiphany) – people worship in church and return for a sumptuous feast. Loukamades is served.
February – Carnival – for the two weeks before Lent, especially in Limassol, there are processions. Bourekia, a pastry with mint flavored cheese and ravioli, and sweets – daktyla and kandaifi are eaten. During the second week, Tyrini "Cheese Week" is celebrated. This ends on Green Monday, the first day of Lent when one indulges in a picnic of cheese, olives, bread, and wine.
Lent – an Orthodox person does not eat meat, fish or dairy products, instead many vegetables and fruit for seven weeks. During Lent wine and olive oil may be forbidden on certain days. Kolokopitta is a favorite pastry with pumpkin, raisins, and cracked wheat; tahinopitta – pastry with sesame seed; or spinakopitta
Easter – avgolemono or mayeristsa soups; flauounes – Easter cakes with special Easter cheese, eggs, spices, herbs in yeast pastry; kokovesti – Easter sausage; stuffed vine leaves; and souvla. Dyed red eggs are placed on the table and decorate breads.
Summer – orange blossoms and rose water are made to flavor pastries. Fruit preserves are made.
Weddings – are mainly held during the summer. Resi – pilaf with lamb and wheat and loukoumia – shortbreads are served.
Fall Harvest – almonds, carobs, olives, and grapes; soutzoukos – almonds dipped in palouzes; carob honey is eaten on bread
All Saints' Day – xerotiana – special donuts

Advent – a pig is smoked and sausage made.
Christmas – kouramiedes – shortbread; memomakaron – buns in honey; koulouria – sesame bread; sesamota (Christ's bread) and kolliva – boiled wheat in memory of the dead
Christmas and New Year's – many sweets made with nuts, honey and cinnamon, and sweet fritters

Beverages

Cyprus has produced wine since ancient times, dating back to at least 3,000 BC, much of it exported to the Egyptians, Greeks and Romans who praised its quality. Dionysis was the god of wine. Mark Anthony gave Cleopatra Cyprus as a gift, mainly for its wine. The oldest recorded wine "Nama" c 800 BC was later renamed "Commandaria" and made by the Knights Hospitallers during the 12-14th c at Kolossi, in the foothills of the Troodos. Richard the Lionheart so enjoyed the wine he called it "The wine of kings and king of wines". It was nicknamed the "Apostle of wines" and is still being produced. This sweet dessert wine is made from grapes picked late for their sugar content and then spread on straw mats for a week to concentrate the sugar. The wine is fermented in open jars with red and white grapes, aged in casks, then bottled.

Several wines had their origins in Cyprus. The Count of Champagne received his cuttings from Queen Alice of Cyprus to plant in Champagne, France. Madeira was introduced to Madeira during the 15th c, later Marsala and Tokay to their respective countries. When the Turks invaded in 1571, the Sultan Selim II drank wine, but those that succeeded him obeyed the Koran, for which wine was forbidden. Wine was still produced on the island, but it was not till the British occupied it in 1878 that wine regained popularity. Many villages and monasteries produce wines. Sherries, ouzo, brandy, vermouth, retsina, cognac, raki, fruit liqueurs, and beer are also produced.

Coffee houses are very popular and one may still see men sitting there, playing cards and other games, sipping away on their coffee. Coffee is brewed very strong with sediment. When offered please sip it slowly, and enjoy this and other signs of hospitality when offered. Glykos is sweet coffee, metrios medium sweet, and sketos no sugar.

Did You Know?

The Stavrovouni Monastery "Mountain of the Cross" was founded in 327 by St. Helena, mother of Constantine the Great. The monastery produces honey, cheese, and sultana grapes, and is known for its icons.
The Church is the wealthiest institution on Cyprus, owning banks, hotels, mining companies, real estate, and breweries, and is tax exempt!
Famagusta, now a government controlled area, was the main potato producing region and popular resort.
The Troodos Mountains are home to the wine growing region, almond, hazelnut and cherry orchards.
Kythrea, founded c 3500 BC, was famous for flour mills, and vegetables such as broccoli and olives, that were exported.
The Cyprus Palestine Plantation Company near Ypsonas, was established in the 1930s to cultivate citrus fruit, sultana raisins, and honey.
Kathikas, Greek for "Chamber Pot", is a grape and sultana center.

Czech Republic

Located in the heart of Europe the Czech Republic occupies the regions of Bohemia, Moravia and Silesia. It 78, 864 sq. km are surrounded by Germany and Poland to the north, Slovakia the east, and Austria the south. The earliest inhabitants were the Celtic Boii tribe which gave Bohemia its name "Boiohaemum". During the 4th c AD Germanic tribes conquered the Boii anfd from the 5th to 10th c West Slavs were present, which became the Great Moravian Empire. In 935 King Wenceslas, patron saint of Bohemia died. The capital, Prague, situated on the river Vltava, was on ancient trading routes and was made an archbisphoric in 1344 under King Charles who became Holy Roman Emperor in 1355. The Jagiello dynasty brought Hungary and Bohemia together, and then under the Augsburg Habsburg rule. In 1918 The Czechoslovak Republic was formed, but overrun by the Germans during World War II. Today the Czech Republic is a parliamentary democracy. Prague, the capital, was settled over 2000 years ago by Celts. Prague Castle was built c 885 AD. The official languages are Czech and Slovak.

Dining Etiquette

Shake hands greeting and departing. A married woman adds "ova" to her husband's name. When entertained in a home please bring whiskey, cognac, coffee, or a gift for the home. Flowers can be brought in an odd number (13 is an unlucky number). Red roses are for lovers! Lunch is the main meal of the day served 12-2. Dinner is often lighter with cold meats and cheese. When entertained, a guest will be offered something to drink – wine, beer or perhaps a whiskey. There are no long cocktail hours! When seated at the table guests should wait for the hostess to start. Please eat with your fork in the left hand, knife in the right. Do not put your hands in your lap, and no elbows on the table. Toasting is done for many occasions. The toast is "Na Zdravi" or "To your health". Please return the toast.

Cuisine

The Czech cuisine has been influenced by Bohemia and Moravia, but many of the dishes are native to this country and have influenced other nearby regions. The Czech Republic brings together vegetables, fruits and meats native to the region. The dishes use dill, tomatoes, sour cream, caraway seeds, sauerkraut, sausage, cheese, potatoes, and plums. The country is known for its excellent breads; game - goose, rabbit, duck; fresh water fish; chicken, mushrooms; pork, ham, sausage, veal, chicken, and thick rich soups. Common vegetables are carrots, celery, parsley, turnip, cauliflower, salad, onion, leek, garlic, cabbage, kale and chives, peas, lentils,   tomatoes, bell peppers, courgettes, pumpkins, melons, sunflowers, poppies, potatoes and beets. Dumplings (*knedlíky*) made from whole wheat or potato-based are served with meals. Noodles, potatoes, and rice are served as the starch. Bread is made from wheat or rye and may contain caraway, poppy or other seeds. Dairy products include Eidam and Niva (blue) cheese, nakladany hermelin (pickled cheese), and sour cream.

Kolache (dough with filling)

3 packages dry yeast
½ cup warm water
2 ¾ cups lukewarm milk
1 tsp. sugar
2 sticks butter, softened
2 egg yolks

1 egg white
6 cups flour
1 tsp. salt
Zest of 1 lemon
Fresh fruit, dried fruit, or fruit preserves

Dissolve the yeast in a cup with the warm water.
Beat together the milk, butter, sugar, eggs, flour, salt and lemon zest. Add the yeast and work into a dough. Cover and let rise until doubled.
On a floured board make the dough into small balls. Place on a greased cookie sheet. Make an indentation in each ball and place a small amount of fruit or jam. Let rise for ½ hour.
Preheat oven to 400°
Bake kolache for 10-15 minutes, or until dough slightly browned. Brush with melted butter when they come out of the oven.
Meat, cheese, or other fillings can be used.

Czech Specialties

Veprova pecene – roast pork
Pecena husa se zelim – duck or goose served with sauerkraut or cabbage and dumplings
Svickova – similar to stroganoff – marinated beef filet, cooked in a sauce with sour cream and vegetables, and served with dumplings and cranberries
Rostenky – roast with onions
Svickova na smetane – beef with dumplings and cream
Lesco – pepper, onion, tomato, stew
Pecene veproves knedliky a se zelim – roast pork, cabbage, and dumplings
Soulet – peas with barley and fat
Pecena kachna – roast duck
Schnitzel – thin veal, chicken or pork with trojobal
Pinene papriky – bell peppers stuffed with mear or rice and vegetables
Dusene teleci na kmine – veal ragout with caraway seeds

Sauerkraut with carraway seeds
Klobasa – smoked meat sausage
Houbovy Kuba – barley, mushroom, fried onion, and garlic dish served at Christmas
Gulas – meat stew with onion and spices
Kapr na cerno – carp in black sauce
Houskove Knedliky – bread dumplings that cannot be touched with a knife, but are sliced with thread
Knedliky (dumplings) - are served in soup, as an entrée, or dessert filled with fruit
Parky - sausage
Polevka – soup, usually potato or vegetable
Cesnecka – garlic soup
Bramboracka – potato soup
Rybi polevka – fish soup
Zelnacka – cabbage (sauerkraut) soup
Kulajda – soup with spices, cream, mushrooms, egg, dill and potatoes
Kyselo – rye sourdough, mushroom, caraway and fricd onion soup

147

Nudles makem – homemade noodles with ground poppy seeds, powdered sugar and butter
Mehlspeisen – warm cake
Dalken – tarts with marmalade
Koprova omacka – dill sauce
Shubanky – dumplings with cinnamon sugar
Povidla – plum jam
Krupicova kase – semolina porridge with sugar, honey, cinnamon and butter
Houska – braided rolls

Palacinky – pancakes
Bramboracky – fried pancakes
Loupak - crescent shaped sweet roll
Palacinky - Egg batter crepes with fillings such as chocolate or preserves – apricot and often served with ice cream
Zemlovka – baked sliced rolls, apples, milk, eggs, cinnamon and raisins
Strudl – pastry with fruit, nuts, or stuffed with meat, cheese, cabbage or spinach
Ovocne knedliky – fruit dumplings

Holidays and Special Occasions

Easter – hot cross buns and lamb-shaped breads (Velikonocni beranek) and cakes are baked at Easter. Lamb is eaten and eggs (kraslice) decorated.
St. Nicholas' Day – gifts brought for children
Christmas – vanocka (braided bread), mazanec (buns), roast goose, fish soup (*rybí polévka*) made with carp; red cabbage, sauerkraut, carp, potato salad or dumplings, apple strudel, plaited cakes, gingerbread, Christmas cookies (*vánoční cukroví*)

Beverages

The Czech Republic produces excellent beer. Pilsner Urquell, from the German "Old Spring Beer" or "The Original Source", was founded in 1842, and is known for its goldenness and bitter taste. Czech beers can be either light or dark, and have an alcohol content of 3-4%. The hops are in the Zatec region. Beers can be sampled in restaurants or at the annual hop festival in Pilzen. 1995 marked the 700th anniversary of the city of Pilzen. The Brewery Museum is located in Pivoraske. A pivnice is a beer tavern. The U Fleku Brewery in Prague dates from 1499. U Svateho Tomase is an old monastery producing beer made by the monks.

Moravia produces good wines. The oldest known is Ludmilla from Melnik, the grapes having been brought there in 1348 by Charles XIV from France. Other drinks are Becherovka, a liqueur from Karlovy Vary; Fernet Stock, a liquor; Zubrovka, a vodka with herbs; and grog, rum with hot water and sugar. Slivovice, plum brandy is the national drink. Mattoni – sparkling water and Kofola are non-alcoholic beverages.

Did You Know?

Ray Kroc, founder of McDonald's, was of Czech descent!
The town of Znojmo has been famous since the 16th c for gherkins.
In 1714 Deodat Damajian opened the first coffee house (the U Tri Pstrosu) "Three Ostriches Inn" in Prague.
It used to be at the time of a wedding a bride is held "hostage" in a pub till her husband arrives to "rescue her".
Bohemia is famous for lead crystal, glassware, porcelain and garnets.

Denmark

Denmark, the oldest kingdom in Europe, lies at the mouth of the Baltic Sea and is made up of the Jutland Peninsula and over 500 islands. Greenland and the Faroe Islands are also part of Denmark. Copenhagen, the capital, was once a fishing village that Vlademar the Great in 1157 presented to Bishop Absalon who then built the castle at Christianborg. During the 15th c Copenhagen was also the capital of Norway and Sweden. Danish is the official language.

Dining Etiquette

When invited out please be punctual. If bringing a gift please bring liquor, wine, wrapped flowers – roses or anemones, chocolates, or something from your own country. Please shake hands greeting and departing. Cocktails or aperitifs are served. The host and hostess will be seated at each end of the table. The male guest of honor will be seated to the hostess' left. Food is served on platters. Courses are soup, meat or fish, vegetables and potatoes with salad, cheese and fruit, dessert and coffee. Please wait for the hostess to start. Food is eaten continental style, fork in the left hand, knife in the right. When finished place the knife and fork facing down. Thank the hostess for the meal "Tak for mad". Wait for the host and hostess to get up to leave the table. Do not leave immediately. Dinner is usually served 6-8 PM. To toast raise your glass, look the person in the eye, say "Skal", and exchange glances again. The host or the highest ranking person proposes a toast first. The male guest to the left of the hostess thanks her for the meal by proposing a toast.

Cuisine

Denmark is famous for its smorrebrod "open sandwiches" and Det koldtbord "cold table" or Hojt smorrebrod "hot table". Smorrebrod means "buttered bread" and eaten with a fork and knife. This dish was invented by the Danes probably to soak up gravy or to be used as a plate. The koldtbord is a cold buffet, while the hojt smorrebrod begins with herring, aquavit and beer, followed by hot fish, cold meats, cheese, fruit and aquavit, each served on a different plate. Vegetables are often served pickled, especially cabbage, cucumbers, and beets. Kringle is a sweet bread with lots of butter and sugar. Danish pastries are world renowned. Denmark is well known too for its cheese – Danablu, Danish blue; Castello; Bla Castello; Havarti; Danbo; Samso; Typo; and other dairy products. During World War I an eye disease, Xerophthalmia, which is a vitamin A deficiency, was attributed to the fact that most butter had been sold to the Germans, at very high prices!

Bornholm, one of the Danish islands, produces grapes, figs, mulberries, spelt, durum, Manitoba grains, herbs, wild garlic, sorrel and mushrooms. Also found here are game – pheasant, hare, roe deer; free range cattle, pigs, sheep and goats; and fish – trout, cod, herring, plaice, and flounder. In Gaarden is Denmark's first Culinary History Center.

Meatballs in a Curry Sauce

"This is a very traditional Danish dish that has been very popular for the last 50 years. Both kids and grownups love these soft meatballs in a curry sauce, and many Danes regard it as one of their favorite meals. The dish also testifies to the fact that food cultures travel and become mixed into each other, and how most of this is an outcome of people trading with each other. This is my own version of the dish. I have modernized it a little bit by adding ginger and vegetables.

This serves 8 people, or 4 people for 2 days, that's the way my family does it, that is, eating it for 2 days.

Meatballs

500 g minced pork	1 tbls. curry powder
500 g minced veal	5 tsp salt
1 small onion, chopped	pepper
2 garlic cloves, crushed	4 eggs
200 ml milk	2 bay leaves
50 g plain wheat flour	

Combine the minced meat, onion, and garlic in a bowl. Add the milk, flour, curry powder, 2 teaspoons of the salt, and some freshly ground pepper and mix together. Add the eggs and mix again for about 5 minutes so that the mixture is as light and fluffy as possible.
Heat 4–5 liters water in a pot. Add the bay leaves and the remaining salt to the water and bring to a boil.
Meanwhile, use your hands to shape half the meat mixture into little balls about 2 cm wide. Plop them in the water and let them simmer for 20 minutes.
Remove the meatballs from the broth with a skimmer and place on a tray. Shape and cook the other half of the meat mixture in the same way. Set all the meatballs aside until the sauce is done, reserving 800 ml of the cooking liquid.

Sauce

30 g butter	200 ml double cream
2 onions, chopped	1 leek, sliced
2 garlic cloves, chopped	2 carrots, peeled and cut into large chunks
2 tbls. curry powder	2 apples, cored and sliced
2 tbls. plain wheat flour	

In a pot melt the butter, add the onions, garlic and curry powder and cook for a couple of minutes. Add the flour and stir well. Add 100 ml of the meatball cooking liquid and stir until smooth. Pour in the rest of the cooking liquid and bring to a simmer. Add the cream and return to a boil. Reduce the heat, add the meatballs, leek and carrots and simmer for 5 minutes. Add the apples and continue cooking for 3 minutes. Season to taste with salt and pepper and serve with rice.
Ms. Trina Hahnemann, author of "The Scandinavian Cookbook", and special thanks to the Royal Danish Embassy Washington, D.C.

Brunsviger

Denmark is a country of islands, and one of the main islands is Funen, where my family on my mother's side comes from. Denmark has lots of different regional recipes, and this is one of them. Brunsviger is a Funen specialty and it is a wonderful tasting tea cake that has to be eaten the same day it is baked. This is my grandmother's recipe. Her name was Marie, and she was a wonderful home cook who taught me and my mother the love of food and about it seasons. For a children's birthday party shape the dough as a girl or a boy, and when it comes out of the oven decorate it with candy.

Ms. Trina Hahnemann, author of The Scandinavian Cookbook and special thanks to the Royal Danish Embassy, Washington, DC

250 ml lukewarm whole milk
50 g fresh yeast
2 eggs
75 g butter, melted

500 g plain wheat flour
2 tbls. caster sugar
a pinch of salt

Glazing

150 g dark brown sugar

100 g butter

Pour the milk into a bowl, add the yeast and stir with a wooden spoon until the yeast has dissolved. Add the eggs and mix well, then add the melted butter.
Sift the flour with the sugar and salt, then stir the dry ingredients into the yeast mixture to make a dough. When the dough comes cleanly from the edge of the bowl, transfer it to a floured work surface and knead for about 5 minutes. Return the dough to the bowl and leave to rise at room temperature for 30 minutes.
Line a 40x50cm ovenproof dish with baking paper and press the dough evenly out in the dish. Cover with a tea towel and leave to rise again for 15 minutes.
Preheat the oven to 200°c.
To make the glaze, melt the brown sugar and butter together in a saucepan, stirring until the mixture is smooth and the sugar is no longer crunchy. Do not let it boil.
Press your fingers down into the risen dough, making small indentations across the surface. Spread the glazing evenly over the dough, leaving a 1 cm border.
Bake for 25–30 minutes, then leave the brunsviger to cool a little before cutting it into pieces and serving.

Danish Specialties

Ebelskiers – puffy pancakes cooked in a special pan and filled with jams, meat, cheese, or at Christmas with raspberry jam and served with glog
Leverpostej – liver pate
Kaernemaelkskoldskaal – buttermilk soup
Gronkalsoppa – kale soup

Lamgkal – braised kale
Gaaseteg med aebler og svedsker – roast goose stuffed with apples and prunes
Morbrad med svedsker og aebler – pork loin stuffed with apples and prunes
Frikadeller – pork meatballs

Sild – herring, can be pickled, in cream, marinated, in salads, sauces, and used in a variety of ways

Agurkesalat – pickled cucumbers
Klenater – fried cookies

Holidays and Special Occasions

New Year's Day – an old tradition includes breaking crockery at doors for good luck and inviting everyone in for doughnuts.
Easter – lamb
Christmas Eve – roast goose or stuffed pork loin, potatoes, red cabbage, bruened kartofler – sugar-glazed potatoes, risengrod – rice pudding with an almond (whoever finds the almond is assured good luck for the coming year), marzipan, ginger cookies, apple cake.
Christmas day – roast pork, pickled beets, cabbage, potatoes, rice and almond pudding (unless you have it Christmas Eve); Julekage – Christmas fruit cake

Beverages

Denmark is noted for beer, liqueurs, and aquavit. Since the 1400s the Royal Court Brewery has produced beer. The Carlsberg Brewery was founded in the 1700s when Christian Jacobsen, a farmer, settled in Copenhagen. His son, Jacob Christian Jacobsen, studied beer making under Gabriel Sedlmayr at the Spaten Brewery in Munich and developed the lager (lighter) types of beer. The brewery produced Denmark's first commercially marketed bottom fermented beer and received a royal license. The brewery was named after his son Carl and berg, a hill. This was one of the first breweries to use a thermometer. Tuborg developed a pale Pilsener style of beer. In 1883 Emil Hansen who worked under the Jacobsens discovered the single-cell yeast culture. In the 1970s Carlsberg and Tuborg merged forming the United Breweries. The Little Mermaid statue in Copenhagen was donated by Carl Jacobsen. Denmark is the 4th largest consumer of beer in the world!

Since the 16th c Akvavit (Aquavit) "water of life" was thought to be a cure for ailments. The drink is made from fermented mash of barley, malt, grain, or potatoes, and seasoned with caraway seed, coriander, fennel, cinnamon, anise, or cardamom. After a year of maturing it is bottled. The colorless alcoholic drink is 80 proof and is serve ice cold, neat and with appetizers. Denmark is the major producer of cherry wines (Cherry Heering), made from sour cherries "langeskov". There is a short aging period, during which the drink is fortified giving it a 17 ½ -19 ½ % alcohol content and sweet taste. Serve chilled. Snaps is served very cold with the smorrebrod. Dansk Glogg (mulled wine) is served at Christmas. Mjod or mead has been drunk even by the ancient Greeks and Chinese, and today is known as honey wine – fermenting hiney and water, sometimes with spices added.

Did You Know?

Early eating habits were quite primitive with the women feeding the men, not sitting down, and all eating from a communal bowl! The first Danish cookbook was published in 1616 for the aristocrats, included recipes for meat pies with live birds and was influenced by the French. In the 19th c Madame Mangor wrote on cooking and etiquette.

Djibouti

Djibouti is a country in the Horn of Africa, bordered by Eritrea in the north, Ethiopia in the west and south, Somalia in the southeast, the Red Sea and the Gulf of Aden at the east. The Somali and Afar peoples have inhabited the region and were among the first on the African continent to become Muslims. The northern region Obock was ruled by sultans, and from 1862 to 1894 signed treaties with France. In 1894 the region became French Somaliland. In 1967 it was renamed the French Territory of the Afars and Issas. Independence was granted in 1977. The capital, Djibouti, is nicknamed the Pearl of the Gulf of Tadjoura. French and Arabic are the official languages; Somali and Afar are also spoken.

Dining Etiquette

It is an honor to be invited to a Djibouti home. When invited for a meal please arrive promptly, or slightly past the time requested. You may have to remove your shoes before entering a home. Please bring a small gift such as pastries, fruit, flowers, something for the home, or if children present something for them. When giving the gift do so with both hands, or the right hand only. Gifts are not opened in front of the presenter. Please shake hands greeting and departing with good eye contact. Good friends may kiss each other three times on the cheeks. Women should extend their hand to a man. When first introduced, use Mr., Mrs., or Miss and the last name. Elders are introduced first. Please bow to an older or more senior person.

The Djiboutians enjoy entertaining friends and are very hospitable. A cup of coffee will be served. Please accept it. Meals might be served to guests using stools, on cushions, or seated on the floor. Families usually sit on the floor and the men and women may dine separately. Before the meal please wash your hands with the water and towel offered. Utensils may not be provided, rather food is eaten with the right hand. The eldest person will take from the communal plate first. Food will continue to be served as a sign of hospitality. Hands will be washed at the end of the meal, and coffee served. Please remember elders are very much respected in this country. Djiboutian women wear a dira (a long, flowing robe) and a shalmat (headscarf). A gorgorat (a long slip with embroidery at the bottom) is worn under the dira. In the afternoon and especially Thursdays men gather to chew khat (qat) which may suppress their appetite for a day or more.

Cuisine

The cuisine has been influenced by the French, Ethiopians, some Italian and Indian (pastas and curries), Yemeni, and Arabs. The Ethiopian influence is the use of injera (fermented flatbread) with sauces. The Yemeni influence is noticed in the way fish are baked, and the use of meat with dates, grains and bananas. The Somali influence comes with the grilled meats in the south. The Arabs introduced spices and pomegranates. Dairy products and local meats are consumed, along with grains, fresh seafood, lentils, fruit such as pineapples, lemons, bananas, oranges, and vegetables – peppers and tomatoes. Over 90% of the country is desert. Cattle, goats, sheep and camels are raised.

Isku Dhex Karis (all mixed together)

10 servings

3-4 lbs lamb cubes (or beef)	Cloves
Vegetable oil	2 hot peppers (remove stems and cut in two pieces each)
3-6 cloves of garlic, minced	
2 tlbs. cumin	Salt and pepper (use lots of pepper)
1 large onion, diced	3 large carrots, diced
Half a bunch of cilantro	2 large potatoes, diced
Cinnamon	White rice

In a hot, dry skillet, heat cumin until it begins to smoke, not burn, set aside in a dish.
Using vegetable oil or trimmed lamb fat, brown lamb in skillet, spicing with cumin, salt, and pepper.
Place the lamb in a Dutch oven. Sauté onions and garlic in a little oil and add to lamb. Simmer a few minutes. Add carrots, peppers, potatoes, and cilantro. Add uncooked non-instant white rice. Prepare white rice according to package directions. Use any broth from the lamb as part of the liquid. A pinch each of pepper, cinnamon, and cloves. Cook until rice is done. Be careful to turn down the burner to simmer while rice is cooking or it will burn on the bottom.
Pile rice-meat mixture onto plates, add salad on top, slice bananas over the salad, and squeeze lime juice over everything.
Serve with: mixed green salad, bananas, fresh limes
Recipe Courtesy of Rachel Jones, Djibouti

Djibouti Specialties

Cabri or riyo – baby goat
Beer –liver, usually sauteed
Foul – white beans with tomato and onin
Halicot – boiled white beans with onion and tomato and oil
Fah-fah – goat, vegetable and hot pepper soup
Bariis – Somali dish of spicy rice
Marak – soup with meat and/or vegetables
Roli, pain, or baguette – French bread
Berbere sauce – groundnut oil, red wine and berbere spices
Harira – beef, lentil, chickpea stew with tomato sauce, spices, and pasta
Banana fritters

Lentils- often cooked with onions, spices, berbere sauce
Soupe djiboutienne – mutton, potato and vegetable soup served to end the fast during Ramadan
Marake Kaloune – fish in a tomato, okra, onion, potato sauce
Samboussa – fried pastry
Skoudchkaris – rice and lamb dish
Yetakelt w'et – spicy vegetable stew
Grilled meats and fish
Doro wat – spicy chicken stew
Nitter kebbeth - sauce

Afar Goat

2-3 lbs. goat, cut into large pieces
2 tbls. fresh, whole cumin
2-3 onions, chopped

1-2 cloves garlic, chopped
5-7 tomatoes, finely chopped
Salt and pepper to taste

Sauté cumin, onions, garlic, tomatoes, salt, and pepper. Add goat pieces and fry until browned. Place in a large pan, pouring sautéed ingredients over the meat. Cover with tin foil and bake at 350 F until meat is tender and falling off the bone.
Serve with rice or couscous.
Recipe courtesy of Rachel Jones, Djibouti

Holidays and Special Occasions

Independence Feast Day – June 27th
Ramadan – fasting from sunrise to sunset
Id al-Fitr – end of Ramadan with feasts
Id al-Adha – Festival of Sacrifice
Christmas is celebrated by Christians
Wear put henna on their hands and feet for weddings and holidays
Religious services - qat is used
Wednesdays and Fridays - no meat is consumed

Beverages

Since most people are Muslim alcoholic beverages are not consumed. Shah is a milky tea.

Did You Know?

Lac Assal is part of the Danakil Depression 155m below sea level and a salt lake

Dominica

The Commonwealth of Dominica is an island in the Caribbean Sea. Guadaloupe is to the northwest and Martinique to the southeast. The Arawaks and Kalinago Carib tribes were the earliest settlers. Christopher Columbus named the island for the Sunday on which he saw it in 1493 Domenica "Sunday". In 1635 the French took over the island, and in 1763 it became part of the United Kingdom. From 1958 to 1962, Dominica was a province of the West Indies Federation. In 1978, Dominica became an independent nation. The capital Roseau is the largest city on the island. English is the official language, though Creole is also spoken.

Dining Etiquette

Please arrive punctually when invited for a meal, though you are on island time here. Please dress conservatively, men in trousers, women in resort dresses. Gifts are not expected, but something from your country for the home is appreciated. Please shake hands greeting and departing. Women will often kiss each other. Men may make a "tap" or fist and tap the other person's fist. Drinks and hors d'oeuvres will be served. Please wait for the hostess to seat you at the dining table. Food may be served on the table or buffet style. Wait for the hostess to begin. After dessert coffee or liqueurs may be served. The host initiates the toast by raising his glass and saying "Cheers". Do write a thank-you note after being entertained.

Cuisine

The cuisine is a combination of French, English, Creole and Caribbean. Curry, Scotch bonnet peppers and coconut milk are used in many of the dishes. Bananas, coffee, fruit are grown on the island. Fruit include tamarind, passion fruit, soursop, coconut, papayas, guavas, pineapples, mangoes, zabwico (similar to an apricot), plantains, cantalopes, and watermelons. Chicken, goat, lamb, beef, and fish – marlin, bream, tuna, lobster, agouti, crab, crayfish, manicou, crapaud (mountain frog), Dorado, kingfish, snapper, octopus, conch, flying fish are used in many dishes. Chicken is fried, roasted, grilled, in gravy, or in soups. Root vegetables grown on the island are dasheen, tania, yams and other vegetables – lettuce, spinach, watercress, celery, cucumber and callalou. Fresh herbs are grown on the island especially parsley and chives. Spices used are cinnamon, thyme, nutmeg, cloves, bay leaves Sauces are served with the food and can be spicy or made from local fruit or vegetables.

Chicken Pelau

3-4 lb. chicken
4 cups rice
Salt and pepper to taste
2 tbls. Worcestershire Sauce
2 tbls. sugar
2 tbls. oil
2 tbls. butter
2 onions, peeled and chopped
2 cloves garlic, minced

1 sweet pepper, chopped
1 hot pepper, chopped
1 sprig celery, chopped
1 sprig parsley, chopped
2 chives, snipped
1 sprig thyme, snipped
Dash of bitters
1 medium bottle Ketchup
10 cups water

Cut up the chicken and season with salt, pepper and Worcestershire Sauce.
Fry in burnt sugar and oil till golden brown.
Melt butter, add the vegetables, herbs, bitters, and ketchup and saute.
Pour vegetable mixture over the chicken and allow to marinate for two hours.
Put the chicken and water in a large pot. Bring to a boil. Stir. Add rice and lower heat.
Pelau is ready when the rice is tender.
Recipe courtesy of the Consulate General of the Commonwealth of Dominica, New York

Dominica Specialties

Pelau – the national dish of Dominica is a one pot rice and chicken dish
Mountain chicken – the national dish made frog legs
Frozen joys – peanut flavored popsicle
Callaloo soup – soup made from dasheen leaves
Pumpkin soup -
Buljow – cod cooked with onions, peppers, onions, tomatoes, bananas in coconut milk
Bakes – fritter stuffed with cod, tuna and cheese
Le roti – tortilla with chicken and curry sauce, onions and potatoes

Goat water – goat stew
Ton pictcho – stuffed tuna
Moro – rice and bean mixture
La bandera dominicana – rice beans and meat
Tostones – fried plantains
Mangu – mashed plantains fried with onions (breakfast dish)
Sancocho – chicken stew with yucca, plantains, spices and vinegar
Tres leches – cake with cream frosting
Palitos de coco – coconut cake
Cocoyucca – yucca flan with coconut

Yam Puffs

Serves 6
1 lb. yams
2 tbls. butter

Pinch of salt
4 eggs

Peel, wash and boil the yams until tender. Mash with the butter and salt. Add the eggs.
Heat hot oil in a frying pan. Drop yam mixture by spoonful in oil. Fry till golden brown.
Recipe courtesy of the Consulate General of the Commonwealth of Dominica, New York

Holidays and Special Occasions

For national holidays smoked or stewed opossum are served with rice, yucca, and pumpkin. The patron saints of each village have a feast day.

Governor Plum Drink

4 cups plums	Piece of mace
5 cups water	Small piece of ginger, crushed
Peel of 1 lime	1 lb. sugar

In a pot bring the plums, 4 cups water, mace, lime peel, and ginger to a boil. Boil for ½ hour. Allow to cool. Add other cup of water. Sweeten with sugar and bottle.
Recipe courtesy of the Consulate General of the Commonwealth of Dominica, New York

Beverages

Lots of fresh water from the mountains provides good drinking water.. Dominica brews its own beer under the Kubuli label. Sorrel blooms around Christmas and is made into a drink. Rum is made from sugar cane grown on the sugar plantations founded by the British. Well known brands are Macoucherie, Soca and Red Cap.

Did You Know?

Fort Cashacrou means "that which is being eaten".
Cabrits National Park is named for the goats which were left by the early explorers.
Breadfruit was brought to the island by Captain Bligh in 1793.
Citronella grass is grown as a base for perfume.
The Spaniards introduced mangos, bananas, cocoa, sugar cane, and coffee.

Dominican Republic

The Dominican Republic shares the island of Hispanola with Haiti in the Caribbean. The Tainos who came from South America c 650 AD, farmed, fished, and were hunter-gatherers. In the 15th c the Caribs settled on the island. In 1496 Bartholomew Columbus, Christopher Columbus' brother built the city of Santo Domingo, the first European city in the "New World", and today the capital of the Dominican Republic. Some French speaking people settled in western Hispaniola, as the island was called, and in 1697 Spain ceded the region to France. In 1808 Hispaniola was returned to Spain. In 1844 the Dominican Republic became independent from Haiti. The official language is Spanish.

Dining Etiquette

Please arrive promptly, or just slightly late when invited for a meal. Please shake hands greeting and departing with good eye contact and a smile. Please bring a gift of candy, pastries, or a gift for the home from your country. Gifts are opened when received. Guests will be served beverages. The hostess will escort the guests to the dining room with the male guest of honor seated to her right. Food is eaten continental style with the fork in the left hand and knife in the right. Food may be passed, buffet style, or served. Please wait for the hostess to start. Please keep your hands at table level and not in your lap and no elbows on the table. When finished please place your utensils face down with the handles facing to the right. The host will begin the first toast and the toast is "Salud". Please thank the hostess when departing. A thank you note or phone call is always appreciated.

The family is very important in the Dominican Republic and most family members live nearby. Elders are shown much respect.

Cuisine

The cuisine has been influenced by the Spanish, Taino and Africans. Onions, garlic, cilantro, hot peppers, oregano, yucca, cassava, sugarcane, sweet potatoes, squash, coffee, bananas, mangoes, pineapples, coconuts, potatoes and seafood – lobsters, shrimp, marlin, mahi-mahi, and conch are available. Lunch may be the main meal of the day and would include rice; chicken, pork, beef, or fish; beans; and salad.

Sancocho

Serves 10

1 lb. pork
1 lb. pork ribs
1 lb. beef
1 lb. goat meat
1 lb. sausage
1 lb. boneless chicken
¼ cup fresh lime juice
½ tsp. ground cumin
½ tsp. oregano
¼ cup fresh cilantro
4 garlic cloves, minced
3 tbls. oil
2 onions, chopped

1 lb. sweet potatoes, peeled and cut into 1 in. slices
4 carrots, peeled and sliced
½ lb. taro
½ lb. cassava
2 corn cobs
1 red or green chili
6 cups beef broth or chicken stock or just water
Cilantro
Avocado slices
Rice

Cut all the meat into small pieces. Coat the meat, except sausage with the lemon juice.

Place the beef in a bowl and combine with the cilantro, oregano, cumin and garlic. Marinate for ½ hour.

Heat some oil in a pot and brown the beef. Add the pork, ribs, sausage, and goat. Simmer for 15 minutes. Add a little water to keep from burning. Add the chicken. Add 2 cups of stock or water. Bring to a boil. Add the onions, sweet potatoes, carrots, taro, cassava, and chili. Continue simmering, adding stock or water when necessary until all the meat and vegetables are thoroughly cooked – about an hour.

Serve with rice, cilantro, and avocado. Hot sauces are often added.

Most sancocho recipes call for using 7 different meats. Other recipes will only use chicken, or other meats. Sancocho means "slow cooking" "long simmering". Yucca and other Caribbean vegetables can be used.

Dominican Republic Specialties

Mangu – mashed and boiled plantain which may be accompanied by fried meat
Mofongo – fried green plantains or yuca with garlic, olive oil, cracklings with broth
Pastels en hojas – tamales made with root vegetables
La bandera – meat and red beans with rice
Sofrito – sauce of onions or garlic, tomatoes, spices, peppers, herbs, and cooked in oil
Chicarrones – fried pork cracklings
Pastelitos – meat turnovers
Carne mechata – braised beef

Molondrones quisados – okra stew
Casaba – yuca bread
Yucca y batatas fritas – fried sweet potatoes and cassava
Chen-chen – cornmeal pudding
Chimichurri – herb, onion and garlic sauce served with roasted or grilled meats
Tostones – fried plantain
Sopa hamaca – fish soup with vegetables
Roast pork and carne de cerdo – ground pork
Roast suckling pig
Beans and rice

Torta de coco – coconut cheese tart
Yanikeiki - johnnycakes
Arroz con dulce – rice dessert
Habichuelas con dulce – beans with coconut milk and sweet potato
Moros de ganduales con coco – rice, peas and coconut milk

Cana – sugar cane
Bizcocho dominicano – Dominican cake
Flan –sweet custard
Frio frio – snow cones

Holidays and Special Occasions

Easter - fish
Christmas Eve (Noche Buena) – roast pork or chicken; potato salad; green salad; Pastelas en hojas – banana leaf with a filling of beef, pork, chicken, fish, cheese, vegetables (first cooked by Dona Isabel Coiscou of San Cristobal); Pan telera –crusty bread; Pudim navidena – Christmas pudding; fruits, nuts; Poncho de huevo – eggnog; Anis de mono- anise drink; Jengibre – drink of boiled ginger root and cinnamon; pigeon peas, boiled chestnuts
Baptism – takes place at a church followed by a lunch or brunch
Girl's 15th birthday – girls dress in fancy dresses; buffet dinner with many types of drinks and a special cake
Wedding – buffet, lots of food and drinks, and a wedding cake

Beverages

Making of rum dates back to to the time of Christopher Columbus. On one of his trips he was accompanied by Don Diego Bermudez who introduced sugar cane to the island. The Bermudez family began full scale production of rum in 1852 with Amargo Panacea. The Brugal Company was founded in 1888 by Andres Brugal Montener which is located in Puerto Plata. Other rum companies are Barcelo, Pedro Justo Carrion, and Ron Siboney. The rum is considered very smooth. The rum may be aged from 18 months to 10 years or more. Rum is drunk with just ice or as a mixed drink. The Rum and Sugar Cane Museum is in Santo Domingo.

Other drinks are Mauby Fizz, Morir Sonando (orange juice, milk and sugar), Mabi 9fermented colubrine bark or fruit), and Mama Juana (dark rum with sticks, leaves). Beer is also produced on the island.

Ecuador

The South American country of Ecuador lies directly on the Equator, and thus its name which means "Equal" with 12 hours of daylight and 12 of darkness. It is bordered by Colombia to the north, Peru, the south, and the Pacific Ocean to the west. The country is made up of four regions – the coastal plain in the west; the Andes Mountains in the center; the Central Valley; and the Galapagos Islands 622 miles at sea. There are two official languages – Spanish and Quechua. The capital Quito lies at the foot of Mt. Pichincha. Ecuador's history dates back more than 4000 years to the Valdivia culture. During the 15th c later tribes were captured by the Inca from Peru. Spanish explorers took over the country in the 16th c. In 1830 Ecuador became an independent nation. Spanish is the official language.

Dining Etiquette

When invited out you do not need to arrive punctually, but may arrive up to 30 minutes late. People shake hands greeting and departing. Men may embrace and women kiss on the cheek if they know each other well enough. Women extend hands first. Appropriate house presents are flowers, wine, liquor or something for the home. You may also send a note and/r flowers as a thank you. Dinner is about 7- 8PM. Drinks and appetizers will be served. The hostess will escort the guests into the dining room. The table is set with a dinner fork to the left of the plate, and to the left of that a salad fork. To the right is the knife facing the plate and a soup spoon. Over the plate is a dessert fork, and a spoon for coffee or tea. The host and hostess will sit at each end of the table, with the guest of honor to the hostesses' right. The meal will be served in courses. It will include a soup, salad, meat, rice or potatoes, bread, no butter, dessert or fruit, and then coffee. Wine and/or juices are served. When finished place the knife and fork together. The toast is "Salud" "To health".

The old boy network is very important in Ecuador - one's social standing, education, business and political connections. Life is centered around the family. Dinners are social occasions where business is not discussed.

Cuisine

The cuisine of Ecuador has been influenced by the Amerindi and Spanis, and the local products. The different regions of Ecuador have their own specialties. In the highlands potatoes, corn, cheese, avocadoes, roasted pigs (hornado), cuy (guinea pig) are grown. In the north coastal region bananas (plantain) are used as banana chips, banana flour for breads and pastries, pureed, and banana desserts. Other ingredients include yucca, coconut, rice, papaya, pineapples, and starfruit. Like most Latin American countries Ecuador has cultivated corn, beans, root crops and fruit for thousands of years. Fish is abundant along the coast. Other favorite dishes are baked guinea pig (cuy); mondongo soup (made with hominy); llapingachos (potato and cheese pancakes: empanadas; locko (stew with potatoes, cheese and avocados); humitas (sweet corn tamale); ceviche (seafood marinated with cilantro, onions, and hot peppers); and Narangilla (a peach like drink).

Among the popular herbs and spices are cilantro,

Until the 1920s Ecuador was the largest exported of cocoa, now replaced by shrimp and bananas. Maqueno bananas have a black and yellow peel, but are pale in color. Other products are coffee, cacao, rice, sugar, corn, wheat, cattle, potatoes, Shrimp and tuna processing plants

Fanesca (Salt Cod)

1 lb. salt cod
1 clove garlic, minced
1 bay leaf
1 cup cooked corn kernels
2 cups chopped, cooked zucchini
1 cup cooked green beans, cut in ½ in.
pieces
1 cup light cream
3 hardboiled eggs, sliced
½ stick butter
¼ tsp. oregano
Fresh ground pepper
2 ½ cups cooked shredded cabbage

1 cup cooked baby lima or fava beans
½ cup peanuts, ground
1 cup Queso Freco or Queso Blaco cheese,
or Munster, chopped
Grated Parmesan cheese
2 medium onions, finely chopped
¼ tsp. cumin
1 cup rice cooked in 1 cup water and 1 cup
milk
2 cups cooked, mashed winter squash
1 cup cooked green peas
4 cups milk
Salt

Soak the cod in cold water to cover for 12 hours or more, changing the water frequently. Drain the fish and put it into a saucepan with fresh water to cover. Bring to a boil, lower the heat, and simmer until the fish is tender, about 15 minutes. Drain, and reserve the fish stock. Remove any skin an bones from the fish and cut it into 1/2-inch pieces. Set aside.

Heat the butter in a large saucepan and saute the onions and garlic until the onions are soft. Add the oregano, cumin, bay leaf, and several grinds of black pepper and saute for a minute or two longer. Add 1 cup water, bring to a boil, and add the cooked rice, corn, cabbage, squash, zucchini, lima or fava beans, peas, green beans, ground peanuts, the fish and fish stock, the milk, and the cream. Stir to mix and simmer very gently for about 5 minutes to blend the flavors. Add the chopped cheese and salt to taste. The soup should be about as thick as a minestrone. If it seems too thick, thin it with a little more milk and simmer for a few minutes longer.

Pour the soup into a tureen and serve in soup plates. Garnish the servings with sliced hardboiled egg. Have the grated Parmesan cheese in a bowl on the table to be used as liked.

Recipe courtesy of the Embassy of Ecuador, Washington, DC

Ecuadorian Specialties

Ilapingachos – fried mashed potato and cheese patties
Seco de chivo – goat stew
Locro de papa – potato and cheese soup with shredded chicken and avocados
Fritada – fried pork
Empanada – pastry with meat or cheese
Puchero – beef stew with peaches, cabbage, rice, sweet potatoes, and other vegetables
Mote- boiled corn
Bizcochos – biscuit from Cayambe
Patacones – plantain that has been fried, pounded and fired again, served with salt
Chifles – deep fried plantain
Maduro con queso –barbecued plantain with cheese

Bolones de verde – plantain balls with cheese
Chupe de corvina - fish stew
Hornado – suckling pig
Encocados –fish or prawns in coconut sauce served with rice and patacones (from Esmeraldas)
Ceviche – seafood with lime or lemon juice, chili and onion
Encebollados – seafood in a tomato sauce with yucca, onion and coriander
Molo – mashed potatoes
Flan – caramelized custard,
Dulces de higos – green figs stewed with molasses or brown sugar, eaten with a white cheese

Holidays and Special Occasions

Lent – fanesca is made with seven types of grain, young white corn, peas, kidney beans, broad beans, roasted peanuts, vegetable marrow, scallions, grated white cheese, cabbage, rice, milk and cream
Easter – the traditional soup is fanesca made with grains, beans, dried salt cod, vegetables, and served with sliced hardboiled eggs, fried ripe plantains, fresco, hot peppers, hot sauce, white onions in lime juice, and empanadas.
All Souls' Day (Day of the Dead) – November 2 – decorated bread dough dolls (guaguas de pan) are eaten and colado morada (black raspberry, blueberry, maize flour, pineapple drink with herbs and spices) is served
Christmas – tamales de Navidad, turkey, lamb, potatoes, brown sugar bread
A girl's 15th birthday is celebrated with a large party.

Beverages

Ecuador produces very good beers – Pilsener and Club, and a few wines mainly from the Labrusca or table grapes. Almost all alcoholic beverages are imported and expensive. Special drinks are aguardiente (anise flavored liquor), paico (aguardiente and lemon), and canelazo (a drink of hot water, sugar cane, spirits, lemon, sugar, herbs, and cinnamon). Chicha Morada is made from fermented boiled white corn, pineapple, other fruit and sugar.

Did You Know?

Tuesday the 13th and Sunday the 7th are considered days of bad luck!
The Yaku Museum of Water in Quito is an old water treatment plant now used a museum to educate about water conservation. The site was once an Inca ceremonial bath.

Egypt

Egypt occupies the northeastern part of Africa, abutted by the Mediterranean to the north, the Red Sea, Libya, The Sudan, and Israel. Egypt's history dates back to at least 10,000 BC. C 8000 BC the land became more desert and the people migrated to the fertile Nile River Valley. C 3150 BC the Upper and Lower Kingdoms were united by King Menes. Later Egypt was once part of Persia, then Greece, Rome, and Byzantine. In 1914 Egypt became a protectorate of Great Britain. Today Egypt is a republic with a legal system based on the Napoleonic code and Islamic law. The capital, Cairo, from "Al Qahira" was founded in 640 AD after an Arab invasion. The official language is Arabic, with English and French also spoken.

Dining Etiquette

When invited to a home please arrive punctually. Please bring a gift which is presented with both hands or the right hand. Or send flowers the day before, or the day after. Shake hands greeting and departing. Men, if they know each other well, will hug or kiss on the right, and then the left cheek. Women should not look men in the eye. Breakfast is a light meal, lunch the main meal from 2-3, and dinner 9-11PM. When utensils are present please eat continental style, fork in the left hand and knife in the right. In rural areas no utensils, or only a spoon might be used in the right hand only. When finished, leave a small amount on your plate. Pointing is an insult. When sitting keep both feet on the ground and do not point the soles of your feet. Do not display affection in public. Family and old ties are very important as is respect for elders.

Chakchouka

Olive oil
1 ½ lbs. ground beef
2 15 oz. cans stewed tomatoes
2 onions, chopped
Salt and pepper
½ tsp. cumin
1 tbls. coriander
1 clove garlic, minced

1 chili pepper, seeded and diced
½ tsp. paprika
6 green peppers, chopped
8 eggs
Cooked rice
Parsley

In a skillet fry the onions in some olive oil. Add the meat until cooked. Add tomatoes, salt, pepper, spices and herbs. Cook for 15-20 minutes. Add green peppers. Cook for 2-3 hours on low heat. Put in baking dish. Heat oven to 325°. Before serving break the eggs on top. Cook until the eggs are set.
Serve with rice and fresh parsley.
Recipe courtesy of a dear Egyptian friend

Koushari

Serves 6

Oil
2 onions, chopped
½ cup mint
Penne pasta
1 cup brown lentils, rinsed
6 tsp. white vinegar

6 cloves garlic, minced
5 tomatoes, chopped
Pepper/salt
Spice
1 cup rice

Heat a little oil in a pan, add 1 onion, turning until it becomes tender and golden. Remove from pan. Add lentils to pan and add some water. Boil for 5-10 minutes, and then add the rice. Add more water, salt and pepper. Cook until all moisture is absorbed.
Cook pasta until tender.
In another pan prepare the sauce mixing tomatoes, garlic and remaining onion, vinegar, salt and pepper. Bring to a boil.
Pour the mixture of rice and lentils with macaroni in a dish. Add the tender and golden onions and the sauce. You can add a bit of spice to the mixture.
Recipe courtesy of Ambassador Mohamed Tawfk, Embassy of Egypt, Washington, DC

Baklawa

Serves 6

1 lb. phyllo dough
1 lb. walnuts or almonds, finely chopped
½ cup breadcrumbs

¼ cup cinnamon sugar
11 oz. butter, melted

Preheat oven to 350º
Mix the walnuts, breadcrumbs, and cinnamon sugar.
Prepare phyllo dough, brushing each sheet with butter. Line a rectangular mold with six phyllo sheets superimposed, spread a layer with nuts, cover with 2 sheets of phyllo, repeat until all is used and last layer is 6 sheets phyllo. Do a few incisions on the top crust with a sharp knife.
Bake for 20 minutes or until crust is golden brown. Cool.

Syrup

4 cups sugar
2 cups water

Juice from a lemon

Boil the sugar, water and lemon juice in a sauce pan for 10 minutes.
Pour the hot syrup over the cooled baklawa.
Let stand several hours before serving. Cut into squares.
Recipe courtesy of Ambassador Mohamed Tawfk, Embassy of Egypt, Washington, DC

Cuisine

Egypt has been inhabited for thousands of years and along the fertile Nile River crops were grown. Grains of barley from Tutankhamen's tomb were found dating back to the 14th c BC. Even in ancient pictures flatbreads were known to have been eaten, and leavened breads made of wheat or barley flour. Dates, honey, grapes, fruit trees, herbs, leeks, onions, mushrooms, cabbage, and okra were grown. Most of the country is desert with a few oases. The Nile's fertile valley and delta provide for the major crops which are maize, peanuts, sorghum, rice, wheat, berseem Egyptian clover, sugar cane, sugar beets, potatoes, tomatoes, and beans. The food is very Middle Eastern using okra, onions, leeks, rice, fava beans, lamb, beef, fish, squab (young pigeon), couscous, potatoes, tomatoes, maize, sorghum, rice, wheat, beans, okra, lamb, chicken, pomegranates, apples, and yogurt. Spices and herbs are used to season the food and may include cumin, caraway seeds, saffron, coriander, mint, garlic, cinnamon, and cardamom. Coriander is a very ancient herb and seeds were found in the Egyptian tombs from the Twenty-First Dynasty.

Egyptian Specialties

Koushari – is Egypt's national dish. It is made with rice, lentils, chickpeas, cardamom, jasmine, hot peppers, a variety of other ingredients, and fried onions. The dish is known to have dated back to the 14th c by Ibn Battuta, an explorer, but has been influenced by Indian, Persian, Italian, and other cuisines using leftovers.

Molohia – similar to spinach (part of mallow family), used as a thick green soup with chicken or meat, vegetables and rice

Couscous – finely ground wheat, served as a side dish or dessert

Fuul medames – fuul medames beans, garlic, oil, onions, eggs used as a dip or spread, perhaps dates back to the pharaohs

Mezza – salad served at the beginning of a meal

Warag anab – grape leaves stuffed with rice and meat

Baba ghanouj – eggplant with tahini (sesame paste), lemon, garlic, and oil

Schawrirma – sandwich similar to a Greek gyro

Hamam Mahshi – braised pigeon

Kofta – ground meat with spices

Gambari – broiled prawns

Aysh – bread

Pilaf – rice often cooked with nuts

Firakh – fish

Shy – tea

Ahwa – coffee

Karkade – hibiscus flower drink

Yansoun – anise drink

Salhleb – a hot cream made with orchids and nuts

Duqqa – pounded spice blend served with olive oil and bread

Falafel – dried beans and spices shaped into a ball and fried

Tamiya – deep fried beans

Tahina – sesame paste

Mezze dishes – small plates

Zalabia – fried dough with powdered sugar

Aish baladi "villege bread" - puffy flatbread

Kahk – cookies that date back to the pharaohs. Tombs depict pictures of women making kahk. They are a round shape like the sun.

Mihallabiya – rice flour pudding with rose water

Esh es seraya "bread of the palace" – bread soaked in sugar syrup, baked, and topped with ishta (cream)

Holidays and Special Occasions

Moulids (pilgrim festivals) – music, ceremonies and food
Muslims celebrate Ramadan (a month of fasting from sunrise to sunset), Eid-al-Fitr and the Birthday of the Prophet.
Christians celebrate Easter and Christmas.

Beverages

The earliest known wines may have originated in Egypt and date back to c 3000 BC. They were made from grapes or dates and came from the Nile Delta and the Kharga and Dahla Oases. Storage was in earthenware jars. Wines played an important role in ceremonial life. Winemaking scenes appeared on tomb walls, and were part of the afterlife. The earliest wines produced were red. Shedeh was considered the most precious wine. Plutarch's *Moralia* relates that, prior to Psammetichus I, the pharaohs did not drink wine nor offer it to the gods "thinking it to be the blood of those who had once battled against the gods and from whom, when they had fallen and had become commingled with the earth, they believed vines to have sprung". This was considered to be the reason why drunkenness "drives men out of their senses and crazes them, inasmuch as they are then filled with the blood of their forebears". Later Christians and monasteries, and then Jews produced wines. By the time of the Muslim conquests in the 7th c wine production declined. Muslims were known to drink *nebit shamsi* wine made from raisins and honey and fermented in the sun; and *booza* local barley beer.

Viticulture was revived in Egypt by Greek-Egyptian tobacco merchant and entrepreneur, Nestor Gianaclis, who founded the country's first modern vineyard south of Alexandria in 1882. In 1963 the government nationalized and merged breweries and vineyards in the country under the previously Belgian-owned Pyramid Brewery, which later came to be known as Al Ahram Beverages Company. The Gianaclis Vineyards again began planting vines in 2004 in Alexandria and Luxor. The main varieties used in red wines are Cabernet Sauvignon, Syrah, Grenache, Bobal and Tempranillo, while Viognier, Chardonnay and Muscat are used for white wines. Koroum of the Nile, a winery based in El Gouna, cultivates an indigenous grape variety known as Bannati which is used in its Beausoleil white wine.

Beer was made from fermented barley, wheat, dates and bread. Other drinks are Zattos, a rum and Zibib, an aperitif.

Did You Know?

In excavating ruins it was found that the tombs contained food, beer and wine casks for the afterlife. Grains of barley were found still intact in the Tutankhamen's tomb and proved white wine was also produced.
Egyptian hieroglyphics dating back 5000 years show cheese making. The tomb of the second king of the First Dynasty, Horus-aha, held pots which were believed to make cheese.
Sia is a western desert oasis that has date palms and olive groves.

168

El Salvador

El Salvador borders the Pacific Ocean on the west, Guatemala to the north, and Honduras to the east. In pre-Columbian times the country was inhabited by the Pipil who had an advanced civilization and built many ancient cities. The Spanish arrived in the early 16th c and by 1520 most of the indigenous population had been killed by smallpox. For a period of time El Salvador was part of the Captaincy General of Guatemala. In 8121 the country was annexed by Mexico, and in 1823 joined the Federation of Central America. It became independent in 1841. The capital San Salvador, was founded near the Pipil capital of Cuzcatian in 1521. The official language is Spanish. El Salvador means "The Savior".

Dining Etiquette

Please arrive punctually when invited, or a few minutes late. Please bring a gift of candies, wine, Scotch, flowers (not white which are for funerals), or something from your country. Men stand when introduced to women. Please shake hands greeting and departing. Close female friends will kiss on the cheek. Some people will nod their head on greeting. If someone puts their arm around you it is a sign of friendship. People may stand quite close when speaking. Beverages will be served. Please wait for the hostess to seat you. Food will be served or buffet style. Wait for the hostess to start. Please leave a little on your plate at the end of the meal. Always compliment the hostess on the preparation of the food. The toast is "Salud". Family ties are still very important.

Pupusa Revuelta

3½ cups masa harina (corn flour)   4 cups water

Place the masa and water in a bowl and knead until a soft dough is formed. Let rest for about 15 minutes. Shape into about 16-18 balls. Make an indentation in each. Place on a cookie sheet and cover with a towel.
Place a spoonful of the filling in each indentation. Wrap dough around to seal. Flatten to about ¼ in. thick.
In a skillet with a little oil brown the pupusa on each side 2-3 minutes.
Serve with tomato or other sauces.

Filling

½ lb. chicharron (finely ground pork)   ½ cup refried beans
1 cup grated quesillo (Salvadoran cheese)

Put the beans in a food processor until smooth. Add the cheese and chicharron.

Cuisine and Beverages

The cuisine has been influenced by the Maya, Lenca, Pipil and Spanish. Corn, squash, tomatoes, frijoles - black beans, refried beans, simmered, grilled or fried chicken, pork, tortillas, rice, eggs, fruit, carrots, pumpkin (ayote), plantain, chayotte, boiled or deep-fried yucca, fruit – mango, banana, pineapple are used in cooking. The most common spices and herbs are cumin, cinnamon, tamarind, and cilantro. Pupusas were first made by the Pipil tribe in Central America. They are made with rice or corn flour and stuffed with quesillo cheese. Other ingredients might be beans, pork, chicharron, squash, or other vegetables. Coffee is produced, exported and drunk in El Salvador. Beer (cerveza) is brewed and popular brands include Pilsener and Suprema. Kolachampan is a local soda; minutas flavored frozen drinks; and licuados minutas with fresh fruit. Horchata is made with morro or other seeds, cinnamon, cocoa, and sesame seeds. Fruit juices; atole de elote (a corn drink); and coconut milk are also drunk. Chocolate caliente – chocolate and hot water is a drink with chunks of chocolate

Salvadoran Specialties

Yucca frites- fried cassava

Pupusa – masa cake (corn masa flour and water) with beans, cheese, pork, or loroco and served with curtido (pickled cabbage) and tomato sauce (eaten at breakfast)

Tamales de elote – corn cakes

Empanadas – pastry with meat or cheese

Pan con pavo – turkey sandwich with tomato and watercress

Sopa de pata – cow tripe, plantain, corn, tomatoes, cabbage and spice soup

Gallo en chicha – corn and chicken soup

Curtido – condiment made with cabbage, carrots, vinegar and other vegetables

Mariscada – seafood soup

Chorizo – spicy sausage

Pollo encebellado – chicken with onions

Salsa roja – cooked tomato sauce

Casamiento – black beans and rice

Queso seco – hard cheese for grating

Relajo sauce – tomato, sesame and pumpkin seed, cinnamon and paprika sauce

Blanco fresco – similar to farmers' cheese, but has banana flavor, eaten at breakfast with fried plantain and beans

Poleads – vanilla custard

Arroz con leche – rice pudding

Platanos fritos – fried bananas

Flan de leche – caramel custard

Semita – pastry with jam, fruit or other filling

Maria Lusia – jam filled cake

Pastel tres leches – three milk cake

Holidays and Special Occasions

Lent – seafood instead of meat eaten on Fridays, often dried red snapper (pargo)

Holy week – fishcake or seafood soup rice, clams, tortillas, dry fruit candy, torrejas – French toast with honey

Easter – cascarones (colored eggs with confetti and small toys that are broken over someone's head as a sign of good luck.

Day of the Dead – November 2 – chicken or pork tamales, ayote en miel (sliced pumpkin with brown sugar)

Christmas Eve – dinner is served after mass. Turkey, chicken, tamales, rice, potatoes, salads, and drinks are served

Patron Saint feasts – celebrated in most towns at different times of the year

England (Great Britain)

England lies off the northwest coast of Europe, separated from it by the English Channel, the Strait of Dover, and the North Sea. England, Scotland, Wales and Northern Ireland form the United Kingdom. The history of England dates back thousands of years. Stonehenge was built c 2800-1800 BC. The Romans built cities such as York. Christian missionaries came in the 3rd c, followed by the Germans, Vikings, and others, until William the Conqueror was crowned at Westminster Abbey in 1066. Her Majesty Queen Elizabeth II began her reign in 1952! London, the capital, dates back to Roman times, the first being Londnium founded in 60 AD by Queen Boadicca. English is the official language.

Dining Etiquette

Always be punctual for meals. Appropriate house presents are flowers, books, food, wine,, or candies. Please shake hands greeting and departing. Ladies extend hands first. If you are introduced to the Queen, she will extend her hand first. Men hold doors for ladies, stand when introduced, and seat ladies. Drinks will be served. The guest of honor will be seated at the head of the table or to the right of the hostess. The fork is used in the right hand, the knife the left. Salad is served with the meal. Hands, not elbows should remain on the table. A host or hostess initiates toasting. An older person, or one of higher rank toasts before a younger person. The toast is "Cheers" or "Cheerio". The toast to the Queen is "To the Queen". Do write or call the hostess to thank her for the meal.

Cuisine

For years England ranked behind many other European countries in the development of its culinary arts. The influence of French and Russian cooking brought to the royal court in the 19th c changed some of this. Now with numerous immigrants, England is a treasure trove of cuisines. Ingredients include salmon and fresh fish, mutton, spices, asparagus, cucumbers, strawberries, and raspberries. Game is very popular ranging from duck, goose, partridge, woodcock, deer, rabbit, grouse, snipe and plover. Accompaniments are mustards, chutneys, jams, horseradish and Hollandaise. Each region of the country is noted for certain foods such as scones and cream teas in Devon; pasties (meat pies) from Cornwall, and Blue Viney cheese from Dorchester.

Steamed Orange Sponge with Marmalade Ice Cream and Hot Orange Sauce

Pudding

4 ozs. unsalted butter	finely grated zest of 1 orange
5ozs sugar	7 ozs. self-rising flour
2 eggs	Juice of 3 oranges boil and reduce by 2/3 (cool)
1 egg yolk	Sprigs of fresh mint

To make sponge – cream butter and sugar together. Mix eggs and yolk together and beat into the butter and sugar mixture. Add zest and fold in sifted flour. Add orange juice
 Line six – 5 fl.oz moulds or 1/12 pint mould with butter and flour. Spoon in sponge mixture to fill ¾ of the way up the mould and cover with buttered paper. Steam individual puddings for 35-40 minutes and larger puddings for 1 1/4 - 1 ½ hours
 Once the pudding is cooked turn out and serve with a spoonful of marmalade ice cream and some hot orange sauce. Decorate with a sprig of mint.

Sauce

1 pint fresh orange juice	1 teaspoon corn flour
2 ozs. sugar	1 tablespoon water

Boil orange juice until reduced by half then add the sugar. Mix cornflour with water – whisk into the simmering juice. Allow to cook for 3-4 minutes
Recipe courtesy of Harry Simpson, chef to Ambassador Sir Nigel Sheinwald, Washington, DC

English Specialties

Yorkshire Pudding – batter cooked in roast beef drippings
Crumpets – pastry served at breakfast or tea
Marlborough Pudding
Bubble and Squeak – roast beef and cabbage dish
Exeter Stew – beef stew
Steak and kidney pie
Cornish pasties – pastries with a meat and vegetable stuffing
Fish and Chips – fried fish and potatoes
Kedgeree or finan haddie – smoked haddock
Potted shrimp - shrimp with clarified butter
Tipsy pudding- egg, sugar, flour and rum pudding
Flummeries – molded desserts with gelatin, sherry and cream

Mincemeat – beef suet, dried and candied fruit, nuts, apples and spices used in a pie crust for Christmas
Shortbread – rich buttery cookies
Scones – pastries served at tea with jam and cloated cream, or lemon curd (butter, sugar and lemon juice)
Madeira cake – served at afternoon tea with a glass of Madeira
Spotted dick – dough with currants, dried fruit and custard sauce
Trifle – pound cake or lady fingers, fruit, custard and whipped cream dessert
Syllabub – macaroon, Madeira and cream dessert
Cumberland sauce – lemon, orange, Port, and red currant jam sauce

Holidays and Special Occasions

Shrove Tuesday – pancakes
Good Friday – hot cross buns
Easter – decorated eggs, hot cross buns, ham or lamb, roast potatoes, Simnel cake
Christmas – wassail bowls, smoked salmon, goose, turkey, stuffing and gravy; roast beef, Yorkshire pudding, mince pies, fruitcake, chestnuts, , plum pudding
Boxing Day (December 26) - day to visit friends and party. Ham, Christmas leftovers,

Beverages

England produces ales, beer, port, beer, sherry, wines, and gin. The earliest wines may have been brought by the Romans. Records show King Edwy gave a vineyard to the Glastonbury Abbey monks in 955 AD. Most vineyards are in Somerset, Cornwall, and Devon. Port was introduced in 1688 when England under William of Orange had a trade embargo with France. The Metheun Treaty allowed England to import Portuguese wines. Port was found to travel best when fortified with alcohol and placed in a stoppered bottle which was developed in 1780. Vintage port matures in the bottle while wood port is put in a cask. At first the English were unwilling to change their drinking habits. Most bottling of ports and sherry was done in Bristol, which continues as a port today. Sherry from Spain was introduced in the 16th c.

Ales are made from hops grown in the southeast counties. During the reign of Charles II (1660-1685) London was a noted ale making district with water coming from the Thames River. Special less fragile glasses were introduced, made from lead. Ale is not filtered or pasteurized, matures in a cask and is served warm. Stout is made from roasted unmalted barley and has a sweet taste to it. Porter is also made from the same and is dark and bitter. Mead, made from honey, comes from Cornwall.

Gin, made from juniper berries, was brought to England from the Netherlands in the 17th c. by William of Orange and the drink was known as Jenever. The Gin Act of 1736 halted the production and sale of gin. London Dry Gin was made during the 19th c in London and is sweeter. Proof was developed by Bartholomew Sykes in the 18th c – 100=57.1% alcohol, over that amount is "overproofed". England also produces fruit brandies and liqueurs. Shandy from Leeds is made from malt, sugar cane, rum, or whisky with lemonade or ginger beer. A mother-in-law is half stout and half beer. Cider or scrumpy is made fermented apples. If asking for whisky you will be served Scotch.

Did You Know?

When tea was first brought from China it was thought to be a drug.
The first printed cookbook was "This is the Boke of Cokery" c 1500. Before the 18th c most cookbooks were written by men.
Cucumbers and eggplant were introduced c 1575.
The first tea house opened in Oxford in the 1650s.
The Puritans forbade spices and rich dishes.
Tobacco, coffee, chocolate and sweet potatoes were introduced from the America's in the 17th c.

King Henry VIII, founder of the Church of England, abolished eating fish on Fridays and holidays. However, it so devastated the fishing industry he made new laws to promote it.

During Medieval times everyone, including lords and children, ate in the same room. Children were often sent away to learn manners.

The first cheddar cheese was made in 1666.

Tom Coryat introduced forks c 1603. Until the beginning of the 20th c the British Navy forbade the use of forks and knives. Fingers or trenchers (dry bread) were used.

In 1682 Denys Papin invented the first pressure cooker.

Lea and Perrins, chemists, concocted Worcestershire Sauce during the reign of Queen Victoria.

Cesar Ritz was invited by D'Oyly Court to open the Savoy Hotel and later stayed on with Escoffier.

A ploughman's platter includes cheese, bread, meat, butter, and relishes.

Black pudding is made from pig's blood. Fagots is a pork liver dish.

Sally Lunn buns are from Sally Lunn's Restaurant in Bath.

Andre Simon founded the Wine and Food Society in 1933.

Grog, a mix of rum, water, and lemon or lime juice, was given to the sailors to prevent scurvy, and thus the nickname "Limeys".

Some of the herbs grown and used are bladder campions (native to England with white flowers), catmint, catnip, chives, cotton lavender, basil, bay, borage, dill, lovage, mints, fennel, oregano, parsley, rosemary, sage and thyme. Doesn't it make you think of *Scarborough Fair* sung Simon & Garfunkel. How English can you get? Perhaps you didn't know Scarborough Fair was a traditional English fair dating back to the Middle Ages and lasting for 45 days. Scarborough Fair originated from a charter granted by King Henry III of England in 1253!

In 1810 merchant Peter Durand patented the "canister" or tin can. He sold the patent in 1813 to John Hall and Bryan Dorkin who opened the first commercial canning factory in England. In 1846, Henry Evans inventd a machine that could manufacture tin cans at a rate of sixty per hour.

McVitie's of London has produced biscuits since 1892 as a digestive aid developed by Alexander Grant. More recently they were used to make Queen Elizabeth's and Prince William's wedding cakes. The company is the largest biscuit factory in Europe and produces 27 million a day!

Cheshire cheese has been produced in Cheshire even at the time of the Roman invasion when the romans protected the city from other invaders.

The Cheshire Cat in *Alice in Wonderland* received its name from the cat molds used to make cheese in Cheshire.

The English Oxford Dictionary listed "hamburger" as salt beef beginning in 1802.

The word 'pickled' or to be very drunk may have come from pickling Admiral Lord Nelson's body in a cask of rum or brandy after his death at Trafalgar in 1805. "Drunk as a lord" may also have come from the same situation!

Equatorial Guinea

Equatorial Guinea is located in the middle of Africa and is divided into two parts: Río Muni which includes the islands of Corisco, Elobey Grande and Elobey Chico; and Annobón and Bioko islands. The country is bordered by Cameroon on the north, Gabon on the south and east, and the Gulf of Guinea on the west, where the island nation of São Tomé and Príncipe is located between Bioko and Annobón. The earliest settlers were Pygmies, only a few survive in Rio Muni. The Bantu arrived in the 18th c followed by the Fang. The Portuguese explored the coast in 1472 naming Bioko Island Formosa "Beautiful" and colonized the region beginning in 1474. In 1778 some of the islands and mainland were ceded to Spain. Equatorial Guinea received its independence in 1968. The capital, Malabo, is situated on the northern coast of Bioko Island, and was founded by the British in 1827. Spanish, French and Portuguese are the official languages; Fang, Bube, Annobonese are also spoken.

Dining Etiquette

When invited for a meal please arrive punctually. Bring a gift of fruit, sweets, whiskey, wine, or something from your own country. Gifts are presented with both hands or the right hand only, and are not opened in front of the presenter. Men shake hands greeting and departing. Close friends may embrace. When greeting elders men may not look them in the eye. Elders are always greeted first. Women may or may not shake hands. When dining men may eat first, followed by the women, then the children. Before dining a bowl and soup will be passed to wash your hands. Each person will be given a bowl to put the food which is taken from a communal platter. The eldest is the first to take the food. Food is eaten with the right hand, although cutlery may be offered. Hands are washed after the meal.

Succotash

Succotash is the national dish!

Serves 4-6

2 cups fresh lima beans	Corn from 4 ears of corn
4 large tomatoes	Salt and pepper to taste
1 tbls. sugar	2 tbls. butter

Cook the lima beans in a small amount of water for about 15 minutes, not soft. Drain water and place in a bowl. Cook the tomatoes and sugar in the pan until tomatoes are just softened, but not mushy. Add the lima beans, corn, salt and pepper, and butter. Cook 10 minutes.

Fish Stew

Serves 4

2 tbls. oil	2 carrots, sliced
2 onions, sliced thinly	1 large green pepper, chopped
2 garlic cloves, minced	2 okra, sliced
1 hot chili, seeded and chopped (more for a spicier dish)	2 tomatoes, chopped
	1 ½ lb. fish fillet

Heat the oil in a skillet. Stir in the onions until translucent. Add garlic, chili, carrots, pepper, and okra. Cook until tender. Add the tomatoes and fish. Cook for about 10 minutes until fish is cooked. Serve over rice.

Cuisine

The cuisine has been influenced by the tribes native to the region, but also the Arabs, Portuguese and Spanish. Fish, cassava, sweet potatoes yams, leafy greens, rice, sauces, okra, peanuts, and fruit – plantains, bananas, mangoes and coconut are the staples of the diet. The fish is often grilled and wrapped in leaves. Chickens are stewed in peanut sauces. Game and bush meat besides fish are part of the cuisine. The meats are grilled, stewed, fried or boiled and served with porridges. Chilies and spices are used. Cocoa trees and sugar cane are grown on Bioko.

Equatorial Guinea Specialties

Gari - cassava flour porridge

Lomandoha – malanga leaves, fish and chocolate

Chicken in peanut butter or cream sauce over rice or boiled plantains

Grilled meat or fish with pumpkin seeds

Holidays and Special Occasions

Holiday foods include roast duck, chicken, and smoked beef.
Abira is a celebration to drive the devil away by cleansing the community.
Balele is a native dance performed on special occasions and at Christmas.

Beverages

Coffee and cocoa are grown in Equatorial Guinea. Osang (African tea) is drunk by the people. They also make their own palm wine, malamba (sugar cane alcoholic beverage, also known as firewater), and local beer.

Eritrea

Eritrea, located on the Horn of Africa is bordered by Sudan in the west, Ethiopia in the south, and Djibouti in the southeast. To the north and east Eritrea borders on the Red Sea. The Dahlak Archipelago and several of the Hanish Islands are part of Eritrea. The land once known as Punt "God's Land" to the Egyptians is known to date back to the 25th c BC. During the 8th and 7th c BC the kingdom of D'mt, located in Eritrea and Ethiopia, developed irrigation, grew millet, and made iron tools. Later smaller kingdoms abounded in the region which was united under the Aksumite Kingdom in the 1st c. The Arabians, Ottoman Turks, Portuguese, Egyptians, the British and Italians colonized the area. Italy invaded in 1869, and in 1890 Eritrea became an Italian colony. By 1936 it became part of Italian East Africa with Ethiopia and Italian Somalialand. In 1950 Eritrea was federated with Ethiopia and received its independence from Ethiopia in 1993. The capital, Asmara, dates back more than 700 years. Arabic and Tiginya are the official languages; English and Italian and other languages are also spoken.

Dining Etiquette

Please arrive punctually for a meal. You may leave your shoes at the entrance. Please bring a gift of pastries, fruit, flowers, or something from your country. Gifts are presented with both hands or your right hand only, and are not opened in front of the presenter. Men will lightly shake hands with direct eye contact. Close friends may kiss three times on the cheek. Women will extend their hands first. Elders are greeted first with a slight bow. You will be offered coffee. Hands will be washed before eating. Meals are eaten at a low table. The meal will be served on a communal platter. The eldest person takes the food first. Food is eaten with the right hand only. Guests are given food in a ritual called "gursa" whereby a person places a small amount of food in another person's mouth. The injera (bread) is torn off in small pieces with the right hand and used to dip in the meat, vegetables or sauces served. Please take the injera that is placed in front of you. Please don't touch your lips with your fingers, or lick your fingers. Being served raw meat is considered an honor. Hands are washed at the end of the meal and coffee is served.

The coffee ceremony is common when visiting friends and on special occasions, and is a sign of hospitality. During the ceremony you will be seated on pillows or on the floor with grass and flowers. Incense will be burning. A women will wash and roast the coffee beans in a pan over a fire. The beans are then ground and added to boiling water in the jebena (coffee pot). The coffee is poured into finjal (small cups without handles) containing sugar. You are expected to enjoy the aroma of the coffee before sipping. Please sip slowly. The eldest will start the awol or first round. After the first round the jebena is refilled with water and the second round or tona starts. Again water is added to the jebena for third round or Baraka. Please remember to drink three cups.

Cuisine

Food has been influenced by local cuisine and Italians, and can be quite spicy. The Italian influence is noticed in the various pasta and tomato dishes. The different regions have their own style of cooking. Injera, the national bread is eaten with stews, sauces and is served on a platter with the stew poured on top. Teff, a very small grain, is used in making injera, porridges, or in alcoholic beverages. Lamb, goat, beef, chickens, pigs, lentils, cereals, peanuts, fruit, fava beans, food from Red Sea – tuna, red snapper, kingfish, sardines, lobster, crab, shrimp, oysters, spices and herbs – cardamom, basil, ginger, hot chilies, garlic, onions, and beans are part of local diet. The food is cooked by the women in large pots over a wood fire, stirring with a long stick. Sowa is the locally brewed beer made from roast corn, barley, or other grains and flavored with Gesho, a leaf. Sowa is drunk in millileek (special cups). Mez (honey wine), araki made with anise, fruit juices, and shai (tea) are also drunk.

Ful

Serves 4

2 tbls. olive oil
1 small onion, peeled and chopped
2 cups chickpeas (canned and drained of liquid)
½ cup water

½ tsp. cumin
2 cloves garlic, minced
1 chili, seeded and chopped
1 tbls. lemon juice

Heat the olive oil in a skillet and stir in onion until just translucent. Stir in water, beans, cumin, garlic and chili. Bring to a boil. Simmer 10 minutes. Sprinkle with lemon juice.
The beans can be served whole or mashed. Serve warm.

Eritrean Specialties

Tsebbi or wot – hot spicy meat or vegetable sauces or stews served with injera
Dorho tsebbi – chicken tsebbi
Basha – breakfast bread
Zigini – stew made from vegetables, meat, or fish in a tomato sauce with spices

Asida – sorghum porridge
Akelet – wheat flour dough with berbere and butter sauce and milk or yogurt
Alicha birsen – lentil curry
Berbere – herb and spice mixture served with food

Holidays and Special Occasions

Christians fast during Lent abstaining from meat and dairy products; and celebrate Easter and Christmas with feasts that will include bread, stews and sowa.
The Muslims celebrate Ramadan – fasting from sunrise to sunset and Eid el-Fitr at the end of Ramadan
Religious celebrations – sheep, ox or goat slaughtered, and the meat and intestines eaten with the injera along with sowa or mez.

Estonia

Estonia is bordered to the north by the Gulf of Finland, to the west by the Baltic Sea, to the south by Latvia, and to the east by the Russia. The area was first settled around 8500 BC. The Danish Teutonic, Swedes, Russians, Danes and Germans invaded the country over many centuries. From 1228-1562 much of Estonia was part of the crusader state Terra Mariana, then part of Ordensstaat, then the Livonian Confederation. During the 16th c it was included in trade with the Hanseatic League. It remained part of Sweden until 1710-21 when it became part of the Russian Empire. In 1918 the Estonian Declaration of Independence was declared, only to be followed by the Estonian War of Independence 1918-20. During World War II Estonia was occupied by the Soviet Union, the Third Reich, and again by the Soviets. Estonia regained its independence in 1991. The capital Talinn, is an ancient city, and may have received its name Qlwn prior to 1154, when it was first named on a map. The official language is Estonian.

Karask – Traditional Estonian Barley Bread

Serves 8

"This is an Estonian folk recipe that I adjusted to include only whole foods and natural sweeteners. The barley flour gives it a distinct, sweet taste."

4½ ounces (125 g) farmer cheese
1 cup (240 ml) kefir or yogurt
1 egg
1 tsp. salt
1 tsp. honey

2 tbls. butter, melted
1 cup (240 ml) barley flour
½ cup (120 ml) whole-wheat flour
½ tbls. baking soda

Preheat the oven to 400°F (200°C).
Line a rectangular baking pan (5 x 10 inches or 12 x 25 cm) with parchment paper.
Combine the farmer cheese, kefir, egg, salt and honey in a bowl and mix until smooth.
Stir in the melted butter.
Combine the flours with the baking soda and add to the batter. Mix well.
Pour the batter into the pan and bake for 30 to 40 minutes. To check whether the bread is ready, insert a wooden toothpick into the center. When the toothpick comes out dry, the bread is done.
Serve with butter or onion butter.
Recipe courtesy of Marika Blossfeldt, "Essential Nourishment, Recipes from My Estonian Farm", published 2011 by Delicious Nutrition, Beacon NY.

179

Dining Etiquette

Please arrive promptly when asked for a meal. Please bring a gift of flowers, chocolates or something for the home from your country. Flowers are given in odd numbers. Gifts are usually opened in front of the presenter. Please shake hands greeting and departing. Always shake hands standing, showing eye contact, and a firm handshake. "Tere" is "hello". Please use titles, and only first names when asked to do so. Please remain standing until invited to sit down. Drinks and hors d'oeuvres will be offered. Meals are eaten continental style fork in the left hand, knife in the right. Please do not begin the meal until the hostess says "head isu" "bon appetite". Please do not rest your elbows on the table and do not put your hands in your lap. Try to finish everything on your plate. Please compliment the hostess on the meal. Please reciprocate any hospitality offered. The toast is Tervist, (Teie) terviseks (to your health), or (Teie terviseks).

Barley Scones with Herbs and Hazelnuts

200 g barley flour	1 tbls. honey
100 g rye flour	1 tsp. salt
2 chicken eggs	0.5 tsp soda
5 dl sour milk	

Filling

3 g chopped fresh thyme
150 g crushed hazelnuts

Butter to grease the baking tin and barley flour or bread crumbs for sprinkling.
Mix the eggs with honey and salt, add the sour milk. Sieve the barley flour and the soda that has been previously added to the flour into the mix until you get an even dough. To make the filling, rinse the thyme, drain carefully and chop. Mix with the crushed hazelnuts and add to the dough. Pour the dough into the several small baking tins that have been greased with butter and sprinkled with flour or bread crumbs and bake in a fan-assisted oven at 180˚C for ca. 20-30 minutes. The scone will be ready after it turns a golden brown and separates from the tin.
Serve sliced with egg butter and green cream soup.

Egg Butter

Makes 200 g

100 g butter	salt
2 eggs	

Soften the butter at room temperature. Hard boil the eggs, cool them, remove the shells and chop in a food processor or with a fork. Add the soft butter and mix until even. Flavour with salt.
Serve the egg butter in a separate bowl and eat with the scone and green cream soup.
Recipe courtesy of the Embassy of the Republic of Estonia, Washington, DC

Cuisine

In Estonia the main foods are potatoes, meat, black bread, pork, dairy products, mushrooms, vegetables, fish (herring, flounder, sprat, perch), berries, herbs, and game. The food available is mostly determined by the seasons. In the jams, preserves, and pickles are used. The cold table is the first course consisting of cold dishes – meats, sausages, potato salad, herring, pirukas (meat pies), and raim (Baltic herring). Soups are eaten before the main course. They are a cream type made with sour cream, yogurt or milk or meat or chicken with vegetables. The entree is usually meat and potatoes with a gravy and served with sauerkraut. Pork can be roasted, cured, grilled or made into sausages. Fish and meat are often dried. Black rye bread is served. Desserts include rhubarb pies, karask, kissel, curd snacks, large pancakes served with lingonberry jam, and kama. Pipparkogid are cookies made from peppercorns, cocoa and cinnamon and served at Christmas. Coffee is served with cream or whipped cream.

Holidays and Special Occasions

New Year's Day was declared an official holiday in 1691.
Vastlapäev – last day before Lent – lots of food, sleigh rides, quaint sayings, wearing of leather shoes
The Christmas Market in Talinn is open the end of November. Traditional Christmas foods can be found there – pork, sauerkraut, blood sausages, blood dumplings, apples, mandarins, gingerbread, marzipan, local honey, cookies, nuts, and pastries. Hot mulled wine is served from barrels.
The Christmas season begins on December 21st (the Feast of St. Thomas) and ends on Epiphany January 6 when people visit each other, eat rest of food left from Christmas and drink beer, and clean the straw or hay from the house. For centuries the leader of Estonia declares Christmas Peace on Christmas Eve. Food that is served on Christmas Eve is left on the table for visiting spirits Beer is drunk. Old customs at Christmas are observed such as covering floors with straw or hay.
A Christmas menu might include Salted Baltic herring with sour cream and dill potatoes, salted mushroom salad with baked goose fillet, blood sausage, pork fillet with dried fruit served with sauerkraut stewed with hazelnuts and cream, bacon baked apple and roast potatoes and cheesecake with cranberry sauce.

Drinks

Popular drinks are kali (root beer), juices, beer, milk, liquors, liqueurs (Vana Talinn), wine, and vodka. Beers are brewed locally and include Saku (1820), A. LeCoq founded in 1807, and Viru Olu. Wine is made from grapes and other fruit. Vodka was distilled beginning in the 15th c.

Rye Rhubarb Mousse

Serves 10 to 12

"This is a traditional Estonian dessert. To anybody but an Estonian, this mousse made of rye must seem rather perplexing. But Estonians have long been successful at making fluffy desserts from grain. My mom used to make a similar dessert using cream of wheat and red currant juice. I got to taste the rye mousse – from Helle Veltman's kitchen – for the first time a few summers ago. Rhubarb is one of the first edible things you can harvest from your garden, so enjoy this dessert in late spring."

3 cups (400 g) rhubarb chunks (stalks peeled and cut into ½-inch (1-cm) pieces)
3 cups (720 ml) water
8 to 10 tablespoons maple syrup

½ teaspoon ground cinnamon
1 pinch salt
¾ cup (180 ml) rye flour
lemon balm leaves or berries for garnish

Boil the rhubarb in the water until it becomes soft and loses its structure. Add the maple syrup, cinnamon and salt.
Slowly whisk in the rye flour. Bring to a boil, continuously whisking, then reduce the heat to low and simmer for 5 minutes.
Allow to cool. With a hand mixer, whip the mixture until its volume has doubled.
Pour the mousse into individual dessert dishes and garnish with a lemon balm leaf or berries.
Serve as is, or with milk or whipped cream.
Recipe courtesy of Marika Blossfeldt, "Essential Nourishment, Recipes from My Estonian Farm", published 2011 by Delicious Nutrition, Beacon NY.

Salted Baltic Herring with Sour Cream and Dill Potatoes

Serves 4

200 g salted Baltic herring
4 tbls. sour cream
4 potatoes

2 tbsp chopped spring onions or chives
2 tsp chopped dill

Peel the potatoes and boil in lightly salted water or steam, sprinkle with chopped dill.
Fillet the fish and serve with the sour cream, chopped onions and dill potatoes.
Recipe courtesy of the Embassy of the Republic of Estonia, Washington, DC

Ethiopia

Ethiopia is bordered by Eritrea to the north, Sudan and South Sudan to the west, Djibouti and Somalia to the east, and Kenya to the south. Homo Sapiens are known to have existed in the region over 400,000 years ago and remains have been found dating back 160,000 years. The Land of Punt, also called Pwenet, or Pwene by the Egyptians, exported gold, aromatic resins, blackwood, ebony, ivory, slaves, and animals. C the 8th century BC, a kingdom known as Dʻmt was established in northern Ethiopia and Eritrea. Its capital was around the current town of Yeha, situated in northern Ethiopia. After the fall of Dʻmt in the 4th century BC, there were smaller kingdoms, until 1st c BC, and the Aksumite Empire united the country. In 316 two Christian brothers exploring the African coast were shipwrecked, but were able to convert the queen to Christianity. From 1137 to 1270 the Zagwe dynasty ruled most of Ethiopia, followed by the Solomonic dynasty. The Portuguese arrived in 1508, but from 1755 to 1855 the country remained isolated, although it was periodically invaded by the Ottoman Empire and the Egyptians. Italy received a small portion of the northern part of Ethiopia in 1899. Emperor Haile Selassi united the country in the 20th c., but from 1936-41 the country was occupied by the Italians. A federation with Eritrea existed from 1952-62. The new constitution was written in 1994. Addis Ababa, the capital, was founded in 1886 by Emperor Menelik II. The name means "New Flower". There are over 80 languages spoken with Amharic and English the official languages.

Dining Etiquette

It is an honor to be invited to an Ethiopian home. When invited for a meal please arrive promptly, or slightly past the time requested. You may have to remove your shoes before entering a home. Please bring a small gift such as pastries, fruit, flowers, something for the home, or if children present something for them. When giving the gift do so with both hands, or the right hand only. Gifts are not opened in front of the presenter. Please shake hands greeting and departing with good eye contact. Good friends may kiss each other three times on the cheeks. Women should extend their hand to a man. When first introduced, use Mr., Mrs., or Miss and the last name. Elders are introduced first. Please bow to an older or more senior person.

The Ethiopians enjoy entertaining friends and are very hospitable. Please accept any beverages or food that is offered. A cup of coffee will be served. Please accept it. Women may offer to help the hostess before or after the meal. Meals might be served to guests using stools, on cushions, or seated on the floor. The injera is served on mesobs – basket tables. Before the meal please wash your hands with the water and towel offered. Food is served on a gebeta (plate) lined with injera and sauces, vegetables, and other side dishes, plus a utensil. The bread is broken off and used in most cases as the utensil. Utensils may not be provided, rather food is eaten with the right hand. The eldest person will take from the communal plate first. Guests are served food through "gursha" someone else placing a small bite of food wrapped in injera in your mouth. It is disrespectful to refuse. Food will continue to be served as a sign of hospitality. Hands will be washed at the end of the meal, and coffee served.

Jebna Bunna (coffee ceremony)

When invited for coffee you may be seated on cushions, small stools, or the floor with incense. A woman washes and roasts the coffee beans over a fire. The beans are then ground and added to boiling water in the jebena (coffee pot). Cups without handles are used to serve the coffee with sugar. Before drinking the coffee please enjoy the aroma. The eldest person is served first during the "awol" or first round. When the cup is finished water is added to the jebena and a second round or tona served. The third round is called the Baraka. Please take your time and enjoy each round.

Cuisine

Ethiopia has not been influenced from the rest of the world in its cuisine which is truly its own, though the Italian influence is found in some cooking. Ethiopian food can be quite spicy, and uses injera (sour flat bread) as a server and utensil. Vegetables, grains (teff), coffee, sugar, sorghum, millet, wheat, and livestock are raised in the country. Because of the large Islamic, Jewish, and Ethiopian Orthodox Christian population almost no pork or shellfish is eaten. Lamb, goat, camel, or chicken are the most common meats. Fish includes tilapia, Nile perch, and catfish. Crops grown are coffee, sugar, maize, teff (grain), sorghum, millet, wheat, livestock, and peppers. Bee keeping is also important. Injera and stews are diet staples. Bal' injera means "companion" or "friend" in Amharic, also translates to "someone with whom one shares bread". Thus the importance of sharing injera, the Ethiopian national bread. The basket table on which the injera platter is set, is known as a messob.

Doro Wat (Chicken Stew)

Serves 6

½ stick butter	3 lb. chicken, cut into pieces
2 large onions, diced	2 red chilies, minced
2 garlic cloves, minced	1 tbls. Berbere
½ tsp. cardamom	2 ½ cups chicken stock
1 tsp. ground ginger	3 hardboiled eggs, peeled
1 tsp. fresh ground pepper	

Melt the butter in a pan and sauté onions for 10 minutes. Add garlic, cardamom, ginger, pepper, chilies and Berbere.
Add the chicken stock and chicken. Bring to a boil. Let simmer at least 30 minutes, or until chicken is cooked. Add the eggs and simmer 5 more minutes.
Serve with injera or rice.
Beef and beef stock can be substituted for the chicken.

Ethiopian Specialties

Berbere – dried ground spice mixture with pepper and salt, used in stews

Awase – spicy chili blend

Tiblo – made from roasted barley flour is eaten in Amhara, Agame, and Awlaelo.

Injera – sour, spongy flat bread that is folded into quarters and then laid on a table with stews ladled on top. Guests then take pieces. No spoons, forks, or knives are needed to eat.

Nit'ir qibe – spicy butter

Wot or wat – spicy pepper stew or sauce made with vegetables, meat, chicken, lentils, chickpeas, or other ingredients

Doro wot – chicken stew in red pepper sauce

Sambusas – fried dough with different fillings

Shiro powder – paste made from dried chickpeas, chilies, garlic, berbere and served with injera

Shiro – chickpea sauce

Kotcho – cake made of ensete stem and root

Ayib – fresh cheese, serve with injera, similar to cottage cheese

Tibs – sautéed, grilled or deep-fried meat and chili dish

Dabo – honey bread

Kitfo – raw beef with spices

Mitmita – hot spice blend of chilies

Teff- gluten-free grain used to make injera

Holidays and Special Occasions

Because of religious traditions there are over 200 fast days, when vegetarian food is consumed.

Timket Festival, January 19th – the festival of the Epiphany – baptisms and drinking of tej (mead) and tella (beer), special breads baked, and sheep slaughtered

When Christians fast they do not eat animals or animal products. No food or drink can be consumed from midnight until 3 PM.

Ethiopian Orthodox Christians do not eat meat on Wednesdays and Fridays, and during Lent.

Maskal – September 27 – discovery of the "Cross of Christ" – is celebrated with dancing, fests, bonfires and gun salutes.

At the time of wedding proposal the groom's elders visit the bride's parents and make decisions on the ceremony. At the time of the wedding the bride and groom's family prepare the food and brew beer.

A person is buried the same day he or she dies, but the mourning period takes place over three days with food provided by family and friends.

Christians have patron saints, and especially celebrate St. Gabriel on the 19th of each month and December 28th.

Buhe – August 21st – buhe means bread or dough and is made on the eve of Buhe and baked the following day. On the eve fires made from chibo (bunches of twigs) are lit. This symbolizes the Lost Children who were found by torches and given bread to eat.

Beverages

Coffee is Ethiopia's major export. Kaffa province is renowned for its coffee. Coffee was discovered by a shepherd named Kaldi who noticed his goats became much more energetic when eating the coffee berry. The beans need to be roasted and then ground, but they were also chewed. Please see above for the protocol of drinking coffee. Tea (shai) is grown in the lowland areas of

Ethiopia. The water is brewed with spices and black tea. Peanut tea is made from peanut butter and hot water.

Ethiopians make a honey wine known as Tej which is served on special occasions. The wine is made with honey and water with gesho plant twigs and leaves. The wine is drunk in round vase-shaped vessels. Mead and beer (talla) are also brewed.

Did You Know?

Salt was once considered a very precious commodity and was known as "white gold". In Ethiopia black salt was cut into 10 inch long slabs and one two to three inches thick could be used to buy a slave. The slabs were originally used by the Amole tribe for currency and for years were called amoles. These bars were used in trade until World War II. Bricks of salt are still cut from the dry lake beds in the Danakil Depression in the Afar region and transported by camel caravans.

The people, especially in rural areas, are still divided into social classes based on the amount of grain and cattle owned.

The most widespread social welfare association in rural areas is the debo. If a farmer is having difficulty tending his fields, he may invite his neighbors to help on a specific date. In return, the farmer must provide food and drink for the day and contribute his labor when others in the same debo require help. The debo is not restricted to agriculture but is also prevalent in housing construction.

Men are responsible for plowing, harvesting, the trading of goods, the slaughtering of animals, herding, the building of houses, and the cutting of wood. Women are responsible for the domestic sphere and help the men with some activities on the farm. Women are in charge of cooking, brewing beer, cutting hops, buying and selling spices, making butter, collecting and carrying wood, and carrying water. Households may contain several generations, and children care for their elders. A child will often take his father's first name as his or her last name. Khat – mild stimulant that is chewed

European Union

The European Union is represented in Washington, DC. This is an economic and political union among 28 countries in Europe. The currency used is the Euro.

I had the privilege of knowing Doreen Merkel when her husband served with the Delegation of the European Union in Washington. She wished to contribute this recipe for the book.

Easy-Peasy Cucumber Salad

1 cucumber
1-2 sachets sweetener or 1-2 tsp. sugar
Salt and pepper

2 tbls. white vinegar
1 tsp. dill

In a bowl put the vinegar, dill and sweetener. Add finely sliced washed cucumber. Mix thoroughly.
Add Salt and pepper to taste.
Best served chilled.
Can be prepared a day or two in advance.

Fiji Islands

The Republic of Fiji is an island nation in Melanesia in the South Pacific Ocean north of New Zealand. There are about 350 islands formed from volcanoes over 150 million years ago. The islands were probably settled 3500-1000 BC. The Melanesians arrived later. The Dutch explorer Abel Tasman visited Fiji in 1643 while looking for the Great Southern Continent. During the 19th c Europeans began to settle on the islands, and in 1874 they became a British colony. Sugar cane plantations flourished under the British. The British granted the islands independence in 1970. The capital, Suva, is located on the southeast coast of the island of Viti Levu. The official languages are English, Bau Fijian, and Fiji Hindi.

Dining Etiquette

The Fijians are warm and hospitable people and on arrival on the islands you will be welcomed with "bula" which means "hello" or "What's happening?" When visiting a village please do not wear a hat. It is considered an insult to the chief. Leave your shoes outside the door. Please do not touch someone's head. Please shake hands greeting and departing. Fijians greet each other with a smile or nodding the head. It is customary to present the "Turaga Ni Koro" (head of the village) with sevusevu (a gift) of kava "yagona". This will be pounded into powder and served with water. Please drink the kava if you are invited to. This is a sign of goodwill, and should not be refused.

A tablecloth is spread on the floor for eating. Food is eaten with utensils, although in Hindi households with your fingers. In Indo-Fijian homes men and women eat separately. Indo- Hindi do not eat beef and Muslims no pork. When you thank someone you say "Cobo" or clap with cupped hands. Folding one's arms while speaking shows respect to the other person. People are beckoned by waving all fingers of the hand with the palm facing down. The people are family oriented and the father the head of the household. Affection is not shown in public.

Cuisine

There are four different Fijian cuisines – continental, Indian, Fijian and Asian, mainly Chinese. Seafood, pork, chicken, dalo (taro), rourou (taro leaf), yams, cassava, sweet potatoes, breadfruit, bananas, pawpaw, pineapple, papaya, beans, passionfruit, oranges, eggplant, bok choy, and nuts from the islands are used in cooking. The Indians introduced chilies, flatbread, rice, curries and tea. Spices and herbs used are curry leaves, chilies, basil and coriander. Local fish include lagoon fish, crab, prawns, mussels, and lobster.

The dishes are often prepared in coconut cream (lolo). Food is mainly steamed or boiled, but it may also be roasted, broiled or fried. A lovo is the underground oven in which meat, vegetables, fish or chicken is cooked. A magiti is the feast after the food is prepared. Food is eaten with the hands only, no utensils. This is followed by a meke, an evening of traditional songs and dance.

Cassava Pudding

Serves 6

4 cups grated cassava
3 ½ cups sugar
1½ sticks butter
6 eggs
3 cups milk
2 cans evaporated milk

1 tsp. cinnamon
1 tsp. nutmeg
1 tbls. grated ginger
½ tsp. ground cloves
2 cups coconut
1 tsp. vanilla

Preheat oven to 350°
Grease 2 baking pans.
Cream the butter and sugar. Beat in the eggs. Add the milk and evaporated milk. Stir in the cassava, coconut, spices and vanilla, mixing well. Divide between the two pans. Bake 40 minutes. Allow to cool before serving.

Fijian Specialties

Kokoda – fresh fish marinated in lime or lemon juice with fresh vegetables
Palusami – meat, fish and vegetables wrapped in dalo leaves and cooked in lolo
Ika vakalolo – fish in coconut milk

Miti – coconut cream with onions, chilies, lemon juice, salt and pepper
Duruka – vegetable similar to asparagus and cooked in coconut cream

Holidays and Special Occasions

Sevu-sevu – welcoming ceremony
New Year's Day – people are showered with water
Muslims, Christians and Hindus celebrate their own holidays
Special occasions, weddings and funerals – lovo
Weddings – ceremonies are performed and with the solevu, the great feast
Ceremonies – whole pig, oxen or turtles are cooked
Christmas – lovo, but may also include a whole pig, chicken, cow, and curries
Boxing Day – December 26 – traditionally celebrated by the British where presents are given to tradesmen and service workers
Sugar Festival in Lautoka – celebrates sugar cane

Beverages

Kava or yaqona is the national drink and is made by pounding the root of the yagona plant which is then mixed with water. Yagona is also used for medicinal purposes to cure illnesses. Water, coconut water, fruit juices, tea, and tropical drinks are drunk. Fiji produces beer including Carlton and Fiji Bitter. The South Pacific Distilleries make rum, vodka, gin, and whiskey. Wine is also made on the islands.

Finland

Finland occupies an area bounded by the Baltic Sea, the Gulf of Finland, the Gulf of Bothnia, Russia, Sweden and Norway. Much of the country is lowlands with 187,000 lakes. One third of the country lies above the Arctic Circle. Beginning in 1154 the Swedes, needing Finland's natural resources and wishing to convert the people to Christianity, commenced a number of crusades. Over many centuries the country's borders changed repeatedly, and in 1809 it became an autonomous Grand Duchy of Russia. Independence was declared in 1917. Helsinki, the capital, was founded in 1550 by Gustav Vasa and is called "The White City of the North" or "Daughter of the Baltic. The official language is Finnish.

Dining Etiquette

Please be punctual when invited out. Please shake hands greeting and departing. Please bring a gift from your own country or a bottle of wine or flowers. Flowers can also be sent afterwards. Shake hands greeting and departing. Drinks or an aperitif will be served. At dinner the hostess will arrange the seating, with the host and hostess at each end of the table. The male guest of honor will be seated at the hostess' right. Eating is continental style, fork in the left hand, knife in the right. Please wait for the hostess to begin. Usually the host will wish everyone "bon appétit" and raise his glass for the guests to begin eating. Do take seconds and finish what is on your plate. Always keep your jacket on. Desserts are often with fruit or a raisin and fruit pudding. When finished, coffee is served often followed by cognac or berry liqueurs. No one leaves before the honored guest. Always thank your hostess, and say good-bye to each guest. Vodka is used as a dinner drink during special occasions such as the crayfish festival. When drunk with a meal vodka is served cold as a schnapps in small glasses. The toast is "skal", "Kippis", or "Marskin ryyppy" with aquavit or vodka. Do not drink until the host proposes a toast. A guest does not propose a toast.

Cuisine

Dining in Finland offers many delights – the use of fresh vegetables, an abundance of fish – perch, herring, crayfish, pikeperch, bream, eel, salmon, turbot, vendance; dark rye bread, pasties, dill, potatoes, mushrooms especially morels and chanterelles, reindeer, smoked meats and berries – cloudberries, raspberries, lingonberries, sea buckthorn, Arctic bramble, currants, strawberries, gooseberries, rowan, and cranberries. Meadowsweet, a flower can be used in cooking. Milk, water, or home brewed beers are usually drunk with meals.

Even though the country is so northerly it is self- sufficient, growing grains – wheat, rye, oats, and barley. The people developed methods of preserving rye crispbread by drying it. The country has numerous lakes, rivers, and ponds and shoreline. Silakka, Baltic herring; salmon; rainbow trout; roe – whitefish, vendance, rainbow trout, and burbot; and crayfish abound.

Families own small farms which are very productive. Pork and lamb were often smoked in the traditional sauna with smoke from the alder branches. Finnish cheese includes Finlandia Swiss Cheese, Brie, Roquefort, and over 30 other varieties. Mushrooms, potatoes, and berries are part of the diet. In addition reindeer meat is served, including Poronkaristys, sautéed reindeer meat.

Tippaleivat (May Day Cookies)

2 eggs
2 tsp. sugar
1 tsp. salt
¾ cup milk

1½ cups flour
½ tsp. vanilla
Vegetable oil

Combine the eggs and sugar. Add the other ingredients, except oil, to make a smooth batter.
Put the batter into a pastry bag with a small nozzle.
Put some vegetable oil in a pan. Squeeze the batter and form a circle, or pretzel shape. Cook until golden brown.
Remove and drain on paper towels.
Dust with powdered sugar.

Finnish Specialties

Voileipapoyta – cold table or smorgasbord. This is set out in an orderly fashion starting with herring, fish, potatoes, and snaps, then meats and salads, followed by cheeses, fruit, and desserts. After enjoying a sauna sausages and beer might be served. A smoke sauna was often used to smoke meats and grains. Obviously the smoke was let out before the bathers entered.

Vorshmack – ground mutton, herring and garlic
Kesakeitto – summer vegetable soup
Kurkkukeitto – cucumber soup
Ekkasilkat – pickled herring
Kulibiaka - salmon and rice pasty
Karelian hot pot – beef and pork stew
Karelian Pasties – small pie with a rice or potato filling, and eaten with butter and chopped hard-boiled eggs
Kalakukko – fish and pork in rye dough

Mrurinpohjaletut – pancakes
Sara – roasted lamb from Lemi
Piirakka – (national dish) - fish pastry with rice
Silakka – Baltic herring
Etikkasilkat - pickled herring
Viili – yogurt
Bliny – pancake eaten with roe
Lohimuhennos – salmon chowder or stew
Mansikkatorttu – strawberry cake

Holidays

Runeberg's Day (February 5, in honor of the national poet) – Runeberg tarts (pastries made from bread crumbs, raspberry jam)

Shrove Tuesday – pancakes and laskiaipulla (white bun with marzipan, jam or cream)

Easter – children color eggs, breads and special pastries, lamb, Mammi (sweet baked malt dish), pasha, mignon eggs (a real eggshell with chocolate nougat)

May 1 – May Day – tippaleipa (deep fried cookies) and sima (mead)

Midsummer (June) – pancakes, Ostrobothnia (red cheese soup), new potatoes, dill, salmon, herring, strawberries

July 21 – beginning of crayfish parties which last through August

November – Martinmas – goose and black soup made of blood

Christmas – cold cuts, herring, freshly salted salmon, roe, smoked whitefish, baked lutefish, dried cod, salads, sausages, ham; vegetables; liver and other casseroles; fruit salad or soup, Christmas rye bread, rice porridge, prune pudding, ginger cookies, raisin cakes, joulutorttu (Christmas tarts). Glogg, a hot spicy red wine drink, is served.

December 26 – visit neighbors and friends

Special dinners are held for family reunions, birthdays (50, 60, 70, 75, 80 and on up)

Drinks

Finnish beer is light, more like a lager and is served cold. Beers are keskiolut, higher alcohol, A-olut, or Sahti – home brewed. The oldest brewery is Sinebrychoff in Helsinki, founded in 1819. Dry vodka is made from grain and 38% by weight. Koskenkorva (koskis) vodka is colorless and 31%. Food should be served when drinking vodka.

Liqueurs are made from cloudberries, cranberries, red raspberries, Arctic bramble, lingonberry, rowanberry and yellow sea buckthorn. A sparkling wine is made from white currants and gooseberries. Apple and pear ciders are also produced. Spring is produced from the sap of birch trees.

Coffee is served every day but is also part of christenings and funerals, and drunk at the end of a meal. Juices are steamed to be used during the winter.

Did You Know?

The Kalevala, the national epic, mentions that even Iron Age Finns drank beer! The oldest breweries in Scandinavia are in Finland.

A 5000 year old piece of gum made from birch bark tar was discovered in Finland in 2007 by an archeological student.

France

The Republic of France on the European continent is surrounded by Belgium, Germany, Luxembourg, Switzerland, Italy, Spain, and to the west the Atlantic Ocean. France's history goes back 40,000 years known through the wall paintings at Lascaux. Later invasions brought the Gauls, Franks, and wars with England. During both World Wars, France was devastated. Paris, the capital, founded in 52 BC by the Romans, was originally named Lutetia. French is the official language.

Dining Etiquette

Please be punctual, or up to fifteen minutes late, when entertained. Please bring flowers in an odd number that morning or with you. Other suitable gifts are something from your country, books, or something for the home. Please stand when introduced. Shake hands greeting and departing. An older person offers their hand first. Drinks will be offered – champagne or an aperitif so that wines may be enjoyed later. The table is set with all utensils (fork and spoon turned down) and wine glasses. The fork and spoon above the plate are for dessert. Food is eaten continental style, fork in the left hand, knife in the right. Hands should be above the table and no elbows on the table. Wait until the host or hostess begins. They will be seated opposite each other at the center of the table, with the guest of honor to the right. Wine and mineral water are always served with the meal. Bread is broken, not cut with a knife. Salads are eaten with a fork, never cutting the lettuce. When finished place the knife and fork together. The host initiates the toast which is "A votre santé" "To your health".

Quiche Lorraine

Serves 4

1 9" pie shell	2 ½ cups half and half
6 strip bacon, cooked and crumbled	3 eggs
1 cup Gruyere cheese, grated	¼ tsp. nutmeg

Preheat oven to 400°
Heat the pie shell for 10 minutes in the oven. Remove.
Sprinkle bacon and cheese on the pie shell.
In a bowl beat together the eggs, half and half, and nutmeg. Pour over the bacon and cheese.
Turn down oven to 350° and bake quiche for 45 minutes, or until set.
Serve hot or room temperature.

Cuisine

France's cuisine is the most famous in the world, dating back many centuries – producing the first cookbooks, culinary delights and rules of table etiquette. The Greeks, Romans and Russians all influenced the style. The Romans enjoyed large banquets, and one specialty was snails. During the Renaissance Italian cooking once again influenced French cooking and setting a gracious table with linens, utensils, and glass vessels.

Each region is noted for its specialties and customs. Dining is taken seriously with each course and wine chosen to compliment. Julia Childs might have brought French cooking to the Americans, but it was Marie-Antoine Careme (1784-1833) and Auguste Escoffier, born in 1847 at Villeneuve-Loubet, who was the master chef at the Ritz and London Carlton who brought French cooking to the world. He was known as the "King of Chefs and the Chef of kings".

What makes French cuisine so special is its use of truffles, foie gras, pates, soufflés, galantines, mousses, aspics, sauces, soups, meringues, breads, and served so appealingly and in moderation. Using only fresh ingredients - fish, game, meat, vegetables, especially mushrooms, herbs and fruit chefs produce. Bread is part of the everyday meal, usually with a good crust and in many shapes. Radishes are eaten with salt and butter. French cheeses are world renowned - Camembert, Port Salut, Roquefort, and Brie, to name a few.

But it is not only the ingredients, but the way they are prepared in copper pots and pans, poissonieres for poaching fish, terrines, molds, and other utensils, often taking days to prepare that make the French cuisine so unique.

A classic French meal often begins with a clear soup, served with sherry; fish with a white wine, meat and vegetables with a red wine, a salad, cheese with red wine, then dessert.

French Regional Specialties

Bretagne (Brittany) – seafood, especially oysters and mussels: Muscadet, and galettes – savory pancakes served with different toppings
Drome – lamb
Normandy – butter, cream, Camembert cheese, Pont-l'eveque, Petit-Swiss and Neufchatel cheeses, and other dairy product, seafood, meat, poultry, game, apples, Calvados
Champagne – Champagne, sausages, seafood, wild boar, cheese
Touraine – trout, pork, prunes, wines (Loire Valley), shallots, dairy products, fish
Ile de France - Paris, fish, fruits, vegetables, wheat, Brie, honey
Savoy and Dauphine - chicken, dairy products, onions, Lyonaise sauce, Comte and Reblochon cheese, wines, fresh water fish, sausages
Languedoc – cassoulets
Foix, Rousillon – omelets, peppers, ham
Provence – Herbes de Provence – rosemary, sage, oregano and savory, garlic, olive oil, tomatoes, bouillabaisse; Anchoiade – sauce of anchovies, olive oil and garlic; Mediterranean influence, Rhone wines, truffles, lamb, beef, rice, pastis

Bordeaux – great wines, sauce bordelaise, cured ham, Cognac, foie gras, Black Perigord truffles, cabbage, goose, oysters, garlic , mushrooms, plums, cassoulet

Bourgogne (Burgandy) – wines, boeuf bourguignon, Bresse chickens, Charolais beef, honey, Dijon mustard, currants for cassi

Alsace and Lorraine – choucroute garnie (sauerkraut with pork), sausage, pork, goose, dairy products – Munster cheese, grains, fruit, Alsatian wines; Kugelhopf – brioche pastry with butter, eggs, raisins, almonds and kirsch; Quiche Lorraine – pastry with bacon, cheese, eggs

Rouergue – Roquefort cheese

The French inspired dishes that are now part of the international cuisine vocabulary:

Quiche Lorraine – tart of eggs, cream, cheese and bacon

Soufflé – baked egg, flour, cream or milk, and cheese dish; but can also be made as a dessert without the cheese adding chocolate, liqueurs, and fruit

Crepes – thin pancakes, invented in Brittany

Haricots verts – green beans

Crepes Suzette crepes with a Grand Marnier sauce

Hollandaise – egg yolk, lemon, and butter sauce

Vinaigrette – olive oil, vinegar, mustard and pepper sauce for salads

Vichyssoise – potato and leek soup

Soup a l'oignon – onion and beef stock soup with crusty bread and Gruyer cheese

Pate – ground meat, butter, herbs and Cognac baked in a terrine. There are also vegetable pates

Quenelles – poached dumplings with meat, fish or fowl

Bouillabaisse – fish stew

Boeuf bourguignon – beef stew with red wine

Coulibiac – pastry with salmon, mushrooms, veloute and crepes

Veloute – sauce made with butter, flour and stock

Bechamel sauce – roux with milk, nutmeg, onion, butter, and other seasonings

Demi-glace – dark roux

Mirepoix – finely chopped vegetables in butter

Croquette – meat, fish or vegetables cone-shaped, dipped in egg and bread crumbs, and fried

Coquille Saint-Jacques – scallops served in a shell

A la Florentine – with spinach

Tournedos – beef tenderloin with truffles, Madeira, and butter

Cassoulet- famous in Carcassone for bean, pork, goose or red partridge, and herb stew baked in a casserole, a clay pot.

Ris de veau a la financiere en vol-au-vent – sweetbreads banker's style

Chartreuse – an elaborate layered dish with cabbage and other vegetables, partridge, sausages, potatoes, and herbs

Gateau Saint-honoree – cream puffs, pastry with liquor, cream, and spun sugar

Canard a l'orange – duck with orange sauce

Selle de veau Orloff – veal with mushrooms, truffles and mornay sauce and soubise sauce (onion sauce)

Filets de sole Marguery – filet of sole with mussels, shrimp and wine sauce

Sole Albert – named for Monsiuer Albert, the former head chef at Maxim's of Paris -

Pate brisee – dough for tarts and other pastries

Croissant – flaky pastry in the shape of a crescent

Brioche – flaky pastry

Petit fours – small cakes dipped in fondant

Crème Anglaise – custard filling

Crème caramel – caramel custard

Bearnaise Sauce – sauce of butter, egg yolks, wine vinegar, shallots and tarragon (from Bearn in the Pyrenees)

Bordelaise Sauce – shallots, pepper, thyme, bay leaf, red wine, and meat drippings

Sauce Mornay – concocted by Joseph Voiron of the Restaurant Durand, the white sauce uses cream, Gruyere and Parmesan cheese

Hollandaise sauce – egg yolk, lemon juice and butter

Pommes Frites – French fries

Mousse – dessert made with whipped cream or egg whites

Fougasse – sweet braided bread with lemon zest and poppy seeds

Holidays and Special Occasions

New Year's – oysters and turkeys

Epiphany– Galette des Rois (puff pastry with almond cream). The pastry is named for the three kings who visited the baby Jesus. Inside is a ceramic baby inside.

Shrove Tuesday – crepes

Easter – lamb

Christmas Eve (revillon) – dinner served after midnight mass

Christmas – oysters, venison, veal or turkey, buche de Noel

In Provence special desserts are prepared for each of the twelve days of Christmas.

Beverages

Many of the finest wines in the world come from different regions in France. When dining, wines are chosen specifically to go with certain dishes, although today attitudes have changed somewhat about red with meat, and white with fish. But it is the soil, the vineyards and wine making process that make French wines so distinct. In order to preserve this, the French government has appellation controlee, each bottle labeled as to district, grapes used, and where bottled. "Premier Cru" "first growth" on a bittle means "vineyard of the first class". The finest red and some white wines come from the Bordeaux region's four districts – the Medoc, Graves, St. Emilion, and Pomerol. Burgandy is particularly known for the hospice de Beaune, a hospital founded in 1443 that is supported by the excellent vineyards surrounding it and its world famous auction held the third Saturday in November. During the Great Depression in the 1930s many vineyards failed, so in 1934 the Confrerie des Chevaliers du Tastevin "The Brotherhood of the Knight's of the Winetaster's Cup" was formed to promote Beaune and its wines.

The Rhone Valley contains the Chateauneuf-du-Pape district, so named because the 14th c Avignon was home to the Roman Catholic Church. Chateauneuf-du-Pape is made not from one variety of grape, but from twelve or more. The Syrah varietal has been produced since Roman times. The Loire Valley is noted for its wine and magnificent chateaux.

After finishing a fine meal a Cognac is often served. This brandy is made in the Charente district using mainly the St. Emilion grape which is distilled twice and then aged in limousin oak barrels. Cognac is a blend and therefore does not contain a vintage year on the label. The Cognac region is also noted for snails, butter, and fleur de sel (sea salt). France also produces other brandies – Armagnac, Marc, Calvados (apple brandy from Normandy), Chartreuse, Cointreau (orange triple-sec from Angers), and Benedictine. Benedictine has been produced at Palais Benedictine in

Fecamp since the 19th c. Kir is a drink made with crème de Cassis (blackcurrant liqueur and wine) and vermouth.

Champagne was first made by Dom Perignon, the blind cellar master at the Benedictine Abbey at Hautvillers, when he corked the bottle of wine adding a dollop of sugar. Champagne is best drunk before a meal and served in a tall fluted glass that holds the bubbles. Make sure it is chilled and only fill half the glass. Early large champagne bottles were names after Biblical personages, the largest being Belshazzar, containing 416 ounces! Today the largest bottle is the Rehoboam holding 156 ounces.

Did You Know?

Bistro comes from the Russian Cossack word for "quick", although others claim it is from the French *bistrouille,* a blend of coffee and brandy.
Peach Melba is a dessert concocted by Auguste Escoffier and named after Dame Nellie Melba, as is melba toast. His cookbook *Ma Cuisine* has been the handbook for cooks for almost 100 years.
La Couronne in Rouen is the oldest tavern in France dating back to 1345.
The first known cookbook *Le Viandier* was written by Guillaume Tirel (Tallevant), chef to several kings in the 14th c.
Forks were not introduced until the reign of Henri III. Before that fingers or the tip of a knife were used.
Not until the 1860s were dishes put on the table Russian style, which is course by course, introduced by Urbain DuBois. Before then all dishes were served at the same time.
Until c 1600 vegetables were not part of the diet which consisted mainly of fish and meat.
Marie Marel introduced Camembert Cheese in 1781.
Francois Pierre de La Varenne, author of *Le Cuisinier Francois*, was one of France's greatest chefs. He organized the first cookbook alphabetically as well as writing the first book on pastry.
Jean Antheleme Brillat-Savarin wrote *The Physiology of Taste*.
Sole Pompadour was named for Madame de Pompadour, Louis XIV's mistress.
Brie de Maeux cheese has been made since c 770. Charlemagne (768-814) stopped one day at an abbey and was served brie by the bishop. He wanted to cut away the blue veins, but was told that was the best part. After that time large quantities of brie were shipped to him yearly.
Marie- Antoine Careme created Crème Russe or Charlotte Russe, a cake with ladyfingers and custard, in honor of Czar Alexander I of Russia's visit to Paris in 1815. He also served as chef to the Czar and is responsible for France's classic style of cooking.
Jules Gouffe (1807-1877) was a protégé of Careme's, chef at the Jockey Club in Paris, and author of *Le Livre de Cuisine.*
Restaurants did not come into being until the late 18th c, one of the first owned by M Boulanger (the baker) on the rue des Poulies. The Grand Vefour in the Palais Royal opened in 1740.
Maxima Gaillard opened Maxim's in 1893.
The Bloody Mary was concocted at Harry's Bar in Paris.
Alexandre Dumas pere, author of *The Three Muskateers*, wrote *The Grand Dictionaire de la Cuisine*, which was more than 2000 pages long, in 1869.
In 1870 Mege-Mouries discovered margarine for a contest to supply the Imperial Navy with longer lasting butter.
Napoleon's chef concocted Chicken Marengo after the Battle of Marengo.

At the time of the marriage of Catherine de'Medici of Italy to Henri II she brought Italian foods and etiquette to France.

Louis Diat, a chef for the Ritz in London and Paris created Vichyssoise (leek and potato soup) on New York at the Ritz Carlton.

It was not until 1840 that yeast was added to bread.

Limoges porcelain has been made since the 12th c.

The term "ritzy" comes from the Ritz Hotel in Paris, founded by Cesar Ritz, where the elite dined and stayed.

Prosper Montagne (1865-1948), an assistant chef at the Gran Hotel in Monaco published *Larousse Gastronomique.*

Phileas Gilbert edited *La Revue de l'Art Culinaire.*

Antoine-Auguste Parmentier introduced potatoes in France in 1786.

Les Halles, the famed Paris market in the 1st arrondissement, dates back to at least 1183, King Philippe II Auguste enlarged the marketplace. It existed there until 1971 when the wholesale part moved to Rungis.

The Guide Michelin – Andre Michelin published the guide for travelers in France, at first a free publication and in 1920 a charge added. In 1926 stars were awarded to the top restaurants, with three stars being the top. Today there are twelve guides. Printed with a red cover.

Le Train Bleu which ran between Paris and the Riviera beginning in 1883 served meals in its dining cars with such gastronomic delights as foie gras, boeuf en gelee, and sole Metternich, The train ran from Calais to the Riviera from 1922 until 1938.

France produces over four hundred cheeses including double and triple crème, Brie (from the Seine-et-Marne area), Chevre, Bleu, and firm textured cheeses.

In the 18th c wild mushrooms were domesticated and raised in limestone caves outside Paris.

In the early 1800s Napoleon offered an award of 12,000 francs to an inventor who could find a way of preserving food for his troops. In 1809 Nicholas Appert won the award for his glass jars boiled in hot water to preserve food.

During the 15th c cheese making in France prompted King Charles VI to enact the first law protecting the process. Roquefort was given the monopoly for curing the cheese of that name.

Marie Harel is credited with making the first Camembert cheese c 1790.

Port du Salut cheese was made beginning in 1815 by Trappist monks at the Abbey of Notre Dame de Port du Salud.

Triple crème cheeses such as Boursin and Boursault were not made until the 1950s.

The Crusaders returning from the Holy Land and Syria introduced plum trees to the Lot-et-Garonne region. Today the town of Agen is known for its production of plums.

Dijon mustard seeds were brought to France from Asia by the Romans. "There is no town like Dijon. There is no mustard like that in Dijon", from a 15th c writer. The word mustard comes from moultarde "burn much". It was formerly made and purchased daily.

Gabon

Gabon is located in west central Africa bordered by Equatorial Guinea to the northwest, Cameroon to the north, the Republic of the Congo to the east and south, and the Gulf of Guinea to the west. The earliest inhabitants were the Pygmy, and later the Bantu. Tools have been found that date from the Stone Age. The Myene arrived in the 13th c. By the 15th c the Portuguese, Dutch, French and English explored the region. The first French settlement commenced in 1830. Libreville, the capital was founded in 1849. At this time the Fang migrated from Cameroon into Gabon. In 1910 Gabon became one of the four territories that formed French Equatorial Africa. The territories became independent of France in 1960. The name comes from "Gabao", the Portuguese word for "cloak". French is the official language with Fang and Myene also spoken.

Dining Etiquette

It is an honor to be invited for a meal. Please bring a small gift for the children or something from your country. Gifts are presented with both hands or the right hand. They are not opened in front of the presenter. Greetings may vary among the ethnic groups, but please shake hands greeting and departing. Please greet elders first. Hands will be washed before and after the meal. Please use your right hand only. Food is taken from a communal bowl and eaten from the section in front of you. Scoop the right hand and form the rice or other food into a ball and then dip in the sauces and stews.

Cuisine

The cuisine has been influenced by the Ba'Aka, Bibayak, Babongo, and Mitsogo tribes, and also the French, mainly in the cities with introduction of bread. The food staples are cassava, rice, yams, peanuts and peanut butter, plantains, tomatoes, eggplant, garlic, onions, spinach, okra, black-eyed beans, corn, sugarcane, and brown beans; spices – ginger, peppers, chilies; and Fruit – bananas, papaya, guava, mangoes, pineapples, coconuts, and avocado. Meat, fish and bush animals such as antelope, boar, monkey, crocodile, warthog provide protein. Fish are smoked, dried, grilled, or made into stews. Sauces are made with hot peppery berbere. Stews are made with fish, meat, tomatoes, onions and spices. Fufu is served with grilled meats and sauces.

Gabonese Specialties

Berbere – hot peppery sauce
Fufu – made from pounded cassava
Bananas are baked and served with sour cream and brown sugar
Gari – cassava flour porridge

Bambara – rice, peanut butter and sugar porridge
Groundnut stew – peanut stew with chicken, ginger, and okra
Injera – flatbread

Nyembwe (chicken stew)

Serves 6

3 lb. chicken, cut into pieces	½ lb. okra, chopped
Salt and pepper	1 hot chili, chopped
2 tbls. oil	3 garlic cloves, minced
2 onions, chopped	½ cup water
1 tomato, chopped	
1 cup palm butter	

Rub the chicken with some pepper and salt, and a little oil. On a grill bbq the chicken. The whole chicken can also be smoked and cut into pieces.
In a large pan sauté the onions, tomato, and okra until tender. Stir in the chili and garlic. Stir in the water, palm butter and chicken. Simmer on low heat for about 1 hour.
Serve with fufu or rice.

Holidays and Special Occasions

For festivals and holidays gari, nyembwe, stews and fufu are served. Eboga, a hallucinogenic root and palm wine are used for death, healing, and initiation. Food and wine are offered to ancestors.
January 1 – New Year's Day – music and dance, people wear new clothes, and evergreen decorations are everywhere symbolizing long life.
March 12 – Renovation Day – parades with people in traditional dress; music, dancing and food.
Easter – cheese wrapped in banana leaves
August 6 – Independence Day – parades, music, dancing, food and drinks
Ramadan is observed by Muslims who fast from sunrise to sunset. Eid al-Fitr breaks the month long fast with feasts and many sweets
November 1 – All Saints' Day – graves are cleaned and decorated
Eid al-Adha – Festival of Sacrifice to celebrate Abraham and the saving of his son. Animals are slaughtered and one-third of the meat is used by the family; one-third for oneself; and one-third to charity.
December 25 – Christmas – families share dinner. Ingredients used at Christmas are cassava, rice, yams, peanuts, plantains, tomatoes, corn and eggplant; chicken, fish, and bush meats; hot berbere sauce; and many fruit – pineapples, coconuts, avocadoes, mangoes, bananas, papaya, and guava.

Beverages

Palm wine is produced in Gabon. Beers are brewed in Libreville and locally.

The Gambia

The Gambia is a country in West Africa surrounded by Senegal except fort coastline on the Atlantic Ocean in the west. The country is situated around the Gambia River. Hanno the Carthagian wrote about Gambia in 470. The country was part of different West African kingdoms including Foni, Kombo, Sine-Saloum, and Fulladou. Beginning in the 14th c Gambia was part of the Mali Empire. The Portuguese arrived in the 15th c.. In 1588 Portugal sold trade rights on the Gambia River to English merchants. In the 1783 the Treaty of Versailles gave England the Gambia River with a small part held by the French on the north side. The boundaries of Gambia were established in 1889 and Gambia became the British Crown Colony of British Gambia. The country received its independence in 1965. The capital, Banjul, was founded as a British trading post in 1816. It is located on St. Mary's Island where the Gambia River enters the Atlantic Ocean. English is the official language, Mandinka, Wolof, and Fula are also spoken.

Dining Etiquette

It is an honor to be invited to a Gambian home. Please remove your shoes on entering a home. Please bring a small gift from your country. Present it with your right hand. Gifts are not opened in front of the presenter. Shake hands greeting and departing. Greet with the words "Slaam Aleikum" "peace be upon you". Women do not shake hands unless they extend it first. Take time to make pleasantries. Before and after eating hands will be washed. Food is served from a communal bowl which has rice or another starch and stews or sauces. The bowl is placed on a mat. Take food that is directly in front of you in the bowl. Eat with your right hand only. Please do not start before your hosts. The rice is shaped in your right hand to use for dipping in the sauces and stews. You might be given a spoon if it is available. Meals are usually eaten quietly, but do thank your hostess for the good food. A slight belch at the end of the meal means you have enjoyed it.

Cuisine

Rice is the staple food eaten with spicy sauces or stews. Other foods are steamed millet, couscous, cassava, okra, palm oil, peanut butter and peanuts, spinach, cassava and cassava leaves, fruit – mangoes, bananas, grapefruit, papaya, oranges; meat – goat, chicken, lamb, beef; and seafood; - lady fish, barracuda, butter fish, prawns, oysters, and crab. Fish may be dried, grilled, fried or boiled.

Domoda (Peanut Stew)

Serves 4

1 cup water	½ lb. pumpkin
1 large onion, chopped	½ cup tomato paste
2 large tomatoes	1 cup (or more) peanut butter
2 lbs. beef, cut into small cubes	Salt and pepper

In a pot boil the onion, tomatoes, beef, and pumpkin for 10 minutes. Stir in the tomato paste, peanut butter, and a little salt and pepper. Bring to a boil, and simmer for 45 minutes. Add more water if too thick.
Serve with rice
Chicken can be substituted for the beef.
Sweet potatoes can be substituted for the pumpkin.

Gambian Specialties

Benachin – jollof rice – rice cooked with spiced meat or fish, vegetables and tomatoes
Domoda – meat stewed in peanut butter sauce and served with rice
Supakanja – okra stew with fish or meat, palm oil, onions and pepper
Chicken yassa – fried chicken with onions, lime and pepper
Chura gerteh – rice and peanut porridge, served with yogurt or sour milk
Chere – millet flour balls

Plasas – meat and smoked fish cooked in palm oil with vegetables
Mbahal – rice with peanuts and dried fish
Chew I Yappa - beef stew
Chew I kong – fish stew
Slavas – spinach stew
Fufu – yam or cassava paste used as the starch in the communal bowl and served with stews and sauces
Chakery – couscous pudding
Lah - sweet porridge mix with baobab fruit, millet couscous and peanut butter.

Holidays and Special Occasions

Muslims observe Ramadan (fasting from sunrise to sunset) and Eid al-Fitr at the end of Ramadan. Christians celebrate Lent, Easter, and Christmas.
For naming ceremonies, betrothals, marriages and death food is served usually meat, jollof rice and fruit.

Beverages

Since 90% of the Gambians are Muslim almost no alcoholic drinks are consumed. Palm wine, wonjo juice made from sorrel, ginger beer, tea, soft drinks and water are mainly consumed.

Georgia

Georgia is bounded to the west by the Black Sea, to the north by Russia, the south by Turkey and Armenia, and to the east by Azerbaijan. The history of Georgia can be traced back to the ancient kingdoms of Colchis and Iberia. It was one of the first countries to adopt Christianity in the 4th century (state religion 337AD), brought by St. Nino. During the reign of King David and Queen Tamar in 11th and 12th c Georgia was a very powerful country. At the beginning of the 19th c, Georgia was annexed by Russia, invaded by the Bolsheviks in 1921 and became part of the Soviet Union in 1922. Independence was restored in 1991. The capital, Tbilisi, located on the Kura River, was founded in the 5th century by Vakhtang Gorgasali of the Kingdom of Iberia. Georgian is the official language.

Dining Etiquette

"The Georgians have a saying "that a guest is a gift from God". The Georgians are very warm and known for their hospitality. Elders are held in high respect.

When invited to a Georgian home please arrive punctually. Please bring flowers (odd number), sweets, chocolates, or something from your country. If you know there are children please bring a gift for them. Gifts may or may not be opened in front of the giver. Shake hands greeting and departing. If people know each other well they will kiss on the cheek. Women will extend their hand first. When seated at a table please eat continental style with use your fork in the left hand, knife in the right. Keep your hands at table level, no elbows on the table. The oldest or honored guest will be served first. Do try all the dishes, taking a small amount of each, as you will be offered more. Clear everything on your plate.

The supra or Georgian table is a dinner party with many toasts. The supra table will have flatbread, khachapuri, shish kebab, roast pig, chicken or turkey with plum sauce, and churchkhela. The tamada (toastmaster) is in charge of the toasts and making guests feel comfortable. A horn (khantsi) full of wine is passed around the table. Or if you are the honored guest you may have to drink it to the bottom! Only wine or brandy is used for toasts. Toasting with beer is considered an insult! When the toast is offered to you wait until the tamada has finished, stand up and thank the toaster. Wait until everyone has drunk and then you may drink. If the tamada says "Alaverdi" continue his toast. Georgians toast parents and ancestors first. The toast is "Gaumarjos" "cheers". Toasting may go on for hours!

"Cooks never die of starvation."
Old Georgian proverb

Khachapuri (Cheese Stuffed Bread)

Dough

2 pkg. dry yeast	3 ½ cups flour
1 tbls. sugar	1 tsp. salt
1 cup lukewarm milk	1 stick butter, softened

In a bowl sprinkle the yeast into ½ cup milk with ½ tsp. sugar. Stir until dissolved. Set aside for 3 minutes. Place in warm place for 5 minutes or until mixture has doubled.

Pour 3 cups flour into a bowl and make a well in the center. Add ½ cup milk, the yeast mixture, and butter. With a large spoon beat the ingredients together into a smooth dough. . Make into a ball and place on a floured board.

Knead for 10 minutes using remaining flour on board, until smooth and elastic. (This can also be done in a Kitchen Aid).

Place in a large buttered bowl. Cover with a towel and let rise for 45 minutes, or until doubled in size. Punch down. Let rise another 30-40 minutes.

Punch down the dough, then roll out on a floured board into a large circle, about 20 inches.

Butter a cake pan, or something larger. Line the pan with the dough, leaving a large overlapping rim over the side of the pan.

Fill with the cheese mixture. Begin to fold over the dough sides to make like pleats, turning the pan. Gather the ends in at the top and tic into a knot. Set aside for 10 minutes.

Preheat oven to 375°

Bake bread for ½ hour or more, until browned.

Turn onto a wire rack and let cool, but still warm.

Serve sliced.

Cheese Filling

2 cup mozzarella or muenster cheese, grated	2 tbls. butter, softened
2 cups parmesan cheese, grated	1 egg

In a large bowl combine the cheeses, butter and egg. Puree in a food processor.

Cuisine

The cuisine has been influenced by what is grown here, but also the Turks in the west and the Iranians in the east. The cuisine of Georgia is differentiated by the regions. In the west walnuts, vegetables, corn for bread and porridges, tarragon, basil, coriander, feuille Grec, pepper, cheese from cow's milk, sulugini and Imeretian cheese, and khachapuri. Khachapuri varies by region and is a buttery, cheese, and egg bread. The food is spicy. Bread is baked in a ketsi (clay frying pan). In the east people eat mutton, pork, beef, wheat for bread, spicy and salty cheese from sheep, and gomi (thick corn flour porridge). The bread is baked in a clay oven. In the mountains khinkali (meat dumpling) is eaten with beer.

The vegetables used in cooking include tomatoes, potatoes, radishes, pumpkins, eggplant, beans, cucumbers, cabbage, and beans. These are eaten raw, stewed, boiled, baked, fried, made into sauces, or marinated. The country has many orchards and vineyards growing grapes, barberries, pomegranates, plums, watermelon, apples, sloes, and tangerines, some of which are dried. Walnuts, watermelon, eggplant, green tomatoes and fruit are made into jams. The region near the Black Sea is noted for citrus groves and tea plantations. Trout and sturgeon are caught in lake and stream waters. Walnuts, hazelnuts, and almonds, plus numerous herbs and spices – basil, savory, fennel, tarragon, parsley, dill, coriander and garlic are used. Sauces are made from nuts and spices and served with meat. Other sauces are made with fruit or tomatoes and mixed with vinegar and spices.

Georgian Specialties

Kubdari – bread stuffed with meat, spices and onions

Themali – wild plum sauce

Tabaka – chicken with breadcrumbs

Matsoni – sour yogurt

Sheat – fish in vinegar with fennel

Sholi – white leavened bread

Pkhali – beet greens or spinach with walnut paste, pomegranate grains and spices

Kharcho – spicy rice and mutton soup

Chikhirtma – chicken soup with eggs

Chizhi-pizhi – liver and spleen roasted in butter and eggs

Tabaka – chicken with satsivi, a sour sauce

Chakapuli – lamb with damson and onions

Chanakhi – braised lamb stew

Kupati – spiced sausages

Khashi - broth of beef entrails and garlic

Khinkali – soup dumplings

Khachapuri – cheese filled bread

Azelila – egg salad – national dish

Kharcho –meat or chicken soup

Lobio – red bean soup

Pkhali - spinach with walnut and garlic sauce

Gomi – corn mash

Chakhokbili - Chicken with Herbs and Tomatoes

Chkmeruli – chicken with garlic

Adjara khachapuri – boat-shaped dough with grated cheese and egg in center with butter

Satsivi – chicken or turkey in walnut sauce

Badrijani nigvzit – eggplant with ground walnuts, vinegar, pomegranates, spices

Soko- mushrooms with herbs and spices

Ispanakhi – spinach with ground walnuts, spices and herbs

Mtchadi – cornbread

Chvishtari – cheese cornbread

Puri – bread baked in ceramic oven

Sulguni – cheese soaked in salt water

Qababi – grilled meat with sumac and onion wrapped in a thin bread

Dolmas – cabbage, grape or other leaves stuffed with meat, herbs and rice

Mtsvadi – shashlik

Adjika – spicy paste served with cucumbers and tomatoes

Svaneti – salt made from spices and herbs

Churchkhela – dessert with walnuts or hazelnuts, dipped into a paste made of boiled grape skins

Gozinaki – nut and honey bar

Pelamushi – grape pudding

Holidays and Special Occasions

New Year's –satsivi (turkey or chicken in walnut sauce); ground walnuts boiled in honey
Lent – Orthodox Christians abstain from meat
Easter – dyed eggs; roast pig or lamb; chakapuli (lamb stew with herbs)
At Easter Georgians visit cemeteries bringing baskets with bread, cheese and hard-boiled eggs. Wine is poured on the grave and a toast made
Mariamoba - Assumption of the Blessed Virgin Mary – August 28th – feasts; people carry a lamb to the church, then walk around the church, and later slaughter the lamb. The lamb is boiled and shared with others.
Barbaroba (St. Barbara's Day) – December 17 – lobiani (bread with bean stuffing)
Christmas is celebrated on January 7th – satsivi
Wedding – much feasting, drinking, and dancing, and the "tamada".
After a wedding the bride and groom break a plate for good luck, and then enter their home and are given a glass of wine. The groom drinks first, dips the wedding ring in the wine, and gives the glass to the bride. She returns the glass and the groom removes the ring.
Wake – rice with mutton; rice with meat and raisins Grains are thrown to the corners of the house to make it prosperous. The bride must also touch the cauldron and go around it three times with oil or wheat as a symbol of the house.
Forty days after a death – wheat porridge with honey and walnuts

Beverages

Georgia is one of the oldest wine producing countries in the world, dating back to between 7000 to 5000BC. It was found that wild grape juice buried in clay vessels (qvevri) during the winter turned to wine. Gold, bronze, and silver objects and wine cups dating from the 2nd millennium BC have vine, grape and wine designs. The main regions are Kakheti, made up of Telavi and Kvareli; Kartli; Imereti; Racha-Lechkhumi and Kvemo Svaneti; and Abhazia. Wine is made in old traditions and a few modern wineries by numerous small farms. The region is ideal – sundrenched summers and mild winters. Natural streams and the Caucasian Mountains provide plentiful water, and the moderate climate and moist air from the Black Sea provide ideal wine growing conditions. A number of varieties are unique to Georgia. Most wines are a blend of two or more grapes.

Georgia also produces cognacs, brandies, sparkling wines, mineral waters, fruit drinks, vodka; Araki, a grape and fruit drink with honey; and tchatcha, a strong alcoholic drink made from grape pomace seeds and skins. Tea is grown in the Dzirula Valley.

Did You Know?

On the hills above Tbilisi is a statue of Mother Georgia, holding a bowl of wine in one hand and a sword in the other.
In the olden days young girls were given a chicken which they had to cut into 17 exact pieces, and if done were considered marriageable!

Germany

Centrally located in Europe Germany is bounded by Poland, the Czech Republic, Austria, Switzerland; France, Belgium, Luxembourg, The Netherlands and Denmark. The earliest history of Germany can be traced back to the Heidelberg Man found in 1907 and was perhaps 500,000 years old. The Celts later moved about the country, which was eventually settled by Germanic tribes. The Romans moved north c 9 BC. Eventually different municipalities were to form the Holy Roman Empire. The name Deutsch was first used in the 9th c and the area was known as Deutschland. Following Germany's defeat in World War II, in 1948 the Soviet Union blockaded Berlin and Germany was divided into East and West Germany. Reunification occurred on October 3, 1990 "Tear Down the Wall". Berlin, the capital, was first mentioned as a city in 1237, made up of Colln and Berlin, straddling the Spree River.

Dining Etiquette

Please be punctual when invited for a meal. Please bring a gift or flowers, which are unwrapped and an uneven number, not 13. Gifts are opened in front of the presenter. Shake hands greeting and departing. Ladies offer their hands to gentlemen. Men stand when introduced to a lady, hold doors and chairs for her. Drinks will be served before the meal. When seated the male guest of honor will be seated to the left of the hostess. Meals are usually served in courses, and place settings will include a fish fork and knife, if fish is served. Food is eaten continental style, fork in the left hand, knife in the right. Keep your hands at table level, not in your lap .Please wait until the hostess begins. When finished place your knife and fork together. Say "Danke" after each serving and "Bitte Sehr" when you hand a dish to another person. Wines are served with meals, and coffee usually after dessert.

The host proposes the toast, sampling the wine, and no one may drink until he has done so. The guest of honor or person of highest rank follows. A lady never proposes a toast to a man and glasses are not clinked, except for special occasions, or wishing good luck. Glasses are refilled when empty. The toasts are "Prosit" or "Zum Wohl" – "To your health". Wine or champagne are used for "Zum Wohl". "Prosit" is a beer toast. Other toasts are made when two men seal their friendship, drink with arms locked, and call each other by first names "Bruderschaft". When a house is completed, the carpenter toasts with a glass of schnapps (a clear distilled grain-based drink served ice cold, often as a chaser with beer) for good luck "Richtfest".

Cuisine

German food has its own distinctive flavors making us of such regional specialties as Westphalian ham; different sausages; fish – eel, pike, perch, herring, carp, and catfish; fruit – cherries, apples, and plums; pfannkuchen – German pancakes; fowl – duck and goose; sugar beets; cabbage; and mushrooms.

German Kartoffelsalat

8-10 salad potatoes
1 onion, finely chopped
½ cup of warm meat broth

White wine vinegar, sunflower oil, .salt and pepper to taste

Steam the potatoes in their skins until tender. If you have any potatoes from the day before, even better as they are easier to slice. Scrape them and let them cool slightly until just warm.
Slice the potatoes thinly with a potato slicer or a vegetable knife. Place in a large bowl.
Add the onion and enough warm meat broth so that the potatoes are quite moist but not sitting in broth and leave to soak for an hour.
Lastly add enough sunflower oil, vinegar, salt and pepper to taste. Again I can`t give exact quantities but I suggest that you start off with a couple of tablespoons of each of the oil and vinegar and then add more to taste. Mix thoroughly. The potato salad should not be too dry, but quite moist.
Serve with your favorite German recipe such as Wiener Schnitzel.
Recipe Courtesy of the German Information Center, Embassy of the Federal Republic of Germany, Washington, DC

German Specialties

Sauerbrauten – pickled beef
Aalsuppe – eel soup
Rollmopes – salt herring dish
Roulade – stuffed beef
Spatzle – small dumplings
Bratwurst – German sausage
Kartoffelpuffer – potato pancakes
German pancakes – large puffy pancakes eaten with jam, often for dessert

Dresdner stolen – Christmas fruit bread
Pfeffernusse- spice cookies
Lebkuchen – gingerbread famous in Nuremberg
Lebkuchen hauschen – gingerbread house made ar Christmas
Schwarzwalder kirschtorte – black forest cherry cake
Rahmbrot – rye bread

Regional Specialties

Black Forest – Black forest ham; Schwarzwalder Kirschtorte – Black Forest cherry cake; Kirschwasser – cherry brandy; and Schwarzwaldgerauchhertes – smoked bacon
Berlin – Eisbein mit sauerkraut – pork knuckles with sauerkraut; rouladen – rolled beef; spanferkel – suckling pig; Bockwurst – sausage; Flammkuchen - ham, cheese, and cream; Pfannkuchen - crepe
Rhineland – The Palatinate grows figs, lemons, chestnuts and grapes. Rabbit pate and pfalzer – sausage with herbs are favorites.

Frankfurt – apfelwein – apple cider, marzipan, and frankfurters
Bavaria and Munich – weisswurst – veal sausage; leberkas – liver cheese; tellerfleisch- boiled beef and horseradish; pork roast; suckling pig; ham hocks; apfelkuchen –apple cake; trout; venison; salmon, carp; catfish, rabbit; asparagus; dumplings; and radishes.
Bodensee – Swiss influence
Franconian/Swabian cuisine – pancakes; Spatzle; roast beef; ravioli; carp; cuttlefish; bratwurst; gingerbread; almond cake; venison; dumplings; duck, pork; and beer
Rhine region – chocolates; pork; truffles; asparagus; rabbit; game; venison; fruit; trout; eels;
Baltic Coast – Gurtzwurst – liver sausage with raisins; Eierbier – egg whites, beer, ginger, cinnamon, and heated; fish; potatoes

German Spaetzle (a dumpling, means "little sparrows")

Side dish serves 8, main course 4

500g wheat flour
4-5 eggs
1 tsp salt

1/8 -1/4 litre water, depending on type of flour
Hot water for tossing the Spätzle

Mix the flour, eggs and salt in a large bowl. Add the water.
Moisten a Spätzlesbrett (a wooden board with a handle on one side and a beveled edge on the other), with water. Spread a small amount of dough on it and scrape with a broad knife thin strips of dough into slightly boiling water. If you are using a Spätzle press or potato ricer, then you need to fill the press with the dough and press down as per instructions.
While scraping, dip the board and the knife time and time again into boiling water. This makes scraping the dough easier. When the Spätzle rise to the surface, remove them from the pan with a slotted spoon and toss them briefly in hot water, so that they won't stick together. Drain well and place them on a pre-heated plate and serve immediately.
Spaetzle can either be served with melted butter and slightly toasted breadcrumbs or with finely sliced, fried onion rings.
Spaetzle also taste excellent if the dough is only prepared with eggs (about 8-9 eggs) instead of water.
Enjoy my Spaetzle recipe with a roast meat dish with a sauce or gravy.

Examples of Spätzle recipes:

Linsen, Spätzle und Saitenwürstle: Spätzle with lentils and frankfurter style sausages.
Gaisburger Marsch: a stew containing Spätzle.
Kässpätzle: Spätzle mixed with a large amount of grated cheese and topped with fried onions. This can be served as a main course.
Recipe Courtesy of the German Information Center, Embassy of the Federal Republic of Germany, Washington, DC

Holidays and Special Occasions

Carnival – Fasching – everything but fasting
Easter – colored eggs,
Octoberfest – Octoberfest was founded in 1810 to celebrate the marriage of Crown Prince Ludwig of Bavaria. Foods include unlimited amounts of beer, chicken, fish, roasted oxen, and wurst.
Wine festivals – during fall in many wine villages
Prior to Christmas - Christkindlmarkt (Christ Child Market) – Christmas fairs with fabulous foods, especially Nurnberg
Christmas Eve – carp; der bunte Teller (dish with apples, nuts, raisins, and cookies)
Christmas – Christstollen (Christmas stolen); Lebkuchen (gingerbread and gingerbread houses); Pfefferkuchen (spice cakes); baumkuchen (Christmas cake in shape of tree); marzipan; goose, hare, or turkey stuffed with chestnuts, apples or onions; venison; red cabbage; mushrooms

Beverages

Germany's unique soil and ideal growing conditions have produced some of the world's finest wines, dating back to Roman times in the Mosel, and to Charlemagne in the Rheingau region. Monasteries also produced wines, one the earliest at Johannisberg (Hill of St. John) founded in 853. The earliest distilled wines were known as Gerbrannter Wein or Brandwein "burnt or distilled", later brandy. During the Middle Ages wine was an expensive luxury, and beer, milk, and cider drunk more often. Much of the Rhine wine was shipped to England during the 18th c and labeled "Hochheimer", which the English shortened to "Hock". Germany is the largest producer of Sekt, sparkling wine. The most commonly used bottles are the long green ones for the young Moselles which should be drunk young and the tall brown bottles which are the golden Rhine wines. Most wine is made in the Moselle and Rhine regions, often with vineyards planted on steep hillsides with short growing seasons, thus producing mainly white wines. Because of the short growing season, sugar was often added to the wine.

Germany has the most breweries in the world, and is the largest producer of hops, mainly in Bavaria. German beer dates back to early times with the Benedictine monks at Weisstephan cultivating hops in 768 and a brewery in 1040. In fact, the earliest producers of beer were Dortmund in 1293 and the Augustiner in the 14th c. Early hops came from the northern cities of Hamburg and Bremen. Seefahrbier, a beer shipped from the above ports, was permitted to ferment at sea. In 1434 the city attempted to ban the brewery and beer, but its popularity won out. In 1516 in Bavaria the Reinheitsgebot "purity law" decreed that beer could only be made of pure water, barley or wheat, hops and yeast with no additives. Lager was first produced in Dortmund in 1843. Bock beer was originally from Einbeck and means "Billy Goat". Alt means "old", uses top fermentation, and is similar to ale. The strongest beer is Kulminator from Eisbock. Lowenbrauerei, Munich, means "Lion Brewery". Hofbrau is "Royal Brew". Gose is a pale, unfiltered wheat based beer with coriander and salt with a low alcoholic content, that undergoes a lactic fermentation, made in Goslar.

Germany also produces many fine liqueurs. Among these are Kroatzbeere – blackberry; Fes – orange; Kirschwasser – cherry; Fraise – strawberry; Danzig Goldwasser – aniseed and caraway with gold specks; Nranntwein – apples or pears; Zitroneneis Likor – lemon juice and peel; Ettaler – herbs; and Quetsch – plums.

Did You Know?

Tacitus, a Roman general in Germanus 1st c AD wrote about the local food. The Romans brought with them gold and silver drinking vessels.

Sauerkraut (sour plant) dates from Roman times, when salt was added to cabbage and allowed to ferment.

Charlemagne c 800 taught the Germans how to plant vineyards and gardens.

Dining etiquette rules were strict, even in medieval times. Though a person ate with his fingers, hands had to be washed before and after a meal.

One of Germany's more famous wines, Bernkasteler Doktor, received its name when the Archbishop of Trier visited Bernkastel in the 13th c. He came down with a very high fever for which there was no cure, until someone suggested the local wine which did the job!

The Jagdshloss Speigelberger (now a restaurant in Halberstadt) has a wine cask that holds 35,080 gallons of wine built in 1594.

The Heidelberger Fass winery contains a barrel that holds 49,000 gallons!

During the Renaissance, cooking became popular among the middle class. Cookbooks were published, among them were *Kuchenmeistere* (Mastery of the Kitchen) in Nurnberg in 1485 and in 1652, a cooking manual by Paul Furst describing table etiquette and recipes.

The Italians and later the French, especially Louis XIV, were to influence the Germans allowing them to begin producing Meissen and other fine china and glassware.

In the 17th c forks with 3 tines, spoons and knives, or all of these as a set, were introduced.

Coffee, tea, and chocolate were brought from the Americas or the Far East.

Nurnberg became a center for the spice trade.

The Rathskeller in Bremen opened in 1408.

The Schiffergesellschaft Restaurant in Lubeck has been serving meals since 1535 with only male waiters. Women were not admitted until 1870.

The first mention of a der Weihncachtsbaum (Christmas tree) is in Alsace in 1605. The tree was decorated with sugar, apples, cakes, candies, and paper roses.

In 1774 Frederick the Great brought potato seeds to Prussia and by law they had to be planted.

The chemist, Frederick Accum, wrote "A Treatise on Adulteration of Food and Culinary Poisons" in 1820 about altering foods.

Ludwig Roselius of Bremen invented decaffeinated coffee (sanka).

Sunday fish markets first became popular in the 18th c before church services.

The earliest baking powder was powdered hartshorn, made from deer and hart's (a breed of deer) antlers

In 1909 Dr. Stepp, a biochemist, discovered the vitamins that were fat soluble.

The Striezelmarkt in Dresden dates from 1434 and the Hauptmarkt in Nuremberg (Christkindlesmarkt) flourish at Christmas with their straw ornaments, the aroma of roasting nuts, cakes, gingerbread, streudel, wines, and sausage such as bratwurst.

2014 marked the 700th anniversary of bratwurst in Nuremberg. They were first mentioned in a city ordinance in 1313!

Ghana

Ghana, located on the west coast of Africa is bounded to the east by the Cote d'Ivoire, Burkina Faso to the north, Togo to the east, and the Atlantic Ocean to the south. The country has been inhabited since the Bronze Age. The Akan settled in Bonoman by the 11th c, but it was not until the 16th c that the various ethnic groups made permanent settlements. By the 19th c the region was part of the Empire of Ashanti. The Portuguese arrived in the 15th c searching for gold. By 1598 the Dutch also arrived and built forts. The English named the area the Gold Coast. The Dutch withdrew in 1874 and the Gold Coast became a British Protectorate. Ghana became an independent nation in 1957. Accra, the capital, is from the word "nkran" "ants" in Akan, for the many anthills around Accra. The city was settled in the 15th c by the Ga people as a fishing village. The official language is English. Akan, Fanti, Akuapem Twi, Akyem, Kwahu, Wassa Nzema, Dagaare/Wale, Dagbani, Dangme, Ewe, Ga, Gonja and Kasem, and others are spoken.

Dining Etiquette

The people are very hospitable and entertaining is a sign of friendship. Please arrive punctually for a meal. You may have to remove your shoes before entering the home. You do not need to bring a gift, but if you know there are children please bring something for them, or flowers or a small gift from your country. Gifts are given with the right hand or both hands. They will not usually be opened in front of the presenter. The host will greet you at the door saying "Akwaaba" "You are welcome". Please shake hands greeting and departing. Elders are greeted first. You will be offered water or another drink. You will be told where to be seated for dining. A bowl is brought out to wash your hands before eating. Grace or a few words may be said. The host and hostess will be at each end of the table or seated next to each other. Food is served from a communal bowl. Your section is right in front of you and only take from there. Please eat with your right hand. Do not start eating until the eldest male starts. You will also wash your hands at the end of the meal.

Yam Fufu

Serves 4

4 yams, peeled and diced

Boil the yams in water until tender.
In a bowl pound with a wooden mortar until smooth.
Serve with a sauce, stew, or soup.
This is eaten with the right hand. Take some of the yam in your hand and form into a ball. Dip into the soup, sauce, or stew. Salt, pepper, or butter can be added for more flavor.

Cuisine

The main crops are cassava, cocoa, coffee, maize, millet, sorghum, rice, plantains, yams, palm oil, copra, cola nuts, peanuts, keneaf and limes. The dishes make use of garlic, chilies, tomatoes, onions, hot peppers, lamb, goat, or chicken, fish, yams, and cassava. An asanka is a small bowl used for mashing vegetables, meat, fish and spices. Some of the food may be quite spicy.

Ghanian Specialties

Fufu – dumpling made with yams, coco, plantains, cassava or other root vegetables and used to eat
Domoda – ground peanut butter stew
Hkatenkwan - groundnut soup
Palava – spinach, pumpkin, prawn, meat and smoked herring stew
Fetri detsi - okra soup
Akrakro – plantain dumplings with black-eyed peas
Shitor din – chili sambal
Banku – cornmeal dumplings
Baked, salted, or fried fish
Aponkyi nkakra - mutton with ginger, chili, tomato and onion.
Banku - maize balls
Egusi – melon seed and spinach sauce or stew served with goat
Kenkey – fermented corn dough served with a stew
Swaakye, - black-eyed beans and wild rice
Jollof rice – rice with tomato, peppers, and onions

Kelewele - deep-fried plantain mixed with spices and served with roasted peanuts, a favorite snack
Kenkey – fermented corn and cassava dough
Yele - deep fried yam
Omo tuo - rice balls
Shito – spicy sauces
Kumasi nkatikwan – chicken in peanut butter sauce
Ground nut soup with rice balls
Abenkwan - palm nut soup
Nkatsenkwan - peanut soup
Kontomire ne momone – spinach and dried salted fish
Ampesi – yams or plantains with pallava sauce
Pallava sauce - vegetable, meat, fish and spices in a stew
Red-red – fried plantains and black-eyed peas
Toogbei – hot fried dough
Kubecake – rum, ginger, coconut, and sugar balls
Fried plantains

Holidays and Special Occasions

Edina Bakatue – a six week ban on fishing, to allow the fish to multiply, followed by a celebration with drums, cowbells, and singing in Elmina.
Oguaa Fetu Festival, first Saturday in September – district chiefs and queen mothers participate, fetish priests, palm wine

Beverages

Palm wine, Pito (millet wine), Akpeteshie (gin), Asana (maize wine), Lamujii (ginger wine) are locally produced. Tea, coffee, water, fruit juices and soda are also drunk.

Greece

Greece is made up of the Greek Peninsula and thousands of islands. Greece's history spans thousands of years from c 3000 BC. Settlements were along the Peloponnese Peninsula and the Cyclades Islands with Crete being the most cultured and advanced. Mycenae was the capital, and city-states were formed. Philip of Macedonia captured Greece in 338 BC. In 146 BC it became a Roman province. Following the 4th Crusade (1202-04) parts of the country were divided between Venice and the Franks, then part of the Turkish Ottoman Empire. Greece won independence from the Turks in 1830. Athens, the capital, received its name from a contest for a patron – Poseidon struck the top of the Acropolis with his trident, producing a salt well and Athena presented an olive tree. Thus the name and the fact that olive trees are in abundance today, and a symbol of peace, virginity, and wisdom. The city was founded c 1581 BC, and was located on ancient trading routes. Greek is the official language.

Dining Etiquette

Please be punctual when invited out for a meal. Meals are social occasions and much talking will take place. Please bring a gift for the hostess – flowers or a plant unwrapped, pastries, or something for the home. Shake hands greeting and departing. Both men and women if they know each other may embrace and kiss on each cheek. Elders are introduced first. Dinner is usually after 8 PM. Drinks are served with hors d'oeuvres. The hostess will seat the guests with the guest of honor to her right. Courses are served with dishes placed on the table. Please wait for the hostess to start. Food is eaten continental style, fork in the left hand, knife in the right with hands kept at table level, and no elbows on the table. Fish, salad, and dessert knives and forks are used. When finished please put your knife and fork together. Wine glasses should not be "topped off", nor should one finish a glass completely. The toast is "To your health", "Yasas", "Yamas", or "Yasau". The host should raise his glass and toast first.

If invited to a home, but not for a main meal, guests are offered preserved fruit and a glass of water as a sign of hospitality after chatting for a while. When it is offered do not refuse. Drink the water first. Later coffee, tea or brandy might be served. In the countryside, Sunday is a women's day off. Bread is baked in communal ovens with the men carrying the bread.

Tomatoes and Peppers Stuffed with Rice

Big tomatoes, not too soft, and peppers
2-3 more tomatoes for their juice: if you stuff, for instance, 5 tomatoes and 5 peppers, you will need the juice of another 2-3 tomatoes
2 big onions (you may use more onion or garlic, depends on what you like)
4 pieces of garlic
Parsley
Mint or basil
Pine nuts

Raisins (you can do without, if you don't like them)
Rice for risotto (Arborio)
4-5 potatoes (depends on your pan), but you have to cut them in larger pieces, not as small as the French fries!
A slashed tablespoon of sugar (you may use slightly more if you don't use raisins)
Olive oil
Salt and black pepper

Cut the upper part of the tomatoes and peppers (be careful not to throw the cover/lid away, because you have to use this a the lid after you stuff them).

Remove with caution the inside of the tomatoes and you keep it separately along with the inside of the 2-3 additional tomatoes. You either blend or cut into small piece.

Remove the inside of the peppers (much easier!).

Wash the parsley and basil and cut them in small pieces.

Cut in small pieces the onion and the garlic. Put them in a larger pan to fry. First put the olive oil in the pan and when it gets hot, pour the onions and garlic. Stir them well till they start drying. Turn the heat down, should be low for the next steps.

Add in the pan where the onion and garlic are, the tomato juice (just keep a little in order to spray the vegetables after you stuff them), the parsley and mint/basil. Stir them for a couple of minutes.

Then add the pine nuts, the raisins, a bit of sugar, salt and pepper and stir them for 2 minutes.

Then add one tablespoon of Arborio rice per stuffed vegetable. Stir for another 2 minutes, switch the heat off.

Heat the oven at 200 degrees centigrade!

Put some olive oil in the pan using a painter's brush.

Fill the vegetables but not to the top, with the mixture and put their "lids" on top. Put the potatoes that you have sliced between the vegetables.

Pour/spray the vegetables and potatoes with the remaining tomato juice, just a little bit of water (half a cup maybe), some olive oil, salt and pepper.

Put them in the oven.

Usually, I have them in the oven covered with aluminum foil for about an hour and then cook them uncovered for about half an hour. You have to make sure that the rice inside the vegetables is ready and that the vegetables are soft. The tomatoes will usually not look great, but this is actually the sign that they are well cooked! But make sure they don't burn on top. Try also the potatoes to see if they are ready.

The stuffed vegetables usually taste better on the following day, as all the ingredient come together. You can serve them with feta cheese! You don't need to warm them up, you can eat them cold. Good luck!

Recipe courtesy of Mimi- Maria Arvaniti, Office of the Ambassador, Greek Embassy, Washington, DC

Burgetto (Fish Soup) from Galaxidi by Stella Senduka

1 ½ kilo different kinds of small size sea fish
¼ kilo shrimp
1 ½ kilo codfish
1 ½ kilo potatoes, cut in half
3-4 red onions, sliced

Half water glass Esti olive oil
Juice from 1-2 lemons
Sea salt
Pepper

Clean the fish and shrimp. Boil the shrimp, fish, and some sea salt in boiling water for 10-15 minutes, or shrimp are pink. Remove from broth. Clean and devein the shrimp.
Add the codfish to the broth and boil 15 minutes. Remove cod and place on a plate.
Add the potatoes and onions to the broth, and boil for 15-20 minutes, or potatoes are tender.
Add olive oil and lemon juice to the broth. If you would like a thicker broth, mash one of the potatoes and add.
Place small fish and shrimp in broth.
In a soup bowl place the cod and ladle the broth over the cod. Pepper can be used sparingly for taste.
Recipe courtesy of George Papageorgiu, Athens   www.esti.com.gr

Cuisine

The Greeks use fresh vegetables, fruits, lamb, fish, and herbs, and each region has a specialty. Examples are Corinth – grapes; Kalamata and Corinth – olives; Patras – currants and artichokes; Chios – Terebinth lantisk or mastic which is made into jams, liqueurs, and gum; Prespa for flat beans, goat, and mutton. Olives have been grown in Greece for thousands of years.

Meals start with meze (appetizers) which might include keftedes (meatballs), hummus; tzatziki (yogurt, cucumber, and garlic dip); taramosalata (carp roe), or cheese; salads; soups; meat or fish, vegetables, and dessert. Breads are served with every meal, and are in various shapes for holidays, births, baptisms, engagement parties and weddings. A farmer's lunch consists of bread, cheese, olives, and perhaps some meat. Coffee is drunk strong in small cups with sugar.

Greece produces an abundance of cheese including Feta, Anthotyro (blossom cheese), Graviera. Kasseri, kefalograviera, Kefalotyri, Ladotyri, Manouri, Metsovone, and Myzithra. Greek yogurt is world famous.

Greek Specialties

Avgolemono – lemon and chicken soup
Avgotaraho – is the roe of grey mullet that is served with olive oil, pepper, and lemon, or with dried fruit
Kakavia – fish soup
Spinakopita – spinach pie
Taramoslata – roe dish

Dolmathes – steamed stuffed grape leaves
Tzatziki - yogurt, cucumber and garlic dip
Salata - salads
Seafood – calamari, octopus, rofos (sea bass), salt cod, squid, sardines, and eel
Spanakopitta – spinach cheese pie
Hortopitta – wild greens pie

Tzoulama – liver and cinnamon pie
Tiropitakia – small cheese pies
Tiganta – frying vegetables such as aubergines, zucchinis, courgette, beans, or peppers; fish, meat or chicken
Kouneli Gemisto Lemonato – stuffed rabbit (recipe from Crete)
Sofrito –veal dish from Corfu
Arnaki - lamb
Souvlaki and kebabs – skewered meats and vegetables
Moussaka – eggplant, lamb and tomato casserole

Pastitio – macaroni and cheese casserole
Keftadakia - meatballs
Yiaourti – yogurt made from cow or sheep's milk, is eaten plain, or served in or with many dishes
Baklava –layered pastry with honey and nuts
Karidopita – walnut cake
Loukoumades – fried fritters with honey
Halva – semolina candy
Kourambiedes – walnut and butter cookies
Trahana- is made with semolina or wheat flour, bulgar or cracked wheat, mixed with yogurt, milk or buttermilk.

Horiatiki (Greek Salad)

¾ lbs. tomatoes, seeded, diced (about 2 cups)
2 cups diced, seeded, peeled cucumber (from about
1 large)
1 cup diced red bell pepper (from about 1 large)
¼ cup Kalamata olives

¼ cup diced red onion
3 tbls. chopped fresh Italian parsley
3 tbls. extra-virgin olive oil
1½ tbls. red wine vinegar
½ teaspoon dried oregano
2 oz. feta cheese

Toss first 9 ingredients in medium bowl to blend. Gently mix in cheese. Season with salt and pepper.
(Can be made 2 hours ahead. Let stand at room temperature.)
Makes about 4 ½ cups.
Recipe courtesy of the Cultural Affairs Office, Embassy of Greece, Washington, DC

Holidays and Special Occasions

Lagana is served on *Clean Monday* (Pure Monday, Ash Monday, Monday of Lent or Green Monday) and garlic eaten as a vegetable. Lagana (white unleavened bread) is never cut with a knife, instead pieces are broken off. This is a time of fasting. The Greek Orthodox Church has strict rules on fasting – no animal products, and on Wednesday, Friday and during Holy Week no wine or olive oil can be consumed. Fasting foods include seafood – octopus and calamari, shellfish, olives, dolmades, lagana, and taramosalata (fish roe spread). On Clean Monday people go on outdoor excursions, fly kites, dance and have music. During *Lent* tahini is used instead of butter in sweet dishes.
Easter – food preparation begins Holy Thursday when eggs are dyed red and eaten after the Saturday midnight mass. Lamb or goat, avgolemono soup and special breads are eaten (Tsoureki – Easter bread and Koulourakia Paschalina – Easter biscuits)
St. Andrew's Day – November 30- loukoumades (honey fritters)

Christmas – turkey with chestnut stuffing, Kourabiedes (cookies rolled in powdered sugar), Melomacarona (honey cookies, and tsourekia (Christmas cakes)

New Year's – Vassilopita (St. Basil's bread with a coin). At midnight the first piece is cut by the head of the house, and set aside for Christ, the second piece for the house, 3rd for himself, the 4th for the mother, and then pieces are given to the others in descending age. The person who finds the hidden coin receives good luck in the coming year.

Weddings – pilaffi tis nifis (Bride's pilaf); kourambiedes (traditional wedding cookies in Sparta)

Funerals and All Saints' Day - Kolyva (boiled wheat, sugar, raisins and spices) which is made 40 days after a death, then on the 1st and 3rd anniversaries. During mourning sweets are not made in a home, but are given as gifts.

Beverages

Wines have produced in Greece since c 5000 BC, originally brought from Asia. The word wine comes from the Greek "oinos". The Greeks were the first to name appellation of origin. Amphora "something that can be carried by two" were used to transport wine, honey and olive oil. They were marked with origin, month, and year, and were transported by boat throughout the Mediterranean. The earliest red wines came from Macedonia and Thrace. Honey was once used to sweeten the wines. Some of the Greek wines are sweeter due to the warm climate and warm fermentation. Water or spices were added in craters to dilute wine. An early wine producing region, Samos, was stripped of its vineyards in 1453 by the Turks. In 1912 the region was taken back by Greece. Achaia Clauss is the oldest winemaker in Greece.

Crete produces about one-fifth of Greece's wine. Most wines were once imported from here to France and Italy and blended as table wines. Malmsey produces a sweet dessert wine. Rhodes exports Muscat, red and white wines. Santorini is famous for its white wines, grown in chalky soil with over ten varieties. Other islands producing wines are Chios, Corfu, Cyclades, Samos, Thasos, Cos, and Lesbos. Much of the red wine is from Thessaloniki. Most wineries are family run, with the harvest in August and September. Wine festivals are held in many towns.

Retsina is made from pine resin, a sealant and preservative known since ancient times to transport the wines in amphora. Retsina is drunk young and cold. Ouzo, a liqueur made from grape stems, is colorless, and flavored with aniseed from Tirvanos, and has been made since the late 19th c. It is served at room temperature, straight up, with water, or on ice. Other drinks are Mastiha, a liqueur made from mastic gum; Metaxa, a brandy; and Kitro, a lemon liqueur from Naxos. Tsikoudia is a clear spirit produced on Crete.

Beer is also produced in Greece. The largest brewery is Hellenic Breweries which produced Kev, a lager.

Did You Know?

Phyllo comes from the Greek "leaf", a wrapping since ancient times.
The ancient Greeks believed strangers might be gods in disguise and were kind to all strangers.
Demeter is the goddess of earth and bread.

Olives have been harvested since c 3000 BC, first on Crete. They were considered sacred and, if someone was caught cutting a tree down, punishment was death! The olive branch is a symbol of peace. Olive oil is used in lamps, cooking, soap, cosmetics, or on the skin as a medicine. Olives, of which there are many types, are packed in brine and preserved. Almost 2000 olives are needed to make one quart of olive oil. All olives start out green and turn to black. They are bitter and not edible unless cured. Olive wood is used in wood carving and for utensils.

Honey, used in much of the cooking and medicinal purposes, is produced from May to November. Honey has been used as a sweetener since ancient times. Walnuts sweetened with honey were offered to bride and grooms at a wedding to sweeten their marriage and act as an aphrodisiac.

Cheese, originally from Crete, is depicted in pictures dating back to 3000 BC.

Formos, the Greek word for cheese, comes from the wicker baskets (formos), used to drain the whey from the curd. It later became formo which we get the Italian "formaggio" and French 'fromage".

In 2004 the European Union granted Greek feta PDO (Protected Designation of Origin) status prohibiting other European countries, other than Greece to use the name Feta.

The ancient Greeks worshipped Aristaeus, the diety of shepherds and cheese-making, bee-keeping, honey, honey-mead, olive growing, medicinal herbs and the Etesian winds cooled the air during summer.

Greek Athletes ate cheese for strength, and the island of Delos had a coin with cheese on it.

Supposedly the first cheesecake was made on Samos, and recorded by Athenaeus.

On the island of Argos cheesecakes were served by brides to friends of the groom, and probably the source of present day wedding cakes.

Even in *The Odyssey* of Homer, Odysseus found cheese in caves.

Corn was first grown on the Thrasian Plain by the ancient Greeks.

The ancient Greeks thought lettuce inhibited sex; arugula, eggs and watercress were aphrodisiacs; and all strange fruits were called apples!

Pastas date back before the 12th c, when macaroni was eaten to honor the dead.

Salads were always eaten after the meal!

Margarine is from the Greek "margaron" or "pearl".

The word symposium means "drinking together".

Plato suggested boys under 18 should not drink wine.

Many places in Italy were founded and named by Greeks who took vines. Marseilles (Massasalia), France was founded in 500 BC.

Hippocrates, the Father of medicine, used wine as a cure for many ills.

Homer's *Odyssey* and *Iliad*, along with Greek tragedy allude to wine throughout their stories.

In August 1992 Coco-Cola ran an ad in Italy that showed the Parthenon with columns shaped like Coke bottles. Following many protests it was withdrawn, having insulted the Greeks who need profuse apologies!

The ancient Greeks chewed something similar to chewing gum, but from the bark of the mastic tree.

The ancient Greeks believed fennel aided dieters!

Santorini is noted for its large cherry tomatoes (Tomataki Santorini) that grow in the volcanic soil of the island. Tomato paste was made from the tomatoes, and today it is honored at the tomato Industrial Museum.

Grenada

The island of Grenada and six smaller islands are located in the southeastern Caribbean Sea north of Venezuela. The earliest settlers probably came from Venezuela c the 1st c AD. The island was inhabited by Island Caribs known as the Kalinago. The islands were sighted by the Spanish in 1498, but the first permanent European settlement was by the French in 1649 who named it Le Grenade. Indigo and sugar cane were raised on the island. The British captured the island in 1762. The French retook the island during the American Revolutionary War, but it was restored to the British in 1783. Grenada received its independence in 1974. St. George's, the capital, was built by the French in 1650. English is the official language. Grenada is also known as the "Island of Spice" as nutmeg and mace are grown here.

Dining Etiquette

Please arrive punctually when you are invited for a meal. Please bring a gift of flowers, chocolates, wine, or something for the home. Shake hands greeting and departing. Drinks will be served. The hostess will escort the guests to the table. Food will either be served or buffet style. Please eat continental style with the fork in your left hand, and knife in the right. Please do not start until the hostess lifts her fork. The toast is "Cheers". At the end of the meal thank your hostess, and call or send a thank-you letter.

Oil Down

Serves 2-4

1 lb. salted beef	1¼ cups coconut milk
1 medium onion, peeled and sliced	1 stalk celery, chopped
1 large green breadfruit	2 sprig thyme
8-10 dasheen callaloo leaves or spinach	Avocado slices

Wash the meat and cut into small pieces. Put into aluminum pot. Add the celery and thyme.
Wash and peel the breadfruit. Cut into 405 pegs. Remove center. Core. Cut pegs in half across. Arrange the breadfruit on the meat.
Wash the callaloo leaves, stems, and break into pieces, add to pot. Spread the callaloo leaves on top of the breadfruit. Add the coconut milk. Cover. Put on low heat and cook until all liquid is absorbed and meat begins to fry. Remove from stove.
Open pot and using a fork and spoon, rolls up the leaves into a ball-like mixture.
Serve on a warm platter with the meat on the breadfruit. Garnish with the avocado.
Salt cod can be used instead of the meat, but soak and boil first.
Recipe courtesy of travelgrenada.com

Cuisine

The cuisine has been influenced by the British, French, African, Indian, and West Indian dishes. Stews are made with beef, pork, goat, chicken, or fish, and served with rice and vegetables. Vegetables include potatoes, tannia (hairy brown potatoes), eddoe, yams, christophene, cassava, and coocoo made from corn. Tannia porridge is a popular breakfast dish. Cocoa, mace and nutmeg are grown on the islands. Organic cocoa is processed by the Grenada Chocolate Company into bars. Grenada is the world's second largest producer of nutmeg. Other spices used are bay leaves, vanilla, allspice, capsicum, pepper, turmeric, cinnamon, ginger and cloves. The Spice Market is located in St. George's.

Grenadian Specialties

Oildown (national dish) – dasheen leaves, breadfruit, root vegetables, and salt pork steamed in coconut milk and spices. The meaning Oildown comes from the cooking process whereby all the coconut milk is cooked until it is absorbed. Oil down may be cooked in a large pot called a karhee or curry pot.
Black pudding – blood sausage
Lambie curry – conch curry. Lambie are also made in fritters, stews, roti, or chowder
Salt fish souse
Pig souse
Salt fish cakes

Callaloo – dasheen with coconut milk and spices
Rice and peas
Baked breadfruit
Curry rice
Curries
Kurma
Guava cheese
Fried plantains
Yam pie
Raisin ice cream
Tamarind balls – candies made from tamarind pods

Holidays and Special Occasions

Easter – decorated eggs, hot Easter buns, fish,
Christmas- ham, rice, pigeon green peas, macaroni pie, turkey, black fruitcake,
March - International Food and Drink Festival

Beverages

Grenada has produced rum for several hundred years. The River Antoine Estate distillery was founded in 1785, and still uses a water wheel to power the mill. Grenada Distillers produces Clarkes Court Rum which is 69% Alcohol by Volume, and 138 Proof! Other island favorites are breadfruit punch, sorrel ginger beer, and fruit drinks.

Did You Know?

Nutmeg can be made into nutmeg syrup, nutmeg jelly, and nutmeg ice cream.

Guatemala

Located in Central America, Guatemala is surrounded by Mexico, Belize, Honduras, El Salvador, the Caribbean Sea and the Pacific Ocean. The history of Guatemala dates back to the Archaic Period (13,000-2000 BC) when the people began the agricultural traditions which raised maize, squash, turkeys, dogs, and basket weaving. From 300 BC on, the Mayans built city states, temples, pyramids, until c 1200 AD when food shortages (overuse of the land by planting corn) and migrations left abandoned cities. The Spanish conquest took place in 1518 and they eventually defeated the Mayans. Their lands were divided into ecomiendas (large estates). Guatemala received its independence from Spain in 1821. Antigua became the capital in 1543. Spanish is the official language, with the Indian groups speaking their own dialect. Guatemala is known as "The Land of the Eternal Spring" because the annual temperature in Guatemala City is 75º.

Dining Etiquette

Be punctual when invited for a meal. Shake hands greeting and departing, and smile. Men will often embrace and pat each other on the back. Ladies, if they know each other, will hug and kiss. Eye contact is important. The Guatemalans are very friendly people, enjoy making new friends, and wish to show off their country, its wares, and have people to their homes. Please bring a gift from your country or a small present. The extended family is still traditional. The hostess will seat the guests, with the male guest of honor to her right. Food is eaten in continental style, fork in the left hand, knife in the right. Hands are kept at table level. The host offers the toast which is "Salud".

Cuisine

The cuisine has been influenced by the Mayans, Spanish, and makes use of the vegetables, fruits and meats of the region. Since agriculture has been the primary occupation for thousands of years, maize (corn first domesticated in the highlands), beans and squash are served in a variety of dishes. The Mayans ate amaranth, a cereal. Tortillas are eaten with almost every meal. On the Caribbean coast one finds seafood, enchiladas, sweet coconut breads, and tapadas. The west coast too is noted for deep sea fishing. Many fruits, vegetables, and fish are exported. Fruits include strawberries, blackberries, lycee, rambutan, melons, papaya, mango, pineapples, apples, plantains, sugar cane and grapes. Vegetables are okra, snow peas, celery, tomatoes, cauliflower, asparagus, garlic, corn, wheat, and black beans (frijoles). Guatemala also grows and exports spices – cardamom, black pepper, sesame seeds, ginger, chilies, allspice, Tabasco pepper, oregano, chicle (for chewing gum). Other exports are cacao, coffee and nuts, especially cashews and macadamia. Shrimp farming has become a major industry, along with cattle ranching.

Breakfast (desayuno) consists of sweet rolls, toast, and coffee. Lunch (el almuerzo) is the main meal of the day with soup, entrée, vegetables, rice, tortillas, dessert and coffee. Dinner (la cena) is the same as lunch, but a lighter meal.

Pepian (Chicken Stew)

Pepian is considered the national dish of Guatemala.

Serves 6

3-4 lb. chicken, cut into pieces
2 chayote, peeled and diced
2 carrots, peeled and chopped
4 potatoes, peeled and diced
2 tbls. oil
2 onions, peeled and sliced
2 tomatoes, sliced
1 green pepper, seeded and chopped
4 cloves garlic, minced

2 red chilies or poblano peppers, seeded and chopped
½ lb. green beans
¼ cup pepita (pumpkin seeds)
1 tsp. coriander seeds
3 tbls. sesame seeds
Salt and pepper
Cilantro
Rice

Place the chicken, carrots and chayote in a large pan. Just cover with water. Bring to a boil and cook 10 minutes. Add the potatoes. Cook 15 minutes. Drain. Save stock for other uses.
In a skillet sauté the onions until just tender. Stir in tomatoes, chilies, pepper, garlic, green beans and coriander.
In a small skillet toast the pumpkin and sesame seeds.
Add the chicken, chayote, carrots and potatoes to the tomato mixture. Stir in seeds.
Cook 15 minutes, or until chicken is thoroughly cooked. Add stock if needed.
Serve hot with rice and garnish with cilantro.

Specialties

Tamales – dough stuffed with meat and tomato sauce
Frijoles are served refried, mashed, or cooked slowly for hours, making them very tender, and served with rice.
Chicken, beef, and turkey are roasted, grilled, fried or served in stews.
Bistec – grilled or fried beef

Churrasco – grilled steak
Mosh – porridge
Donas - donuts
Chilies rellenos – chilies stuffed with meat and vegetables
Fried plantanos – vegetable bananas with honey, cream, or black beans
Licuado – fruit juice with water or milk

Holidays and Special Occasions

Tamales are served for birthdays, first communions, Christmas, Sunday breakfast, and many other festive occasions. Fiestas are held almost daily, and each town has a patron saint
Carnival is held before Lent
During Holy Week large processions with figures representing Christ, worship of saints and incense
Holy Week and Easter – fish, spicy vegetables in vinegar, chickpeas, candied fruit, drinks made from hibiscus and rice, torrejas – sweet pastries.
Christmas celebrations begin December 7th when people begin to clean their homes.
Christmas – tamales, pavo (turkey), chicken with stuffing, fish, bunuelos (corn dessert with honey), ponche (fruit punch); firecrackers are set off Christmas day and New Year's
Cofradias – religious brotherhoods with patron saints. They have processions in costumes on Sunday mornings and religious festivals

Beverages

Guatemala has produced alcoholic drinks for several centuries. German immigrants founded the breweries in the 19th c. Types of beer are Moza (dark), Gallo (rooster), and Cabro (goat). Most beer is served at room temperature or ask for ":una cerveza fria" (cold beer). Local wines are produced from sugar cane. Aguardiente is a sugar cane liquor; Zacapa Centenario, a rum made in Zacapa that is aged for 23 years, for sipping only! Chicha, a strong drink made from distilled corn has been served since the Mayans.

Did You Know?

Golden skinned bananas were brought to Guatemala in 1516 by a monk from the Canary Islands. President Manuel Estrada Caberra (1998-1920) turned over much land in the country to the United Fruit Company for growing bananas.
Corn is still planted as it was thousands of years ago through the sacred ritual of planting the seed and setting fire to the soil for ash. The site and soil are important, and the family will often move to be near the crop.
From early Mayan times cacao was used in drinks and its kernels for currency.
The Mayans had no metal tools or draught animals. All work in the fields and for building was done by hand.

Guinea

Guinea is a country in West Africa formerly known as French Guinea (*Guinée française*) and today also Guinea-Conakry. It is bordered by the Atlantic Ocean to the west, Guinea-Bissau, Senegal and Mali to the north, Sierra Leone, Liberia, and Cote d'Ivoire to the south. The source of the Niger River is in the Guinea highlands. The region was inhabited by the Ghana, Mali, and Songhai empires from the 10th to 15th c. Europeans began exploring the area in the 15th c, and the French in 19th c. Guinea's boundaries, along with the present Sierra Leone, Guinea-Bissau and Liberia were negotiated in the late 19th and early 20th c as part of the Territory of Guinea within French West Africa. The country became independent in 1958. Conarky, the capital was originally settled on Tombo Island and later spread to neighboring areas after 1887. The name is supposed to have from the name "Cona", a wine producer of the Baga people and "nakin""the other bank" in Sosso. Conarky became the capital in 1904. Guinea has several ethnic groups – the Peuhl (Foula) who live in the mountains, Malinke (Mandinko) in the savannah and forest, the Soussou (Susu) in the coastal regions, and others including the Gerze, Kissi, and Toma. The official language is French, with Fula (Peuhl), Mandinka, Susu, and over 30 others. 85 % of the population is Muslim.

Dining Etiquette

Please arrive punctually when invited for a meal. It is an honor to be invited into a home. Please bring a small gift from your country, or something got the children. Gifts are presented with both hands or the right hand only. Please shake hands greeting and departing with many pleasantries. Good friends may hold hands while they are speaking. You may also bow your head slightly, especially to elders as a sign of respect. In some cases the people will place their left hand under the forearm during the handshake. Female friends will shake hands, but may also give two kisses on the cheek. Please wait for a woman to extend her hand. Beverages may be served. Basins or bowls will be offered to wash your hands before and after the meal. Dishes are served in communal bowls. Food is eaten only with the right hand. Use either your fingers to form a ball with the fufu or rice, or a spoon may be offered. In some families men will eat from one bowl and women from the other. The main meal is usually served mid-day.

Cuisine

The staples of the diet are rice, millet, cassava, sorghum, bananas, mangoes, sweet potatoes, peanuts and peanut sauce. Sauces are served made with groundnuts (peanuts), okra, tomatoes, and spices. The sauces may contain fresh or smoked fish, meat or poultry. Because this is a Muslim nation almost no pork or alcoholic beverages are consumed. In some places milk is made into yogurt and used as a sauce.

Poulet Yassa (Chicken with Onions and Peppers)

Serves 6

3-4 lb. chicken, cut into pieces
1 cup lemon juice
4 onions, peeled and sliced
4 cloves, minced

2 red chilies
4 - 6 tbls. palm oil
Bay leaf
Salt and pepper

In a bowl combine the lemon juice, onions, garlic and 2 tbls. oil. Add the chicken. Marinate for at least 2 hours.
Preheat oven to 350°
Remove the chicken. Grill until browned.
Drain onion and garlic. Keep marinade.
In a Dutch oven or covered baking dish heat the remaining oil. Sauté the onions until tender. Add garlic, chicken, chilies, bay leaf, salt and pepper to taste. Cover and bake in oven 1 hour, basting with remaining marinade. Serve over rice.

Guinean Specialties

Fufu – made from cassava, yams, or bananas into a paste
Maffi tiga – peanut sauce
Yassa chicken – chicken with lemon juice, onions and other vegetables, and spices

Jollof rice – rice with tomatoes, spices and other vegetables and meats
Coupe coupe – smoked bbq meat in a sandwich

Holidays and Special Occasions

Ramadan – fasting from sunrise to sunset
Eid al-Fitr – the feast ending Ramadan – yassa chicken
Tabaski – slaughter goat, sheep or chicken
Easter, Christmas for Christians
Baptisms, weddings and funerals – elaborate meals
Weddings – the groom pays bride wealth to the bride's family with cash, clothes, and livestock

Beverages

Palm wine, fruit juices, hibiscus drink, ginger beer, and beer are among the beverages served.

Did You Know?

Yams received their name when the Portuguese asked what they were and the people replied "nyami" "something to eat".
The seeds of the Guinea pepper, also called paradise or melagueta pepper, were once shipped to Europe and used to flavor sausage and beer. It is a member of the ginger family.

Guinea - Bissau

Guinea-Bissau is a country in West Africa bordered by Senegal to the north and Guinea to the south and east, and the Atlantic Ocean to the west. Guinea-Bissau was once part of the kingdom of Gabu, and later part of the Mali Empire. The region was explored by the Portuguese in 1446-47. In 1588 Cacheu from Cape Verde started arriving and for a time the region was under the Captaincy of Cacheau. The Dutch occupied Cacheau from 1624-30. Bissau was founded by the Portuguese in 1687. In 1753 Bissau became a separate Portuguese colony subject to Cape Verde. In 1879 Bissau and Cacheu were united as Portuguese Guinea. The independent state of Guinea-Bissau was declared in 1973 and in 1977 became the Republic of Guinea-Bissau. The capital, Bissau, founded by the Portuguese in 1687 was a port and trading center. The official language is Portuguese, with Kriolu, Fula, Bijago, and almost 20 others spoken.

Dining Etiquette

Please arrive punctually for a meal. Bring a small gift from your country. Shake hands greeting and departing. Food is served from a communal bowl and eaten with the right hand. Please take food from the section in front of you.

Fish Stew

Serves 6

2 lbs. fresh fish, cleaned and filleted
¼ cup flour
2 tbls. palm oil
1 tsp. fresh ground pepper
4 small onions, peeled and sliced

2 tomatoes, sliced
1 green pepper, seeded and chopped
2 red chilies, seeded and chopped
1 tsp. salt
1 cup water

Dredge the fish in the flour.
Heat the oil in a skillet. Fry the fish on both sides until just browned.
Remove fish and fry onion, pepper, chilies, and tomatoes. Add water. Simmer 10 minutes.
Add fish, salt and pepper.
Cover and simmer for 20 minutes.
Serve with rice or boiled dough.

Cuisine

The staple foods are rice, maize, millet, cassava, fish, beef, goat, pork, chicken, okra, peppers, squash, yams and coco yams, peanuts, black-eyed peas, onions, tomatoes, plantains, bananas, oranges, grapes, coconuts, mangoes, papaya, and melons. Native animals such as deer, monkey and others are eaten. The food is served with sauces made from onions, tomatoes, and other vegetables, peanuts, meat and fish. Palm oil is used in cooking. Milk, curd, and whey are also available. Hot spices such as peppers and chilies are used to season the food. Dried fish is fried sometimes with chicken, vegetables and spices. Each ethnic group has its own specialties. Guinea-Bissau grows cashews which are used in cooking and wine. The cuisine also has been influenced by the Portuguese.

Specialties

Fufu- paste made from yams, cassava, grains, or plantains

Egusi – seafood stew

Yassa – chicken or fish stew

Jollof rice – ham, chicken, rice, vegetables and spices

Groundnut soup – peanut soup

Yassa – marinated chicken with mustard and onions

Holidays and Festivals

Amilcar Cabral's birthday, also National Day – September 12 - yassa
Birth, circumcision, weddings and funerals are occasions to sacrifice livestock and drink palm wine.
About 30% of the population is Muslim who observe Ramadan fasting from sunrise to sunset and Eid al-Fitr the feast breaking the Ramadan fast.
Christians celebrate Easter and Christmas.
Carnival takes places four days before Lent in February.

Beverages

Warga is a sweet green tea. Palm wine and cashew wine are produced and drunk. Beer is again being produced at the Pampa beer factory which was originally opened by Portuguese investors in 1974.

Guyana

The Co-operative Republic of Guyana is on the northern coast of South America, bordered by the Atlantic Ocean to the north, Suriname to the east, Brazil to the south and west, and Venezuela to the west. The region was inhabited by Arawak and Carib tribes. In 1498 the Dutch founded the colonies of Essequibo, Berbice, and Demerara, followed by the British in the 18th c. In 1831 the colonies became British Guiana. The country became independent in 1966 and a republic in 1970. The name Guyana is from the Amerindian "Guiana" meaning "land of many waters". The capital Georgetown, founded in the 18th c was originally the capital of the Demerara-Essequibo colony, and was located on Borselen Island in the Demerara River. The official language is English, but Portuguese, Hindi, Spanish, Akawaio, Macushi, Wai Wai, Arawak, Patamona, Warrau, Carib, Wapishiana and Arekuna are also spoken.

Dining Etiquette

Please arrive 15 to 30 minutes late when invited for a meal. Please bring a gift from your country or send flowers before. Shake hands greeting and departing with good eye contact. Close female friends will shake hands and kiss on the cheek. Beverages will be served. The hostess will seat the guests with the male guest of honor to her right. The food will be served or buffet style. Please eat continental style with the fork in your left hand and knife in your right. Please keep your hands at table level, and no elbows on the table. When finished place your knife and fork together. The toast is "Cheers". Please send a thank-you note.

Cuisine

The cuisine has been influenced by the Amerindian, British, Dutch, African, Indian, Chinese, Portuguese, and Caribbean cultures. Among the popular seafood are catfish, hassa, gilbaka, tilapia, and crab. Staples in the diet are cassava, sweet potatoes, edoes, fresh fruit, seafood, okra, green peppers, onions, celery, and avocados. The country produces sugar, rice, and rum. There were once large cattle ranches. Muslims do not eat pork and the Hindi no beef

Chicken Curry

Serves 4-6

2-3 breasts of chicken, cubed can deboned
2-3 medium potatoes
½ cup water
1 hot pepper
2-4 drops hot pepper sauce
2 fresh thyme leaves
½ onion, chopped

4-5 garlic cloves, minced
2 tsp. salt
2 tbls. garam masala
3 tbls. curry powder
½ cup oil
Boiling water

Wash cubed chicken in vinegar and rinse. Peel, rinse and quarter potatoes. Put potatoes in bowl with the chicken.

In a blender, make a paste of water, hot pepper, thyme, onion and garlic. Add salt, garam masala, and curry powder to the paste.

In a saucepan, heat oil until quite hot. Add 2/3 of the paste mixture to the hot oil. Cook for 1 minute.

Add potatoes and chicken pieces. Stir to coat all the pieces. Cook for 5-10 minutes on low heat.

Add boiling water to cover the chicken and potatoes. Simmer for about ½ hour.

Serve with roti, bread, or salad, and sweet mango chutney for the ultimate experience!

Recipe courtesy of the late Mrs. Sarah Insanally, Embassy of Guyana, Washington, DC

Guyana Specialties

Cookup rice – rice and peas
Pepperpot – cassareep (cassava) stew
Metemgie – edoes, yam, cassava, and plantain soup cooked in coconut milk and grated coconut with dumplings
Cassava bread
Roti

Curries – made with chicken, goat, seafood, lamb
Chicken in the ruff- fried rice and chicken
Cheese roll
Pine – pineapple tart
Fried plantains
Patties – beef patty
Foo-foo – plantain cakes

Holidays and Special Occasions

Christians celebrate Easter and Christmas; Muslims Ramadan, the month of fasting, Eid ul-Fitr, Eid ul-Azah, Youman Nabi; and Hindi Phagwag (Festival of Colors), Deepavali (Festival of Lights).

Masharamani – February 27 – Independence Day

Curry, roti, garlic pork, dhol-puri and chow mein are consumed on special occasions.

Easter –hot cross buns, kite flying

Christmas morning – pepperpot

Christmas – black cakes are prepared by soaking fruit in rum long before Christmas; garlic pork; chicken or turkey, pickled onions, ginger beer, mauby, sorrel drink
Hindi wedding – seven curry (seven vegetable curries)

Garlic Pork

Serves 6

3 lbs. lean pork (with a little fat)
1 lb. pork (finger ribs), optional
2 pts. white vinegar
1-2" piece orange peel (fresh or dried)
1-2" piece tangerine peel (fresh or dried)
4 pieces mace
2" cinnamon sticks (broken into small pieces)
2-3 bay leaves, whole

12-15 wiri wiri peppers (red, green or yellow)
4-6 cloves
1 bunch thyme (6-12" pieces fine leaf)
3-4 leaves broad leaf thyme
½ lb. garlic
1 small sprig basil (about 6 leaves)
4 tsp. salt, or to taste
2 tbls. brown sugar
Juice of 1 orange or 2 tangerines, strained

Cut pork into finger pieces. Steep in a solution of ¼ pint vinegar and water. Lift out pork with two forks and put into a large jar that has been washed and sterilized.
Strain off as much liquid as possible from the pork in the jar. Add citrus peel cut into small pieces, mace, cinnamon, bay leaves, and two stalks (cut in two) of fine leaf thyme. Blend together garlic, and the remaining peppers, basil and thyme with the rest of the water and vinegar. Add salt and sugar to taste. Pour over pork, making sure there is enough liquid to cover pork completely. Stir to make sure seasonings and pork are mixed well.
Cover jar and soak for 2-3 days.
Put pork into a pan and add a little liquid. Boil until liquid evaporates and pork is cooked. Add citrus juice and fry pork in its own fat until lightly browned. Serve hot.
This recipe can be frozen before the final cooking stage. Strain off most of the liquid, then put in Ziploc bags. Thaw and cook as usual.
Recipe courtesy of the late Mrs. Sarah Insanally, Embassy of Guyana, Washington, DC

Beverages

Beverages include local fruit drinks such as lemonade, banana, pineapple, orange and other citrus, pawpaw, and coconut water punch. Other drinks include mauby (tree bark), a sorrel drink made from hibiscus, ginger beer, and peanut punch (peanut butter, sugar, and milk). Beer is brewed and coffee grown.

Along the Demeerara, Europeans founded plantations to grow sugar cane, mainly for rum. One of the famous rums to come from here was the Royal Navy Rum which later became Pusser's Rum. Today Demerara Distillers Limited is the only rum producer in the country, bottling under the El Dorado and other labels.

Haiti

Haiti occupies the western portion and the Dominican Republic in the east on the island of Hispaniola in the Greater Antilles between the Atlantic Ocean and the Caribbean Sea. The original inhabitants were the Taino who probably came from Venezuela c 2600 BC. Christopher Columbus landed on the western side of the island in 1492, and 39 of his men founded La Nanidad, later moving to the eastern portion. Gold was found to be on the island. The French settled in the western part and began growing tobacco and later sugar plantations. In the Treaty of Ryswick in 1697 France received the western part and Spain the east. Independence was achieved in 1804 and called Ayti. The name comes from the Taino "Ayti" "land of high mountains". The United States occupied Haiti from 1915-34, becoming an independent country in 1934. The capital Part-au-Prince, dates from early Spanish settlements, but became the capital of Haiti in 1804. The official languages are French and Haitian Creole.

Dining Etiquette

Please arrive punctually when invited for a meal. Please bring a gift, something for the home, something from your country, wine, or flowers. Shake hands greeting and departing. Close female friends will kiss on the cheek. Beverages will be served. The hostess will seat the guests. Food will be served or buffet style. Please eat continental style with your fork in the left hand and knife in the right. Please wait for the hostess to start. Keep your elbows at table level. The host will initiate a toast. The toast is "A votre santé". When finished place your knife and fork together. Please thank the hosts, and send a thank-you or call.

Cuisine

Sugar cane and coffee plantains date from the 18th c. The cuisine is a blend of French, African, Spanish, and Creole. The dishes are spicy, but not hot. Among the staples are peppers, yams, rice, beans, tomatoes, oregano, cabbage, avocado, sweet potatoes, manioc, corn, sugarcane, millet, wheat, peas, taro, mirliton (chayote), coconuts, fish – red snapper, shrimp, lobster, salted codfish; Meat- goat, mutton, chicken, beef; and fruit – guava, papaya, mango, limes, oranges, and ackee.

Riz et Pois (Red Beans and Rice)

Serves 6

1 cup dried red kidney beans
Salt and pepper

3 tbls. lard or butter
2 cups uncooked rice

Rinse the beans with water. Heat a pan with 6 cups water. Bring to a boil. Simmer until beans are tender about 1 hour. Drain and reserve 4 cups liquid.
Melt 1 tbls. lard in saucepan. Stir in rice for 2 minutes. Stir in reserved liquid (add water if needed to make 4 cups). Cook until rice has absorbed all liquid and is tender. Season with salt and pepper.
Melt the 2 tbls. lard in a skillet. Add beans, and stir until warmed.
Make a mound of the rice on a platter. Place the beans on top. Serve immediately.

Haitian Specialties

Riz et pois – (national dish) rice and beans
Riz djon – rice with black mushrooms
Mayi moulen –cornmeal mush served with different sauces made from peas, beans, kidney, garbanzo, pinto, pigeon peas, or with fish
Banana pese (tostone) – fried plantain
Tassot – deep fried goat
Griot – deep fried or braised pork

Sauce ti-malice – chili, onion, lime juice sauce
Pain patate – sweet potato, fig and banana pudding
Rapadou – sugar paste
Pikliz – pickled vegetables
Calalou – crabmeat, salted pork, spinach, onions, okra, peppers
Boukanen – Bbq'd meats
Pain Haitian –bread with spices and coffee

Holidays and Festivals

New Year's Day – jomou (pumpkin soup) for good luck
Easter - turkey, eggs
All Souls' Day (Day of the Dead) – November 2 – a day to honor those who have died with stories, food and drink, and placing food at graves
Christmas – Christians go to Mass, followed by dinner – fried goat or pork, pikliz, fried plantains, pain patate
Baptisms, first communions, weddings – colas, cake, keleren, kremass
Sunday dinners – jomou
Harvest festivals in November
Manger - Yam – "eat yam" day

Beverages

Popular drinks are fruit juices; shaved ice topped with a fruity syrup, *Juna* (a locally produced orange squash drink), and even sugarcane. Both adults and children enjoy chewing on the stalks to extract the sweet juice. Kremas is evaporated or condensed milk, cinnamon, and tar anise. Haiti produces rum. The best known is Societe du Rhum Barbancourt. Kleren is a spiced rum. Brana S.A. in Port-au-Prince brews Prestige the national beer.

Holy See/Vatican

The Holy See is an independent sovereign state bounded by the city of Rome, Italy and covering 108 acres. The word "see" comes from the Latin "sedes" for chair or Residence of the Bishop. The history dates back to Ager Vaticanus, belonging to Agrippina, and later by her son, Caligula who used it as a circus and hippodrome. The Basilica di San Pietro was the first building erected in 90 AD by Pope St. Anacletus in honor of St. Peter. Constantine began building St. Peter's, the Santa Maria Maggiore and San Giovann c 319-22. The wall surrounding the City was built by Leo IV (847-55). In 1929 the Lateran Treaty recognized the sovereignty and independence of The Holy See within Italy. The Pope is head of the Roman Catholic Church.

Pope Francis, the present Pope, was born in Argentina and is said to prefer food from his homeland such as mate, empanadas, steak, ice cream, alfajores (round cookies with fillings), and membrillo (gelatinous quince pasta). He enjoys homegrown foods and much is raised at Castle Gandolfo, the summer villa of the popes. Most popes originally came from Italy, but today a pope can be elected from all over the world.

Dining Etiquette and Cuisine: Please see the chapter on Italy. A good reference is *The Vatican Cookbook!*

Honduras

Honduras, located in Central America, is bordered to the west by Guatemala, to the southwest by El Salvador, to the southeast by Nicaragua, to the south by the Pacific Ocean at the Gulf of Fonseca, and to the north by the Gulf of Honduras. Honduras was once part of Mesoamerica, the Mayan culture with its headquarters in Copan. In 1502 explorer Christopher Columbus landed on the Honduran coast, and this region became part of the Spanish Empire within the Kingdom of Guatemala. Honduras became independent of Spain in 1821 and for a while was part of the Mexican Empire, becoming fully independent in 1838. The capital, Tegucigalpa, was founded by Spanish settlers as Real Villa de San Miguel de Heredia de Tegucigalpa in 1578. Spanish is the official language. English is spoken in the Bay Islands and Caribbean coastal cities. Indigenous languages include Misquito, Garifuna, Pech and Tawahka.

Dining Etiquette

Please arrive slightly late when invited for a meal. Please bring a gift of flowers, especially roses, liquor or wine, or something for the home from your country. If the family has a fifteen year old girl her birthday is celebrated with a party and gifts. Gifts are opened when received. Please shake hands greeting and departing. Women will often pat another woman on the right shoulder or forearm. Close friends may hug and kiss on the right cheek. Men extend hands to women. Please use Senor or Senora until you are invited to call a person by the first name. Drinks will be served and the hostess will escort the guests to the table. The male guest of honor will be seated to her right. Guests will be served first. The host will propose a toast "Salud", after which you may drink. Do look your host in the eye when the toast is made. If you do not wish anything more to drink, please leave some wine in your glass. Food is eaten continental style with the fork in the left hand and knife in the right. Both hands, not elbows are kept above the table. After the meal please plan to stay for a while longer. Please reciprocate the invitation. A thank you note or phone call is appreciated as a thank you. Family ties are still very strong in Honduras. Soccer is the national sport.

Cuisine

The Honduran cuisine is a blend of indigenous American, African, and Spanish. The main staples are coconut, plantains, yucca, cabbage, banana leaves, peppers, tomatoes, manioc, beans, rice; fruit – papaya, pineapple, guava, breadfruit, mangoes, avocadoes, sapodilla, plums, passion fruit, and bananas. Corn (maize) was sacred to the Mayans. Tamales are a popular dish made of ground corn and filled with meats and sauce. Along the coast fish is in abundance. Meals often start with coconut bread.

Breakfast is usually a large meal – eggs, beans, sour cream, cheese, avocado, plantains, tortillas, and strong coffee. Lunch is a large meal with rice, tortillas, meat, salads or soup, and dinner lighter

Conch Chowder (Sopa de Caracol)

Serves 10

2 lbs. conch
2 cans of coconut milk
¼ cup chopped onion
1 garlic clove
1 ½ chopped ripe medium size tomato
½ cup finely chopped red bell pepper
2 tbsp corn oil

1 cup each one of the following julienne sliced vegetables: yucca, sweet potatoes, White potatoes, baby corn, ripe plantains *
1 tsp hot chili sauce (optional)
1 tsp "achiote" **
1 tsp oregano powder
1 fish stock cube
Salt and pepper to taste

Clean the conch by taking off the darkish skin with a sharp knife. Cut into one inch pieces. Season the conch with salt, pepper and oregano. Refrigerate.

In a pan, heat the oil and cook the garlic, the onion and the red bell pepper for 3 minutes. Add the tomatoes and cook 5 minutes. Season with salt and the remaining pepper.

In a 4 quart pot, place the coconut milk, add the fish stock cube dissolved in 2 tbps of hot water and the "sofrito" mixture prepared above. Add 5 cups of hot water. Cook for 5 minutes. Add the vegetables and cook at medium heat for 20 minutes or until well cooked.

Puree 6 oz. of the yucca and the potatoes and add them to the soup. Dissolve the "achiote" in a bit of hot oil and add to the soup to obtain a light yellowish red tint.

Right before serving the soup, boil again and add the conch, cooking at medium heat for 5 to 7 minutes. Make sure not to over boil or the conch will become rubbery.

You can garnish the soup dishes with cilantro leaves and serve with lime wedges and hot chili sauce on the side for those who like it hot!

(*) Plantains are ripe when its yellow skin has large black spots. Some people like to add green plantains to this soup.

(**) Achiote (*Bixa Orellana*) is a small tropical tree from which a vegetable coloring is extracted from its seeds. It is a basic ingredient in the traditional Honduran cooking which is used to give the typical yellowish red color to a great variety of foods, such as tamales, rices, soups, and meat based stews. Achiote can be purchased at most Latino markets.

Recipe courtesy of his Excellency Jorge Ramon Hernandez Alcerro, Embassy of Honduras, Washington, DC

Honduran Specialties

Fried fish – along the coast
Yojoa Lake fish – salted and fried, served with pickled onions, red cabbage, and platantanos
Rice and beans are cooked in coconut milk, cilantro and spices
Tamales – steamed cornhusks with meat
Nacatamales – meat and vegetables
Tajaditas – fried plantain chips
Carneada – marinated meat that is grilled and served with chimol sauce (tomato, cilantro, onion, lemon), roasted plantains, chorizo, cheese, guacamole, refried beans
Carne asada – roasted meat
Ticucos – corn flour dough and beans in a corn husk that is boiled
Pupusas – dough stuffed with beans, meat or cheese and fried
Chorizo – spicy sausages
Balaeadas – flour tortillas topped with eggs, meat, beans, cheese, or sour cream

Chilaquiles – tortillas with egg and deep fried, then layered with cheese, chicken, hot sauce and baked. Served with sour cream.

Chicken with rice and corn

Bean soup

Tapado – beef, vegetable and coconut milk stew

Mondongo – tripe and beef knuckles

Nacatamales – made of meat and vegetables

Torrijas – similar to French toast

Sopa marinera – soup using crab, fish, or shrimp

Mondongo soup –tripe soup

Corn tortillas – flat corn bread

Tacos fritos – tortillas filled with ground meat or chicken and then fried

Catrachitas – deep fried tortilla chips with refried beans, cheese and hot sauce

Enchiladas – tortilla with meat or chicken, cabbage or lettuce, tomato sauce, hard boiled egg, rolled up and deep fried served with a sauce

Tortilla con Quesillo – tortillas with melted cheese, deep fried and served with tomato sauce

Anafre – claypot with melted cheese or sour cream, beans or chorizo, served with tortilla chips

Olanchano cheese

Montuca – corn husks with pork chops, raisins and spices

Plantain pancakes

Yucca is served with cabbage and lemon

Mantequilla – semi-sweet cream

Torrijas – "French" toast

Leche poleada – cornstarch, milk, egg custard used in desserts

Holidays and Special Occasions

Semana Santa – Holy Week before Easter; Good Friday – dried fish soup

Christmas night (Noche Buena) is celebrated December 24th by going to mass and then with a feast. – roasted pork, stuffed turkey or chicken; tamales; yucca; arroz con pollo – chicken and rice; Rompopo – eggnog; red grapes, apples; rice; Ponche infernal – warm Christmas drink; torrejas, a fried white bread and then boiled with cinnamon and brown sugar; nacatamales, similar to tamales, but in banana leaves with rice and meat

Horchata, rice drink

Patron saints days are celebrated in each town

Birthdays – candies and chocolates

Beverages

Coffee is drunk with every meal, and soft drinks at lunch or dinner. Other favorite drinks are horchata, made with milk, rice and cinnamon; licuados, milk with fruit; frescos, fruit sugar, and water; topogios, frozen fruit juice; and atol, made with corn, beans, and red food coloring.

Alcoholic beverages include aguardiente; guaro, made from sugar cane; and giffity, made on the islands with spices and herbs. Beers are brewed in Honduras including Barena, Port Royal, Salva Vida, and Imperial, plus others.

Did You Know?

Corn grinding stones were found at Copan dating back to 1300 BC.

The song "Sopa de Caracol" "Conch Soup", written by Hernan Chico Ramos and Juan Pilo Tejeda, was released in 1991 and made number one in the Billboard Top Latin Songs.

Hungary

Hungary, located in Central Europe, is bordered by Austria, Slovakia, Ukraine, Romania, Serbia, Croatia, and Slovenia. The Celts settled here c 450 BC, followed by the Romans 9AD to c 430 AD. The Kingdom of Hungary lasted for over 900 years, until the Ottomans occupied the country from 1541 to 1699. Hungary then became part of the Hapsburg Empire, later known as the Austro-Hungarian dual monarchy (1867-1918). After World War I Hungary lost 70% of its territory, and from 1947-1989 was a Communist country. Straddling the Danube River is the magnificent capital city of Budapest, and first known as Aquincum during Celtic times. In 1873 the towns of Buda, Pest and Obuda united to form Budapest. Hungarian is the official language.

Dining Etiquette

Guests are expected to arrive on time when asked out. A gift of liquor or chocolates makes a good present. If bringing flowers, do not bring chrysanthemums as they are for funerals only, or given in odd numbers. Please shake hands greeting and departing. Good friends will hug and kiss. A woman extends her hand first. Dinner is usually served about 7 without cocktails. Wine or tokay may be served. Elders are still very much respected and are given the seat of honor. Men always wear a coat and tie. The host and hostess will be seated at opposite ends of the table. Always wait for your hostess to pick up her fork before eating. Food is eaten continental style, fork in the left hand and knife in the right. Do not rest your elbows on the table. Do not add salt and pepper to your food before tasting. This is an insult to the hostess. Water is not served at meals and must be asked for. Fish is eaten with a fish knife and fork. When finished place your knife and fork parallel on your plate. The male guest of honor proposes the toast during the first course. The toast is "egesczegedre" "to your health". At the end of the meal dessert and/or cheese and fruit will be served. There may be coffee, but always espresso, though this is usually drunk in the morning or afternoon. The guest of honor will toast the host at the end of the meal to say "Thank you". Remember to leave wine in your glass if you do not wish it to be refilled. Do not clink glasses if drinking beer.

Cuisine

The cuisine has been influenced by the gypsies and the Ottoman Empire. The earliest records of Hungarian cooking date back to King Mathias (1458-90) and his wife Beatrice d'Este, daughter of the King of Naples, who imported cheese, onions, and garlic from Italy, and used sauces in cooking. Austrian, French, German, and Polish cooking also influenced the Hungarian style. The French introduced tortes and tarts, the Austrians rich pastries. The Turks introduced paprika, phyllo, stuffed peppers, eggplant, and coffee. Lard, teifol (sour cream), onions, bacon, cabbage. Potatoes, caraway seeds, and paprika (ground red peppers) are the main ingredients. Gypsy music played an important role at meals. Noodle desserts, cabbage, sauerkraut, stuffed peppers, cucumbers, strudels, and tortes are all Hungarian favorites. Goulash is made from chicken or beef and sweet or hot Hungarian paprika. Liptoli is a paprika cheese. Paprika bacon is made with salt bacon which is dipped into a paprika/water mixture, dried, then smoked. The modern Hungarian cuisine was developed by Karoly Gundel born (1883-1956) and the chef at the City Park Restaurant and author of many books.

The different regions of Hungary are known for their specialties:
Trandanubia is home to Lake Balaton which suppies fogas (pike-perch), a fish famous in Hungary; white wines; fruits, grapes, vegetables, mushrooms, aspics, sausages; river crabs; truffles; and chestnuts. In the north game, Paloc (joy cake) a braided yeast dough for weddings; and wines; (Puszta) - gray horned cattle whose beef is used in goulash
Alfold (The Great Hungarian Plain) grows rice, barley, wheat, corn, fruit – plums and apples, sheep, and vineyards.

Paprika Chicken

1 large onion, peeled and sliced in rings	1 green paprika pepper, sliced
1½ tbls. Hungarian paprika	1 tomato, sliced
1½ lb. chicken, cut up, washed and salted	4 tbls. oil

Saute the onion rings in a 3 quart pot until transparent. Remove the pot from the heat and add the paprika, chicken, half of the paprika pepper, half of the tomato. Put the pot on to heat. Cover with a lid and simmer slowly for 1½ hours. Occasionally turn the pieces over so that they evenly cook. If necessary add a small amount of water. When meat is tender transfer to a baking dish. Scrap the onion in the pan and add a little water to it and pour on the chicken. Garnish with remaining pepper and tomato. Cover with foil and keep warm until you are ready to serve.
Sour cream can be added to the gravy if you wish.
Spatzle is the usual side dish, but buttered noodles can also be served.
Recipe courtesy of the late Judith Hadnagy, Bonita Springs, Florida

Hungarian Specialties

Gulyas – goulash
Gulyasleves – goulash soup
Paprikas csirke – chicken paprika
Halazzle – fish poached and used in soup
Korozptt – cheese spread with cream cheese and caraway seeds
Vadas – game stew
Porkolt – pork, veal or beef goulash
Tokany – hearty pork stew
Sertesporkolt galuskaval – pork stew with spatzle
Csirke paprikas – chicken paprikash
Toltott kaposzta - stuffed cabbage
Kolozvari – layered cabbage

Lecso - tomato, green pepper, onion, bacon and paprika dish
Megy leves – cold cherrty soup
Ujhazi – noodle and chicken soup
Tesztak – dumplings
Nokedli - dumplings
Palacsinta – crepes with meat or dessert fillings
Palacsintak - pancakes
Langos – fried bread, often rubbed with garlic and topped with parmesan cheese
Retesk – strudels
Dobos torta – first served by Jozsef Dobos in Budapest in 1887, torte with chocolate filling

Rigo Jancsi – chocolate cake with chocolate whipped cream filling and a chocolate glaze
Almas pite – apple tart
Mezekalacs – honey cake
Szilvas gombac – plum dumplings
Gesztenyepure – chestnuts with sugar, rum and whipped cream

Gundel Dios Torta - gundel nut torte – walnut torte
Strudels are made with cheese, poppy seeds, jams, nuts, fruit, cabbage, mushrooms, chocolate, and even potatoes.

Hangover Soup

"Usually this soup is served the last day of the year from midnight until morning. Great if you have a hangover."

Serves 4-6

3 slices of bacon
1 small onion, chopped
1 tsp. Hungarian paprika
4 cups water
1 to 2 ham hockes
1 green pepper, sliced

1 tomato, sliced
1 16 oz. can sauerkraut, washed
1 tbls. all purpose flour
½ pint sour cream
½ lb. Polish sausage

Brown the bacon in a 3-quart pan with a tight fitting top. Remove the bacon and brown the onion in the bacon drippings until transparent. Add paprika, water, ham hocks, green pepper and tomato to the pot. Simmer 1 ½ hours, or until the meat is tender. Add the sauerkraut and cook for 20 minutes. Be careful not to overcook.
Combine flour and the sour cream and add to the soup mixture, along with the sausages. Debone the ham hocks and add to the soup. Bring to a boil. Serve hot with sour cream.
Recipe courtesy of the late Judith Hadnagy, Bonita Springs, Florida

Holidays and Special Occasions

Lentil or bean dishes are served on New Year's Day to bring wealth. Pork is eaten on New Year's Eve.
During Lent meat is forbidden. The day before Ash Wednesday is called "hushagyo kedd" "meat abandoning Tuesday." On Holy Saturday, the day before Easter takes baskets with kalacs, red eggs and salt to the church where it is blessed. For Easter eggs are painted, ham, lamb, poultry or rabbit, stuffed cabbage, beigli (sweet cake with walnuts or poppy seed are eaten.
August 20th, St. Stephen's Day, celebrates the harvest and St. Stephen, the first king of Hungary who converted its inhabitants to Christianity.
On December 31st, Szilveszter Day, superstitious Hungarians entertain and hope to see a better future. Part of the ritual at midnight is to take a key, melt a plumb and then pour the plumb through the keyhole into water, which hardens it. You then hold the hardened bit in the light against a wall. With that pattern a prediction can be made for the next year. Following this "conversational piece" much partying goes on until the wee hours when "Hangover Soup" is served.
During baptisms in Zala fomu, a gingerbread figure of a baby and braided bread are used.

Beverages

Hungarians are very proud of their agricultural heritage and production of good wines. Wine was first introduced in the 13th c by King Bela IV who imported French vines. Wine growing began in the Tokaj region (northeastern Hungary) by Walloons from Belgium in the 13th c. The best known was Takaji Aszu, a dessert wine. Egri Bikaver or Bull's Blood is from the town of Eger. During the 18th c under the Habsburgs the vineyards were replanted, mainly around Lake Balaton. The six wine regions are North-Transdanubia, Lake Balaton, South-Pannónia, Duna-region or Alföld, Upper-Hungary and Tokaj-Hegyalja. The Tokaji wines have been celebrated in poems, by composers, emperors and kings. Fruit brandies are producing including Palinka made from apricots or cherries and szilva from plums. Beers are brewed and the main brands are Borsodi, Soproni, Arany Ászok, Kõbányai, and Dreher. The liqueur Zwack Unicum has been made for over 150 years blended with 40 herbs. This bitter liqueur is drunk as an aperitif or after a meal to aid in digestion. Marc is a caramel honey drink

Did You Know?

Gulyas dates back to the Magyars who cooked and dried meat. They could then heat the meat with onions and water for a meal. It was not until many years later that paprika was added.

During the reign of King Stephen (1000-1038) monasteries were built and provided travelers with food. Landowners could also provide guests with food, similar to an early inn. The first mention of this dates to a deed of sale in 1279.

In 1414 Ferenc Eresztvenyi, the court chef of King Sigismund, was awarded a "patent of Nobility". He was born in the village of Nemesszakacsi, which means Noble Chef. The village provided royal chefs for more than two centuries.

One of the earliest Hungarian cookbooks is The Book of Mihaly Szent-Benedeki written in 1601. The first Hungarian language cookbook was printed in 1695 by Miklos Kiss de Misztotfalu.

A kocsma was originally a drinking place, but might also serve food. A csarda or place for travelers serving food and drink was first recorded in 1720. A kisvendeglo served food and perhaps drinks. During the summer one visited a zoldvendeglo, or garden restaurant.

During the time Hungary was dominated by Vienna, coffee houses or cukraszdak, devoted to the enjoyment of coffee, tea, pastries and other confections became popular. St. Sebastian Kaffee-Conditorei was the first pastry shop opened in the 18th c. The Gerbeaud cukraszda at Vorosmarty ter, in Budapest was founded in 1858 by Henrik Kugler.

Dobos Torta was first sold publicly in 1887, made by Jozcef C. Dobos, who owned a food specialty store in Budapest.

A poem written in 1823 by Ferenc Kolcsey became the national anthem and includes the love of wine in the country "For us let the golden grain Grow upon the fields of Kún, And let Nectar's silver rain Ripen grapes of Tokay soon."

Paprika, thought to be authentically Hungarian had its origins from the Spanish conquerors in the New World who brought back to Europe the capsicum chili seed pods. These were introduced into Hungary by the Ottoman Turks. Today the paprika peppers are grown on the Great Hungary Plain and readied for markets in Szeged. There are three varieties of paprika. The mildest is rozsa (noble rose) or sweet paprika. Feledes or half sweet paprika is a blend of sweet and hot paprika. Finally eros, or hot paprika has fire to it as the seeds and veins are ground in with the spice.

Iceland

Iceland lies 500 miles off the European continent and is comprised of rugged mountains, volcanoes, geysers, fjords, icebergs, glaciers, waterfalls, and other islands. The history of Iceland begins c 575 AD when St. Brendan of Ireland is thought to have sighted the island. The first settlements were made during the 8th and 9th c by Irish monks. The Norwegian Ingolfur Amarson arrived in 874 and founded Reykjavik, the capital. For many years following them the first sagas, or great stories, were written about Iceland. Iceland became part of Norway in 1262, and in 1387 under Danish rule. Iceland became an independent republic in 1944. The name means "Smoky Bay", the steam rising from geothermal springs. Icelandic is the official language.

Dining Etiquette

When entertained at home please bring flowers, candy, or whiskey. Please arrive promptly. Remove your shoes when entering a home. Please shake hands greeting and departing. Icelandic names are difficult as a son or daughter takes the father's first name and adds son or dottir. Women keep their natal surnames. Lunch is eaten around noon, and dinner 7-8 pm. When one enters a home, or is seated at the table the hostess says "Gerdu svo vel", the equivalent of "Please". The continental style of eating is used, fork in the left hand, knife in the right. When thanking the hostess please say "Takk fyrir mig". The toast is "Skal". Family is still very important with a matriarchal society.

Cuisine

The Icelanders are hardy people and their cooking still resembles what their ancestors might have indulged in. Fish – salmon from the rivers, cod, halibut, plaice, herring, haddock, arctic char, and trout, are smoked, dried, boiled, pickled or salted. Lamb is often pickled and served with red cabbage and sugar potatoes. Potatoes, usually boiled, are served with most meals. Skyr, a skimmed milk curd with whipped cream, is a favorite dessert. Surmjolk, soured milk with brown sugar is eaten for breakfast. Rye bread and flatkokur – rye pancakes are made from locally grown rye. Hverabraud, a sweet bread, is baked in the ground. Many berries and wild mushrooms grow in abundance. Iceland is self-sufficient in meat, fish, and dairy products. As an island nation it has survived for over a thousand years. Even the cow herds are descended from cows brought by the Vikings in 874 AD. Greenhouses are now used to grow vegetables and fruit.

Lamb Shanks

Serves 4

4 lamb shanks	½ lb. mushrooms, halved
2 tbls. flour	1 cup white wine
1 tbls. olive oil	½ -1 pint lamb or chicken stock
1 tbls. butter	1-2 branches fresh sage
6 plum tomatoes	Salt
4 shallots, chopped	Fresh ground pepper
2-3 carrots, sliced	4-6 cloves garlic, minced
1-2 stalks celery, chopped	½ cup fresh parsley
Zest of 1 lemon	

Preheat oven to 300° F

Pierce each tomato and drop in boiling water for 30 seconds. Quickly transfer to cold water. Peel and slice the tomatoes. Arrange in ovenproof dish.

Place the lamb shanks and flour in a plastic bag and shake, so shanks are evenly coated.

Melt the oil and butter in a skillet. Saute shanks until browned. Salt and pepper to taste. Remove shanks.

In skillet sauté the carrots, celery and shallots until tender. Add the mushrooms. Deglaze the pan with white wine and stock.

Put the shanks on the tomatoes, and pour the vegetables and stock on top. Sprinkle with sage.

Bake for 1½ - 2 hours, basting with stock. When 20 minutes are left sprinkle with garlic, parsley and zest.

Recipe courtesy of Chef Siggi Hall and the Embassy of Iceland, Washington, DC

Specialties

Svid – boiled brains
Hakarl – fermented shark
Hangikjot - smoked lamb
Salted cod
Graflax – raw salmon with herbs
Grilled fish or lamb
Thorramatur - preserved foods usually salted, dried or smoked eaten during the winter months

laufabrauð - deep-fried bread
kleinur - Icelandic doughnut
Brauðsúpa - bread soup
Flatbraud – flatbread
Fjallagrasamjolk – moss milk
Eggjamjólk - Egg soup
Síldarsalat - Herring salad

Holidays and Special Occasions

Thorrablot – in February, dates from pagan times. Hakarl (rotten shark); singed sheep's head with mashed turnips; pickled ram's testicles; and blodmore (blood pudding); Brennivin (carraway seed flavored drink, drunk very cold, and called the "Black Death". Beware!

Bolludagur – Monday before Shrove Tuesday – bollur (pastry with cream)

Sprengidagur – Shrove Tuesday "Explosion Day – salt lamb and split peas
Ash Wednesday – children collect money for sweets
Sun Coffee – served when the sun's rays again appear after the long winter
Christmas Eve – smoked lamb
Christmas and New Year's - hangikjot (sheepshead with potatoes, white sauce and peas); vinarterta – seven layer cake with fillings of apricots, prunes, vanilla, cardamom

Beverages

Brennivin, meaning "black death" is a bitter schnapps made from fermented potato pulp and caraway seeds and angelica. Reyka vodka is produced with spring water that runs through a lava field. Topas is a sweet herb liqueur. Isafold gin is produced by the Olgeroin Brewery in Reykavik. Other drinks are Birkir, a snaps and Bjork, a liqueur; and Fjallagrasa Icelandic Schnapps, made from moss and is considered medicinal in healing sore throats, viruses, and bacteria. Until 1989 beer was banned in Iceland but today Viking Gold and other brands are brewed.

Did You Know?

The Vikings were thought to consume 10-12 pints of mead a day!
Prohibition lasted from 1915-89. A ban was lifted on wine in 1021 and strong beer in 1989.
Midsandur, located northeast of Reykjavik was the site of the last whaling station in Iceland.
The Westman Islands' economy is based on fishing. The salmon and trout season is from June to September.

India

The Republic of India dominates the south Asian continent, and is the seventh largest country in the world. It is bordered to the northeast by China, Bangladesh, Nepal, and Bhutan; the northwest Pakistan; the east the Bay of Bengal; the south Sri Lanka; and the west the Arabian Sea. The country contains the high peaks of the Himalayas, the fertile Ganetic Plain, and the rest of the peninsula the Deccan Plateau. The Indus Valley civilization dates back over 5000 years to the Harappas. Hinduism was founded c 1500 BC. From the 7-5th c BC kingdoms developed in the Ganges Plain. In 540 BC Mahavira founded Jainism and in 566 BC Buddha Buddhism. In the 4th c AD the north was united under the Gupta dynasty. The Moguls invaded the country 1506-1707. Vasco de Gama, the Portuguese explorer, arrived in Calcutta in 1498. The British East India Company was founded in Bombay in 1600. In 1857 all of India came under the British Crown. In 1947 India and Pakistan became independent countries. The capital New Delhi was designed in the 1920s by Sir Edward Lytyens. English and Hindi are the official languages with over 300 languages spoken in this vast country.

Dining Etiquette

Please be punctual when invited for a meal. Indians are very warm and friendly, and you may receive many invitations for hospitality. Please remove your shoes on entering a home. Please shake hands greeting and departing, or with folded hands (Namaste). Women do not usually shake hands, and men may not offer hands to a woman. When greeting a superior or to show respect, a slight bow can be used. Drinks will be offered, probably beer and whisky along with a snack, except in Muslim homes where tea is served. You may be seated at a table for the meal, or on cushions where you will cross-legged. In some cases men and women may be separated. Never enter a kitchen. Meals will be served with all courses on the table, or separately on silver or brass trays. Always wash your hands before eating. The hostess will serve the food to the guests and men first, followed by the women. Food is eaten with the right hand. A fork, fingers, or bread can also be utilized. Watch how the hostess eats. Food is passed with the right hand. Men may share food from their own plate. For Hindus food is only eaten with those in their caste or religion. At the end of the meal thank-you's are not usually said, but please reciprocate the meal. Never leave in a group of three as it is considered bad luck. Please drink bottled water, wash and peel all vegetables and fruit. If you are an overnight guest in a home, do tip the servants. The toast is "cheers" or "To your health". The host initiates toasting and the guest of honor reciprocates.

Family is important, as are obedience, faithfulness, and sincerity. A nod of the head means a person has heard you. Shaking the head from side to side means "Yes". Avoid direct eye contact, especially with someone of the opposite sex. Lowering one's head when listening is considered respectful. Never touch another person's head. To beckon someone, do so with the palm down.

Because of the sacredness of cattle, leather products are never given as gifts to Hindus. The same is true of pigskin for Muslims. When entertained at home please bring pastries, fruit, candies, flowers which are a sign of prosperity, especially marigolds, jasmine and roses. If children are present please bring gifts for them. Guests when greeted may be adorned with a garland of flowers, which should be removed and held in the hand as a sign of humility.

Cuisine

India is such a vast country with numerous religions, ethnic groups, culinary styles it is difficult to define one cuisine, or even begin to cover the whole country. Therefore I have picked out some main regions to highlight. Some of the spicy foods are cooled with cucumbers, tomatoes, and yogurt.

Kolkata (Calcutta) (Bengal) is India's center for cloth, silk, lacquer, rice, betel nuts, tobacco, tea, and jute. Cochin is India's major port in the southwest and one of the oldest European settlements, founded by Vasco de Gama in 1500, and who is buried here. Formerly it had been a Jewish settlement as early as the 6th c BC. Fishing, rope, spices, ginger, peppers, and tropical fruits are exported from here. The state of Orissa is known for cashews, rice, mangoes, sugar cane, jute, casarina, teak, sandal and bamboo forests. The Phoenicians once traded with Kerala for spices sandal wood, and ivory. Later it was a trading post for the Chinese, then settled as the Dutch East India Company in 1602, and the British East India Company in 1795. Even today it is known for tea, timber, rubber, cashews, teak, palm, spices – peppers, cardamom, ginger, and turmeric. Alleppey is known for carpets, black pepper, and fishing. Goa founded in 1510 on the Arabian Sea is a blend of Portuguese and Indian cultures. From here spices, silks, pearls, and porcelains were shipped to Europe.

Northwest – influence of Persian, Turkish and Moghul cooking, use of ginger, lemon, turmeric, and saffron. Tandoori cooking makes use of marinated meats (in yogurt, turmeric, and spices) baked in hot clay ovens.

Kashmir – sticky rice; meat, chicken, fish, vegetables, mutton, turnips; rista – mutton meatballs; rojan josh –red curry; lamb kebabs, and apples

Lucknow – kebabs, lamb, fish, beef, chicken, roomali roti bread

West Coast (Bombay and Goa) - vindaloo (from the Portuguese "vinegar") – spicy curries using ginger, garlic, cumin, chilies, peppercorns, cloves, mustard, cinnamon, and usually contains tomatoes. Fish, lamb, lentils, yogurt and rice are part of the diet. Calderirada – fish stew; rabbit cabidela; pork vindaloos. Konkan – coconut, fish, duck, mutton, kombdi vade – chicken curry with dumplings; sol kadhi – drink of kokum fruit and coconut milk

Northeast (Bengal) – use of mustard oil; coriander; ginger; seafood – prawns, and freshwater fish; jackfruit; paanch phoron – five spice mix; yogurt; poppy seeds; mishit doi – yogurt with vanilla or jiggery; paan – shredded coconut and rose petal preserve wrapped in a betel leaf; bananas; pumpkins; British influence; and chutneys

Arunachal Pradesh – Apatani salt (a black powder pressed from a local grass); pike pilla (pork stew); rice paddies; fresh water fish; sudu (fish steamed in a hollow bamboo stalk and placed over open coals); rice beer and rice liquor;

Central India (mainly Madhya Pradesh) – okra, eggplant, green beans, sesame oil, spinach, yogurt, coriander, lentils, sanwal (fresh water fish), and biryanis (spiced rice with chicken or meat)

South – mainly vegetarian. Use of green herbs (dill, basil, mint, sorrel, and oregano). The Bengal region uses black mustard seed and mustard oil. The word for mustard in Assam and Bengal is rye. Madras curries are very spicy. Bengal - fish – carp, catfish, prawn, dried fish; rice, mung beans, red lentils, mango. Temil Nadu – rice flavored with coconut or lemon; dosas – thin pancakes; idlis – steamed dumplings; vada – fried fritters. Chettinid – chicken, mutton; paniyaram – fried rice flour pancakes

Kerala – Syrian influence with chicken and potato stews with cinnamon, green chilies, lime juice; meen molee – fish stew with spices; coconuts; dosas – pancake of ground rice and urad dhal and accompanied by coconut curry and sambar, a vegetable stew; thoren – vegetable stir-fry with shredded coconut and mustard seeds; iddyappam, rice noodles; and toddy, a coconut drink; rasam, a peppery soup; idlies, rice cakes; oroti, rice powder, cumin and coconut pancakes; appams – rice flour pancakes; puttu – steamed rice flour with grated coconut; wadas, ground lentil fritters; parottas, round breads

Eastern India – machher jhol (curries rice), loochi (bread), malai (curry with prawns and coconut)

Andhra Pradessh – kabobs, pulao (rice pilaf), haleem (wheat with meat and onions), nahai (stewed lamb trotters), kulcha (bread cakes)

North (Delhi) – lamb, poultry, ghee (clarified butter), tandoori, naan (bread), karma (lamb and cashew curry), pulao, curries, dahls (lentils). chilies, pork

Venison Korma

3 venison chops (6-7 oz)	1 medium onion, sliced
1 tbls. ghee (clarified butter)	Oil to fry
1" piece cinnamon	1 cup yogurt
4 cloves	¼ tsp. garam masala powder
1 bayleaf	¼ tsp. nutmeg powder
2 cardamom	½ tsp. saffron
4 cloves garlic, peeled	Salt to taste
1" piece ginger, sliced	¼ cup rice
¼ tsp. red chili powder (deghi mirch)	1 tsp. butter
1 tbls. almond	1 tsp. shredded almonds

Heat oil, fry the onions till golden. Strain the oil.
Blend the onions, almond with yogurt to make a fine paste. Make ginger – garlic paste.
Soak the rice.
Dissolve the half saffron in warm water & half in warm butter.
Toast the shredded almonds.
Heat the ghee, fry cinnamon, clove, bayleaf & cardamom.
Add ginger garlic paste, fry little. Add chili powder. Add the onion- almond paste. Cook for 10 - 15 minutes.
Add both the powders, saffron & salt.
Boil the water, put in the rice & cook till soft. Drain out the water.
Mix the rice with saffron butter.
Heat the pan, put little oil, grill the chops both sides for few minutes till the blood dries up.
Place the chops on the plate, pour over the sauce. Make a mould of rice & demould on to the plate near top left to the chops. Garnish with toasted almonds.

Tawa Baigan

Serves 4

Eggplant Marinade

2 Holland eggplant
6 cloves garlic
4 tbls. olive oil

1 tsp. crushed black pepper
Salt to taste

In a bowl, mix the olive oil, chopped garlic, black pepper and salt, keep aside.
Cut the eggplant into 5mm thick round slices, mix in the marinade and keep aside.

Potato Mixture

1 tbls canola oil
¼ tsp. cumin seeds
1 oz. chopped red onion
1 tsp. chopped ginger
¼ tsp. chopped Thai green chili
½ tsp. red chili powder

½ tsp. turmeric powder
2 medium Idaho potatoes
½ tsp. Chaat Masala
1 tbls. lemon juice
Salt to taste

Boil and grate the potatoes and keep aside.
Heat the oil in a sauté pan, add the cumin seeds and let them crackle. Sauté the onions till soft.
Add the ginger, green chilies along with the tomatoes and turmeric powder.
Cook till the tomatoes are mashed, add the chili powder and cook a little more. Mix in the grated potatoes along with the chaat masala and lemon juice. Add salt to taste. Keep aside.

Sauce

2 oz. Jaggery
¼ tsp. red chili flakes
½ cup coconut milk

1 oz chopped peanuts
½ tsp. lemon juice
Salt to taste

Melt the jaggery in a sauce pan over a low flame.
Add the red chili flakes, coconut milk and bring to a boil.
Finish off with lemon juice, salt and chopped peanuts.

To Assemble

Cook the eggplant slices on a hot flat griddle on both sides till golden brown.
Heat the spiced potato mix separately
Sandwich the eggplant slices (at least 4 slices to a portion) with the potato mix.
Drizzle the warm jaggery and peanut sauce over the eggplant.
Garnish with chopped cilantro.
Recipe courtesy of Rasika, Washington, DC

Indian Specialies

Thalis – several small dishes

Kitchari – grain, usually long-grain white rice and legume (yellow moong dal), and other vegetable dish with spices that is made throughout India. The name comes from the Hindi "a mess" or "all mixed up".

Sabudana kitchari – made with tapioca and served on fast days

Murg – chicken; murg kari (curried chicken)

Chapati – similar to a tortilla, fried –southern India

Channa masala – chickpea curry

Breads –naan, roti – whole wheat bread, puri, parathas, pappadam, luccis

Samovar- used to brew green tea – northern India, Kashmir

Ghee – clarified butter

Pulau – pilaf, made from rice with spices, meat, poultry, or seafood

Falooda – drink using rose syrup, vermicelli and tapioca seeds

Lassi – Drink from yogurt with sugar, herbs or spices

Samosas - fried dough with meat orvegetables

Dahi – yogurt

Kofta – ground meatballs

Pongal – sweet rice dish served during Pongal (rice) festival with mustard seed, spices and cashews

Rayta – yogurt with raw or cooked vegetables, herbs and spices

Chaat – snack of chickpeas, diced potato, fruit, meat, or vegetables, and chaat masala

Tandoor – clay oven

Rice – red (color from bran wrapping around kernel), white, puffed rice

Karanjias – pastries with grated coconut and sugar

Rangoli – decorative pattern using beans, rice, lentils, chick-peas and wheat – used on feast day of Ganesha

Thali – tray to serve food, carefully arranged

Korma – curried lamb

Kabab – grilled skewered meats and vegetables

Phuchkas – (Kolkata) – spicy potatoes and fried bread with tamarind water

Biryani – rice dish that can be made with lamb, prawns, or many other combinations

Parantha – sweet breads

Momos –steamed dumplings with chicken and vegetables

Dal – term for lentils, beans, or split peas

Pappadams – lentil wafers

Pachadi – yogurt salad

Pappyasam – sweet pudding

Rasam – dahl and lentil soup

Palak paneer –fresh cheese and spinach

Holidays and Special Occasions

Shraaddam – anniversary of a death with an elaborate feast

Spring and harvest festivals occur between January and March with dancing, feasting and often fireworks.

Pongal Rice Harvest – cattle are bathed and thanks is given for their milk. Ven Pongal is a rice and lentil dish with cashews, and spices. Sarkarai Pongal is made from sweet rice, fried lentils, cashews, molasses, raisins, coconut, and spices.

Divali is celebrated in November on the darkest night of the year, and lights are everywhere. For Hindi it is the beginning of the New Year. Sweets are sent to friends, neighbors, and almost everyone!

Holi – colored waters and powders are thrown on people to mark the triumph of Lord Krishna over Holika

Dasehra – 10 day celebration of the triumph of Prince Rama over the monster Ravana with lots of dishes, beginning with *payasam* a sweet with rice, followed by *thovey* a green vegetable with masala. Other dishes might be *pachadi* yogurt with coconut and spices; *rasam* spicy lentil soup; *modak* dumplings with coconut and molasses; and *chitranna* rice with lime and saffron.

Weddings and festivals – lamb biryani

Auspicious occasions – colored powder used to make rangoli to decorate thresholds

Beverages

The consumption of tea in India dates back thousands of years and was first recorded in the *Ramayana* (750-500 BC). Jan Huyghen van Linschoten, a Dutchman, noted in 1598 that the Indians drank Assam tea and also used it as a vegetable with garlic and oil. During the 1820s the British East India Company produced large amounts of tea in Assam. This black tea is familiar to many as English Breakfast, Irish Breakfast or Scottish Breakfast tea. Assam is the largest producer of tea in the world. Darjeeling tea is considered the finest of black teas. Tea was first planted here in 1841 by Dr. Campbell, a civil surgeon in the Indian Medical Service, who had brought the seeds from China. One of the world's most expensive teas comes from Makaibari Tea Estate in Darjeeling.

Coffee plantations are part of the landscape in Coorg (Kodagu), planted by the British. After independence the British sold the plantations to the Kodavas, the original inhabitants of the regions and other southern Indians. The two main varieties of coffee grown are Arabica and robusta. Cardamon and oranges are also grown here.

The earliest drinks were made from fuit, sugar cane, jaggeri, or honey. Rice beer was an early drink, and later Madhuparka, a honey drink given to priests, suitors in asking for a wife, or a woman five months pregnant. Wine has been produced for thousands of years, probably introduced by the Persians in the 4th millennium BC. Wine made from rice or millet have been made for centuries. Goa improved wine making under the Portuguese and produces sweet wines. The British encouraged wines production and vineyards were planted in the Baramati, Kashmir and Surat regions. The phylloxera epidemic and religious beliefs hindered the growth of the wine industry until the early 1980s with the founding of Chateau Indage in the state of Maharashtra. Other wine regions are in Karnataka (Bangelore- Blue grape) and Himachal Pradesh.

Beer is brewed in Hyderabad and Calcutta. Mohan Meakin Brewery in Lucknow was India's first commercial brewery. Vodka, rum and whiskies are also produced. Feni is a liquor made from cashew nuts; toddy from coconut palm flower; and Arak, a distilled rice liquor. No alcoholic beverages are permitted in some of India's states. Vegetarian restaurants do not serve liquor. The English learned to drink "punch", a word from Sanskrit that means "fire". Punch contains alcohol, tea, lemon juice, water, sugar or honey.

Did You Know?

Cucumbers have been grown in the northwest for over 3,000 years.

The Indians have grown rice and citrus fruits for thousands of years. Rice is the symbol of fecundity

In the 2nd millennium BC the Aryan brought in cattle, and also raised goats, horses, sheep and water buffalo for food. The cow is sacred to the Hindi and no part of it may be eaten. Water buffalo is eaten instead. Muslims eat no pork or shellfish. Most Buddhists ate vegetarians, but may eat lamb or goat.

By the 1st millennium BC many foods were thought to be unclean. They could be purified by pouring ghi, water, or curds over them. Hygiene was very important. Leaves were used as plates, so they could easily be thrown away.

Beginning in the 1st c AD the Code of Manu specified food measurements, recipes and other codes of conduct for the Hindi. Rules were set on how much one should eat – 32 spoonfuls at a meal, and a wife was to serve her husband first.

Wine was even mentioned in the Kama Sutra

Curries from "kari" "sauce" are made of spices such as turmeric, cumin, ginger, paprika, cayenne, and saffron, Garam Masala "mix of spices" are used for the curry sauces. Curries can be *white* made with coconut milk; *green*, coriander and mint; dark brown from spices; brown with onions, garlic, and spices.

Sugar cane was introduced in the 5th c BC.

India is the largest producer and exporter of tea in the world.

India produces 60% of the world's mangoes.

The Jagannath Temple's kitchen feeds over 10,000 daily, and at least 25,000 during festivals.

Salt is still a government monopoly. In 1930 Gandhi marched to Dandi for the sea salt protest.

Jains are strictly vegetarians and will not eat meat, onions, garlic, and root vegetables.

Saffron is made from crocus blossoms, 75,000 to make one pound!

Kashmir is known for its elaborate wedding feasts .Wazas, wedding chefs, cook 36 course meals including lamb, mutton, and chicken cooked over open fires;

Kochi (Cochin) has been the capital of the spice trade for over 1500 years.

Urdu, the Moslem Indian language, has long used the word chiz for cheese, meaning thing from which we get "big cheese".

Chutneys can be made from various fruit and vegetables, and be very spicy or quite mild. Major Grey's Chutney was created in the 19th c by a British officer stationed in India, and uses mangoes as its base.

When you enter a temple you may be given saffron, water from the Ganges, and Prasad, food from the lord. Please accept all of these.

Indonesia

The Republic of Indonesia is the world's largest archipelago, made up of more than 17,000 islands, extending along the equator from the mainland of Asia to Australia, spanning over 3,000 miles. The main islands are Java, Sulawesi, Kalimantan, Sumatra and Irian Jaya. The 1,266,905 sq. miles are made up of mountains, jungles, volcanoes, rich soil, and coral reefs. Eugene DuBois discovered Java Man in 1891 in Trinil, and is thought to date back 250,000 years. People were known to have inhabited the islands 40,000 years ago. Approximately three thousand years ago the Dongson culture brought rice, domesticated animals, used copper and bronze. Wet rice cultivation and adat (the law of communities) came into prominence. Marco Polo visited the area in 1292 and Kublai Khan attacked in 1293, the year the Majapahit Kingdom was founded. The Portuguese arrived in 1512, influencing the music, language, introducing tobacco and shipbuilding. The Portuguese were followed by the English, Dutch, and Spanish. The Japanese invaded in 1942. Indonesia proclaimed its independence from the Dutch in 1945. The capital, Jakarta "Ibu Kota" or "Mother City" was founded on the Ciliwung River in 1619, even though it may date from c 500 AD. The official language, Bahasa Indonesia, is a combination of Malay, Sandskrit, and Arabic. Almost 600 dialects and other languages are spoken.

Dining Etiquette

Please be punctual when invited for a meal. Being invited to a home is a privilege. Please bring a gift from your country, flowers or a cake to be served later. Receive a gift with the right hand. Men and women may be separated. Coffee, tea, fruit drinks, or beer are served with the meal. Before a meal "Silahkan Minum" "Please begin" is said. Food is eaten with the right hand using a fork and spoon. Watch what the hostess uses. Wait for the host to begin. Always accept food with your right hand. Take a small amount, then a second helping if you wish. Conversation may be non-existent until the end of the meal. If you do not wish more food, leave some food on your plate. Breakfast is a light meal consisting of nasi goring; lunch and dinner full meals.

Men shake hands and bow heads slightly. Elders are well respected and are greeted with a bow. Stand when elders enter a room, let them go first, introduce them first, and hold doors for them. Names are usually one word, though in Sumatra two names or a clan name may be used. When seated keep your feet together on the floor, and do not point the sole of your shoe at anyone. Never show anger, displeasure, yawn, or raise your voice. Face is important. Malu, to make someone lose face, reaches beyond that person to his family and business. Do not touch another person's head as it is considered the highest part of the body and sacred. Men may touch or hold hands with each other as a display of friendship. Do not use red ink in correspondence. When summoning someone, do so with the palm down and wiggling all fingers. A clenched fist is a sign of fertility. Don't stare at someone or look someone directly in the eye.

Gado-Gado (Vegetables with Peanut and Coconut Sauce)

Serves 6-8

4 small potatoes, cubed
1 lb. fresh baby spinach
1 lb. green beans
1 lb. fresh bean sprouts

1 large cucumber, peeled and sliced
2 hard-boiled eggs, sliced

Boil the potatoes in water until just tender.
Steam or boil the beans.
Steam the spinach.
All vegetables should be just tender.
To serve, place the spinach on a platter. Arrange the the potatoes, green beans, bean sprouts, and eggs on top and around the spinach. Line the edges of the plate with the cucumber.
Serve the sauce over the vegetables.
Other vegetables such as cabbage or lettuce can be substituted for the spinach, carrots and vegetables can be used.
Tamarind water can be added to the sauce or the vegetables.

Sauce

½ cup finely chopped onion
1 tbls. oil
1-2 cloves garlic, finely chopped
2 cups water
1 tsp. shrimp paste
2 tsp. brown sugar
1 tsp. lemon juice

1 tsp. soy sauce
¼ tsp. dried red pepper, or 1 tbls. fresh chopped hot chili
½ tsp. fresh grated ginger
½ cup peanut butter
½ cup finely chopped peanuts
2 cups coconut milk

Heat the oil in a skillet and sautee the onion. Stir in garlic. Add the water and then stir in shrimp paste. Stir in the rest of the ingredients, except coconut milk. Add coconut milk and simmer 15 minutes.

Cuisine

Indonesia's rich history in the spice trade lends itself to an interesting array of national dishes and customs. Most dishes are hot and spicy, and served around rice. Indonesian cuisine makes excellent use of native vegetables, fruit, and seafood that are so abundant. The most common ingredients are bamboo, papaya, palm oil, rice, coconut, tea, sugar, coffee, cassava (tapioca), chilies, ginger, peanuts, beans and lentils. Spices include lemon grass, lais, cardimon, tamarind, mace, cloves, nutmeg, mace, peppers, and turmeric. The food is a mix of Indian (curries), Chinese (stir-fried), Arabic (spices), and each island has its own cooking methods and cuisine.

Indonesian Specialties

Sambal – hot chili sauces. Padang and West Sumatra make very hot sambals. Central Java sweeter; and East Java salty and hot
Satay – grilled meat or fish dipped in sauces
Sayur lodeh – vegetable coconut stew
Rijsttafel – rice table with many dishes and condiments developed by the Dutch
Prasmanan – buffet of many dishes
Nasi goring – fried rice
Soto –coconut soup
Rending – beef in coconut milk
Kekap – hot soybean sauce
Gado – gado – steamed salad with peanut sauce
Gulai – curry
Rendang – small bits of beef in a coconut and spice sauce
Tahu – soybean cake
Tempe – fermented soybeans that are highly nutritious and can be fried, or used in a number of dishes. Tempe was originally from Java
Sate – grilled skewered meat
Tea – manis (with sugar) or pahit (no sugar)
Coffee is thick with grounds in the bottom
Fish will be served salted and dried, fresh, smoked, or as a paste
Tropical fruits include mangoes, pineapples, papayas, bananas, rambutan, mangosteen, and durian
Desserts:
Ketan – rice pudding with coconut milk and sugar syrup
Coconut cakes; ice cream; fried bananas
Lentil pastis
Longtong – rice in banana leaves
Bujang didaialum selimaut "bachelor wrapped in a blanket" – a pancake wrapped around palm sugar and coconut
Dodol – sweet made from coconut milk, palm sugar and glutinous rice

Regional Specialties

N. Sumatra – palm oil, coffee
Sumatra – pepper, nutmeg, cloves
Maluku- fish, cloves
East Java – salt, grapes, mangoes, coffee, cattle, sheep, goats, coconut
Madura – salt, cattle, fishing, poultry, goats, spices, pineapples, cassava, and taro
Cirebon (West Java) – rice, sugar, pepper, dried and processed shrimp
Central Java – cloves

Holidays and Special Occasions

Asjura – bubur asjura – rice porridge with peanuts, eggs and beans
Tumpeng – rice cone or "holy mountain" offered by Muslims which is eaten by men, but cannot be touched by women
Bebanten is a temple food offering. Women carry on their heads, then blessed and placed at the foot of the priests. It is made up of flowers, cakes, fruit, sweets, and later consumed.
The tumpeng, rice cone or holy mountain, is used by the Muslims on holy days. Originally ceremonial, it can now be eaten by men.
Weddings and funerals are very formal occasions and vary from island to island.

Beverages

Beer was first introduced by Heineken. Other drinks are tuak – palm wine; brem – wine made from glutinous rice and coconut milk; badeh – from fermented rice; and arak – a rice spirit. Sap from coconut trees can be allowed to ferment to produce a strong wine. Cendol is a drink made from coconut milk and sweet bean bits. Coconut water is the juice that runs out of the coconut and coconut milk is made from shredded coconut. Drunkenness is frowned upon.

Did You Know?

The United East India Company was founded in 1602. Jsn Pieterzoon Coen was to monopolize the spice trade. Unfortunately almost native Indonesians were killed or forced into slavery to harvest cloves and nutmeg, and later the Dutch were to destroy much of the Indonesian culture! The Dutch introduced corn in the 17th c in Madura. In 1830 the Dutch forced the Culture System of agriculture on the people, using forced labor to raise indigo, coffee, and rice. In 1870 the Agrarian Law was passed, and rubber, tea, cinchona, and sugar were introduced. Until World War II Indonesia supplied most of the world's quinine, pepper, rubber, coconut, tea, coffee, sugar, and oil.
The largest restaurant in the world is the Jalan Malioboro in Yogyakarta.
 The palmetto cabbage or hearts of palm when cut out of a tree kills the tree.
The coconut received its name from the Spanish "coco" or "clown" because of its three black spots or eyes.
Women in Bali are forbidden to touch a coconut tree. Clove trees blossom only every 2-4 years.
Mace is the red covering of the nutmeg fruit. Nutmeg comes from a black shell.
Chilies used in so much of the cooking came originally from the West Indies.
Rice is revered.
Clove trees only blossom every two to four years.
When the palmetto cabbage or hearts are cut out of the tree, the tree is killed.
Chew betel nuts if you want bloody looking lips!
Peppercorns were once so valuable they were used as currency in Germany and England.
Coconut is from "coco" the Spanish word for clown, because of the three spots or eyes on the coconut. Brown coconuts are the ones that have dropped and dried out. Monkeys can be trained to fetch the ripe ones. Women in Bali are forbidden to touch coconut trees.

Iran

Iran is bordered on the north by Armenia, Azerbaijan, Turkmenistan, the Caspian Sea; Kazakhstan and Russia; to the east by Afghanistan and Pakistan, the south by the Persian Gulf and the Gulf of Oman, the west by Iraq and on the northwest by Turkey. The Elamite kingdom dates back to 2800 BC. In 625 BC the Medes unified Iran as an empire, followed by the Achaemenid, the Hellenic Seleucid, the Parthians, and the Sassanids. The Muslims arrived in 651 AD. In 1501 the Safavid dynasty promoted Islam as the official religion. The first parliament was founded in 1906, and in 1979 Iran became an Islamic Republic. Tehran, the capital, once known as Ray, was a village in the 9th c, and probably dates back further than that. The official language is Persian (Farsi), but there are also many other languages and dialects spoken.

Dining Etiquette

Please arrive punctually when for a meal. Please bring flowers or a flowering plant, sweets, or some other elegantly wrapped gift. Gifts are not usually opened when received. If when entering a home the host(ess) is not wearing shoes, please remove yours or remove them in the carpeted areas. Dress conversantly. Shake hands greeting and departing. Women will extend their hand first to a gentleman. Men may kiss men they know, and women kiss female acquaintances A slight bow or nod of the head is a sign of respect. Please stand when an older person or another person enters a room. Women socialize separately from men.

Please accept drinks and food when offered. Most meals are served at a table which is covered with a tablecloth (sofreh) or spread out on a Persian carpet. Please wait to be told where you may sit. The main dishes will be placed in the center with side dishes (mokhalafat) near those dining. Always eat with your right hand. Most food is eaten with a spoon or fork, though a knife may be offered. If there is a knife and fork, eat continental style with the fork in the left hand and knife in the right. Leave some food on your plate when finished, although you may be offered seconds. When passing food or objects please pass with both hands. Alcohol consumption and pork are forbidden by the Muslims. During Ramadan Muslims go without food from sunrise to sunset. During the evenings there are large meals with families and friends.

Iranians are very family oriented. Friendship is extremely important. There is respect for elders who are cared for by their family. Tarof defines social behavior through politeness and hospitality, and is unqiue to Persia. Never point the soles of your feet at another person. Do not cross your legs when seated. Men do not maintain eye contact with women, unless a family member.

Fresh Herb Kuku

"This kuku brings back golden memories of my childhood in Iran. On the eve of the Persian New Year, our kitchen would be buzzing with activity as my mother and other members of the family were busy preparing kuku sabzi, an essential dish for the New Year feast. The tantalizing aroma of the herbs floating around the house would drive us children crazy with the desire to have some of the kuku. A *kuku* is a baked omelet somewhat similar to an Italian *frittata* or an Arab *eggah;* it is thick and rather fluffy, and stuffed with herbs, vegetables, or meat. It may be eaten hot or cold — it keeps well in the refrigerator for two or three days — as an appetizer, side dish, or light main dish with yogurt or salad and bread. *Kukus* are traditionally made on the stovetop, but my oven version is much simpler. A fresh herb *kuku* such as this one is a traditional New Year's dish in Iran. The green herbs symbolize rebirth, and the eggs, fertility and happiness for the year to come.

½ cup vegetable oil, butter, or ghee
5 eggs
1 teaspoon baking powder
2 teaspoons Persian spice mix *(advieh)* (see Tips, below)
1 teaspoon salt
1 teaspoon freshly ground black pepper
2 cloves garlic, peeled and crushed

1 cup chopped fresh garlic, chives, or leeks
1 cup chopped fresh parsley
1 cup chopped fresh coriander (cilantro)
1 cup chopped fresh dill
1 tablespoon all-purpose flour
1 tablespoon dried fenugreek or 2 tablespoons dried barberries, cleaned (optional)

Preheat oven to 350°F. Pour the oil into an 8-inch baking dish lined with parchment paper.

Break the eggs into a large bowl. Add the baking powder, *advieh,* salt, and pepper. Lightly beat in the garlic, chopped herbs, flour, and fenugreek. Adjust seasoning.

Pour the egg mixture into the dish and bake uncovered for 45 to 50 minutes, until the edge is golden brown.

Serve the *kuku* from the baking dish, or unmold it by loosening the edge with a knife and inverting the dish onto a serving platter. Remove the parchment paper. *NUSH-E JAN!*

Advieh, a mix of ground cinnamon, cardamom, and cumin and dried rose petals •Dried barberries, which add a sour flavor to many Persian dishes, are available online at www.sadaf.com. "I like to use the dried fenugreek leaves in the batter, and also some red barberries on top for color," says Batmanglij. "Sauté them with a little oil and a teaspoon of sugar, then sprinkle them on top of the kuku just before serving."

Recipe courtesy of Najmieh Batmanglij, Washington, DC

Cucumber and Rose Petal Dip

Makes 4 servings
Preparation time: 15 minutes plus 10 minutes to 1 hours' refrigeration

1. In a serving bowl, combine cucumbers, raisins, yogurt, spring onions, mint, dill weed, oregano, thyme, tarragon, garlic, and walnuts. Stir thoroughly and season to taste with salt and pepper.
2. Cover and refrigerate for 10 minutes before serving.
3. Garnish with mint, rose petals, and raisins. Just before serving, stir gently, and serve as a side dish or as an appetizer with bread. *Nush-e Jan!*

Variations:

Shirazi-Style Yogurt and Cucumber Dip *(Mast-o khiar-e Shirazi)*—Add the following to the garnish: 1 teaspoon toasted sesame, 1 teaspoon toasted nigella seeds, 1 teaspoon toasted coriander seeds, and 1 teaspoon toasted cumin seeds. Stir well just before serving.
Yogurt, Cucumber, and Rose Petal Soup *(Abdugh khiar ba gol-e sorkh)*—This dip can be transformed into a refreshing cold soup by adding 1 cup of cold water (or more to taste) and 2 or 3 ice cubes to the mixture. Add more salt and pepper to taste. Toast flat Persian bread or pita bread, cut into 1-inch squares, and add to the soup, just before serving, as croutons.

Mast-o khiar

4 Persian cucumbers, or 1 long seedless, peeled and diced
1 cup green raisins
3 cups plain whole-milk drained yogurt
1 cup chopped spring onions
2 tablespoons chopped fresh mint
2 tablespoons chopped fresh dill weed

2 tablespoons chopped fresh oregano
1 tablespoon chopped fresh thyme
2 tablespoons chopped fresh tarragon
2 cloves garlic, peeled and grated
W cup shelled walnuts, chopped
1 teaspoon sea salt
1 teaspoon freshly ground pepper

Garnish

1 teaspoon dried mint
2 tablespoons dried rose petals
1 tablespoon green raisins

Recipes from "Food of Life: Ancient Persian and Modern Iranian Cookery and Ceremonies; Najmieh Batmanglij and Mage Publishers. www.mage.com

Dolmeh (Grape Leaves with Rice and Meat)

Makes 30

½ cup rice
¾ cup water
¼ cup olive oil
1 onion, chopped
½ lb. ground lamb
4 green onions, chopped
¼ cup parsley, chopped

¼ cup fresh dill, chopped
4 leaves mint, chopped
2 tbls. lemon juice
½ tsp. turmeric
½ tsp. oregano
30 grape leaves
Lemon

Place the rice and water in a pan. Bring to a boil. Simmer until water evaporates. Fork rice. Cover.

Heat the olive oil in a skillet and saute onions until golden. Stir in the lamb and cook until pink. Drain off excess oil. Add rice, green onions, parsley, dill mint, lemon juice, turmeric, and oregano.

In a large pot bring water to boil. Blanche the grape leaves for 1 minute. Pour off water and run leaves under cold water. Separate the leaves and place on paper towels.

Taking each leaf place a spoonful of the rice mixture in the center. Starting with the stem roll up the leaf, then sides and top into a cylinder. Press with fingers to keep shape.

Place the leaves seam down in a casserole. Sprinkle with a little olive oil and water.

Bake covered for 10 minutes, or until warmed.

Serve on a platter or in the casserole garnished with lemon wedges.

Cuisine

The different regions of Iran each have their own distinctive cuisine. Rice is served with meat, chicken, fish, vegetables, nuts, herbs, yogurt, and fruit. Northern Iraq rice is usually served with meals and bread in other regions. Sadri rice, an extra long-grained rice, is grown in fields bordering the Caspian Sea. Properly cooked rice is washed several times to remove the starch, boiled in salted water, drained and then steamed with melted butter. Saffron is often added to the rice.

The country is noted for its fruit – plums, pomegranates, quince, prunes, apricots, raisins, dried limes, dates, figs, apricots, peaches, cherries, apples, grapes, melons; and its use of herbs and spices – saffron, cinnamon, parsley, cloves, turmeric, dill, parsley, mint, and cardamom. The flavors are subtle, but very pleasing to the palate. Vegetable dishes include garlic and onions served raw or pickled; aubergines, tomatoes, cucumbers, spring onions, pumpkin, spinach, green beans, courgettes, squash, carrots, sweet peppers, and cabbage. Salads are served with olive oil, lemon juice, salt, pepper, and garlic. The finest caviar comes from the Caspian Sea. Yogurt is used in cooking and in drinks. Panir (feta cheese) comes from goat and sheep's milk. Pistachios have been grown in Iran for centuries. Breakfast consists of flatbread, butter, white cheese (tabrizi), feta cheese, cream, fruit and jams.

Iranian Specialties

Chelo – steamed rice
Chelo khoresht - rice topped with vegetables and meat with a nut sauce
Khoresht beh – quince, lamb and yellow split pea stew served with rice
Khoresht e-fesenjan is one of the earliest recorded recipes in Persia and is made with duck in a pomegranate and walnut sauce and served over rice
Advieh – spice blend with dried rose petals, cinnamon, cardamom, angelica powder, nutmeg, cumin, coriander, and dried lime
Haleem - wheatmeal served with lamb or turkey
Chelo kebabs – grilled skewered meat served over rice
Kofte – ground meat form into a meatball
Abgusht – stew
Polo chele – pilau rice
Polo sabzi – pilau rice with herbs
Polo chirin – rice with raisins, oranges, and almonds
Reshteh polow – rice with noodles
Adas polo – rice, lentils, meat
Margh polo – pilau rice and chicken
Tah-chin – saffron rice cake with a filling, often chicken
Qaymeh –lamb stew
Nan – bread – nan-e-lavash (thin crisp bread); nan-e-sangak (yeast bread)
Dolma – vegetable or fruit stuffed with rice and/or ground meat, often grape or cabbage leaves

Ice cream made with rose water, saffron, and cream
Bastani-e – ice cream with saffron
Faludeh – sorbet with noodles and rose water
Shrini tar – "moist sweets" made with whipped cream, fruit, tarts, éclairs, custards, cakes often with saffron, pistachio, and walnuts
Shirini khishk – cookies made of rice, chickepeas, raisins, and saffron; cupcakes, muffins
Bamieh – deep fried dough with honey or syrup
Zulbia – similar to bamieh, except twisted dough
Goosh-e-fil – dough in shape of elephant's ear, fried and covered with powdered sugar
Halvardah – tahini – sesame paste
Sabzi – dish of fresh herbs served at meals consisting of basil, cilantro, fenugreek, tarragon, watercress
Panir- Persian cheese similar to feta
Kateh – (northern Iran) – rice cooked in water with butter and salt, can be eaten at breakfast
Gaz – nougat made from angebin, a sap only found near Esfahan
Baklava is made with cardamom, walnuts and sugar

Holidays and Special Occasions

Ramadan – fasting from dawn to dusk A feast is held at the end of each fast (iftar).
Nowruz "new day"– spring equinox - clean homes, dress in new clothes, burn incense to welcome departed spirits, visit friends and family for 12 days and make bonfires. On the 13th day "Nature Day" usually a picnic is held with sprouted wheat or lentils that are thrown into the water to symbolize letting go of problems from the last year. Some of the New Year's dishes are: sabzi polow (rice with herbs and fish); rice with herbs; ickled vegetables; ash reshteh – bean, noodle and herb soup; reshteh polow (rice with noodles); dolme barg (meat, rice and vegetables cooked in grape leaves); kookoo sabzi (vegetable and herb soufflé); zeytoon parvardeh – olive spread; and

painted eggs. Haft-seen is a table set to await spring with seven (lucky number) items beginning with S in Farsi. These will include sabzah (wheat, barley, lentil sprouts) to symbolize rebirth; samanu (wheat germ pudding) to symbolize wealth; senjed (dried oleaster fruit) love; seer torshi – sweet and sour garlic cloves; sib (apples) health; somaq (sumac berries) sunrise; and serkeh (vinegar) age.

Weddings – couples are wed in front of a Sofrehye Aghd whose ornaments symbolize their bond – eggs for fertility, candelabras for energy and a mirror of faith. After the ceremony the bride and groom dip their fingers in honey to symbolize the marriage with sweetness and love. Rice with fruit, nuts and spices, noghl – sugar coated almonds, served at weddings

On leaving for Mecca or a son's leaving house – ashe-e reshteh, a noodle soup is served.

First prayer meeting of the month – noodle soup is served

Beverages

Vines have been grown in Iran since ancient times to make wine, use grapes and grape leaves in cooking. Archeological digs in the Zagros Mountains have found pottery dating back to 5400 BC. Tablets found dating from c 500 BCE in Persepolis built by King Darius, provide for the distribution of wine to its citizens, including large amounts to the royal family. The earliest known wine vessel is from Hajji Firuz.

Shiraz was originally cultivated here. In August the wine is placed in large earthenware vessels, and then buried in cool cellars. The wine is then filtered into long necked bottles, covered with straw. Other wine regions are Ispahan, Tabriz, Yezd, and Teheran. Grapes include Kishmish from Ispahan, Damas, Kishbaba, Askeri, Shahoni, Imperial, and Samarkand.

Tea (chai) is served with dried fruit, pastries and sweets. When offered tea, at first decline, and then accept. Dough is a yogurt drink with water and dried mint. Other popular drinks are carrot juice with cinnamon and nutmeg; sheer moz – banana milkshake; aab talebi – cantaloupe juice; aab hendevaneh – watermelon juice; aab anaar – pomegranate juice; and sekanjebin, a syrup of carbonated water with mint, vinegar and sugar, to which rose water may be added

Did You Know?

Iran is the world's largest producer of saffron

Marzipan came originally from Persia.

The Gilani variety of rice is considered one of the best in Iran, where it has been in use since the fourth century BCE.

Pomegranates were grown in ancient times in Iran, Egypt, India, and then transported to Africa, Southeast Asia, and eventually to California. The name comes from the French "seeded apple".

During the 14th c the poets Hafez and Jahan Khatun wrote about the delights of wine.

The earliest cookbooks from Persia date to the Safavid period and include the *Kār-nāmeh dar bāb-e tabbākhī va sanat-e ān* ("Manual on cooking and its craft") by Ḥājī Moḥammad-ʿAlī Bāvaṛčī Baḡdādī and *Māddat al-ḥayāt, resāla dar ʿelm-e ṭabbākī* ("The substance of life, a treatise on the art of cooking") by Nur-Allah.

Iraq

Iraq is bordered by Jordan to the west, Syria to the northwest, Turkey to the north, Iran to the east, and Kuwait and Saudi Arabia to the south. Iraq's history dates back to at least the 6th millennium BC, home to the Sumerian civilization in the fertile Tigris-Euphrates River valley, Mesopotamia (meaning "the land between the two rivers". In the 7th c CE the country came under Ottoman rule and Islam was introduced. During World War I the Ottomans sided with Germany and the Central Powers. The British invaded the country but were defeated by the Turkish army. In 1917 the British captured Baghdad, and in 1918 Iraq under the Sykes-Picot Agreement was no longer a part of the Ottoman Empire. The British granted Iraq independence in 1932. The capital city, Baghdad located on the Tigris River, was founded in the 8th century and became the capital of the Abbasid Caliphate. The Mongols destroyed much of the city in 1258, but by the 18th c under the Ottomans grew as a major city in the Middle East. The official languages are Arabic and Kurdish.

Dining Etiquette

This is a country where family, honor, and hospitality are very important. Please arrive promptly when invited for a meal. Check to see if you need to remove your shoes before entering a home. Please bring a gift of pastries, chocolates, or something special from your country. Present the gift with both hands. Gifts are not opened in front of the presenter. Men shake hands with other men, keeping good eye contact. Only shake hands with a lady if she offers her hand. Good friends, of the same sex, will shake hands and kiss on each cheek, beginning with the right cheek. Tea or strong, bitter coffee will be served. You will be served three cups, and then shake the cup showing you have had enough. If the meal is served on the floor, kneel on one knee or sit cross-legged not exposing the soles of your shoes. Otherwise you may be seated at a table, or low tables. Use the right hands only for eating. If you are not given utensils, take some rice in your right hand, make it into a ball, put it into your mouth, or use it for soaking up the sauces or other dishes in front of you. Leave a small amount of food on your plate when finished.

Cuisine

The Iraqi cuisine dates back at least 10,000 to the Sumerians, Akkadians, Babylonians, Assyrians, and Persians. Nineveh was the capital of the Assyrian Empire and its people were known to eat meat or fowl, pomegranates, dates, pears, apricots, apples, radishes, beets, lettuce, onions, garlic and leeks. They cultivated emmer wheat, now known as smelt and from which we get durum, used in making pastas. Kasu was a wild licorice used in cooking and making beer. Ancient tablets even had recipes and pictures of these foodstuffs! The Ma'dan lived in Mesopotamia in the marshlands c 4000 BCE, and in ancient cities like Uruk, Ur, and Larsa. There they raised water buffalo for their milk, yogurt, meat and dung for fuel, and lived in reed houses. Much of the excellent cuisine now enjoyed was developed in Baghdad, under the Abbasid caliphate, but also has Turk, Iranian and Syrian influences. But they were also very sophisticated and had water mills to grind wheat into flour, sugar refineries to make sugar, and distillation for making essence from rose and orange petals, olives pressed into olive oil, and grew many types of vegetables, fruits, and herbs. Spices were imported from India, Africa, and Asia.

Dishes use local products: vegetables - aubergine (eggplant), tomatoes, okra, onions, potatoes, courgette (zucchini), garlic, peppers, chilies, lentils, chickpeas, cannellini; grains – rice, bulghur, barley; fruit - dates, raisins, apricots, figs, grapes, melon, pomegranate, lemons, and limes. Other ingredients used in cooking include olives and olive oil, butter, tamarind, tahini, pistachios, almonds, honey, bulghur wheat, yogurt and rose water. Herbs and spices are used generously – cinnamon, cardamom, fenugreek, za'atar, cumin, oregano, saffron, babarat, and sumac. Chicken and lamb are the most common meats. Rice is grown in southern Iraq and is used with most dishes. A meal begins with meze, an assortment of appetizers.

Iraqi Specialties

Masgouf – grilled fish with tamarind and pepper
Kebab – meat marinated with garlic, lemon, spices and grilled
Quiz – stuffed roasted lamb
Pastirma – air dried beef
Shawarma – grilled meat sandwich
Kibbeh – minced ground meat
Keema – minced meat, chickpea and tomato stew
Margot baytinijan – aubergine and tomato dish with meat
Bamia – lamb, okra and tomato stew
Maqluba – rice, lamb, tomatoes and aubergine
Dolma – stuffed vegetables with rice and meat
Ouzi – lamb with rice, almonds, raisins and spices
Falafel – fried chickpea patties
Kofta – minced meat with spices and onions
Fattoush – vegetable salad with pita bread
Makhlamah – breakfast dish with tomato, minced meat and eggs

Bagila bil dihin – breakfast dish with flat bread with oil and beans topped with egg
Tabbouleh – bulghur, tomato, parsley, scallion salad
Tbiet – stuffed chicken with rice (cooked before Sabbath by Iraqi Jews)
Turshi – pickled vegetables
Baba ghanoush – aubergine appetizer
Hummus – garlic, chickpea, tahini appetizer
Sambusak – fried pastry
Fasouilia – white bean soup
Tashrib - lamb or chicken soup
Tepsi baytinijan – aubergine, meatballs, tomatoes, onion and garlic dish with potato slices
Harissa- spice mixture
Shorbat rumman – pomegranate soup
Burek – baked or fried pastry with cheese
Baharat –spice mixture of allspice, peppercorns, cardamom, cloves, coriander, cumin, nutmeg, dried chili
Kleicha – national cookie with a date or other filling

Tabsi'l Betinjaan (Eggplant Casserole)

In addition to its great taste, this baked dish demonstrates the many layers of Iraqi history. Note the use of pomegranate syrup - a decidedly Persian touch. The Abbasid Caliphate, which ruled Iraq from 786-809AD, derived a great deal of culinary inspiration from the Persians. The tomatoes and peppers were introduced after the 15th century from the Americas. Curry powder was probably brought back from India with the British, who ruled Iraq as recently as the early 20th century.

Serves 4-6 people

2 large eggplant
Oil, for frying
Pinch of salt
2 large onions, diced
2 tbls. olive oil
2-3 garlic cloves, thinly sliced
½ tsp. curry powder

1 medium bell pepper, sliced, seeded, and membranes removed
1 small hot pepper, sliced
1 lb. cubed lamb or ground beef
2 large sliced tomatoes (canned or diced are OK)
For Garnish: chopped parsley and lemon slices

Sauce

3 heaping tbls. tomato paste, diluted in 3½ cups hot water, or 4 cups tomato juice
½ tsp. salt
¼ tsp. black pepper

1 tbls. fresh basil, chopped or ½ tsp/ dried
1 tbls. pomegranate syrup, optional
½ tsp. sugar
1 cup cooked chickpeas, optional

Preheat oven to 400F degrees.
Cut off stems of the eggplant and peel. Cut into ¼ " slices crosswise
Soak the slices in warm salted water for 30 minutes
Drain and fry them in oil until they are light golden. Remove from oil and place on a platter.
In a big skillet, saute onion in olive oil. Add the garlic and curry powder. Stir in the bell and hot pepper. Cook a few minutes, or until they start to soften.
Add meat, salt, and pepper. Pour hot water in pan until the meat is barely covered. Let the meat simmer until tender. Drain meat and reserve liquid for sauce.
In a glass baking dish, place cooked meat on the bottom. Layer the eggplant over the meat, and then top with the onion mixture. Arrange the sliced tomato on top.
Make the sauce by combining all sauce ingredients in the same skillet that was used to cook the meat. (If leftover cooking liquid was reserved, this may be added back into the pan).
Bring sauce to a boil over high heat, reduce to medium low and simmer for 5 minutes. Pour liquid over the casserole.
Bake for 40 minutes, or until vegetables are tender and sauce has thickened.
Garnish with parsley and lemon slices.
Recipe Courtesy of the Embassy of Iraq, Washington, DC

Holidays and Special Occasions

Ramadan – no food is consumed from sunrise to sunset. Suhur is the meal before sunrise and contains grains and fruit. The Ifitr after sunset begins by eating a date.
Feast of Ramadan (Şeker Bayramı) – coffee, stuffed chicken, pilaf, borek, baklava, kadayf, and other sweets
Feast of the Sacrifice (Kurban Bayramı) – animals are sacrficied and eaten including kidneys, liver and intestines, sweets, coffee
The Month of Muharrem (Aşure Month) – wheat pudding
Weddings – aşure (wheat pudding) is served the day after in the groom's home
Kandils - lokum, halva, borek

Beverages

Very strong, bitter coffee is served as a sign of hospitality to guests. Tea (chai) is also served, often brewed with cardamom. Arak is a clear aniseed drink.

Did You Know?

Lalish is believed to be the site of the Garden of Eden.
The aqueduct at Jerwan brought water to the ancient city of Ninevah, and is thought to be the oldest aqueduct in the world.
Jarmo in Kurdistan is known to have been inhabited over 9,000 years ago.
The Sumerians (3500 to 2800 BC) of Mesopotamia produced stone pictures of cows being milked and dairy products.
The word for rice comes from Aramaia "ourouzza", and was originally brought by the Persians from India to Iraq.
Lettuce was known to be the source of water dating back to at least the 3rd millennium BC and was first recorded as growing on terraces in the gardens of Babylon.
Citrus fruit (citron) is also known to have been grown here since the 3rd millennium BC.
The first surviving cookbook in Arabic was compiled by Ibn Syyan al-War-raq and was known as the Kitah-al-Tabikh (Book of Dishes) and dates to the 10th c. Very early recipes inscribed in cuneiform date back thousands of years.

Ireland

Ireland is an island located off the west coast of Europe. The earliest occupants settled about 6000 BC. Later tribes arrived from Europe establishing a well-defined culture with magnificent gold and silver ornaments, and huge stone monuments. The Celts arrived c 4th c BC, and divided the country into five kingdoms. St. Patrick arrived in 432 AD to convert the Celts to Christianity. From the 8th to 11th c Vikings invaded and in the 17th c England took over. The United Kingdom of Great Britain and Ireland was established in 1801. During the 1840s famine devastated the island forcing many to flee to the United States and Australia. Northern Ireland is part of the United Kingdom and Eire and an independent republic. The capital, Dublin, founded in 795, was preceded by Kilkenny, the site of Parliament 1642-48. Gaelic and English are spoken.

Irish Stew

Serves 8

8 gigot lamb chops, trimmed of excess fat	2 onions, chopped
2 large carrots, chopped	2 sticks celery, chopped
8 medium potatoes, peeled	1 tsp. of chopped rosemary and thyme
Salt and pepper	1½ to 2 pints chicken stock
Oil for frying	

Preheat oven to 350° F, gas mark 4
Brown the chops in a frying pan and transfer to a large ovenproof casserole with lid.
Toss the onions, carrots, and celery in the pan for a few minutes and add to casserole.
Cover with the stock and add herbs, salt and pepper, and place the potatoes on top.
Cook for about 1 ½ hours or until meat is tender.
Liquid can be thickened with 1-2 tsp. cornflour mixed with water and added to the casserole.
Recipe courtesy of Helen Waide, Youghal, County Waterford, Ireland

Dining Etiquette

The Irish are very warm and friendly people. They love to entertain. Send or bring flowers, chocolates, or a gift for the home. Please be punctual when invited for a meal. Shake hands greeting and departing. Women extend their hands first. Men or younger people stand when a lady enters a room, hold a chair and doors for her. Drinks such as Irish whiskey, wine, or sherry will be served. A starter is a hors d'oeuvres, a sweet a dessert. When seated the host and hostess will be seated at opposite ends with the male guest of honor to the hostess' right. Courses are usually served starting with fish for which a fish knife and fork will provided, or soup. Eating is continental style with the fork in the left hand, knife in the right. Meat with vegetables and potatoes, then cheese, ending with dessert and coffee round out the meal. Port or other brandies may be served. Medieval banquets, which are prearranged, are held on some country estates with food eaten in the hand and mead served. A ceilidh is a traditional Irish meal with dancing and singing. The toast is proposed by the host who raises his glass and says "Slainte" "To your health". Always say "Cheers" before drinking.

Salmon Kiev in a Crust

Serves 4

4 x 175g salmon fillets, skinned and boned (each one at least 2.5cm thick)
100g butter, softened
2 tbls. fresh tarragon, chopped
1 tbls. fresh chives, snipped
1 small garlic clove, crushed

500g packet puff pastry, thawed if frozen (all butter, if possible)
A little plain flour, for dusting
50g tender young baby spinach leaves
Good Pinch freshly-grated nutmeg
1 egg, beaten
Salt and freshly-grated black pepper

Preheat the oven to Gas Mark 6, 200°C (400°F).

Place the butter in a small bowl and beat in the tarragon with the chives, garlic and a little pepper and salt to taste. Spoon on to a sheet of cling film or non-stick parchment paper and shape into a roll about 2.5cm thick, then wrap tightly. Chill in the freezer for at least 10 minutes to firm up (or keep in the fridge for up to 48 hours until required, if time allows),

Cut the pastry into 8 even-sized sections and roll each one out on a lightly floured surface to a 23cm x 15cm rectangle, trimming down the edges as necessary. Place a salmon fillet in the centre of 4 of the pastry rectangles. Unwrap the tarragon butter, cut into slices and arrange on top, then cover with the spinach leaves. Season the spinach and add a little nutmeg.

Brush the edges of the pastry bases with a little of the beaten egg and lay a second sheet of pastry on top, pressing down to seal. Crimp the edges by gently pressing the edge of the pastry with the forefinger of one hand and between the first two fingers of the other hand. Continue all the way around the edge of the parcel, then repeat until you have 4 parcels in total. Using a sharp knife, make light slashes across each parcel but take care not to cut right through.

Place a baking sheet in the preheated oven for a few minutes. Meanwhile, brush the pastry parcels with the remaining beaten egg. Transfer to the heated baking sheet and bake for 25-30 +minutes or until the pastry is cooked through and golden brown. Arrange the salmon parcels on warmed serving plates.

Delicious served with steamed samphire or green beans and hollandaise sauce.

Recipe courtesy of the Bord Bia (The Irish Food Board)

Cuisine

Ireland's rich soil provides many crops and livestock, sad when you think millions starved a little over a century ago. The potato was introduced to Ireland during the 16th and 17th c by the English. The "lumper" potato grew well in Ireland's cool and wet climate, and when served with milk provided a meal for the poor. During the famine food was readily available but the land was owned mainly by wealth Englishmen and Anglo-Irish who basically did not take interest in their lands and shipped the produce to England. Thus when the potato blight struck the poor either perished from starvation, or if able migrated out of the country.

Sheep, fish, potatoes and cabbage are staples. Ireland is renowned for its cheeses – Cashel Blue, Blarney, Lough Caum, St. Killian, Burren Gold, and Ring. Favorite seafood are salmon, hake, mussels, clams, Galway oysters, crab, trout, lobster, prawns, eel, sea urchin, sole, herring, cockles, periwinkles, and cod. Common berries are gooseberries, raspberries, blackberries, and strawberries. The Irish are very particular about their tea which must be made with boiling water, loose tea, and steeped for at least five minutes! Do start the day off properly with an Irish breakfast of eggs, bacon, sausages, toast or scones, and perhaps a finnan haddie, smoked salmon or kippers.

Beef in Guinness

Serves 4-6

2 lbs. braising steak, cut into 2 inch squares approximately	Olive oil
2 onions, chopped	2 crushed garlic cloves
1 tbls. plain flour	Few fresh thyme sprigs
2 bay leaves	Salt and freshly milled pepper
	1 pint Guinness

Saute onion and garlic with oil until soft and transfer to a large ovenproof casserole with a lid. Next fry the meat in hot pan in batches until browned and remove to plate and when done return to pan. Lower heat and add flour. Stir until all the flour has been absorbed into the juices.
Now gradually stir in the Guinness and let it all come to simmering point. Add salt, pepper, and bay leaves. Transfer to the casserole and place in oven for 2 ½ to 3 hours hours at 300° F, gas mark 2, until beef is tender.
I often add beef stock cube for extra flavor.
Recipe courtesy of Helen Waide, Youghal, County Waterford, Ireland

Irish Specialties

Irish cream and butter – oh, so rich!	Colcannon – potato and cabbage dish
Irish soda bread	Bubble and squeak – roast beef with potatoes,
Black pudding- sausage with pig's blood, oatmeal, milk and bread that is baked, cut in circles, and then fried	cabbage and a sauce
	Dulse – dried seaweed
	Potato pancakes

Holidays and Special Occasions

St. Patrick's Day – Irish soda bread, corned beef, colcannon or potatoes and cabbage. St. Patrick's day is the traditional day to plant potatoes and peas.
Easter – young lamb
The Galway International Oyster and Seafood Festival is held in the fall.
Christmas – goose, turkey, ham, plum pudding, trifle

Strawberry Sundae

Serves 3-4

450g strawberries
2 tbls. red currant jam

1 x 500g carton of fromage frais (whipped cream or crème fraiche can also be used)

Wash and hull the strawberries, reserve two to decorate the glasses.
Put the remainder of the strawberries in a pan with 2 teaspoon water and the redcurrant jam.
Bring to the boil and stir until the jam is dissolved.
Remove from the heat and allow to cool.
Layer this mixture with the fromage frais in individual glasses, finishing with fromage frais.
Decorate with the reserved strawberries, sliced in half
Recipe courtesy of the Bord Bia (The Irish Food Board)

Beverages

One of Ireland's best known products is whiskey made from barley which is dried in kilns, then placed in pot stills, continuous stills and oak barrels where it is allowed to age for three or more years. The word whiskey comes from the Gaelic "usice beatha" "the water of life". The earliest producers were probably the Celts. In 1820 heavy taxes were imposed on whiskey as Ireland was the leading world exporter. In turn illicit whiskey (poteen) was produced in pot stills at home. The world's oldest distillery is Bushmill's founded in 1608. Ireland also produces Irish Mist, a whiskey with honey; Bailey's Irish Cream, whiskey and cream which is drunk as an aperitif. Blended whiskey is 35%, malt whiskey 65% grain.

Breweries were founded in the 18th c. often in monasteries, the one at Smithwick in 1710, once a 12th c Franciscan monastery. Stout was first made in Dublin in 1759 by Arthur Guinness. This was a dark ale, made from barley, kiln dried with yeast added, giving it a very distinct flavor. Other types brewed are ales, lagers, and mead. The Guinness Brewery in Dublin is the world's largest exporter of beer. Beers and lagers are served at room temperature.

Apples have been grown since Celtic times. Apple cider was first mentioned in 1155. Today hard cider has become very popular. Apples are also used for vinegar, brandy, gin, vodka, and syrup.

Did You Know?

The first potatoes were brought to Ireland in the 17th c by Walter Raleigh from North Carolina.
The oldest pub still in operation in Dublin is the Brazen Head founded in 1688.
Poteen "little pot" was thought to have been a liquor distilled from potatoes by the Leprechauns.
The shamrock represents the Cross and Holy Trinity.

Israel

Israel is located in the Middle East bordered to the east by the Mediterranean Sea, Lebanon to the north, Syria the northeast, Jordan and the West Bank in the east, Egypt and the Gaza Strip on the southwest. *Eretz Yisrael* has existed for the Jewish people since Biblical times. The first kingdom was established c 1100 BCE. Later the Assyrian, Babylonian, Persian, Greek, Roman, Sassanian, and Byzantine ruled. The Jews revolted in 610 CE and allied themselves with the Persians. In 628-29 CE the Byzantine emperor massacred and expelled the Jews. In 1516 Israel became part of the Ottoman Empire which ruled until the 20th c. Beginning in 1881 Jews began fleeing the pogroms in Eastern Europe. The modern state of Israel was declared in 1948. The official language is Hebrew. The capital is Jerusalem.

Dining Etiquette

The Israelis are warm and wish to entertain their guests often taking 2-3 hours for meals. Please arrive promptly and bring a gift. Do not bring food, except Kosher if the family is Orthodox. Men should wear a dress shirt and slacks, women skirts or a dress. Please shake hands greeting and departing, although some may not shake hands with the opposite sex. If a person is known to you, a hug whether male or female will probably be expected. The usual greeting is "Shalom", which means "peace", and also used when saying good-bye.

The guest of honor is seated at the head of the table. Before a meal a blessing may be said, candles lit, wine drunk or washing of hands. Please wait for the host or hostess to start. A blessing or prayers may be said at the end of the meal. "Mazal tov" – "good luck"; L'chim" "to life", or "to health" is the toast. All raise their glasses and clink.

Cuisine

Israel's cuisine dates back to Biblical times. The agricultural products still reflect foods from Biblical times – olives and olive oil, wine, figs, grapes, pomegranates, barley, wheat, eggplant, tomatoes, okra, dates, nuts, lemons, and honey.

For those who follow strict kosher dietary laws (from Leviticus and Deuteronomy in the Bible), a rabbi oversees kosher food. Kosher means "fit" or "suitable". The dietary laws are known as kashrut.

For meat and fowl to be considered kosher it must be killed by a "shohet", a person trained in the slaughtering, then examined so as to be "clean", and the blood removed. Fish must have fins and scales, no shellfish. One cannot mix milk and meat – including dishes and utensils; cannot eat at

270

same time (usually three to six hours). Pareve foods do not contain milk or meat. Non kosher can serve shellfish, pork, and dairy and meat dishes are not separated.

The Bible says one must observe the Sabbath day, and the Jewish Sabbath begins at sundown on Friday to sundown on Saturday. Cannot mix seeds in a field – from Bible; also cannot graft fruit trees or vines.

Meals might include salad, hummus, falafel, breads, soups, stuffed vegetables, desserts such as baklava and halvah.

Middle Eastern Style Chicken

Filling

4 tbls. olive oil
Whole chicken to be filled
1 medium onion, diced
250 gr. ground meat (beef or turkey ½ lb)
Salt and pepper
1 cup basmati rice
1 tsp. cinnamon
Soak the rice for ½ hour.

1 tsp. bharat
30 gr. pinenuts (.60 oz)
2 cups water

Heat the olive oil in a large skillet. Add the onion and cook until golden. Add the ground meat. Stir in rice for 30 seconds. Add salt, pepper, cinnamon and bharat. Stir for 30 seconds. Add the pine nuts and water. Cook for about 20 minutes or until all the water is evaporated. Let cool.
Fill the chicken cavity with the filling and close with toothpicks.

Marinade

Olive oil
Salt and pepper

Paprika

Combine the ingredients and rub over entire chicken. Cover the chicken with foil.
Preheat oven to 200° F
Cook the chicken slowly for 4-5 hours until the meat is softened.
Recipe courtesy of Shlomit Hochner, Embassy of Israel, Washington, DC

Israeli Specialties

Matzoh – unleavened bread – bread could not rise as the Jews fled from Pharaoh (now celebration of Passover). Matzoh is made of wheat, spelt, barley, oats, and rye.

Matzoh brei – leftover matzoh soaked in hot water or milk, liquid drained, and then fried. Can be served with salt, pepper, or sweet condiments
Matzoh ball soup

271

Gefilte fish – eaten on Friday nights and holidays. These are fish balls cooked in fish stock.

Brisket – made with boneless beef and slow cooked

Cholent – beans, potatoes, and other vegetables cooked for a long time

Latkes – pancakes that can be made with buckwheat, potato, cheese, vegetables or other ingredients. During Hanukkah they must be fried in oil to symbolize the fact that oil lasted for eight days when the Jews recaptured Jerusalem in 165 BC.

Borscht – red beet soup

Chicken soup

Noodle or potato kugel – baked pudding

Vegetable salad – salad with olive oil, lemon juice and spices

Challah – braided bread

Kugel – baked noodle or potato pudding

Kabab – meat and vegetables on a skewer

Ugat drash – honey cake decorated with almonds

Leben – made from skim milk, similar to yogurt or sour cream

Soufganiyot – fried jelly donuts

Holidays and Special Occasions

Shabbat (Sabbath dinner) is held every Friday night by observant Jews. The women cover their heads, light candles and serve challah (braided bread) and on Saturday cholent (stew).

Tu Bishvat – Jewish arbor day when fruit is eaten and trees planted

Seder during *Passover* begins at sundown with much cleaning for the last touch of leavened bread, and preparation for the Seder, reading the Haggada, cleansing of chametz - all crumbs, crackers, cakes, legumes, and grains. When entering a home please say "Shabbat Shalom" Wines blessed by a rabbi will be served. Four cups of wine will be drunk, plus one for the prophet Elijah.

The Seder plate holds roasted egg, lamb shank, matzoh, bitter herbs, haroset – apples, nuts, raisins and walnuts) and wine; greens, matzoh-ball soup, gefilte fish, matzoh balls, and borscht

Purim – the children dress as Queen Esther, pastries served such as oznayhaman (filled cookies with fruit or poppy seeds "Haman's ears".

Sukkot- the Feast of Booths, the end of the harvest season – in honor of celebrating in booths at harvest time over 8 days. Sukkot is "dining in a booth". Dried fruits and nuts are eaten.

Shavuot – the Feast of First Fruits; dairy products such as cheese blintzes; also the giving of the Law on Mount Sinai

Rosh Hashanah - ten "Days of Awe" (penitence) – New Year when abstinence of food and drink continues from dawn to dusk. Challah is eaten on the eve of Rosh Hashanah, known as the Seder from the Hebrew word for "order". The round loaf symbolizes the full year, and is dipped in honey to promise a sweet and fruitful year. Small dishes are served, each for a wish for the New Year. Simanim is Hebrew for the special foods eaten such as carrots and pomegranate seeds symbolize blessings for the New Year. Among other foods that carry symbols are leeks, garlic, dates, to name a few.

Tashlich – ceremony where bread is thrown into the water before Yom Kippur to wash away one's sins

Yom Kippur – Day of Atonement – is celebrated on the 10th day, a day of fasting, penitence, and prayer when the Ram's horn (shofar) is blown as a reminder of Abraham's faithfulness to God.

Hanukkah – candles on a menorah are lighted for eight nights, in commemoration of the Maccabees' victory over the Syrian Greeks in 165 BC, who rededicated their temple in Jerusalem and found they only had oil for the menorah for one night, but lasted for eight days. Potato latkes, sufganiyot (jelly donuts), and fried (in oil) foods are eaten

Bar mitzvah – boy's coming of age at 13 – "Man of Duty" – boys are study religious works in preparation; singing from Torah scroll; tefillin – black leather thongs laced on forehead and arm. On the day of the Bar Mitzvah the boy reads from the Torah. Large and elaborate parties are given in celebration.

Bat mitzvah – is given for girls when they turn of age

Weddings – Before the ceremony the bride and groom fast that day, breaking the fast after the ceremony. Two cups of wine are used during the wedding ceremony blessed during the betrothal blessings recited by the rabbi. The wine must be drunk by the bride and groom. The groom will smash the first glass symbolizing a break with the past and their new life together. Seven glasses will be drunk during the event. At the beginning of the wedding feast a blessing said over a loaf of challah. Kosher food is served – bread, meat or poultry and wine, and might include stuffed cabbage or poached salmon. Cakes may or may not be served.

White clothing is worn to symbolize purity on Yom Kippur, at weddings, and the Passover Seder.

Beverages

Vines were cultivated in Judea since early Biblical times (7500 BC). Vessels from the Middle Bronze Age (c1700BC) have been found at Tel Kabri. Wines were flavored back then with honey, spices, and herbs which were in the archeological dig. Wines are used during the Jewish Seder and at the Last supper. The Christian monasteries also produced wine. Near the end of the 19th c Baron Edmond de Rothschild introduced French style grapes. Wines are grown in Zichron-Jacob, Nes-Ziona, Gedara, Rishon-le-Zion. Kosher wine can be red or white but must adhere to strict Rabinical law – pure, natural, and not mixed with other wines. The same wines can be used in the synagogue or home. On the two nights of Seder during Passover each person drinks four glasses of wine.

Israel also produces Arak, distilled spirits from rice, palm sap, yams or dates; brandies; and Carmei-Zion, a liqueur. Beer is brewed at the National Brewery.

Tea, coffee, fruit juices, especially orange; and drinks made from tamarind, dates and almonds are drunk. Sahlab is made with milk, sugar, raisins, rose water, sahlab powder and coconut.

Did You Know?

Archeological work on the ancient city of Gath dates it back at least three millennia when the Philistines arrived from Greece. The Philistines ate grass pea lentils, pigs, and dogs, the latter were considered unclean by the Israelites. Today the city is a national park.

There are references in the Bible to cheese – David delivering the ten loaves to the Hebrew army fighting the Philistines (1Samuel 17:17-19), and in Job 10:10 who said "Did you not pour me out like milk, and curdled me like cheese."

Rosh Hashanah dates from the Babylonian Talmud (3rd to 5th c) which describes the laws and customs relating to the Jewish holiday. The original was in Aramaic, and there are many translations for some of the words. Rubia can be black-eyed peas, green beans, fenugreek, or sesame seeds. Silka could be beets, Swiss chard, or spinach. Pomegranates are also used.

Italy

Tiramisu and Zabaglione

"Tiramisu is one of the most famous Italian desserts, in Italy and throughout the world. It belongs to the layered cake category, such as trifle. The originality of the recipe lies in its ingredients, which include zabaglione, mascarpone cheese and ladyfingers."
His Excellency Giulio Terzi, Embassy of Italy, Washington, DC

Tiramisu, a dessert from Venice, means "to pick me up".

Serves 8

450 grams mascarpone cheese	3 tbls. unsweetened cocoa powder
230 grams whipping cream	200 grams ladyfingers
350 grams espresso coffee	

Prepare the zabaglione in accordance with the directions below. Allow it to cool, add the mascarpone, then whip the cream and delicately stir it into the mixture.
Quickly, to avoid complete saturation, dip the ladyfingers into the coffee and place them in a single layer in a baking dish.
Spread a layer of the cheese mixture over the ladyfingers, repeat the layers, ending with the cheese mixture.
Sprinkle the final layer with the unsweetened cocoa powder and refrigerate for at least six hours before serving.

Zabaglione

120 grams Marsala wine	100 grams flour
4 egg yolks	660 ml of milk
100 grams sugar	

For each egg use 1 tbls. sugar, 2 tbls. of Marsala wine, 25 grams of flour, and about 170 ml milk.
Pour the ingredients into a heatproof bowl and place it in a saucepan which is larger than the bowl itself and which contains hot water.
Place all of this on a heated stove and whisk the zabaglione until it trebles its volume.
Recipes Courtesy of His Excellency Giulio Terzi, Embassy of Italy, Washington, DC

Italy is located in south-central Europe. To the north it borders France, Switzerland, Austria and Slovenia. To the south it consists of the Italian Peninsula, the islands of Sicily and Sardinia and other smaller islands. Italy was settled by the Etruscans c 1000 BC, though the Anatolians were probably in the south c 3500 BC. As early as the 11c BC the Greeks were known to write myths about this area. Later invasions were by the Gauls c 600 BC, Hannibal with his elephants, and Julius Caesar in 49 AD. Rome in turn invaded Europe as far west as the British Isles. In 1796 Napoleon conquered Rome. Rome "The Eternal City", the capital, was founded on seven hills on the Tiber River in central Italy by Romulus and Remus in 753 BC. Italian is the official language.

Dining Etiquette

When invited for a meal guests usually do not arrive on time. At least one half hour late is permissible. Please send flowers (in an uneven number), a plant or something for the house the day after. Shake hands greeting and departing. Men may hug each other. A lady extends her hand first. Do stand when an older person enters a room. Cocktail hours are not long. Liquor may not be served, rather wine or an aperitif such as Campari. The male guest of honor will be seated to the left of the hostess, the female guest of honor to the left of the host. Food is served in course, each with wine/ Never cut pasta, but rather twirl it on the fork using the plate or a spoon. Salads are to be eaten with forks only. When finished place your fork and knife together. Both hands should be kept above the table during the meal. Coffee and liqueurs may follow. The toast is "Salute" or "Chin-chin". Ladies should never make a toast!

Cuisine

Italians for centuries have cultivated their own cuisine and from ancient times knew about crushing olives for oil, making cheese, using grapes for wine and vinegar, leavening for breads, grains for cereals, and salt for seasoning and preserving. The ancient Romans ate extremely well and contributed to the dishes still used today. During the Dark Ages barbarians from the north invaded, but in the 9th c the Arabs arrived in southern Italy and brought with them their culture sugar cane, spices, raisins, candied fruit, and later pasta in the 12th c. During the Middle Ages rice and spices arrived from the East. The Renaissance brought elegant meals. With the European discovery of the Americas beans, tomatoes, squash, chilies, cacao, corn, peppers, turkey, and potatoes were introduced.

Italian food is known the world over with many dishes named after famous cities or personages. The food is prepared with fresh ingredients coming from the different regions. In the north butter, polenta, risotto, and fresh pastas are more readily used, while in the south olive oil, tomato sauces and dried pastas are eaten. Along the coast seafood is in abundance, lemon, fig and olive trees dot the hillsides.

Italy is made up of 20 regions, separated into 103 provinces, each with its own food and wines. The south, the Mezzogiorno, is made up of Sicily, Sardinia, Calabria, Basilicata, Apulia and Campania. The region produces olive oil. Sicily is known for oranges, olives, fish, especially sardines, currants, fennel, pine nuts, wine, pasta, wheat, almonds, cattle and sheep, and chocolate. Puglia, on Italy's "Spur" grows oranges and lemons. Central Italy is made up of Molise, Abruzzi, Latium, Umbria, Tuscany, and the Marches. Produce includes spelt, chestnuts, wheat, olive oil, artichokes, peas, white beans, black cabbage, lentils, chickpeas, truffles, seafood, pecorino cheese, pork and other meats, and of course wine. Northern Italy is comprised of Emilia-Romagna, Liguria, Lombardy, Piedmont, Valle d'Aosta, Veneto, Friuli-Venezia Giulia, and Trentino-Alto Adige. Grain, corn, rice, vineyards, cattle and dairy farms provide an abundance of food for the region. Among the popular foods are fresh pasta, polenta, gnocchi, prosciutto, Parmagiano-Reggiano and Grana Padano cheese, wines, and grappa, and along the coast seafood. Each region also produces its own pastas – agnolotti, cappelletti, casonsei, ravioli, tortellini, tortelli, some filled, some flavored, and grouped by dried, egg, or fresh pasta. Pasta is made from water, flour, sometimes eggs, and then kneaded. Spelt, which has been known since ancient times in Central Italy is also used to make pasta.

Salumi (cured meats) can be made into prosciutto, salame, sausages, mortadella, and bresaola. Well known cheeses are Parmgiano-Reggiano, Gorgonzola, Grana Padano, Fontina, Provolone, Cacaicavallo, Pecorino Romano, Sardo, and Mozzarella. Water buffalo are grown in southern Italy where they are used to make creamy mozzarella cheese which is shaped into braids or spheres. Mozzarella was first mentioned in 1570 in a cookbook by Bartolomeo Scappi, a papal chef. Mozarella comes from the word"mozzare" "to chop".

Italian Specialties

Caponata – eggplant appetizer

Zuppa di pesce – fish soup

Minestrone – vegetable soup

Minestra – soup or first course

Calzone – pizza dough stuffed with cheese and/or meats and baked or fried

Porchetta – roasted suckling pig with herbs

Gnocchi – dough of flour or potatoes that is boiled.

Tortellini – half circle pasta with fillings

Ravioli – round pasta that can be stuffed with different fillings

Risotto – Arborio rice that is slowly cooked with stock to which vegetables, fish, or any number of items are added and topped with grated hard cheese

Alla marinara – with tomato sauce

Polenta – cornmeal and water that can be served as a porridge or baked

Lasagne – large (lasagna) noodles with meat or vegetables

Cannelloni – rolled dough stuffed with meat, cheese or other fillings

Fettuccine – pasta made with eggs

Risotto – braised rice

Spaghetti all carbonara – spaghetti with eggs, bacon, cheese and cream sauce

Parmigiana di Melanzane – eggplant parmesan

Ragu Bolognese - northern Italan meat sauce

Scampi – grilled shrimp with garlic

Pollo alla Cacciatora – chicken with olive and anchovy sauce

Calamari – squid

Alla diavola – "devil's style" – spicy foods

Frutti di mare – raw or cooked seafood

Vitello Tonnato – veal with tuna

Scaloppini al limone – veal with lemon

Braciola – veal, lamb or pork cutlet, or stuffed rolled meat or fish in southern Italy

Osso buco – braised veal shanks

Insalata - salad

Prosciutto – very thin cured Parma ham

Mortadella – very thin sliced sausage from Bologna

Pancetta – salt cured pork

Insalata di pomodori – tomato salad

Gelato – ice cream or frozen dessert

Granite – flavored ices

Panettone – coffee cake with fruit and raisins (often served at Christmas)

Bigne – pastry with creams
Biscotti – biscuits or cookies
Ameretti – almond cookies
Cannoli – fried and filled with ricotta cheese confection

Mascarpone – whipped cream, sweetened or unsweetened

Holidays and Special Occasions

Lent – Maritozzi quaresimali (buns with raisins, fruit and nuts)
St. Joseph's Day (March 19th) – Sfingi di San Giuseppe (deep fried pastry) – St. Joseph's Cream Puffs
Easter – during Holy Week in southern Italy baccala (salted cod) is served each day. On Easter eggs (symbolizing rebirth), real or chocolate are everywhere and may be filled with gifts. Pasta, lamb or pig and special pastries are served.
Pasquetta (the day after Easter – is a holiday for picnicking
Saint John's Eve (Midsummer night) – snails
During the fall there are numerous wine festivals
Christmas Eve – roasted eel, salt cod, fish, shellfish, pasta, risotto, panettone and torrone. At midnight sausage and champagne may be served.
Christmas – lasts for twelve days and on the twelfth (Epiphany) children are visited by La Befana who brings gifts and food which might include dates, figs, honey and oranges. In Tuscany befanini cookies are baked with anise, yeast and cut into various shapes with colored sprinkles.
Christmas day dishes may include minestra maritata (vegetable soup), eels, venison, quail, wold boar, vegetable tortellini, cauliflower,

Beverages

Since earliest times Italy has produced excellent wines, knowing they were a healthy part of the diet and complimented the dishes prepared. The first wines were probably brought by the Etruscans and Greeks before 800 BC, though wine production dates back to 7000 BC. The wines were a mix of honey and grapes, and even in Roman times were very expensive. By law women could not drink wine. Each region produces wine.

Some facts you might want to know about Italian wines:

Pier de'Crescenzi wrote the earliest known book on wine in the 13th c.
The Tuscans were the first to use glass wine glasses. Previously they had been made of silver or pewter.
In 1320 the citizens of Rome were taxed for their production of five million gallons of wine to finance the building of the Signoria Palace.
Vino Santo, a dessert wine, means "saintly wine".
A wine tasting is a degustazioni.
The Alto Adige in northern Italy produces German style white wines.
The Wine Museum of the Fondazione Lungarotti is located near Perugia and Assisi in Umbria and traces the history of wine making in Italy.
Lachrima Christi meaning "Tear of Christ" is a wine produced near Mt. Vesuvius.

Sagredo invented the termoscopio to measure liquids through the use of Chianti. Chianti is derived from the word "Clango" "Sounding of horns".

Salerno had a medical school to study wine for medicinal purposes.

The wine region Valpolicella's name comes from the Latin "val polis cellar" "valley of the "cellars". Since early Roman times the region has produced sweet wines.

Italy also produces several liqueurs and beer. These include Grappa made from leftover wine; Sambucca from anisette; Strega with an almond flavor; Marsala, a sweet red wine produced on Sicily; Vermouth made from wine and spices; and Campari, concocted by Gaspare Campari and his son c 1890. Vermouth comes from the German "wermut" or wormwood for making absinthe. Vermouth was known even in Etruscan times, but became popular after it was commercially produced by Benedetto Carpano in Turin in 1786.

Did You Know?

Bartolommeo de' Sacchi wrote the oldest cookbook *De Honesta Voluptate ac Valetudina* (Concerning Honest Pleasure and Wellbeing) in c 1474.

In Puglia, the "toe of Italy" is one of the oldest olive trees, "Il Grande Vecchio" "the Great Old One" which was planted by the Romans about 3000 years ago.

The ancient Romans celebrated the end of the planting season by honoring Saturn, the god of agriculture, with Saturnalia. They decorated their homes with wreaths, gave gifts, drank much wine and ate tremendous amounts of food with a lot of merrymaking!

The Tatars brought the first pasta to Italy in the 13th c. Early pasta was eaten with the fingers, but when tomato sauces were introduced, forks became part of the table setting.

Potatoes were introduced by Napoleon and were used to make gnocchi.

Macaroni was a German dish brought to Genoa.

Pasta fresco literally means fresh pasta, and should always be used promptly. This usually made with durum or all-purpose wheat. Pasta secca is the dried pasta and only made with durum flour.

Pasta is from the Latin meaning "dough" "paste" or "pastry cake".

Forks were first used in Venice.

Paella means "pot".

In 1533 Catherine de' Medici married the future king of France Henri II, bringing recipes, dishes, wines, and herbs to France from Italy.

White truffles from Piedmont sell for over $1000 per pound.

Saltimbocca, a dish with veal, wine, ham, and sage means "jump in the mouth".

A Mr. Tortoni of Naples invented biscuit tortoni – granite and gelati "ice cream".

Maria de Cleofa invented the double boiler.

Italy is the largest producer of rice in Europe.

Focaccia is from the Latin "focus" or hearth, since the bread was once cooked on hot stones before the invention of ovens.

Brutti ma buoni cookies translates into English "ugly but good" and are made in Lazio.

Crostini, small toast rounds, are a sign of hospitality.

Risotto Milanese was first concocted by a Mr. Zafferano, a stained glass maker in Milan. He added saffron, a very expensive spice to the rice to make it look golden, in honor of his daughter's wedding.

Calzone, a folded over pizza, comes from the word for trousers.

Emperor Maximus was thought to consume 40 pounds of food and 40 quarts of wine a day!

Salt, once very expensive, was used for barter.

Sicily is known for marzipan (an almond and sugar paste made into candies of various shapes) and bottarga (also found on Elba and Sardinia), dried tuna or gray mullet roe.

Marco Polo was one of many explorers to bring back spices from the Far East and sell them at exorbitant prices. Eventually Spain and Portugal were to corner this market.

Parma is known for Parmesan cheese and Parma hams.

The best olive oil comes from Lucca, and is best sampled in late summer or early fall after the pressing.

Cannoli, a pastry from Sicily, comes from "capello di turco" "Turkish hats", after Turkey invaded that island.

"Candy" is derived from 'canna melis" Latin for sugar cane. These hard candies date back to ancient times and were made by cooking sugar with fragrances and essences.

Knights returning from the Holy Land to Milan founded the Bakery of "Quattro Marie", one of the oldest charitable organizations. Its specialties were Panettone and Colomba, cakes for Christmas and Easter. Tre Marie Panettone is still located in Milan.

Pimentos, turkeys, tomatoes, potatoes, and tobacco were brought from the Americas.

The word cereal comes from Ceres, goddess of agriculture.

Pizza was invented in Naples, probably in the 1700s. At that time it was a flat bread with garlic, butter and salt.

Mantua is noted for its tortelli di zucca, pumpkin filled pasta; Luccio in salsa, poached pike; and the Gonzaga family chef who wrote his own cookbook.

Naples is noted for chocolates.

Abruzzo has vineyards, olive trees, sheep and famous dried pasta.

Gusto comes from the Roman word "to taste".

Apicus wrote what is thought to be the first Italian cookbook *De Re Coquinaria*. The book included recipes for vegetables, seafood, meats, mushrooms, truffles, fruits, nuts, cakes, wine, herbs and spices.

Caeseus is the Latin word for cheese. Other countries use similar words – Kase in German; Kaas in Dutch; cais Gaelic; caws Welsh; queijo Portuguese; queso Spanish; and cese Old English from which we get cheese.

Documents show Rome has had a Jewish community since 159BC located on the Tiber River and still known as the Ghetto. Following Jewish dietary laws theey used local ingredients, and may have influenced much of the early Roman cuisine.

Pretzels were thought to have been first made in Italy by monks in the 7th c.

Coffee has long been favored by the Italians, especially espresso. Coffee was first brought here c 1600. Café Florian on the Piazzo San Marco in Venice has been serving coffee and pastries since about 1720. Cappuccino is named for the Capuchin monks who wear brown hooded robes, thus the name "monks head" for the coffee with white crema foam and a brown ring!

Strawberries were thought to have first been cultivated in Rome.

Pietro Ferrero, an Italian pastry maker invented Nutella in the 1940s during World War II when chocolate was rationed. He mixed cocoa with toasted hazelnuts, cocoa butter, and vegetable oils. This was called pasta gianduja or hazelnut paste. The name was changed to Nutella in 1964.

A ristorante offers a full meal, a trattoria is a neighborhood restaurant serving local foods and wines, and an osteria provides food and lodging.

Jamaica

Jamaica is an island of the Greater Antilles in the Caribbean Sea, about 90 miles south of Cuba, and 119 miles west of Hispaniola, the island with Haiti and the Dominican Republic. Jamaica was settled by the Arawak and Taino indigenous people of South America between 4000 and 1000 BC. The Arawaks called the island "Xaymaca" "land of wood and water" "Island of the Springs". Christopher Columbus claimed Jamaica for Spain in 1494. In 1655 it became a British colony and sugar cane plantations were started. Jamaica is still part of the British Commonwealth achieving its independence in 1962. Kingston is the capital. English is the official language.

Stamp and Go (Codfish Fritters)

Makes about 24 fritters

½ lb. salted cod
1 cup flour
1 tsp. baking powder
1 small onion, peeled and chopped
1 egg, lightly beaten
¾ cup milk
1 tbls. melted butter or vegetable oil

1 clove garlic, minced
½ red or jalapeno chili, or Scotch bonnet, seeded and finely chopped
1 tsp. hot sauce
½ tsp. dried thyme
Vegetable oil for frying

Place the cod in a bowl of water overnight. Drain, wash and cover with water in a saucepan. Bring to a boil. Drain
Combine the flour, baking powder in a bowl. Make a hole and add the egg, milk, and butter. Mix until smooth. Add fish, onion, chili, hot sauce, and thyme.
Heat some oil in a skillet.
Make the mixture into balls and drop into hot oil. Cook until browned. Drain on paper towels.
Serve hot.

Dining Etiquette

Jamaican families are very close knit. When invited for a meal please be punctual. Dress conservatively men in trousers, ladies in dresses, skirts, or dressy slacks. Please bring a small gift for the home, perhaps something from your country, or flowers. Shake hands greeting and departing. Men may pat each other on the shoulder or arm. Women may hug and kiss on each cheek, starting with the right. Please use titles with names until you get to know someone. Drinks and hors d'oeuvres will be served. Please wait for the hostess to seat you, and start after she has, or the host invited you to start. Meals may be served with dishes on the table or buffet style. Eat continental style with your fork in the left hand and fork in the right. Please try a little of everything and try to finish what is on your plate. The toast is initiated by the host "cheers". Soccer and football are popular sports.

Tropical Guava BBQ Chicken

1 whole chicken - quartered & cleaned
1-2 tbls. Walkerswood Mild Jerk Seasoning
3 tbls. Walkerswood Guava Jam
1 tbls. olive oil
1½ cups orange juice

1 tsp. fresh Jamaican ginger - minced
1 clove garlic - minced
1 tsp. fresh thyme leaves
1 tbls. tomato ketchup

Rub chicken with Jerk Seasoning and olive oil, allow to marinate for 1 hour (preferably overnight)
To make tropical guava BBQ sauce - combine remaining ingredients into a sauce pan and simmer on medium heat for 15 minutes
Cook chicken on BBQ grill for 45 minutes until cooked through
Baste chicken repeatedly during the final 10 minutes of cooking.
Recipe courtesy of Walkerswood Caribbean Kitchen Cookbook; Chef/Author Virginia Burke; and Sean Garbutt

Cuisine

The cuisine is a combination of Arawak, French, Dutch, Spanish, British, African, Indian, Middle Eastern, and Chinese cultures. Native to the island are tropical fruits, fish, goats, sugar cane, cocoa, bananas, yams and vegetables. The Arawaks preserved meat with peppers, allspice, and sea salt to make what we now call Jamaican jerk spice. Common dishes are curry goat, fried dumplings, akee and salt fish (cod), fried plantains, jerk, rice and beans, and steamed cabbage. Some of the ingredients used in the food are pimento (allspice), avocado, breadfruit, callaloo, cassava, chayote, coconut and coconut milk, bananas, ginger, plantain, pineapple, Scotch Bonnet Peppers, taro, jerk spice, yams, garlic, dried and salted cod and beef, thyme, oxtail, okra, guava, passion fruit, cho-cho (christophene), soursop, sugar cane, ketchup and vinegar, onions, and beans. The food is often cooked outdoors. Jamaican All Purpose Seasoning is a blend of allspice, coriander, paprika, garlic, onion, ginger, celery salt, thyme, oregano, black pepper, cumin, hot red pepper, salt, sugar, and citric acid made by Grace, Kennedy and Co.

Jamaican Specialties

Saltfish and ackee (a red fruit) – salt and dried cod, onions, and Scotch bonnet is the national dish and served for breakfast
Curry goat – curried goat with Scotch Bonnet peppers
Jamaican patty - pastry with meat, chicken, vegetables or other ingredients

Jerk seasoning – chili peppers, garlic, onion, cinnamon, ginger and allspice blend
Jerk chicken – grilled chicken with jerk spices; also jerk pork
Escovitch – poached or fried fish dish with pickled vegetables and Scotch bonnet peppers
Brown fish stew – fried fish with gravy

Jamaican spiced bun – spicy bun
Coconut rundown – boiled coconut and water to make a custard
Fish tea – fish, yam, pumpkin, cassava, potato and spice soup
Festival – fried cornmeal snack
Pilau – chicken, pork, shellfish and vegetables
Callaloo – soup made from dasheen leaves
Pepperpot soup – callaloo, okra, beef, coconut milk, yams and spices
Solomon Gundy – pickled fish pate
Mannish water – goat soup
Rice and peas (kidney beans)
Spinners – flour dumplings

Coco bread – like a bun, can be stuffed
Bulla cakes – pastry with molasses, ginger and nutmeg
Bammy - cassava flatbread
Mango and sour sop ice cream
Irish moss – dessert made from seaweed
Gizzada – tart with coconut filling
Banana fritters
Coconut drops
Bustamante Backbone – dessert named for the first Prime Minister Alexander Bustamante, grated coconut and sugar candy
Grater cake – grated coconut in sugar fondant
Toto – coconut cake
Matrimony – Otaheite apple dessert

Holidays and Special Occasions

Good Friday – eggs are used to predict the future. In a clear glass three quarters filled with water the albumen (white of an egg) is placed. Two pieces of a stick forming a cross representing a crucifix are rested on the rim of the glass. At 11 AM the glass is placed in a garden so the sun shines on it directly. The sun's heat is supposed to make shapes appear. They might be a ship, coffin, bride, motor car, or something else. If a ship then travel may be in the works, a coffin suggests death.
Easter – escovitch, ackee, callaloo, codfish, jerk chicken and pork, rice and peas, curried goat, Easter buns made with raisins and spices, cheese; rum punch
Christmas – roast beef or turkey, glazed ham, dark fruit cake; rum soaked fruits, sorrel drink, eggnog
New Year's Eve – Mannish Water, a goat soup

Beverages

In 1655 when the British captured Jamaica the Navy decided to give as liquor rations rum instead of French brandy! Rum was first produced when the British developed large sugar cane plantations on the island. Appleton Estate rum has been made on Jamaica since 1749. Rum is not only used as a drink but in cakes, meat, vegetable, fruit and dessert dishes. But it is not only rum that is produced on the island. There are also fruit and vegetable juices, ginger beer, sour sop, and of course tea is consumed in large quantities.

Did You Know?

According to superstition if a Physic Tree is chopped down on Good Friday near noon it bleeds.
Scotch Bonnet peppers (red, yellow or orange hot chilies) got their name because they look like a Scotsman's tam-'o-shanter (hat). They are related to the Mexican habanero.
Pickapeppa Sauce was created by Norman Nash in 1923 and is only slightly hot! It is used in Jamaican cooking.

Japan

Japan, "The Land of the Rising Sun", or in Japanese "Nihon", is formed by an archipelago of about 3300 islands off Asia in the Pacific Ocean. The four main islands are Honshu, Hokkaido, Shikoku, and Kyushu. Only about 16% of the land is arable. Japan has been inhabited since Paleolithic times with the first society c 10,000 BC, and the world's first pottery; c 6000 BC agriculture; and rice cultivated in the 3rd c BC. The Yayoi Culture c 300 AD brought farming and metallurgy with bronze and iron. Later Buddhism was introduced, and Japan went through periods with emperors, shoguns, and the courts were constantly moved. The Portuguese arrived in 1543, but all doors to trade, except to a few Dutch were closed from 1635 to 1853 when Commodore Matthew C. Perry arrived. Beginning in the 1930s Japan invaded China and in the 1940s much of the Pacific. In 1945 Japan surrendered, with the U.S. occupying the country until 1952. Tokyo, formerly Edo, became the official capital in 1686, when Emperor Meiji moved it from Kyoto. Japanese is the official language.

Dining Etiquette

Please be punctual when invited for a meal. Please take candy, cakes, flowers (in an uneven number and not arranged), or a gift for the home. Remove your shoes on entering a home. The Japanese may bow (ojige) slightly or will offer to shake hands, but limply. The deeper the bow, the more respect. An informal bow is with hands at one's side and bowing about 15 degrees. A more formal bow is with hands together, about 30 degrees. The Saikeirei is the most honorable bow executed very slowly and to a 45 degree angle. Do not bow with your hands in your pockets. Stand well apart and do not look the other person directly in the eye. If seated place your feet together or cross them at the ankle. The Japanese are very polite. Laughter can mean embarrassment or not understanding.

Drinks will be served. The host or hostess will seat the guests at the table, which will be low and one will sit on cushions or mats. The host and hostess will be seated next to each other. The place of honor is in front of the tokonoma (alcove). Hot towels will be distributed to wipe one's hands and mouth, and then is used as a napkin. Sake, poured by the host, and then the guests, is served before the rice, which is eaten as the last course. At each place will be a rice bowl on the left, a soup bowl with a covered lid on the right, and chopsticks placed horizontally in front of them. Before the meal say "Itadakimasu", and at the end Gochiso-sama deshita". Dishes are served at the same time. Take a small amount. Lift the bowl to eat from, and drink your soup. When starting don't wait for the host, just start. Never pass food with chopsticks from one person to another, or cross your chopsticks on an empty bowl, which signifies death. Don't stick them in the bowl, or point them at anyone. Sushi may be eaten with your fingers. It is OK to slurp noodles. Don't blow your nose at the table.

Toasting is profuse and never ending. As soon as one's glass is emptied it is refilled. One must always pour for someone else with your right hand, supported by the left, and not one's own glass. Never spill from your glass or bottle. People of lower rank or age pour for more senior or elder. To make a toast raise your glass, make eye contact, and say "Kampai" "Cheers". All then drink at once. At the end of the evening, finish by saying "Ekey" "Bottoms up".

Japanese Style Fried Chicken

3 lbs. chicken wings or drum sticks   3 tbls. toasted sesame seeds
Salt and pepper
½ cup corn starch

In a plastic bag, combine corn starch, chicken (seasoned with salt and pepper)
Put the chicken pieces in the bag, a few at a time, shaking to coat.
Deep fry the chicken in heated oil until the chickens are golden brown.
Soak the chicken immediately to the sauce.
Pull out the chicken from the sauce and sprinkle the toasted sesame over the top.

Sauce

1 cup water   ½ tsp. salt
½ cup soy sauce   ½ tsp. black pepper
½ cup sugar   3 cloves garlic crushed

In a small pan, combine all the ingredients for the sauce.
Stir over medium heat until sugar dissolves completely. Set aside.
Recipe courtesy of Mayu Nakamura, Embassy of Japan, Washington, DC

Cuisine

The staples of the Japanese diet are rice, fish, seaweed, salt, fruit and vegetables. Each island has its specialty, though the most traditional and noted is from Kyoto. Food, like other parts of Japanese life, depends on harmony. The food presentation, room, decorations in the tokonoma (alcove), serving dishes, the seasons, and diners are all taken into account. Contrasts of color, shapes, and texture dominate the presentation. Each dish has importance. Most food is not spicy, and strong flavors are added at the last moment. Few sauces are used. Decorations on plates using flowers and carved vegetables add to the elegance. Portions are small. The food is always made from fresh ingredients, and is very healthy. A grilled dish is served before a steamed one, steamed before simmered. A square dish is used to serve round food. A bento (box lunch) will contain rice, pickles, grilled meat or fish and vegetables. An o-bento is the lovely lacquered box that carries the bento.

Japanese Specialties

Sashimi – raw fish

Tempura – vegetables or fish dipped in batter and fried

Sukiyaki – stir-fry vegetables and strips of beef dish

Teriyaki – broiled or grilled slices of marinated fish or meat

Yakitori – grilled chicken skewers

Shabu-shabu – thin beef, dipped in a broth, and then a sauce

Kaiseki ryori –tea ceremony cooking, with influence on dining etiquette

Tofu – soybean cake

Mochi – rice cake

Senbei – rice cracker

Daikon – large white radish

Wasabi – Japanese horseradish

Dashi – basic clear soup stock, made with katsuo, dried fish and kombu, dried kelp, and is the base for many Japanese dishes, especially soup

Sushi – rice, vinegar, vegetables and fish rolled in seaweed

Miso – fermented bean paste

Tonkatsu – fried, breaded pork cutlets

Fugu – blowfish that must be very carefully prepared, or can cause sudden death

Noodles – soba (buckwheat), ramen (yellow), or udon (white wheat)

Seafood is grilled, steamed, fried, stewed or eaten raw

Vegetables are steamed, sautéed, blanched, or pickled

Holidays and Special Occasions

New Year's – mocha (rice cakes), tangerines (passing of generations), lobsters (old age), zoni (broth), herring roe, black beans, dried water chestnuts, seaweed, sake, and offerings for the gods

Doll Festival – kusmochi- green for spring

Children's Day – special candies, shrimp that look like samurai helmets

Weddings, birthdays – kyogashi (colored, pastel candies); red dishes (happy food); sea bream (brings good luck); Rice with beans is eaten on one's birthday. The 61st birthday is very important.

Weddings – the bride and groom take 3 sips of sake from each of 3 cups. Clam soup is served to symbolize the union.

Funeral – special cake with leaf of lotus; tea is given in times of sorrow. Salt is given to each attendee, and another person should sprinkle it on you before entering a home.

The Tea Ceremony

The tea ceremony (Chanoyu) has many special meanings, is beautiful to watch, and fulfills the Japanese embodiment of harmony. It is part of the Zen path to enlightenment. There are no decorations. Instead the utensils, actions, and conversation are governed by the participants. The utensils consist of a furnace, ladle, tongs for charcoal, slop bowl, trivet, water vessel, kettle, kettle stand, tea caddies, and tea bowls. When invited for a ceremony the host(ess) enters the room last. Dress very conservatively as you will be seated on the floor. Koicha, thick green tea is brewed. Sweet cakes are usually served. The tea bowl is passed from person to person on a silk cloth placed on the left palm. Take 3 ½ sips, set down, wipe the edge of the bowl with the cloth, and pass to the next guests. The tea ceremony was perfected by Sen No Rikyo, the Grand Master. He later was assassinated by Toyotomi Hideyoshi in 1590. Some of his family have continued the tea ceremony tradition founding special schools.

Beverages

Japan's national drink is sake, a rice wine, and dates back over 1200 years. Sake is 17% alcohol, made from rice that is polished, washed, steeped and steamed. Mold is then added which converts starch to sugar, then stirred for 38 hours, and yeast mash turns the sugar to alcohol. Lastly, the mash, mold rice and water are mixed for four days, then allowed to ferment for three weeks. The sake is finally filtered, pasteurized and bottled. Akita is said to grow the best rice for sake and its springs produce the purest water. The best sake is served cold. Sake can also be served hot in small cups from a flask. Please drink using the right hand. Sake is drunk at festivals, rituals, and for everyday drinking. Amarake is sweet sake; otoso, sake with rice. The largest brewery is the Gekkeikan Sake Company in Kyoto, founded in 1637.

The plum tree was introduced to Japan by a Chinese envoy in the 6th c. The imperial family found the plum flowers extremely beautiful. By the 17th c plum wine was being produced. Wine is produced on three of the four islands.

Shochu is a distilled liquor made from rice, wheat, sweet potatoes, sugar cane, and fermented. Made in Kyushu, it has an alcoholic content of 25-35%. Serve it on the rocks, or with water. Japan also has produced whiskey since the 1920s, including the 18 year old Yamazaki made by Suntory and single malts produced by Nikka. Suntory is one of the world's largest liquor makers. Its whiskey is blended with Scotch whisky, and aged in oak casks. The Germans found hops in Japan and taught the Japanese how to brew beer. They are mainly light lagers.

Did You Know?

Soy sauce was brought from China about 500 AD and tea c 800.
The Portuguese introduced the tempura (frying) style of cooking in the 17th c.
Meat appeared in the 19th c, but was forbidden by the Buddhists.
The largest fish market in Asia is located at Tsukiji in Tokyo. The fish arrives by truck to an area of 54 acres, 15,000 employees, and auctions took place daily.
The hocho is a special knife for designing flowers, etc. out of flowers and fruit, or slicing sashimi, raw fish.
By the 3rd c BC Korea was growing rice which was brought to Japan by the Yayoi.
Rice farming has its own rituals. Sake is poured on the field at the beginning of the year as an offering to the rice paddy god. Inar is the goddess of rice.
Rice was used for paying taxes and wages until the mid 19th c.
In 1993 Japan, for the first time permitted imported rice, and in 1995 apples from the U.S.
Matsuzaka beef from Kobe is world famous and the most expensive.
Butter was introduced by the Europeans, who were called eaters of animal fat "batakusai", or "butter stinkers".
Noritake China in Nagoya is the world's largest porcelain maker.
Sushi was once used as a method to preserve fish. Dried fish was placed between vinegared rice. Seaweed did not become part of the dish until later. Today sushi rolls can be made with almost anything, but will always include rice. Sashimi is the raw fish used in sushi.

Jordan

Jordan is a country on the east bank of the River Jordan bordered by Saudi Arabia to the east and southeast, Iraq to the northeast, Syria to the north, and the West Bank and Israel to the west. Much of the country is desert, but there is arable land and forests, and it is part of the Fertile Crescent. The history of Jordan dates back to ancient times as part of the Babylonian and Canaanite civilizations. The country was part of different kingdoms – Edom, Moab, Ammon, and Petra, and at times part of Egypt and Israel. The later rulers were the Greek, Persian, Roman, and Byzantine Empires. In the 7th it was controlled by the Arab Islamic Empire, and in the 15th c the Ottoman Empire until 1918. In 1922 Jordan was recognized as a state under the British mandate, and in 1946 became the sovereign state of the Hashemite Kingdom of Jordan. Amman, the capital, has been settled since at least 10,050 BC, destroyed by earthquakes, and other disasters, and in the late 19th when a railroad was built between Medina and Damascus, was on trade and pilgrimage routes. The official language is Arabic.

Dining Etiquette

It is a sign of hospitality to be invited to a Jordanian home. When invited for a meal please arrive punctually. Shoes may or may not be removed when entering. Please bring a gift – an odd number of flowers, chocolates, pastries, or something from your country. Men will be greeted by the host, and female guests by the hostess. Men will shake hands with other men. A lady will extend her hand first. Good female friends will kiss several times on the cheek. Strong, bitter coffee will be offered in a handleless cup. A pitcher of water will be offered to wash your hands over a basin and then a towel. You may be seated at a low table with cushions, on the floor, or at a dining table. Eating is always with the right hand, and a spoon or other utensils may be provided. Always pass or accept things with the right hand or both hands. When bread is served, you may use it like a utensil. If a communal dish is served, please take only the food right in front of you. Water is usually offered only at the end of meal. Please wash your hands on finishing the meal. Coffee will then be served.

If tea is offered please accept at least two glasses, though three may be offered. Please place your hand over the glass if you are finished. If you are offered coffee please shake the cup "no more" before returning it, so that the cup is not refilled. Jordan is an Islamic country and no pork or alcohol are served.

When visiting the Bedouin you will be seated on the floor. Please sit cross-legged, and never show the sole of your shoe. The Bedouin are known for their hospitality, and appreciate it being returned either with a gift for the host, hostess or children, or doing something else special such as reciprocating a meal. At a mansaf banquet only men will dine, and the women and children will eat what is left. Shrak, a whole wheat bread is placed on a platter, topped with rice and lamb placed on top. After the meal is finished, coffee, or perhaps tea will be offered.

287

Mansaf (rice with stewed lamb)

Mansaf is the national dish.

10 lbs. lamb or chicken	Onions
2 ¼ lbs. whey, yogurt or ayran	Pine nuts
Margarine	Roasted almonds
4 ½ lbs. rice	Flat bread

Wash whey and soak in water for an hour. Mash in blender, then let dry. Wash meat and put on a tray. Cover with water and let soak. Add diced onion, then boil until partially cooked. Remove meat saving broth. Mix whey juice with the broth and let boil (thicken with cornstarch as desired). Add meat and simmer until meat is thoroughly cooked.
Cook rice.
Please 2 or 3 flat loaves of bread on a tray. Put rice on the bread in a pyramid, then arrange pieces of meat on top. Garnish with pine nuts and almonds.
Recipe Courtesy of the Royal Jordanian Embassy, Washington, DC

Cuisine

The cuisine has been developed over thousands of years using the local ingredients. Much of the land is desert, with mountains in the west, and the Dead Sea forms a border. Meats are baked, sautéed, roasted, or grilled. Mountain regions grow lentils, chickpeas, bulgur, olives, and grapes, and the valleys – citrus fruits – oranges, lemons, kumquats, vegetables, and sumac. The Bedouin make use of camel's milk and dates. Staples include wheat, barley, tomatoes, eggplant, cabbage, yogurt, dates, olives and olive oil, limes and lemons, lamb, and mutton. Herbs and spices used are cinnamon, saffron, garlic, nutmeg, allspice, and pepper. Common nuts are almond and walnuts. Tomato sauces are frequently served. Mezze – small plates (appetizers) are offered before large meals.

Jordanian Specialties

Laban – yogurt
Jameed – yogurt sauce, served with mansaf
Maglouba – rice, meat, and vegetables cooked in layers
Makmora – chicken baked in dough with olive oil
Musakhan – chicken with onions, olive oil, pine seeds, and seasonings
Kofta b'tahini – ground meat baked in tahini with potatoes and pine nuts and served over rice
Meshwi - kebab – grilled skewered meats

Galayet bandore – stewed tomatoes with garlic, olive oil, salt and pepper and eaten with pita bread
Shwarma – lamb or chicken served in a thin bread
Hummus – chickpea, tahini paste and garlic dip
Foul maddamis – mashed fava beans with lemon juice, olive oil, parsley, other herbs
Falafel - mashed chickpeas with lemon juice, garlic and olive oil
Saniyat dajej – baked chicken with potatoes, tomatoes, onions and spices

Shankish – spiced goat cheese

Chacheel – flour, eggs, and herbs in a yogurt sauce

Athan al-shayeb – wheat dough stuffed with ground beef and spices and cooked in jameed

Zarb – meat and vegetables cooked in an underground pot

Kubbeh – fried minced meat mixed with bulghur

Shrak – whole wheat bread

Burghul ahmar – bulghur in tomato sauce and served with chicken

Freekeh – fried meat that is braised and cinnamon bark and coriander added

Dawali – stuffed grape leaves

Bamya – okra with tomato sauce and served with meat

Moutabal – pureed eggppant or potato with garlic

Sambusak – fried dough stuffed with meat, pinenuts and onions

Tabouleh – bulghur, tomato, onion and parsley salad

Manakeesh- pastry with thyme, often eaten at breakfast

Fattoush – chopped vegetable salad with flatbread

Karadeesh – corn bread

Baklava – phyllo pastry with walnuts and honey

Holidays and Special Occasions

Holidays and special occasions – mansaf, quzi (stuffed spring lamb)

During Ramadan Muslims fast from sunrise to sunset - qatayef – sweet pastry with cream of nuts

Eid el-Fitr – the feast at the end of Ramadan

Eid-al-Adha – Feast of the Sacrifice that comes after the pilgrimage to Mecca

Birth, weddings, funerals and birthdays are celebrated with feasts

Beverages

Strong coffee and tea with na'na or meramiyyeh are drunk. Qahwah Saadah (Bedouin coffee) is bitter and frunk from small cups. Arabic coffee is sweeter. Other drinks are shaneeneh (goat milk yogurt); juices – lemon and mint, apricot, tamarind; and salhab (boiled milk with coconut and cinnamon).

Cave paintings in Petra depict winemaking over two thousand years ago. However with the arrival of the Muslims winemaking ceased in the 7th c. In 1996 Omar Zumot planted vineyards and wine has been produced at Madaba in southwest Jordan, under the Saint George brand. Since 2015 Haddad Estates & Vineyards in northern Jordan has been producing wines under the Jordan River label. The vines were first planted in 2002. Eagle Distilleries is the largest winery and wine cellar in the country.

Did You Know?

One of the earliest known places to grow sugar cane was at Tawahin es-Sukkar on the River Jordan. Today archeological digs have found evidence of millstones, water chutes, and other equipment used in the refining process. At one time it was a large part of Jordan's economy with many sugarcane plantations.

Baba Ghanouj (Roasted Eggplant Appetizer)

1 medium eggplant
Juice of 1 lemon
2 or 3 large cloves garlic
2 large tbls. tahini paste (sesame seed paste)

Salt to taste
Summak or parsley for garnish
2 tbls. olive oil
Pita bread

Preheat oven to 350°
Pierce eggplant in several places, and set on baking sheet. Bake for 1 hour. Cool.
Strip off and discard peel. Cut eggplant into chunks and place in food processor.
Add lemon juice, garlic, tahini and salt. Blend until smooth.
Place in a bowl. Garnish with summack or parsley. Drizzle with olive oil.
Serve with pieces of pita bread.
Recipe courtesy of the Royal Jordanian Embassy, Washington, DC

Falafel

1 cup dried chickpeas, or 1 can chickpeas or garbanzo beans
1 large onion
2 cloves garlic, chopped
1 tsp. coriander

1 tsp. cumin
3-5 tbls. flour
Salt and pepper to taste
Oil for frying

Place dried chickpeas in a bowl. Cover with cold water. Soak overnight. Drain.
If using canned beans, drain.
Place chickpeas in a saucepan with water, bring to boil for 5 minutes. Simmer for one hour.
Drain and cool for at least 15 minutes.
In a bowl combine chickpeas, garlic, onion, coriander, cumin, salt and pepper. Add flour.
Mash till a thick paste forms. Can also be done in a food processor.
Form into small balls.
Fry in oil until golden brown (about 5-7 minutes).
Serve hot.
Recipe courtesy of Royal Jordanian Embassy, Washington, DC

Kazakhstan

The Republic of Kazakhstan, is located in Central Asia, and is the world's largest landlocked country. It borders Russia, China, Kyrgyzstan, Uzbekistan, and Turkmenistan, and also adjoins a large part of the Caspian Sea. The country has been inhabited since the Neolithic Age and was mainly nomadic and horses are thought to have been first domesticated here. The Cumans came to the steppes in the 11th c. Several important cities such as Taraz and Hazrat-e Turkestan were located along the Silk Road. Genghis Khan invaded in the 13th c. By the 16th c the Kazakhs emerged as the distinct group, and in the 18th c the Russians advanced into the Kazakh steppe. By the 19th c it was part of the Russian Empire. The Russians later brought in collectivization and during the 1920-30s mass starvation through famine led to the population depleted by 38%. Kazakhstan received its independence in 1991. There are 131 ethnic groups including Kazakhs, Russians, Uzbeks, Ukrainians, Germans, Tatars, and Uyghurs. The majority of the population is Muslim. The state language is Kazakh with Russian also spoken. The capital was Almaty "Father of Apples" but since 1997 has been Astana . The word "Kazakh" means "a free and independent nomad" in ancient Turkish.

Dining Etiquette

The Kazakhs have traditionally been made up of family groups since early times to protect themselves against the environment and to protect their cattle and was called "ata-balasy" 'joining of one's grandson into one tribe". Families are hierarchical, and there is respect for elders and those in position.

The Kazakhs enjoy entertaining and there will always be an abundance of food. Please arrive on time, and no later than thirty minutes and dress conservatively. Shoes are removed and left by the door. When invited to a home please bring a gift for the hostess, pastries or other sweets, or if they drink alcoholic beverages vodka. Gifts are opened when received. When meeting a person please shake hands, sometimes with both hands and a smile. Since much of the country is Muslim men to do not shake hands with women. If she extends her hand it may be shaken. Women on greeting each other will usually hug. Do not call someone by there first name unless asked to do so. On arrival tea and bread will be served as serving bread is a sign of respect. The teacup will only be half filled. Filling it means the host would like you to leave. If the host drinks, vodka and appetizers may be offered. Seating could be at a table or seated on the floor. A soup and 1 or more main dishes will be offered. Food is eaten continental style with the fork in the left hand and knife in the right. Some foods will be eaten by hand. Use only your right hand. A bowl is given to the guest to drink a broth or tea. Turn your bowl upside down if you do not wish any more. Meals are a time to enjoy company and may take many hours. Leave something on your plate when you are finished eating, otherwise you will be served more! Kumys or tea will be served at the end of the meal. Since this is mainly a Muslim country alcoholic beverages or pork may not be served. If alcohol is, there is usually a lot of drinking and toasting. During the toast please maintain good eye contact.

In the countryside an honoured guest is served a boiled sheep's head on an elegant plate. The guest divides the parts of the sheep. The smallest child is given an ear so he or she will listen to and obey their elders; the eyes to the two closest friends so they will take care of their guest; the upper palate to the daughter-in-law, and the tongue to the daughter so they will hold their tongues; the pelvic bones to the second most respected guest; and the brisket to the son-in-law. You might also be offered kumys mare's milk during the summer.

If you are entertained in a yourta (a felt dwelling with a round wooden frame) please take off your shoes on entering and you will be taken to the place of honour. You will be seated opposite the entrance on a bright satin quilt, with your legs crossed. The other people sit according to the precedence of age. On your left will be a samovour, and tea is prepared. In the center will be a colored linen tablecloth, the dastarkhan "a meeting of friends". Sweets, cookies, apples and grapes are part of the first stage of serving. Before eating wash your hands. Tea may be served with sweets, but also hard drinks and toasts proposed.

Manti (Lamb Dumplings)

Makes about 20 dumplings

1½ lb. ground lamb	½ stick butter, softened
1 medium onion, peeled and finely chopped	Yogurt
Salt and pepper	Mint

In a bowl combine the ingredients.
Place a spoonful of the meat mixture in the center of the dough rounds. Bring the edges of the dough up and pinch shut. Using a little water seal the dough.
Place a colander in a pan with 1 inch water. Put the dumplings carefully in the colander. Cover. Bring to a boil. Simmer for 15 minutes.
Place dumplings in a serving bowl and garnish with the mint. Serve with yogurt.
The dumplings can also be deep-fried.

Dough

3 cups flour	1½ cups water

Combine the water and flour into a smooth dough. Make into a ball and place on a floured board. Roll out until very thin. Using a large cookie cutter cut into about 20 circles.

Cuisine

Kazakhstan is mainly an agricultural country and is known for its grains, potatoes, vegetables, melons and livestock. Dairy products, leather, meat and wool come from the livestock. The major crops are wheat, barley, cotton, and rice. The apple may originally have come from the Almaty, a name meaning "rich with apple". Mushrooms, carrots, and onions are quite common in cooking.

The cuisine is mainly native to the region but has also been influenced by the Russians, Ukrainians, Uzbeks and Turks. Most meals include bread, a starch such as potatoes or noodles and meat – goat, sheep, horse, which are also used for milk. Since the country is landlocked the only fish comes from rivers or lakes, and the North Aral Sea. The Sea almost dried up but now has over 22 species of fish including carp and pike. The winters are cold, so that there is a short growing season. Many of the vegetables are root vegetables that are hardier.

Destrakan refers to a table full of food. Bausak, the deep fried bread is strewn over the table, which is always more than copiously filled to show respect and prosperity.

Specialties

Plov/Pilaf – rice dish made with carrots, mutton, garlic, and oil
Lagman – stew with noodles
Borscht – beet soup with cabbage, meat and served with sour cream
Pelmeni – dough with meat and onions
Manti – dough with meat and onions, but may also have pumpkin
Leipioskka – round, flat bread
Shaslik – marinated meat grilled on a stick
Beshbarmak – means "five fingers" and is the national dish – boiled horse, goat, cow, or sheep meat, or sausage on the bone served over noodles with a meat broth called souppa. If it is sheep the honored guest is given the head. The rest of the meat is then divided as mentioned above.

Mypalau – sheep brain with broth and garlic
Ulpershek – horse heart, fat and aorta
Kazy – horse meat sausage
Bausak – deep-fried bread in the shape of a triangle or circle.

Holidays and Special Occasions

Nauryz – is a New Year festival celebrated at the time of the spring equinox. Lamb, horse, and bread are served to celebrate the arrival of spring after the long winter.

Beverages

Shay (hot black tea) is always served to guests on arrival in a home. Russians drink their tea filled up in teacups and the Kazakhs in wide-mouthed cups called kasirs that are only filled partway. Tea should always be hot and refilling showing respect..

Ayran, shubat, and kumys are drinks made with milk. Kumys is the national drink made from fermented mare's milk. It is also drunk on special occasions. Milk can come from camels, cattle, sheep and horses.

Though this is mainly a Muslim country vodka is drunk before a gathering, for ceremonies, and is drunk in large quantities. Toasts are given before drinking vodka. Wine is produced in the mountains to the east of Almaty. Beer is also brewed.

Kenya

Kenya is located in East Africa on the Equator. It was inhabited by hunting groups – Dorobo or bushmen who lived on the plains. They mixed with the Bantu from western Africa. The Coast was settled in 7th c by Persians and Arabs. The Portuguese came in the 15th c and established trading posts, but were driven out by the Arabs in 1729. C 1740 the Arabs ruled the coast. The British East Africa Company leased the coast from the Sultan of Zanzibar in 1887. Kenya became a British protectorate in 1895 and a crown colony in 1920. It received its independence in 1963, but remained a member of the British Commonwealth. The capital, Nairobi, was founded in 1899 as a railroad depot linking Mombasa to Uganda. English and Swahili are the official languages, plus more than 40 tribal languages are spoken.

Dining Etiquette

Please arrive punctually when invited for a meal. Please remove your shoes. Bring a gift of chocolates, something from your country, or for the home. Flowers are only given for condolence and wine is given for weddings. Please shake hands greeting and departing. Close female friends will kiss on the cheeks. Please wash your hands before and after meal. There will be no glasses on the table as beverages are served after the meal. Guests are served first, and please take some food as it is considered rude not to. Please wait until everyone has been served, and the oldest male starts, to eat. Food is eaten with the right hand, or may be eaten with your hands and no utensils. If passing, use your right hand or both hands. Please finish the food on your plate. Dessert is not usually served, but fruit might be at the end of the meal. A toast is proposed by the host "Cheers" and the guest of honor is expected to reciprocate. Socializing is after the meal. In some homes men may eat first, followed by the women and children. In Muslim homes, women if they wish to shake hands will extend a hand first. Men and women may dine separately. Please eat with your right hand. Muslims do not eat pork or drink alcohol. Afternoon tea is a daily custom and you might be invited for tea instead of a meal. Ugali is served from a large dish from which all eat.

Cuisine and Beverages

The Great Rift Valley has been home to very old civilizations and is very fertile with tea and cattle grown. Predominately the Kalenjin and Maasai live here. C 1000 AD cattle herding was introduced. The Maasai and Turkana eat beef and goat. The Kikuyu and Gikuyu raise corn, potatoes, bananas, yams, beans, greens, and irio is the main dish prepared. The Abaluhya eat ugali, and in the morning a thinner version called uji. Near Lake Victoria fish stews, vegetables, and rice are mainly eaten. The Maasai people herd cattle (a sign of wealth), sheep, and goats. Milk is served in decorative gourds, often mixed with cow's blood. The Maasai do not believe in the cultivation of land.

294

The cuisine comes from the Portuguese, English and the various ethnic groups in the country. The Portuguese introduced maize, bananas, chilies, pineapples, peppers, sweet potatoes, cassava, lemons, oranges, limes, and pigs; the British curries, chutneys, puddings and cream; the Indians samosas and other Indian dishes. The main staples are corn, maize, kale and other leafy greens, cabbage, tomatoes, avocados, potatoes, beans, grains, meat, chicken, mutton, fish along coast, fruit – mangoes, pawpaw, pears, papaya, pineapple, watermelon, oranges, guava, bananas, coconuts, and passion fruit. Crops grown include tea, coffee, sugarcane, pineapples, sorghum, cassava, beans, livestock – goats, cows, sheep, chickens, fish, peppers, fruit – passion fruit, oranges, limes, mango, papaya, pineapple, coconuts, wheat, greens - collards, tomatoes, cabbage, pumpkins, garlic, and squash. Pilli pilli (bird's eye peppers) and cilantro are used as seasonings. Much of the farming is still done by hand or with oxen. Some wild meat such as crocodile and ostrich may be included in the meals. Meals are served with ugali or potatoes, vegetables, and meat.

Tea (chai) – the tea is boiled with water, milk and sugar and is quite sweet. Coffee (kahawa) is grown in Kenya and has been a major export, especially Arabica. The after-dinner beverage is Maziwa Ya Kuganda (sour skimmed milk). Other popular drinks are lemonade, squash, punch and iced tea. Beer is brewed and the local beer is called muratina. Tusker is brewed by the East African Breweries and is known for its slogan "My Beer, My Country". In the 1990s the South African Breweries closed, but has now been bought by Kenya Breweries. Wine is produced in the Rift Valley along the slopes of Lake Naivasha.

Kuku Paka (Chicken and Coconut Milk)

Serves 6

3 lbs. chicken, cut into parts
2 tomatoes, chopped
1 onion, peeled and chopped
3 hot chilies, seeded and chopped
2 tbls. fresh grated ginger
4 garlic cloves, chopped
1 tbls. curry powder
2 tsp. ground cumin

1 tsp. ground coriander
2 tbls. coconut oil
2 cups coconut milk
Salt and pepper to taste
Lemon juice
½ cup cilantro, chopped
Rice or flatbread

In a food processor combine the tomatoes, onions, garlic, chilies, ginger, curry, cumin, and coriander until a paste forms.
Rub ½ the mixture over the chicken in a bowl. Reserve the remaining paste for the sauce.
Heat the coconut oil in a large pot, and add the remaining paste. Cook until thickened. Add the coconut milk and cook until thickened.
The chicken can be added to the mixture and cooked for about 30 minutes, or grilled and then added to the mixture.
Season with salt, pepper and a little lemon juice.
Serve garnished with cilantro and with rice or flatbread.

Matoke (Green Plantains and Beef)

Serves 4

1 lb. green plantains, peeled
1 lb. beef, cut into small cubes
1 tsp. lemon juice
1 tbls. fresh grated ginger
1 jalapeno or other hot pepper, chopped

1 large red onion, chopped
2 tbls. oil
1 tsp. curry powder
1 large clove garlic, minced
1 cup coconut milk

Boil the plantains in water for about 20 minutes, but not mushy. Drain water. Boil the beef in water with the lemon juice and ginger. Save the broth. Saute the onions in a skillet with the oil until just browned. Add the garlic and beef until it is just browned. Stir in a small amount of the broth and curry. Add coconut milk. Serve the beef with the plantains.

Kenyan Specialties

Ugali – (national dish) - maize porridge (light ugali is made from cornmeal and dark ugali from millet flour)
Nyama choma – (national dish) – roasted or grilled meat, usually goat or beef
Chapati- flat bread
Irio - mashed vegetables used to dip into meat or vegetable stews
Nyama choma – grilled or roasted meat
Posho – stiff dough
Red bean stew
Kitumbura – fried bread
Wali – coconut rice
Rice pilau – rice with spices
Kachumbari – tomato, onion, pepper, cilantro, lemon juice

M'baazi – pea beans
Kuku paka- chicken with coconut curry sauce
Karanga – meat and potato stew
Kunde – black-eyed peas and tomatoes
Samosas – fried meat pies
Githeri – boiled beans and corn
Ingoho – chicken dish eaten by Luhya
Matoke – mashed plantains
Sukuma wiki – vegetable stew
Samaki wa kupaka – grilled fish with coconut sauce and chilies
Sukuma wiki – collards, onions, chilies
Egg-bread – fried eggs and minced meat wrapped in a wheat flour pancake
Mandazi – sweet doughnut
Ndizi – bananas cooked in coconut leaves

Holidays and Special Occasions

Lent – meat is not eaten
Easter – people will often sleep in a church overnight. Chapati is served.
Easter Monday – nyoma choma
Christmas – family and friends visit and food is served. Christmas dinner will be fish, nyoma choma made of beef or goat, vegetables, fruit, chapati and chutneys. A cow or goat may be killed and roasted
Muslims do not eat or drink from sunrise to sunset during Ramadan. Idul-Fitr is the 3 day feast celebrated at the end of Ramadan
Weddings – cow or goat killed and roasted

Kiribati

The Republic of Kiribati is an island nation in the central Pacific Ocean comprised of 33 atolls and reef islands and one raised coral island, Banaba. Kiribati became independent from the United Kingdom in 1979. The South Tarawa, consists of a number of islets, connected by a series of causeways. The name *Kiribati* was adopted at independence in 1976 and is the local enunciation of *Gilberts*. This name derives from the main archipelago of three forming the nation. It was named the Gilbert Islands after the British explorer Thomas Gilbert who sighted he islands in 1788 while mapping out the Outer Passage route from Port Jackson to Canton. The islands have been inhabited by Micronesians since c 3000BC. Austronesians, European, Chinese, Polynesian, Fijin, Tongans, and Samoan stopped here for trading, whaling, and political interests. Some of the islands were occupied by the Japanese from 1941-43. English is the official language.

Dining Etiquette

The oldest male is considered head of the house. There is respect for elders. Please do not have direct eye contact is not appropriate especially with an older person.

Please arrive promptly. Shake hands greeting and departing. Please bring a gift from your ohme country. Unlike in many places bringing food to a meal is an insult to the hostess as it means she has not prepared enough food. The host will seat you at the table. Guests may be seated in the middle. There may or may not be cutlery. If the host eats with his fingers, please follow even though there may be a fork or spoon at your place. If eating with your fingers a bowl of water will be passed before and after the meal to wash your hands. Take only one serving as it is considered rude to take seconds. Do try every dish. Please wait for the host to start and after a blessing has been said.

Cuisine

Since the islands are mainly coral reefs there is little soil, plant life, and animals. However it is from the sea the population feed itself on crabs, turtles, shrimp, crayfish, giant clam, fish – lobster, tuna; and birds – noddies and terns. Coconut has been a staple food used for its milk and flesh. Settlers over the years brought in animals and plants for survival. They included pigs, rats, dogs, rice, taro, yams, breadfruit, bananas, lemons, and sugarcane. Later the British brought cattle, chicken, wheat, potatoes, cassava, watermelons, pineapples, papaya, oranges, mangoes, onions, tomatoes, pumpkin, cabbage and spices such as curry powder, garlic, and ginger. Today some food is imported, including canned goods and non-perishable items. The most common foods used in cooking are breadfruit, coconuts, panadanus (screwpine), rice, taro, a native fig, and yams. Coconut is very important for its toddy (sap) cut from the flower spathe which has many vitamins.

Toddy is used in children's drink, as a base for syrups, soured for vinegar, or fermented into an alcoholic drink. Food is cooked with rocks that are heated and then placed in the ground. Food is wrapped in banana leaves, placed on the hot rocks and then covered with dirt. Fish is served fried, broiled, battered and deep fried, and baked.

Breakfast may consist of bread, fruit, coffee, and tea. In many places lunch was the largest meal of the day, then naps taken in the heat of the day. Today dinner is the larger meal with many people working.

Palu Sami

Serves 4

2 lbs. fresh spinach	2 tbls. butter
1 can (#3) corned beef, break into pieces	2 cans coconut milk
1 medium onion, peeled and chopped	

Preheat oven to 350°
In a skillet heat the butter and sauté the onions until tender. Add corned beef.
Place the spinach leaves in a baking dish. Cover with the corned beef mixture. Top with the coconut milk. Cover.
Bake for 45 minutes.

Specialties

Poi – taro root
Pandanus – boiled, sliced and served with coconut cream
Palu sami – coconut cream, onion and curry powder wrapped in banana leaves, spinach or taro leaves served with pork, corned beef or chicken

Holidays and Special Occasions

The most important holiday is the annual celebration of independence on July 12th, which includes sports competitions, parades, and feasts. Other national holidays include New Year's Day, Easter, Christmas, and Youth Day (4 August).
Yap Day Festival – first weekend in March – traditional dancing, costumes, and food

Beverages

Fruit juices are common, along with coffee and tea. Kava is made from the kava root, which is ground for its liquid and water added. Beer, alcohol, and wines are all imported.

Kosovo

Kosovo is a landlocked country in southeastern Europe that borders Albania to the southwest, Macedonia to the southeast, Montenegro to the west, and Central Serbia to the north and east. Most of its terrain is mountainous. The country has been inhabited for over 10,000 years by various tribal ethnic groups. It was originally part of the Dardanian Kingdom and later the Roman province of Dardania. The region was inhabited by Illyrian tribes, and during the Middle Ages was part of the Byzantine, Bulgarian and Serbian Empire. From 1455 to 1912 it was part of the Ottoman Empire. Eventually it was within the republic of Serbia in the Federal Republic of Yugoslavia. Kosovo declared its independence from Serbia in 2008. The capital is Pristina. Languages spoken here are Albanian, Serbian, Turkish, Romani, and Bosnian.

Dining Etiquette

Please shake hands greeting and departing. Men and women may kiss if they know each other well. Gift giving is very important, and if you are given something, please return with your own gift. Never give money as it could be misconstrued as a bribe! Flowers are not usually presented. Instead take a small painting, book, or something from your own country. If there are children present, please bring something for them. Drinks will be served, mainly grape rakia. The hostess will seat the guests at the table. Dishes will probably be served by the host. There may be an abundance of food, even though the family may not have much. Please do not start eating until the hostess does.

Burek (pastry with cheese)

½ lb. feta cheese
1 lb. phyllo pastry leaves
2 sticks butter, softened

½ cup milk
2 eggs
Small bunch of parsley or dill

Using your fingers or a brush grease about 1 tbls. butter on a cookie sheet.
In a pan heat the butter and milk until the butter is melted.
Beat the eggs in a small bowl. Add to milk and butter.
Chop the cheese and parsley.
Take out half the phyllo. Wrap the rest in a damp cloth so it won't dry out.
Take out several phyllo leaves at a time and place on cookie sheet, each time brushing with butter mixture. Spread the cheese and parsley on the top layer. Open the rest of the phyllo and layer with butter mixture. Cut the pastry in squares.
Preheat oven to 300-325°.
Bake for about 30 minutes, or until golden brown.

Cuisine

The cuisine of Kosovo has been influenced by the cuisines of Albania, Montenegro, Greece, and Turkey. Common dairy products are milk – cow and goat, yogurt, ayran, spreads, Sar cheese, cheese, cottage cheese, and kaymak. Meat is mainly beef, chicken and lamb Vegetables are used seasonally - cucumbers, tomatoes, mushrooms, garlic, onion and cabbage are pickled, nettles, ajvar – hot or mild red peppers, and beans. Stuffed peppers are a favorite dish. Many medicinal herbs and teas are grown in the country, some of which are now exported as dried herbs, essential oils and extracts. Fruits include apples, quince, plums, bilberries, blueberries, strawberries, and raspberries. Pita bread, potatoes and rice are part of diet. Traditional Kosovan desserts are often made with sherbet - water cooked with sugar with either lemon or vanilla flavor. Pies in Kosovo are known as "trejte"or "pite".

Kosovo Specialties

Kullpite – pie with yogurt
Bakllasarm – pie with yogurt and garlic
Leqenik – cornbread filled with spinach or cheese
Flija – thin pastry layers served with cream and kaymak
Kaymak – thickened cream
Kebab – meat and/or vegetables cooked on skewers over the grill
Resenik – cabbage pie
Purrenik – leek pie
Hithenik – nettle pie
Sujuk – traditional sausages
Sarma – cabbage or vine leaves wrapped around meat
Tarator - salad of cucumbers, garlic and yogurt

Shope salad – tomato, cucumber, onion and white cheese salad
Tave prizreni – casserole of lamb, eggplant, green peppers, onions, tomatoes,
Tave kosi – baked lamb and yogurt
Tave krapi – carp dish with garlic, bay, tomato and parsley
Burian – vegetable dish with rice, spinach and eggs
Baklava - phyllo pastry with nuts and honey or sugar syrup
Sultjash – rice with water or milk, raisins and cinnamon
Kajmacin – baked eggs with sugar and oil
Sheqer Pare – pastry with sherbet
Kadaif – phyllo with vanilla sugar and walnuts

Holidays and Special Occasions

New Year's Day – national holiday
Orthodox Christmas Day is celebrated in January with candlelit mass, processions from the churches, family feasts and gifts
Independence Day – February 17
Hazu Jehon – folk festival in May with native costumes, crafts and food
Prizren Cultural Fair – Held during Ramadan to break the fast in the evening with food, crafts, and traditional dress.
Bayram is held at the end of Ramadan and llokuma "wedding donuts" are served
New Year's Eve – parties, fireworks, and family reunions

Tomato and Cucumber Salad

Serves 6

Lettuce
1 green pepper, chopped
1 red pepper, chopped
1 cucumber, chopped

4 tomatoes, chopped
3 green onions, chopped
8 oz. feta cheese
½ cup black olives

Combine the ingredients in a salad bowl. Toss with the dressing.

Dressing

¼ cup olive oil
¼ cup fresh lemon juice
2 cloves garlic, grated

2 tbls. fresh parsley, chopped
2 tbls. mint, chopped
Salt and pepper

Combine the ingredients in a bowl.

Beverages

Wine has long been produced in Kosovo, but after the breakup of Yugoslavia and the infrastructure destroyed by war, the industry floundered. Pinot noir was the premier grape. The wineries were state-owned, but later privatized. The largest winery is Stone Castle in Rohovec, the main winemaking region in the country with an average of 270 sunshine filled days. Much of the wine is exported to Germany, but growing internationally. Vranac grapes, largely grown in the Balkan region have achieved some success. Sideritis, also known as ironwort, mountain tea and shepherd's tea, is an herbal tea. Strong Turkish style coffee is drunk. Other drinks include Rasoj – cabbage drink; Boza – malt drink made from maize and wheat, drunk during the summer; Kompot – drink made from fruit boiled with sugar and served in the autumn; Ajron – yogurt, water, and salt; and Rakia – alcoholic beverage made from fruits and mainly grapes. Local beers are produced – Birra Peja, Birra Erueniku, and Birra Prishtina.

Kuwait

Kuwait from the Arabic word "Kut", means fortress neat the water. The country lies between Iraq and Saudi Arabia in the northwestern corner of the Arabian Peninsula. Since ancient times Kuwait has been a stopping point for caravans and prospered with a large merchant class. Archeological finds date back to 5000 BC. In 1913 the Kuwait and Iraqi border were established. Kuwait received it independence from Great Britain in 1961. Kuwait City, once a fishing village, is the capital. Arabic is the official language.

Dining Etiquette

Family and business connections are very important. Please arrive punctually when invited out. Please bring fruit or a gift for the home. Flowers are for someone in the hospital. Shake hands greeting and departing, with women offering their hand to men first, or not shaking at all. Women do not take their husband's name. A man's second name is connected with al (and the father's name), then al (and the grandfather's name). Liquor might be served, though it is not legal. Men and women may dine separately. Please use your right hand only. Many side dishes will be served, as well as water. All utensils needed for the meal will be on the table. Guests are served first, then the eldest. Honored guests may be given a sheep's eye or head. You cannot turn it down. Please leave some food on your plate when finished, or it will be refilled. The meal is ended when the host stands.

Cuisine and Beverages

The Kuwaitis proximity to the sea provides them with an abundance of seafood. Seafood, rice, dates and buttermilk are part of each meal. Kuwaitis blend spices such as cardamom, cinnamon, cloves, coriander, cumin, ginger, nutmeg, black pepper, and paprika. Since Kuwait is a Muslim country the beverages are mainly fruit and vegetable drinks. Tea and coffee are also served.

Kuwaiti Specialties

Tabeekh – Bedouin cooking – large pots of meat, vegetables, rice, wheat and water are simmered over charcoal.

Marag – meal also cooked in a large pot, but the meat and vegetables are first fried or boiled with spices, then served with rice or wheat.

Kouzi - roasted lamb stuffed with rice, chicken, eggs

Gers Ogaily - cake made of eggs, flour, sugar, cardamom, and saffron that is served with tea.

Harees - barley cooked with meat and topped with cinnamon sugar.

Jireesh – bulgur with chicken or lamb and tomatoes.

Gabout - stuffed flour dumplings in a thick meat stew.

Biryani - rice with chicken or lamb.

Mutabbaq samak - fish served over rice.
Balaleet - sweetened noodles
Ghuraiba - cookies usually served with coffee.
Mumawwash - rice with black lentils and shrimp
Kabsa – rice with herbs and spices served with meat

Lugaimat - fFried dough balls soaked in sugar, lemon and saffron syrup
Fūl is a paste of fava beans, garlic and lemon
Aish – rice with almonds, raisins and saffron
Kharoof – grilled lamb
Samak – grilled or stewed fish

Machboos Dyaay (Chicken and Rice) (The National Dish)

Serves 8-10

4 cups rice
Water
1 tsp. saffron
100 gr. rose water
2 whole chickens
200 gr. chickpeas
200 gr. raisins
5 onions, chopped
Olive oil

3 tbls. mix of dried parsley, marjoram, sage, thyme, basil, mint and savoury
2 tsp. loomi (black limes)
2 tsp. cardamom
5 cinnamon sticks
2 tsp. fresh ground pepper
Salt (to taste)
6 cups water

Wash the rice and soak in the water for half an hour. In a bowl combine the saffron and rose water. Stuff the chickens with the chickpeas, ½ of the onions, 1 tsp pepper, some of the mixed herbs, 100 gr. raisins, 1 tsp. loomi. Sew up the chicken. Pour a small amount of olive oil in a Dutch oven and sauté the remaining onion until just browned. Add the cardamom and cinnamon sticks. Add the six cups of water. Bring to a boil. Add chickens and cook for 1 ½ hours, or until tender. Remove the chickens and cinnamon sticks. (Save the stock). Sprinkle half of the saffron water on the chickens. In some oil fry the chickens until just browned.
In a skillet with a small amount of water add the remaining onions, herbs, loomi, and raisins. Bring the stock to a boil. Stir in rice and cook until fluffy.
On a platter mound the rice, top with the chickens, the onion mixture and finally the remaining rosewater and saffron blend. Serve immediately.
Recipe courtesy of the Embassy of Kuwait, Washington, DC

Holidays and Special Occasions

During Ramadan Muslims fast sunrise to sunset, then take a meal to break the fast. On the 13, 14, and 15 nights of Ramadan mother present children with candy and nuts.
Al-noon – baby's first teeth or steps – a mother spreads a carpet in the courtyard and then throws candy and nuts to the guests
Daq Al-Harees – "grinding wheat" – women grind wheat before Ramadan
Weddings – family and friends prepare the food
Spring – many picnics

Kyrgyzstan

Kyrgyzstan, a landlocked and mountainous country located in Central Asia., is bordered by Kazakhstan to the north, Uzbekistan to the west, Tajikistan to the southwest and China to the east. "Kyrgyz" is believed to have been derived from the Turkic word for "forty", in reference to the forty clans of Manas, a legendary hero who united forty regional clans against the Uyghurs. Literally, Kyrgyz means *"We are forty"*. At the time, in the early 9th century AD, the Uyghurs dominated much of Central Asia (including Kyrgyzstan), Mongolia, and parts of Russia and China. In the 7th century, Muslim Turkic traders initially introduced Islam to Central Asia, including what is now Kyrgyzstan. The Kyrgyz defeated the Uyghur Khaganate in 840 and continued to expand, but by 1207 were part of the Mongol Empire. Issyk Kul Lake was a stop on the Silk Road. The Kyrgyz tribes were overrun by the Mongol Oirats in the 17th c; the Manchu Ming in the 18thc; and Uzbek Khanate of Kokand in the 19th c. Much of what is today Kyrygstan was ceded to the Russians in the 19th c and was known as Kirgizia. Some of the population moved to the Pamir Mountains and Afghanistan, and after the 1916 rebellion against Russia to China. On 5 December 1936, the Kirghiz Soviet Socialist Republic was established as a full republic of the Soviet Union. It received its independence on August 31, 1991 as the Republic of Kyrgyzstan. Bishkek is the capital. The country is 80% Muslim; 17% Christian – Orthodox. Russian and Kyrgyz are the official languages.

Dining Etiquette

The Kyrygs are very hospitable and enjoy inviting others to their homes. Please bring a gift of pastries, or if they are not Muslim an alcoholic beverage. On arrival please leave your shoes by the door. In the south men and women greet their own gender by shaking hands and putting the left hand over the heart. Older women and female friends will kiss on the cheek while shaking hands. In the north only the men shake hands with each other. "Assalom aleikum" is said by a younger man to an older as a sign of respect. The host will show you to a seat, and there will be ceremonies, often beginning with a toast with vodka. Please return the toast and thank the host for his hospitality.

A white cloth "dastorkhwon" is placed over the eating area (a table or the floor). When seated at a table, men and women are seated on opposite sides with the oldest or most respected person seated at the head of the table, and farthest from the door. In the south men and women may be placed in separate rooms for special occasions. There will be an abundance of food often with the host serving. You will be served tea with appetizers, bread, dried fruit, dairy products such as butter, then the main course is served. You must eat everything you are served. If mutton is used instead of horse meat in besbarmak, a boiled sheep's head is placed on the table in front of the most honored guest, who cuts bits and parts from the head and offers them around to the other guests at the table Cutlery may be on the table usually a fork and knife. Please eat continental style with the fork in the left hand and the knife in the right. For some food, or in some places food is eaten with the right hand only. Bread is considered sacred and should never be placed on the ground or turned upside down. Bread is never thrown away, but can be given to animals. Tea is served at the end of the meal. Also a prayer is said to honor ancestors and thanksgiving to God. Hands are held out with palms up, everyone then covers their faces and say "omin". Respect for elders and those in authority is very important.

Cuisine

The early people were nomads. The Turkic people introduced pasta, plov, kebabs, and pastries. As Kyrygstan was located on the Silk Road other foods were introduced, including spices and rice. The Russians introduced pelmani, peroshski, and borscht. Bread is usually flat bread served with each meal.

Farmland cannot be owned by individuals, but a person can hold rights for up to ninety-nine years. Much of the country is mountainous, and being landlocked, there is only a short growing season. Less than 8& of the land is cultivated mainly in northern highlands and the Fergana Valley. The most important crops are wheat, potatoes, sugar beets, tobacco, cotton, and silkworms for silk. Other foods used in cooking are berries, mushrooms, carrots, and onions. Goats, sheep, and horses are used for their meat, milk, and skins, and the horse intestines for sausage. Lakes and rivers do have fish which are dried or smoked. Nuts, especially walnuts and honey are part of the diet.

Specialties

Besbarmak/Beshbarmak "five fingers" - the national dish, is boiled mutton, horse meat or beef with noodles and broth sprinkled with coriander and parsley and eaten with the hand

Lagman/Laghman - noodles with vegetables in a spicy vinegar sauce

Manti - steamed dumplings filled with ground meat and onions

Samsa – flaky pastry with meat and vegetables baked in an oven known as a tandyr, and eaten with the hands

Plov/Paloo - rice fried with meat or chicken, carrots, garlic, and hot peppers

Shashlyk: grilled mutton, pork, or chicken sometimes served with raw onions, parsley, and/or a vinegar sauce

Pelmeni – meat dumplings

Shorpo – meat soup

Qattama and boorsoq – fried breads

Lepyoshka – round flat bread which is broken not cut and never placed upside down

Boorsok – deep fried dough that is spread over the table for celebrations

Kalama – flattened unleavened bread, baked on top of a stovekattama – flat bread baked for guests

Kuimak – dough fried in warm oil and eaten with sour cream

Chuchuuk – horsemeat sausage

Kuirook- boor – sheep fat and liver served with spices

Besh Barmak

Besh barmak is the national dish. When it is served, the honored guest is given the head of the sheep.

Serves 4

1.5 k lamb, beef, or horse	2 onions
4 liter water	

Put the lamb in a sauce pan with enough water to cover. Bring to a boil. Remove foam. Cook 1 ½ hours. Save broth. Cool. Cut into small pieces. Put on a platter and cover to keep warm.

Dough

200 mil water	2 cups flour
1 tsp. salt	1 egg

Combine the ingredients in a bowl to form a dough. Divide into two equal parts. Wait 15 minutes. Roll each
Bring the lamb broth to a boil. Drop in the dough. Simmer for a minute. Remove and let drain. Put on a platter.
Cut the onions into rings and drop into boiling broth for 1 minute. Remove from broth and put on dough. Place the meat on the onions.

Sauce

1 onion, peeled and finely chopped	500 mil broth
Salt and pepper	

In a pot bring the broth to a boil. Add the onions and some salt and pepper.
Pour over the meat and noodles.

Broth

1 tbls. dill	3.5 liter broth
2 bay leaf	

Bring the broth to a boil and add the bay leaf.
Pour the broth into 4 serving bowls. Sprinkle with the dill

Each person is given a bowl with the broth and the Besh barmak is placed in the middle of the table and each person takes some.

Holidays and Special Occasions

Nauryz – New Year celebrated at the time of the spring equinox. Dishes include lamb and mare's milk. Horse games are held.

Birthday or anniversary – sheep is killed which is used to make soups, meat, milk, and sausage

Funerals and weddings – horse eaten

Birth, death, or important birthday – besh barmak

Brides have dowries of clothing, sleeping mats, pillows and a rug. The groom pays a bride's price with cash and animals, which may be eaten at the wedding feast. Weddings last three days. After a burial every Thursday for forty days the family must kill a sheep in remembrance of the dead. At the end of the forty days a feast called kirku is held when a horse or cow is killed. On the first anniversary of a death a feast ash or jildik takes place over two days. The first day is for grieving, the second for games and horse races. Ancestors are given food in prayers, and water poured on graves so they will not be thirsty.

January 7 is observed as the Christian Orthodox Christmas, and Orozo Ait and Kurman Ait as Muslim holidays.

Beverages

Kymyz, made from fermented mare's milk is a traditional drink served only during the summer. Chai is a tea brewed with boiled water. Maksym is a fermented carbonated drink made from grains usually malt. Jarma is made from ground cereals and mixed with ayran, as is Chalap. Jarma has salt, but the nomads also might add sugar, honey, buckthorn, barberry, or other ingredients. Sheep and camel milk are also drunk. Yoghurt is also made. Shoro "salty" is made of animal fat and wheat. Although this is a Muslim country vodka is extremely popular as is beer. Chagyrmak is a vodka made of kumys. Bozo is an alcoholic drink made from wheat.

Laos

The Lao People's Democratic Republic, is a landlocked country in Southeast Asia, bordered by Burma and the People's Republic of China to the northwest, Vietnam to the east, Cambodia to the south and Thailand to the west. Laotian culture dates back at least 10,000 years when the country contained present day Laos and part of northern Thailand. More than 2/3 of the country's people are ethnic Lao (lowland people) who migrated from China in the 1st millennium AD. The hill tribes of Laos are considered an endangered people. From the 14th to the 18th c Laos was the Kingdom of Lan Xang, the *Land of a Million Elephants*, which was founded in 1353 by Fa Ngum. In the 18th c the kingdom was divided into 3 principalities which eventually became part of Siam (Thailand). During the 19th c Luang Prabang became a protectorate of French Indonesia, which was later to include the Kingdom of Chamasak and the territory of Vientiane. The Japanese briefly occupied Laos during World War II. The country became independent from France in 1954. The capital, Vientiane, situated on the Mekong River, was originally a Lao meuang (city-state) c 1000 AD. In 1560 King Sayasetthathirat made Vientiane the capital of Lane Xang. The official language is Lao. Nearly 85% of the population is Buddhist.

Tam Mark Houng (Papaya Salad)

"Laotian women enjoy Tam Mark Houng during a summer afternoon get together. We have this kind of dish almost every time we get together and normally women choose this food for their diet."

Serves 2

½ lb green papaya, peel and shred in food processor
2 small red hot peppers
1 clove garlic
½ tbls. shrimp paste

5 cherry tomatoes, quartered
1 ½ tsp. fish sauce
1 tbls. sugar
1 tbls. lime juice

Please the shredded papaya in a bowl.
Combine the hot peppers, garlic and shrimp paste in the mortar (Kork) and mash/
Add the tomatoes, fish sauce, sugar and lime juice.
Combine all ingredients until well mixed and soft.
Transfer to a serving plate and accompany with sliced green cabbage or lettuce.
Serve as an appetizer or side dish with grilled chicken, steak, or pork and sticky rice.
Recipe courtesy of Mrs. Bouapha Phommaseng, Lao Embassy, Washington, DC

Dining Etiquette

Please be prompt when invited for a meal. Dress conservatively. It is not customary to bring a gift. Please remove your shoes before entering a home (and a Buddhist temple). Place your hands together and bring them close to the chest, slightly bowing your head when greeting (nop). Tea or fruit may be offered. Food will be served with several dishes on a table, each person receiving a plate, and a wicker container with sticky "glutinous" rice. Spoons are mainly used for soups and rice and held in the right hand; chopsticks for noodles, and a fork is held in the left hand. Rice is rolled into a ball with the hand. In more traditional homes and in temples diners are seated on a reed mat around a ka toke (raised platform) where the dishes are arranged. The meal will usually consist of soup, grilled food, steamed greens, a stew or other dish. Soup is eaten during the meal. No beverages are served. Food is always in abundance, otherwise humiliating for a host not to serve enough. Place the cover on the rice to show you have finished eating. Coffee is drunk during the day, followed by green tea.

Always respect another person, so as not to shame him or her. Please do not show affection in public. Families are very close knit, and more than one generation may live in the same dwelling. The oldest man is the patriarch of the family. Elders and parents have great respect. Remember feet are considered the lowest part of the body and one should never point with your toes. The head is considered sacred, and one should not touch another's head.

Cuisine

Lao food is quite spicy and has influenced the cuisine in Thailand and Cambodia. The staple food is sticky (glutinous or sweet) rice. The rice is steamed for hours in a basket over boiling water. It is served in a basket or dish, and eaten with the fingers after being shaped into a ball. The rice is then dipped into a hot sauce. Sticky rice can also be ground into flour for rice noodles. Dried salted meat sliced thin is covered with fish sauce and allowed to dry in the sun. Fermented salted fish is used to flavor many dishes. The different regions of Laos have their own dishes using the available fresh local fruit, vegetables and fish. Vientiane is still influenced by the French. Hamjeongsik is a feast with small plates of smoked fish, grilled meat, noodles, soup, and other dishes. Various vegetables include pumpkin, corn, cucumbers, tomatoes, and herbs. Fruit include watermelon, pineapples, apples, longan, mango, bananas, jackfruit, rambutan, coconuts, oranges, tamarind, papaya, durian, sugar cane, pomelo, sapodilla, guava, grapes and soursop. Noodles, rice, meat and fish depending on the region are staples. Ginger and garlic are used in many dishes. The main crop is rice, but corn, vegetables, tobacco, and other foodstuffs are grown.

Lao Specialties

Bibimbap – rice, vegetable and beef dish
Khaonaio - steamed sticky rice
Nam khao – coconut rice and pork served on lettuce leaves
Lap – marinated meat or fish with herbs, greens, and spices is the national dish
Laap pa – fish salad

Tammakhung – spicy green papaya
Padaek – Laotian fish sauce
Jeow mak khua – roasted eggplant dip
Jeow marg len – roasted tomato dip
Jeow bong – paste made with roasted chilies, pork skin, galangal
Kaipen – fresh water algae snack

Som moo- pickled pork
Som khai pa – pickled fish roe
Som phak kad – pickled greens
Som pa –pickled fish
Pon – spicy pureed fish
Ping pa – grilled fish
Mock pa – fish steamed in banana leaves
Mok gai – chicken steamed in banana leaves
Titi gai – beef steamed in a banana leaf
Ping sin – grilled beef
Tam padaek – fish cooked in padaek
Tam mak taeng – cucumber salad

Kaeng kalee – curry
Khao khua – fried rice
Khao ping – baked sticky rice with eggs
Khao piak khao –porridge
Khao piak sen – noodle soup
Khao soi – tomato and ground pork soup
Pad Lao – fried noodles
Khao tom – steamed rice in a banana leaf
Khanom maw kaeng – coconut custard cake
Feu - noodle soup with meat and vegetables
Tom –som – chicken soup

Larp Kai (Savory Chopped Chicken Salad)

Serves 2

"The chopped chicken is mixed with shallots, spring onions, lime juice, cilantro, chilies, fish sauce and ground roasted rice, and served with fresh vegetables. The original recipe is from the Norther Provinces of Laos. Larp means "lucky" in the Lao language. Lao people eat Larp occasionally at Lao New Year, wedding ceremonies and other important functions to bring luck to their families and friends."

1 ½ cups chicken, finely sliced
2 tbls. spring onions, sliced
1 tbls. coriander, chopped
2 tbls. mint leaves
2 tabls. Sliced shallots or fried sliced shallots
½ tsp. hot and dried chili flakes
2 tbls. roasted sticky rice

½ tsp. salt
2 tbls. fish sauce
2 tbls. lime juice
1 tbls. sliced lemon grass (fresh or fried)
½ tsp. finely chopped galangal leave kefir
5 long beans, finely sliced

Fry the chicken in a pan with hot oil, adding a pinch of salt. Transfer chicken to a mixing bowl. Season with chili flakes, fish sauce, lime juice and lemon grass, mixing well. Add sticky rice and stir.
Add spring onions, shallots, mint leaves, and coriander.
Spoon onto a serving dish, garnish with mint sprig, dried chillies, spring onion, Chinese cabbage, and shallots.
Serve with fresh vegetables, long beans, and sticky rice.
Fish, beef or pork can be substituted for the chicken.
Recipe courtesy of Mrs. Bouapha Phommaseng, Lao Embassy, Washington, DC

Holidays and Special Occasions

The Lao New Year Songkarn is celebrated April 13-15th. Water is poured over Buddhas and elders. Laotians return to their home villages.
The Rocket Festival is celebrated with homemade rockets, boat races, and folk dances.
Most Laotian men spend at least three months as a monk, putting on a robe, shaving his head, and renouncing worldly things. Food is brought to the temples (wat) to feed the monks.
Thanks and prayer are used for the blessing of nature. Prayers are used for festivals concerning rain and harvest. The basi or sukhwan ceremony was developed to share the different stages of life such as birth, marriage, and moving when people sit in a circle and touch each other with threads from the altar. Offerings, food and wine are part of the ceremony.

Beverages

Coffee grown in Lao is called Pakxong. It is drunk in glasses with condensed milk in the bottom, followed by a glass of green tea. Both coffee and tea are grown on the Bolovens Plateau. Other drinks are made from coconut and fruit juices.

Alcoholic beverages are made from rice. Makkoli is a rice wine. Lao hai means jar alcohol and is served from an earthen jar. Lao lao is similar to whiskey. Beerlao, the state owned brewery, produces beer.

Latvia

The Republic of Latvia is located in the Baltic region of Northern Europe. It is bordered to the north by Estonia, to the south by Lithuania, to the east by Russia, and to the southeast by Belarus. Beginning c 9000BC the Balts settled on the Baltic Sea, eventually trading with Roma and the Byzantine Empire. Amber found along the shores of the Baltic was traded for precious metals. During the 13th c AD part of present Latvia was conquered and Estonia became part of Livonia. In 1282 Riga, now the capital, along with several other cities became part of the Hanseatic League and important trading centers. During the 16th c Livonia was ruled by Poland and Lithuania, and then Swedish rule. In the 17th c the region now called Latvia became part of the Russian Empire. In 1918 Latvia proclaimed its independence. In 1940 the Soviet Union occupied Latvia. Latvia again received full independence in 1991. The official language is Latvian.

Dining Etiquette

Please be prompt when invited for a meal. Dress conservatively. Please bring a small gift for the home, or wine, liquor, flowers (in an uneven number), or chocolates. On entering a home you may be asked to remove your shoes. Shake hands greeting and departing. Please use Mr., Mrs. or Miss until by mutual agreement first names may be used. Do not sit down until asked to. Beverages may be served. Please wait for your host to seat you at the table. Dining is continental style with the fork in the left hand and knife in the right. Do not start eating until the hostess does. Please keep your napkin on the table. Eat all that is placed on your plate. Latvians are known for their love of singing and a meal may end with singing. The toast is "Priekaa" "Cheers".

Cuisine and Beverages

Latvian cuisine is based on local agricultural products, meat, fowl, wild game, dairy products, and fish, especially herring, eel, flounder, lamprey and cod. The fish is often smoked. Ingredients include potatoes, grains – rye, oats, millet, wheat, barley; cabbage, peas, beans; berries – strawberries, bilberries, raspberries, loganberries, cranberries; apples, plums, turnips, black radishes, linseed, carrots, garlic, dill, onions, eggs, pork, caraway seeds, white mustard, honey, nuts, sour cream, yogurt, and almost no spices. Black bread, sauerkraut and pork are popular. Because the winters are long, porridges, hot soups and baked dishes are popular. Cheese is often made with cumin and curdled milk. Latvians drink tea, coffee, fruit juices, spring water, ruguspiens (curdled milk), kvass (a yeast based drink), and beer. Beer is brewed from barley and hops. Medalus is beer made from honey. Other additives are juniper berries and wormwood. Riga Black Balsam, first produced in the 18th c by Abraham Kunze, a Riga pharmacist, is a dark liqueur with herbs. Van Talinn, a rum with spices such as cinnamon and vanilla, was first concocted in 1962 by Ilse Maar. Abavas Abolu Pommo is a refreshing drink matured in French oak barrels. Vodka is also drunk.

GREY PEAS WITH BACON

"The very first thing that foreigners get to know in Latvia besides beer, are the grey peas with bacon that is considered to be the traditional Latvian meal. Some might say that is very nourishing, but that is where the magic hides, you cannot eat too much so that you won't get bored with the meal and will come back to eat it once more the very next day. It is easy to prepare the meal, unfortunately it is hard to find grey peas. But when you find them, do not get too cheery since you have to find curdled milk as well because without *rūgušpiens* it is not complete." *(Latvian Institute)*

200 g (7oz) grey peas
60g (2.1oz) smoked or unsmoked streaky bacon

40g (1.4oz) onion
Salt.

Soak peas, then cover with hot water and boil until tender.
Dice bacon and onion and sauté. Serve drained peas in individual clay bowls, adding fried bacon mixture to each serving.
Serve with a drink of *rūgušpiens* (curdled milk).
Beans with fresh bacon are also prepared in this way.
Recipe courtesy of the Latvian Institute, Riga, Latvia (www.latvia.lv)

Specialties

Rupjmaize – dark rye bread
Kimenu siers –caraway cheese
Biesu zupa – beet soup
Aukstais galds – similar to a Swedish smorgabord
Piragi – crescent shaped pastry with chopped onion and bacon usually eaten on special occasions
Sauerkraut – onions, cabbage, apples, caraway seeds
Borscht – beet soup
Skaba putra – fermented barley and buttermilk soup served with sour cream, herring, bread, and butter
Skabu Kaposti Zupa – sour cabbage soup with meat
Pilditi Pipari – bell peppers stuffed with ground meat, rice, onion, vegetables, and spices, then boiled in a cream, tomato and spice sauce

Rasols – potato salad with beets, smoked pork, pickles, hardboiled eggs, cucumbers,
Salad Olivier – cooked potatoes, carrots, hardboiled eggs, pickles, peas
Speck – field peas with bacon
Solianka – fish stew
Kartolianki – baked mashed potato balls, then topped with fried onions and sour cream
Kurzemes pork – fresh ham simmered with onions, beef broth, and later sour cream and mushrooms
Ligzdinas – beef with pork and bread and hard boiled whole egg
Kotletes – fried ground beef or pork patties
Sipolklopsis - baked beef or pork with onion, and then covered with sour cream
Debessmanna – blueberry cake with milk
Kliņģers (Saffron Birthday Bread) - a bread with raisins and covered in drupacas or streusel and almonds for birthdays or Name Days

JĀŅU CHEESE

"*Jāņu* cheese is prepared specially for the celebrations of summer solstice holiday that in Latvia is called *Jāņi*. It tastes the best with Latvian beer and Latvian songs all around, nevertheless, it may be prepared at home as well. The cheese itself is not complicated, what makes this cheese special is the caraway seeds and the incredible mood that surrounds you during the celebrations of summer solstice fest." *(Latvian Institute)*

1kg (2lb., 3oz) skim milk dry cottage cheese	100g (3.5 oz) butter
5l milk	Salt
100g (3.5oz) sour cream,	Caraway seeds.
2 eggs	

Heat milk, stirring occasionally, until the temperature reaches 90-95°C (194-203°F). Grind or process cottage cheese and add to milk. If the cottage cheese is sweet, mix with rūgušpiens (curdled milk) for the whey to separate more easily. Continue to heat at 85-90°C (185-194°F) for 10-15 minutes. When a clear whey separates, remove from heat, and allow cheese to sit. Pour off liquid. Place cheese into a dampened linen cloth. Holding corners of the cloth together, roll cheese back and forth to allow any extra liquid to separate out before the cheese cools down. Put cheese in a bowl. Mix sour cream with eggs, salt and caraway seeds and gradually add to cheese, mixing with a wooden spoon. Add the mixture to a saucepan with melted butter, and stir continuously over a low flame for 10-15 minutes, until cheese is smooth and shiny, and has a temperature of 75-80°C (167-176°F). (The lower the temperature and shorter the heating time, the softer and more crumbly the cheese will be. A higher temperature and a longer heating time will make the cheese harder). Place cheese in a dampened linen cloth. Gather corners of the cloth together and tie, smooth out any folds, and place under a weight in the refrigerator. When cheese is cool, remove from cloth, place on a shallow dish and slice. *Jāņu* cheese is served with butter or honey or as a snack with beer. If you wish to store the cheese for a longer period, rub with salt, wrap in paper or plastic wrap and store in a cool, dry place. The cheese can also be spread with butter and baked in a hot oven until brown.
Recipe courtesy of the Latvian Institute, Riga, Latvia (www.latvia.lv)

Holidays and Special Occasions

The Jani (summer solstice) marking the shortest night of the year, is celebrated with folk songs, floral wreaths and bonfires. Foods include caraway cheese, piragi, Janu cheese, breads, and beer. Easter eggs are colored with brown onion skins and then decorated.
During the autumn farmers celebrate the harvest with a festival. Weddings are held at this time of the year. Pork, sauerkraut and bread figure prominently in the meal. Sausage would be prepared from the pig not used. Piragi are eaten for most festive occasions.
Christmas is celebrated with boiled gray peas with fried meat and bacon and blood sausage with pearl barley. Ruguspiens (curdled milk) or kefirs (cultured milk) are served. Sklandu (tarts with mashed potato and carrot), roast pork and sauerkraut, goose, carp, and gingerbread are prepared.
Latvian weddings are known for their abundance of food. They include piragis, sweet breads, salads, soup, pork or veal, boiled potatoes, sauerkraut, sauces, desserts, herbal teas, and beer, Guests after midnight are presented with a "new wife's torte" and coffee.

Lebanon

Lebanon located on the eastern Mediterranean, is bordered by Syria to the north and east, and Israel to the south. Lebanon has been inhabited for over 7000 years. The earliest settlement was at Byblos which dates back to before 5000 BC. From c 3000- 539 BC the Phoenicians flourished. The region was part of the Persian Empire, and later Alexander the Great burned the city of Tyre. Other empires included the Egyptian, Assyrian, Hellenistic, Roman, Eastern Roman, Arab, Seljuk, Mamluk, Crusader and Ottoman. After World War I five provinces that now make up Lebanon were mandated to France. On 1 September 1926, France formed the Lebanese Republic, and the country became independent in 1943. Beirut, the capital, is first mentioned by the Egyptians in the 15c BC, and successive cities have been built on the site. Arabic is the official language.

Dining Etiquette

The Lebanese are very hospitable people, and it is an honor to be invited to a home. Please arrive punctually. Bring a gift of flowers, pastries, or something from your country. Gifts are presented with the right hand or both hands. Please shake hands greeting and departing with direct eye contact. Close female friends will greet each other with three kisses on the cheek. If the woman is Muslim she may or may not extend her hand. Please greet elders first. You will be served coffee or tea. The hostess will seat the guests at the table. Food is eaten continental style with the fork in the left hand and knife in the right. Please wait for the hostess to begin. Do not take too much food as you will be offered second and third helpings. Please take some of each to show respect for your hostess' cooking.

Cuisine

The cuisine is a blend of Middle Eastern, European and North African influences. The Ottoman Turks probably had the greatest influence on Lebanese cooking, influencing the use of lamb and spices. The French introduced rich breads and desserts. The staples are lamb, dates, rice, nuts, sesame seeds, fruits – pomegranates, oranges, figs, apricots, mulberries, vegetables - okra, spinach, green beans, onions, lentils, eggplant, potatoes, fish, chickpeas, yogurt, chicken, goat, garlic, olive oil, lemon juice, honey, phyllo, orange blossom water, mint and other herbs and spices – cumin, coriander, parsley, allspice, black pepper, cinnamon, cloves, fenugreek, nutmeg ginger, and thyme. Meat and fish are grilled, baked or sauteed. Mezze are the small dishes served before the meal, and may include more than thirty dishes.

Man'oushe (Lebanese Flatbread)

2 ½ cups flour
1 cup cake flour
2 tsp. salt
1¼ cups lukewarm water

1 tsp. yeast
1 tsp. sugar
1 tbls. olive oil

Put the yeast and sugar in a bowl with ¼ cup water. Stir. Set aside for 15 minutes.
In a food processor or bowl combine the flours and salt.
Add the yeast mixture and 1 tbls. olive oil to flour mixture. Add remaining cup of water. If combining in food processor let a ball form. If mixing in a bowl knead dough until elastic.
Oil a bowl and add the dough. Cover with a cloth and let rise until doubled.
Punch the dough. Shape into 4 balls. Cover and let rise 20 more minutes.
Preheat oven to 400°
On a floured surface roll out each ball until ¼" thick, rolling by starting in center, turning dough and containing until the desired thickness.
Place each on a baking stone in the oven. Cook 6-10 minutes, or until golden brown.
Serve hot by breaking off pieces.
Serve with tomatoes, mint, cucumber and olive oil, or za'atar and olive oil.
The za'atar can be spread on the dough as it is baking, or afterwards.

Kofta (grilled lamb with herbs)

1½ lbs. ground lamb
1 onion
2 tbls. fresh parsley
2 tbls. cilantro
2 tbls. mint

½ tsp. cumin
Salt and pepper
Skewers
Lemon slices
Yogurt

Place the lamb in a food processor with the onion, parsley, cilantro, mint, cumin and some salt and pepper until smooth. Chill for 1 hour.
Mold the meat into balls and place on skewers.
Cook on a grill until desired pinkness.
Serve with lemon slices and yogurt.

Lebanese Specialties

Kibbeh – (national dish) – ground lamb with crushed wheat
Shawarma – skewered marinated meat served in pita with tomatoes
Siyyadiyeh – spiced fish served on rice
Douma – lamb with rice
Dolma – stuffed grape leaves
Yakhnehs - stews

Hummus - chickpeas and tahini dip
Baba ghanouj – roasted eggplant appetizer
Balila – cumin chickpeas
Labneh –yogurt garnished with olive oil and salt
Fattoush – vegetable salads with pita bread
Batata harra – spicy potatoes
Makdous - stuffed eggplant

Tabbouleh – bulghur, tomatoes, mint and parsley salad
Soujok – sausage made with garlic and spices
Shankleesh – seasoned aged cheese
Tahini – sesame paste
Falafel – fried chickpea patties
Za'atar – dried thyme and sumac
Kishk – wheat with yogurt
Fool mdammas – dark beans cooked with olive oil and lemon and eaten at breakfast with bread

Yakhnit – vegetables stews with a small amount of meat
Nammoorah – semolina cake
Ma'moul – semolina cookies with walnuts or pistachios
K'nafeh – phyllo pistachio squares
Gh'raybeh – shortbread cookies
Halva – sesame paste with fruit and nuts
Kunafi – pastry with cheese, nuts and syrup
Baklava – phyllo pastry with honey and nuts

Holidays and Special Occasions

Lent – kibbeh (dish made of burghul, lentils or beans, mint) and dels al remann (pomegranate molasses)
Good Friday – fasting
Easter – turkey or chicken stuffed with nuts, rice, couscous with lamb, kibbeh, stuffed eggplant, mamool
Christmas –tabbouleh, kibbe, turkey, sfouf (aniseed and turmeric cake)
Muslims fast sunrise to sunset during Ramadan. The early morning meal is known as suhoor and the evening meal iftar.
Birth – meghli (spice cake)
Weddings – can be buffet or seated with lamb dishes, rice, vegetable dishes, wedding cake

Beverages

Strong coffee is served in small cup from a rakwe (long handled coffee pot), often flavored with cardamom. Sugar is added before being served, if one so wishes. Tea, Sharab ward – lemon and rosewater drink, and fruit juices are also drunk

Vineyards have been cultivated in Lebanon for thousands of years and with the Phoenecians wine could be transported throughout the Mediterranean. The wines of Tyre and Sidon were especially well known. Vines grew in Canaan as recorded in *The Bible* and wines from Byblos were exported to Egypt during the time of the Old Kingdom (2686-2134 BC). Under the Ottomans winemaking ceased, but in 1857 Jesuit monks started growing vines once again. Today the major wineries are in the Beqaa Valley. Beer is also brewed in Lebanon with Almaza Beer the best known. Arak is an aniseed flavored liqueur.

Lesotho

Lesotho is a landlocked country in southern Africa completely surrounded by South Africa. The earliest inhabitants were Khoisan hunter-gatherers and later the Wasja of the Bantu and Sotho-Taswana people who colonized the region from the 3rd to 11th c AD. Basutoland, the area we now know as Lesotho, was united in 1822. Boer farmers moved in from South Africa beginning in the 1830s. In 1868 Basutoland became a British protectorate. Basutoland gained its independence from Britain and became the Kingdom of Lesotho in 1966. The capital, Maseru, was once a police boot camp and became the capital under the British. English is the official language with Sotho also spoken

Dining Etiquette

It is an honor to be invited for a meal with the Lesotho. The people are very friendly. Please arrive punctually and bring a gift of flowers, sweets, wine, or something from your country. Greetings are usually speaking pleasantries, nodding the head, or waving. Some may shake hands greeting and departing with good eye contact. Women may or may not shake hands, or just nod their head. Guests may be presented with a chicken or a sheep. The skin, head and legs are given back to the owner.

Chakakala (Vegetable Stew)

Serves 4

2 tbls. oil
1 carrot, peeled and sliced
1 medium onion, finely chopped
2 red hot chilies, finely chopped

1 red bell pepper, chopped
2 medium tomatoes, finely chopped
Salt and pepper

Heat the oil in a skillet. Stir in the carrots and onions until just tender. Add chilies and bell pepper. Saute for 5 minutes. Stir in tomatoes. Cook until stewed. Add salt and pepper to taste. Serve with Pap-Pap

Pap-Pap

1 cup cornmeal

1½ cups water

Bring the water to a boil in a pan. Slowly stir in cornmeal until thickened.

Cuisine

The Lesothan cuisine has been influenced by South African, European, Indian, Asian, and Malay cuisines. The Indians and Malays introduced hot curries, chutneys, pickled fish, kebabs and stews. Staples are maize, greens, cassava, rice, plantains, millet, peanuts, aubergine, tomatoes, cabbage, celery, potatoes, grains, milk, seafood, meat, and wild game. Seafood includes crayfish, prawns, tuna, mussels, oysters, mackerel, and lobster; wild game – ostrich, impala, and warthog; fresh fruit- grapes, mangoes, bananas, papayas, and avocado. The dishes are quite spicy. The land is not owned but held in trust by chiefs and headmen who permit certain areas for grazing animals. Cooking is done outside.

Lesothan Specialties

Lekhot loane – mutton
Landjager – beef and pork sausages
Kitozer – dried beef strips
Akodo sy voanio – chicken in coconut milk
Braai – grilled meats
Inyama yenkukhu – fried chicken
Nyekoe – beans, sorghum, pumpkin
Mocha-hlama – steamed bread
Pap – maize porridge

Chakalaka – sauce made with tomatoes, peppers, onion, chilies, and carrots and served with rice or pap
Peanut and fish stews
Cured and smoked hams
Kebabs – lamb or pork
Papa – corn mush
Sauces – tomato, eggplant, spinach, peanut
Smoked fish – freshwater fish
Makoenya – donuts

Holidays and Special Occasions

Moshoeshoe Day/Christmas – cabbage and bacon
Mealie, mealie, braai, landjager, kitoza and Akodo sy Voanio are eaten on holidays and special occasions.

Beverages

Mahleu is a fermented sorghum drink. Local beers are brewed, ginger beer made, and pure mineral water comes from the Maluti Mountains

Did You Know?

Lengana is a shrub used to cure common colds. Parsnip (paper bark tree) has many medicinal uses.

Liberia

Liberia is a country in West Africa, bordered by Sierra Leone to the west, Guinea the north, and Côte d'Ivoire the east. The region has been inhabited since at least the 12th c. The Mende came from Sudan, followed by the Dei, Bassa, Gola, and Kissi. The peoples moved closer to the coast growing cotton, sorghum, and rice, and built canoes for trading along the African coast. Later peoples were the Manes and the Vai. Beginning in 1461 the Portuguese, Dutch and British also explored and traded with the local people. The Portuguese named the area "Costa da Pimenta" "Pepper Coast" In 1820 the American Colonization Society began sending representatives to find suitable land for a colony to be established for freed American slaves. In 1847 the settlers adopted a Declaration of Independence and created the Independent Republic of Liberia. Monrovia, the capital, was founded in 1822 and named in honor of U.S. President James Monroe. English is the official language with Kpelle, Bassa, Ku and more than 20 other languages spoken.

Dining Etiquette

It is an honor to be invited into a Liberian home. The host(ess) will greet the guests by shaking hands and taking that person's middle finger of the right hand between his thumb and third finger and then snapping it. Otherwise please shake hands greeting and departing. There will be a number of dishes set on the table. Plates and glasses will be turned over on the table and the napkin covering the plate. Utensils may be used, but people also eat with their hands. Soup is served in a tureen with small bowls for the guests. Everything is served at once and the food remains on the table throughout the meal. Ginger beer may be drunk with the meal. Coffee is not usually served. Fruit is often served later and not during meal

Cuisine

The staples are cassava, rice, sugarcane, peppers, sweet potatoes, tomatoes, ginger, palm oil, beef, chicken, collards, adores, hot peppers, yams, green bananas, cabbage, eggplant, okra, coconut, seafood- fish and shrimp, goat, peanuts, and onions. Fresh fruit include alligator apple, mango, avocado, pineapples, plantains, bananas. Common spices are cloves, mint, nutmeg and pepper. Potato and cassava leaves are boiled. The cooking is done on a three stone hearth. Rice is eaten at least twice a day

Goat Soup

Serves 4

2 lbs. boneless goat meat, cubed	2 medium tomatoes, chopped
2 tbls. oil	1 red pepper, seeded and chopped
1 onion, peeled and chopped	1 hot red pepper, seeded and chopped
2 yams, peeled and chopped	½ tsp. dried oregano
2 carrots, peeled and sliced	½ tsp. thyme
2 cloves garlic, minced	Salt and pepper to season

In a skillet heat 2 tbls. oil and brown the goat.

Place all the ingredients in a large pot. Cover with water, about 4 cups.

Cook for 1 hour or until all the ingredients are tender, and have thickened. Add more water if necessary.

Pumpkin can be substituted for the yams, and lamb or beef for the goat.

More hot pepper can be added for a spicier soup.

Liberian Specialties

Goat soup (national dish)

Kanya – rice, peanut, and sugar snack

Fufu (Foofoo) – dough made from cassava, rice, plantain, corn, or yams, and served with palm butter, or eaten with a spicy soup

Dumboy – fufu that is boiled before mashing

Palava sauce – dried fish or meat stew with okra in palm oil

Country chop- meat, fish and greens dish in palm oil

Rice bread – mashed bananas

Fish cooked in coconut cream

Fried plantains

Eggplant and chicken stew

Beef internal soup – beef, dried codfish, tripe, smoked fish, hot peppers and cayenne peppers

Jollof rice - chicken, beef, bacon dish with vegetables and rice

Check rice – rice and platto or okra

Monrovian collards and cabbage – bacon, onions, pepper and greens

Sweet potato pone

Coconut pie

Plantain gingerbread

Pineapple nut bread

Palm Butter

Palm butter is made from palm nuts, the bright red and yellowish fruit of the palm tree, *elaeis guineenis*. The nuts are washed and boiled until the skin comes loose from the kernels. The kernels are removed and the rest is put in a mortar and beaten well to form a pulp. This pulp is placed in a pot with enough cold water to cover it. This liquid is then put through a sieve to remove all the fibers and kernels. What comes through is palm butter. It can be cooked with meat or fish, onions, pepper, and salt. It is cooked until it gets thick and served over rice. Palm butter is processed and canned in West Africa and can be bought in many ethnic food specialty shops.

Mary Moran

Joseph's Palm Butter

½ lb. meat
1 can prepared palm pulp (about 3 ½ c.)
1 bouillon cube (Maggi Cube)

½ tsp. black pepper
1 or 2 pods of very hot pepper
1 medium onion, chopped

While smoked meat is usually used in Liberia, fresh meat may be substituted. Cut meat into bite-sized pieces and season with chopped onions and black pepper.

Steam meat with onion in ¼ cup water for 5 minutes. Stir in palm pulp and rinse can with 1/3 cup of water and add to stew. Add bouillon cube and hot pepper pods. Cook over medium heat in an uncovered sauce pan for 10-12 minutes. Stir and adjust seasonings to taste. Simmer on very low heat until mixture condenses to a thick sauce. Serve with rice.

Caution: *Palm butter splatters. Use deep cooking pot and cover with splatter shield. Putting on the cover is not recommended. It waters down taste and consistency.*

Recipe courtesy of Joseph Barchue, Friends of Liberia's Liberian Cookhouse Cooking

Holidays and Special Occasions

Easter and Thanksgiving are celebrated and at Christmas – fufu, palm butter, collard greens, potatoes, sweets are eaten.

Special occasions – goat soup and coffee

Beverages

Monrovia Breweries brews Club beer. Ginger beer is very popular with meals. Palm wine is also made. Other drinks are made from fruit, and of course soft drinks and coffee are drunk.

Libya

Libya is located in North Africa, bordering the Mediterranean Sea to the north, Egypt to the east, Sudan to the southeast, Chad and Niger to the south, and Algeria and Tunisia to the west. The name comes from Libu Berber tribesmen. Thousands of years ago the Saharan Desert was lush green land. Libya has been inhabited since c 8000 BCE by nomadic Berbers who domesticated cattle and grew crops. Later the Garamantes developed underground irrigation systems. The Phoenicians developed trading posts in Libya. By the 5th c BC Carthage had extended into much of northern Africa, and Punic settlements in Libya. In 630 BC, the Greeks conquered Eastern Libya and founded the city of Cyrene. In 525 BC the Persians took over Cyrene, and in 106 BC the Romans conquered Tripolitania (Tripopli), which became a major exporter of olive oil. Cyrene was known for its wines. The Vandals overran northern Africa in the 5th c AD, causing mass destruction. In the 6th C the Byzantine Empire took over. Islamic Arabs ruled Libya from 642-1551, and the Ottoman Regency from 1551-1911, when it came under Italian rule. In 1951 Libya gained its independence as the United Kingdom of Libya. The capital, Tripoli, was founded in the 7th century BC, by the Phoenicians, who named it "Oea". The official language is Arabic.

Sharba Libya (Libyan Lamb Soup)

½ lamb meat cut into small pieces	1 lemon
¼ cup oil or "samn" (vegetable ghee)	½ cup orzo
1 large onion, chopped	Salt
1 tbls. tomato paste	Red pepper
2-3 tomatoes, chopped	Libyan spices (Hararat) or cinnamon

Saute the onion with the meat in oil. Add the parsley and saute until meat is browned.
Add the chopped tomatoes, tomato paste, salt, spices, and stir while sizzling.
Add enough water to cover meat, simmer on medium heat until meat is cooked. Add more water if needed, and bring to a boil.
Add orzo, simmer until cooked.
Before serving, sprinkle crushed dried mint leaves, and squeeze fresh lemon juice to taste.
More parsley can be added at the end when the orzo is almost cooked to give a fresher parsley flavor.
Spices may be added to the meat while sauteing so it will absorb the salt and the spices. Then add the tomato and simmer longer for the tomato to be cooked in the oil.
Substitute chicken or beef or lamb
Add uncooked soaked chick peas with the meat
Add cilantro with parsley.
Recipe courtesy of Naima Bseikri, Libyan Embassy, Washington, DC

Dining Etiquette

Family is very important, and respect for elders. Please be prompt when entertained, or just a few minutes late. Please bring a gift of pastries, fruit, or something from your country. Gifts are given with both hands or the right hand, and are not opened in front of the presenter. Men shake hands greeting and departing, and women will shake hands if they extend theirs first. The greeting is "Aalaamu alaikum" "Peace be with you" to which one would respond with "wa alaikum salam" "and Peace be with you". Please accept the offer of tea or coffee. No alcohol is permitted in the country. In some parts of the country women and children may eat separately. Before a meal a bowl of perfumed water may be passed. Using three fingers on your right hand please use for washing them. A prayer may be said before the meal. Guests will serve themselves first or be served by the host. Food is only eaten with the right hand. There will always be an abundance of food. Always leave a small amount of food on the plate to thank you host for abundant food. Black tea may be served after the meal. A second glass, then a third glass with peanuts or almonds will be offered. Please accept all three. Drinking tea is a daily ritual. Tea leaves are added to boiling water, and then sugar. The tea is strong. Since the country is Muslim no alcoholic beverages are served.

Cuisine

Olives, grains, dates, milk, lamb, chicken, beef, beans, nuts, dried apricots, melons, herbs, figs, garlic, lemons, eggplant, and unleavened bread are all part of the Libyan diet. The Libyan cuisine culture is a mixture of Arabic and Mediterranean, with a strong Italian influence. Italy's legacy from the days when Libya was an Italian colony can be seen in the popularity of pasta on its menus, particularly macaroni. A famous local dish is couscous, which is a boiled cereal (traditionally millet, now fairly often wheat) used as a base for meat and potatoes. The meat is usually lamb, but chicken is served occasionally. Sharba is a highly-spiced Libyan soup. Bazin, a local specialty is a hard paste, made from barley, salt and water. Fish is in abundance in Libya, and fresh fish is available. Libyans have all sorts of traditional desert dishes, one of the most popular being the Asida, usually eaten on Eid day. It consists of dough eaten with melted butter and honey. Fruit, mostly oranges, but not only, is also in abundance in Libya and foreigners are usually impressed by its large size, juiciness and deliciousness. Libyans prefer to eat at home, except on Fridays, when they enjoy family beachside picnics, or go to restaurants. Many of the eating places have sections specially reserved for family parties. Fruit juices, particularly orange, can be bought in season from street stalls. Then there's Libyan tea, which is a thick beverage served in a small glass, often accompanied by mint or peanuts.
Special thanks to Fatima Aujali, Libyan Embassy, Washington, DC

Libyan Specialties

Za'atar – sesame and spice blend
Sharba Libiya – lamb soup
Bureek – spinach, meat, potato, or other types
of dumplings
Hassasa – gravy
Zemeeta- dried barley and spices

Ghreyba – butter cookie
Mhalbiya – rice pudding
Slatha – summer salad
Lebrak – stuffed vine leaves

Mb'atten – served on special occasions is sliced potato stuffed with minced meat, herbs and fried

Mbekbka – macaroni boiled in a sauce

Megetta – homemade spaghetti

O's'b'an – sausage stuffed with meat, liver, herbs, onions, and rice

Leka'ek – ring- shaped pasrty which can be salty or sweet

Magrood (semolina and dates sweet)

1 lb. dates (paste)

1 tsp. cinnamon
3 Tsp. oil

Mix all ingredients together. Take a handful of the mixture, and begin shaping into a ball. Roll out the date ball into a long, finger-wide "snake."

Dough

3 cups semolina
1cup oil
½ cup flour

1tsp. baking powder
½ cup sesame seeds
1½ cups warm water

Mix semolina, flour and baking powder in a bowl. Add oil and mix well.

TEST: Take a handful of the mixture, and try to roll it in a ball by bouncing it gently on the work surface. If it crumbles you need to add a little more oil. The ball should be able to hold together.

Take about 1-1/2 cup of the mixture in another bowl.

Sprinkle a little bit of warm water and mix with hands, almost kneading; and repeat until it forms soft dough.

Shape the dough into a long loaf. Press on the center of the loaf with your fingertips to form a grove along the length of the loaf. Place formed date roll into the grove, and smooth the dough over it. Cut the loaf diagonally into 1 ½ in. pieces.

Decorate (engrave) the top of each piece by using a fork or the special tool "mangasha" (wide tweezers with a serrated edge) and arrange on baking sheet.

Bake in a preheated oven at 375-400 ƒF (190-200 ƒC) for about 40 minutes, or until golden brown.

Dip each piece in a boiling sugar syrup and garnish with sesame seeds.

Recipe courtesy of Naima Bseikri, Libyan Embassy, Washington, DC

Holidays and Festivals

Libya celebrates Ramadan, the month long fast from sunrise to sunset. The Iftar table breaks the fast. Eid al-Fitr is celebrated at the end of Ramadan. Eid al-adha commemorates Abraham's willingness to sacrifice his son.

Liechtenstein

Liechtenstein, located in Western Europe, is bordered by Switzerland to the west and south and by Austria to the east, an area over 61.7 square miles. The country was once part of the Roman province Raetia. The Liechtenstein dynasty came from Castle Liechtenstein in Lower Austria from at least 1140 until the 13th century, and from 1807 on In order to hold a seat in Reichstag (parliament) the family purchased the Herrschaft ("Lordship") of Schellenberg and county of Vaduz (in 1699 and 1712 respectively) from the Hohenems, and then became a member of the Holy Roman Empire. The country's constitution was adopted in 2003, and this small country has prospered with low corporate tax rates, and a very high standard of living and a blissful winter Alpine paradise. The capital, Vaduz, located on the Rhine River, was founded by the Counts of Werdenberg in the 13th c. The official language is German.

Dining Etiquette

Please be punctual when invited for a meal. Please bring chocolates, or something for the home. Shake hands greeting and departing. Drinks will be offered. The hostess will lead the guests to the dining room. Please put your napkin in your lap. Food is eaten continental style, fork in the left hand, knife in the right. Please wait until the hostess says "mahlzeit" or "Guten Appetit" to begin. Please place your knife and fork together when finished. The host proposes the toast, everyone clinks their glasses, and says "Prost". The male guest of honor offers a toast to the host at the end of the meal.

Feldsalat (field salad served with kasenopfle)

Four good handfuls of Mache salad greens	2 tbls. wine vinegar
2 hard-boiled eggs, chopped	Salt and pepper
¼ cup olive oil	

The mache should be lightly coated in the vinaigrette (so as not to weigh down and overwhelm the delicate greens), with no excess in the bottom of the bowl. Mix the chopped egg in at the same time as mixing in the vinaigrette.
Recipe courtesy of the Embassy of Liechtenstein, Washington, DC

Käsknöpfle (Cheese Dumplings)

1 serving

300 grams flour
1 ½ tsp. salt
3 eggs
15 ml water
1 large onion

150 grams mixed grated cheeses (use sharp cheese such as Gruyere, mild cheese such as Emmental and, if possible, add sour cheese)

Place flour and salt in a mixing bowl.

Mix eggs and water in a separate bowl and then add to the dry ingredients. Mix until bubbles rise in the batter. The batter is the correct consistency when it is thick. Cover the batter with a cloth and let stand for approx. 30 minutes.

Bring salted water to a boil in a large pot. Drop small bits of the batter into the simmering water or put through a sliding cutter or colander. When the dumplings come to the surface, remove and drain them with a sieve.

Place them on a plate and mix with the grated cheese.

Garnish the cheese dumplings with toasted onions and serve with salad or applesauce.

Recipe courtesy of the Embassy of Liechtenstein, Washington, DC

Cuisine

The cuisine of Liechtenstein consists of small dumplings with cheese, brawn and ribel grain; cheese dishes; pork; smoked bacon, ham, schnitzels, green beans, tomatoes, asparagus (especially in the spring), sauces, pears, apple, sauerkraut; pancakes with fruit or nuts; fondues; pork and sauerkraut stews. Liechtenstein is the world's largest producer of sausage casings.

Liechtenstein Specialties

Rebi – cornmeal or mix of cornmeal and semolina
Saukerkas - a local cheese
Hafalaab - a dish made from wheat flour and cornmeal dumplings, with smoked bacon or ham in a broth.

Spatzli – egg noodles
Alperrosti – fried potato cake with bacon or ham and Gruyere cheese with a fried egg

Beverages

Growing vineyards in Liechtenstein dates back over 2000 years, first with the Celts who settled in the region, and later the Romans. During the 4th c monks grew vines at the monasteries. Blauburgunder (Pinot Noir) was introduced by Henri, duc de Rohan (1579 – 1638). Today mainly white wines are produced with over 100 wine growers.

Lithuania

Lithuania is the largest of the Baltic countries in central Europe bounded on the west by the Baltic Sea and Poland, north Latvia, and south Belarus. Lithuania's history dates back at least 12,000 years. Approximately 5000 years ago "cord-ware culture" was spread over most of Eastern Europe between the Baltic Sea and the Vistula River in the west to Moscow in the east. The first written mention of Lithuania was in the Annales Quedlinburgenses in 1009 AD. Germanic monastic military orders spread in the 13th c. Grand Dukes ruled the country. Russia attempted to push into the country in the 16th c, and Poland and Lithuania were united in 1569. Much of Lithuania became part of Russia in 1795. In the 1890s crop failures forced many Lithuanians to emigrate to Germany, Scotland, England and the United States. During World War I Lithuania was occupied by Germany, and in 1939 became part of the Soviet Union. Today it is an independent country. Vilnius, the capital, was founded in 1316 by Duke Gediminas, although it was known to have been settled just before the birth of Christ. Lithuanian is the official language. The name comes from lieutiva "little river".

Dining Etiquette

The Lithuanians love to entertain, and no matter how rich or poor, will put out everything they have from their best linens to a table brimming with food. Please be punctual when asked to dine. Shake hands greeting and departing. Guests will be served drinks, often vodka and served appetizers. The hostess will seat the guests with the guest of honor to her right. Dishes are usually passed or will be placed on the table and served from there. Good breads and salads are often eaten with the meal, rather than before or after. Please wait for the hostess to start. Eat continental style with the fork in the left hand, knife in the right, keeping your elbows at table level. Dessert or fruit will be served at the end of the meal. To toast, raise your glass and look the person you are toasting in the eye and say "Sveikata" "To your health".

Cuisine

Lithuania's rich soil produces excellent agricultural products. Potatoes; breads, especially rye; cottage cheese; sour cream; cream; cheese; honey; cucumbers; cabbage; sorrel; beets; apples; pork, bacon, and sausages are all used in cooking. Fruit is eaten fresh or in jams and puddings. The Tatar influence is in the use of spices – black pepper, marjoram, and nutmeg. Potatoes were introduced in the 18th c by the Germans and can be boiled, fried, or used in such dishes as potatoes pancakes. Cakes are made with honey, poppy seeds, and rich in dairy products.

Cepelinai (Zeppelin or Potato Meat Dumplings)

Serves 4 or more

Meat Filling

1 lb. ground meat (mix of pork, beef or veal, or combination of any of these)
1 medium onion, peeled and finely chopped

Salt and pepper
1 egg, beaten

In a bowl combine the ingredients.
Cover and refrigerate.

Dumplings

8 large potatoes, peeled and grated
2 large potatoes, peeled, boiled and riced

1 medium onion, peeled and finely chopped
Salt to taste

Place the grated potatoes in cheesecloth. Squeeze over a bowl to rid of any liquid. Pour off liquid but reserve potato starch at bottom of the bowl.
Add the grated potatoes, riced potatoes, onion and salt, and combine well.
In a large pot boil water with a tsp. of salt
Take about 1 cup of the potato mixture and pat it in your hand. Add about ¼ cup of the meat mixture and pat potato mixture around the meat until it is sealed and a ball is formed. Continue to use all the mixtures.
Carefully spoon the balls into the boiling water. Bring to a boil and cook 25 minutes.
Remove with a slotted strainer, drain on towel and place on a platter.

Gravy

½ lb. bacon, diced
1 large onion, chopped

1 cup sour cream
Salt and pepper to taste

Fry the bacon and onion in a skillet until onion is tender and bacon cooked. Drain fat.
Stir in sour cream, salt and pepper.
Serve with the dumplings.

Lithuanian Specialties

Pig's stomach stuffed with potatoes and herring and baked
Fried black bread with garlic
Leistinuku sriuba – dough pieces soup

Virtiniai – boiled dumplings of noodle dough that are stuffed and served with sour cream and butter
Kotlety – fried ground meat patty
Verderai – groat sausage
Pirozhki – meat or vegetable pastries

Kugelis – potato pudding
Dzukiska bulvine banda – potato pie
Saltibarsciai – cold sour cream and vegetable soup
Kijevo Kotletas – chicken Kiev
Baked fish in cream sauce
Apples are eaten raw, in cakes, canned, applesauce, candies, syrup or as wine
Grybu salotos su grietine – mushroom salad in sour cream
Kastinis – butter and sour cream seasoned with salt, pepper, onions, and served bread and potatoes

Balandale – stuffed cabbage
Serniena – wild boar
Briediena – elk
Blynia – pancakes; blyneliai – small pancakes
Varske – curd
Grietine – sour cream
Silke – herring
Karbonadas – grilled meat

Holidays and Special Occasions

Some of the holidays celebrated are New Year's Day, Lithuanian Independence Day (February 16), St. Kazimiera's Day (Patron Saint of Lithuania),and Easter
Midsummer – spicy cheese, picnics
Fall is a favorite time for weddings which can last 2-3 days with much dancing, feasting, and drinking.
Christmas – poppy loaf bread, mushrooms, fish, chicken or goose, Avizine kose – fermented oatmeal pudding served with poppy seed milk (boiled syrup with poppy seeds, chopped, almonds, milk and sugar)

Beverages

The national drink is krupnikas which is made of many spices – cloves, cinnamon, ginger, caraway, cardamom, nutmeg, and saffron. It is often used in cakes, on cheese, or vegetables. Apple cheese is krupnikas with apples and spices. Lithuania produces vodka, wine, beer, mead, and fruit liqueurs made from grapes, cherries, apples, and black currants. Beer is the usual drink, and beer bars are very popular. Aguonu pienas is poppy milk.

Luxembourg

The Grand Duchy of Luxembourg is centrally located in Europe, landlocked by France, Belgium, and Germany. The earliest settlers were Celts, Franks and Romans. The area remained an autonomous region until the 14th c when it became part of the German Empire, then the Duchy of Burgandy, followed by the occupation of Spain, France, Austria, and France again. It became an independent duchy in 1815. The capital, Luxembourg City, was founded in 963 as Lucilinburhuc by Siegfried, Count of the Ardennes. Luxembourgish is the official language. French and German are also spoken.

Dining Etiquette

Please arrive promptly when invited for a meal. Please send or bring flowers, chocolates, or a gift for the home. Shake hands greeting and departing. Ladies are introduced first and precede men through doors. Men and younger people stand when a lady enters a room, and hold her chair when seated. Meals are still very family oriented. Fathers and children may come home for lunch, the main meal of the day. Before dinner drinks, often wine or beer, will be served. The hostess will seat the guests with the male guest of honor to her right, the female guest of honor to the host's right. Please wait for the hostess to begin. Food is served in several courses. A separate knife and fork are used for fish. Food is eaten continental style. Wrists are to be kept at table level and no elbows on the table. When finished place your knife and fork together. Coffee (kaffi) and liqueurs (plum) will be served after dinner. A toast is made by clinking the glasses and saying "Gesonthet", "Prost", or "May it be good for you". Most toasts are made with wine or beer.

Cuisine

Luxembourg has long been known for game – wild boar, venison, fowl; river fish – trout, crawfish, pike; fruits- apples, grapes, and plums; marzipan and chocolates. The earliest foods and wines were influenced by the Romans. Today they are a mix of French, German and Belgium dishes. Some specialities include ham, freshwater fish – pike and trout, sausages, potatoes, cheeses and dairy products, and sauerkraut.

Luxembourg Specialties

Traipen – black pudding (meat dish)
Ardennes ham, sauerkraut and sausages
Fierkeljhelli – jellied suckling pig
Kachkeis – cooked cheese
Judd Mat Gaardebounen – smoked pork with beans is the national dish

Quenelle – calves liver dumplings
Quetschentaart – plum tart
Mettwurscht – spicy sausage
Quenelles – calves liver dumplings
Bou'neschlupp – green bean soup
Brennesselszopp – nettle soup

Gromperekniddelen- potato dumplings
F'rell am Rèisleck –trout in Piesling sauce
Friture – fried fish
Moulen – mussels in white wine
Hiecht mat Kraïderzooss – pike in green sauce
Kriibsen – crayfish on wihte wine

Hong am Rèisleck – chicken in wihte wine
Stäerzelen – buckwheat dumplings
Huesenziwwi – jugged hare
Jhelli – pork in aspic
Gromperekichelcher – potato fritters
Äppelkuch – apple cake
Quetschentaart – plum tart

Gromperenzopp (Potato Soup)

4-5 leeks
1 tbls. butter
4-5 potatoes, diced
3 cups boiling water
1 tsp. salt
3 cups boiling milk

1 tbls. butter
2 egg yolks
½ cup cream
Salt
Pepper
Chopped parsley

Remove green stalks and roots from the leeks. Wash well and cut into small pieces. There should be approximately 1½ cups.
Melt the butter in a heavy soup pot.
Add leeks and sauté slowly on a low heat until leeks are soft and transparent
Add potatoes to leeks along with boiling water and salt. Cook for 30 minutes.
Strain mixture through sieve or food mill and return to the pot.
Add boiling milk, stirring constantly and add butter. Then add egg yolks blended with the cream slowly to hot soup (sour cream may be used).
Add salt and pepper and finely chopped parsley if desired.
Recipe courtesy of the Luxembourg Embassy, Washington, DC

Verwurrelt Gedanken (A Special Pastry served during Carnival)

750 gr. flour
2 eggs
4 oz butter
½ teaspoon bicarbonate

½ teaspoon salt
½ teaspoon sugar
½ cup milk
1 grated lemon rind

Prepare dough and put on a pastry board, leave for one hour. Then roll out and cut into thin strips, approx. 4-5 inches long, knot them and put on a lightly floured board, cover with a cloth for about 10-15 minutes to allow mixture to settle. Deep fry in hot fat until golden brown, drain and sprinkle with icing sugar. One could use yeast instead of bicarbonate in which case the pastry would not be as crisp.
Recipe courtesy of the Luxembourg Embassy, Washington, DC

Holidays and Special Occasions

February 2 –The Fest of St. Blasius – children go to homes asking for treats
Sunday after Shrove Tuesday – Buergsonndeg – bonfire built and wooden cross often added. Barbeque and mulled wine might be served
Easter – decorated eggs; a woman gives her husband or boyfriend a praline filled Easter egg
Bratzelsonndeg - Pretzel Sunday - a man gives his girlfriend or wife a pretzel, a symbol of love
The Schueberfouer – market, now fair during the summer – fouerfesch (whiting fried in yeast) with fritten (French fries)
Gingerbread men – Boxemännercher served on December 6, St. Nicholas Day
Families attend midnight Mass on Christmas Eve and dine afterwards. The meal might include black pudding, potatoes, applesauce, and Mettwurscht, and spice wine.

Beverages

Since the early Roman conquest, white wine of the Moselle type, has been made. Others grapes used are Riesling, Rwaner, Auxerrois, Pinot, Rulander, and Traminer. Grevenmacher, on the Moselle River, is the center of the wine growing region. Luxembourg also produces sparkling wines (vins mousseux) and liqueurs such as Mirabelle, Kirsch, Prunelle, Cassis, and Quetsch. Beers are German style of the pilsener or lager types. The beer motto is "pure malt and hops".

Did You Know?

The Caves Cooperative at Wormeldanze has storage for 3 million liters of wine.

Madagascar

The Republic of Madagascar is an island nation in the Indian Ocean off the southeastern coast of Africa. The original inhabitants, according to Malagasy mythology, were the Vazimba. However settlement of the island was probably about 200-500 AD with seafarers from Southeast Asia. Later immigrants were Bantu, Arab and East Africans. Chiefdoms existed and Madagascar served as a coastal trading post. The Portuguese arrived c 1500 and began trading with the country. The British also provided military and financial assistance. France invaded in 1883. During the 19th c Madagascar was ruled by the Merina kingdom and part of the French empire. It received its independence in 1960. The capital, Antananarivo, is located in the Central Highlands and was settled about 400 years ago. The official languages are Malagasy, French and English. It is often referred to as "The Great Red Island".

Dining Etiquette

Men should wear dress shirt and slacks, women dresses or skirts not above the knee. Please be punctual when arriving and shake hands greeting and departing. Please bring a small gift for the home, preferably something from your country. Before a meal drinks or hors d'oeuvres are not usually served. Instead a meal is served on one plate for each person. Eating is with a spoon. Family and respect for the dead are important.

Cuisine and Beverages

The cuisine has been influenced by the Arabic, Chinese, French, African and Indian cultures. The French founded clove, coffee, vanilla and sugar plantations. Madagascar produces 60% of the world's vanilla. C 1793 vanilla vines were smuggled from Mexico to Reunion Island, then called Ile Bourbon. Today these beans are still called Bourbons. Vanilla pods are the fruit of an orchid. Rice is the staple food and eaten at all three meals – breakfast, lunch and dinner. Rice is cooked so that the bottom part is burned. One removes the unburned rice, and water is added to the burned rice. This is boiled and then served as a beverage at the meal, and is known as ranonapango. Rice is served with sauces, meat, chicken or seafood, and spicy seasonings such as hot peppers may be used. At breakfast rice might be served with sugar, fruit, eggs, or sausage. The dishes served with rice may vary by season and what is available. Fruits include coconut, bananas, fig, persimmon, berries, passion fruit, avocados, lychee, apples, lemons, watermelon, oranges, limes, cherries, strawberries, mango, pineapple, guava, longans, "pok-pok", tamarind, sakoa, and the fruit of the baobab tree (the national tree); seafood – crab, lobster, fish; vegetables – sweet potato, cassava, beans; meat – goat, Zebu beef, pork, and chicken. Vineyards and tea plantations are located near Fianarantsoa. Beverages include tea, coffee, fruit juices, wine, water, and beer. Ranonpango is the traditional drink. Others include: Tichel – lychee aperitif; Toaka gasy – distilled sugar cane and rice; Ravin'oliva – an herbal tea; Three Horses Lager and local rums.

Akoho Sy Voanio (Madagascar Chicken and Coconut Stew)

Whole chicken (12 pieces)
2 coconut powder (sachets)
3 medium tomatoes, chopped
2 onions, chopped
2 cloves garlic, diced

20 grams yellow curry powder
Olive oil
Salt and pepper
Water
Soy sauce

Cut and sprinkle the chicken with salt and pepper. Add a small amount of olive oil to a skillet. Saute the chicken until done. Add garlic and onions to the pan until onions are browned. Add tomatoes and curry powder. Sautee briefly. Add coconut powder, soy sauce, and 1-2 cups water. Simmer over low heat for 30 minutes. Serve with rice, coconut rice, and rogay tomato.
Recipe courtesy of Mrs. Erna Radifera, Embassy of the Republic of Madagascar, Washington, DC

Rogay Tomato (Tomato Salad)

2 medium tomatoes, finely chopped
Fresh chives or 1 small onion, finely chopped
1 tsp. salt

1 tsp. vinegar
A few drops of Tabasco or Malagasy sakay (chili)

Combine the ingredients and chill.
Recipe courtesy of Mrs. Erna Radifera

Madagascar Specialties

Sakay – very hot chili, garlic, ginger sauce
Vary sosoa – soupy rice
Vary amin 'anana – rice, leaves, herbs, meat or shrimp
Kitoza – smoked, cured meat
Akoho sy voanio – chicken with rice and coconut
Foza sy hena-kisoa – stir-fried crab, pork and rice
Koba – (the national snack) – mix of sweet rice paste, ground peanuts, and brown sugar, and wrapped in banana leaves
Koba akondro - a batter of ground peanuts, mashed bananas, honey and corn flour wrapped in banana leaves, then steamed or boiled as cakes

Vary – rice
Voanjoory – peas and pork
Ro – beef and pork marinated in vinegar, water and oil. It is cooked with leaves, onions, pickles, pimento, and other vegetables
Ravitoto – cassava leaves with peanuts or meat
Romazava – beef or pork with leaves or greens, sautéed with ginger, tomato and onion
Akoho – chicken with ginger
Mofo gasy – Malagasy bread made of sweetened rice flour
Godro-godro – coconut milk pudding

Hena Omby Ritra (Beef Saute)

500 grams beef with fat, cubed
4 tomatoes, chopped
2 onions, chopped
3 cloves garlic

Salt and pepper
3 cups water
Soy sauce

Place the water and beef in a pressure cooker. Cook about 20 minutes. Add tomatoes, onions, garlic, salt, pepper and soy sauce. Saute over medium heat. Mix well. Reduce heat and cook for 10-15 minutes, or until sauce becomes thick. Serve with coconut rice and rogay tomato.
Recipe courtesy of Mrs. Erna Radifera

Vary Amin'ny Voanio

3 cups rice
1 coconut powder

Salt
2 cups water

Wash the rice. Add a small amount of salt, water and coconut powder. Cook until rice is tender. Serve with Madagascar chicken and coconut stew, beef sauté and rogay tomato.
Recipe courtesy of Mrs. Erna Radifera

Hot Chocolate Ice Cream

6 egg yolks
2 tsp. vanilla extract
¼ tsp. cinnamon
2 tsp. ancho chili powder
Pinch of salt

1 ½ cups heavy cream
1 ½ cups whole milk
5 oz. bittersweet chocolate

Beat together the egg yolks, vanilla extract, cinnamon, ancho chile powder, and salt in a small bowl. Break the chocolate into pieces. Pour the cream and milk into a medium-sized saucepan and add chocolate pieces. Heat very gently on low. Stir continuously so chocolate does not burn on the bottom. Heat until just barely simmering. Remove from heat. Pour about one cup into the egg mixture and stir for about a minute. Slowly add the rest of the chocolate/milk to the eggs and stir until combined. Pour the mixture into a clean pot and stir over low heat until thickened. Pour into a clean bowl. Cool for several hours or overnight in the refrigerator. Process in an ice cream maker according to the manufacturer's instructions. Chocolate from Madagascar is recommended.
Recipe courtesy of Kelly Brooks, www.cooklocalthinksocial.com and Joe Salvatore, Madecasse Madagascar pure vanilla powder

Holidays or Special Events

For Independence Day, Easter, Christmas and New Year's Eve the family dines together. Rice and chicken are served. Only poultry, no meat is served the week before New Year's.

Malawi

Malawi is a landlocked country in southeast Africa formerly known as Nyasaland and bordered by Zambia to the northwest, Tanzania to the northeast, and Mozambique on the east, south and west. The country is separated from Tanzania and Mozambique by Lake Malawi. The earliest inhabitants were hunter-gatherers. In the 4th c Bantu speaking people arrived and formed tribes. By the 15th c these tribes established the kingdom of Maravi that stretched from the Zambezi River in the north and what is now Zambia. In the 17th c Portuguese traders explored the region. In 1859 Scottish explorers reached Lake Nyasa, followed by British missionaries and a British consul in 1883. In 1889 the British formed the Shire Highlands Protectorate and in 1891 much of Malawi was formed into the British Central African Protectorate. Malawi became independent in 1964. Lilongwe, located on the Lilongwe River, became the capital in 1975. English and Chichewa are the official languages.

Dining Etiquette

Malawians live on their own time, but if invited for a meal please be punctual. Please shake hands greeting and departing. If meeting someone of importance bend your knee slightly and use your left hand to hold the right arm. The food is served on a low table. A bowl and pitcher of water will be extended to wash your hands before and after the meal. Prayers will probably be said before the meal. Food is eaten with the right hand, by taking a small amount of the nsima, forming it into a bowl, and then dipping it into the relishes. Please thank the hosts for their hospitality after the meal.

Cuisine and Beverages

Malawi is basically a farming country with fertile plains in the south, but also is part of the Great Rift Valley. The staples of the diet are millet, sorghum, maize, cassava, peanuts and peanut butter, chilies, rice, potatoes, sweet potatoes, spinach, tomatoes, peppers, onions, ; fruit – mangoes, melons, oranges, bananas, pineapples; fish – tilapia, mlamba (catfish), mpasa, usipa, kampango, and chambo from Lake Malawi; chickens, goats, pigs, and cattle.

Tea plantations are located near Mount Mulanje and tea is exported, and use for local consumption. Beer is brewed at Malawi Carlsberg Brewery in Blantyre and at home. Chibuku is a drink made by women and served in milk cartons. A variety of fruit wines are produced by Linga Country Wine.

Mtedza (Ground Nut Chicken)

Serves 6

3 lb. chicken, cut into pieces
¼ cup flour
Salt and pepper
¼ cup oil
3 hardboiled eggs, sliced or quartered
2 cups peanuts, minced

1 large onion, chopped
3 tomatoes, chopped
2 cups chicken stock
1 hot chili, chopped
Salt and pepper

Preheat oven to 350°
In a bowl coat the chicken with the flour and some salt and pepper.
Heat the oil in a skillet and sauté the chicken pieces until brown. Place in a casserole
In a bowl mix the peanuts and stock until smooth. Add the tomatoes, onions and pepper. Pour over the chicken.
Bake for 30 minutes, or chicken is cooked.
Serve with egg garnish and boiled rice, or nsima.

Malawian Specialties

Nsima – national dish - maize porridge served with beans, meat, or vegetables; pumpkin leaves with groundnut flour and chicken may also be served
Ndiwo – relishes, dishes served with nsima
Fufu – fermented cassava
Futou – mashed plantain and cassava
Ntochi – banana bread
Mbtata pudding – sweet potato pudding
Mbtata biscuits – sweet potato biscuits
Mtedza – peanut puffs

Futali – pumpkin and peanut flour dish
Curried chambo – chambo (fish) with lemon juice, flour, onions, curry, chutney, and carrots
Wali wa samaki –salmon, pasta, onion, carrots, rice
Ana a njuchi – dried wild bee larvae that are fried
Bwamnoni – dried bush crickets, also fried
Nsensenya – fried shield bugs

Holidays and Special Occasions

Weddings – Dowries are given by the bride's parents to the groom and will include livestock, grain, or land.
Weddings and funerals – food and alcoholic beverages
End of harvest season – thanks given to ancestral spirits and food is offered to the gods.
Food is served on holidays which include New Year's Day, Martyr's Day, Easter, Freedom Day, Republic Day, Mother's Day and Christmas.

Malaysia

Malaysia occupies the southern half of the Malay Peninsula and the northwestern coast of the neighboring island of Borneo in Southeast Asia. A range of forested mountains runs north and south along the center of the peninsula, flanked on the east and west by coastal plains. The earliest known inhabitants were Negritos, followed by the Malays, and from 2500-1500 BC settlers from southern China. Over the years it was part of the Sri Vijayan Empire, the Javanese kingdom, Siam, the Portuguese, the Dutch, the British, the Japanese. The British colonies of Sarawak, Singapore and Sabah joined the federation of Malaya to form Malaysia on September 16, 1963, with Singapore withdrawing in 1965. The capital Kuala Lumpur (muddy river mouth) was founded as a trading post and later a center for rubber export by the British. Putrajaya is the administrative capital, located about half an hour from Kuala Lumpur. Islam is the official religion. Bahasa Malaysia (Malay) is the national language, but English is widely spoken. Islam is the official religion.

Dining Etiquette

Please be punctual for meetings and meals. When greeting people bow slightly, and shake hands lightly. Bring hands to your chest and say "Salaam" "I greet you by heart". Women may not shake hands, and only do so if she offers hers. Women bring their hands to their lips, and then the breast. Elders, superiors, and women are introduced first. Please stand when introduced to an older person or when he/she enters a room. When seated do not show the soles of your feet, keeping your feet together on the floor. Women should dress modestly.

When arriving at a home please remove your shoes. One will be offered tea or juices, which you should accept with the right hand. Dining is on cushions on the floor. Men sit cross-legged, women side-saddle. Hands are washed before the meal with a bowl and towel offered. At the beginning of the meal the hosts says "Will you join me?", and then you may start. Dishes, usually 5-6 are served together on the table. Rice is placed in separate bowls. Juice and water are served beverages. Drink using the left hand, as the glass will be placed to the left of the rice. Food is eaten with the right hand only. If you are left handed, apologize to the host before eating. The left hand is used for toilet oblations. Malays and Indians eat with their hands and spoons; the Chinese with chopsticks and spoons. If using the hand so as a scoop. Food is served with the left hand, and passed right to left with spoons. If you do not wish something, please put your hand over your plate and say "No thank you". Don't refuse food or drink, even if you only finish a small amount. Dipping one's forefinger in a salt dish is a sign of friendship.

Do's and Don't's:

Because Malaysia is mainly a Muslim country no pork, liquor, knives, images of humans or toy dogs are given as presents. Present a gift with both hands. Gifts are opened in front of the presenter. If visiting and staying overnight in Iban long house, please bring gifts and cigarettes. If you admire something too much it will be given to you. Never give too much praise to a child or he/she will acquire an "evil eye". Never touch the head of another person. Don't step over the crossed legs of someone seated. Anger and emotions are not shown in public. Do not raise your voice. Placing one's hands on the hips shows anger. People may laugh when shy or embarrassed. Do not touch a member of the opposite sex. Never point with the index finger, use the whole hand. To gesture to someone use the palm down. "No" can mean many things, and is not used to save "face". Do not shame or embarrass a person. Remember Ramadan is celebrated for one month and fasting is all day.

Satay (Grilled Meat)

Serves 6

1 tsp. coriander seeds	3 tbls. ground peanuts
1 tsp. cumin seeds	1 tbls. fresh lime or lemon juice
4 cloves garlic, grated	1 tsp. soy sauce
½ tsp. sea salt	2 lb. boneless leg of lamb, cut into 1 in. cubes
1 tbls. grated ginger	Bamboo skewers, soaked in water for 30 minutes
½ tsp. cayenne	
1 tsp. turmeric	2 tbls. vegetable oil

In a skillet heat the coriander seeds for 1 minute. Put in a bowl. Do the same for the cumin seeds. Place the seeds in a spice grinder and place back in the bowl.

Pound the garlic and salt together to make a paste in a bowl. Add the seeds, ginger, cayenne, turmeric, ground peanuts, soy sauce, and lime juice. A food processor can also be used for these steps. The marinade can be stored in the refrigerator if not using immediately.

Place the lamb in a bowl or plastic bag and coat on all sides with the marinade.

Place the meat on the skewers. Baste with the vegetable oil.

Cook the meat on a BBQ 3-4 minutes, or more, depending on how you like your lamb.

Serve immediately with rice and condiments. The rest of the marinade can also be used.

Beef, chicken, pork or fish can be substituted for the lamb.

Cuisine

Malaysian food is a wonderful blend of fresh vegetables, fruit, herbs and spices. It makes use of coconut milk, tamarind, screw-pine, onions, pandan leaves, cinnamon, coriander, ginger, lime and lime leaves, cumin, cardamom, curry, lemon grass, shrimp paste, chili peppers, and garlic. Others include mustard greens, bean sprouts, durian, jackfruit, crabs and shrimp. Local fish include marlin, wahoo, sailfish, grouper, snapper, coral trout, and yellowfin tuna. A number of tropical fruit are grown here. Cashews are popular nuts. Many dishes are simmered slowly. Each of the ethnic groups has its own style of cooking. The customs and cooking have also been influenced by the Dutch, English, Indians, Arabs, and Portuguese who used the islands on the "Spice Routes". On Penang Nonya cooking with influences from the Chinese, Malay, Indian and Thai cultures prevails, using pork, fried noodles, sambals (sauce of chilies and shrimp paste) and achars (pickled fruit and vegetables). Sabah is known for its tea, coffee, greens, and many fruits and vegetables. Sarawak is a leading producer of pepper, pineapples; in the Kelabit Highlands Bario rice; the Ba'Kelalan highlands apples; and exporting Swiftlet's nests. Two favorite dishes from Sarawak are kaksa, a noodle dish served with a tangy soup; and Sarawak layer cake, a cake that looks like a mosaic. Labuan is noted for seafood – prawns, crabs, lobster, shellfish and fish. Coconut pudding is made on Labuan from coconut water and jelly.

Breakfast is served 7-8AM, and usually consists of nasi lemak (rice with coconut milk and fish). Lunch is 12-1:30 and consists of rice, curry, vegetables, water and tea. Dinner is 7 or 8, similar to lunch, but may also include fruit. Many families have kitchen altars dedicated to food deities.

Malaysian Specialties

Satay – the national dish - small pieces of meat, skewered and basted with soy sauce, oil, grilled, then dipped in sauces of chilies, spices and peanuts.

Rendang – beef cooked in spices and coconut milk

Sambal – hot paste of pounded chilies, prawn paste and lime juice

Nasi lemak – rice cooked in coconut milk with spices such as ginger, star anise, and cinnamon. It is eaten with fried anchovies, poached eggs, sliced cucumber, groundnuts, sambal gravy and rending

Nasi Campur – rice with accompanying dishes

Nasi Goreng – fried rice with meat, seafood and vegetables

Hinava – raw fish or prawn salad with grated seeds of wild mangothat is indigenous to Sabah

Tuhau – salad made from ginger-like plant with lime juice, onions, and chillies. Can be served by itself or with rice

Chicken rice – rice with steamed, roasted or poached chicken with ginger paste, chilli sauce and soy sauce

Laksa – noodle soup

Tuaran mee- egg yolk and flour batter stir-fried with vegetables and garnished with chicken or pork and eggs

Pasembor – shredded vegetable salad with curried squid and deep fried crab with a spicy sauce

Rojak buah – fruit salad in a sauce of fermented shrimp paste

Lemang – glutinous rice cake

Blacan (belcacan or blacang) – shrimp paste used in cooking

Heh kian taugeh – bean sprout and shrimp fritters (Nonya)

Opor – chicken cooked in coconut milk

Nasi ulam – rice with herbs and coconut (Nonya)

Pisang goring – fried battered banana

Kelupis – glutinous rice wrapped in daun nyirik leaf and cooked coconut milk

Cheng tng – dessert made with brown soup, lotus seeds, white fungus and nuts

Agar-agar – "jelly" – boiled seaweed jelly with fruit and sugar

Aiskrim potong – ice cream made with coconut milk or milk in various flavors

Bubur cha-cha – sweet potato and yam cooked in coconut milk

Cendol – flour noodles with palm sugar, coconut milk and shaved ice

Kuih – small steamed pastries with various flavorings
Pulut hitam – black glutinous rice with sago
Tau fa fah – soybean curd in syrup
Roti canai – crisp wheat pancake and served with lentil or chicken curry
Dodol – coconut milk, rice flour, jiggery, and fruit sweet
Ketupat – rice dumpling

Air batu campur – shaved ice with red beans, groundnuts, corn and fruit, sweetened with condensed milk and sugar syrup
Ambuyat or nantung – thick sago, tapioca or rice porridge which is rolled or twisted around a chopstick
Coconut pudding – steamed coconut water and jelly
Jelurut – rice flour, sugar, coconut milk jelly-like dessert

Holidays and Special Occasions

Ramadan – fasting from sunrise to sunset after which the fast is broken (iftar) eating dried or fresh dates. The supper (moreh) follows prayers with snacks and tea. Bubur lambuk (rice porridge with sweet potatoes, prawns, beef and herbs) is served.

Hari Raya Aidilfitri (Eid ul-Fitr) – the end of Ramadan – special dishes are prepared – ketupat, dodol, opor, rendang, lemang, and cookies

Hari Raya Aidiladha – marks the completion of a pilgrimage to Mecca with prayers said and cattle, goats or ram are sacrificed and the meat distributed to the poor

Chinese Lunar New Year – family reunion dinners

Dccpavali celebrated by Hindus as the Festival of Lights with a ritualistic oil bath and prayers, and feasting

Mid-autumn Festival (Lantern and Mooncake Festival) - mooncakes

Birthdays – mee (egg noodle stew with shrimp, crab, chicken and pork)

First anniversary after a death – a special meal is prepared

Beverages

Bandung is a drink made with condensed milk and rose syrup. Soya cincau is a soybean and grass jelly drink. Teh tarik (means "stretched tea") is made with tea and condensed milk and frothed. Ais batu campur (mixed ice cubes) is made from red beans, peanuts, grass jelly, cendol, agar-agar, sweet corn, and shaved ice. Malaysians also drink tea and coffee. Kopi tongkat ali ginseng is made with coffee, and aphrodisiac, ginseng, and served with condensed milk. Fruit juices and milo (chocolate drink) are also served. Drinks served might be rose water, kopi – coffee, the – tea, air tebu – sugar cane juice, or kelapa muda – coconut juice. Muslims do not drink alcohol, but alcoholic beverages are available. Local rice wine is produced. Tea is grown in the Cameron Highlands; tea and coffee in Sabah.

Did You Know?

Bananas once grew in the wild, had large seeds and were inedible. C 50,000 years ago during the Stone Age probably in Malaysia, a banana grew without seeds and could be eaten. Later people carried the shoots to new lands in the tropics and bananas flourished. Bananas stay green until they are picked.

Maldives

Maldives is a South Asian island country, located in the Indian Ocean, and lies southwest of India and Sri Lanka. The chain of twenty-six atolls comprising 1192 islands stretches from Ihavandhippolhu Atoll in the north to the Addu City in the south. The earliest written history of the Maldives was marked by the arrival of Sinhalese people in Sri Lanka and the Maldives (*Mahiladvipika*) circa 543 to 483 BC. Since ancient times, the Maldives were ruled by kings (Radhun) and occasionally queens (Ranin). The Maldives had a strategic importance because of its location on the major marine routes of the Indian Ocean. The Maldives' nearest neighbors are Sri Lanka and India, both of which have had cultural and economic ties with Maldives for centuries. Middle Eastern seafarers had just begun to take over the Indian Ocean trade routes in the 10th century and found Maldives to be an important link in those routes as the first landfall for traders from Basra sailing to Southeast Asia. Trade involved mainly cowrie shells – widely used as a form of currency throughout Asia and parts of the East African coast – and coir fiber. In the 12 c Arab traders converted the king to Islam. During the 16th and 17th c the Portuguese, Dutch, and French explored the region, and in the 19th c Maldives became a British protectorate. They received their independence in 1965. The capital is Male and the official language Maldivian.

Dining Etiquette

The people are warm and friendly. If invited to a home remove your shoes upon entering the home and leave them by the front door. Please shake hands on greeting, or nod your head or bow slightly. Women offer their hand first. If nod just nod your head. Please bring a gift preferably something from your country. The host or hostess will seat the guests at a table. Please wait till you are seated to begin eating. Please try everything. Eat and pass with your right hand. Leave a little on your plate, otherwise your host will think you did not get enough. Because this is a Muslim country no pork or alcohol is served.

Cuisine

The cuisine has been influenced by what is available on the islands, India and Sri Lanka, and the Muslims arriving in the 11th c. Seafood – yellowfin, skipjack, and frigate tuna, tunny, bigeye and mackerel scad, mahi mahi, and wahoo is readily available. These are boiled, grilled, deep-fried, dried, or processed. Curries are often made with fish. Curries can also be made using chicken, eggplant, tora, pumpkin, and bananas. Banana leaves are used in cooking. Curries are eaten with rice or roshi (flat bread).

Tuna are caught using pole fishing. They are then processed so they do not need to be refrigerated. Tuna are gutted, and the head and spine removed. The fillets are cut in half lengthways and cut into four pieces called ari. The fillets are processed by being boiled, smoking and sun-dried. The fish is used in many dishes such as curries, soups, pastes or relishes. Among the ingredients used are rice – boiled or made into flour, root crops such as taro, sweet potatoes, cassava; and fruit – breadfruit and screwpine and coconuts. Coconut is grated, made into coconut oil or coconut milk (kaashi kiri). A hunigondi is used to grate the coconut. Root crops and breadfruit are boiled; screwpine is sliced. Since Maldives is a Muslim country alcoholic beverages are not drunk. Mainly fruit or coconut drinks are served.

Mas Huni (tuna and coconut)

Serves 4

3 cans tuna with water, or smoked, drained, or dried tuna, or fresh tuna
2 jalapeno, seeded and chopped
4 green onions, chopped, including tops
Juice of 2 large limes
Zest of 2 limes

¼ cup shredded coconut
¼ cup coconut milk
¼ cup cilantro leaves, chopped
2tbls. olive oil
Salt and pepper

Combine all the ingredients in a bowl. Make into molds on 4 plates with lettuce. Serve chilled.

Specialties

Gulha – fried dough balls with mas huni
Kulhi bokiba – fish cakes
Bajiya – roshi with dried tuna and spices
Fathafolhi – noonles and tuna
Garudiya – clear fish broth made from fresh or dried tuna
Rihaakuru – fish paste made from tuna and salt used in cooking, and eaten with rice or other starches, or roshi.
Curries are made with coconut milk, curry paste, onions, chilies, herbs, and spices. Vegetable curries are also prepared with pumpkin, potatoes, sweet potatoes, beans, or other vegetables
Mas riha – tuna curry with onions, chilies, coriander, fennel, cumin, garlic, and lime juice
Kukulhu riha – chicken curry
Baraboa mas huni - pumpkin, coconut, chilis, curry
Roshi – flatbread eaten with mas huni and curries
Mas roshi – flat dough balls with mas huni

Holidays and Special Occasions

Ramadan – Muslims fast from sunrise to sunset.
National Day – first day of Rabee-ul Awwal in the third month of the Islamic calendar – parades and marches
Independence Day – July 26 – parades, performances, food
Republic Day – November 11 – marks second independence in 1968 – parades and other celebrations
Prophet's Birthday – 12 day of Rabee-ul Awwal – celebrated in mosques
Eid Festival – held at end of Ramadan with elaborate feasts

Mali

Mali, located on the west coast of Africa, is bounded to the west by Mauritania, Guinea, Algeria and Niger to the east, and Burkina Faso, Niger, and the Cote D'Ivoire to the south. Mali is located on ancient trading routes of the Sahara and once part of the Sahelian kingdoms, the earliest the Ghana Empire. The Soinke, Mande speaking people, expanded throughout West Africa from the 8th c to 1078, when they were conquered by the Almoravids. The Mali Empire formed on the Niger River and the cities of Djenne and Timbuktu were trading centers. The Songhai Empire was the third empire to make up present day Mali. In the late 19th c The French took over the region and Mali became part of the French Sudan. The French Sudan joined with Senegal in 1959, and in 1960 became independent as the Mali Federation. After the withdrawal of Senegal from the Federation the Sudanese Republic became the Republic of Mali. Timbuktu was founded in the 11th c. The capital Bamako, has been inhabited since Paleolithic times as the Niger River Valley provided agricultural products. Kola nuts, salt, gold and ivory were traded. Mali is from the Mandingo word for hippopotamus. French is the official language with Bambara, Fula, Tamashek (Tuareg), Songhai, Dogon, and approximately 50 other languages spoken.

Dining Etiquette

When invited for a meal please arrive punctually. Please do not bring a gift as the host is to provide for the guests. Men shake hands greeting and put their right hand to the chest to show respect. Good friends may hug. Bow your head slightly when greeting elders. Women will greet other women with a handshake, and if they want to shake hands with a man will extend their hands. Otherwise a man should just bow his head slightly or nod to the woman. Women greeting elders should bend their knees. Food is eaten with the right hand only. Being a Muslim country most people do not drink alcoholic beverages. Instead fruit juices (watermelon, banana, mango, guava, tamarind, and lemon), te (tea), café (coffee), dablenin (sorrel drink), djinimbere (ginger drink), and bissap (boiled hibiscus leaves). Drinking tea is done three times, the first tea is sweet for life, the second very sweet for love, and the third bitter for death. Please accept all three cups.

Cuisine

Each of the different ethnic groups has its own cuisine. The main staples are corn, millet, rice porridges served with sauces, sorghum, sugar, oil, fonio (cereal), peanuts (groundnuts), cereals, kola nuts, maize, vegetables – eggplant, peas, onions, peppers, okra, tomatoes, cassava, yams, chilies; fish – fresh water from the Niger which is grilled or dried; chicken; cattle; goats; and sheep. Two thirds of the country is desert or semi-arid. In the north milk, dates, and wheat are part of the diet. Sauces are made with peanuts, okra, baobab, tomatoes, or sweet potato leaves to which other vegetables or meat might be added and then served over porridge, rice, or couscous. Food is cooked outside on an open hearth. Sikasso has a large fruit and vegetable market. Huge veins of salt once existed in the Sahara near Taghaza and Taoudeni. Salt slabs were brought by camels to the markets in Timbuktu, Mopti and other towns along the Niger. Because Mali was on the Trans-Sahara trade routes salt and gold found in the north made early Mali prosper. In fact it was said 1 pound of gold was equal to one pound of salt as both were so valuable. Salt was used for currency.

Tiguadege Na (Meat in Peanut Butter Sauce)

Serves 6

3 tbls. oil	4 cups beef broth
2 lbs. beef, lamb, or goat	¼ cup peanut butter
2 onions, peeled and chopped	½ tsp. thyme
3 garlic cloves, peeled and minced	½ tsp. marjoram
Salt and pepper to taste	2 carrots, peeled and sliced
4 medium tomatoes, chopped	2 potatoes, peeled and cubed

Heat the oil in a large pan. Brown the meat on all sides. Add the onions until translucent. Stir in garlic, salt and pepper. Add the tomatoes. Bring to a boil and let simmer for 10 minutes. Stir in the broth, peanut butter, and herbs. Add the potatoes and carrots. Cover and cook for ½ hour or until potatoes and carrots are tender. Serve over rice.

Mali Specialties

Poulet yassa- chicken with onions, chilies, mustard, and lemon juice
Poulet kedjennou – chicken or fish with peppers and tomatoes
Saga saga – meat in sweet potato leaf sauce
Larho – millet porridge
Degue – yogurt porridge
Riz yollof – meat with tomatoes and vegetables and rice
Tcheke – fish with plantains
Tigadèguèna ni Djèguè Woussou - Smoked fish in peanut sauce
Nsaame – rice with meat and vegetables
La capitaine sangha – Nile perch with hot chili sauce, fried bananas and rice

Tiga diga na – peanut butter sauce
Mafe – beef with tomatoes, onion, garlic, peanut butter, and stock
Foutou (fufu) – mashed yams, yucca, or potato and served with meat
Couscous – semolina pasta
Seri – sweet porridge
To – millet or cornmeal porridge with okra
Meni – meniyong – sesame seed, honey, and butter dessert
Kyinkyinga – meat and capsicum (peppers) dish
Akara – fried bean, chilies, onion balls
Kulikuli – groundnut biscuits
Maasa – millet fritters

Holidays and Special Occasions

Naming ceremonies, weddings and other occasions – nsaame and dabileni (water, sugar and sorrel drink), and jinjinbere (water, sugar, and lemon drink)
Crossing of the Cattle (December) – in Diafarabe – the herders bring the cattle from the grazing lands to the river, where families are reunited, and then the cattle taken to new pastures.

Malta

Malta and the islands adjoining (Gozo and Comino and two other smaller islands) are located in the Mediterranean, made up of safe harbors, rocky coastlines and low hills. The history of Malta dates from the 5th millennium BC when the first settlers, probably farmers arrived at Skorba from Sicily. Throughout its history it has been occupied by Carthage, Romans, Byzantine rule, united with Sicily in 1284, the Turks, Napoleon, and the British. Malta finally became a democratic republic within the British Commonwealth in 1974. The capital Valletta, was established by the Knights of St. John in the 1500s and is a walled city.

Dining Etiquette

Shake hands greeting and departing. Men stand when ladies are introduced, and hold doors and chairs for them. Many people still take lunch at home. Dinner is a time for socializing. Please arrive promptly. When entertained in a home please take wine, whiskey, flowers, or candies. Drinks and appetizers will be served. The hostess will escort her guests to the table with the guest of honor to her right. Food is served in courses. Please wait for the hostess to begin, and eat continental style – fork in the left hand, knife in the right, using these at the same time with elbows at table level, hands not in your lap. When finished please place the knife and fork together.

Maltese Baked Macaroni (mqarrun fil-forn)

Serves 8

1 kilo (2lb8oz) macaroni (choose from the wide assortment available)
Best Bolognese sauce made with ½ kilo meat.

4 eggs, beaten
Salt and pepper
150g (6oz) parmesan cheese grated

Lightly grease a good oven dish with butter or margarine
Cook macaroni in lots of boiling salted water. When just tender, drain and then mix well with the warm Bolognese sauce, the cheese, and eggs. Season well with salt and pepper.
Spoon into the prepared oven dish and bake in a fairly hot oven 190°/375f/gas mark 5 for about 45 minutes, until the dish is cooked and the macaroni tinged with black crispy tops!
Serve immediately, or wrap in foil and newspapers and take on a picnic!
Recipe courtesy of Pippa Mattei "25 Years in a Maltese Kitchen" and the Embassy of Malta, Washington, DC

"After Easter we launch into full spring, the countryside is lush with Oxalis and other wild flowers, and our wonderful citrus trees are all in blossom, giving out a heady smell. Gardens look their best at this time of year and Birthday parties, Christenings and Holy Communion celebrations can be held outside. This flurry of celebration calls for an assortment of Maltese tea time treats."
Pippa Mattei

Biskuttini tal-Magħmudija "Christening Biscuits"

Makes 30

4 eggs
350 g (14oz) caster sugar
¼ teaspoon ground cinnamon
¼ teaspoon ground cloves

25 g (1oz) candied peel, finely chopped
300 g (12oz) plain flour
1 teaspoon baking powder

Separate yolk and whites of the eggs and beat whites until stiff, whisk in the yolks and slowly add the sugar and the cinnamon and ground cloves. Add the chopped candied peel and fold into the mixture.
Sift the flour and the baking powder and again fold into the egg mix. Do not beat.
Grease paper on baking sheets, and sprinkle with 1 tablespoon flour and one tablespoon sugar.
Now place oval tablespoons of the biscuit mixture onto this, leaving space between each mound.
Pre-heat oven (preferably fan oven) to 180°C/350°F/gas mark 4, and bake biscuits for 15 minutes until firm but still light in color.
Cool on racks and when cold decorate with swirls of white and pink royal icing.
To decorate: Royal icing
Baking sheets lined with greaseproof paper
Extra sugar and flour to sprinkle on greaseproof paper on baking sheets
Recipe courtesy of Pippa Mattei "Pippa's Festa - A Celebration of Food in Malta'

Cuisine

Malta's history and geography had an important influence on its cuisine. Having to import most of its foodstuffs, situated along trade routes, and controlled by other countries, Maltese cuisine highlights Italian, English, French Maghrebin, and Mediterranean influences. The Knights of St. John came mainly from France, Italy, and Spain and introduced aljotta, a fish broth with garlic, herbs, and tomatoes; and brought foodstuffs from the Americas such as tomatoes, potatoes, and chocolate. The British brought mustards, Bovril, HP Sauce, and Worcestershire Sauce. From Gozo foods include ġbejna t'Għawdex - cheese and ftira Għawdxija - flatbread with potatoes and ġbejniet - eggs, grated cheese, tomatoes, anchovies, olives, ricotta and sausage. Fruit – oranges, grapes, strawberries, melons, tangerines, mulberries, and pomegranates are all grown on the islands

348

Maltese Specialties

Soups – aljotta (fish); brodu (beef and vegetable); minestra (vegetables with beans and pork); kawlata – vegetable with pork

Pasta – kusku (pasta stuffed with vegetables); ravjul (ravioli); timpana (pastry with ricotta cheese, macaroni, tomato puree, aubergines, onions, and eggs)

Ros il-forn – baked rice

Fenek – marinated rabbit with roasted vegetables, the national dish

Fish – torla tal (fish in pastry with vegetables); qarnit (octopus or squid); perch; catfish; or red sea salmon

Meats – bragioli (meat, bacon, eggs, onions, and breadcrumbs in the steak that is rolled and fried); brungiel mimli (eggplant stuffed with ground meat and vegetables; bzar ahdar mimli (stuffed peppers)

Vegetables – Bigilla (beans with herbs and garlic)

Desserts – prinjolata (sponge cake with butter, cream, almonds, topped with chocolate and cherries – eaten at carnival) and kwarezimal (cake with fruit and nuts, eaten during Lent from quadragesima, the forty days of Lent). Other sweets eaten at special times are karamelli tal-ħarrub, ftira tar-Randan, figolla and qagħaq tal-għasel

Cheese – gbejna (from goat or sheep's milk)

Holidays and Special Occasions

During festas quabbajt (nougat) and mqaret (hot fritters with dates) are served.

Most Catholics fast during Lent eating mainly fish such as Lampuki, whitebait and salted cod; stewed snails (bebbux), stuffed artichokes (qaqoċċ mimli), fritters (sfineġ), broad beans, and kusksu (a vegetable and pasta dish).

During Holy Week bakers also bake a large bagel with some almonds on top called qagħqa tal-appostli (lit. apostles' bagel).

At Easter lamb and figolla (a pastry with marzipan, colored icing, and a whole egg, usually in the shape of a lamb or basket) are served. Eggs are also dyed.

On Christmas people attend midnight mass after a large meal. On Christmas day turkey, vegetables, rich desserts, and fine wines are served.

Beverages

Wine has been produced on Malta for many centuries, though during the Turkish occupation and the Muslim influence, production dwindled. Charles V and the Knights of St. John revived the industry after 1533. Many of the wines are sweet with a high alcohol content (16%). Liqueurs are also produced including Tamakari, an herb liqueur. Light beers, lagers and stout are brewed on island. The toast is "Cheers" or "to your health". Fruit juices and squashes are popular drinks.

Did You Know?

The luzzus are the brightly painted fishing boats with eyes on either side of the prow to ward off evil spirits.

Marshall Islands

The Republic of the Marshall Islands is an island country located near the equator in the Pacific Ocean and is spread out over 29 coral atolls, comprising 1,156 individual islands and islets. The islands share maritime boundaries with the Federated States of Micronesia to the west, Wake Island to the north, Kiribati to the south-east, and Nauru to the south. Micronesian colonists gradually settled the Marshall Islands during the 2nd millennium BC. Islands in the archipelago were first explored by Europeans in the 1520s with the islands' current name coming from British explorer John Marshall (1788) who visited with Thomas Gilbert. The European powers recognized the islands as part of the Spanish East Indies in 1874. However, Spain sold the islands to the German Empire in 1884, and they became part of German New Guinea in 1885. In World War I the Empire of Japan occupied the Marshall Islands, which in 1919 the League of Nations combined with other former German territories to form the South Pacific Mandate. In World War II, the United States conquered the islands in the Gilbert and Marshall Islands campaign and along with other Pacific Islands, they were then consolidated into the Trust Territory of the Pacific Islands governed by the United States. Self-government was achieved in 1979, and full sovereignty in 1986, under a Compact of Free Association with the United States. The most populous atoll is Majuro, which also acts as the capital.

Dining Etiquette

When invited for a meal please arrive promptly. Shake hands greeting departing. The host will show you to your seat at the table. Please do try everything, which shows how much it is appreciated. Knives, forks and spoons may be provided, but the people mostly eat with their hands. If using cutlery do so the continental way – fork in the left hand and knife in the right. Children are fed first.

Cuisine and Beverages

The earliest settlers came to this region about 3000 years ago and brought with them pigs, rats, and dogs. Later taro, rice, yams, breadfruit, bananas, lemons, and sugarcane were introduced. The land is quite fertile as the islands are volcanic in origin. Few plants are native to the islands, most imported by early settlers or traders. It was not until the 1800s that the Spanish and Germans brought cattle, chickens, potatoes, wheat, pineapples, papaya, and mangoes. Later during the Japanese occupation the Japanese brought in their own foodstuffs. Among the seafood are crabs, clams, turtles, and various fish. Seabirds are also used for food. Lavish feasts may be held roasting whole pigs in dirt and leaves. Most agricultural products are produced on small farms. Coconuts, tomatoes, melons and ulu (breadfruit) are the main crops. Macadamia nuts, bananas, pandan leaves, cabbage, potatoes, pumpkins, papaya, and yams are also grown. Coconut are utilized in many different ways - milk and cream, meat, palms for clothing, coconut lumber to build houses, burn coconut husks or shells for fuel, coconut oil lamps, and copra- the dried meat of the coconut. Copra can be made into coconut oil which can be used for cooking, soaps, perfumes, face creams and many other uses. Sago is a starch extracted from palm stems which is made into flour which when mixed with water can rolled into balls, formed into a paste, or eaten as a pancake. Pearls, similar to tapioca, can also be made which are boiled with milk or water and sugar as sago pudding. Fruit juices, tea, and coffee are drunk. Kava is a drink made from the ground roots of the kava plant to release a liquid, and then water is added.

Barramundi (Cod in Banana Leaves)

Serves 6

2- 4 large banana leaves
2 chilies, seeded and chopped
1 cup fresh grated coconut
2 tbls. fresh grated ginger

2 lbs. fresh cod fillets, cut into 6 pieces
Sea salt
2 limes

Trim the banana leaves so they are about 10 inches square and have six to work with.
Line a baking dish with the banana leaves. Place the chilies, coconut, ginger, sea salt and lime in the center of each leaf. Top with a fish fillet. Fold the edges of the leaves over the fillets, then tuck in each end so that you have six packets.
Place in 350° oven for 20-30 minutes to steam but not overcook fish.
Serve immediately with rice or other condiments.
The banana leaves are not edible. This dish can be made using tinfoil to bake the fish.

Holidays and Special Occasions

For national holidays people prepare traditional dishes such as, fruit bat soup, Chicken, banana cakes or banana pancakes, rice pudding, lemon cheese cake, and macadamia nut pie.
Before Christmas homes, streets and churches are cleaned. Gifts for the performers are prepared with bottles of coconut oil, bags of coconut, and other items. Pigs are slaughtered for the Christmas feast. Fish are caught and coconuts gathered. The women make rice, doughnuts, and bread. Costumes are made for the *jeptas*, and the baskets prepared for another family or the *jeptas*. The jeptas visit the minister's home, sing for the family and give them presents. The minister serves tea or coffee.
Christmas (Kurijmoj) - December 25 – people attend church and baskets of food are exchanged. They watch *jeptas* (different groups) perform songs, dances, and skits. With them they bring food and other gifts. Sometimes the women steal the men's food! Competition between the female jeptas is known as *karate*. During Advent jeptas perform in front of churches and build a *wojke*, similar to a Mexican pinata that contain presents for God. The *wojke* are opened on Christmas day. The day ends with prayers and singing.
New Year's Eve – gifts are also given, and much partying takes place. At midnight children visit neighbors, sing, and are given presents. On New Year's Day people attend church and there are softball games.

351

Martinique

Martinique, an island in the eastern Caribbean Sea, is an overseas region of France To the northwest lies Dominica, to the south St Lucia, and to the southeast Barbados. The island was occupied first by Arawaks, then by Caribs and charted by Christopher Columbus in 1493. It was claimed by France in 1635. In 1946, the French National Assembly voted unanimously to transform the colony into an overseas department. The island was called Madiana by the Carobs, meaning "Island of Flowers". The capital, Fort de France, lies at the entrance to Fort de France Bay on Martinique's western coast. The official language is French, with English and Creole spoken.

Dining Etiquette

Please arrive promptly or a few minutes late when invited for a meal. Please bring flowers, chocolates, wine, or a gift for the home. Shake hands greeting and departing. Drinks and hors d'oeuvres will be served. The hostess will seat the guests with the male guest of honor to her right. Food is eaten continental style with the fork in the left hand and knife in the right. Please wait for the hostess to begin eating. When finished place your knife and fork together.

Accra L'en Mori (Fish Cakes)

½ lb. boneless fish fillets (cod or other fish)	1 pkg. yeast
½ medium onion	1½ cups lukewarm water
2 cloves garlic, minced	2 cups flour
½ tsp. thyme	1 ½ tsp. salt
¼ tsp. fresh ground pepper	Oil

Grind the fish and onion in a food mill. Add the garlic, thyme and pepper.
Combine the yeast and ½ cup of the water in a bowl. Let sit for 5 minutes. Add the remaining water. Combine the flour and salt in a bowl. Add the yeast and stir until a batter is formed. Add the fish mixture, stirring until smooth. Cover and set aside for 2 hours.
Heat the oil in a skillet. Drop the fish mixture by spoonful, and cook until just browned.
Serve hot.

Cuisine

The cuisine of Martinique is a blend of French, African, Carib Amerindian and Southeast Asian traditions. Coconut milk, rice; local fruits- oranges, lemons, limes, grapefruit, plantains, bananas, coconuts, guava, pineapples, mangoes, carambole, love apples, passion fruit; vegetables –

breadfruit, Chinese cabbage, cassava, tamarind, hot pepper (piment), spring onions, tomatoes, peas, chilies, yams and sweet potatoes, pumpkin and squash, christophenes, avocados, gumbo, manioc; seafood – salted cod, lambi (conch), octopus, crabs; and livestock contribute to a healthy diet. The fish may be dried and salted, smoked, stewed or fried. The food can be quite spicy, and bread (pain) is served with the meals. The French government subsidizes banana, sugar, and pineapple plantations. Exports include sugar, rum, tinned fruit, and cacao, banana, and pineapples

Martinique Specialties

Colombo – curried chicken, meat (goat or mutton) or fish with vegetables, spices, tamarind, wine, coconut milk, cassava, and rum, served with rice
Blaff – boiled fish with chives
Court-bouillon – fish in tomato sauce
Chadron – sea urchin, octopus
Metete de crabs – rice with crabs, shallots and chives

Rice and peas
Cakes often will contain pineapple and rum
Beignets de banana – banana fritters
Gateau Mais – cornmeal and raisin cake with caramel sauce
Snowballs- coconut sorbet served in a cone
Gateaux-pays – coconut, guava, or banana pastries

Holidays and Special Occasions

All holidays - boudin, pig's blood sausage; calalou (gumbo and vegetable soup with crab or salted meat; bananas flambé; fruit salads; gratins de bananas jaunes; and Court bouillon.
Easter –matoutou (crab and rice dish)
Pentecost - matoutou (crab and rice dish)
Christmas – spicy seafood
Saint's days – acras (vegetable or fish cakes)

Beverages

Sugar cane has been grown here for hundreds of years and rum distilleries are located throughout the island The St. James Distillery in Sainte-Marie is home to the Musee du Rhum; Fonds Saint-Jacques Distillery the Musee du Pierre Labat, a monk who distilled rum from 1693-1705; and the Maision de la Canne Museum in Trois-Ilets all showing exhibits on rum, sugar, cane and its production. Rhum agricole is made from sugar cane juice and rhum industriel from molasses. Old Rum Martinique is aged in French brandy casks for at least three years.

Special drinks include ti-punch (a colorless white rum with a twist of lemon with sugar cane); planteur (fruit juice and rum), and shrubb (rum with marinated orange or tamarind rinds, served at Christmas). Local beers are produced.

Did You Know?

The gommier (a wooden fishing boat carved from the gommier tree, a gum tree out of a single log) symbolizes a society surrounded by water. The gommier and yole boats now are often used for racing.

Mauritania

Mauritania is bordered by Senegal to the south, Mali to the south and east, the Western Sahara, Morocco and Algeria to the north. The name comes from the Moors who speak the Hassaniya dialect of Arabic. The region was on ancient caravan routes. The earliest people the Bafours were agriculturalists, having emigrated from a nomadic lifestyle in the north. Central Saharans emigrated and in 1076 Moorish Islamic warrior monks conquered the Ghana Empire. For 500 years Arabs dominated what is today Mauritania. The Berbers continued their influence by producing the Marabouts those who preserve and teach Islamic traditions. During the 19th c France took over the region. French rule later extended to other emirates, and in 1920 Mauritania became part of French West Africa. Mauritania gained its independence in 1960. The capital, Nouakchott "The Place of the Winds", was originally a fishing village known as Ksar. The official language is Arabic, with French, Fula (Pulaar), Soninke, and Wolof also spoken. In the north are White and Black Moors, and in the south many indigenous groups.

Dining Etiquette

Please arrive punctually when invited for a meal. Please bring a small gift for the home – chocolates, pastries, fruit, or something from your own country. Gifts are presented with both hands, never just the left. Gifts should be wrapped, and may not be opened in front of the presenter.. The different ethnic groups have their own way of greeting, but most men do shake hands greeting and departing. Being a Muslim country, women do not shake hands with men, unless they extend their hand. Close friends may hug each other, and kiss three times on the cheeks beginning with the left cheek and alternating. When greeting an elder the greeter takes the elder's right hand and places it on his head and bows his head slightly. Clan names rather than family names are used. Wait to be shown to your seat as it may be done according to hierarchy. If seated at a low table or on the floor, please sit cross-legged. Do not let your feet be near the food. A basin with water will be used to wash your hands before dining. Men and women may be seated at separate tables, or dine in separate rooms. People do not eat with their in-laws. Please wait until the oldest male begins eating. Food may be served from a communal bowl known as a calabash. Eat from the section of the bowl in front of you. Never reach across to the other side. Please eat only with your right hand. If utensils are not provided use your hand and fingers to make the couscous or rice into a ball to dip into the communal dish. Leave some food in the bowl, so the host knows you have been well taken care of. Stay only a short time after the meal is finished.

Zrig, a mixture of milk, water, and sugar may be offered during or after a meal. Other drinks are water, hibiscus flower juice and baobab juice. If tea is served it will be by a younger person or the women. Tea is presented three times. The first is a small cup with no sweetener and represents the difficulty of life. The second cup is sweetened and with mint representing life is better when one is married. The last cup is also sweetened and with mint and represents the sweetness of life when one has children. Please accept all three cups.

Vindaloo

Serves 4

1 tsp. ground cumin
1 tsp. ground coriander seeds
1 tsp. ground cardamom
½ tsp ground cloves
2 star anise
1tsp ground pepper

2 sticks cinnamon
4 cloves garlic, minced
3 tbls. fresh grated ginger
2 jalapeno or hotter chilies, seeded and chopped
½ tsp. turmeric

In a small bowl combine all the ingredients.

3 tbls. butter
2 onions, finely chopped
2 tbls. tomato sauce

2 cups chicken broth
1½ lbs. fish fillets, boneless chicken breasts or pork

In a skillet melt the butter and saute the onions until translucent. Remove. Add the fish to the skillet and just brown. Stir in tomato sauce and broth. Stir in spice mix. Bring to boil. Simmer until slightly thickened, about ½ hour.
Serve with rice, lentils, pickles, and chutney.

Cuisine and Beverages

The cuisine has been influenced by the different ethnic groups that inhabit the country. The food is a combination of native African, French, Chinese, and Indian dishes. Much of the country is desert. Foodstuffs grown naturally include couscous, millet, rice, sweet potatoes, potatoes, dates, meat – mutton, camel, lamb, chicken; and fish. Dried meat is served with couscous and spiced meat with vegetables. Meat and fish are often dried. Both are then prepared with spices. Alcoholic beverages are forbidden by Islamic law. Zrig (sweetened milk) and tea (see above) are served along with fruit juices. Tea is served after meals or for guests.

Mauritanian Specialties

Thieboudiene – fish and rice served with a sauce
Mechoui – roast whole lamb
Maffe - peanut stew with goat or camel meat, tomato paste and okra served on rice

Yassa poulet – roasted chicken and vegetables served on French fries or rice
Hakko – ground bean leaf sauce served over couscous

Holidays and Special Occasions

At the end of Ramadan, name giving, birthdays, initiation, marriage, or funerals a lamb or other animal is offered and couscous served.
At the harvest a feast is given and farmers marry.

Mauritius

The Republic of Mauritius is an island nation off the southeast coast of the African continent in the southwest Indian Ocean, about 540 miles east of Madagascar. In addition to the island of Mauritius, the Republic includes the islands of Cargados Carajos, Rodrigues, Tromelin and the Agalega Islands. Mauritius Island is part of the Mascarene Islands, with the French island of Réunion Rodrigues. Mauritius was uninhabited when visited by Arab sailors during the Middle Ages who named it Dina Arobi. In 1507 Portuguese sailors visited the island and established a visiting base. In 1598 the Dutch Admiral Wybrand Van Warwyck named the island Mauritius in honor of Prince Maurits van Nassau. The Dutch introduced sugar cane, domesticated animals and deer. In 1715 France which already controlled Reunion Island took over Mauritius. The French increased sugar production. Port Louis, now the capital, became a naval base and boat building center. In 1810 the island became part of Great Britain and received its independence in 1968. English is the only official language but the lingua franca is Mauritian Creole.

Dining Etiquette

The Mauritanians are very hospitable people and enjoy entertaining. There is great respect for elders, and many homes are occupied by several generations. When invited to a home bring a gift from your country, or something for the children, if you know they are present. Or send flowers afterwards. Men will shake hands and women will kiss on one cheek or both. Hindu will say "namaste" with hands held together and perhaps with a slight bow. Tea with sugar and milk may be served. Drinks will be offered and the meal served. Please accept and try all the food. Forks, knives and spoons are used, though some Hindu may eat with their right hand. Please pass or receive items with the right hand. Hindu do not eat beef, and Muslims do not eat pork or drink alcoholic beverages.

Heart of Palm in Sauce

2 cups heart of palm, cooked or canned, and drained
½ stick butter
¼ cup flour
1 cup light cream

1 cup grated cheddar or parmesan cheese
2 green onions, chopped
Dash cayenne or Tabasco
½ cup bread crumbs

Preheat the oven to 350º
In a saucepan melt the butter. Stir in the flour. Slowly add cream until thickened. Stir in cheese, green onion and cayenne. Place the hearts of palm in a round baking dish. Pour the sauce over the palm. Sprinkle with breadcrumbs. Bake for about 20 minutes, or until bubbling.
Serve as a side dish, or as an appetizer with thinly sliced French bread or crackers.

Cuisine and Beverages

The cuisine is a blend of Chinese, Indian, Creole, African, British and French. Rice is the main staple. Because of the French influence French breads are popular. Indian, Creole and Chinese cuisine are the most often used. Spicy dishes such as curries are made from meat, chicken, fish or vegetarian; and served with rice. Common fish are squid, shrimp, oysters, prawns, octopus; fruit – bananas, mango, pineapples, coconut, palm; vegetables – chokos, red pumpkins, squash, greens, tomatoes, onions, pickles, shallots, muranga leaves, curry leaves, lentils, beans, kidney beans, olives are all used. Seafood is baked, grilled, fried, sautéed or made into curries. Spices include mustard seeds, turmeric, chilies, garlic, ginger, mustard seeds, thyme, parsley, coriander, saffron, cinnamon, cardamom, and cloves. Chutneys are made from fruit, tomatoes, and coconut. St. Aubin grows vanilla beans. Sugar cane has been grown here for years on plantations, and there is L'Aventure du Sucre, a sugar museum. The Dutch introduced sugar cane in 1638, and first made arrack, then c1700 rum. In 1850 Pierre Charles Francois Harel began making locally distilled rum. Today there are three main distilleries – Grays, Medine and St. Aubin. Phoenix Beer is brewed on the island. Bois Cheri tea estate is located on the south of the island and grows black tea.

Mauritius Specialties

Biryanis – made from meat or chicken and rice

Rougaille – stew with meat or fish, tomatoes, garlic, onions, and thyme

Mine frites – Chinese fried noodles served with chutneys (chatini)

Samosas – fried pastries with vegetables or other fillings

Boulettes – meat or fish balls

Fish vindaye – fish with mustard, garlic, ginger, turmeric, and onion served with lentils and chutney

Dipain Frire - chick pea battered bread

Roti – flat bread

Gajaks – fried snacks usually made from vegetables

Gateaux patat douce – sweet potato cakes

Mazavaroo – chopped chilies or chili paste eaten with most meals

Rougaille – tomato paste served with fish

Hakien – spring rolls

Boulet – dim sum – vegetable or fish dumplings

Alouda – pink sweet drink made with tapioca and syrup

Bouillons – made with fresh greens

Touffes – vegetable stir-fry

Dholl puns – flat bread with peas

Gateaux piments – pea balls with spices

Mithai – Indian sweets

Holidays and Special Occasions

Chinese Spring Festival – Chinese New Year much food, red predominant color and wax cake

Thaipoosam Cavadee – Tamils fire-walk and sword-climb. The cavadee is a wooden arch with flowers and a pot of milk at each end (Hindu)

Maha Shivratree – Hindu festival where people dress in white and carry kanwar (wooden arches with flowers) to Grand Bassin for the holy water.

Ramadan – Muslims do not eat or drink from sunrise to sunset. Eid ul-Fidr marks the end of Ramadan, and great feasts are prepared

Christians celebrate Lent, Easter, and Christmas.

Mexico

Mexico is a bounded to the north by the United States and Guatemala and Belize to the south. There are mountain ranges, volcanoes, plateau, coastal regions and jungles. The earliest settlers were located in the Valley of Mexico about 10,000 years ago. The people c 1200 BCE domesticated maize, tomatoes, and beans and formed villages. Before that time they hunted game and were gatherers of plants including chili peppers and roasted agave. Corn was treated with lye to soften it for grinding, and the people began to make tortillas and flat breads. Amaranth, turkeys, insects, iguanas, turtle eggs, squash, chilacayote, jicama, and edible flowers became part of the diet. Chile peppers were used in cooking, for rituals, and in medicine. The Olmec along the Gulf Coast developed a highly cultured civilization, followed by the Maya, Zapotec, Teotihuacan, Toltec, Mixtec, Mexica, and Aztec. The Spanish began their conquest in 1519 with the arrival of Hernan Cortez. Sadly the native population was ravaged by disease brought by the conquerors. The capital, Mexico City was founded in 1524 on top of the ancient Mexica capital of Mexico-Tenochtitlan and is located on Lake Texcoco. Spanish is the official language.

Dining Etiquette

Please be prompt when invited for a meal. The main meal is "comida" meaning "meal" for dinner or supper. Dinner is not usually served until 8-9 PM. Please bring flowers or send them ahead, or bring something from your country. Shake hands greeting and departing. Please stand close to each other while talking. Remember the middle name is the surname. Dinner is preceded by drinks, much made in Mexico such as wines, beer, rum or tequila. The host(ess) will seat the guests. Food is eaten continental style with the fork in the left hand and knife in the right. Please wait for the host(ess) to start. Please try some of everything. When finished please place your knife and fork together. The toast is "Salud" "Cheers".

Cuisine

Most of today's Mexican food is based on pre-Columbian traditions, including Aztec and Maya, combined with culinary trends introduced by Spanish colonists. At the time of the Aztec Empire Mexico had very highly sophisticated culture and agricultural techniques. They lived on corn, beans, chili peppers, turkey, fish, game, insects, a variety of fruits and vegetables, seeds, mushrooms, tomatoes, avocados, vanilla, chilies, cocoa, squash, amaranth, plantains, zucchini, cauliflower, potatoes, spinach, mushrooms, cactus, edible flowers, and herbs. The Spanish introduced olive oil, rice, vinegars, wheat, onions, sugar cane, garlic, oregano, coriander; spices such as cinnamon, cloves, and saffron; and brought with them pigs, cows, chickens, goats, and sheep, which flourished and could be grilled. Cheese and other dairy products became part of the diet. Among the popular cheeses are Queso fresco – farmers' cheese; ranchero, cuajada, requeson, mennonita, and asadero (smoked cheese). Most of the early food was fried.

During the 19th century French, Lebanese, German, Chinese and Italian immigrants influenced the cuisine. Chef Tudor was brought to Mexico by Emperor Maximilian of Hapsburg, and along with French breads and sweet breads became popular such as bolillos and conchas. The Germans brewed beer. Tex-Mex came from Mexican and American influences.

Even though rice and wheat are eaten, corn is used in most cooking. Corn can be eaten fresh or dried, treated with lime and fashioned into masa dough. The corn be used fresh or fermented to make drinks, tamales, tortillas, and a variety of dishes. Chilies are also used in cooking and range from very mild to very hot.

In the north ranches with mainly dairy cattle which were raised for meat and dairy products especially cheese, goat, and ostrich. Wheat was grown, and used in flour tortillas. Food was preserved through dehydration, canning and drying – meat, chilies, squash, peas, corn, lentils, and fruit. The northeastern part of Mexico was settled during Spanish colonization by Cryto- Jews who developed their own cuisine introducing Pan de Semita "Semitic Bread", made without leavening; cabrito – baby goat; and capirotada – bread pudding. Other groups that have influenced the northern cooking are the Chinese, Mormons and Mennonites.

In Oaxaca vegetables grow in the central valley and seafood is found along the coast. Oaxacan cooking was influenced by the Mixtec and Zapotec. Corn from Oaxaca is used to make blandas "tortillas"; empanadas; and tamales. Beans, chili peppers, and herbs flavor the foods. Chocolate is drunk or ground with almonds and cinnamon. The Spanish brought mozzarella cheese now called Oaxaca cheese. Moles here come in a variety of colors and flavors – Negro (black), rojo (red), verde (green), Amarillo (yellow), Coloradito (little red), mancha manteles (table cloth stainer), chchilo (smoky stew). They are made with dried chili and spices such as peppercorns, cloves, and cinnamon with garlic and onion. Mole probably came from the Nahuatl "molli" "mixture of ingredients ground together".

The Yucatan cuisine was influenced by the Mayan, Caribbean, Central Mexican, Europe, and Middle Eastern cultures. Corn is used to make beverages and in cooking. The achiote or annatto seeds tinges the food with a red color. Recado paste made with achiote or habanero and charcoal are used with chicken and pork. Cochinita pibil is a dish made with recado rojo, wrapped in banana leaves and baked in a pit. The Mayan word "p'ib" means "buried". The Yucatan grows many tropical fruits such as tamarind, mamey, avocado, orange, and plums. Along the coasts seafood dishes use fish, conch, shrimp, snails, and whatever is available.

To the west, the cuisine of Michoacan is based on the Purepecha culture with freshwater fish, corn, tamales wrapped in corn husks, cactus, rice, pork, spices, wheat, sweets and the local drinks charanda and tejuino made from fermented corn. Jalisco produced tequila; and Jalisco and Colima are noted for agriculture and raising cattle. Along the Pacific coast seafood – marlin, swordfish, snapper, tuna, shrimp and octopus are prepared with spices and chilies. Tropical fruits are also found here. Dishes made in Veracruz combine the native Mexican, Afro-Mexican and Spanish cultures and use corn, vanilla, herbs, tropical fruits and fish. Africans introduced peanuts, plantains, yucca, and sweet potatoes. Rice is used more than corn. Tamales are wrapped in banana leaves. Beef, pork, chicken and cheese are also part of the diet.

Pollo Mole Poblano (Chicken in Chili and Chocolate Sauce)

Serves 8

½ cup toasted bread crumbs
1 tbls. chili seeds
½ tsp. coriander seeds
½ cup peanuts
½ tsp. anise seeds
3 tbls. sesame seeds
¼ cup pepitas (pumpkin seeds)
4 peppercorns
4 dried pasilla chilies
4 dried mulato chilies
6 dried ancho chilies
¼ cup raisins
½ tsp. ground cinnamon or ½ in. cinnamon stick

½ tsp. cloves
½ cup almonds
3 tbls. oil or lard
1 medium onion, chopped
4 cloves garlic, minced
3 tomatoes, finely chopped
2 tbls. powdered cocoa
4 large boneless chicken breasts, cut in half
Sea salt
3 cups chicken broth

Combine the chili seeds, coriander seeds, peanuts, anise seeds, sesame, and pumpkin seeds in a skillet. Do not add oil. Cook until golden.
In a blender combine the bread crumbs and spice mixture.
Add the peppercorns, pasilla, mulato and ancho chilies, raisins, cinnamon, and cloves to the blender.
Heat the oil in the skillet and saute onions until golden. Stir in garlic. Add the blender mixture. Stir and cook for about 5 minutes. Stir in tomatoes.
Add the cocoa and chicken broth. Cook 10 minutes.
Add the chicken. Cook until chicken is tender 20-30 minutes.
Serve with black beans and rice.
Turkey is used in Mexico to make mole poblano.
A rock mortar and pestle is more commonly used to grind the spices together.

Mexican Specialties

Cecina – very thin beef, salted and air dried that is eaten for many meals with warm tortillas, crema and fresh lime. Can also be made from pork (cecina enchilada)
Gorditas – corn tortillas filled with cheese
Chicharron – pork rind
Chiles en nogada – dish with colors of Mexican flag
Mole poblano – a dish developed by the nuns at the Convento de Santa Rosa in the 16th c for the visiting archbishop

Canole – candy made from sweet potatoes and fruit
Capirotada – fried bread with honey, nuts, raisins, cheese
Enchiladas – corn tortilla is dipped in oil and enchilada sauce, then wrapped around a filling of meat, cheese, etc, topped with enchilada sauce and then baked
Flautas – overlapping two corn tortillas, filled, rolled, and fried

Nachos – pie-shaped tortillas that a fried and served with a cheese sauce (chile con queso)
Burritos – flour tortillas warmed to room temperature and filled
Chimichangas – deep fried burritos
Quesadillas – tortillas with cheese or other fillings that are fried or baked
Tortillas – thin flatbread made from corn or flour
Taco shells – tortillas that are folded in half and deep fried and then filled with meat, beans, or any filling. Taco means "snack"

Tostadas –tortillas are fried flat with fillings on top
Birria - a stew of goat, beef, mutton or pork with chilies and spices.
Cevishe – seafood marinated in lime juice
Salsas – sauces
Huitlacoche – corn fungus used in cooking
Chilies en nogada – meat stuffed chilies in a walnut sauce with pomegranate seeds

Holidays and Special Occasions

Fiestas and holidays are times for families and friends to get together and cook together as many dishes take a great deal of time to prepare. Mole is the most important food. This is served on Christmas, Easter, Day of the Dead, birthdays, baptisms, weddings, and funerals. Tamales can be made from corn or wheat, and wrapped in corn husks, cornstalk, reed, or banana leaves.

Feast of the Epiphany – gifts are brought to the children by the Three Kings
Candlemas – tamales; bullfights and fiestas
Lent – no meat
Semana Santa – week before Easter – fruit drinks, ice cream, paletas (fruit ice bars), raspados (shaved ice cones), roscas (cookies), mugueganos (nut bars)
Easter - Capirotada - spiced Mexican bread pudding filled with raisins, cinnamon, cloves and cheese that is popular during the Easter period. It's said that each ingredients carries a reminder of the suffering of Christ - the cloves being the nails on the cross, the cinnamon sticks the wooden cross and the bread the Body of Christ himself.
Dia de los Muertos - Day of the Dead – tamales, mole and other foods are placed on altars for the deceased and living.
Before Christmas – neighbors exchange tamales at posadas (parties)
Christmas – tamales, mole poblano de guajolote (turkey with a sauce of chilies, raisins, sesame seeds, and chocolate), salads

Margaritas

Makes 1 cocktail

1 slice lime
Coarse salt
½ oz. fresh lime juice

1 ½ oz. tequila
1 oz. Triple Sec or Cointreau
3-4 ice cubes

Rub the rim of the glass with the lime slice. Put salt in a dish and dip the rim of the glass in the salt.
Combine the lime juice, tequila, Triple Sec and ice cubes in a shaker. Shake vigorously. Place a strainer on top and pour into the glass.

Beverages

Corn is not only eaten but made into a number of drinks. Atole is a hot drink flavored with fruit, chocolate, rice, blackberry, cascabel chili, and other flavors. Fermented corn is made into cold drinks such as tejuino and pozol. Aguas frescas are flavored drinks made with fruit, water, and sugar. Others drinks include ingredients such as hibiscus, tamarind, rice "horchata"; coffees including café de olla coffee with cinnamon and raw sugar.

Besides corn, cocoa and chocolate date back to very ancient civilizations. The word "chocolate" originated from Mexico's Aztec cuisine, derived from the Nahuatl word *xocolatl*. Chocolate was first drunk rather than eaten. It was also used for religious rituals. The Maya civilization grew cacao trees and used the cacao seeds it produced to make a frothy, bitter drink. The drink, called *xocoatl*, was often flavored with vanilla, chile pepper, and *achiote*. In the Yucatan honey was used long before the arrival of the Spanish to sweeten foods and to make a ritual alcoholic drink called balché. Today, a honey liquor called xtabentun is still made and consumed in the region.

Tequila dates from the 16th c. Tequila is made from blue agave that is cooked and then fermented. Other alcoholic beverages include pulque, aguardiente, mezcal, and charanda with brandy. Wine, rum and beer also produced. The most common alcoholic beverage consumed with food in Mexico is beer (cerveza), followed by tequila. A classic margarita, a popular cocktail, is composed of tequila, cointreau and lime juice, and the glass rims are frosted with salt. Most is from the southwestern state of Jalisco. The three types are plata (not aged, reposado (aged for 11 months), and anejo (aged for at least a year).

Did You Know?

Corn has been grown in the valley of Tehaucan for over 7000 years!
The Mayans chewed chicle, made from the sapodilla tree, mixed with tar and insect grease, similar to today's chewing gum.
For many years the vanilla pod was only found in Mexico, and only the Totonaco Indians knew of its existence. When the Aztecs defeated the Totonaco, they demanded the pods known as the Tlilxochitl vine. Along with cacao beans the pods were used to make "chocolatl". In 1520 when Hernando Cortez conquered the Aztecs he was served this drink. On his return to Spain he brought with him cacao beans and vanilla pods which the Spaniards called "vanilla" or "Little Scabbard". The famous floating gardens in Mexico City provided food for the Aztecs and were made up of fifty square miles of canals and lakes. Fish, chilies, cactus, herbs, frogs, and fowl were harvested here. Axoltl, foot long salamanders, once populated the lakes, but are almost extinct. Now only flowers are grown in the polluted waters. The Aztecs also grew avocados, from the Aztec "ahuacatl" for testicle and also known as the "fertility fruit".

Micronesia

Micronesia is a region of Oceania, comprising thousands of small islands in the western Pacific Ocean with four main archipelagos. Micronesia is divided politically among several sovereign countries - the Federated States of Micronesia "Micronesia" and four other sovereign, independent nations—Kiribati, Marshall Islands, Nauru, and Palau—as well as three U.S. territories—Guam, Northern Mariana Islands, and Wake Island. There are four main groups; the Caroline Islands, the Gilbert Islands, the Mariana Islands, and the Marshall Islands.

The earliest archaeological traces of civilization have been found on the island of Saipan c1500 BCE. Micronesian colonists gradually settled the Marshall Islands during the 2nd millennium BC. Construction of Nan Madol, a megalithic complex made from basalt lava logs in Pohnpei began as early as 1200 CE. The earliest known contact with Europeans occurred in 1521, when Ferdinand Magellan reached the Marianas. In the early 17th century Spain colonized Guam, the Northern Marianas, and the Caroline Islands creating the Spanish East Indies, which was governed from the Spanish Philippines. During the Spanish-American War Spain lost many of its remaining colonies The United States took possession of the Spanish Philippines and Guam. This left Spain with the remainder of the Spanish East Indies, about 6,000 tiny islands. The Spanish government therefore decided to sell the remaining islands and transferred the Caroline Islands, the Mariana Islands, Palau and other possessions to Germany. The islands were then placed under control of German New Guinea. Nauru had been annexed and claimed as a colony by Germany in 1888. The United States took control of Guam, and the British the Gilbert Islands. Today, most of Micronesia are independent states, except for Guam and Wake Island, which are U.S. territories, and for the U.S. Commonwealth of the Northern Mariana Islands.

Dining Etiquette

Micronesians are very hospitable people. They have much respect for elders, family, political rank and, and religious title. Brothers and sisters should not meet in public, and women walk behind their husbands, and show respect by serving them first during a meal. Public displays of affection are rare. During church and on social occasions women will occupy different space from men. Elders are fed first, and may be given special seats of honor, as are guests.

Being invited to a home for a meal is an honor as sharing food is a sign of warm hospitality. When invited to a home please bring a gift, preferably something from your country. Shake hands greeting and departing. The host will seat guests. Eating all the food on your plate shows appreciation to your host. Eating is continental style with the fork in the left hand and knife in the right. Some people will eat with their hands depending where you are. Please compliment and thank your host for the food.

Breadfruit Salad

Serves 4-6

3 cups oven roasted or boiled breadfruit
1 cup green beans, cooked
1 cucumber, sliced
2 green onions, sliced

2 cups cooked meat, chicken, or fish
2 large tomatoes chopped
½ head cabbage, shredded

Combine the ingredients in a salad bowl. Toss with the dressing

Mayo Dressing

½ cup mayonnaise
1 tbls. mustard

1 tsp. hot pepper sauce

Combine the ingredients in a bowl.

Vinagrette

½ cup olive oil
2 tbls. red wine vinegar
1 tbls. mustard

1 tbls. sugar
Sea salt and pepper to taste

Combine the ingredients in a bowl.

Cuisine

Even though Portuguese and Spanish explorers came to the region, it was probably not till the 19th c that cattle, chickens, wheat, potatoes, pineapples, papaya, and mangoes became part of the diet. Later the Germans introduced their cuisine, followed by the Japanese. The islands are mainly volcanic, quite fertile allowing plants to grow. However few plants and animals are native to the islands, having been brought later by people probably about 4000 years ago. They would have brought taro, rice, yams, ulu (breadfruit), bananas, lemons, sugarcane, and coconuts. Coconuts are used for their flesh, milk, cream, and husks and shells for fuel, palms for mats and clothing. Breadfruit can be steamed or baked, fried as chips, grated or mashed, and made into salad. Rice is an important part of the diet and is served with most meals. Seafood is found in abundance and includes shellfish, turtles, crab, shrimp and fish. Fish is often uncooked and marinated, grilled or stuffed with onions and wrapped in banana leaves. Raw fish is also served with a spicy sauce. Many meat, vegetable, fruit, and fish dishes contain coconut and coconut milk. Other ingredients are breadfruit, taro, sweet potatoes, yams, cassava, pigs, and chicken. Various fruit are grown such as bananas, mangos, pandanus, wild apples, star fruit, papaya, guava, sour sop and citrus fruits – oranges, limes, tangerines, and mandarins. Breads are fried or baked. Pohnpeian pepper, *sakau* (kava), betel nut, and citrus fruit, and copra (dried coconut flesh) are exported in limited quantities. The Pohnpei pepper blooms and bears fruit all year, and is quite spicy. Betel nuts are also grown on the island. They are cut open, covered with lime, wrapped in pepper plant leaves, and used as chewing tobacco. Coconuts are used in cooking especially desserts.

Grilled Marinated Chicken Breasts

Serves 4

4 boneless chicken breasts
Juice of 2 lemons
4 garlic cloves, sliced thin
2 tbls. olive oil

3 tbls. soy sauce
½ cup beer
1 medium onion, chopped
Salt and pepper

In a large bowl combine the lemon juice, garlic, olive oil, soy sauce, beer, onion, salt and pepper. Add the chicken. Marinate covered at least 1 hour or overnight.
Remove the chicken and save marinade. Cook the chicken on a grill. Serve with remaining marinade.
The chicken can also be cooked in an oven in the marinade.
Herbs such as thyme and rosemary can be added.

Holidays and Special Events

Yap Day Festival – held on the first weekend in March in every village featuring dances, traditional costumes. It is a symbol of friendship, hospitality, and respect. Food served are rice, meat or seafood, lumpia, adobo, sinigang, bistek, and lechon.
Pigs, taro or breadfruit, sugarcane, and coconuts are eaten at funerals, weddings, other celebrations and ceremonies.
During feasts on Pohnpei pigs, yams, and sakau are served.

Beverages

Sakau or kava is made from the pounded kava (piper capsicum) plant roots. The juice is filtered with hibiscus bark and water added. It is considered a very relaxing drink. The drink was once served only to high chiefs and nobility. Toddy is a fermented sap from the palm blossom. Other drinks are made from citrus fruit, especially lime juice with water. Beer is produced from pepper shoot roots.

Moldova

The Republic of Moldova is a landlocked country in Eastern Europe bordered by Romania to the west and Ukraine to the north, east, and south. Flint tools are known to date back 800,000-1.2 million years ago. The region was inhabited over 44,000 years ago and is included in ancient records of Greece. The Cucuteni-Trypillian culture that stretched east beyond the Dniester River in Ukraine and west up to and beyond the Carpathian Mountains in Romania. The people of this civilization, which lasted roughly from 5500 to 2750 BC, practiced agriculture, raised livestock, hunted, and made intricately-designed pottery. Later it was inhabited by Dacian tribes. Between the 1st and 7th centuries AD, the south was intermittently under the Roman, and then Byzantine Empires. Due to its strategic location on a route between Asia and Europe, the territory of modern Moldova was invaded many times by Goths, Huns, Avars, Bulgarians, Magyars, Pechenegs, Cumans, Mongols, Tatars, and Bolohoveni, a Vlach population, the Brodniks, the Poles, and Crimean Tatars. In 1538 it became a tributary to the Ottoman Empire, and then a vassal of the Polish-Lithuanian Commonwealth, followed by the Ottomans, and then part of Russia. Independence was declared in 1991. The capital is Chişinău. Moldovan is the official language.

Dining Etiquette

Please be prompt when invited for a meal. Shake hands greeting and departing. Men and men, women and women may embrace and kiss if they are good friends. Men stand when introduced to ladies, hold doors and chairs for them. Being a guest in a home is an honor. Please bring flowers in an odd number and wrapped. Tuica (plum brandy, often homemade), wine, or other drinks are served before the meal. The guest of honor sits at the opposite end of the table from the host. Please eat continental style – fork in the left hand, knife in the right. Do try all the food, even if only taking a small amount. Salad is served with the meal. Food is served in courses – soup, appetizers, entrée and vegetables, then desserts. Silverware and dishes are cleared with each course. Keep your hands table level, not in your lap. The host initiates a toast, touch glasses, and say "Sanatate" "to health".

Cuisine

Moldova has very fertile black soil and is an excellent region for raising vegetables – tomatoes, peppers, aubergine, cabbage, beans, garlic, onion, and leeks; fruit, especially grapes; grains, meat and dairy products. Vegetables are murături (pickled), salted, marinated, or baked and used in salads, soups, and sauces. Meat is served as an appetizer or first course. Lamb, beef and pork are most common. Meat and fish are marinated and roasted or grilled.

Sarmale (Cabbage Rolls)

1 onion, chopped
Vegetable oil or lard
3 lb. cabbage
½ lb. ground pork
½ lb. ground beef
½ green or red pepper, chopped
1 carrot, sliced thinly

1 cup cooked rice
Paprika
Salt and pepper
1 cup beef stock
1 cup tomato puree, tomato soup or 1 large tomato, chopped
Sour cream

Preheat oven to 350°. Parboil the cabbage in salted water for 5 minutes. Separate outer leaves. Return cabbage to boiling water and cook another 5 minutes, or until all leaves can be removed. Cut the stem off the cabbage. Heat a small amount of the lard or oil in a skillet and saute the onion. Add the pork and beef, and saute until just slightly pink. Add rice, pepper, and carrot, and season with paprika, salt and pepper. Place a spoonful of the meat filling on each leaf. Roll up the leaf. Repeat, placing the rolls next to each other in a baking dish. Cover with beef stock. Bake in oven 1 hour. Top with tomato puree. Bake ½ hour more. Serve hot with sour cream.

Specialties

Mămăligă - cornmeal porridge served with stews, meat, fish, cheese, sour cream, or garlic, which is cut with a string not a knife
brânză -a brined cheese
ghiveci - lamb or goat stew
pârjoale - meatballs
zeamă – chicken soup with noodles and vegetables, served with bread, salt, and perhaps sour cream

(ciorbă (bors) – is used for its sour taste and is made from bran to season vegetable, meat, and fish soups
Tochitură - beef or pork stew
Placinta - fried bread with a filling such as brinza (homemade cheese), varza (cabbage) or cartofi (potatoes), boston (pumpkin), visine (sour cherries), apples, or meat

Holidays and Special Occasions

For holidays, sarmale, chicken, pilaf, pork jelly, noodles, pastries and buns with fillings are served.
New Year's – coltunasi (dumplings filled with cheese, meat or cherries); shuba (herring), and Olivier salad (potato salad).
Masa is a celebratory meal and placinta is always eaten

Beverages

Wine has been produced in Moldova since ancient times. The most commonly used grapes are Sauvignon, Cabernet, and Muscat, Fetească, Rara neagră, and Busuioacă albă. Sparkling wines are made in the Cricova winery. The best known are Negru de Purcari, Moldova, Chişinău, Cricova, Muscat spumant, National, and Nisporeni. They are made from Chardonnay, Pinot blanc, Pinot gris, Pinot menie, Sauvignon, Aligote, Traminer pink, Muscat blanc, Cabernet Sauvignon, and Pinot noir, and Feteasca Albă. Divin (brandy) and beer are also produced.

Monaco

Monaco is bordered by France on three sides and the Mediterranean Sea, an area less than 2 km. The name comes from a 6th c Greek colony Monoikos single house". In 1228 Monaco was a colony of Genoa. The House of Grimaldi has been in power since 1297. In 1793 French troops captured the country and it remained part of France until 1814. Monaco became an independent country with a constitution in 1911. It was occupied by the Germans during World War II. French is the official language

La Fougasse (pastry with nuts and aniseed)

Serves 20

600 g type 55 flour (chick pea flour)	Water
20 g yeast	Egg yolk
150 cl warm water	Almonds
200 g sugar	Pine nuts
10 g salt	Hazelnuts
1 tbls. rum, curacao, and anisette	Dragees (sugar coated almonds)
2 tbls. green aniseed	Red and white aniseed
4 tbls. orange blossom water	Confectioners' sugar
2 tbls. olive oil	Orange blossom water
Zest of one lemon	Rum, curacao, or Mesccia
220 g butter	

Two hours beforehand prepare the leaven; in a fairly large bowl, add warm water to the yeast and dissolve using a wire whisk. Take a little flour and mix with the water to form a firm ball of dough. Let it rise; it should double in volume. Add the rest of the flour to the leaven, along with the liqueurs, olive oil, orange blossom water, green aniseed, sugar and butter in small pieces, and finally the salt. Knead energetically. Cover the dough with a cloth. Let rise two hours, and keep in the refrigerator. The next day spread the dough in a thin layer using a rolling pin and arrange it in a lightly oiled pie dish. Brush the top of the fougasse with egg yolk diluted in water.

Decorate with almonds, pine nuts, hazelnuts, dragees (sugar coated almonds), and red and white aniseed. Let rise for 1 hour

Heat oven to 340°. Bake fougasse for approximately 20 minutes. Lift with spatula to see it is cooked. Sprinkle with confectioners' sugar and dampen lightly with a mixture of orange blossom water, rum and curacao, or with Mesccia. Turn off the oven and let the fougasse dry with the oven door ajar. Serve with aniseed liqueur "A mescia".

Recipe courtesy of Paul Mullot, author of "Savuers de Monaco" and the Embassy of the Principality of Monaco, Washington, DC

Dining Etiquette

Please arrive punctually when invited for a meal. Shake hands greeting and departing. Drinks will be served. Please wait for the hostess to seat the guests. The male guest of honor is to her right. Dining is continental style, fork in the left hand, knife in the right. Please wait for the hostess to begin. When finished place your knife and fork together. The host will initiate the toast which is "A Votre Sante" "To your health".

Cuisine

Monaco's cuisine was influenced by the French and is very Mediterranean, using olive oil, tomatoes, onions, garlic, black olives, eggplant, anchovies, lemons, oranges, seafood - sea bass, red mullet, and daurade. Smoked ham may also be included in dishes. A popular onion dish is made with onions, olive oil, white wine vinegar, currants, sprigs, potatoes and parsley.

Specialties

Barbagiuan - Pumpkin or spinach pastry with rice, cheese, and leek
Socca - pancakes made of chickpea flour
Stocafi – dried cod cooked in a tomato sauce with chilies

Machete – anchovy paste
Bouillabaisse – fish stew
Ratatouille – eggplant, tomato, pepper and onion dish

Holidays and Special Occasions

Candlemas (February) – Catholics attend church, have seeds and figs blessed, and then make a beverage with cloves, apple and cinnamon to cure sore throats.
Ash Wednesday – chickpea soup
Easter – goat, pasqualina (chard pie), dyed eggs,
Day after Easter – picnics in the countryside
Christmas Eve – brandaminciun (salted cod), cardu (cardoon in white sauce), friscioer (apple fritters), and La fougasse
Christmas – pan de Natale (round loaf of bread with four nuts in the shape of a cross, an olive branch, orange tree and fruit are in the center; 13 desserts (mainly fruits) that remained until Epiphany to bring abundance to a home. Mariote are cakes made from leftover La fougasse pastry in the shape of dolls for the girls, u galu in the shape of a cock for the boys.
The royal family still includes its citizens in events such as christenings, weddings, and engagements at the royal palace. Children under 12 are invited to the annual Christmas party.

Beverages

Fine wines and other alcoholic drinks from France, Italy and other countries are available in Monaco. They also drink milk, hot chocolate, coffee, and many fruit drinks.

Mongolia

Mongolia, the Mongolian People's Republic, is a landlocked country in central Asia. Its 604,103 square miles are bounded on the north by Russia, and to the south China. Mongolia is known for its mountains, lakes, extinct volcanoes, prehistoric caves, hot springs, and the Gobi Desert. Many species of wildlife are unique to the area, and hunting is protected. The capital Ulaanbaatar "The Red Hero". Mongolia has a long history of invasions, tribal life, being the center of ancient trading routes, and for having conquered lands are far away as the Middle East, Poland and Hungary, and into China. The Republic was established in 1924.

Booz (Buuz)

Buuz are stuffed dough pockets (dumplings)
Other types of meat, shrimp or ingredients can be substituted for the mutton. Mongolians do not eat many vegetables, but vegetables could also be substituted. *Banshi* are dumplings boiled in water.

The Pocket

3 cups flour   1½ cups boiling water

In a bowl mix the flour with the water until a soft dough is formed. Knead until smooth.. Cover let stand for ½ hour. Flour a cutting board and roll dough out with hands into a snake, about 1 inch in diameter. Cut into 1 inch pieces. Shape each piece into a circle with the center slightly thicker than the sides. Place a 1 tsp. of the filling in the center. Fold into a crescent and seal with water. Or fold one side and shape so you are sealing in all sides.
Place buuz on a steamer rack. Do not layer. Add water to bottom of pan. Cover pan. Steam for 15 minutes.

Filling

1 lb. minced mutton   ½ tsp. salt
1 medium onion, finely chopped   1 tsp. fresh ground pepper
2 cloves garlic, minced   1 tsp. or more caraway seeds

Combine the ingredients in a bowl.

**"Happy is he who often has guests;
cheerful is the home near where stand the horses of visitors"**

Dining Etiquette

Entertaining in Mongolia is mainly done in restaurants or homes. These can vary from small apartments, often with no refrigerators, to dining in a yurt, a felt tent. Dinner is the main meal of the day. Much tea is served, often mixed with butter and millet, butter and salt, or with preserves. When tea is very hot, smack your lips. To do so is polite. Milk products called *tsagan-ide* or sweets and biscuits are served with the tea. Mongolian vodka may be served, and is drunk straight. The diet relies a great deal on meat, potatoes, cabbage and dairy products. These would include cheese, yogurt, and airag – fermented mare's milk. Airag is served to a guest in a silver cup (mongen ayaga) and is presented with the right hand. The host says a few words, or many of respect and happiness. The guest takes the cup with the right hand, and supported with the other hand drinks from the cup. The milk is very healthy, and can sustain a person for a long period of time.

During the summer, in the country, meat is not usually eaten. Instead cheese and other dairy products are consumed, starting the day at sunrise. During the winter, much tea is drunk for warmth, and almost no food consumed during the day.

Dishes are served with both hands, or the right hand supported at the wrist or elbow. For a guest of honor the host will present a sacrum of a sheep with a tail. If a guest is offered this special portion of meat, he must slice it and serve some to the other guests. To say "thank you" for food, the guest touches it with his right hand, supported by the left hand with his palm up.

To make a toast, the host stands, raises his glass, and makes a short speech "We are honored to have you, and may there be peace, and thanks to you". A traditional toast is "for the good", or "your well-being", or very poetic prose. Please leave a small bit in the cup.

Gifts are given during the lunar New Year, for weddings, old age celebrations (85), and if you are a guest. They should always be accepted when presented, and words of respect said as a "thank you". A most special present is the hadag, a long light blue silk scarf. This presented with both hands. Other appropriate gifts are (depending on the occasion) money and livestock (horses are very highly regarded, and even songs have been written about them). White, blue and green are colors for funerals.

Both men and women wear trousers and a robe (deel) made of cotton or silk. A woman's is often of brighter colors. In the winter these are lined with sheepskin, goatskin, or other furs. Cloaks, hats, often fur trimmed, and boots with upturned toes make up traditional Mongolian garb. The shape of the hat will vary according to one's tribal connections. Hats are worn even in greeting. A family's wealth is often found on the wife through her display of jewelry.

Cuisine

The food is high in protein and fat to sustain the people in the extremely cold climate. The cooking uses mutton, yak milk, horse milk, dried milk curd, reindeer milk, horse meat, mamot, and almost no vegetables as they can't be grown here. The mutton is boiled, stewed or cooked with oil and flour and served with noodles.

Drinks

Nermalike is made from yoghurt and similar to vodka. Airag is fermented horse's milk. Suutei Tsai is a tea made from hot water, butter, rice, salt, yak milk and tea.

Holidays and Special Occasions

There are many folk festivals each with their own ceremony and colours.
Tsagaan Sar "White Month" celebrates the Mongolian New Year. Bituuleg is celebrated the evening before on Bituun "to close down". The people serve meat covered with dough and a ceremonial layered bread Boov. After this games are played and oral histories recited. Bituun Baldanlham, a god, rides her mule three times to each family, and three pieces of ice are placed on the ger, or a balcony for water. On Tsagaan Sar children honor their older relatives with white food, pastries, and gifts. Khadag, white and blue scarves are presented to the honored guests. The celebration usually lasts for three days.

Did You Know?

The Tsaatan in Western Mongolia move camp six times a year to find grazing land for their reindeer. The reindeer provide milk, cheese, yogurt, meat, clothing, and are used to transport people and goods.

Montenegro

Montenegro meaning "Black Mountain" borders on the Adriatic Sea to the south-west, Croatia to the west, Bosnia and Herzegovina to the northwest, Serbia to the northeast, and Albania to the south-east. In 9 AD the Romans conquered the region. Slavs colonized the area in the 6th century, and by the 10th century formed a semi-independent principality called Duklja in suzerainty to the Byzantine Empire. Duklja gained its independence from the Byzantine Roman Empire in 1042. By 1186 it was conquered by Stefan Nemanja and incorporated into the Serbian realm as a province named Zeta. It fell to the Ottomans in 1496. In the 17th the Montenegrins century defeated the Ottomans in the Great Turkish War. The republic was succeeded by the Austrian Empire in 1797 and in 1787 became independent. In 1918 Montenegro merged with Serbia and in 1929 as part of Yugoslavia. In 2006 the Montenegrin Parliament declared its independence. The capital is Podgorica. The official language is Montenegrin.

Dining Etiquette

Please arrive promptly when invited for a meal. You may be asked to remove your shoes before entering. Please bring wine, chocolates, flowers (in an uneven number as even numbers are for funerals), or a gift from your home country. Shake hands greeting and departing. Close female friends will kiss alternating three times on the cheek. The host(ess) will seat the guests. Meals are to be enjoyed with lively conversation. Please eat continental style with the fork in the left hand and knife in the right. The meal begins with a soup and salad and may be followed by many courses. When you are full leave a little food on your plate, and your glass half full. People toast with home-made *rakija* (grape brandy), by clinking glasses and saying *"Živjeli!"*, and good eye contact.

Cuisine and Beverages

Early Montenegrin cooking was in clay pots over a fire, and in some remote places this is still done. The Slavs and Turks influenced the cuisine. The Turks brought samra, musaka, pilav, pita, biscuits, and cakes; Austrians – bread; and the Hungarians – goulash, sataras, and duvec. Along the coast Italian cuisine has influenced the cooking – bread making, cured and dried meats, cheese, wines, soups, stews, noodles, and polenta. Common foodstuffs used in cooking are olives, citrus fruits, fish, cereals, tomatoes, onions, cabbage, walnuts, honey, plums, quince, pomegranates, yogurt, buttermilk, sour cream and other dairy products; meat- lamb and sausage. Along the coast are an abundance of fish – squid, octopus, tuna, cuddlefish, shrimp, mussels, and inland fresh water fish. The lowlands make use of fish and dairy products; in the mountains – fruit, berries, dairy products, and various meats. Bread is served with every meal. They are made from barley, rye, wheat or corn. Rice or pasta are added to soups or stews to make a heartier dish. Rastan has been grown in this region for over 2000 years! Rastan is similar to cabbage and the leaves are cooked with potatoes, carrots, and cheese as a hearty winter dish.

Montenegrens drink kisjela – mineral water, sok od sopka - pomegranate syrup, and a lot of strong coffee. Montenegro produces wine in the south from Vranac and Krstac grapes. Vranac is known as black wine, a red wine. Rakija is a brandy made from distilled grapes. Other brandies are made from apples, plums (sljivovica), pear (krusku), juniper, and figs. Brandy is served as an aperitif with "meze" or with fruit, and is used for toasting. Many people still make their own brandy. Niksic beer is made from barley, mountain water, and bitter and aromatic hops with about 5% alcohol.

Brav u Mlijeku (Lamb in Milk)

The national dish!

Serves 4

3 cloves garlic, minced	6 small white or red potatoes, peeled
½ cup parsley, chopped	2 carrots, peeled and sliced
1 tsp. fennel seeds	3 cups milk
¼ cup extra virgin olive oil	2 tbls. rosemary
2 lbs. boneless lamb, cut into small cubes	Fresh parsley
Salt and pepper to taste	

Combine the garlic and parsley into a paste.
Heat the oil in a skillet and cook paste for 1 minute. Add the lamb and brown on all sides. Remove and season with salt and pepper.
Add ½ cup milk to pan and deglaze drippings in pan. Add rest of milk, rosemary, lamb, potatoes and carrots. Bring to a boil. Simmer for 1 hour. Remove lamb. Bring milk to a boil and reduce by 1 half. Add the lamb.
Serve the lamb in the milk sauce and garnished with parsley, or rosemary.
Serve with bread.

Specialties

Cicvara – stewed cornmeal with cream
Prigance – fritters served with homey, cheese or jam
Kacamak – wheat, barley, or corn flour, or potatoes in skorup (fresh salted cream) served with milk, buttermilk or yogurt
Kajmak – also made from wheat, barley or corn flour but is stirred for a long time
Karp – smoked fish, usually carp
Popara – bread with milk, oil, and cheese
Japraci – rastan leaves served with mashed potatoes
Sarma –sauerkraut rolls with minced pork and rice, and served with mashed potatoes
Krofne –doughnuts with jam

Prsuta – smoked ham that is dried on beech logs for several months from Njegusi. It is served with grape brandy and cheese
Popeci – veal rolled in cheese and fried in oil
Cevapi – kebabs
Zelje u kokote na kastradinu - cooked cabbage with mutton
Corbast pasulj – bean stew with pork and salami
Gralak – beef and pea stew
Balsica tava – fried veal with vegetables
Cufte – meatballs
Pilav – rice with nuts and/or vegetables
Gulas – stew
Sataras – minced and roasted vegetables

Morocco

Morocco is bounded in the north and west by the Mediterranean Sea and the Atlantic Ocean, east and south by Algeria and Mauretania. The history of Morocco dates back c1200 BC when the Phoenicians arrived to trade. They salted and preserved fish, made anchovy paste, grew wheat and introduced grapes. Beginning in the 6th c BC the Carthaginians, then the Romans 33 BC who built aqueducts and reservoirs, the Berber tribes inhabited the land. During the 20th c Spain and France were given the right to "police" Morocco jointly. In 1956 an agreement was signed with Spain, and Morocco received its independence from France. Today Morocco is ruled by a hereditary king. The capital is Rabat (from ribat, a monastery), founded in the 7th c BC and Fez the religious center. Casablanca "White House" acquired its name in 1781 when Mohammed III granted a Spanish shipping company permission to export corn. The official language is Moroccan Arabic, with French and Berber languages.

Dining Etiquette

Moroccans love to entertain, and are most gracious hosts. Being invited to a private home is a special honor. You must not refuse hospitality. Please be punctual. Please bring a gift of chocolates, flowers, or something for the home. If children are present, please bring a gift for them. Please remove your shoes. Shake hands greeting and departing, touching the heart with the right hand. People, if they each other well, will kiss each other, brushing the cheek, or with many small kisses. Women should not have direct eye contact with men.

You will be seated on low banquettes or pillows at low tables with a tablecloth and napkins. When sitting do not cross your legs, or point the bottom of your shoes at others. Mint tea and milk with dates are served as a symbol of hospitality. Tea is served with "loaf sugar". You will be served three glasses. Please accept them. A bowl with water, soap, and a towel will be set before you. Always wash your hands before eating. Eat with your thumb and 2 fingers of your right hand, unless utensils are given to you, then also use only your right hand. Bread is for scooping or soaking. The host will say "bis m'Allah" "In the name of God", and invite you to start the meal. A variety of salads, which are passed, may begin the meal. Soups or flaky pastries might also be served. Always pass with your right hand.

The first course is often mechoui, a whole roasted lamb or part of it, or a tangine. Then there are more courses. If you are an honored guest you will be served pastille. Couscous is wrapped into a ball with your fingers, or eaten with a spoon. Sweetmeats and fruit are then served. Hands and faces are washed after the meal, water often mixed with orange blossom or rose water. Three glasses of tea are then served. Please leave following the meal.

During the meal food is to be enjoyed and savored, and most conversation will take place before or afterwards. Take only small amounts of each dish. Meal often will be large gatherings, mainly with extended family. Do not admire something too much as your host may feel obligated to give it to you.

Tea ceremonies are held serving green tea. One sits cross-legged on the floor. A tray is brought with a silver teapot, glasses and 3 silver boxes containing green tea, mint, and sugar lumps. The tea is placed in the teapot with boiling water, mint, and sugar. When it has steeped, please taste it. You will be offered three glasses.

Date and Fig Salad

Serves 4 (can be served as a salad or dessert)

4 large oranges, peeled, pith removed and cut into slices
16 dates, pitted and halved
¼ cup orange flower water

¼ cup lemon juice
½ cup pistachio nuts, shelled
8 figs

Combine the dates and oranges in a bowl with the orange water and lemon juice. Let sit for at least an hour. Serve on plates with the nuts and figs.

Cuisine

The cuisine is a blend of foodstuffs native to Morocco, African, Andulsian, Arab, Berber, and Muslim influences. They use lovely spices, dried and fresh vegetables and fruit, and herbs. Moroccan cooking makes use of spices – coriander, cumin, mint, saffron, ginger, black pepper, verbena, cloves and cinnamon; plentiful fruits - dates, strawberries, cherries, lemons, pomegranates, limes, apples, pears, oranges and dried fruits; vegetables – chickpeas, aubergines, peppers, zucchini, tomatoes, lentils, carrots; meats – sheep, goats, and lamb; olives and olive oil; nuts – almonds, walnuts, pistachios; fish – shrimp, sardines, prawns, squid, octopus, whiting, sea perch, mullet, tuna, lobsters, and crayfish; and rose water.

In many places communal ovens are still used. Each loaf has a family symbol to distinguish the bread. Erfoud is noted for dates, and a festival is held annually in October. The largest palm groves are in Figuig, irrigated by artesian wells. Fruits and vegetables are harvested in Oualida. Safi is famous for sardine canning. Taliouine produces saffron which is harvested at the beginning of winter.

A diffa is a family banquet or ceremonial meal to celebrate the return from the Hadj, wedding, or other special occasions. Numerous dishes are served such as couscous, pastille, along with dates, nuts, and raisins. During Ramadan no eating, drinking, smoking or sexual intercourse is permitted during daylight hours for Muslims. Many businesses are closed. At the time of a wedding the couple is given amlou – thyme, wild lavender, honey, arganoil, and ground almonds for good luck.

The Berbers, farmers with herds and of various tribes, live in the High Atlas Mountains. Some are established in one location, others nomadic. Towns are centered around a collective granary – igherm or a fortified house – ighermt.

Markets, such as the one in Marrakech, have probably changed little since ancient times. There you can buy carpets, jewelry, clothing, and food, all while watching snake charmers, dancers, and other exotic pleasures.

Tagine

Serves 6

3-3 ½ lb. chicken, cut into pieces
1 medium onion, chopped
3 cloves garlic, minced
½ tsp. turmeric
1 tsp. cinnamon
½ tsp. ginger
½ tsp. nutmeg
½ tsp. cayenne
½ tsp. cloves
2 cups water

2 tomatoes, chopped
½ cup red bell pepper, chopped
½ cup yellow bell pepper, chopped
2 large carrots, peeled and chopped
½ cup raisins
¼ cup almonds
½ lb. dried apricots
¼ dates, pitted
1 cup uncooked couscous

Preheat oven to 350°
Place all ingredients in a covered baking dish or tagine.
Cook for 1 hour, or until chicken is tender.
Lamb can be substituted for the chicken.
Other dried fruits such as prunes can be used.

Moroccan Specialties

Couscous – is the national dish. Couscous is also the name of the pot it is cooked in. Couscous is usually served with lamb, vegetables, condiments, and extra broth. It can also be sweetened and served as a dessert. It is always served warm, and eaten communally.
Bisteeya (Bastila or Pastilla) – almond and pigeon pie with cinnamon and sugar
A bisteeya can also be made with shrimp, fish, noodles and spinach
Tagines- slowly simmered meat or poultry stews cooked in earthenware pots with prunes or other dried fruits, nuts, lemons, olives, and spices.
Mechoui – lamb rubbed with cumin and garlic and roasted over an open fire
Briouattes –meat pastries
Harira – soup with lamb, spices, chicken, and broth served to break the fast during Ramadan
Pastilla – pie of paper thin pastry filled with pigeon, onion, eggs, almonds, and herbs topped with cinnamon and sugar
Ras el hanout –"head of the shop", a mix of 27 spices including chili peppers, coriander,

cardamom, cumin, clove, nutmeg and turmeric.

Charmoula – marinade of cilantro, parsley, hot pepper, tomatoes, lemon, preserved lemon and olive oil

Harissa – red paste made with piri piri chiles

Kefta – well seasoned ground beef or lamb cooked over charcoal

Msir – pickled lemons used in cooking

Salads- mainly use tomatoes and cucumbers, sometimes greens

Cornes de gazelle – croissants with almonds, honey, then rolled in sugar and nuts

Qa'b el-ghazal – crescent shaped pastry with almond and sugar filling

M'hencha – an almond filled pastry

Khobz dyal snida – bread cooked on a grill

Salted and preserved lemons

Holidays and Special Occasions

Mimouna – is a Jewish celebration held on the last night of Passover and the end of the eating "chametz" or leavened foods. Tables are covered with white clothes, wheat represents abundance, flowers for spring, dates and honey for a sweet life, fish for fertility, milk and flour for purity; eggs, bean stalks, dates and coins for a good new year. Foods served are mofleta (flour and water fritter dipped in honey), grilled fish, couscous, nuts, raisins, preserves, pastries, "mahiya", a licorice liqueur, wine, and mint tea.

Weddings, birthdays – bisteeya and meshwi whole lamb or goat is roasted in a pit

Beverages

Even though Morocco is a Muslim country, alcoholic beverages are readily available. Beer and wine are produced. Wine is grown in three districts – Berkane near Oudja, Boulaouane, and Meknes. Agourai is a center for vineyards and wines. Boulaouane is known for red and rose wines. Claret de Meknes is a light, red cabernet. Vin Gris, a rose is also from Meknes. Some local beers are Stork and Flag. Almond milk is made of roasted ground almonds, sugar, water, milk, and orange rind. Fruit drinks include watermelon juice, fresh orange juice.

Did You Know?

The Western Sahara (capital Laayoune), formerly ruled by Spain, became part of Morocco in 1975. The Mamora forest near Rabat is the world's largest cork forest. Cork forests are also found in the Rif and Atlas Mountains.

Mozambique

Mozambique is located in southeastern Africa, bordered by the Indian Ocean to the east, Tanzania to the north, Malawi and Zambia to the northwest, Zimbabwe to the west and Swaziland and South Africa to the southwest. From the 1st to 5th c AD Bantu speaking peoples occupied the region. Later Swahili and Arabs founded the ports along the Indian Ocean. In 1498 the Portuguese explorer Vasco de Gama sailed along the coast, and in 1505 Mozambique became a Portuguese colony. It did not receive its independence until 1975. The capital Maputo, formerly known as Lourenço Marques, the name of the Spanish explorer in 1544, and also later as the City of Accacias, has existed as a town since 1850. The official language is Portuguese with Swahili, Makhuwa and Sena also spoken, along with many other languages. The name Mozambique is thought to have come from Swahili Musa al Big, an ancient Arab sheik.

Dining Etiquette

Please arrive promptly when invited for a meal. People greet each other warmly and take their time in doing so inquiring about family and health. They will stand close to each in speaking. Drinks, often alcohol will be served. Guests will be seated at a table set with a tablecloth and napkins, utensils and wine glasses. Soup may be served first, followed by salad, meat or fish with rice and sauces, followed by dessert. The hostess will serve or pass the food. After the meal coffee, tea and/or liqueurs will be served in the living room.

If dining in a rural area, one would wash your hands before and after a meal. Food is eaten with your hands, usually rice that is then rolled in a sauce.

Cuisine

The earliest people in Mozambique were hunter-gatherers, the Bushmen, who traveled to find wild animals, fruits, seeds, or root vegetables. Agriculture was introduced by the Bantu c 300 AD. Later Arab merchants brought salt which was used to preserve meat. The Portuguese introduced crops such as cassava, cashews, onions, peppers, sugarcane, rice, millet, maize, garlic, sorghum, herbs and spices. Since then the food has also been influenced by other African traditions and Indians. The cuisine uses rice, piri-piri, cashews, coconut milk, cornmeal, millet, hot stews, peanuts, vegetables - corn, beans, squash, tomatoes, cucumbers, cassava and cassava root (mandioca), peppers, onions; fruits – avocados, oranges, limes, coconuts, pineapples; watermelon; seafood- lobster, shrimp, prawns, mussels, oysters, crabs, clams, calamari; fresh water fish – mackerel, anchovies, prawns; meat and chicken. In rural areas cassava is pounded to make a porridge.

Matapa (Cassava leaves in coconut and peanuts)

Serves 4

1 lb. young cassava leaves, pounded
2 cloves garlic, crushed
1 large onion, finely chopped
2 tbls. oil
1½ lbs. fish fillet or cooked shelled shrimp, chopped

¾ cup peanuts
1¼ cup coconut milk
4 Maggi cubes
Salt to taste
1 tsp. crushed red pepper

In a pot of boiling water cook the cassava leaves and garlic until tender. Drain.
Heat the oil in a skillet and saute onion until tender.
Add the fish, peanuts, coconut milk, Maggi, and red pepper. Bring to a boil and let simmer until warmed. Add the cassava leaves. Cover and cook 15 minutes.
Serve with rice or xima (corn flour porridge)
Peanut butter can be substituted for the peanuts.

Mozambique Specialties

Piri-piri - hot pepper sauce (Swahili for hot chili)
Frango – chicken rubbed with piri-piri and roasted over hot charcoal
Caril – curries
Manga achar – mango chutney
Bedgia – fried bean patty
Xima – maize and water
Arroz de coco – white rice in coconut water
Bau – locally baked bread
Bifel – steak

Pregos – steak sandwiches
Cassava chips
Batata fritas – French fried potatoes (chips)
Posho – maize porridge
Macaza – grilled fish kebabs
Bacalhao – salted cod
Chocos – squid cooked in squid ink
Galinha zambezia – chicken with lime sauce (Quelimane and Zambezia provinces)
Lulas – fried, stuffed or grilled calamari
Malasadas - doughnuts

Holidays and Special Occasions

For holidays and other rituals elaborate feasts may be prepared though in rural areas these may consist of the food used daily. Bolo polana (cashew and potato cake) is served.
Christmas – children dance, decorations are hung on trees, and a meal prepared with meat, chicken with piri-piri, or seafood (along the coast), rice, chips, cabbage and other vegetables, fruit, and dessert such as watermelon and filhos de natal (Christmas fritters), beer and wine. Christmas Day is called Family Day.

Beverages

Beer is locally brewed using maize. Nipa is a beer made from the fruit of the cashew, cassava, mango, or sugarcane. Beers include Manica, Laurentina, and Dois M (2M) Sura is a drink made from coconut fronds (palm wine). Coffee, tea (Cha) and fruit juices are also served.

Myanmar (Burma)

Myanmar is a country in Southeast Asia, bordered by the People's Republic of China in the northeast, Laos in the east, Thailand on the southeast, Bangladesh on the west, India on the northwest, and the Bay of Bengal to the southwest. The earliest people were hunter-gatherers in Shane State, and the Mon the first to migrate into the Irrawaddy valley before the 10th c BC. In the 1st c BC the Tibeto-Burman speaking Pyu established city states, including Sri Ksetra. Both the Mon and Pyu were on trade routes between China and India. The Nanzhao invaded in the 9th c AD. The Mongol Kublai Khan invaded northern Burma in 1277, followed by the Tai-Shan from Yunnan who established Shan states. Later small kingdoms. – Ava (the Burmans) in Upper Burma; the Mon kingdom of Hanthawady Pegu in Lower Burma; and the Rakhine kingdom in the west came about. King Alaungpaya founded Yangon in 1755. During the 18th c the Qing Dynasty of China invaded four times. In 1852 the British named its territories Lower Burma. King Mindon founded Mandalay in 1859, making it the capital. In 1885 the British occupied Upper Burma, and by 1886 the entire country had become the British Raj, finally receiving its independence in 1948. In 1989 the name was changed to Myanmar. The capital Naypyidaw was a planned city founded in 2006. The official language is Burmese with Jingpho, Kayah, Karen, Chin, Mon, Rakhine, and Shan also spoken. There are about 125 ethnic groups in the country.

Dining Etiquette

Please be punctual when invited for a meal. Please bring a gift from your country. Remove your shoes before entering the home. The people are very friendly and are always trying to feed you. You will dine at low tables, seated on reed mats. The meal will be set on the table as there are no courses and you will eat from the various bowls. Food is eaten with the right hand, and if no utensils are available, using the fingers. The left hand serves dishes from the middle of the table. Soup is served in bowls, each person receiving his own spoon. Salad and soup are served with the main course. Appetizers and desserts are served on special occasions. At a party it is impolite to eat and drink while standing. Please sit on a mat, or a chair if provided.

When visiting tea and fritters or sweets are served. Do not touch anyone on the head, including children. Do not point the bottom of your soles at anyone. Do not show emotions and especially displays of affection. Several generations may live together.

Cuisine

The cuisine has been influenced by the Chinese, Thai, and Indians, and much of the food is vegetarian. The meals are centered around rice or rice noodles with some meat, fish, chicken, duck and vegetables. Many spices and herbs are used - chilies, curries, turmeric, paprika, garlic, ginger, cloves, nutmeg, cumin, lemongrass, Coriander is used as a sedative. Cabbage, okra, watercress, long beans, chayote, gourd squash, banana leaves, yams, chutneys, peanuts, potatoes, sesame, beans, chilies, maize, sugar cane, mushrooms, eggplant, and chinbaung (used in many dishes and similar to rhubarb) are used in cooking. Over 100 varieties of rice are grown – pink, black, long grain, and glutinous. Rice flour is made. Asparagus is grown in the highlands. Among the popular fish are catfish, shrimp, dried fish, crab, shad, hilsa, and fish paste. All parts of the fish including the head are eaten. Salads with condiments are often served as main dishes. Soup may be served as a beverage instead of tea or water. Many fruits are grown among them strawberries, avocados, limes, banana leaves. At breakfast rice, fish soup, curry, coconut chicken noodles, or glutinous rice are served.; midday – meat or seafood, vegetables, soup, rice, bread, fruit; and dinner includes soup. Soups are served at room temperature because of the heat. Food is cooked in sesame or peanut oil. Meals end with lephet; fresh ginger salads or fruit. Sweets are served at other times, often with tea. The desserts are made with coconut milk, sesame seeds, and glutinous rice. Betel nuts are chewed and can be slightly intoxicating.

Mohinga (Fish Soup)

Mohinga, the national dish, is a lemon grass fish soup with onion, garlic, ginger, turmeric, black pepper and other seasonings, fish sauce, rice, and core of banana plant which is served over rice noodles and garnished with browned onion and cilantro; usually eaten at breakfast

Serves 6

2 tbls. oil	3 cups fish stock
2 chilies, green or red for very hot, seeded and chopped	1 lb. fresh rice vermicelli, cooked according to directions and drained
1 tsp. turmeric	2 tbls. fish sauce
2 tbls. fresh grated ginger	2 lb. fish fillet (cod, catfish, or other)
4 scallion, finely chopped including greens	2 tomatoes, chopped
2 cloves garlic, peeled and minced	1 bunch cilantro, chopped
2 tbls. lemon grass	Lime wedges
1 tbls. tamarind paste	

In a large pan heat the oil. Stir in the chilies, turmeric, ginger, scallion, garlic, lemongrass, and tamarind. Cook for about 5 minutes or until softened.
Stir in stock, and simmer for 10 minutes. Add vermicelli, fish, and tomatoes. Cook for 10 minutes. Serve in bowls and garnish with cilantro and lemon wedges.
The soup can also be served over the vermicelli, instead of included in the soup.

Specialties

Ohnokaukswe – coconut noodle soup	Nanpyar – flat bread
Sanbyoke – rice soup	Tohu – Burmese bean curd
Kyarzan chet – bean thread soup (for special occasions)	Kaungnyin paung – glutinous rice and black-eyed peas
Hin lay – pork curry	

Oh-no-khauk owe – rice, noodles, chicken, spices, and coconut milk
Curried stews
Paratha – fried pancake
Rice with stir fried vegetables
Lingyo – clear soup with vegetables
Kauk hnyin boung – glutinous rice and coconut sweet

Kaukswe – chicken or meat, noodles, coconut milk and spices
Panthay khowse – noodles and chicken
Nga-pi-gyet – garlic and shrimp sauce
Ngapi – fish paste
Peiyarkyaw – pea fritters
Ghin thoke – pickled ginger salad (dessert)
Beikmoke – cake
Own thee moant – coconut cake

Holidays and Special Occasions

There are many special festivals during the year each highlighted by the food served. On most occasions rice with coconut milk is served. Pedi chin (fermented bean sprouts) are served on special occasions with pork and balo chong (shrimp). Coconut is also eaten on special occasions
Rice Harvest – htamane (glutinous rice with sesame seeds, peanuts, ginger, coconut, and oil). Rice is given to the monks and special dishes prepared.
Water Festival - nga-nitu kyaw (fried dried fish); water throwing is celebrated at same time as
Thingyan (New Year) – smoked rice, mango and many salads, fried dried fish
During Lent the monks remain in their monasteries and no weddings are held.
Seven days after birth guests are invited for naming the child using an astrologer.
Shinpyu ceremony– young boys 7 or older enter the monastery
At death a coin is put in a person's mouth so ferryman can carry him across the river to the next life.

Beverages

King Alaung Sithu introduced tea in 1113 AD in Pagan which had been brought from China. Lephet, fresh tea leaves brewed and stored in underground jars, is served at the end of meals. It is eaten by crushing the leaves with salt and oil or as a salad. Tea is served quite strong.

Sugar cane juice is used in beverages. Burma also produces Mandalay Beer, Shan Whiskey, Manadalay Gin, Manadalay Rum, Shwe le maw – orange brandy from the mountains near Kalaw and Taunggyi, Ayet piu – "white liquor" – distilled rice or palm sap, and Taw ayet – "jungle liquor".

Did You Know?

The monks beg each day going from home to home offering covered bowls. The nuns cook their own food.
Before World War II Burma was the worlds' largest exported of rice.

Namibia

Namibia, located in southern Africa, is bordered to the west by the Atlantic Ocean, to the north Angola and Zambia, to the east Botswana, and South Africa to the south and east. Namibia has been inhabited by Bushmen, Damara, and Namaqua, and since c14th century AD by Bantu. It became a German Imperial protectorate in 1884 and remained a German colony until the end of World War I. In 1920, the League of Nations mandated the country to South Africa. Namibia gained independence from South Africa in 1990. The driest country in sub-Saharan Africa, Namibia only has permanent rivers on its northern and southern borders. The capital is Windhoek. English is the official language with Afrikaans, German, and Oshiwambo also spoken.

Dining Etiquette

Please arrive promptly when invited for a meal. Please bring a small gift of food, a beverage, or something from your country. Shake hands greeting and departing. Meals are served at a table with the guest of honor seated to the right of the host or hostess. The table is set with cutlery for each course. Food is eaten continental style. Please wait for your hostess to start. In some rural areas spoons and/or fingers are still used for eating. When asked for a meal in a village, please make a donation to the tribe to thank them.

Cuisine

The early inhabitants were gatherers and hunted wild game, and ate what was abundantly grown such as fruit, nuts, and bulbs. The Khoisan domesticated cattle about 2000 years ago giving them dairy products and meat. Along the Atlantic the Namid desert dunes drop right to the coastline. In the Namib-Naukluft National Park Sossuvlei is a dry salt flat lake. Near Angola the Epupa Falls are baobab, fig and palm trees. The Himba tribe has herds of cattle and goats. The women rub butter fat and mud into their skin and hair. The cuisine has been influenced indigenous people, German, and Afrikaan. There are 11 different ethnic groups in the country, and all have played a role in the cuisine. Much of the country is arid, and each region has its own produce and animals. The Germans introduced dishes such as Wiener schnitzel. Swakopmund has excellent green asparagus, and Swakopmund, Luderitz and Windhoek are famous for German pastries and chocolates - Schwarzwalder, Kirschtorte, and Kalahari Truffles. Omajowa produces very large mushrooms. The common game meats include kudu, springbok, gemsbok, oryx, wildebeest, frog, ostrich, zebra, crocodile, and game birds; plus domesticated animals – sheep, goat, chicken, pork, and beef. Along the coast is abundant seafood kabeljou, rock lobster, oysters, mussels, and crayfish. Corn or millet porridge is served with meat or fish stew. Common vegetables are potatoes, cabbage, celery; fruit – oranges, bananas, kiwi, avocado, mandarin oranges, and pineapples; and nuts, peanuts. In the south corn is used in making bread. Shellfish, tomato sauces, chicken, Wiener schnitzel, goat, beef, bush rat, rice, beans, and couscous. In the west beans and rice are served.

Braaivleis, barbecue and potjiekos, a hot meat, chicken or fish stew cooked in a three-legged cast-iron pot are very popular. Chakalaka is a spicy sauce served with breads, stews, and curries.

Hake Casserole

3 tbls. olive oil	8 slices (Pereira) hake, skinless
1 clove garlic, minced	Parsley
½ onion, finely chopped	6 asparagus
1 tomato, chopped	2 peppers, chopped

Poach the onion, garlic and tomato in an earthen pan in the olive oil over modest heat.
Add the hake. Add parsley. Season with salt and pepper. Garnish with asparagus and peppers.
Serve with baked or fried potatoes.
Recipe courtesy of Sacky P. Kadhila Amoomo, Pereira, Walvis Bay, Namibia

Braaivleis Sauce for Meat

Good for at least 2 lbs. meat. Braai is red meat with vegetables and dried fruits and herbs; or with chicken, pork, or other meats and barbecued

1 cup vinegar	2 cups tomato sauce
1 cup oil	2 tbls. Worcestershire sauce
1 tsp. salt	1 tsp. Tabasco sauce or ground red pepper
1 onion, finely chopped	2 cloves garlic, minced

Place ingredients in a jar and shake well. Refrigerate overnight.
Marinate the meat for at least one hour or overnight in the sauce.
Grill on the BBQ.

Holidays and Special Occasions

National Day, March 21 – braai and potjie
Manherero Day, August – in Okahandja – to honor ancestors with parades
Other holidays are Workers Day, Cassinga Day, Ascension Day, Africa Day, Heroes Day, Women's Day, Christmas day and New Year's Day with special dishes served
For special occasions stews are made with seafood, tomatoes, onion, and hot sauces.

Beverages

German influenced beer is produced including Windhoek and Hansa Lager. The annual Octoberfest is in Swakopmund.

Nauru

Nauru is an island country in Micronesia in the Central Pacific. Its nearest neighbor is Banaba Island in Kiribati, 186 miles to the east. Nauru was first inhabited by Micronesians and Polynesians at least 3,000 years ago. There were traditionally 12 clans or tribes on Nauru, which are represented in the 12-pointed star on the country's flag. The name "Nauru" may derive from the Nauruan word *Anáoero*, which means "I go to the beach." The British sea captain John Fearn, a whale hunter, became the first Westerner to visit Nauru in 1798, calling it "Pleasant Island". From around 1830, Nauruans had contact with Europeans from whaling ships and traders who replenished their supplies particularly fresh water. Around this time, deserters from European ships began to live on the island. The islanders traded food for alcoholic palm wine and firearms. Nauru was annexed by Germany in 1888 and incorporated into Germany's Marshall Islands Protectorate. Kings were established as rulers of the island. In 1914, following the outbreak of World War I, Nauru was captured by Australian troops and in 1942 Japan occupied Nauru. Nauru became self-governing in January 1966, and independent in 1968.

Dining Etiquette

When invited for a meal please arrive promptly. Shake hands greeting and departing. Please bring a gift from your country. Do not bring food as it may mean the host does not have enough. The host will seat the guests often in the middle of the table so they can talk to others. Flatware is usually available, though some people eat with their hands. A prayer may be said at the beginning of the meal. Try a little bit of everything. If there is food left over from the meal it may be offered to you, though it is better to finish everything on your plate.

Younger people honor and show respect for their elders. This is a matriarchal society and mothers are very much respected.

Cuisine

Inhabitants practiced aquaculture: they caught juvenile *ibija* fish, aclimatised them to fresh water, and raised them in the Buada Lagoon, providing a reliable source of food. The island has almost no soil and little grows on it except coconuts and pandanus. The surrounding Pacific Ocean provides plentiful seafood – crabs, clams, turtles, and fish, and birds. Some early settlers began arriving over 4000 years ago did bring vegetables, fruit, and animals but because of the conditions many of these did not survive. Among them rice, taro, yams, breadfruit, bananas, lemons, sugarcane, pigs, dogs, and rats. When the Europeans arrived in the 1800s they brought wheat, potatoes, pineapples, cattle, and chickens. In the early 1900s phosphate was discovered, but strip mining and over mining further depleted the soil. Imported food helped provide needed nourishment and a variety of food. However in the early 2000s when the phosphate ran out imported food became too expensive. Today the people grow what they can and eat mainly fish coconuts for milk and their flesh, and rice.

Coconut Fish

Serves 4

1½ lbs. tuna or other fish or shrimp
¼ cup olive oil
2 tbls. butter
4 cloves garlic
4 green onions

2 tbls. fresh grated ginger
2 jalapeno or other hot chili pepper
2 tbls. lime juice
1 cup coconut milk

In a skillet heat the olive oil and butter. Stir in the green onions, ginger, garlic, and jalapeno until softened. Add lime juice and coconut milk.
Add fish and cook for about 10 minutes or until fish is cooked.
Serve over rice.

Special Occasions and Holidays

January 31 – Independence Day – flags, speeches, fishing competition, and other sports events
Christmas - banana and coconut cakes, or coconut mousse.
May 17 – Constitution Day – sports, competitions, parades
September 25 – National Youth Day – sports competitions
Angam Day – to celebrate the fact the island must maintain a population of 1500 citizens, as so many had perished during World War II and from famine. *Angam* translates to "celebration" or "homecoming" in English.

Beverages

Juices, soft drinks tea, coffee and iced coffee are served. Kava is made from kava plant roots, which are ground to form a liquid and water is added. Beer and alcoholic beverages must be imported.

Nepal

Nepal is a landlocked central Himalayan country in South Asia, bordering China in the north and India in the south, east, and west. The territory of Nepal has a recorded history since the Neolithic Age, over 11,000 years in the Kathmandu Valley. Tibeto-Burman-speaking people probably lived in Nepal 2500 years ago. The name "Nepal" is first recorded in texts from the Vedic Age, the era which founded Hinduism, the predominant religion of the country. Around 500 BCE, small kingdoms and confederations of clans arose in the southern regions of Nepal. From one of these, the Shakya polity, arose a prince who later renounced his status to lead an ascetic life, founded Buddhism, and came to be known as Gautama Buddha (traditionally dated 563–483 BCE). By 250 BCE, the southern regions came under the influence of the Maurya Empire of North India and parts of Nepal later on became a nominal vassal state under the Gupta Empire in the fourth century CE. Beginning in the third century CE, the Licchavi Kingdom governed the Kathmandu Valley and the region surrounding central Nepal. In the early 12th century, leaders emerged in far western Nepal whose names ended with the Sanskrit suffix *malla* ("wrestler"). These kings consolidated their power and ruled over the next 200 years, until the kingdom splintered into two dozen petty states. Another Malla dynasty beginning with Jayasthiti emerged in the Kathmandu valley in the late 14th century, and much of central Nepal again came under a unified rule. In 1482 the realm was divided into three kingdoms: Kathmandu, Patan, and Bhaktapur. In the mid-18th century, Prithvi Narayan Shah, a Gorkha king, set out to put together what would become present-day Nepal. Kathmandu is the nation's capital and largest city. Nepal is a multiethnic nation with Nepali as the official language.

Dining Etiquette

The Nepalese are very warm and hospitable. When invited for a meal please arrive promptly. Dress is conservative, and legs and arms should be covered. Shoes should be taken off on entering. Please bring a gift from your country, or gifts for children, if you know they have them. The right hand is used for giving and receiving items. Shake hands greeting or departing. Namaste is the proper form of greeting where one places one's palms together in front of the chest and bow slightly. Please wash your hands before eating, and in some cases a bowl will be passed around. The host will show you to your seat. When seated in a chair or at a table do not point the bottom of your shoe, but keep both feet on the floor. Please try all the food. If you are serving yourself do not touch the plate with the serving utensils. If there are no spoons, forks or knives, please eat with your right hand as the left is considered unclean. There may be places where chopsticks are used. Naan bread or rice can be used to scoop up food or eat sauces. Leave some food on your plate so that your host knows he has served you a bountiful amount. Since the country is mostly made up of Buddhists and Hindus many people may be vegetarian. Hindus do not eat beef, buffalo, or yak.

Hindus observe *jutho* (ritual impurity) where food and drinks are not shared with the same plate or utensils. Also do not touch another person's head or shoulders.

Dal Bhat (Lentil Soup Served over Rice)

Serves 4

1 cup masoor dal (lentil)
3 cups water
1 tbls. fresh grated ginger
1 clove garlic, grated
2 fresh green chilies, chopped

1 tsp. turmeric
¼ cup ghee
1 large onion, thinly sliced
1 tsp. cumin seeds
Cilantro

Boil the masoor with the ginger, garlic, turmeric, and chilies for 15-20 minutes or until lentils are soft. Mash the mixture.
Heat the ghee in a pan and fry the onions and cumin seeds for 6 minutes, or until soft and golden. Add to lentils.
Serve over rice garnished with the coriander.
Dried red chilies can be substituted for the green chilies.
To make a thinner dal, add more water.

Cuisine

The national cuisine is Dhindo and Gundruk. The cuisine of Nepal varies according to the region of the country, the customs and religion, and what is available. When the Indians arrived in Nepal they introduced Hinduism and beef could not be consumed. They also introduced curries, pulses, and naan. Nepalese food has also been influenced by Tibetan and Chinese dishes. Later with the British and expansion of the spice trade spices were more frequently used, and potatoes introduced. Mustard oil is used in cooking. Spices include sesame seeds, cumin, coriander, black pepper, turmeric, garlic, ginger, fenugreek, bay leaves, cloves, cinnamon, chilies, and mustard seeds. Lentils, yogurt, chickpeas, buckwheat, red rice, barley, millet, and beans are used in many dishes. Yak is used for its meat and milk. Vegetables include spinach, fresh greens, white radish, potatoes, green beans, cauliflower, cabbage, taro, and pumpkin. Local fruits are mandarin orange, kaffir lime, lemons, Asian pears, bayberry, apples, litchi, papaya, bananas, jackfruit, and mangoes. Chicken, pork, beef, yak, buffalo, sheep, goat, fish, wild boar, blood sausage and other dried meats, and snails are eaten, depending on the person's religion and where one lives.

Specialties

Tarkari – curried vegetables
Masu - meat curry served over rice
Achaar – spicy fermented or fresh pickles
Chutni (chutney) – spicy condiment
Momo – steamed dumplings with meat or vegetables

Curries – meat or vegetable
Naan – thin round bread served at meals
Aloo tama – curried bamboo shoots with potatoes
Pulao (pilaf) - rice with turmeric, cumin and vegetables

Chatamari – naan with meat, vegetables, eggs
Gundrook-dheedo – wheat, corn and vegetables
Thukpa – soup with noodles, vegetables, and chicken
Kwati – soup made from nine varieties of sprouted beans

Chhoyla – water buffalo marinated and grilled
Sel roti – fired round rice bread sweetened with sugar and honey, served at religious festivals
Tsampa – flour ground from toasted grain
Taruwa – fried vegetable batter
Bagiya – rice and lentil dumplings
Ghau - yogurt

Holidays and Special Occasions

Festivals are held almost daily throughout Nepal. On these days the Nepalese take a ritual bath, worship, visit a temple, fast or feast. Many local festivals are celebrated where dishes include sekuwa, goat, and rice. During the Hindu festival of Tihar sel roti and patre are served.
Navavarsha (New Year) - first day of first month of Baisakh (usually second week in April)
Losar is celebrated for 15 days. On the first day changkol, a beverage, is served. On the second day is King Losar.
Teej – takes place in August/September. Hindu married women wear red saris with glass beads, sing and dance, fast, and pray to Lord Shiva for good and prosperous lives with their husbands. Unmarried women observe the festival and hope they can find good husbands.
Dashain – in September/October – a festival mainly celebrated by Hindus. For nine days the Goddess Durga is prayed to. Family members return to their homes for this. On the 1st day "Ghatansthapana" seeds of corn are placed in a vessel with clay and water, and placed in a prayer room to pray to the Goddess Durga. Temples are visited. On the 10th day children take tika and blessings from their elders. Sel roti served
Tihar "Festival of Lights" – October/November – During this festival people worship Laxmi, the Goddess of Wealth for 5 days. Houses are cleaned and decorated, lamps lit. Crows, dogs, and cows are worshipped with vermilion and food; crows as messengers; dogs as obedient; and cows a symbol of wealth and the national animal. During Tihar Mha puja, worshipping one's body, is observed. Children dress up and give performances, receiving candy and money
Maha Shivarati – February – festival in honor of Lord Shiva
Fagu Prunima – March – colored powders and water balloons are thrown
Saraswati Pooja – spring festival to honor Saraswati, Goddess of learning
Indra Jatra – a festival to thank Indra, King of Heaven and rains
Gai Jatra – cows are brought out by families to commemorate the spirits of their ancestors, showing respect for ancestors and gods

Beverages

Tea (chiya) is the most common drink, usually black tea with sugar and milk; or salted butter tea. Sarbat, a drink made from sugarcane; and mahi buttermilk are also drunk. Alcoholic drinks are tongba and rakshi, made from fermented millet; jard, a beer made from rice; thwon, rice beer, and ayla, a local drink from the Newars.

The Netherlands

The Netherlands is bordered by the North Sea, Belgium and Germany. The original name was Holtland "Soaked Land". Much of the country's 16,464 sq. miles lie below sea level. The earliest known inhabitants (c 2500 BC) were from the fishing village of Vlaargingen. The Romans started trading with the country in 12 BC. Later inhabitants were the Franks, Vikings, and in 1548 Belgium, Luxembourg, and the Netherlands became one state under the Treaty of Augsburg. Napoleon made it part of France, and in 1940 it was invaded by the Germans. Amsterdam, the capital, received its city charter in 1275. The Hague, the seat of government, comes from the word Gravenhage "Count's Hedge". Dutch is the official language.

Dining Etiquette

Please be punctual when invited out. Shake hands greeting and departing. Please send or bring flowers (roses are for lovers, white lilies for funerals). Drinks and light hors d'oeuvres will be served. The guest of honor will be seated to the right of the hostess. Men stand until the ladies are seated. All dishes are served, rather than placed on the table or buffet style. Please wait till the hostess picks up her fork to eat. Food is eaten continental style with the fork in the left hand and knife in the right. Hands are kept above the table, no elbows on the table. When finished put your knife and fork together. Dessert is served with coffee, followed by brandy. The toasts are "Op Je Gezondheid", "Prost" or "To your health".

Cuisine

The early Dutch mainly ate bread and herring. The Dutch East India Company was founded in 1602. After this Dutch, food made much use of spices from Asia, and later many Indonesian dishes became quite popular –nasi goring (fried rice), fried spring rolls, satay, and peanut sauce. Potatoes were introduced in the 18th c. The wealthier families made use of spices, fruits, cheeses, nuts, meat, fish and wines. In the north fish, game, meat, sausages (metworst) and smoked sausage (rookworst), pastries, cookies, pancakes are eaten. The western region is noted for dairy products – cheese, butter and buttermilk, seafood – herring, mussels, eels, oysters, and shrimp, pastries and cookies. The southern region of The Netherlands is known for pastries, soups, stews, vegetable dishes, sauces, fried potatoes, and asparagus. The country grows vegetables – potatoes, kale, beets, beans, carrots, celery, onions, cabbages, Brussels sprouts, cauliflower, endive, spinach, asparagus, tomatoes, cucumbers, peppers, and lettuce, plus many others and herbs. Fruits are eaten raw or processed into jams or drinks and include apples, pears, cherries, berries, and plums. Being a coastal country seafood is in abundance – cod, herring, lobster, sole, mackerel, eel, oysters, shrimp, mussels, tuna, salmon, trout and sardines. Willem Beukelszoon of Bievliet discovered the method for curing herring. The color "Royal Purple" comes from crushing small crabs to powder. The Dutch were the first to use drift nets for fishing c 1416.

The Dutch are known for their cheese – Limburger, Edam, Gouda, Leyden - cheese with cumin, Leerdammer, and Beemster which are made from cows' milk. The cheeses may be flavored with herbs or spices. Boerenkaas – "farmers' cheese" is Farmhouse Gouda and Bitterballen – "cheese balls to go with bitters" are served with gin.

Dutch Apple Pie

Dough

10.5 oz self-rising flour
6 oz cold butter
5.5 oz white sugar

1 tbls. vanilla sugar or vanilla extract
1 whisked egg
Pinch of salt

Mix flour and sugar in a bowl. Whisk the egg, adding most of it to the flour (keeping about 1/3 of the egg behind to brush the pie with later). Add the cubed butter, the vanilla sugar and salt. Knead by hand until the dough comes together into a ball. Put the dough in foil and place it in the refrigerator.

Filling

2.2 lb peeled and diced sour apples
1 tbls. lemon juice
0.5 oz white sugar

2 ts. cinnamon
2 oz raisins

Peel and core the apples, cut them into bite-sized pieces and mix with the lemon juice, cinnamon and 0.5 oz. sugar.
Soak the raisins in hot water. Dab the raisins and add them to the apple mixture.
Grease a large spring form pie dish Use 2/3 of the dough to cover the bottom and sides of the dish. Add the apple mixture to the pie dish and firmly press down. Use the rest of the dough to make the topping. Make 5 strips of the remaining dough. Put three strips on horizontally and two strips vertically. Brush the pastry with the egg wash and place in the oven to bake for approximately 70/80 minutes in a preheated oven on 335 degrees. The pie should be cooled in the spring form and then carefully turned out.
An extra treat is to serve the Dutch Apple Pie with whipped cream.
Recipe courtesy of the Royal Netherlands Embassy, Washington, DC

Dutch Specialties

Hutspot – stew with potatoes, carrots, onions and meat, bacon, or smoked sausage
Hachee – beef and onion stew

Boerenkool, a sausage, cabbage and potato dish is known to have been mentioned in cookbooks dating back to c1661, before potatoes were used.

Andijviestamppot – endive with mashed potatoes and bacon

Zuurkoolstamppot – sauerkraut mashed with potatoes and served with bacon or sausage

Boerenkoolstamppot – kale and potatoes with gravy, mustard and rookworst

Hete bliksem - boiled potatoes and green apples

Patat – French fries

Gehaktballen - meatballs

Snert – pea soup with sausages served with roggebrood (rye bread)

Stamppot – vegetables, potatoes, and meat stew with gravy and other vegetables

Poffertjes – puffed pancakes served with sugar and butter

Patatje met – fries with mayonnaise

Haring – herring

Liquorice – liquorice that can be sweet or salty

Engelse drop – liquorice with coconut fondant

Hagelslag – chocolate sprinkles on a sandwich

Stroopwafel – flat waffle with caramel syrup

Pannenkoeken – pancakes

Wentelteefjes –French toast

Broeder - cake

Vla – vanilla custard

Vlaai – pie with fruit filling

Broodpap – bread pudding

Rijstebrij – rice pudding

Peperkoek - gingerbread

Holidays and Special Occasions

Easter – eggs

Sinterklaas (Saint Nicholas) visits on December 5th leaving gifts for the children. Chocolate milk and spice cookies and marzipan are eaten

Christmas – marzipan, fondant, speculaas – ginger cookies, taii-taii- cakes, and banketletter – pastry with almond paste. Brunch is celebrated with kerstsol (raisin bread with fruit). Dinner is served with pork or game.

New Year's Eve – oliebollen – doughnuts without holes. Coin are hidden in them, or special cakes with the finder having to give everyone a treat. Also served are appelflappen, appelbeignetz, and knieppertjes.

Birth of a baby – beschuit met muisjes – rusk covered with aniseed

Birthdays – cakes, cookies, pies

Drinks

The Dutch are known for their beers, the oldest brewery having started in 1340 in Wijlre, Limburg. There are several types – Pilsener, light, Bock, and stout. The top fermenting beers are brewed for 2-3 months to produce a distinctive flavor. Gin was invented by a Dutch doctor, Franciscus de la Boe in the 17th c. Gin is made from redistilled malt spirits and the juniper berry and is called genever or Hollands gin. This is a distilled mash of malted barley and other grains that is heated, redistilled with juniper berries or other flavors. Gin is served cold, drunk in one gulp; and served with green herring or eel. Borrel is Dutch gin and bessert red currant gin. Kleine angst "little terror" is jenever and bitters. Bitters include Beerenburg. Jenever is a distilled malt wine; Kandeel is a liquor made from white wine; Kraamanijs, an aniseed liquor, and Oranjebitter, an orange flavored brandy. Franciscus de la Boie is thought to have made the first gin in the 17th c. Liqueurs come in many flavors from Pisang Ambon (banana), Kummel (caraway), chocolate, Advocaat (egg, sugar and brandy)or Goudwasser (liqueur with gold specks).

New Zealand

New Zealand is an island nation located in the southwestern Pacific Ocean and consists of the North and South Islands, plus smaller islands. Polynesians settled on the islands in 1250-1300 CE and developed the Maori culture. Europeans arrived in 1642 with Dutch explorer Abel Tasman. Europeans did not appear again until 1769 when British explorer James Cook mapped the coastline. Following that New Zealand was visited by Europeans and Americans who looking for whales and seals and traded with the Maori. The Europeans introduced potatoes and muskets. In 1840 the British and Maori signed a treaty which established New Zealand as a British colony. Today New Zealand is a member of the British Commonwealth. The capital, Wellington, is named after Arthur Wellesley, the first Duke of Wellington, and victor of the Battle of Waterloo. The town may have been settled as early as the 11th c. The official languages are English and Maori.

Dining Etiquette

The New Zealanders are very friendly and enjoy entertaining. Please be prompt when invited for a meal. Please bring a small gift, flowers, chocolates, or something from your country. Gifts are opened when received. Shake hands greeting and departing. They are very informal and first names will probably be used. Lunch is served around 12:30, dinner 7:30-8 pm. Drinks are served before dinner. Please wait to be seated. Keep your elbows off the table and your hands above the table. Food is eaten continental style fork in the left hand and knife in the right. Salads are always eaten with the meal. The toasts are "Cheers", "Down the hatch", "Here's how", and "Here's looking up your kilt". When finished with your meal place your fork and knife parallel on the plate with the handles facing to the right. Coffee may be served following the meal.

Afternoon tea is still enjoyed and may include scones, tea sandwiches, and other pastries.

Maori Customs

Visitors to a Marae are given a welcoming ceremony, with speeches, singing, and a formal feast or several meals will follow. Before eating a prayer "karakia" is always said. Remember the head is sacred and must never be touched. Death is a public matter and three days of mourning are observed. Much food is served, and on the final day a feast, and water is sprinkled where the body had lain in and around the house. "Kai" is the Maori word for "food".

Cuisine

The cuisine has been influenced by the Maori which brought with them kumara, taro, ti plants, dogs, rats, and other edible products. Foodstuffs already growing on the islands were fernroot, birds such as moa and wood pigeons, seafood, and grubs that formed part of their diet. The Maori cooked their food in earthen ovens known as hangi. Stones were heated by the fire and then food wrapped in leaves was placed on the hot coals. They were covered with leaves or cloth. Other foodstuffs might be roasted, or boiled. Two Maori dishes used today are the boil-up (potatoes, kumara, dumplings, and pork; and puha).

The Europeans brought food with them and introduced pork, sweet potatoes, potatoes, mutton, wheat, pumpkins, sugar, fruit, alcoholic beverages such as beer, and tea. At that time the Maori had not produced alcoholic drinks. Besides the Brits, Scots also settled in New Zealand bringing with them sweets recipes – cakes, scones, and muffins.

Today New Zealand produces lamb, cheeses and other dairy products, olives, and grapes for wine. As New Zealanders traveled more they brought with them cuisines from every part of the globe, especially Southeast Asia, China, India, Japan, but also European influences as well. During the summer barbecues are popular

Fish and seafood are trout, salmon, toheroa – green clam, pipis – a shellfish; pauas – abalone, oysters, crayfish, whitebait, mussels, and scallops. Local meat includes lamb, mutton, beef, and pork. Common vegetables are kumeras (sweet potato), kumi kumi (similar to pumpkin), rauriki (milkweed greens); and fruit - kiwi, feijoa, tamarillo, and manuka.

Pavlova

"Pavlova is a meringue-based dessert named after the Russian dancer Anna Pavlova. Colloquially referred to as "pav" it has a taste and texture similar to a cross between meringue and chewy marshmallow. The dessert is believed to have been created in honor of the dancer either during or after one of her tours to Australia and New Zealand in the 1920s. The nationality of its creator has been a source of argument between the two nations for many years, but formal research indicates New Zealand as the more probable source. The dessert is a popular dish and an important part of the national cuisine of both countries, and is frequently served during celebratory or holiday meals such as Christmas dinner or New Year's Day brunch."

6 egg whites, at room temperature	1 tsp. vanilla extract
Pinch salt	2 tsp. cornstarch
1½ cups superfine sugar	1 tsp. malt vinegar

Heat oven to 350° and line a baking tray with parchment paper. Place egg whites in the bowl of an electric mixer. Add the salt and whisk to soft peaks. Continue mixing and slowly incorporate the sugar 2 tbls. at a time. Beat for 15 minutes or until mixture is shiny and glossy and very thick. Whisk in the vanilla, cornstarch and vinegar.

Spoon the mix onto the baking tray and spread with a spatula into a 6 inch circle. Bake 5 minutes then reduce oven temperature to 250° and cook for 75 minutes and leave to cool completely with the oven door slightly ajar.

To serve: Pavlova is traditionally served with whipped cream, kiwi fruit and fresh berries although you could use any fruit of your choice.

Recipe courtesy of Nathan Bates, New Zealand Embassy, Washington, DC

Braised Lamb Shanks

"Braised lamb shanks are extremely easy to make. Anyone can follow this recipe and have it turnout with succulent lamb that falls off the bone. It's basically a throw it all in the oven recipe but with stunning results. The recipe doesn't require exact amounts either. Great for a low fuss hearty meal in winter."

Serves 3

3 lamb shanks (a shank per person but just add more for more guests)
5 cloves garlic roughly chopped
1 cup red wine
2 cups beef stock
2 tbls. tomato paste

1 large carrot roughly diced
1 large stick of celery roughly diced
1 large onion roughly diced
4 tbls. oil
1 tbls. rosemary leaves finely chopped
1 tbls. thyme leaves

Preheat oven to 325°

Place oil in a pan and heat until mid-high. Brown lamb shanks on all sides, remove from pan and put to one side. In the same pan add the onion, carrot, and celery and cook until the vegetables start to brown then add the garlic and cook for a further minute. Add the tomato paste and then deglaze the pan with the red wine.

Transfer the vegetables to a casserole dish then cover with the lamb shanks, herbs, and beef stock. Cover and place in the oven for approximately 3 hours or until the meat starts to fall off the bone. Serve with mashed potatoes and steamed vegetables.

Recipe courtesy of Nathan Bates, New Zealand Embassy, Washington, DC

Kiwi Specialties

Fish and chips
Meat pies
Colonial goose – roast leg of lamb
Custard squares

Lamingtons - sponge cake with chocolate frosting or strawberry jam and coconut
Anzac biscuits

Holidays and Special Occasions

Easter – hot cross buns, lamb or ham; dyed eggs, chocolate eggs and bunnies. People attend church and shops are closed Good Friday and/or Easter Day

Christmas – turkey, ham, roasted vegetables, Christmas cake, mince pies, Pavlova, and may include barbecues as it is summer here

Boxing Day – day after Christmas. Visits with friends and entertaining

Kiwifruit Caprioska

"It's so simple to make so you can't really get it wrong. It's tangy and refreshing and perfect as a summer cocktail."

1 lime cut into 8-16 pieces
1 kiwi fruit peeled and thickly sliced
1 tsp. brown sugar
8 cubes ice

60mil of 42 Below Kiwi Vodka
1 tbls. sugar syrup (equal quantities of water and castor sugar heated until sugar is dissolved)

Place the lime, kiwifruit and brown sugar in a cocktail shaker then muddle with a rolling pin.
Add the ice, vodka and sugar syrup, shake vigorously
Serve!
Recipe courtesy of Nathan Bates, New Zealand Embassy, Washington, DC

Beverages

New Zealand produces some excellent wine, much of it exported. The first vines are thought to have been introduced by missionary Samuel Marsden, and planted in 1817 by Charles Gordon, superintendent of agriculture for the missionaries. James Busby is credited with producing wine at Kerikeri in 1833, and Charles Darwin noted the winery in his diary when he visited Kerikeri in 1835. Small vineyards were also planted by French settlers in Akaroa in the 1840s. Aided by the deregulation of the economy in the 1980s and 1990s, domestic wine consumption increased and New Zealand wine won increasing accolades internationally. There are 10 major wine-producing areas in New Zealand, with Marlborough famed for its sauvignon blanc, Gisborne for its chardonnay, and Central Otago and Martinborough for pinot noir and pinot gris. Hawkes Bay is known for cabernets and Auckland's Waiheke Island is home to cabernet blends. Marlborough and Hawkes Bay are New Zealand's two premium wine-growing regions. Beer and ale are also brewed.

Nicaragua

Located in Central America Nicaragua is bordered by Honduras to the north, Costa Rica to the south, the Pacific Ocean to the west, and the Caribbean Sea to the east. In pre-Columbian times, the indigenous people were part of the *Intermediate Area*, between the Mesoamerican and Andean cultural regions, and within the influence of the Isthmo-Colombian area. Ceramics and statues were made from volcanic stone. The *Pipil* migrated to Nicaragua from central Mexico after 500 BC. By the end of the 15th century, western Nicaragua was inhabited by several indigenous peoples related by culture to the Mesoamerican civilizations of the Aztec and Maya, and by language to the Mesoamerican Linguistic Area. They were primarily farmers who lived in towns, organized into small kingdoms. The Caribbean coast of Nicaragua was inhabited by other peoples, mostly Chibcha language groups. They lived a life based primarily on hunting and gathering. In the west and highland areas, occupying the territory between Lake Nicaragua and the Pacific Coast lived the *Niquirano and* the *Chorotega* lived in the central region. In 1502, Christopher Columbus was the first European known to have reached what is now Nicaragua, but it was not until 1524 that the first Spanish permanent settlements were founded. Managua is the capital and Spanish the official language.

Dining Etiquette

Please be prompt when invited for a meal. Please bring flowers or send them ahead, or bring something from your country. Shake hands greeting and departing. Please stand close to each other while talking. Remember the middle name is the surname. Dinner is preceded by drinks. The host(ess) will seat the guests. Food is eaten continental style with the fork in the left hand and knife in the right. Please wait for the host(ess) to start. Please try some of everything. If tortillas are served instead of bread, place them on the side of your plate. When not using your utensils keep your elbows above the table, not on the table. If passing something pass with the left hand. When finished please place your knife and fork together. The toast is "Salud" "Cheers" and is offered by the host at the beginning of the meal.

Cuisine

The cuisine of Nicaragua dates back to pre-Columbian times and is a mix of those cultures, the Spanish, and Creole. In the 19th century, Nicaragua attracted many immigrants from Germany, Italy, Spain, France and Belgium who set up businesses with money they brought from Europe. They established many agricultural businesses, such as coffee and sugar-cane plantations, and also newspapers, hotels and banks. Corn used in cooking and drinks, beans, tomatoes, garlic, onion, rice, flour, tropical fruits– jocote, mango, tamarind, bananas, pipian, avocado and coconut; vegetables – yucca and quequisque; herbs – cilantro, oregano, achiote; and peppers. Almost all parts of animals are used. Meats include pork, cattle, chicken, goats, lizards, armadillos, boas, and turtles including their eggs. Each region has its own specialty dishes. There are many cattle farms in the country.

Arroz Con Pollo (Chicken and Rice)

Serves 4-6

2-3 lb. young chicken, cut into pieces
2 medium tomatoes, chopped
1 medium onion, chopped
1 green pepper

1 cup rice
4 oz. capers
8 oz. olives
1 red pimento

In a large pot boil the chicken, tomatoes, green pepper and onion for about an hour, or until chicken is tender. Add the rice, and cook until tender. Add the other ingredients.

Gallo Pinto "Spotted Rooster"

Gallo pinto is often served at breakfast and considered the national dish – rice with onion and sweet pepper and red beans with garlic that are fried together and served with scrambled or fired eggs

2 tbls. olive oil
1 large onion, chopped
2 cloves garlic, minced

2 cups red beans
2 cups cooked rice
¼ cup cilantro

Heat the oil in a skillet and saute the onions until translucent. Stir in the garlic and beans. Lastly add the rice.
Garnish with the cilantro.
For a spicier dish add a jalapeno or two, seeded and chopped

Specialties

Rosquillas – corn dough with eggs, cheese, butter and lard that is baked
Nacatamal – dough made with ground corn and butter and filled with pork or chicken, rice, potatoes, onions, and pepper in plantain leaves, toed with thread and boiled
Vigoror – plantain leaf with yucca, chicharron, and cabbage and tomato
Indio viejo – shredded meat with onions, garlic, pepper and tomato. Tortillas are softened in water and made into a dough. The meat is fried with the vegetables, dough, orange juice to which broth is added
Quesillo – quesillo cheese is placed in a tortilla, onions, vinegar added with cream and salt on top
Sopa de Mondongo – mondago soup with onion, pepper, garlic, rice, corn, chayote and other vegetables

Rondon – meat, turtle, or fish cooked with peppers, nargan, onions, banana, yucca, and quesquisque

Tres leches – cake with milk, tres leches - condensed milk and cream, and topped with a meringue
Cajeta de coco – coconut, coconut water, yucca and dulce

Holidays and Special Occasions

Most Nicaraguans are Catholic, Evangelists, or Moravians, and celebrate those holidays.
New Year's Day - parties
For forty days before Easter, people and do not eat meat. The week before Easter is celebrated with processions. Santa Entierro or Service of Darkness is held on Good Friday.
Easter –
Dia de los Muertos – Day of the Dead- November 2 – families honor their ancestors with flowerds, bread, fruit and candy in their homes and at the cemeteries
La Purisima – December 7 - honors the Virgin Mary with singing and prayers, children going to homes and offered treats such as rosquillas, leche de burra "donkey's milk" candy, oranges, and sweets
Before Christmas – manger scenes – prayers are held each evening in homes with Christmas carols and food, Christmas trees, Santa Claus
Christmas Eve – Mass followed by a feast of stuffed chicken, nacatamal, rice, bread, and bizcocho (sponge cake) and everyone greeting each other with "Feliz Navidad!"
Quinceanera- party with fancy dresses and food held for girls when they turn 15

Beverages

Arroz-con-pina is a boiled rice and pineapple drink to which sugar, rum, or other ingredients are added. Chichka-de Maiz uses softened and ground corn to which is added red coloring, then dulce, water, and sugar. Gaubal is made of mashed green bananas, milk, coconut water and sugar. Chicha and pinol are corn - based drinks.

Niger

Niger is a landlocked country in Western Africa bordered by Libya to the northeast, Chad to the east, Nigeria and Benin to the south, Burkina Faso and Mali to the west, and Algeria to the northwest. Over 80% of its land area lies in the Sahara Desert. In prehistoric times the climate was wet and good for agriculture and livestock. By the 5th c BC Niger was on the trans-Saharan trade route with Berber tribes in the north using camels for transportation. Islam was introduced in the 7th c AD. Empires and kingdoms existed during this time period. The Songhai Empire was located in the bend of the Niger River in what is present day Niger, Mali and Burkina Faso from 600-1591. The Hausa kingdoms flourished from the mid 14th c to 1808 between the Niger River and Lake Chad. The Mali Empire was a Madinka empire founded c 1230 to 1600 that extended from present day Senegal and Guinee Conakry to western Niger. The Kanem Bornu Empire existed from the 9th c to 1900 in what is now Chad, Nigeria, Cameroon, Niger, and Libya. During the 19th c French and German explorers traveled to Niger and in 1922 Niger became a French colony. The Republic of Niger was created in 1958. The capital city is Niamey, located in Niger's southwest corner. The official language is French, with Hausa, Fula, Djema/Songhai, Tamashek and eight other languages spoken.

Dining Etiquette

It is a privilege to be invited for a meal. Please arrive promptly and clap your hands when approaching the home. Bring a gift from your country. Do greet your host shaking hands. The right hand is used for touching people, to hand something to someone, and for eating. Do ask about the family and then engage in conversation. If you are offered something to drink please accept it. Tea will be offered three times. Please accept each glass. Food is shared from a common platter, take from in front of you. Sharing is part of the dining ritual. Men, women and children may eat separately. Please just do as your host offers. Hands will be washed before and after the meal. Most of the population is Muslim so pork and alcoholic beverages are not consumed.

Dodo (Fried Plantains)

Serves 6

6 or more ripe plantains, sliced thin lengthwise
Palm oil, coconut oil or peanut oil

Heat oil in a skillet and deeply fry or saute bananas.
Serve as a side dish, snack or dessert.

Cuisine

The cuisine of Niger has been influenced by local, Arabic, and French traditions. Since much of the country is desert it has often been difficult to grow crops and raise livestock here. There is some farmland along the Niger River. Millet is the main grain. It is pounded into flour and made into a porridge or dough and served with stews or sauces. Rice or couscous is served on special occasions. Other basic foods include cassava, sorghum, groundnuts, maize, black-eyed peas, and beans. Goat and camel are used for their milk and meat products. Meat is grilled. Fish are found in the Niger River and guinea fowl, chicken, but not in abundance. Spices may include ginger, cloves, saffron, nutmeg and cinnamon but these are used sparingly. Salads start a meal followed by a starch served with a sauce or stew.

Specialties

Shinkafa – rice balls
Tattabara – grilled pigeon
Jollof rice
Deguidegui – tomato stew
Efo – greens stew

Palm nut soup
Foura – ground fermented millet with sugar, milk and spices
Millet porridge
Laban – frozen yogurt

Holidays and Special Occasions

Tabaski – Feast of Sacrifice
Mouloud - Prophet's birthday – roasted camel and goat –gathering of families
Eid al Adha – commemoration of Abraham's sacrifice – lamb or goat
Ramadan – no eating from sunrise to sunset for Muslims
Eid al Fitr – end of Ramadan to break fast
La Cure Salee – at the end of September in In-Gall west of Agadez, the salt flats are flooded with rainwater and the nomadic herders come to feed their animals and look for wives. Gathering of the Tuareg and Fulani clans
Guerewol – Fulani matchmaking festival for young men at the end of the rainy season
Hotoungo - at Gangui – farmer's festival
Fishermen's Festival at Karay-Kopto

Beverages

Serving tea follows a ritual where it will be offered three times. The tea will use the same leaves for each round, but the amount of sugar is increased.

Nigeria

Nigeria is a republic in West Africa, bordering Benin in the west, Chad and Cameroon in the east, and Niger in the north and the coast in the south lies on the Gulf of Guinea in the Atlantic Ocean. The Nok civilization of Northern Nigeria flourished between 500 BC and AD 200, producing life-sized terracotta figures that are some of the earliest known sculptures in Sub-Saharan Africa. Hausa kingdoms and the Kanem-Bornu Empire prospered as trade posts between North and West Africa. The Kingdom of Nri of the Igbo people consolidated in the 10th century and continued until it lost its sovereignty to the British in 1911. The Yoruba kingdoms of Ife and Oyo in southwestern Nigeria became prominent in the 12th and 14th centuries, respectively and the oldest signs of human settlement at Ife's current site date back to the 9th century. Oyo, at its territorial zenith in the late 17th to early 18th centuries, extended its influence from western Nigeria to modern-day Togo. The Edo's Benin Empire is located in southwestern Nigeria. In the 16th century, Spanish and Portuguese explorers were the first Europeans to begin significant, direct trade with peoples of modern-day Nigeria, at the port they named Lagos and in Calabar. The Europeans led to the cultivation of many agricultural products including palm. In 1901 Nigeria became a British protectorate and in 1914, the British formally united the Niger area as the Colony and Protectorate of Nigeria and achieved independence in 1960. The capital, Abuja, was built beginning in 1981. The country is mainly Muslim in north and Christian in the south. The official language is English with Yoruba, Hausa, Igbo, and more than 400 other languages spoken.

Dining Etiquette

Please arrive promptly or just slightly late when invited for a meal. Please bring a gift from your country. When entering a home remove your shoes. Older people enter first into a home or room. Please shake hands greeting and departing. Tea will be served three times. During the first tea is not sweetened, the second has some sugar added, and the third sweet tea is served as a symbol of friendship. Always accept the tea when it is passed to you. People of the same sex when talking may stand or sit close to each other. Hands are washed before and after the meal. Food may be eaten with the right hand, or if utensils are provided please use your right hand for the fork. Do not use your left hand or pass something with your left hand. During the meal please eat first and drink something. Wait to be served and do not pour your own drink. Men, women and children dine separately with the men offered the best food first. The honored guest is served first. Do not eat until the oldest man has been served and starts to eat. If communal bowls or plates are used for serving eat only from the one in front of you. You may be seated on low stools or on the floor. The guest of honor is next to the host. Make sure your toes and feet are not pointing to the food or other diners. At the end of the meal a small burp shows you are satisfied. Muslims do not drink alcohol or eat pork.

Efo Riro (Meat and Vegetable Stew)

Serves 6

2 lbs. lamb or beef, cubed
2 cups water
½ palm or peanut oil
1 large onion, finely chopped
1 large green pepper, finely chopped

Red peppers (as many as you want for seasoning)
2 fresh tomatoes
½ lb. fresh spinach or kale
¼ lb. smoked fish
2 oz. dried shrimp

In large pan or Dutch oven, cook the meat for 15 minutes. Add water, oil, onion, and pepper. Bring to boil and simmer for 10 minutes. Add tomatoes, spinach, fish and shrimp. Season with salt to taste. Add red pepper for flavoring and make as hot as you want. Boil for 5 minutes.
Serve with rice.

Cuisine and Beverages

The most common products used in cooking are cocoa, coffee, palm oil, livestock, poultry, sorghum, maize, rice, millet, yams, groundnuts, okra, fish, and cassava. The food may be hot and spicy such as pepper sauce with chicken, fish or meat. The Niger River is important for fish and transportation. Kunu, a beverage, is made from millct, sorghum or maize. Fura da nono is a drink made of cooked pounded millet or sorghum to which is added cow's milk; zobo made from roselle juice; and soya bean milk from soya bean seeds. Palm wine is produced. Regional dishes in the north which is mainly Muslim – beans, sorghum, brown rice; east – Ibo speaking - gari, yams, dumplings; southeast – seafood, yams, yam stew; and southwest – Yoruba people - gari, okra, stews and soups, and spinach.

Nigerian Specialties

Okro – okra soup
Gari – coarse cassava powder
Moi moi – steamed bean and vegetable dish
Chinchin – hot fried dough
Goat or beef kebabs
Eba - hot pepper soup with a cassava flour dumpling
Dodo – fried plantains
Eja gbigbe – fried catfish on a stick
Coconut rice – rice cooked in coconut milk
Jolloff – rice with tomatoes and peppers
Pate – ground dry corn, rice or acha with vegetables, tomatoes, peppers, eggs, beans, groundnuts and may have meat
Tuwo shinkafa – rice pudding eaten with miyan kuku, a thick soup, goat stew, miyan

Taushe, a pumpkin stew with spinach, meat, and smoked fish
Suya – grilled meat with chili and peanut powders prepared on a stick
Kilishi – dried thin meat with paste of chili pepper, spices and herbs that is grilled
Balangu – meat grilled over a coal or wood fire
Nkwobi – cows' legs cooked in a sauce
Banga – palm nut soup
Ofe akwu – palm nut stew eaten with rice
Miyan kuka – powdered baobob leaves and dried okra
Pepper soup - meat and fish soup with herbs and spices

Maafe – groundnut, tomato, and onion stew which may or may not have meat or fish ground
Groundnut stew – ground dry groundnuts, vegetables, meat, fish, and palm oil
Afang – vegetable soup
Omi ukpoka – dry corn and smoked fish soup
Okoroenyeribe – okra or ogbono seed soup
Atama – palm kernel soup
Egusi – ground melon seed and leafy vegetable soup
Miyan taushe – groundnut and pumpkin leaves with pepper and Knorr cubes
Ogbono soup – ogbono seeds with leafy greens, spices, and meat eaten with mashed yams or fufu
Ofe onugbu – bitterleaf soup
Ofada stew – palm oil, peppers, tomatoes, beef, and locust beans
Funkaso – millet pancakes
Iyan – pounded yams

Lafun – cassava dish
Asaro – yam porridge with tomato, chili and red pepper sauce, and palm oil
Mosa – fried fermented ground corn paste served with sugar
Moin moin – steamed black-eyed pea pudding in a leaf
Okpo ogede – plantain pudding
Okpo oka – corn pudding
Masa – ground rice to which yogurt is added, fermented, and poured into clay forms and heated. This served with miyan taushe or honey for breakfast and lunch
Alkubus – steamed bread made of wheat, flour, yeast and water and steamed in molds
Chin chin – fried wheat flour, egg and butter dough
Dun dun – fried slices of yam
Ojojo – grated water yam, pepper, onion beignet

Amazing Quality's Moi Moi

3 medium onions, peeled and chopped
5 red chili peppers
5 cloves garlic
1 tbls. minced fresh ginger
2½ oz. tomato paste
1 tbls. vegetable oil

4 cubes chicken bouillon
1 kg. bean flour
5 liters warm water
2 eggs, beaten
1 tin sardines, chopped

In a food processor blend the onions, peppers, garlic, and ginger to form a paste. Add tomato paste and blend to combine. Heat oil in a large sauce pan over medium heat. Add onion mixture and bouillon cubes. Saute 5 minutes, stirring occasionally. Set stock aside. Pour bean flour into a large bowl. Discard dry peppers included in package. Add warm water and mix well to combine. Stir in reserved stock mixture, eggs and sardines. Scoop mixture into 8-10 greased ramekins. Stack ramekins in a large stock pot with 1-2 inches of water. Cover and steam over low heat for 50 minutes, replenishing water as necessary. Remove from heat and cool 10-15 minutes. Unmold by turning upside down on a plate and shaking gently. Serve warm.
Recipe courtesy of Grace Ekpenyong, Uyo, Nigeria

Holidays and Special Occasions

Ramadan – during Ramadan Muslims fast from sunrise to sundown
Kano durbar – end of Ramadan – much feasting
Weddings, christenings, Christmas, birthdays – chinchin, sweet puffs

405

North Korea

North Korea is located on the northern part of the Korean Peninsula bordered by China and by Russia along the Amnok (known as the Yalu in China) and Tumen rivers; and to the south by South Korea. The history of Korea dates back 600,000 years when the peninsula was first settled. In 2333 BC Tankun founded Ko-Chosen "Land of Morning Calm" at P'yongyang. Successive kingdoms followed. The Mongols invaded in the 13th c, the Japanese in the 16th c., and the Chinese the 17th c. The Yi Dynasty in order to protect the country from invasion adopted an isolationist attitude and the country became known as the "Hermit Kingdom". In 1910, Korea was annexed by Imperial Japan. After the Japanese surrender at the end of World War II in 1945, Korea was divided into two zones, with the north occupied by the Soviet Union and the south occupied by the United States. Negotiations on reunification failed, and in 1948, separate governments were formed: the Democratic People's Republic of Korea in the north, and the Republic of Korea in the south. Pyongyang is the capital. Korean is the official language.

Dining Etiquette

Please be punctual when invited for a meal. The Koreans love to entertain at home or in a restaurant, for which it is an honor to be invited. Please remove your shoes before entering a home. If bringing a gift present it with both hands. Please shake hands greeting and departing. Bow, with a slight nod of the head, and more deeply to elders or superiors. Women offer their hand first. Speak softly and have little eye contact. The most common names are Kim (Gold), Lee (Plum), and Park (White). Women keep and often use their maiden name. Rice wine or beer are served before the meal with panch'an (appetizers). You will probably be seated on cushions around low tables. The men sit crossed legged, the women side saddle. Do not step on these cushions. Before the meal "mulsugun", a moist warm clothe, is handed to each guest to wipe one's hands. Food is always served together, not in courses. On the table will be bowls for serving the rice and accompanying dishes. Do not lift the bowl to your mouth, or even pick up. Please do not use your fingers. Chopsticks and flat spoons are used. Rice and soup are eaten with the spoon, while the chopsticks are used to take the food from the various serving dishes and are left with them. When finished lay them together on the table. Do not leave the chopsticks in the bowl. If something is to be passed, do so with your right hand only.

If dining in a private home, the hostess will often prepare and serve the food, not seated with the guests. A usual meal is meat, rice or noodles, soup, side dishes and tea. Tea is often served after the meal. Meals are considered solemn occasions, and not much talk transpires. Desserts, if served, are sweets, cakes, or fresh fruit such as strawberries, persimmons, plums, or apples. Shikye is a sweet rice drink served following the meal.

Naengmyeon (Cold Noodle Soup)

Serves 4

3 cups beef broth
1 lb. dried naengmyeon noodles, or clear noodles
1 cucumber, halved and sliced lengthwise
2 Korean pears, sliced
4 oz. pickled radish

½ tsp. salt
1 tsp. sugar
1 tbls. vinegar
1 tsp. spicy yellow mustard powder
2 hardboiled eggs, peeled and sliced in half lengthwise

Place the beef broth in a plastic or other container and freeze for 3-4 hours.
Cook the noodles according to the directions. Drain and place in a bowl.
Remove broth from freezer. It should be slightly slushy.
Add salt, sugar, vinegar and mustard powder.
Pour the broth over the noodles.
Garnish with cucumber, Korean pears, pickled radish, and sliced eggs.
Serve cold.

Cuisine

Hansik (Korean cuisine) uses native vegetables, rice, fruits, fish and meat. Cooking combines the five tastes – bitter, salty, sour, sweet, and hot; and the five colors – red, green, yellow, white, and black. Rice is the mainstay of each meal, eaten with side dishes such as kimchi; grilled beef or fish; and vegetables. Food is chopped into small pieces, and each dish must compliment the others – hot and fiery with rice for example. Most meat is cooked in "hot pots" or grilled. Some is cooked right at the table. Pork is basically for the poor; beef for the well-to-do. The Koreans make use of sesame seeds, soybean paste, ginger root, green onions, mung beans, dried chili peppers, and garlic. Seafood includes sea cucumbers, sea urchins, octopus, squid, pollock, herring, mackerel, tuna, bass, sole, halibut, cod, croaker, and skate. Breakfast is a hearty meal; lunch light; and dinner filling.

Specialties

Kimchi – the national dish, Cabbage is seasoned with red pepper powder, garlic, ginger, and anchovies, then put in earthernware jars and allowed to ferment. Each region has its own version.
Hanjeongsik – feast with small plates that might includesmoked fish, beef, noodles, and soup
Samgyeopsal – grilled pork belly
Mandu – stuffed dumplings
Hobakjon – summer squash pancakes
Bibimpap – rice with vegetables and beef

Sinsullo – sliced beef served in a brass pot with vegetables, nuts and hot broth
Haemultang – sea food stew
Galbijjim – braised short ribs
Pajon – is a favorite snack –spring onion pancakes
Nanuls – salads or freshly steamed vegetables
Bulgogi – beef marinated in soy sauce
Kalbi – barbecued beef ribs
Chigae – a thick stew
Bibimbap – mixed vegetables with rice

Jon – batter fried fish and vegetables
Pokkum – stir-fried dishes
Dak-bokkeum-tang – spicy chicken stew
Han-gwa – sweets, often made of puffed rice.
Hodu kwaja – walnutshaped cake with bean paste
Gamja-sujebi – soup with dough flakes and vegetables

Topokki – stir-fried rice cake
Fruits represent different things – oranges, happiness; pomegranate, fertility; apples, peace; and pears, prosperity.

Holidays and Special Occasions

New Year's – dishes prepared for the family and ancestors – duck kook (duck soup), rice cake soup, kimchi, rice, tteok (rice cakes), fruit, benne (sesame) or ginger candy

First full moon of the year – it is traditional to drink wine to prevent deafness. People visit 12 homes and are feed a great deal of food. A traditional dish consists of plain and glutinous rice, millet, corn, and red beans.

Spring – kimchi is made with white radishes, no garlic or chilies.

Summer - Koreans eat noodles for strength, as they are a symbol of longevity, and are cut with scissors.

Fall- kimchi is made at this time to get families through the long winters.

Chusock (Thanksgiving) – people visit family tombs and bring ancestors food.

Longest night of the year – red bean curd is served

Birth of a son – red peppers are hung on a doorway

100 days after a birth – a feast and rice cakes are prepared for family and friends, and if shared with 100 people the belief is the child will have a long life.

Birthdays – the 1st and 61st are most important. A 70th birthday (kohi) means "old and rare" is celebrated with a large party.

Rice cakes are served for a first birthday, New Year's and weddings

1st and 2nd anniversary of a death – serve five kinds of soup; 5 types of meat, fish or vegetables with wine, rice, noodles, rice cakes, and pickles

Drinks

Tea is a very important part of the meal. Rice wine and rice liquor (makkoli) have been produced for hundreds of years. Makkoli is often served from tubs.

North Macedonia

North Macedonia borders Kosovo to the northwest, Serbia to the north, Bulgaria to the east, Greece to the south, and Albania to the west. The country's earliest inhabitant were the Paonians and Dardani. In the 6th c BC it was captured by Darius, the Persian king; the 4th c by Alexander the Great; and the 2nd c BC by the Romans. Slavic peoples settled in the Balkan region including Macedonia by the late 6th century AD. In 1014, the Byzantine Emperor Basil II defeated the armies of Tsar Samuil of Bulgaria, and within four years the Byzantines restored control over the Balkans (including Macedonia) for the first time since the 7th century. However, by the late 12th century, Byzantine decline saw the region contested by various political entities, including a brief Norman occupation in the 1080s. In the 14th century, it became part of the Serbian Empire. Gradually, all of the central Balkans were conquered by the Ottoman Empire and remained under its domination for five centuries. By the 19th c there were movements to establish an autonomous Macedonia. Following the two Balkan wars of 1912 and 1913 and the dissolution of the Ottoman Empire, most of its European-held territories were divided between Greece, Bulgaria and Serbia. The territory of the modern Macedonian state was annexed by Serbia and named *Južna Srbija*, "Southern Serbia". In 1929, the Kingdom was officially renamed the Kingdom of Yugoslavia, later the Republic of Yugoslavia Macedonia in 1991, and today North Macedonia. The capital is Skopje and the official language Macedonian.

Dining Etiquette

Please shake hands greeting and departing. Men and women may kiss if they know each other well. Gift giving is very important, and if you are given something, please return with your own gift. Never give money as it could be misconstrued as a bribe! Flowers are not usually presented. Instead take a small painting, book, or something from your own country. If there are children present, please bring something for them. Drinks will be served, mainly grape rakija. The hostess will seat the guests at the table. Dishes will probably be served by the host. There may be an abundance of food, even though the family may not have much. Please do not start eating until the hostess does. The toast is "Na zdravye!"

Cuisine

Macedonian cuisine has been influenced by Roman, Slav, Greek, Bulgarian, Serb, and Ottoman cooking. The relatively warm climate in Macedonia provides excellent growth conditions for a variety of vegetables – eggplant, peppers, tomatoes, onions, garlic, herbs and fruits – apples, plums, blackberries. Peppers are hung out to dry to make ajvar. Being a landlocked country the fish is mainly fresh such as trout. The country has a rich variety of dairy products.

Tavce Gravce (Bean Casserole)

6 cups dry white beans
3 onions, peeled and chopped
3 chile peppers, seeded and chopped
3 tbls. oil

Salt and pepper
Parsley
Mint

Soak the beans in water overnight. Drain.
Bring a pan of water to a boil. Add the beans, until just slightly softened. Drain water.
Heat the oil in a skillet and sauté the onions until translucent. Add the beans and chiles.
Preheat oven to 350°
Place beans in an earthenware ovenproof pot. Sprinkle with salt, pepper, mint and parsley.
Bake for 20 minutes-30 minutes, but do not let beans dry out.
Mint and parsley can be added after baking instead of before.
Tomatoes, leeks, or other vegetables can be added to the casserole.

Moussaka (ground lamb casserole with sliced eggplant)

Serves

3 large aubergine (eggplant)
¼ cup olive oil
1 large onion, finely chopped
2 cloves garlic, minced
2 lbs. ground lamb

2 large tomatoes, finely chopped
½ cup red wine
½ tsp. oregano
½ tsp. cinnamon
2tbls. parsley, chopped

Preheat oven to 350
Wrap the eggplant in tin foil. Bake in oven until soft, at least ½ hour. Cool, slice and season with a little salt.
Heat the oil in a pan and saute the onions until softened. Add garlic and lamb. Cook until lamb is just pink. Add the tomatoes, wine, oregano, cinnamon and parley. Simmer for 15 minutes.
Grease a baking dish. Arrange half the aubergine in the dish. Top with meat sauce, and rest of aubergine. Pour the béchamel sauce on top.
Bake for 30-40 minutes.
The aubergine can also be salted and floured and fried in oil.

Bechamel Sauce

¼ cup butter
¼ cup flour

4cups hot milk
¼ tsp. nutmeg

Melt the butter and stir in the flour. Slowly add the hot milk until thickened. Add nutmeg.

Macedonian Specialties

Burek - Dough with meat, cheese or spinach filling

Simit pogacha – burek without a filling

Makalo – garlic sauce

Shirden – stuffed lamb stomach

Shopska salad – side dish of tomatoes, cucumbers and salty cheese

Tarator – sour cream or yogurt salad with cucumbers, garlic, walnuts, and oil

Yogurtlitava – rice, meat and yogurt dish

Ajvar – roasted red pepper, eggplant or tomatoes, garlic, chili relish that is served with bread, as a condiment or salad

Kashkaval – yellow sheep milk cheese

Kora – baked flat dough with fillings- spinach, cheese, potato, cheese, cabbage or eggs

Sarma – stuffed cabbage or grape leaves

Podvarok – sauerkraut casserole

Kompir mandza – potato stew

Zlenik – pie filled ground meat, spinach or cheese

Pastrmajlija – pie made from dough, meat and eggs (from pastrma – salted or dried meat); fried eggs are served on top

Skara – grilled meats

Pindzhur – roasted peppers, eggplant, and tomato dish

Piperki polneti – stuffed peppers

Kacamak – corn porridge

Kozinjak – braided sweet bread with raisins

Lokum – "Turkish Delight" – melted sugar with cornstarch and nuts in a cube shape

Sutlijach – rice pudding

Ravanija – coconut and egg sponge soaked in syrup

Tulumba – fried pastry with syrup

Holidays and Special Occasions

Kolede (January 5th) – people sing carols, and are given nuts, fruit and coins, then gather around bonfire and feast. A Christmas bread is served with a coin. Whoever receives the coin will have good luck in the coming year.

Christmas Eve (January 6th) meal "posna" - no dairy, meat or animal products are served. Instead fish, nuts, fruit, bread, kidney bean soup, potato salad, ajvar, sarma, pickled vegetables, and a cake with a coin will be served. Straw may be on the floor or under the tablecloth.

Orthodox Christmas (January 7th) – people attend church after which the Christmas dinner is served. This will include roasted meat, cheese pies, salads, breads, cakes and other treats

Great Lent – people fast for 40 days before Easter

Good Friday – people fast and eat nuts, fruit and vegetables

Easter Eve – people attend church, greet each other at midnight, and tap eggs symbolizing Christ's resurrection and breaking the fast

Easter – eggs are dyed red, Easter bread with a dyed red egg, lamb soup, sarma, salads, cakes and perhaps Kukurec, a lamb intestine dish prepared in a clay pot

Beverages

Macedonia has produced wine since ancient times. The Tikves Valley is especially known for its wines. Rakija is made from distilled fermented fruit, or walnuts. Mastika is a liquor made from the resin of the mastic tree and contains 45% alcohol. This may contain raisins, grapes, plums or figs, and is served with meze (small dishes). Beer is produced from barley malt; unmalted cereals; hops; and brewers' yeast. Fermented milk is popular in some parts of the country.

Norway

Norway, "The Way to the North" located on the Scandinavian Peninsula is bordered by Sweden, Finland, Russia, and the North Atlantic. The earliest people date back to the last Ice Age 11,000-8,000BC and tools dating back to 9500-6000BC have been discovered. Rock carvings depict deer, reindeer, elk, bears, birds, seals, whales and fish were prevalent and most likely part of their diet. By 3000BC Indo-European farmers arrived and grew grain, cows, and sheep. Later the Romans influenced the culture. From the 8-10th c AD Vikings colonized the region and traded with the rest of Europe. In the 14th c Sweden and Norway were united under King Magnus VII, with Denmark joining later. Sweden left the union in 1521, and in 1905 Sweden became a separate country. The capital, Oslo, is basically a new city, much having been destroyed by fire. Norwegian is the official language.

Dining Etiquette

Please be punctual when invited out. Take a small gift of chocolates, wine, liquor or send flowers ahead. Shake hands greeting and departing. Drinks will be served. The host and hostess will sit at opposite ends of the table, the male guest of honor to the left of the hostess. The Norwegians love to toast and will do so on all occasions. This is called skaaling and is never done with beer or water. The host skaals first, all raise their glasses, the host catches the eye of each guest, and then all drink. In earlier times the host and hostess might also sing before skaaling. Each guest may then skaal and/or drink. At the end of the meal the guest of honor should thank and toast the host. Thank-you is said again on leaving.

Cuisine

Even though Norway is situated in the very north of the world, they can still grow many of their foodstuffs, livestock and seafood and fresh water fish are readily available. Sour cream is used or served in many dishes, as are eggs, butter and sauces. Vegetables consumed are rutabagas, cauliflower, spinach, caraway sprouts, spring nettles, and cucumbers. Seafood includes shrimp, langoustes, herring, mussels, cod, trout, salmon, haddock, mackerel, and coalfish. Because of long winters much fish is dried, pickled, and salted. Meats are lamb, mutton, pork, goat, whale, reindeer and seal. The most commonly used herbs are caraway seeds, dill, thyme, and horseradish. Fruit includes blueberries, cloudberries, ligonberries, pears, plums, morello cherries, and rhubarb. Stews are eaten during the long winters.

Surkal (Sauerkraut)

1 head cabbage, shredded
2 tbls. oil
2 cups water
2 tbls. flour
1 tsp. salt

2 tsp. caraway seeds
1 apple, finely chopped
1½ tsp. vinegar
2 tsp. sugar

Heat the oil in a pan and add the cabbage, water, flour, salt, caraway seed, and apple. Bring to boil and simmer for 1 hour. Add vinegar and sugar. More vinegar or sugar can be added for taste.

Julekake (Christmas Cake)

Makes 2 cakes

2 pkg. dry yeast
½ cup warm water
1 cup milk, scalded
½ stick butter, softened
1 egg, beaten
½ cup sugar

1 tsp. salt
1 tsp. ground cardamom
¾ cup diced citron
¾ cup raisins
5 cups flour
1 egg, beaten

Dissolve the yeast in the water.
Mix milk, butter, and egg in a bowl. Let cool. Stir in yeast. Add sugar, salt, cardamom and 2 cups flour. Beat well.
Stir in fruit and remaining flour. Turn onto a floured surface and knead 8-10 minutes. Shape into a ball and place in a greased bowl. Let double, about an hour. Punch down dough. Divide into 2 equal parts.
Grease 2 cake pans. Place the dough in each pan. Cover and let rise 45 minutes.
Preheat oven to 350°. Brush with beaten egg.
Bake 35-40 minutes, or until toothpick comes out clean.
Serve with butter.

Holidays and Special Occasions

Christmas Eve – lutefisk, torsk (cod), rullepolse (rolled spiced beef), surkal, sylte (head cheese), sotsuppe (fruit soup), risgrot (rice pudding), rommegrot (sour cream porridge)
Christmas – fattigmannbakkels "poor man's pastry" (fried rich butter cookies with brandy), krumkaker – pastry cones with peppermint whipped cream
Weddings, confirmations – kransekake – a tiered cake made with rings of almond paste and egg whites

Weddings go on for three days – cakes, rommerot (sour cream porridge with cinnamon and sugar served in rural areas)

Brudlaupskling – wedding cake

Aquavit is often consumed during festive gatherings such as Christmas, New Year's, and weddings.

Norwegian Specialties

Lefse – potato flatbread baked on a griddle

Rakorret – fermented trout

Spekemat – salt cured meats

Spekeskinke – cured ham that is thinly sliced

Far I kal- mutton and cabbage stew

Puss puss – mutton, cabbage, potato and carrot stew

Lutefisk – lye-cured cod

Torrfisk – dried fish

Klippfisk – salted and dried fish

Fiskudding – fish pudding

Fiskesuppe – fish soup

Gammelost (gammel "old" and ost "cheese" – cheese made from sour milk

Gronn Genser – green sweater cake, a cake with green marzipan frosting

Kakebord – dessert table for special occasions

Rabarbragrot – rhubarb compote

Lefser – thin bread made of potatoes served with butter and folded over

Beverages

Beer has been brewed for over 1000 years. The most popular are Pilsner, a pale lager; Bayer, a dark malt; Juleol and Bokko. The national drink is *Akvavit* (Aquavit), an alcoholic beverage made with potatoes and grain with herbs and spices – caraway, cumin, or fennel. *Mead* is made from fermented sugar derived from honey and has been called "honey wine", and is mainly drunk during the cold winters. *Cider* is produced from apple juice, spices and herbs, and can be served hot or cold. Cider is also known as apple wine. *Brennevin* "burn-wine." is a strong liquor distilled from potatoes and grains with an alcohol content of 30 to 38 percent. Punsch is made with alcohol, water, sugar, fruit, and spices. It is sometimes flavored with liqueur to produce a chocolate, almond or banana flavor, and is served hot during the winter. Vodka is also produced in Norway, the best known being Vikingfjord using water from the Jostedalsbreen glacier with an alcohol content of 40! Most wine is imported into Norway with its cold climate, but wines and other drinks are made from blackberries and apples.

Oman

Oman is a country on the southeastern coast of the Arabian Peninsula with the United Arab Emirates to the northwest, Saudi Arabia to the west, and Yemen to the southwest, and it shares marine borders with Iran and Pakistan. In 2011 a Nubian complex was discovered that dates back over 100,000 years ago. Baat had wheel-turned pottery, hand-made stone vessels, a metals industry, and monumental architecture. Over the centuries tribes from the west settled in Oman, making a living by fishing, farming, herding or stock breeding. From the late 17th century, the Omani Sultanate was a powerful empire. In the 19th century, Omani influence or control extended across the Strait of Hormuz to modern-day Iran and Pakistan, and as far south as Zanzibar. As its power declined in the 20th century, the sultanate came under the influence of the United Kingdom.¹ Historically, Muscat was the principal trading port of the Persian Gulf region and the Indian Ocean. In 1497–98, the Portuguese arrived in Oman and occupied Muscat for a 143-year period, from 1507 to 1650. The Ottoman Turks captured Muscat from the Portuguese in 1581 and held it until 1588. Rebellious tribes eventually drove out the Portuguese, but were themselves pushed out about a century later, in 1741, by the leader of an Omani tribe, who began the current line of ruling sultans. Muscat is the capital and the official language is Arabic.

Dining Etiquette

It is an honor to be entertained in a home. Please bring a small gift, never alcoholic beverages or anything made of pigskin. Please present the gift with your right hand. Please greet your host by saying "Salaam Alaykum", then shake hands and say "Kaif Halak". Women extend their hands first, or may not. The host may put his left hand on the shoulder of another male. And when you get to know him better may kiss you on each cheek. Holding hands is a sign of a warm friendship. Strong coffee or tea will be served with dates, nuts or raisins. When seated please keep both feet on the ground, do not show the soles of your shoe, or point it at someone. Men and women may dine separately. Before a meal hands are washed and a prayer "in the name of God" is always said. Only the right hand is used for eating, though fingers are used when no utensil is available. When served wait for your host to start. Never leave your plate empty, or it will be refilled. If you pass something do so with your right hand. If you are the guest of honor and a feast is served, a whole sheep might be served including the eye which is considered a delicacy. Please eat the eye when presented to you. Hands are also washed after the meal. Do write or telephone a thank-you.

Cuisine and Beverages

The food of Oman has been influenced by Arab, Persian, Indian, Asian, Mediterranean and African cuisines. As mentioned above it was in the center of major trading routes, so spices, herbs, sauces, and many dishes came from all over. Chicken, fish, lamb, rice, curries; vegetables, especially smoked aubergine; and soups are the more common ingredients. Oman is a Muslim country and alcoholic beverages are consumed. Fruit drinks, tea, and coffee are drunk. Tea or kahwa, coffee with cardamom is served to guests as a sign of hospitality. These are served with dates and halwa. Laban and yogurt drinks are also served.

Albadhinajan Mae Tawarikh (eggplant, date and onion cake)

2 large eggplant	¼ cup olive oil
2 large onions, finely chopped	1 tbls. rose syrup
12 dates, finely chopped	Salt

Preheat oven to 200° C
Wash the eggplant and cut into cubes. Place in a bowl with 3 tbls. olive oil and combine. Or until tender. Saute the onions in 1 tbls. olive oil until just softened. Add dates and sugar syrup. Add eggplant. Pour into a mold. Unmold and serve over couscous or bulgur.

Halwa (Semolina Candy)

1 cup olive oil	3 cups milk
3 cups semolina	1 cup water
2 cups sugar	

Heat the olive oil in a pan. Pour in the semolina, stirring constantly. Reduce heat and stir 20 minutes until oil is absorbed. The color should be slightly brown. Add the sugar, and stir in the milk and water. Cook 10 minutes, constantly stirring. Do not let it burn, but it should be thickened. Pour into a square baking dish. Let set until firm. Cut into squares.

Specialties

Muqalab – tripe cooked with spices
Harees – wheat with meat or chicken to form a paste, and eaten with a spoon or your fingers
Kebab – skewered and grilled meat

Mashuai – spit-roasted kingfish with lemon rice
Machboos – rice cooked in meat or beef stock and flavored with saffron

Holidays and Special Occasions

Ramadan – fasting from sun up to sunset. After breaking the fast sakhana, a soup made of wheat, molasses, dates and milk is served
Eid al-Fitr - the feast at the end of Ramadan
Eid al-Adha - the Feast of Sacrifice
Holiday meals will include dates, raisins, nuts, soups, lamb or chicken, stuffed vegetables, bean or bulgur wheat salads, hummus, rice, flat breads, and desserts.
Festive occasions – shuwaa is a meal of goat, sheep, cow or camel marinated in a date spice mixture and wrapped in dry leaves. This is cooked in a ground pit.

Pakistan

Pakistan is northwest of India and was part of the partition of India in 1947 with a large Muslim population. Its earliest inhabitants lived in the Soan Valley where early stone tools have been found. In the Indus region were the Neolithic Mehrgarh, and during the Bronze Age the Indus Valley civilization (2800-1800 BC), followed by the Vedic Civilization (1500-500 BC). Taxila in the Punjab had some of the earliest centers of learning in the world. Hindu, Indo-Greek, and Greco-Buddhist cultures flourished. The Pala Dynasty was the last Buddhist empire and stretched across South Asia from what is now Bangladesh, northern India, and Pakistan. The Arabs conquered the Indus Valley in 711AD, and much of the population was converted to Islam. The Moghul Empire (1526-1857) introduced Persian influences. The East India Company established coastal outposts in the 18th c with the British taking over most of India in the 1800s. The capital is Islamabad. The official languages are Urdu and English.

Dining Etiquette

Please be punctual when invited for a meal. Please shake hands greeting and departing, or with folded hands (Namaste). Women do not usually shake hands, and men may not offer hands to a woman. When greeting a superior or to show respect, a slight bow can be used. Drinks will be offered, probably beer and whisky along with a snack, or in some homes where tea is served. You may be seated at a table for the meal, or on cushions where you will cross-legged. Many Pakistani eat sitting on a cloth known as a Dastarkhān, which is spread out on the floor, or at a takht, a raised platform, where people eat their food sitting cross-legged, after taking their shoes off. In some cases men and women may be separated. Never enter a kitchen. Meals will be served with all courses on the table, or separately on silver or brass trays. Always wash your hands before eating. The hostess will serve the food to the guests and men first, followed by the women. Food is eaten with the right hand. A fork, fingers, or bread can also be utilized. Watch how the hostess eats. Food is passed with the right hand. Men may share food from their own plate.

Cuisine

The Pakistani cuisine has been influenced mainly by Indian, Arabic, and Persian food. Sesame, eggplant and humped cattle were known to have been domesticated c3000BC in the Indus Valley, and spices used such as turmeric, cardamom, black pepper and mustard. Later wheat and rice were grown. With the arrival of Islam pork and alcohol consumption were forbidden. Beef, chicken, mutton, goat, fish, vegetables, fruit and dairy products became more prevalent.

Pakistani dishes can be spicy, but are rich in flavor due to the use of cardamom, cinnamon, cloves, nutmeg, mace, black pepper, cumin, chili, bay leaves, and coriander. Garam masala, a spice mixture is often used. In the Pashtun region rice, kebabs, and lamb are most often eaten. The Sindhi cuisine can be quite spicy and uses chicken in its dishes. Common fruit are mangoes, melons, apples and bananas. Lentils, basmati rice, chickpeas, black-eyed peas, honey, nuts, yogurt and pickles are incorporated into meals. Curries and stews may or may not contain meat, and use vegetables such as eggplant, okra, cabbage, potatoes, bitter gourd, cauliflower, rutabaga, saag, and chili peppers. Grilled meat is common, and especially kebabs.

Main courses are usually served with wheat bread (either roti or naan) or rice. Salad is generally taken as a side dish with the main course, rather than as an appetizer beforehand. Assorted fresh fruit or sometimes desserts are consumed at the end of a meal.

A Glimpse of Karachi by Ambrin Hayat, Lahore, Pakistan

Karachi, a city of 18 million people is the southernmost city of Pakistan. The city sits on the shores of Arabian Sea and meanders into the mainland, gushing with people. Karachi has many layers of history and many layers of culture. Its diversity makes it a dynamic city. Named after a woman named Kolachi, in its humble origins it was a sleepy fishing village, over many centuries Karachi evolved into an amalgamation of varied thoughts and customs and a center of commerce and trade. It's a city of many languages and many cuisines. One of its very ancient residents are the ethnic Sindhies, forbearers of the Indus civilization who after 5 thousand years still show signs of their ancient, enigmatic past. The crafts, the customs, all have evidence of millenniums gone by. Karachi lives in many centuries at the same time. The Sindhi community takes pride in their rich cultural heritage and enjoys their cuisine. The Daal bhaji is a common snack served with tea.

Daal Bhaji (Lentil Balls)

200 gm Moong Daal, lentils	Water as required
6 chopped green chilies	5 tbls. oil
½ tsp. cumin seeds	Salt to taste
1 tbls. chopped coriander leaves	

Soak the lentils in water for 2-3 hours. Throw most of the water and grind the lentils.
Add chilies, coriander leaves, cumin seeds and salt. Mix the paste.
Shape the paste into small balls.
Heat oil in a pan and shallow fry the 'balls' on medium flame, until they are golden brown.
Serve with green chutney.

As with many ancient cities of the world, Karachi has had its share of wandering mistrals, saints, traders, warriors or conquerors or just simple immigrants, seeking a new life. At the partition of the Indian Sub-Continent, Karachi accommodated millions of people from states across the newly formed border. That wave of immigrants brought swathes of Old Delhi residents who left their Mughal city behind but not their culture and traditions. The Cuisine, of the Delhi Court carrying Persian and Central Asian traditions had absorbed the best of the local customs and spices producing a unique aroma, this cuisine was thus introduced to the nooks and cranny of Karachi, by these unaware carriers of tradition. Many accomplished cooks of the cuisine who cooked for the aristocracy of Delhi set shops along Burns Road, an unlikely venue that has now become the center of Mughal Cuisine in Karachi. 'Biryani' a favorite of the Kings and Queens and their subjects is still a favorite of Karachites.

Chicken Biryani

4 tablespoons vegetable oil
2 large onions, finely chopped
2 cloves garlic, minced
1 tablespoon minced fresh ginger root
1/2 teaspoon chili powder
1/2 teaspoon ground black pepper
1/2 teaspoon ground turmeric
1 teaspoon ground cumin
1 teaspoon salt
2 medium tomatoes, peeled and chopped
2 tablespoons plain yogurt
2 tablespoons chopped fresh mint leaves
½ teaspoon ground cardamom

1 (2 inch) piece cinnamon stick
3 pounds boneless, skinless chicken pieces cut into chunks
2 1/2 tablespoons vegetable oil
1 large onion, diced
1 pinch powdered saffron
5 pods cardamom
3 whole cloves
1 (1 inch) piece cinnamon stick
1/2 teaspoon ground ginger
1 pound basmati rice
4 cups chicken stock
1 1/2 teaspoons salt

In a large skillet, pour 4 tablespoons vegetable oil and fry onion, garlic and ginger until onion is soft and golden. Add chili, pepper, turmeric, cumin, salt and the tomatoes. Fry, stirring constantly for 5 minutes. Add yogurt, mint, cardamom and cinnamon stick. Cover and cook over low heat, stirring occasionally until the tomatoes are cooked to a pulp. It may be necessary to add a little hot water if the mixture becomes too dry and starts to stick to the pan. When the mixture is thick and smooth, add the chicken pieces and stir well to coat them with the spice mixture. Cover and cook over very low heat until the chicken is tender, approximately 35 to 45 minutes. There should only be a little very thick gravy left when chicken is finished cooking. If necessary cook uncovered for a few minutes to reduce the gravy.

Wash rice well and drain. Then soak the rice for at least 30 minutes. In a large skillet, heat vegetable oil (or ghee) and fry some more onions until they are golden. Add saffron, cardamom, cloves, cinnamon stick, ginger and rice. Stir continuously until the rice is coated with the spices.

In a medium-size pot, heat the chicken stock and salt. When the mixture is hot pour it over the rice and stir well. Add the chicken mixture and gently mix into the rice. Bring to boil. Cover the saucepan tightly, turn heat to very low and steam for 20 minutes. Do not lift lid or stir once you have covered the pan. After 20 minutes serve with yogurt.

Recipe courtesy of Ambrin Hayat, Lahore

Specialties

Roti, chapati, paratha, kulcha, puri, sheermal, and naan– flat breads
Taftan – leavened bread with cardamom

Maakai ki roti – cornbread
Khatchauri – sweet pastry with cheese
Siri-payay – head and feet of lamb or cow

Aloo gosht – meat and potato curry
Korma – chicken or mutton curry
Pulao – rice pilafs with vegetables, spices, dried fruit, nuts, or meat
Tandoor – dishes prepared in a clay pot
Shami kebab – curried meatballs
Chicken tikka (grilled chicken)
Shish kebab – skewered meat
Chapli kabab – ground meat cakes
Biryani – beef or chicken with rice and spices
Haleem – chicken, lentil and grain stew
Nihari - stew

Pasanday – curried beef
Jalebi – dough with syrup
Shami kebab – curried meatballs
Chicken tikka (grilled chicken)
Chapli kabab – ground meat cakes
Haleem – chicken, lentil and grain stew
Pasanday – curried beef
Jalebi – dough with syrup
Gajraila – sweet made with grated carrots boiled in milk, sugar, cardamom with nuts and dried fruit
Halvah – sesame paste candy

Holidays and Special Occasions

Ramadan – fasting from sunrise to sunset
Eid-ul-Fitr (breaking of fast after Ramadan) – vermicelli in milk, korma curries of chicken, beef or lamb, dals, pollaus, shawi – dessert with rice noodles fried in butter, and boiled in milk and sugar
Id-uz-Zaha (from the Koran and Bible the sacrifice of Isaac by Abraham) – sacrifice lambs, goats, rams, cows, or camels. Three days of feasting – pollaus, curries, raytas, curries, barbequed meats
Shab e Baraat – fireworks and feasting to celebrate God's riches
Muharram – celebrates the saint Hussain who fell in battle against Yazid over 1400 years ago. – zarda (rice with saffron) and kheer (milk and rice pudding)
Basant – kite flying; parties (banned at the time of the printing of this book)
Sheermal is a saffron flatbread made with milk, butter, and candied fruit served at marriages with taftan, a leavened bread with saffron and cardamom baked in a tandoor.
Sweetmeats such as gulab jamun, barfi, ras malai, kalakand, jalebi and panjiri are consumed on various festive occasions.
Kashmiri chai or "noon chai", is a pink, milky tea with pistachios and cardamom, is consumed primarily at special occasions, weddings, and during the winter.

Beverages

Pakistan is mainly a Muslim country and alcoholic beverages are not drunk. Instead fruit, yogurt, herb, and milk drinks are popular. Sattu is made from barley seeds, water, milk, sugar, fruit, or lemon. Sweet lassi is made of yogurt, sugar, milk while salty or regular lassi has salt instead of sugar. Qahva is an extract of an herb in water. Sardai is made from almond, milk, sugar and pistachio. Sugarcane juice is known as "Rrouh" or "ganney ka ras". Almond sherbet is made with almonds; gola ganda, ices; and lemonade are also popular drinks. Pakistanis drink chai "tea", black (with milk) and green tea. In Gilgit-Baltistan and Chitral, as well as areas near the Chinese border, salty Tibetan-style butter tea is consumed. Doodh Pati Chai is made by cooking tea leaves with milk and sugar, and often served with cardamom. "Sabz chai" or "kahwah", a green tea with saffron and nuts, is often served after every meal in Kashmir, Khyber Pakhtunkhwa, and the Pashtun belt of Balochistan. Sulaimani chai is black tea served with lemon.

420

Palau

Located in the western Pacific, the Palauan archipelago is the westernmost portion of the Caroline Islands. East of Mindanao in the Philippines, Palau is 722 miles southwest of Guam. Palau has three hundred volcanic and raised coral islands and atolls rise up from the Philippine Plate, with a total land area of 191 square miles. Only 11 islands are inhabited. Descendants of the Carolinean atolls, especially Ulithi, settled on Palau's southern atolls of Hatohobei, Sonsorol, Fannah, Pulo Anna, and Merir. The capital Ngerulmud is located on the nearby island of Babeldaob, in Melekeok State. The country was originally settled approximately 3,000 years ago by migrants from the Philippines and sustained a Negrito population until around 900 years ago. The islands were first explored by Europeans in the 16th century, and were made part of the Spanish East Indies in 1574. Following Spain's defeat in the Spanish–American War in 1898, the islands were sold to Imperial Germany in 1899 and were administered as part of German New Guinea. The Imperial Japanese Navy conquered Palau during World War I, and the islands were later made a part of the Japanese-ruled South Pacific Mandate by the League of Nations. Along with other Pacific Islands, Palau was made a part of the United States-governed Trust Territory of the Pacific Islands in 1947. Having voted against joining the Federated States of Micronesia in 1979, the islands gained full sovereignty in 1994. The capital is Ngerulmud on the island of Babeldaob. English and Paluan are the official languages.

Dining Etiquette

Family is still very important to Palauans, whether it be on the mother or father's side. When invited for a meal please bring a gift from your country. Shake hands greeting and departing. Please stand when an elder enters or exits a room. The host will show you to your seat. Please try all the dishes served to you in appreciation of the hard work the hostess has shown in preparing them. Some people may eat with their hands, but in most cases forks and knives are used, continental style, fork in the left hand and knife in the left. When finished place the knife and fork together at a five o'clock angle. Please thank your hostess for the meal when leaving.

Cuisine

Palauan cuisine has been influenced by the Philippines, Indonesia, Malaysia, Japan and the United States. Staple foods include root vegetables – pandan and taro; pumpkins, yams; rice; fruit – plantains, pineapples, passionfruit, breadfruit, dragon fruit, papaya, mango, soursop, coconut, and rambutans. Coconuts are used in most dishes whether it be stews, soups, desserts, and drinks. Seafood include tuna, shrimp, clams, crab, turtles, and even sea birds are eaten. Cured and smoked ham, chicken, goat are the most common meats.

Pichi- Pichi (Cassava and Coconut)

2 cups cassava, grated
1 cup sugar

2 cups water
1 cup coconut, grated

In a mold combine the cassava, sugar and water.
Place in a steamer for 45 minutes.
Unmold. Roll or top with the coconut.

Specialties

Tinola - chicken soup with papaya and ginger
Broiled fish with ginger, garlic, soy sauce, sesame oil, and lime leaves, steamed in banana leaves
Ulkoy - squash and shrimp fritters

Fruit Bat soup –fruit bats, coconut milk and spice soup
Taro cakes, taro chips
Halo-halo – drink made with fruit, ice cream, ice and flavorings

Holidays and Special Occasions

Easter and Christmas are celebrated with roast suckling pig and/or beef with garlic sauce, yams, and vegetables, and desserts made from bananas and coconut.

Beverages

Popular drinks are made with different fruit. Red Rooster Beer is brewed. Kava juice is made from the root of the kava plant, and has a very calming effect.

Palestine

Palestine is a sovereign state in the Middle East bordered by Israel and the Mediterranean. Palestine became part of the Ottoman Empire in 1516. Following the Crimean War in 1855 Bosnians, Greeks, French and Italians settled in the region. East Jerusalem is the capital and Ramallah, the administrative center. The official language is Arabic.

Dining Etiquette

Please arrive promptly if asked for a meal. Men shake hands. Only if a woman extends her hands are hands shaken. Guests are served coffee or tea along with fresh or dried fruits, sunflower or pumpkin seeds, nuts – especially pistachios and cashews, dates, roasted and salted watermelon, and squash. There are usually two courses served, followed by coffee, fruit and sweets. Meals are family time or for friends and can last for over an hour or more.

Breakfast may consist of eggs, olives, labeneh, olive oil, za'atar, jams and tahini. Lunch may be a large meal with rice, lamb, and vegetables. During the afternnoon one may have a snack of fruit. Dinner is served 8-10 and is a light meal. Many dishes served communally and may be eaten with the fingers. Khubz is a bread that will take the place of utensils. It is torn into bite size pieces and used for dips such as hummus.

Mezzeh is a variety of appetizers that includes hummus, baba ghannooj, fattosh, tabbouleh, olives, pickled vegetables, cabbage salad, cheeses, and flatbreads.

Cuisine

The cuisine has been influenced by Arab, Persian, Turkish, and other Middle Eastern cuisines. Rice is not served as a side dish but with meat, vegetables and soups. Stews are popular as they can serve a large number of people. Rice, kibbi, tomatoes, wheat, fish – sardines, red mullet, sea bass, sea bream, crab, shrimp, squid; red tahini, lentils, chili peppers, lamb, yogurt, dates, olives and olive oil, figs, pomegranates, watermelon, raisins, carob fruit, apples, grapes for jam and wine, apricots are some of the ingredients used in cooking. The most common spices and herbs are cinnamon, oregano, sage, mint, parsley, watercress, jute leaf, cilantro, garlic, cardamom, turmeric, allspice, and nutmeg. Bread was baked in a communal oven known as a taboon. Pastries are often filled with cheese, dates, and nuts – pistachios, pine nuts, walnuts, and almonds. Zibdiyit is the clay bowl used for cooking, serving, and eating.
There are three regions in Palestine and each has its own cuisine:

In Galilee beef, lamb, bulgur,
West Bank – rice, flatbreads, roasted meats
Gaza Strip - fish – grilled or fried, chili peppers, dill seeds, garlic, chard

Mutabbal (Eggplant Dip)

2 large eggplant
2 tbls. tahini paste
4 tbls. lemon juice
2 cloves garlic, minced

½ jalapeno pepper, seeded and minced
Salt and olive oil to taste
½ cup pickled vegetables
Pita bread

Preheat broiler.
Remove the eggplant stems and cut two horizontal slits on each side of the eggplant. Place on a foil-lined baking sheet and broil. Turn occasionally until the skin is charred.
Place the eggplant on a plate and slice in half lengthwise. Scoop out pulp and place it in a large bowl. Mash with a fork.
In a small bowl mix the tahini and lemon juice until smooth. Add to eggplant along with garlic and jalapeno. Add salt and oil to taste.
Garnish with the pickled vegetables and serve with pita bread.
Recipe courtesy of info@thetasteofpalestine.com and info@nakheelpal.ps

Palestinian Specialties

Kubbi bi-siniyee – minced lamb or beef with pepper, allspice, wrapped in a bulgur crust and baked
Kubbi neyee – raw meat with bulgur and spices
Kibbi balls – fried kubbi
Pita – flatbread
Sfiha – flatbread with lamb, red peppers or tomatoes
Manakish – flatbread with za'atar and olive oil
Ikras – dough stuffed with meat or spinach
Sambusac – fried dough stuffed with meat and onions or pine nuts
Markook – very thin unleavened bread
Musakhan – roasted chicken served over taboon bread topped with fried sweet onions, sumac, allspice and pine nuts.
Maqluba – rice, eggplant, cauliflower, carrot and lamb or beef dish

Mansaf - lamb served on taboon with yellow rice and jameed, goat's milk yogurt, and garnished with pine nuts and almonds. Mansaf is eaten with the right hand, and pieces of lamb torn and given to the person next to them.
Zibdieh – shrimp, olive oil, garlic, hot peppers, and tomatoes cooked in a clay pot
Shatta – hot red pepper paste
Sumaghiyyeh – sumac mixed with tahina, slice chard, beef, garbanzo beans, dill seeds, garlic and hot peppers
Rummaniyya – pomegranate seeds, eggplant tahina, garlic, hot peppers, and lentils
Fukharit - lentil stew with red pepper, dill seeds, garlic and cumin
Qidra – rice, lamb, garlic, garbanzo beans, cardamom, turmeric, cinnamon, allspice, nutmeg and cumin cooked in a clay pot in the oven

Fatteh ghazzawiyyeh – rice cooked with chicken or meat broth and spices.

Maqluba – (means "upside down" in Arabic) – Meat is placed in a large pot, with a layer of vegetables and topped with rice. After this is cooked it inverted so the meat is at the top. This is served with salad and yogurt.

Quzi – rice with vegetables and roasted meat served in a sidr, and garnished with parsley, pine nuts or almonds

Zarb – similar to quzi but made with dough

Ruz ma lahma – rice, ground beef, nuts and spices

Mloukhiyeh – stew of Jew's mallaw, lemon juice, and water, served with sliced lemon and rice, chicken or lamb

Shish kebab – grilled meat on skewers

Adas – lentil soup served with sliced onions and bread

Laban – yogurt soup

Musakham – roasted chicken, fried onions, sumac, allspice, saffron, and pine nuts served on taboon and lemon slices. This is eaten with the hands.

Mahshi – vegetables stuffed with rice

Waraq al-'ainib – stuffed grape leaves

Hummus – beans, tahini paste, lemon juice

Baba ghanoush –eggplant dip

Jibneh arabieh –white cheese served with many dishes

Tabbouleh – parsley, bulgur wheat, tomato, and cucumber salad

Salatah arabieh – lettuce, tomato, cucumber mint and parsley salad

Baklava – phyllo pastry with walnuts and honey

Muhalabiyeh – rice pudding with nuts

Kanafeh – shredded pastry with honey cheese and pistachios

Sumagiyya – stew with sumac

Roasted watermelon salad

Dagga – tomato salad

Maftul – couscous?

Kishik – mix of yogurt and bulgur or wheat berries

Rumaniyya – eggplant and lentil stew

Fogaiyya – beef or lamb stew with spices – allspice, cardamom, cinnamon, cloves, bay, mastic, and nutmeg, chard and chickpeas

Zibdiyit Gambari – shrimp stew with onions, peppers, tomatoes, spices and nuts

Tabikh bamia – oxtail stew with okra

Molukhiyya – mallow soup

Filfil mat'houn – ground red chile peppers in oil

Quidra – meat and spice dish

Dukka – legumes and spice dish

Mahshi – stuffed vegetables

Knafa arabiya – walnuts and toasted semolina breadcrumbs with cinnamon and nutmeg in warm syrup

Holidays and Special Occasions

Mansaf is served at engagement parties, weddings, baptisms, and circumcisions. The dish contains bread, laban, rice, nuts, parsley and lamb and is served on a sidr, a large platter. People each from the communal platter without dinnerware.

Roasted lamb with rice, spices, and garnished with parsley and nuts is also served on special occasions.

At the time of Ramadan people fast from sunrise to sunset. Before sunrise they may eat labaneh, cheese, bread, eggs, and liquids before fasting.

During Ramadan dates, tamarind and carob juices, and qamar deen, an iced apricot drink are served at sunset to break the fast. Tamar hind is a licorice flavored drink. Qatayef is a folded dough filled with unsalted goat cheese or ground walnuts and cinnamon that is baked and with a syrup or honey. Ka'ak bi 'awja is a shortbread with ground dates or walnuts served at the end of Ramadan and at Easter for Christians.

Mawlid – honors birth of Prophet Mohammed- zalabieth, deep fried dough dipped in syrup is
Birth of child and at Christmas – meghli, a dessert of ground rice, sugar, and spices, with nuts.
Child's first tooth – sweetened wheat or barley
Child's circumcision – baklava and burmna
Christian family in mourning – rahmeh, a sweet bun served in remembrance of dead

Beverages

Coffeehouses serve hot and cold beverages. They are used mainly by the men who play cards, games, and smoke. Coffee is often served throughout the day. Fruit juices are common. Rose or mint water are added to Palestinian dishes, or as a drink. Herbs can also brewed into drinks. Slhlab is a warm drink made from sweetened milk with saleb and served with walnuts, coconut and cinnamon. Tea with mint or sage is usually drunk in the evening. Fruit juices include tamarind, licorice, carob, and Qamar Eddine – dried apricots.

Arak is a clear anise-flavored alcoholic drink that is mixed with water, and consumed during special occasions such as holidays, weddings, and gatherings or with the mezze. Beer is brewed in Taybeh and Birzeit.

The Bedouins drink qahwah sadad, bitter coffee, which is served to guests as a symbol of hospitality. The host or oldest son moves clockwise around the guests who are seated according to status and age, and pours coffee into small cups from a brad pot. Three cups are poured and then the guest says "daymen" "always".

Panama

Panama is located in Central America bordered by Costa Rica to the west, Colombia to the southeast, the Caribbean to the north and the Pacific Ocean to the south. The earliest known inhabitants were the Paleo-Indians. Pottery has been found dating back to the Monagrillo cultures 2500-1700 BC. The Chibchan, Chocoan, and Cueva people settled the region. In 1501 Rodrigo de Bastidas sailed from Venezuela and was the first European to explore the Isthmus of Panama. Other Spaniard arrived in the 16th c some trekking to the Pacific coast. Gold and silver were brought from South America, taken across the Isthmus and then by ship to Spain on the route known as the Camino Real (Royal Road). The Cuevas and Cocle tribes fled into the forests and islands, but many died from European diseases. Spain ruled Panama 1538-1821 as part of the Viceroyalty of Peru. Besides the Indian tribes, cimarrons "freed Africans" lived in the interior and on some of the Pacific coast islands. The Spanish built plantations, but Panama was mainly important for the isthmus and getting products from one coast to the other. After 1821 Panama was a department of Colombia. In 1903 Panama proclaimed its independence and the Hay-Bunau-Varilla Treaty which gave the United States a zone to build the Panama Canal. The capital and largest city is Panama City.

Dining Etiquette

When invited for a meal arrive promptly or a little later. Please bring a gift from your country. Shake hands greeting and departing. Drinks are served. A toast "Salud" may be offered. You will be shown to your seat by the host(ess). Spouses are usually seated separately. Food will be served and before starting the host will say "buen provecho". Hands should be kept with the wrists on the table. Food is eaten continental style with the fork in the left hand and knife in the right. Tortillas or other food may be eaten with your hands. Take a small amount of food to start, then ask for seconds as this a compliment for the hostess. When finished place your knife and fork together on the right side of the plate.

Cuisine

Many varieties of produce are grown in Panama, some dating back to very early times. The Mayan influenced eating corn and beans as part of the diet. The Spanish brought rice, spices, animals such as sheep, goats, chickens, and cows, cheese and dairy, and their own cooking methods. In the 1800s the cross continent railroad and later the building of the Panama Canal brought in French, Americans, and Chinese. The French introduced sauces and pastries.

Beans, rice, plantains, potatoes, onions, peppers, zucchini, pineapple, cassava, coconuts, and maize are commonly used ingredients. Along the coast seafood includes conch, lobster, crabs, and many types of fish. The food is not highly spiced. Fresh or ground corn are used in many dishes. Mushrooms grow in the mountain region.

Carimanola (yucca with meat)

Makes 8-10

2 lbs. yucca	Salt and pepper
Vegetable oil	½ tsp. cumin
2 cloves garlic, minced	1 tbsl. tomato paste
½ red or green pepper, chopped	½ lb. ground beef
1 small onion, chopped	¼ lb. Mozzarella cheese, grated

Cook the yucca in a pan with a little salt and covered with water until tender, about 15 minutes. Remove any fiber and mash.

Heat 1 tbls. vegetable oil in a skillet. Add the red pepper and onion, and cook until onion is transparent. Add the garlic, salt and pepper, cumin, and beef. Stir until beef is slightly pink. Add tomato sauce and cheese.

Divide the yucca into 8-10 pieces and roll into a ball. Make a hole in each and add the meat mixture. Seal and shape into an oval shape.

Heat oil. Drop in carimanola until browned.

Remove with slotted spatula.

Serve hot.

These can be made with meat or cheese, or a combination.

Panama Specialties

Red or black beans with coconut rice
Rice cooked in coconut milk
Arroz con camarones y coco- rice with shrimp and coconut milk
Arroz verde – green rice
Arroz con puerco y vegetables – rice with pork and vegetables
Arroz con pollo – rice with chicken
Arroz con chorizo - rice with chorizo
Tortillas – corn flat bread, served at most meals
Bollos – corn dough wrapped in corn husks or plantain leaves and then boiled. Can be stuffed with beef or pork (bollo prenado "pregnant bollo"

Empanadas – corn or flour dough stuffed with meat, vegetables, cheese, or as a dessert with fruit or manjar blanco (dulce de leche)
Torrejitas - corn fritters
Tortilla changa – a thick fresh corn tortilla
Almojabanos – "s" shaped corn fritter
Hojaldres – fried bread "tostones"
Carimanola – yucca dough stuffed with beef
Mondongo a la culona – beef tripe stew
Pernil de pueco al horno – roasted pork leg
Ceviche – seafood marinated in lime juice
Tamales – masa dough wrapped in corn husks
Ropa Vieja – "old clothes" stew with beef and vegetables

Mole – cooked sauces
Posoles –heart pork or chicken soups
Golleria - sweetened plantain fritters
Manjar blanco – milk custard
Tres leches – sponge cake made with 3 different milks

Cocada – coconut candy
Mazamorra – sweet corn dessert
Crema de coco – coconut and sweet potato dessert
Bocado pernambucano – coconut milk, egg, parmesan cheese and sugar pudding

Holidays and Special Occasions

Fat Tuesday (Mardi Gras or Carnival) – people eat very fattening foods and drink lots of alcohol
Semana Santa – Holy week before Easter. There are processions. Among the foods eaten are bacalo (dried codfish) which is made into soup for Friday and Saturday. Chiverre, a large pumpkin, is made into jams to be eaten on its own or used in empanadas. Pan casero, a sweet flat bread; encuritos, vegetables pickled with vinegar, mustard, and bay leaves; heart of palm salad; and tuna salad with seashell macaroni are served. Other preparations are enyucado – grated yucca, anise seeds, coco, and white farmers' cheese; cocada- cashew, coconut, sugar cane syrup, and cinnamon balls; dulce defrijoles – beans; bon – circular bread with dried fruit, raisins, cheese, orange rind with molasses, and a cross on top; bienmesabe – rice flour, cane sugar, and milk cooked for a long time and shaped into patties.
Easter – Easter eggs; families have new clothes, attend Mass; ham; lamb
Christmas – chicken tamales, arroz con pollo, pork, pavo (turkey), relleno, fruit, fruitcake. Ron Ponche eggnog is served. This is made from condensed and evaporated milk, eggs, rum, and nutmeg.
Beef and seafood are served for birthdays, anniversaries, and weddings.

Beverages

Coffee has been grown in Panama since the 1800s mainly in the Boquete and Volcan regions of the country. Panama is famous for its Geisha/Gesha coffee variety. A favorable climate with cold air currents through the mountains stimulates the coffee growing. Fruit drinks are very popular made from pineapple, papaya, orange, and passion fruit to mention a few. The juices may be sweetened or condensed milk or water added. Fresh coconut milk; chicheme, made from corn; and chichas a fruit drink are also drunk. Rum is produced in Panama, as are beers – Atlas, Balboa, Panama and Soberana. Seco is distilled from sugarcane and may be served with milk over ice. Sorrel is a drink made from sorrel sepals, ginger, cinnamon, cloves, sugar, water and rum.

Papua New Guinea

Papua New Guinea occupies the eastern half of the island of New Guinea and its offshore islands in Melanesia in the southwestern Pacific Ocean north of Australia. Archaeological evidence indicates that humans first arrived in Papua New Guinea around 42,000 to 45,000 years ago. They were descendants of migrants out of Africa, in one of the early waves of human migration. Agriculture was independently developed in the New Guinea highlands around 7000 BC, making it one of the few areas in the world where people independently domesticated plants. Traders from Southeast Asia had visited New Guinea beginning 5,000 years ago to collect bird of paradise plumes. A major migration of Austronesian-speaking peoples to coastal regions of New Guinea took place around 500 BC with the introduction of pottery, pigs, and certain fishing techniques. In the 18th century, Portuguese traders brought the sweet potato to New Guinea where taro had played a prominent role. Beginning in 1884 Germany controlled the northern half of the country known as German New Guinea and the British the southern half, British New Guinea. In 1914 Australia occupied the country. After World War II and the victory of the Allies, the two territories were combined into the Territory of Papua and New Guinea. This was later referred to as "Papua New Guinea", receiving its independence in 1975, but is a member of the British Commonwealth. The country has over 1000 cultural groups and 852 known languages. The capital, on its southeastern coast, is Port Moresby.

Dining Etiquette

When invited to a home arrive on time or slightly late. Please bring a gift from your country. Please shake hands greeting and departing. The host will show you your seat. When seated at the table eat continental style with the fork in the left hand and the knife in the right. In some homes you may be seated on the ground and eat with your hands. Try everything that is served to you. They are very hospitable people. If you are dining with Chinese you may be given chopsticks. Leave a small amount on your plate when finished.

Cuisine

The land is very fertile and crops such as coconuts, sugarcane, breadfruit, taro, bananas, yams, and lemons are very much part of the diet. Early settlers brought pigs and rodents, and of course seafood was in abundance. The people learned to cook in underground earthen ovens. Europeans introduced chickens, sheep, cattle, wheat, potatoes, pineapples, rice, and cocoa. Today the cuisine uses pork, chicken, fish, kau kau – sweet potatoes, avocado, taro roots, guava, watermelon, papaya, paw paw, mango, bananas, coconut, rice, and vegetables. Sago palm a starch to make puddings and bread. Lunch is usually the largest meal at home with family.

Mumu (roasted pork, rice, yam and greens dish)

The national dish is cooked in an underground oven in Papua New Guinea

Serves 6-8

Taro, banana, or spinach leaves
4 sweet potatoes or yams, peeled
2 lbs. pork butt, cubed
2 lbs. boneless chicken breasts, cubed
1 pineapple, cut into cubes
3 bananas, peeled, and cut into 4 or more pieces

1 papaya, peeled and cut into cubes
3 carrots, cut into 1 in. pieces
1 mango, peeled and cut into cubes
1 yucca, peeled, and cubed
2 garlic cloves, minced
2 cups coconut milk

Preheat oven to 200°
In a Dutch oven or large covered baking dish layer all the ingredients topping with the coconut milk and finally the leaves. Cover tightly.
Cook 4 hours. Do not stir or uncover.
Spices or herbs can be added when cooking.

Specialties

Kokoda – fish cooked with limes and coconut
Dia – sago and bananas cooked in coconut milk

Barramundi cod cooked in banana leaves
Chicken pot – chicken with vegetables and coconut milk

Holidays and Special Occasions

Frangipani Festival in Rabaul – celebrates rebirth of vity after 1994 volcanic eruption. Dancing, bands, fireworks and canoe races
Warwagera Mask Festival – importance of history of masks in culture
On national holidays – New Year's Day, Good Friday, Easter Monday, Queen's Birthday, Remembrance Day, Independence Day, Christmas and Boxing Day - mumu, kau kau, taro, yams, sago, and pork make up traditional feasts.

Beverages

Juices, soft drinks, tea and coffee are popular. Kava "waild koniak" is made from ground kava roots to release the liquid to which water is added. It is considered a very relaxing drink. Some beer is brewed locally.

Did You Know?

Sugar cane was first grown in New Guinea and is thought to date back over 8000 years. From there sugarcane spread to Asia and eventually the Middle East.

Paraguay

Paraguay is a landlocked country in central South America, bordered by Argentina to the south and southwest, Brazil to the east and northeast, and Bolivia to the northwest. Indigenous peoples have inhabited this area for thousands of years. The Paraguay River was roughly the dividing line between the agricultural Guarani people to the east and the nomadic and semi-nomadic people to the west in the Gran Chaco. The Guarcuru nomads were known for their warrior traditions and were not fully pacified until the late 19th century. These indigenous tribes belonged to five distinct language families, which were the bases of their major divisions. Differing language speaking groups were generally competitive over resources and territories. They were further divided into tribes by speaking languages in branches of these families. Today 17 separate ethnolinguistic groups remain. The first Europeans in the area were Spanish explorers in 1516. The Spanish explorer Juan de Salazar de Espinosa founded the settlement of Asunción on 15 August 1537. Paraguay was a colony of the Spanish Empire, receiving independence from Spain in 1811, Following the Paraguayan War (1864–1870), the country lost 60 to 70 percent of its population through war and disease, and about 54,000 sq. mi, one quarter of its territory, to Argentina and Brazil. The capital is Asuncion. Spanish is the official language with Guaraní also spoken.

Dining Etiquette

Please be slightly late when invited for a meal. Men should wear a jacket and tie. Dinner is served late, usually around 10 PM or later. Please shake hands greeting and departing using good eye contact. Women will kiss friends on the cheek. The oldest or guest of honor will be introduced first. Please bring a gift for the hostess such as something for the home, flowers, candy, or liquor which has high import taxes. Gifts are opened immediately. Drinks and hors d'oeuvres will be served. The hostess will seat the guests. Do not begin eating until the hostess picks up her fork. Food is eaten continental style with the fork in the left hand and knife in the right. Keep your hands at table level, and no elbows on the table. If passing a dish do so to your left. Never cut your lettuce. Instead use your knife and fork to pick it up. Please wait for a toast before drinking your wine or beverage. The host will pour the wine. The toast is "Salud". Please leave a small portion of food on your plate when you are finished. When finished place your knife and fork face down with the handles to the right, or crossed. The fork and spoon at the top of your place setting are for dessert. Brandy and coffee may be served at the end of a meal. Please call or write a thank you note to your hostess to thank her for the meal.

Cuisine

The cuisine of Paraguay has been influenced by the Spanish and the indigenous cultures. Meat, vegetables, manioc maize, and fruits are common in Paraguayan cuisine. Barbecuing is both a cooking technique and often a social event, and are known as the *Asado* (from Argentinian influence). Many dishes are based on corn, milk, cheese and meat, and fish caught in rivers are also eaten. There are about 70 varieties of chipa (cake) in Paraguay. Most chipas are made from manioc flour, which is derived from cassava, and cornmeal. The tatakua is a brick adobe oven still used in some places.

Chipa Guasu (Corn Souffle)

Serves 4-6

6-8 fresh ears of corn
1 onion, finely chopped
1 stick butter

4 eggs, separated
1 cup grated cheese
1 cup milk

Preheat oven to 350°
Remove the corn from the cob. Grate the corn and save juice. Place in a bowl.
Beat the butter and the egg yolks. Add the cheese, onion, corn, and milk.
In a separate bowl beat the egg whites until fluffy. Gently stir into corn mixture.
Pour into an ovenproof dish. Bake for 50-60 or until set.

Specialties

Mandioca - yucca or cassava which are eaten with most meals

Chipá – round bread with a hole in the middle made with yucca starch, cheese, eggs, milk and aniseed

Mbejú – cake with mandioca and cheese and cooked in a frying pan. In the Guarani language *mbejú* means cake.

Arró Quesú – rice and Quesú Paraguai (Paraguayan cheese)

Asado - barbecue

Bifé Koygua - beef with fried onions and fried eggs on top

Bori Bori - a thick soup to which dumplings (or small balls) of cornmeal and cheese and sometimes chicken are added.

Chipa Guazú - corn cake with cheese, eggs, oil and milk, and cooked in a Tatakua

Empanadas – fried pastries filled with egg, meat, chicken, corn, cheese and ham

Guiso popó – chicken, rice, sweet pepper and garlic dish.

Milanesa - crumbed meat filets.

Pastel mandi'o – fried dough made from mandioca filled with meat

Pira Caldo - Pira means fish in Guaraní and caldo broth - fish soup with milk, Paraguayan cheese, onions, tomato and sunflower oil.

Puchero - stew made with meat, vegetables - carrot, pumpkin/squash and onions).

Sopa Paraguaya - soup made of ground corn, cheese, eggs and milk

Vori vori is a thick, yellow soup with little balls made of cornmeal, corn flour, and cheese.

Sopa So'o – Sope Paraguaya with a layer of ground beef

Dulce de Guayaba - guava jam

Dulce de Mamón – papaya dessert with caramel.

Kaguyjy - corn and sugar dessert

Ka'i ladrillo - peanut and molasses candy cut cubes that look like bricks. *Ladrillo* is Spanish for brick.

Kosereva – sour orange candy cooked in black molasses

Kamby arró - rice pudding
Mbaipy-he-é - dessert made with milk, molasses and corn

Kivevé - corn flour and pumpkin dessert
Dulce de leche – sweet milk for cakes
Mazamorra – corn mush

Holidays and Special Occasions

Chipá is consumed during holidays, celebrations and Easter.

Semana Santa – Holy week – on Holy Wednesday women begin preparing chipa (Easter breakfast bread) made from fresh ground mandioca flour, cheese, eggs, pig fat or butter, and anise. The dough is baked in a tatakua (Guarani for brick oven). The bread is consumed through the rest of week to Easter, often dipped in coffee of cocido (hot tea) as the bread becomes very hard.

Viernes Santo – Good Friday – fasting, other than eating chipa. Some families bathe in cold water.

Pascua - Easter – family gathers for church and a large meal is prepared. Beef (asado) may be barbequed, a pig roasted, potatoes, rice and mandioca served

End of June – Fiestas de San Juan – Alambreado - meat is cut in long thin strips, Chicharö trenzado – meat in braided strips, Payagua mascada – ground beef and mandioca.

October 1 – Jopara (bean, carrot, pumpkin and mandioca) dish eaten to keep away "Karai Octubre" (Mr. October), a myth about rural man in a straw hat that brings sadness, misery, hunger and disgrace to the home he enters.

Nine days leading up to December 8 – families attend church to celebrate novenario – Virgin of Caacupe

Noche Buena - Christmas Eve – families gather and attend church. A large meal is served with asado (beef bbq), drinks, salads, and Sopa Paraguaya (corn pastries)

Christmas – food from the night before is eaten

Beverages

Carrulim is a drink that contains *caña* (sugar cane alcohol), *ruda* (rue - herb with yellow flowers) and *limón* (lemon in Spanish) and is drunk on August 1, usually the coldest time of the year, to stimulate a person's blood and protect from harm. Mosto is a non-alcoholic beverage. Tereré, the national drink, is an herb beverage usually drunk first thing in the morning. Mate Cocido (*yerba mate)* is a mixture of herbs in boiled water that is strained and poured into cups with sugar.

Peru

Peru is a country in South America, bordered on the north by Ecuador and Colombia, on the east by Brazil, on the southeast by Bolivia, on the south by Chile, and on the west by the Pacific Ocean. Civilization dates back to at least 11,000 BC when hunting tools were used. Between 3,000 and 1800 BCE the Norte Chico civilization prospered along the Pacific coast. This was followed by the the Cupisnique, Chavin, Paracas, Mochica, Nazca, Wari, and Chimú cultures. During the 15th c the Incas became dominant. Agriculture using irrigation and terracing, hunting and fishing provided food for them. In 1532 the Spanish conquistador Francisco Pizarro conquered the Inca and established the Viceroyalty of Peru. Peru became an independent country under Jose de San Martin in 1821. Lima, the capital, is located in the Chillón, Rímac, and Lurín river valleys and was founded in 1535 by conquistador Pizzaro. Spanish and Quechua are the official languages.

Dining Etiquette

The Peruvians are warm and hospitable, and enjoy entertaining. If asked for dinner it will probably be 9 PM or later, and you may arrive up to a half hour late. You may bring a small gift or flowers. For birthdays and Christmas always bring a gift. Please shake greeting and departing. Close female friends will kiss on the cheek. Close male friends will greet each other with an abrazo (hug). Youth are greeted with a pat on the back. Greeting elders or officials please use their title and last name. Drinks and hors d'oeuvres will be served before dinner. People will stand close to each while conversing. Eye contact is important. The hostess will seat the guest with the male guest of honor to her right. Eating is continental style – fork in the left hand, knife in the right. Hands are kept above the table, not in your lap. Please eat all that is on your plate.

Ceviche (Marinated Fish)

Serves 6-8 as an appetizer

2 lbs filleted sea bass, or other firm white fish, cut into cubes
1 red onion cut into long strips
1 red pepper cut into thin strips
2 tsp chopped parsley
4 tbls. olive oil

1 celery stalk, finely chopped
1 tsp hot pepper sauce, or jalapeno, finely chopped
1 cup lemon juice
Salt & Pepper

Combine all the ingredients in a bowl.
Serve on a bed of lettuce on individual plates, or a martini glass.

Cuisine

Amerindian and Spanish influences together with native ingredients, and the influence of Chinese, Japanese, African, and Italian cuisine have made Peruvian cooking a blend of diverse cultures. During the Incan Empire the rulers controlled the land, allowing each family a small property and then working the common property to feed the court. Corn (maize), potatoes, tomatoes, beans, sweet potatoes, peanuts, chocolate, papaya, yucca, quinoa, pineapple, kiwicha, chili peppers, airampo cactus (red used for food coloring), tumbo and other fruits, and other roots and tubers are used in the cooking. The Incas have used quinoa and lima beans in their cooking for over five thousand years. The different regions produce specialty dishes using local crops, seafood, and meats. Along the coast different types of fish and seafood are prevalent; in the Andes trout, alpaca, guinea pigs, sheep and pigs; and in the jungle freshwater fish such as the paiche, piranha, and turtles. In the Andes a pachamanca or special banquet is prepared using various meats, pork, and beef, herbs, vegetables and cooked underground on a bed of hot coals. The ancient ritual of planting maize involved the Indians knowing where to tap water and to gather guano (bird droppings) for fertilizer from the islands. Purple corn is originally from Peru. The native cooking is known as criolla, a combination of the Indian and Spanish. The Spanish brought to Peru citrus fruit, wheat, rice, and cattle. The Chinese introduced soy sauce, fresh ginger, and stir-frying. The Japanese introduced Japanese methods of cooking fish

Peruvian Specialties

Tamales rellenos – mashed corn with onion, pork, hardboiled eggs, olives and ahi (Peruvian chile), wrapped in banana leaves and steamed

Empanadas – pastry with stuffing of chicken, beef or chicken, cheese, hardboiled eggs, raisins, and olives

Anticuchos – skewered grilled beef hearts

Aguadito de pollo – chicken and rice soup

Tacu – tacu – beans, rice, steak and onion salsa

Arroz con pollo – chicken and rice

Chupe de pescado (cheviche) – raw fish or other seafood marinated in lime juice, onions and chilies

Humitas – corn husk leaves with spices, sugar, onions, olives, and pork

Papas a la huancaina – boiled potatoes, lettuce, and cheese sauce

Cioppino – seafood cooked with wine and vegetables and served over rice or with crusty bread

Butifarras – ham sandwich with onions, chili peppers, lime

Causa – potato dumpling served with hard boiled eggs and olives

Carapulcra – pork and chicken stew

Aji de gallina – chicken with chili sauce

Escabeche criollo – fish with onions, vinegar, chili

Causa – layered torte with mash potato, tuna or other filling and covered with a mayonnaise sauce

Cau cau – tripe stew and rice

Yucca chupe – cassava soup

Crema de tarwi – tarwi soup

Chairo – red chili pepper, sweet potato, and meat soup

Chicharrones – deep fried salted pork

Copus – fried bananas, sweet potatoes, poultry or meat, cooked underground

Shambar – wheat and pork soup

Seco de cabrito – goat stew

Upka pikanti – potato, beet, chili, mint, and peanut dish

Cuy chactado – fried guinea pig from Andes

Olluquiti – alpaca, llama or sheep stew with rice

Rocoto – very spicy chilies

Tocosh – fermented potato pulp made by Quechua
Chalona – cured meat usually from alpaca
Alfajores - pastry with flour, key lime, butter and powdered sugar with a filling
Turrones – nougat
Tejas – filled candy
Picarones – pumpkin fritter

Mazamorra –purple maize dessert with cinnamon and cloves
Arroz con leche – rice pudding
Suspiro a la limena – dulce de leche with meringue and port
Helados – ice cream

Holidays and Special Occasions

On Good Friday meat is not eaten and fish served. Chupe de Viernes (Friday soup) is made with crayfish, cheese, milk, and vegetables.
On Easter in Arequipa caldo blanco (seven meats soup) is served made from beef, lamb, chicken, pork, charqui (dried meat), goat and potatoes.
For Easter (Doce Platos) or the Easter feast is made up of twelve courses. Sweets might include mazamorra morada (jelly with fruit and purple corn); rice pudding; besitos (small sweets).
Festival of the cross (May) – chichi (corn beer) is drunk
Senor de los Milagros (Lord of Miracles) (October) – turrones (nougat) are served
Christmas is celebrated on December 24th (Noche Buena) with roasted turkey, or chicken; apple sauce; salad; tamales; fruitcake; panetonne; champagne for adults and hot chocolate for children. Many have families have large parties that night after the children have gone to bed.
The week before Christmas groups organize "chocolatadas" giving hot chocolate and gifts to poor children.

Beverages

Wine is produced in the Ica, Locumba, and Lima regions and the Sicamba River Valley. The vines were the first in the Americas dating back to the 16th c and included Pas or Criolla grapes.

Well known drinks include Chicha morada – a clove or herb flavored maize drink with pineapple, sugar and ice added. Chicha de jora is homemade corn beer. Inca kola is a sweet flavored yellow soda; kola inglesia is a cherry flavored soda that has been around since 1912. Other drinks are refrescos (juices with water and sugar); and te de una de gato (tea from the Amazon).

Pisco, the national drink, is a distilled beverage made from grapes. Pisco Muscat Brandy is distilled from wines in the Ica region. The Pisco Sour is a cocktail made with pisco, key lime juice, egg white, and sugar. Guinda is a cherry brandy and Aguardiente sugar cane alcohol.

Local beers include Pilsen, Crisral Arequipena, and Cuzquena. Often men will share one glass, with the bottle being passed on.

Did You Know?

The last supreme ruler of the Incas was Atahualpa and his uncle Hualpa. Hualpa in the Quechua language means "chicken".

The Philippines

The Philippines is an archipelago located in the Pacific Ocean, comprising 7,107 islands about 500 miles off Southeast Asia. The earliest people to settle here were the Callao Man whose remains date back 67,000 years. The earliest settlers were Austronesians from Taiwan who migrated c 4000 BC. By 1000 BC there were four main groups of people – hunter-gatherer tribes, warrior societies, plutocracies, and maritime harbor principalities. Trade was established with China, India, Brunei, Indonesia, Malaysia and Japan, plus other islands in the pacific. Later Arab traders found the islands and introduced Islam. In 1521 the Portuguese explorer Ferdinand Magellan claimed the islands for Spain. Manila became the capital in 1571. From 1565 to 1821 the Philippines were governed as a territory of the Viceroyalty of New Spain, and many of the people were converted to Christianity. British forces occupied Manila from 1762-64. In 1898 The Spanish-American War which began in 1898 in Cuba spread to the Philippines. The islands were then ceded to the United States. In 1935 the Philippines were granted commonwealth status. The Japanese invaded during World War II. In 1946 the Philippines became an independent republic. The country is named in honor of Prince Philip of Spain, later King Philip II. The capital is Manila. Spanish is the official language.

Dining Etiquette

It is an honor to be invited to a Filipino home. Please arrive promptly and remove your shoes. Elders enter rooms first. The honored guest will be seated to the right of the host or hostess. Forks, knives and forks will be at each place setting. Please eat continental style with the fork in the left hand and knife in the right. Is some homes chopsticks may be used, no utensils or just a fork and spoon. Always eat and pass food with your right hand. The oldest man at the table will begin to eat first. You will be offered more food, at least two or more times. If you do not wish more please leave a little on your plate. The same is true of your beverage glass. Do not refill your glass, but let the person next to you. Some food may be served on a banana leaf with no utensils, and is eaten with the hands. Please take some rice, roll it between your index, middle finger and thumb into a ball. Dip it into the sauce on the banana leaf, and mix it with the vegetables or meat also. Then eat it. Before eating this way wash your hands before and after eating. Do not take the last bite of food on the leaf. At the end of a meal you may be given pabaon, leftover food, which is a sign of hospitality.

If alcohol is served before the meal it may be beer or rice wine, with beer or wine served during the meal. You should never pour a beverage into your glass, but have your neighbor fill or refill it. Toasts are made by the honored guest after the host or at the end of the meal. Please thank your host at the end of the meal.

Adobo (marinated meat in a sauce)

Adobo (the national dish) is made with chicken, pork or other meats, or fish marinated in soy sauce, vinegar garlic, bay leaves, and peppercorns. Meat is boiled, fried and then simmered in broth

Serves 6-8

1 cup distilled white vinegar
1 cup water
1 tbls. finely chopped garlic, mashed to a paste
1 tsp. salt
½ tap. Fresh ground pepper
1 2½ -3 lb. chicken, cut into 10-12 serving pieces

2 ½ lbs. pork butt or shoulder, trimmed of excess fat and cut into 2 in. cubes
2 tbls. soy sauce
Vegetable oil for frying
2 firm ripe tomatoes, cut into 6-8 wedges
Parsley

Combine the vinegar, water, garlic, salt and pepper in a 5-6 qt. pan and stir until the salt dissolves. Add the chicken and pork, turn to coat with mixture. Bring to a boil over high heat. Cover tightly and simmer for 30 minutes.
Stir in the soy sauce. Cover again, and simmer for 10 minutes or longer, or until the pork is tender. Transfer the chicken and pork to a plate. Increase the heat to high. Boil the liquid for 10 minutes, or until sauce is thick and reduced to about 1 cup. Remove from heat. Skim off fat. Pour the fat into a skillet. Taste the sauce for seasoning and keep warm.
Add enough vegetable oil to the skillet to make a layer at least ¼ in. deep. Place pan over high heat. Brown the chicken and pork, turning them frequently, so that they are richly colored but not burned. If necessary add more oil. Transfer the meat to a platter. Cover with foil to keep warm.
To serve, pour the sauce over the meat and garnish with tomato wedges and parsley.
Adobo is accompanied by rice.
Pork, beef, fish or squid can be substituted.

Rice

Place 2 cups rice and 3 cups water in a saucepan. Bring to a boil. Stir with a fork. Cook until water is almost gone. Turn off heat, cover and let steam.

Cuisine

The cuisine has been influenced by the Malay, Chinese, Indian, Spanish, spices from neighboring countries, and American dishes. The Austronesians from southern China introduced boiling, steaming and roasting. They used local livestock – cows, chickens, pigs, and kalabaw (water buffalo); introduced rice cultivation, and vegetables. 14th c Chinese, Indonesian and Indian traders introduced tofu, soy sauce, tofu, bean sprouts, noodle dishes called pancit, lumpia, fish sauce, spring rolls, coconuts, peanuts, puttu, biryani, kurmah, satti, and stir-fry. Malacca and Srivijaya in Malaya and Java introduced patis, puso, rending, kari-kari, bagoong, and cooking with coconut milk. The Spanish brought corn, tomatoes, chili leaves and peppers, chocolate and pineapples. They introduced sautéing with garlic and onions; paella; tamales; and chorizo.

In the south, which is more Muslim the food is hotter and spicier, and uses coconut milk. Most of the Philippine food is less spicier than other Asian cuisines. Much cooking is with vinegar, tamarind pods, coconuts, rice, papaya, bananas, pineapples, kamias; guava; green mango; seafood – shrimp, oysters, crab, catfish, milkfish, tilapia, grouper, sea bass, grouper, prawn, swordfish, mussels, clams, tuna, cod, eels, abalone, and squid. Fish is broiled, grilled, or mixed with vegetables; smoked, sun-dried, or marinated. Seaweed is used in many dishes. Steamed rice is served with meals, and leftover rice can be mixed with garlic to serve with sausages or eggs for breakfast. Rice flour is used to make cakes, pastries and other sweets.

Filipino cuisine is held together with a pairing of flavors tamis (sweet); asim (sour) and alat (salty) flavors called counterpoint. Among the ingredients used are salt, vinegar, garlic, sides – soy sauce, vinegar, shrimp paste, fish sauce, and sugar cane. Tamarind is used in boiled fruit to make sour taste in food; also can be sweetened for drinks or dessert. Dipping sauces for fried food include vinegar, bird's eye chilies, soy, and garlic. Among the common fruit are kalamansi, a sour lime; tabon-tabon used in Kinilaw dishes; batuan round with a soury taste, acid pulp with seeds from Visaya, mangoes, guava, papaya, and pineapple, bananas and banana leaves. Vegetables include water spinach, Chinese and Napa cabbage, eggplant, long beans, potatoes, carrots, taro, cassava, yams, tomatoes, garlic, and onions. Coconut meat is used in desserts, coconut milk in sauces, and coconut oil for frying. Among the nuts is pili, which is milky and used in desserts and as a merienda. Tultul is a rock salt made in Guimaras to use on cooked rice. It is made of reeds, twigs, and bamboo, which are soaked in saltwater, burned and the ashes strained, and then cooked. The most common meats are chicken, pork, and beef.

Philippine Specialties

Rice – glutinous for desserts or toasted and pinipig, a green rice pounded into flakes or used for a dessert topping

Bagoong sauce – fermented fish sauce, usually made from shrimp or anchovies

Tapsilog – marinated meat with garlic, rice and eggs

Patis – fish sauce

Kinilaw or paksiw dishes – fish marinated in vinegar, ginger

Bagoong – fish paste

Pangat – fish cooked in broth of tomatoes or tamarind

Daing – salt dried fish

Kare- kare – beef or oxtail, peanut butter, and bagoong

Lumpia – fried spring roll with cooked ground meat, poultry or shrimp, chilies, vegetables and served with a garlic vinegar sauce or sweet peanut and garlic sauce

Ukoy – shredded papaya shrimp fritters served with vinegar seasoned with garlic, salt and pepper

Balut – cooked egg with a partially developed chick or duckling inside

Meriendas – sweet snacks served during the day

Sinigang – meat or fish cooked with fruit, tomatoes, and vegetables

Sinampalukan – fish or chicken, with vegetables in sour broth

Bucayo – coconut dessert

Ukoy – vegetable and shrimp fritter

Caldereta – goat stew

Chicken relleno – chicken stuffed with hard-boiled eggs, pork, sausage, spices

Puchero – beef, chicken, vegetable stew in banana and tomato sauce with garlic

Embutido – spicy sausage

Camaro – crickets cooked in soy sauce, salt in vinegar

Carabao cheese – made from carabao (water buffalo) milk

Pancit – noodle dishes signifying long life, served at birthday parties and other special occasions

Puto maya – sweet glutinous rice

Halo-halo – shaved ice, coconut milk, fruit, sweet preserves

Champorado – chocolate sticky rice porridge made with coconut milk and served with dried salted fish flakes

Bibingka – hot rice cake

Biko – rice sweets made with butter, sugar, and coconut milk

Gulaman – pineapple and coconut dessert

Holidays and Special Occasions

For special occasions people gather to do the cooking and table preparations. The main dish is the lechon, a whole roasted pig, suckling pigs, or half a cattle can be used. This is served with lechon sauce. Other dishes might include hamonado (honey-cured beef, pork or chicken), relleno (stuffed chicken or milkfish), mechado, afritada, caldereta, puchero, paella, menudo, morcon, embutido, suman (a savory rice and coconut milk concoction steamed in leaves such as banana), and pancit canton., sweets and pastries such as leche flan, ube, sapin-sapin, sorbetes (ice creams), totong (a rice, coconut milk and mongo bean pudding), ginataan (a coconut milk pudding with various root vegetables and tapioca pearls), and gulaman.

Santacruzan (Festival of the Holy Cross) – seafood

Birthdays – pancit luglug (long noodles, garlic, shrimp sauce, pappers, patis, calamansi)

Christmas Eve (Noche Buena) – ham, queso de bola (Edam cheese)

Christmas - Bibingka – rice cake with coconut milk and baked on a banana leaf and topped with salted eggs; and puto bumbong- purple yam puto

Christmas to New Year's – mango float made with Graham crackers, mangoes, cream and milk

Beverages

Much of the Philippines is quite warm, though there are mountains. The people enjoy cold fruit drinks or shakes made from mando, melon, papaya, avocado, watermelon, strawberry, durian, mandarin oranges, pomelo, pineapples, bananas, and soursop. Sago't gulaman is a drink made with gulaman (dried seaweed) and agar (tapioca pearls).

Coffee is widely drunk and comes from mountains of Batangas (kapeng barako) and civet coffee (kape motit) in the Tagalog region. Tea is made from Philippine wild tea; pandan tea from pandan leaves and lemongrass; and salabat is made with ginger root. Tsokolate is a type of hot chocolate made from pure cacao beans that are dried, roasted, ground and formed into tablets.

The Philippines produce beer or serbessa with San Miguel beer the most popular, though there are many types produced. They also produce rum, gin, tuba (a hard liquor made from the drippings of a young palm which is consumed immediately or it becomes sour). The remainder is stored as palm vinegar. Lambanog is a sweet palm wine with a high alcoholic content. Tapuy is made from fermented glutinous rice.

Poland

Poland, from the word "Polanie" "Plains People" is bounded to the north by the Baltic Sea, the south the Carpathian Mountains, the rest mainly rolling plains ideal for agriculture. The history of the Polish region dates to Lusatian culture of the early Iron Age c 700 BC. Slavic groups would form Poland c 500AD and into a recognizable entity in the middle of the 10th c under the Piast dynasty. Krakow became the capital in 1038 by Casimir I the Restorer. In the 13th c Mongols invaded the country when the country was divided into dukedoms. In 1320 the country was unified under Wladyslaw I. Lithuanian Grand Duke Jogaila formed the Polish-Lithuanian Union with the Jagiellon dynasty 1386-1572. Poland developed as a feudal state with an agricultural economy. The 1596 Union of Lublin established the Polish-Lithuanian commonwealth. In 1772 the First Partition of the Commonwealth by Prussia, Russia, and Austria took place. A Second Partition took place in 1793, with a final one in 1795. In 1807 Napoleon I of France created a Polish state as the Duchy of Warsaw, but this was split again in 1815 at the Congress of Vienna. The eastern part was ruled by the Russian tsar who eventually annexed all parts of Poland. In 1918 after World War I Poland regained its independence as the Second Polish Republic. Nazi Germany invaded Poland in September 1939. The Molotov-Ribbentrop Pact divided Poland into 2 zones, one occupied by Nazi Germany and the other including Kresy in the control of the Soviet Union. The People's Republic of Poland was officially declared in 1952. Polish is the official language. Warsaw, the capital, was completely destroyed during World War II.

Dining Etiquette

Family is still very important and elders treated with respect. Please be punctual when entertained. If bringing a gift, flowers in an uneven number are appropriate. Red and white carnations and chrysanthemums are for funerals only. Shake hands greeting and departing. The lady extends her hand first. A married woman takes her husband's surname and changes the last letter to an "a". Meals are preceded by an aperitif, or whiskey, gin and tonic, wine or beer. White vodka is always offered. Light cold hors d'oeuvres (herring in cream, fish in aspic) may also be served. Drinks should not be brought to the table. The guest of honor is seated at the head of the table. The host(ess) begins eating first and hands should be kept above the table at all times. When served seconds, say "No" twice and then "Yes" if you want more. Leave a little something on your plate or it will be refilled. Wine will be served with the meal. Tea rather than coffee is served after the meal.

Toasting is very much enjoyed and will be initiated by the host, who will clink a glass for attention. The toast is" Na Zdrowir" "To your health". Then the guest of honor returns the toast. If a person flicks his fingers against his neck you're invited to join in the drink. Ladies do not toast. Remember the Poles love their vodka and love to drink. Vodka is served straight, without mixers or ice. Drink slowly as your glass will be refilled as soon as it is emptied. If you really want to seal your friendship "Bruderschaft" have a special drink together!

Bigos (Sauerkraut and Meat Stew)

The national dish!

Serves 6

2 kielbasa rings, sliced into 1" rounds, or 2 lbs. cooked meat – lamb, beef, or pork	¼ cup water
6 potatoes, boiled and sliced thick	2large onions, peeled and sliced
2 lb. sauerkraut	2 tbls. butter or oil
4 dried mushrooms	1 tbls. carraway seeds
	Salt and pepper

In a pan soak the mushrooms in the water for 2 hours. Bring to a boil. Slice the mushrooms. Save the liquid.

Wash the sauerkraut and squeeze it. Add the mushrooms and liquid to sauerkraut.

In a skillet brown the sausage. Remove from pan. Using same skillet heat butter and sauté onions. Stir in the meat, sauerkraut and mushrooms, potatoes, and caraway seeds. Heat until warmed.

There are many variations on "Hunter's Stew". It was a hearty dish served on festive occasions, or could be made to use up "leftover" meats.

Cuisine

Polish cooking is a mixture of German, Austrian, Hungarian, Jewish, French, Russian, Italian, and Turkish cuisines. The French influence is seen in the use of mustards and cream sauces. Even back in the 10-12th c the country was rich in "grains, meat, honey and fish' noted by Abraham ben Jacob. The Turks introduced spices such as black pepper and nutmeg. Later the people relied on spices, mushrooms, berries, and nuts. Bona Sforza, the Italian queen and second wife of Sigismund I of Poland, brought Italian chefs to Poland after 1518. Her cooks imported oranges, lemons, pomegranates, olives, figs, tomatoes, potatoes, corn, chestnuts, raisins, almonds, rice, cane sugar, olive oil, herbs, and spices. Spices and herbs included black pepper, fennel, saffron, ginger, nutmeg, cloves, and cinnamon which had not previously been used in Poland. Lettuce, leeks, celeriac, beets, turnips, carrots, peas, cauliflower, and cabbage became more common in the diet. Pickled cucumbers, a sour, or sweet and vinegary pickle were preserved in wooden barrels became popular. Later kings married French women who brought in their own chefs, craftsmen, and staff. Game, fish, snails, various fruits, Italian and French wines and Champagne were introduced. Very elaborate meals were prepared for the aristocracy. Lithuanian, Jewish, German, Hungarian, Ottoman Empire, and Armenian cuisines influenced the Polish cuisine before the 17th c. Potatoes replaced the traditional grains. In 1682 Stanislaw Czerniecki published *Compendium feruculorum, albo Zebranie potraw* "Collection of Dishes" in Krakow, the oldest known cookbook. The book contained Russian, German and Austro-Hungarian traditions.

Chicken, pork, sausages, beef, root vegetables, noodles, grains, eggs, and cream are used in many of the dishes. Among the grains grown arc millct, ryc, and whcat. Fruits and vegetables include apples, plums, currants, berries, onions, potatoes, cabbage, celeriac, cucumbers, carrots, beets, parsnips, radishes, squash, and zucchini. Each region has its own specialties. Trout, venison, eel, duck, and wild boar are also popular. Mustards and horseradish add to the flavor of the dishes. Breads and rolls are made from rye or wheat. In past times guests were welcomed into a home with bread and salt as a sign of hospitality. A 17th century Polish poet, Wespazjan Kochowski, wrote in 1674: "O good bread, when it is given to guests with salt and good will!" Today the tradition is mainly observed on wedding days, when newlyweds are greeted with bread and salt by their parents on returning from the church wedding.

Zupa Wisniowa (cherry soup)

Good for a hot summer day! Other berries or fruit can be used instead of the cherries.

Serves 4

4 cups water
2 pints cherries without seeds and stems
½ tsp. cinnamon
¼ tsp. ground cloves

1 tbls. cornstarch
¼ - ½ cup sugar
¾ cup sour cream

In a saucepan bring the water to a boil and add the cherries, cinnamon and cloves. Simmer until cherries are softened 10-15 minutes. Pour through a sieve into another pan. Stir in the cornstarch. Bring to a boil and add enough sugar to sweeten soup. Cool and add sour cream.

Polish Specialties

Pierogi – stuffed noodles
Kasza - cereals
Barszcz – beet soup
Zurek – sour rye meal mash
Kotlet schabowy – breaded pork cutlet
Flaki – tripe soup
Golonka – pork knuckles with vegetables
Golabki – stuffed cabbage
Kolduny – meat dumplings
Szmalec – spread made with fat and spices
Zrazy –stuffed slices of beef
Surowka – shredded carrot, celeriac or beetroot with lemon and sugar

Kapusta kwaszona – fermented cabbage
Chlodnik – chilled beet or fruit soup
Makowiec – poppyseed pastry
Drozdzowka – yeast cake (dessert)
Kapusta kiszona – sauerkraut
Ogórek kiszony - salted sour cucumber
Kiełbasa - Polish sausage
0scypek – sheepsmilk cheese
Pierniki - gingerbread
Sernik – cheesecake made with twarog, a fresh cheese
Mazurek – cake with fillings, fruit, walnut paste or chocolate

Holiday foods

Fat Thursday is celebrated by Catholics on the last Thursday before Lent and the last day of Carnival. On this day sweets and cakes are consumed including – paczki (Polish donuts with rose petal jam or apple with icing) and makowiec (poppy seed rolls)

Easter – The Saturday preceding Easter people take decorated baskets of food (swieconka) to be blessed at the churches. The baskets may include hard-boiled eggs, ham, sausage, salt, horseradish, fruit, bread and cakes. These will not be eaten till Easter morning after Mass when parishioners return home and tables are set with white tablecloths. Eggs are decorated with symbols such as a lamb. Polish Easter soup "zurek" is served garnished with hard-boiled eggs and sausage. The blessed eggs are shared with family for good health the rest of the year.

Easter breakfast – cold cuts, beet salads, bigos, Zurek, smoked salmon, Easter salad with chopped eggs, and cakes

On Easter Monday people splash each other with water, also for good luck.

Christmas Eve – Wigilia- Before the meal guests share an oplatek – a Christmas wafer symbolizing love, friendship and forgiveness. In earlier times an extra place was always set in case someone either a stranger or family member might appear. White tablecloths are always used, and poppyseeds and honey served with the meal. The meals are usually meatless. The meal may start with red borsch, uszka – noodles stuffed with mushrooms, or herring. These will be followed by pierogi – dumplings stuffed with sauerkraut and mushrooms, carp are usually fried or jellied. Desserts are kutia – poppy seed cake, and cheesecake

Christmas - goose, duck or chicken is served. Other dishes include herring, rollmops, pierogi with sauerkraut and mushrooms, fish soup, kielbasa, hams, bigos, and vegetable salads. Desserts served are gingerbread, cheesecake, fruit, poppyseed cake, and kutia, a sweet grain pudding, plus coffee, nuts and candies.

Day after Christmas – a hunter's stew is made with sausage and leftover meats

Beverages

Early alcoholic beverages were beer and mead. Every day drinks were milk, whey, buttermilk, kvas, and beverages made with herb infusions. In the 13th c mead was so popular Prince Leszek I the White told the Pope that his men could not participate in the Crusades as there was no mead in the Holy Land. In the 16th c Hungarian and Silesian wines were imported into Poland. Vodka is thought to have originally been distilled in Poland, and the *Akta Grodzkie*, dating to 1405 makes mention of the drink, although it may have been produced as early as the 8th c. Cider (cydr) was also produced.

Today beer is produced and drunk. Local grape wines in small vineyards are made in the Lesser Poland, Subcarpathia, Silesia and West Pomerania regions. Polish vodka is traditionally prepared from grain or potatoes. Tea with lemon and sugar, coffee, buttermilk, kefir, mineral waters, juices, and soft drinks are consumed.

Did You Know?

Bona Sforza, a 16th c Italian born queen, is thought to have brought the first soup vegetables and tomatoes to Poland.

Portugal

The Republic of Portugal occupies the western part of the Iberian Peninsula with Spain, and the offshore islands of The Azores and Madeira. The country is divided by the Tagus River, the north being mountainous and cooler, the south hills and valleys. Lisbon, founded by the Phoenicians who called it "Alis Ubbo" "Delightful Shore", became the capital in 1298. During the 15th and 16th c Lisbon was a major port, and one of the richest in the world. The Azores were settled by the Carthaginians c 4th c BC and later colonized by the Portuguese and Flemish. A peace treaty was signed in 1382 between Portugal and the Spanish kingdom of Castile. Philip II of Spain was crowned King of Portugal in 1581. In the 19th c whaling became a major industry. Madeira was founded in 1419 by the explorer Joao Goncalves Zarco for Henry the Navigator. Christopher Columbus' wife Isabel Moniz came from here. Today the island supports dairy farms, fishing and vineyards. Portuguese is the official language.

Dining Etiquette

Most entertaining is done at restaurants or at home. If invited to a home please bring something for the home, chocolates or flowers (chrysanthemums are for funerals). Please be prompt on arrival. Use first names only with good friends. Address people are Senhor (Mrs.) or Senhora (Mrs.). Elders and rank are important. Please shake with everyone greeting and departing. Men hold doors for women, and stand when introduced to a woman or when she enters a room. Aperitifs, wine or liquor will be served. At dinner the host and hostess will be seated at each end of the table, the male guest of honor to the right of the hostess. Bottled mineral water and wine will usually be on the table. A soup – caldo verde; garlic; vegetable or seafood will start the meal. Grace or a few words of welcome are said before eating. Food is eaten continental style with the fork used with the left hand, the knife in the right. Dishes will be passed or served in courses starting with an entrée that includes meat, vegetables, potatoes or rice, and salad on the same plate. Dessert, cheese and fruit are served with Port. Keep your hands above the table, no elbows on the table, and do not stretch or yawn. When finished put your knife and fork together. Since dinner is not till 8 or 9, please plan on leaving by 11-11:30. The toast is initiated by the host and is "Saude" "To your health".

Cuisine

Portuguese cooking uses fresh vegetables, fruit, seafood, garlic and olive oil, sheep cheese, butter; linguica and chorizo – smoked pork sausages made with garlic, wine, and paprika; hazelnuts, coriander; Portuguese allspice, blend of paprika, garlic powder, salt, pepper, turmeric, and orange peel; fresh lemon juice on meats; fresh and dried figs. Vineyards and orchards grow olives, chestnuts, pomegranate, oranges, and grapes. Early on the people learned to salt and dry cod

(bacalhau), often using it with potatoes and onions in their cooking. Seafood includes scallops, octopus, cod, scabbardfish, grouper, monkfish, clams, tuna (some come from the Azores).
Each region has its specialties:
Alentejo – breadbasket of Portugal; mushrooms
Oporto – tripe
Lisbon – liver
Melgaco –ham
Costa de Prata – eels, mussels and suckling pig
Minho – caldo verde; rice dishes
The Algarve – fruit orchards, olives, orange groves, tangerines, apricots, figs, pears, melons, prawns, sea bass, mussels, tuna, sardines

Prince Henry the Navigator was the first to colonize the islands of Madeira and Porto Santo in the 15th c. Forests were burned and the soil mixed with volcanic ash was found to produce excellent crops such as grapes, sugar cane, olives, fruit, fennel and bay leaves. The Portuguese brought spices – cinnamon, turmeric, cumin; and introduced potatoes, tomatoes, peppers, fava beans and rice which are used in the cooking today.

Almost 1000 miles from Portugal is the Azores archipelago, made up of nine volcanic islands. The volcanic heat can be used to heat dishes. The people grow goats, cattle, vineyards for wine, make cheese, and use of the bounty of the sea - kingfish, hake, parrotfish, mackerel, porkfish, neru, and cherne.

Caldo Verde (kale and potato soup with chorizo or linguica)

Serves 6-8

1 lb. chorizo or linguica sausage	4 potatoes, peeled and sliced
1 lb. kale or collard greens, stems removed	4 cloves garlic, minced
¼ cup olive oil	6 cups chicken stock or water
2 large onions, chopped	Salt and pepper to taste

In a pot with water cook the sausage for 5 minutes. Remove from liquid. Drain. Cut into pieces.
Roll up the greens and slice into strips.
Heat the olive oil in the pot and saute the onions until translucent. Add the potatoes and cook until just tender. Add the garlic and stock. Cook for 20 minutes.
Remove about half the potatoes, and mash. Return to pot. Add the sausage and cook 5 minutes. Add greens and cook 3 minutes. Season with salt and pepper.
Serve in a soup tureen or soup bowls. Drizzle with a little more olive oil.
Serve with broa (cornbread)

Ameijoas a bulhau pato – clams cooked in olive oil and garlic)

Serves 4

2tbls. olive oil
¼ tsp. crushed red pepper
2cloves garlic, minced
1 leek, sliced

1red pepper, chopped
32 clams
Salt and pepper
Cilantro

Heat the olive oil in a pan. Add the red pepper, garlic, leek, and red pepper. Saute for a minutes, or just a little more to make sure leek is tender. Add the clams. Serve hot garnished with cilantro. The clams can be chopped or left whole.
Serve with crusty bread and a salad.
Mussels can be substituted for the clams.

Portuguese Specialties

Broa – sweet potato muffins
Ameijoas e porco na cataplana – clams with pork and ham
Caldeirada de peixe – seafood dish with potatoes, green peppers, sardines, and garlic croutons
Arroz de pato – duck rice
Alheira de mirandela – fried sausage or other meat with eggs
Acorda alentejana – bread, eggs, olive oil, and coriander
Rojoes a modado – pork loin cooked in garlic and wine and served with potatoes
Feijado transmontana – bean stew
Presunto- cured ham
Bacalhau Assado – roasted salt cod
Bacalhau a bras – salted cod, onions, straw potatoes, egg, parsley and olives

Bolinhos de bacalhau – cod fritters
Cataplana – fish stew cooked in a copper pan
Cachaco de porco – pork neck with potatoes
Arroz doce - rice pudding
Cakes with Madeira
Castanhas assadas- roasted chestnuts
Pudim flan – caramel custard
Toucinho do ceu – dessert made with lard, sugar and eggs
Malassadas – deep fried dough with sugar
Fatias dourades - toasted bread with cinnamon and sugar
Sonhos – fried dough rolled in cinnamon and sugar
Sonhos de abobara – fried dough with pumpkin
Azavias do grao e amendoa – fried chickpea and almond turnovers

Holidays and Special Occasions

Easter Sunday; Feast of the Resurrection – lamb; cozidoa a Portugueza – beef, pork and chicken stew
Vespera de Natal (Christmas Eve) – bacalhau da consoada (cod with potatoes, cabbage, carrots, and hard-boiled eggs with olive oil) or bacalhau a Gomes Sa – salt cod with onions, garlic, potatoes, hard-boiled eggs, olives and parsley; polvo – roasted octopus
Missa do Galo – midnight mass
Pai Natal (Santa Claus) arrives with gifts which may be opened Christmas Eve or after mass

Feliz Navidad (Christmas) –Consoada dinner - roast turkey and stuffing; roast goat, chicken, pork, or lamb; Bolo Rei (King Cake is filled with fruit and nuts and topped with candied fruit and powdered sugar) and Bolo Rainha (Queen Cake, a nut and raisin cake); filhoses or coscoroes – fried dough with cinnamon and sugar; broa; lampreia de natal – sugared egg yolks in shape of lampray

Between Christmas and New Year's there is much singing. Fireworks are set off New Year's Eve preceded by dinners and family get togethers to ring out the old year.

Dia de Reis – King's Day – Epiphany – children put out shoes with carrots and straw to attract the three kings bringing gifts. Bolo Rei is eaten today.

Beverages

Portugal's wines, port and Madeira are world renowned. Since Roman times wine has been produced, most of the vineyards in the north in the Estrmadura region. In 1756 the wine region was demarcated by the Marquis of Pombal (who designed much of modern Lisbon) and the better wines labeled. The Dao region in central Portugal produces red wines. Port first became popular c1688 when William of Orange of England wished to destroy the French economy and placed heavy duties on wine. The 1703 Metheun Treaty permitted Portugal to ship wine to England in casks where it was bottled. The reaction was not favorable. In 1780 a bottle was developed for transporting the wine to England. Vintage port is aged for two years in casks, shipped to England, refortified, and then allowed to mature for 10-40 years in the bottle. Crusted port ages 4-5 years in the cask and "throws a crust". Some vintage ports may need to be decanted. Most are served after dinner, the host first serving the person to his right, then left, and the bottle is passed clockwise. Port is produced in the Douro valley and matures in Oporto where it is shipped. Port is not necessarily red. There is white port, pink and rubio.

The grapes for Madeira were first brought to Madeira from Crete in the 13th c. Madeira is drunk as an aperitif or dessert wine. Four types are produced – sercial and verdelho – light dry, served as an aperitif and bual or boal and malmsey – which are full-bodied dessert wines. Madeira gets its distinct flavor from aging in a hot room (estufa) for 3-6 months, then allowed to mature 18 months to 2 years, blended, put in new casks and refortified. Madeira ages well and lasts for a long time.

Beer has been produced in Portugal since the 1600s and in the 19th c was influenced by the Danes. The beers are mainly lagers served cold. Other drinks are Ginjinha, a sweet sour cherry liqueur; Vinho verde "young wine" green wine made from young grapes; and Medronho – white alcohol distilled from arbutus berries. Bica is strong coffee served in a small cup.

Did You Know?

Olive trees can live up to 260 years or more.

Much of the world's cork comes from 1.8 million acres planted with cork trees. The land is protected by a law that dates back to 1209. Cork is made from the tree bark which is stripped from the trees, and it takes 8-10 years for it to grow back. Cork has been harvested since Roman times. The aqueduct in Elvas was built in the 1400s, not by early Romans.

Qatar

Qatar is located on the Qatar peninsula on the northeastern coast of the Arabian Peninsula. The peninsula has been inhabited for over 50,000 years as tools and artifacts date back to the Stone Age. Kassite Babylonian material dating back to the second millennium BC includes crushed snail shells and potsherds. Pliny the Elder, a Roman writer, referring to the inhabitants as the *Catharrei*. In 224 AD, the Sasanian Empire gained control over the territories surrounding the Persian Gulf. Qatar played a role in the commercial activity of the Sasanids, contributing at least two commodities: precious pearls and purple dye from shellfish. Qatar was also a famous horse and camel breeding center. In 628 the Arab tribes converted to Islam. Much of Eastern Arabia was controlled by the Usfurids in 1253, but control of the region was seized by the prince of Ormus in 1320. In 1515, Manuel I of Portugal vassalised the Kingdom of Ormus and seized a significant portion of Eastern Arabia in 1521, followed by the Ottomans in 1550. In 1783 Bani Utbah tribes annexed Bahrain and had jurisdiction over Qatar. In 1871 the Al Thani tribe came again under Ottoman rule. The Ottomans renounced all their rights to Qatar and in 1916 it became a British protectorate. Qatar became independent in 1971. Doha is the capital and Arabic the official language.

Dining Etiquette

It is an honor to be entertained in a home. Please bring a small gift, never alcoholic beverages or anything made of pigskin. Please present the gift with your right hand. Punctuality is very important, though the Saudis may take their time. Please greet your host by saying "Salaam Alaykum", then shake hands and say "Kaif Halak". Women extend their hands first, or may not. The host may put his left hand on the shoulder of another male. And when you get to know him better may kiss you on each cheek. Holding hands is a sign of a very warm friendship. Strong coffee or tea will be served with dates, nuts or raisins. When seated please keep both feet on the ground, do not show the soles of your shoe, or point it at someone. The men and women may dine separately. Before a meal hands are washed and a prayer "in the name of God" is always said. Only the right hand is used for eating, though fingers are used when no utensil is available. When served wait for your host to start. Never leave your plate empty, or it will be refilled. If you pass something do so with your right hand. If you are the guest of honor and a feast is served, a whole sheep might be served including the eye which is considered a delicacy. Please eat the eye when presented to you. Hands are also washed after the meal. Please write or telephone a thank-you.

Cuisine and Beverages

The cuisine has been influenced by the Arabs, Indians and Persians. Yogurt, cheese, olives, eggplant, tomatoes, bulghur wheat seafood, dates, rice, meat – lamb, camel, chicken, and fish; spices- cardamom, saffron and cinnamon are used in preparing dishes. Qatar is a Muslim country and alcohol is not served. Coffee is brewed from dark roasted coffee beans with cardamom and served with dates. Karak "tea with milk" is a tea with cardamom, saffron and sugar with evaporated milk. Another drink is made with mint and lemon.

Harees (ground lamb and burghul patties)

Makes 8

1½ cups burghul
1 lb. ground lamb
½ tsp. allspice
¼ tsp. nutmeg

Fresh ground pepper
Taste of salt
¼ cup olive oil
1 onion, chopped

Place the burghul in a bowl. Cover with water. Soak 10 minutes. Drain in a sieve pushing out all water. Place back in the bowl and add lamb and seasonings. Combine all the ingredients. Divide the lamb into 8 balls and flatten into patties. Make an indentation in each patty. Pour a small amount of the oil and onion into the indentation. Serve with flatbread.

Specialties

Harees – wheat with meat to break the fast at Iftar during Ramadan
Balaleet – noodles with cinnamon, saffron and cardamom served with a saffron omelet
Saloona – tomato, aubergine, carrot and potato dish served with rice
Machbus or kabsa - rice dish with spices, chicken, lamb, shrimp, camel or fish
Madhruba – rice, milk, butter and cardamom served during Ramadan
Luqaimat – butter, milk, flour, sugar, saffron and cardamom fried dumplings dipped in honey or sugar syrup and served during Ramadan
Ghuzi or shuwaa – whole roasted lamb with rice, vegetables and nuts
Thareed – lamb or chicken with spices, carrots, beans, onions, and potatoes in a tomato sauce served on bread during Ramadan
Kousa Mahshi – baked zucchini stuffed with lamb, mint and garlic

Margoog – zucchini, carrot, eggplant, tomato, potato, and meat dish layered with thin dough
Foul - mashed beans
Waraq enab – vine leaves stuffed with lamb and rice
Hummus – tahini, chickpea, and garlic dip
Nichee – hummus without tahini
Motabel – spicy eggplant dip
Tabbouleh – burghul, tomato, and mint salad
Muhammara – spicy red pepper dip
Mehalbiya – pistachio and rose water pudding
Umm ali – bread and rice pudding with nuts and raisins
Esh asaraya – cheesecake with cream
Sago – gelatin pudding with saffron and cardamom
Baklava – phyllo with honey and nut dessert
Kanafeh – cheese pastry in syrup
Qatayef - pancake with sweet cheese or nuts served during Ramadan

Holidays and Special Occasions

During Ramadan people fast from sunrise to sunset. See above food to break the fast.
Qatar National Day (December 18) – thareed, machbus, hares, balaleet, and mchalbiya are served.

Romania

Romania is bordered by Hungary and Serbia to the west, Ukraine and the Republic of Moldova to the northeast, and Bulgaria to the south. Its 91,699 sq. miles are made up of the Carpathian Mountains, the Transylvanian Alps, part of the Danube Basin, and low plains. Archeological excavations reveal that settlements have existed since c 600,000 BC. European migrations passed through in the 2nd millennium BC, then the Thracians, Dacians, Greek colonists along the Black Sea, and the Romans, and many others. In the 20th c Romania was a Communist country, but in 1989 student demonstrations finally led to democracy. The capital, Bucharest, was founded in the 11th c by a legendary shepherd, Bucur, on the Dimbovita River. The earliest historical records of the city date to a document signed by Prince Vlad Tepes (Vlad the Impaler), best known as Dracula. The official language is Romanian.

"Sarmale în frunză de viță" (Stuffed Grape Leaves)

2 lbs. of ground pork (or 1.5 lbs. of ground pork and 0.5 lbs. of ground beef)	1 can (15 oz. or so) of crushed tomatoes
	1 can of tomato sauce
4 onions (large size)	Oil to cook the onions, salt, pepper
1.5 cups of rice	

Chop the onions. In a large skillet, brown the onions, but very lightly. Set aside, in a large bowl. Add some more oil and very lightly brown the rice (very carefully, not to burn it, stirring continuously). Mix with the onions, ground meet and rice. Add half of the crushed tomatoes to the mixture, and salt and pepper to taste. I also add some dill, but this is optional.

Meanwhile, take the grape leaves out of the jar, separate gently and let stay in water for about 45 minutes, to get rid of excessive salt.

Roll the "sarmale", a little of the mixture in each leaf, and close the ends, pushing them inwards with your thumb and pointer. Arrange them nicely, in circles, in a large pot. Separately, mix the remaining crushed tomatoes with the tomato sauce and a little water, to make a very light and "watery" sauce. Taste for salt. Pour over the sarmale, so that it covers the last layer. If needed, add more water. Cover and cook. When it starts boiling, reduce the heat to medium/ low, and occasionally sort of "shake" the pot by the handles, sideways, to make sure they don't stick to the bottom of the pot.

Cook for about 45 minutes. When it starts smelling "yummy", taste one of them, to check for the rice to be fully cooked. Cook more, if needed, but make sure you don't over cook.

Recipe courtesy of Diana Pruteanu

Dining Etiquette

Please be prompt when invited for a meal. Shake hands greeting and departing. Men and men, women and women may embrace and kiss if they are good friends. Men stand when introduced to ladies, hold doors and chairs for them. Being a guest in a home is an honor. Please bring flowers in an odd number and wrapped. Tuica (plum brandy, often homemade), wine, or other drinks are served before the meal. The guest of honor sits at the opposite end of the table from the host. Please eat continental style – fork in the left hand, knife in the right. Do try all the food, even if only taking a small amount. Salad is served with the meal. Food is served in courses – soup, appetizers, entrée and vegetables, then desserts. Silverware and dishes are cleared with each course. Keep your hands table level, not in your lap. The host initiates a toast, touch glasses, and say "To your health", "Good luck", "Noroc", or "Salut".

Eggplant Salad

4 large eggplant
¼ sunflower oil (do not use olive oil, doesn't taste good in this salad)

½ onion, chopped
Salt to taste

You can either grill the eggplant or bake them in the oven at 375°, by placing them on a cookie sheet, poke some holes in the eggplant. "This is a very important step, once I forgot to poke holes in the eggplant, and they literally exploded in the oven. So just bake them in the oven, make sure they are baked well, and you'll have to turn them from side to side. Once they are done, let them cool off."

After they are cooled off, remove the peel, using a knife, if you've cooked them enough, the peel should come off easily. You may wash them, to remove any of the dark peel, but make sure you use paper towels to soak up the excess water.

Place them in your food processor, add the onion and the salt, and pulse a few times, slowly add the sunflower oil.

Recipe courtesy of Madalina Iacobita, Embassy of Romania, Washington, DC

Cuisine

The early inhabitants the Dacians ate vegetables such as lentils, peas, spinach, garlic) and fruits (grapes, apples, raspberries) and produced wine. The Romans made pastry from cheese, and introduced millet porridge. Later Maize and potatoes became staples of the Romanian diet. Wallachia and Moldavia were strongly influenced by the Ottoman Empire which introduced eggplant, bell peppers, *chiftele* (deep-fried meatballs, a variation of kofta) and *mici* (short sausages without casings, usually barbecued); *ciorbă/borş* (sour soups) and meat-and-vegetable stews, such as *iahnie de fasole* (beans), *ardei umpluţi* (stuffed peppers), and *sarmale* (stuffed cabbage). The Romanian tomato salad is a variation of the Turkish *çoban salata*. There is a unique procession of sweets and pastries combining honey and nuts, such as *baclava, sarailie* (or *seraigli*), *halva*, and *rahat* (Turkish delight). The Greek influence was also felt with musaca; and the Austrians snitel. Cheese *branza* has been made since early times. Most of the cheeses are made from cow's or sheep's milk.

Once the breadbasket of Europe, Romania fell on hard times. During the last regime almost all foodstuffs had to be imported to help pay the national debt! The country is a major exporter of poppy seeds, mint, coriander, and marjoram. Foodstuffs frequently used in cooking are eggplant, cucumbers, cabbage, carrots, garlic, rice, cornmeal, noodles, potatoes, tomatoes, pork and chicken. Breakfast is usually a light meal with tea or coffee and rolls. Both lunch and dinner are full meals.

Holidays and Special Occasions

During the seven weeks preceding Christmas and Easter, fasting from meat and animal products is observed. Fasting is also observed before Peter and Paul – June 29th. Dormition – August 15th. Funerals - special cakes are baked and given to priests, then on the 3rd and 7th days. 6 months, 1 and 7 years to commemorate the dead. Wine and Coliva – whole wheat boiled with sugar and then sprinkled with crushed nuts and syrup is blessed in the church and then given to the priest and guests. Coliva is also given the last Saturday in March.

On March 9th and St. Stephen's Day – mucenici (boiled donuts covered with syrup, nuts and spices) are eaten

Easter – lamb is served: the main dishes are *borş de miel* (lamb sour soup), roast lamb, and *drob de miel* – a Romanian-style lamb haggis made from minced offal (heart, liver, lungs), lamb meat and spring onions with spices, wrapped in a caul and roasted. The traditional Easter cake is *pască*, a pie made from yeast dough with a sweet cottage cheese filling at the center, chocolates, red dyed eggs

Before Christmas, on December 20 (Ignat's Day or *Ignatul*) a pig is traditionally sacrificed by rural families and a variety of foods for Christmas are prepared from the slaughtered pig

Christmas Eve – turta (cake with sugar or honey and walnuts; Christmas cakes; sauerkraut; pork or carp

Christmas - *cozonac*, a sweet bread made from nuts, poppy seeds, or *rahat* (Turkish delight) , and thin wafers with honey or syrup, representing the baby Jesus' swaddling clothes

Weddings – corn was thrown as a fertility charm

Romanian pancakes, called *clătite*, are thin and can be prepared with savory or sweet fillings: ground meat, cheese, or jam for special occasions.

Beverages

Romania has produced wines for thousands of year. Both the Greeks and the Romans were aware of its qualities, and archeological excavations have uncovered amphorae, frescos, jewelry, and other artwork depicting wine rituals. The wine regions are Tarnava (dry whites); Cotnari (sweet whites) – the Cotnari vineyard dates back to 1448 and was known as the "Pearl of Moldavia; Dealu Mare (red wines); and Murfatler (red and white wine). During the fall pine boughs decorate doorways to celebrate the new wine. Romania also produces Tuica (plum brandy), vodka, fruit brandies, and uses the Methode Champenoise for sparkling wines. Beer is brewed in Azuga in the Carpathian Mountains and Cluj.

Russia

Russia is bordered by Norway, Finland, Estonia, Latvia, Lithuania, Poland, Ukraine, Georgia, Azerbaijan, Kazakhstan, the People's Republic of China, Mongolia, and North Korea. Russia was known to be inhabited over 36,000 years ago along the Don River. The country was inhabited by Slavs from the 3rd to 8th c AD. The first ruler, Rurik, came from Scandinavia and ruled the city state of Novogorod. The region known as Kievan Rus' became a number of smaller states. These were later taken over by the Mongols and absorbed into the Golden Horde. The Grand Duchy of Moscow reunified the surrounding Russian states and gained independence from the Golden Horde. By the 18th century the Russian Empire stretched from Poland to Alaska. Tsars ruled the country until the Bolshevik Revolution in 1917. The Soviet Union was formed in 1922 with a planned economy and collectivization of agriculture. The USSR was dissolved in 1991. Moscow, the capital, was founded by Prince Yuri Dolgoruky in 1147, and is situated on the Moskva River. Russian is the official language.

Dining Etiquette

Russians eat three or four meals a day, starting with *zavtrak* (breakfast) usually porridge and tea. Lunch lasts from 12 noon until 1 p.m and kasha or a salad is served. Dinner may include four courses - The first course *zakuski* or "little bite' is comprised of appetizers and will almost always include herring. The first course is usually soup, although soup may be served as an entrée. The main course is often roast meat, with potatoes and root vegetables followed by dessert. Another meal may follow around 9-10PM with a samovar for tea or coffee and cakes.

When invited for a meal please be prompt and no more than 15 minutes late. Dress in good clothes, so as to show respect for your host. Please bring a small gift – a cake, candy, a bottle of wine, and men may bring flowers, though not yellow. Please shake hands firmly. Women who know each other will kiss three times on the cheek beginning with the left one. Men may hug or give a pat on the back. The oldest or honored guest is served first. Food is eaten continental style with the fork in the left hand and knife in the right. Do not begin eating until your host raises his fork or invited you to start. Do not rest your elbows on the table and keep your hands at table level, not in your lap. You may use your bread to soak up gravy or sauces. Second helpings will be offered. Leave a small amount on your plate to show that your host has provided enough food. Please thank your host for the meal. The host will ask the guests to adjourn from the table.

Men pour drinks for the women seated next to them. Please do not drink your vodka until a toast has been made. Keep your glass raised, then clink glasses. Vodka is drunk straight and in one gulp in a small glass. Do not sip. Do propose a toast to your hosts.

Kulebiaka (Fish, Rice, and Salmon in Pastry)

Serves 8

Pastry

4 cups flour
1 stick butter, cut into small pieces
6 tbls. chilled vegetable shortening

1 tsp. salt
10-12 tbls. cold water

In a large bowl combine the flour, butter, shortening and salt. Add 10 tbls. water. If too crumbly add more water. Divide dough in two, dust with flour, and wrap in wax paper. Refrigerate 2-3 hours.

Filling

2 cups dry white wine
1 large onion, chopped
1 stalk celery, finely chopped
1 carrot, peeled and finely chopped
12 whole peppercorns
1 tsp. salt
3 lbs. salmon, boned and skinned
1 stick butter + 2 tbls.
½ lb. mushrooms, sliced

¼ cup lemon juice
Fresh ground pepper
2 large onions, finely chopped
½ cup rice
1 cup chicken stock
½ cup fresh chopped dill
4 hard-cooked eggs, finely chopped

Combine 3 quarts water, wine, onion, celery, carrots, peppercorns and salt in a large casserole or poacher. Bring to a boil. Carefully add salmon. Simmer 10 minutes, or fish is firm to touch. Transfer fish to a bowl and break into small pieces. Melt 2 tbls. butter in a skillet, add mushrooms, and saute until soft. Place mushrooms in a bowl and toss them with the lemon juice. Melt 4 tbls. butter, and add the onions sautéing until soft. Add to mushrooms. Melt 2 tbls. butter and add rice and chicken stock. Bring to a boil. Cover and simmer for 10 minutes until rice is tender. Stir in the dill. Add the mushroom and onion mixture, rice, eggs, and salmon. Toss.
Preheat oven to 400º
On a floured surface roll out 1 ball of the dough into a rectangle about 7x16 inches. Coat a cookie sheet with 2 tbls. butter. Place the pastry in the cookie sheet, leaving a 1 in. edge. Brush the pastry with ½ egg mixture. Top with salmon mixture. Roll out other half of pastry dough to same size rectangle. Save a little pastry from each half to make into leaves. Place on top of salmon. Garnish with leaves. Brush with remaining egg mixture. Refrigerate for 20 or more minutes. Bake 1 hour or until golden brown. Serve with melted butter or sour cream.

Egg Mixture

½ stick butter, melted

1 egg yolk mixed with 1 tbls. cream

Combine the ingredients.

Cuisine

There are over 160 different ethnic groups in Russia making for a diverse cuisine which include Russian, Slav, Tatar, Bashkirs, Muslims, Caucasus', Finno-Ugric, Siberian, and many other cultures. Much of the food comes from peasant traditions. The north of Russia is largely unpopulated, cold and a vast region. Here one finds mushrooms, berries used in preserves or drinks such as kisel, potatoes, cabbage, carrots, apples, and dried and salted fish. The inhabitants mainly live on stews and soups for warmth. Southern Russia is much warmer. Wheat, buckwheat, livestock, dairy animals, meat, fish, fruits, especially fresh berries, and root vegetables – beets, turnips, potatoes, onions, and cabbage are cultivated. The Mongols captured much of the southern region in the 11th C and introduced tea (the samovar), fermented cabbage, curd cheese, honey pastries, dried fruits, pastries, and lamb. The Caspian Sea once had an abundance of sturgeon, famous for its roe or caviar. The part of Russia closest to the Baltic was influenced by the Scandinavians, the Caucus region used many spices, and in the Far East the culture is more Chinese. Ivan III built numerous buildings with Italian craftsmen who introduced pasta, gelato, sherbets, and pastries to the aristocracy. At the height of the Russian empire during the 16th-20th c dishes were introduced from France, Italy, Austria and other European countries. French chefs were widely sought after. They introduced the country to fine wines and liquors, ice cream, cream sauces, chocolate, and other fine foods. These included Veal Orloff, Beef Stroganoff, Chicken Kiev, and Salade Russe. During the reign of Peter I "The Great" his French chef introduced courses rather than serving food at one time.

Beginning in the 19th c well to do Russians set a zakuska, a table elaborately set with food, always fish, caviar, herring, meats, vegetables, pates, cheeses, pickles, and vodka, before dinner.

The finest caviar came from the Beluga, Sevruga and Osetrova sturgeon and was served on lightly toasted bread. Red caviar comes from salmon and is served on pumpernickel bread with scallions and chopped eggs.

Fish, poultry, games, lamb, beef, beets, honey, berries, poppy seeds, caraway, dill, dumplings, yogurt, raisins, prunes, hazelnuts, walnuts, almonds, cherries, apples, plums, cabbage, sour cream, cucumbers, curd cheese, cinnamon, lemons, and mushrooms are traditionally used in cooking. For Russians finding mushrooms is an art that they enjoy while the mushrooms are in season. Porcini mushrooms, known as the czar's mushrooms and chanterelles are highly prized. Mushrooms should be served raw in salads or just slightly roasted. Rye, wheat, barley and millet are used for cereals, pancakes, puddings, and breads kvass, beer and vodka. Salads do not use many greens, but will contain pickled vegetables, herring, cucumbers, beets, onions, a vinaigrette dressing and perhaps   eggs.

Russian Specialties

There are so many cultures in Russia, only a few items are listed.

Kasha – made from grains or groat and water
Smetana – heavy sour cream
Pirozhki – skewered grilled meats

Syrniki – sweet cheese fritters
Pokhlobka – potato soup
Okroshka - chilled vegetable soup with meat

Botvinia - vegetable soup with fish
Borscht – beet soup
Shchi – cabbage soup
Ukha – fish soup
Shashlyk – grilled meats on skewers
Kulebiaka – salmon or cabbage in pastray
Pirozhki – meat or cabbage pastries
Kholodets – jellied meats
Beef Stroganov – beef with sour cream served over noodles
Pelmeni – dough wrapped meat dumplings
Kotlety – meatballs
Fish – carp, sudak, sturgeon, salmon, and trout. Fish is preserved by salting, smoking, or pickling Pirozhki – buns stuffed with potatoes, meats, fish, rice, cabbage or other fillings
Zharennyi Porosenok - roast pig
Rybnaia Solianka - fish soup with onions, cucumbers and tomatoes
Ukha - clear fish soup with lime and dill
Miasnaia Solianka - meat soup with tomatoes, onions and cucumbers

Golubtsy - stuffed cabbage rolls in sour cream sauce
Blini – thin pancakes, often with caviar and sour cream
Syrniki – fried curd fritters
Tvorog – curd cheese
Olivje – potato salad made with mayonnaise
Kisel – stewed fruit thickened with cornstarch and milk poured over it
Kurnik - Chicken and rice pie
Tushenaia Kuritsa Pod Sousom iz Chernosliv - Chicken with prune sauce
Kotlety Pozharskie - ground Chicken cutlets
Babka - sweet bread
Kulich - a tall dome shaped Russian sweet yeast Easter Bread
Krendel - sweet yeast bread
Bulka: sweet yeast bun/cake
Mazurka – rich cake
Kvhorost – small cakes
Sharlotka - apple cake
Chebureki – fried pastries with meat filling

Holidays and Special Occasions

New Year's Day – presents for children brought by Ded Moroz (Grandfather Frost) and ginger cakes
Anniversaries and name days – vodka, champagne, hot chocolate, food – krendel, a sweet bread
Maslentisa – carnival preceding Lent. On the last day hot bliny with butter and vodka is served
Lent – fasting observed
Orthodox Easter – Attend church; Easter cakes are blessed at churches; they include Kulich – yeast cakes with raisins, candied fruit and nuts and iced; and Pashka made from cottage cheese, cream, eggs, raisins, almonds and candied fruit.
Easter dinner includes vodka, appetizers, ham or roast pork, kolbase (sausage), pickles, bliny, herring, and dyed Easter eggs. At one end of a table the eggs are set with the pashka and kulich at the other.
Eggs were always an important part of Easter, but it was Czar Alexander III who had Karl Faberge, the court jeweler create the spectacular enameled eggs with jewels, gold, and holding different scenes. The Cyrillic letters *XB* on eggs or cakes is Cyrillic for *Christos voskres* (Christ is risen).
Christmas – Christmas trees were brought to Russia by Czar Peter the Great in the 17th c. Goose is served.
New Year's Eve – kutya (sweetened grain porridge with dried fruit), zakuski; a toast of champagne is opened and doors flung open to herald the New Year; blinys; and vodka. Olivier Salad, named for a French chef who lived in Moscow in the 1860s, is made with chopped apples, pickled cucumbers, boiled potatoes, carrots, hardboiled eggs, peas and covered with mayonnaise. Also

served in seledka pod shuboi "herring in a fur coat" – layered with grated boiled potatoes, sliced herring, chopped hardboiled eggs and topped with grated boiled beet and mayonnaise. This is followed by zakuski "starters" - narezka "sliced meats"; and caviar on buttered bread.

Weddings, anniversaries. And name days – surprise parties, feasts, vodka, toasts, hot chocolate and krendel – pretzel with fruit and nuts

Beverages

Beer has been produced since the 9th c. Kvass is a black rye bread based drink Medovukha is a mead made from kvass. Vodka has been produced since the 14th c and can be distilled from potatoes or grain, such as corn with wheat added. Serve ice cold and in a small glass. Today vodka is flavored with many added ingredients. Zubrowka is a vodka with zubrowka grass added, to give it a bitter flavor. It is also served cold.

Grape vines have been grown around the Caspian, Black and Azov seas for thousands of years and trade with other ancient civilizations has been .Modern winemaking probably starts with Prince Leo Galitzine (1845-1915), who made the first Russian champagne wines at his Crimean estate of Novyi Svet. After the Russian Revolution in 1917 many of the winemakers fled Russia, but began making a comeback in the 1940s and 50s. Beginning in 1985 Mikhail Gorbachev founded a campaign against alcoholism, but after the fall of the Soviet Union and farms were privatized grape growing resumed mainly in the Krasnodar, Stavropol and Rostov regions between the Caspian and Black Seas. Most of the wines are table wines made from Cabernet Sauvignon, Riesling, Aligote, Muscat, Rkatsiteli, and Saperavi grapes. Port, Madeira, Sherry and sparkling wines are also produced.

Medovukha is a sweet, low-alcohol drink, made with fermented-honey and spices. Stavlenniy myod is also a honey based drink with berry juices. Sbiten is a non-alcoholic drink, made of honey, water, fruit juices and spices

Did You Know?

Rurik introduced cream sauces and rich fruit pastries
Mongols introduced grilled meat, yogurt, curd cheeses, preserved cabbage, and tea
Bread and salt were offered to guests as a sign of hospitality.
The Nenets, an indigenous nomadic people of western Siberia, still hunt and herd reindeer, using the dried meat for food, the hides for teepees and clothing. They live on a vast tundra, moving as the climate changes, and living in mya, or teepees.
Beef Stroganov is named for the 19th Count Alexander Grigorievich Stroganov, Governor-General of Novorossilisk and the founder of several banks and universities. He traveled a great deal, but also loved to entertain, even if not at home. His chefs came up with Beef Stroganov as an easy dish to fix.

Rwanda

Rwanda, located in Central and East Africa, is bordered by Uganda, Tanzania, Burundi and the Democratic Republic of the Congo. The earliest inhabitants date from c 8000BC, hunter gatherers during the Stone Age, and during the Iron Age those who produced pottery and iron tools. These early inhabitants were the ancestors of the Twa, aboriginal pygmy hunter-gatherers who remain in Rwanda today. Between 700 BC and 1500 AD, a number of Bantu groups migrated into Rwanda, clearing forest land for agriculture. During the Bantu migrations the first settlers were Hutu, while the Tutsi migrated later to form a distinct racial group. The earliest form of social organization in the area was the clan (*ubwoko*) and most included Hutu, Tutsi, and Twa. From the 15th century, the clans began to form into kingdoms and by 1700 around eight kingdoms existed in present-day Rwanda. One of these, the Kingdom of Rwanda, became increasingly dominant from the mid-eighteenth century. The Berlin Conference of 1884 assigned the territory to Germany as part of German East Africa. Belgian forces took control of Rwanda and Burundi in 1916, during World War I. Rwanda became independent from Burundi and Belgium in 1962. The capital is Kigali. The official languages are Kinyarwanda, French and English, with Swahili also spoken.

Dining Etiquette

It is a privilege to be invited for a meal. Dress appropriately ladies in a skirt or dress, and no shorts for men or women. Please arrive punctually and bring a gift, perhaps something from your country. Please shake hands greeting and departing, though a woman extends her first. The host(ess) will often taste a drink or food before the guests. Please eat or drink whatever is offered to you. Men are usually seated in chairs and served first. Others sit on the floor, and women and children eat after the men. Guests of honor will be seated in chairs and served first. Food may be given as a gift at the end of a meal. Respect, extended families; and many children as a sign of wealth are part of the culture.

Cuisine

Most of the Rwandan diet consists of locally grown foodstuffs. The food is not spicy. The country is mountainous and is known as the "land of a thousand hills". Common vegetables are sweet potatoes, potatoes (introduced by the Germans), beans, corn, peas, cassava, spinach; grains – millet, wheat; fruit – iboteke (plantains), cassava, green bananas, bananas, avocado, mango, pineapple, and papaya. Beef is not usually eaten as it is very expensive. Chickens, pigs, goat, rabbit, fish – tilapia and sambaza are available. Meat is roasted or barbecued. Dairy farms are located near Kigali. The Tutsis own the cattle and are herders; the Hutu known for cultivation, and the Twa for hunting. Cattle are considered a status symbol.

Igisafuliya (chicken, vegetables and plantain, means *pot* in Kinyarwanda)

Serves 4

Oil
2 large boneless chicken breasts, cut in half
2 onions, chopped
2 peppers, finely chopped
2 celery stalks, chopped
2 tomatoes, chopped

1 cup water
4 plantains, peeled and sliced
½ lb. spinach
1-2 hot peppers, chopped, seeds removed
Salt and pepper for taste

Heat a small amount of oil in a pan and brown chicken on all sides. Add onions and pepper. Cook 10 minutes. Add tomatoes and celery. Cook 10 minutes. Add water, salt and pepper and cook for 15 minutes. Remove chicken. Place plantains and spinach in pan. Put chicken on top with hot peppers. Add more water if necessary. Cook 25 minutes.

Specialties

Mizuz - fried bananas
Matoke – baked or steamed plantains
Ugali – maize ball used for eating food
Sombe – leafy greens
Akabanga – hot chili oil
Ibiraya – deep fried potatoes
Samosas – meat, cheese, or vegetable filled fried pastries

Chapatti – flat bread
Mandazi – deep fried dough
Isombe – mashed cassava leaves with spinach and eggplant, and served with dried fish
Ubugari – cassava or maize porridge
Brochettes – skewered goat, tripe, beef, or fish are often served with grilled bananas

Holidays and Special Occasions

Holidays observed are January 1 – New Years; January 2; February 1 – National Heroes Day; Good Friday, Easter, and Easter Monday; April 7 – Genocide against Tutsi Memorial Day; May 1 – Labor Day; July 1- Independence Day; and Christmas. There are many festivals. On important occasions such as weddings and funerals only a small amount of food is served, usually a small piece of meat and roasted potato. A container with sorghum beer is placed in the center of a room with straws for all to drink. Banana beer is also served.

Beverages

Coffee and tea are major exports. Men may drink alcoholic beverages; women drink *Icayi* (black tea with milk and sugar). *Ikivuguto* is fermented milk or yogurt. *Ikigage* is a beer made from sorghum and *urwagwa*, made from bananas, which are part of traditional rituals and ceremonies. Bralirwa manufactures soft drink products from The Coca-Cola Company and beers including Primus, Mützig, Amstel, and Turbo King In 2009 Brasseries des Mille Collines (BMC) opened, manufacturing Skol beer and Skol Gatanu. BMC is now owned by Belgian company Unibra. East African Breweries also operate in the country, importing Guinness, Tusker, and Bell, as well as whisky and spirits.

461

Samoa

The independent State of Samoa governs the western part of the Samoan Islands in the South Pacific Ocean. The two main islands of Samoa are Upolu and Savai'i. The Austronesian inhabitants began arriving from Southeast Asia and Melanesia between 2500 and 1500 BCE. Jacob Roggeveen (1659–1729), a Dutchman, was the first known European to sight the Samoan islands in 1722. This visit was followed by French explorer Louis-Antoine de Bougainville who named them the *Navigator Islands* in 1768. At the turn of the twentieth century, the Tripartite Convention partitioned the Samoan Islands into two parts: the eastern island group became a territory of the United States (the Tutuila Islands in 1900 and officially Manu'a in 1904) and is today known as American Samoa; the western islands became known as German Samoa after Britain vacated all claims to Samoa and accepted termination of German rights in Tonga and certain areas in the Solomon Islands and West Africa. From the end of World War I until 1962, New Zealand controlled Samoa as a Class C Mandate under trusteeship through the League of Nations. In 1997 the constitution was amended to change the country's name from *Western Samoa* to *Samoa*. The capital is Apia.

Dining Etiquette

When invited to a home please arrive promptly. Shoes are left outside the home. Please bring a gift which may at first be declined. The person accepting the gift bows his(her) head slightly and places the gift above the head with both hands. Never bring food as it implies the host has not provided enough. If people are sitting on the floor mats around the room, please greet the eldest or highest ranking person first and then greet others in the room. The best floor mats are for guests. When seated sit cross legged or with your feet behind you. Never point your toes at anyone. Do not speak to someone while standing as it is considered impolite. Talk with your eyes lowered especially to an older person. The host will welcome the guest(s) who respond to him. Food and drinks may be offered. If seated at a table the host will seat you often at the middle of the table. Prayers are said before a meal. Elders eat first, and do not begin eating until told to do so. Flatware may be provided but many Samoans eat with their hands. Do try everything, and eat what is on your plate. Respect is very important. Never touch a person on the head as it is considered sacred. Dress conservatively and women should cover their knees and shoulders. In many villages there is an evening prayer curfew which should be observed by all.

Cuisine and Beverages

The land is primarily volcanic and very fertile although few animals or plants are native. Tongans arrived in the 900s and brought their language, religion, foods, and culture. They were brought by settlers and included pigs, dogs, rats, chickens, cattle, taro, rice, yams, ulu (breadfruit), pineapples, papaya, mango, wheat, potatoes, bananas, and lemons. The Germans introduced large plantations mainly growing copra, sugarcane, and cocoa bean. The staple foods are coconut, oil and cream, noni, bananas, and copra. Seafood is in abundance being an island nation – crabs, octopus, turtles, tuna, and also sea birds. Food is prepared in heated rocks in the ground that is wrapped in banana leaves and topped with dirt. Large families get together for an *Umu* or large meal on Sundays. The dishes might include pig, rice, coconut, and taro. Fruit juices including watermelon, coffee, and tea are popular drinks. Kava is made from kava roots which are ground for the juice, then water is added. The drink is considered very relaxing. Vailima is the locally brewed beer.

Oka – (raw fish or other seafood served with coconut cream)

Serves 4

2 lbs. white fish fillets, cut into small pieces
1 tsp. salt
Juice of 2 lemons or limes
2 tomatoes, finely chopped

1 medium onion, finely chopped
1 cup coconut cream

In a bowl combine the fish salt and lemons. Cover and chill for at least 2 hours.
Add the onion, tomatoes and coconut cream. Served chilled.
Cucumbers can also be added. Green onions or leeks can be substituted for the onion.

Samoan Specialties

Alaisa fa'apopo - coconut rice
Fa'alifu - coconut sauce
Fa'apapa - coconut bread
Keke pua'a - bao (pork buns)
Koko Samoa - Samoan cocoa
Miti - Coconut condiment
Palusami - taro leaves in coconut cream
Supasui – beef, soy sauce with ginger, garlic, and onions
Supoesi – coconut cream and pawpaw soup usually served for breakfast
Suafa'i - banana soup
Sua i'a - fish soup

Chicken and taro leaves
Mamma Jamma Pancakes
Esi Fafao - stuffed papaya
Keke Koko - koko cake
Fa'ausi - coconut caramel smothered
Fa'apapa
Keke Fa'i - banana cake
Paifala - half-moon pies
Panipopo - sweet coconut buns
Pisua - tapioca in coconut caramel
Poi - banana pudding

Holidays and Special Occasions

An 'ava ceremony is held during holidays and special events when 'ava (kava) is drunk. Along with the drinking there are speeches and other rituals. Umu, the underground cooking, is also part of these occasions. Holidays celebrated are Good Friday, Easter, Easter Monday, Anzac Day (April 25), Mother's Day, Independence Day (June 1-3), White Monday, Arbor Day, and Christmas. Eunice Viridis (palola reef worm) is celebrated in the lunar calendar when people bring lanterns and nets to capture this delicacy.

San Marino

The Republic of San Marino is surrounded by Italy, situated on the Italian Peninsula on the northeastern side of the Apennine Mountains. The country derives its name from Saint Marinus, a stonemason originating from the Roman colony on the island of Rab, in modern-day Croatia. In AD 257 Marinus, according to legend, participated in the reconstruction of Rimini's city walls after their destruction by Liburnian pirates. Marinus then went on to found an independent monastic community on Monte Titano in AD 301; thus, San Marino lays claim to be the oldest extant sovereign state as well as the oldest constitutional republic. The official date of the founding of what is now known as the Republic is 3 September 301. In 1320 the community of Chiesanuova chose to join the country. In 1463 San Marino was extended with the communities of Faetano, Fiorentino, Montegiardino, and Serravalle, after which the country's border have remained unchanged. In 1631, its independence was recognized by the Papacy. The capital is the City of San Marino. The official language is Italian.

Dining Etiquette

When invited for a meal guests usually do not arrive on time. At least one half hour late is permissible. Please send flowers (in an uneven number), a plant or something for the house the day after. Shake hands greeting and departing. Men may hug each other. A lady extends her hand first. Do stand when an older person enters a room. Cocktail hours are not long. Liquor may not be served, rather wine or an aperitif such as Campari. The male guest of honor will be seated to the left of the hostess, the female guest of honor to the left of the host. Food is served in course, each with wine/ Never cut pasta, but rather twirl it on the fork using the plate or a spoon. Salads are to be eaten with forks only. When finished place your fork and knife together. Both hands should be kept above the table during the meal. Coffee and liqueurs may follow. The toast is "Salute" or "Chin-chin". Ladies should never make a toast!

Cuisine

Sammarinese cuisine is similar to the Italian cuisine, especially that of the adjoining Emilia-Romagna and Marche regions. San Marino's primary agricultural products are cheese, wine and livestock, with cheese making a primary economic activity.

Specialties

Fagioli con le cotiche – bean and bacon soup served at Christmas
Pasta e ceci - chickpea and noodle soup with garlic and rosemary
Nidi di rondine, a baked pasta dish with smoked ham, beef, cheese, and a tomato sauce

Roast rabbit with fennel

Erbazzone – spinach with cheese and onions

Piada - flatbread with various fillings

Torta Tre Monti ("Cake of the Three Mountains/Towers"), based on The Three Towers of San Marino, a layered wafer cake covered in chocolate

Torta Titano, a layered dessert made with biscuit, hazelnuts, chocolate, cream and coffee, also inspired by San Marino's central mountain, Monte Titano

Verretta, a dessert made of hazelnuts, praline and chocolate wafers

Cacciatello, a dessert made with milk, sugar and eggs

Zuppa di ciliegie, cherries stewed in sweetened red wine and served on white bread

Bustrengo (honey, apple, and nut cake)

Serves 6-8

½ cup cornmeal	5 tbls. honey
2 cups flour	2 large apples, peeled, cored, and chopped
1½ cup breadcrumbs	4oz. dried figs, chopped
½ tsp. salt	3oz. raisins
3 eggs	Zest of 1 lemon
¼ cup olive oil	Zest of 1 orange
2 cups milk	½ cup walnuts or almonds

Preheat oven to 325°

In a bowl combine the cornmeal, flour, breadcrumbs, salt, eggs, and oil. Stir in milk and honey, then apples, figs, raisins, lemon and orange zests, and nuts.

Grease a 9x13 baking dish. Pour mixture into baking dish and bake 50-60 minutes.

Holidays and Special Occasions

Lent – fasting

Dec. 8, Feast of Immaculate Conception and Christmas - Bustrengo, a Christmas cake with honey, nuts and dried fruit

Beverages

The region produces a number of wines such as Brugneto and Tessano (cask-aged red wines) and Biancale and Roncale (still white wines). Wine in San Marino is regulated by the San Marino Wine Association, which is also a wine producer. Liqueurs include the aniseed-flavored Mistrà, the truffle-flavored Tilus and the herbal Duca di Gualdo.

Sao Tome and Principe

São Tomé and Príncipe is an island nation in the Gulf of Guinea, off the western equatorial coast of Central Africa consisting of two archipelagos around the two main islands of São Tomé and Príncipe. The islands were uninhabited until their discovery by Portuguese explorers c1470. The rich volcanic soil and close proximity to the Equator made São Tomé and Príncipe ideal for sugar cultivation, followed in the 19th c by crops such as coffee and cocoa. Large plantations called "rocas" sprang up and by 1908 São Tomé was the world's largest producer of cocoa. Today other export crops are copra, palm kernel, and coffee, though the country must import most of its needs. Its people are predominantly of African and mestiço descent. The capital is São Tomé. The official language is Portuguese, with Forro, Angolar, Lingwa-uye and Principense also spoken.

Dining Etiquette

It is a privilege to be invited to a home. When invited to a meal please arrive on time and bring a gift from your country. Shake hands greeting and departing. Elders are treated with respect. When seated at a table eat continental style with the fork in the left hand and knife in the right. Please try a little of everything.

Chicken with Coffee

Serve 4

2 tbls. butter
4 boneless chicken breasts, cubed
2 cloves garlic, minced
4 red chilies
1 bay leaf

¼ cup coffee
¼ cup white wine
¼ cup heavy cream
2 cups cooked rice

Heat the butter. Saute the chicken until just browned. Add the garlic, chilies, bay leaf, coffee, wine, and cream. Cook for 15-20 minutes.
Serve over rice.

Cuisine

The cuisine has been influenced by the Portuguese and nearby African nations. The country has easy access to fish being an island nation, but also grows root crops, plantains, breadfruit, beans, taro, maize, papayas, guava, citrus, bananas, coffee, cocoa, indigenous greens, corn, citrus trees, and pineapple. Fruit bats, monkey, chickens are the more common meats. Rice and wheat are imported. Food is cooked in red palm oil. Coffee is used for drinking and as a spice. Palm oil stews are considered the national dish. Breakfast is often food from the evening meal with tea and bread.

Specialties

Barriga de neixe – grilled fish with rice, breadfruit, or cassava
Arroz doce – sweet corn and coconut served for breakfast
Cachupa – green beans, broad beans, and corn
Calulu – dried smoked fish, prawn, tomato, okra eggplant, onion, spices
Banana pap – porridge
Banana seca – dried banana with smoky flavor
Palla-palla – banana cocoyam crisps
Broa – corn bread

Sonhos de banana – banana fritters
Fios – corn flour and banana snack
Piri-piri - hot sauce made with malagueta peppers
Bobo frito – bananas fried in coconut oil
Sigumba – peanut brittle
Acucarinhas – coconut and sugar patties fried in coconut oil
Aranha – dessert with coconut, sugar, and food coloring
Canjica – canjica maize, egg, sugar, and cinnamon porridge
Chocolate desserts

Holidays and Special Occasions

For baptisms, weddings and wakes, and funerals elaborate feasts are held with roasted goat, chicken, and beef dishes, stews, vegetables, desserts and beverages. Feijoada, a meat and vegetable stew, may also be served on these occasions and Sunday dinners.
Estufa de morcego is a bat stew that is served on saints' days and during fiestas.
Among the holidays celebrated are Easter, Independence Day, Armed Forces Day, All Saint's, Sao Tome Day, and Christmas.
Djambi is a religious ritual in villages where people gather for protection, health restoration, or divination.
The people believe spirits of the dead remain on the islands.

Beverages

Palm wine is made locally. National and Criollo Beers are brewed. A local cane alcohol is cacharamba. Aquardente is a distilled sugar cane beverage. Ponche is a drink with honey and aquardente. Gravana rum is also made from sugar cane. Coconut milk, soft and fruit drinks are also popular.

Saudi Arabia

The Kingdom of Saudi Arabia "Arabia of the Sands" occupies much of the Arabian Peninsula, and is bounded by Jordan and Iraq on the north and northeast, Kuwait, Qatar, Bahrain and the United Arab Emirates in the east, Oman in the southeast, and Yemen in the south. The Persian Gulf lies to the northeast and the Red Sea to the west. The region dates back thousands of years. The Wadi Hanifah was settled by a tribe known as the Banu Hanifah who farmed the fertile land and were traders. The Saudi dynasty began in central Arabia in 1744. Muhammad ibn Saud, the ruler of the town of Ad-Dir'iyyah near Riyadh, joined with a cleric, Muhammad ibn Abd-al-Wahhab, to create an alliance. Since 1932 the regions of Saudi Arabia have been united under the leadership first of King Abdul al-Aziz Al-Saud, and the present king, who is also Custodian of the Two Holy Mosques. Arabic is the official language. Riyadh, the capital, was called Hajr, founded by the tribe of Banu Hanifah. Al-Riyadh means "The Gardens".

Dining Etiquette

It is an honor to be entertained in a home. Please bring a small gift, never alcoholic beverages or anything made of pigskin. Please present the gift with your right hand. Punctuality is very important, though the Saudis may take their time. Please greet your host by saying "Salaam Alaykum", then shake hands and say "Kaif Halak". Women extend their hands first, or may not. The host may put his left hand on the shoulder of another male. And when you get to know him better may kiss you on each cheek. Holding hands is a sign of a very warm friendship. Strong coffee or tea will be served with dates, nuts or raisins. When seated please keep both feet on the ground, do not show the soles of your shoe, or point it at someone. The men and women may dine separately. Before a meal hands are washed and a prayer "in the name of God" is always said. Only the right hand is used for eating, though fingers are used when no utensil is available. When served wait for your host to start. Never leave your plate empty, or it will be refilled. If you pass something do so with your right hand. If you are the guest of honor and a feast is served, a whole sheep might be served including the eye which is considered a delicacy. Please eat the eye when presented to you. Hands are also washed after the meal. Please write or telephone a thank-you after being entertained. "Bil Hana Wal Afia" "Bon Appetit".

Cuisine

Each region in Saudi Arabia has its own cuisine. The food has been influenced by what is grown in the regions, the tribes, spices that arrived on trade routes, and the Koran. Food is always cooked in abundance, and often more than enough if an extra person should arrive. Flat bread, chicken, lamb or fish, falafel, rice, lentils, chickpeas, cracked wheat, tomatoes, onions, yogurt, honey, and dates are all used in cooking. The most common spices are black pepper; cumin; and cardamom, which is used also in coffee.

468

Jobnia (cheese dessert)

½ tsp. dry yeast
¼ cup warm water
Pinch sugar and flour
1 lb. sweet cheese
1 tsp. ground cardamom
1 tsp. baking powder

2 cups flour
2 tbls. vegetable oil or shortening
2 eggs
3 cups syrup
½ cup warm water
4 cups oil for frying

Dissolve the yeast in the warm water with the sugar and flour.

In a bowl crumble the cheese, add the cardamom, flour and baking powder and mix well with the fingertips. Add the yeast and mix well. Then add the oil and eggs, and mix, adding the warm water gradually to make a soft dough. Pat it in the bowl and cover, setting aside in a warm place for one hour.

On a flat surface, pat out the dough into about ¼ inch thickness and cut out with a cookie cutter. Heat the oil and fry the jobnia, gently spooning hot oil onto the top as you fry. When golden remove from oil with a slotted spoon and drain off the oil, then into a bowl of the syrup and onto a plate.

Do not place jobnia on top of each other until they are cooled, then arrange onto a serving plate. Sweet cheese can be found at Middle Eastern markets.

Syrup

2 ½ cups sugar
1¼ cups water

1 tbls. lemon juice
½ tsp. rose water

In a sauce pan bring the sugar, water and lemon juice to a boil, and boil until the temperature reaches 220°. Add the rose water. Remove from heat and cool.

Recipe courtesy of Nahla Al-Zuhair (Brig. Gen. Amin Shaker, Defense Attache, Washington, DC)

Specialties

Al-Kabsa – rice with meat or chicken is considered the national dish
Samak we ruz we adass – fish and rice with lentils
Balilah – chickpea salad
Mahallabia – rice pudding, served at lunar new year
Al-Mandi – chicken or lamb cooked with rice, water, and spices in a covered hole in the ground
Mathbi – grilling lamb or chicken on a stone on hot embers
Jarish – wheat with milk and spices

Mufallaq – jarish with meat, onion, tomato
Qursan – wheat loaf with gravy
Selek – lamb with milk and rice
Mathlutha – rice and jarish
Saleeg – rice and milk dish served with butter
Al-Sayadiah – fish with rice and onions
Kubez – flat bread
Aysh abu Iaham – dough with fennel and caraway filled with meat, onion and topped with tahini sauce
Kultra – meat on skewers
Mezzeh– may include forty dishes

Kubbat maraq – rice balls with turmeric, pepper, cumin, dried lime with fried ground meat in the center and a tomato sauce

Fi qa'atah – layered dish with rice, meat, almonds

Kharuf mahshi – baby lamb stuffed with rice, nuts, raisins and rubbed with onion, cinnamon, cloves, and cardamom

Holidays and Special Occasions

Ramadan – fasting from sun up to sunset
Eid al-Fitr - the feast at the end of Ramadan
Eid al-Adha - the Feast of Sacrifice
Holiday meals will include dates, raisins, nuts, soups, lamb or chicken, al-kabsa, stuffed vegetables, bean or bulgur wheat salads, hummus, rice, flat breads, and desserts.

Beverages

Saudi Arabia is a Muslim country and alcoholic beverages are not consumed. Fruit drinks, tea and coffee are drunk.

Did You Know?

Until 1700 almost all coffee came from Saudi Arabia.
Dishonor for one family member is dishonor for the whole family.
Hospitality is part of Arabian life. They must take someone in, even a stranger, and feed that person for three days.
A camel can go six weeks without drinking. Every part of the camel is consumed – the meat, the udder for milk, the liver is rubbed in salt, the hoofs ground into powder, the urine used to wash hair or as a purgative.
When essence is passed, it is a gesture of warm friendship. It will be passed three times.

Scotland

Scotland, part of the United Kingdom, lies north of England, bordered on the west by the Atlantic Ocean, and to the east the North Sea. The history of Scotland dates from at least 3000 BC. The earliest settlers were either Irish or Iberian Celts who were later called Picts by the Romans. From 82-208 AD the Romans occupied the country, and then four kingdoms (tribes and then clans) until 1034. England and Scotland were united in 1603. Edinburgh, the capital, may have been built on an ancient volcano.

Dining Etiquette

Please arrive punctually. Please bring flowers, wine, a gift for the home, or chocolates. Shake hands greeting and departing. Ladies extend hands first. Drinks are served before dinner. The guest of honor is seated at the head of the table, or to the right of the host. Eating is continental style with the fork in the left hand, knife in the right. Butter plates are placed on the table. Meals will be served in courses starting with soup or an appetizer, entrée, and dessert. Please keep your hands at table level. When finished place the knife and fork together. Coffee is served following the meal. Men may withdraw to another room without the ladies. Toasting is initiated by the host who stands, raises his glass, says a few words, and all drink. The toast is "Cheers". Do not toast a person of higher rank or age before the host does.

Kedgeree (Smoked Haddock and Rice)

Serves 4

½ stick butter	4 hard cooked eggs, chopped
2 cups cooked rice	2 tbls. parsley, chopped
1½ lbs. smoked haddock, flaked	Salt and pepper
¼ cup cream	1 tbls. curry powder

In a large pan melt the butter. Add the rice and haddock. Stir in 2 of the eggs, some salt and pepper, and the curry powder.
Place in a bowl or on a platter and garnish with the remaining eggs and parsley.

Cuisine

Over the years Scottish cuisine has developed a distinct flavor. From early times cooking was done in a simmering pot over a peat fire, griddles, smoke cured or salted meats and fish. Oatmeal, black pudding (made from the blood of animals); porridges and haggis are part of the Scottish tradition. Cattle have been a mainstay of the culture, and a man's wealth was known by the number of cattle he had. Cattle were used to pay rent, in dowries, and as ransom during war. Drovers brought the cattle. Fishing has always been important to Scotland, especially herring. In the 1880s cured herring accounted for about 90,000 barrels and reached its peak in 1907 with 2½ million barrels.

Haggis is usually made from a sheep's stomach as the casing. The ingredients include oatmeal, onions, salt, pepper, spices, chopped meat, and minced organs. This is accompanied by "neeps and tatties". Neeps are mashed turnips with pepper and tatties, mashed potatoes. Robert Burns' "Address to a Haggis" was written in 1786.

Scotland is known for smoked salmon, lamb, Aberdeen Angus beef; cheese; game – hare, red grouse, duck, pheasant, and venison; seafood – shrimp, crabs, sea trout, oysters, cod, halibut, mussels, herring, scallops, whitefish; fish and chips; brambles – blackberries; shortbread; mushrooms, and mince. A full Scottish breakfast will get your day off to a good start with eggs, black pudding, porridge, kippers, bacon, or sausages, oatcakes, scones and other pastries, and cooked tomatoes.

Balmoral Fruit Cake

Balmoral Castle in Aberdeenshire is the Queen's favorite summer residence. The castle was built in c1390 and was bought by Prince Albert in 1852 for Queen Victoria. Thought to be too small the original building was torn down and another castle replaced it. Here the royal family spends time outdoors - hiking, riding, picnics, especially grilling, and just relaxing. In 1997 it was here Prince William and Prince Harry learned that their mother had died. The castle is open to the public from March until July, but you will need to check the website for exact dates.

1½ sticks butter	¼ cup citron
¾ cup sugar	½ tsp. fresh grated nutmeg
3eggs, separated	½ tsp. caraway seeds
2 ½ cups flour	½ cup blanched almonds
1tsp. baking powder	2tbls. brandy
½ cup candied orange peel	

Preheat oven to 325°
Cream the butter and sugar. Beat in the egg yolks, one at a time.
Combine flour, baking powder, orange, citron, nutmeg, caraway seeds, and almonds. Add to butter and sugar.
Beat egg whites until stiff. Fold into batter. Add brandy (can be more like ¼ cup!)
Grease a loaf pan. Line with paper and greased again. Add batter.
Bake 1 hour until toothpick comes out clean.

Scottish Specialties

Finnan haddie - named for Findon, where a fire once destroyed racks of drying fish, turning some golden brown, creating a new dish

Smokies - fresh haddock that is cured and smoked
Kippers - cured and smoked herring
Cockaleekie – chicken and leek stew

Tatties – ground meat and potatoes
Haggis – made from sheep's stomach with innards, spices, oatmeal and suet
Scotch eggs – eggs with sausage and breadcrumbs
Fish and chips – fried fish and French fries
Skirlies – onion and oatmeal dish

Colcannon – cabbage and potatoes
Cranachan – dessert of whipped cream, oatmeal, honey and whisky
Scotch trifle – sponge cake, jelly, sherry, fruit, and whipped cream
Dundee cake – fruit cake
Selkirk Bannock – fruit loaf for teas

Black Bun (fruitcake served on New Year's Eve)

Pastry

3 cups flour
½ tsp. salt
½ tsp. baking powder

1 stick butter
1 egg

In a food processor combine the ingredients. Add a little water if the pastry is too thick. Refrigerate for 2 hours.
Divide into 2.
Roll ½ out on a floured board.
Line a large buttered pie plate or bowl with the pastry.
Roll out other ½ pastry.

Filling

3 cups flour
½ cup sugar
2 cups currants
2 cups raisins
1 cup almonds, blanched and coarsely chopped
1 cup mixed chopped peel
2 tsp. cinnamon

1 tsp. ginger
¼ tsp. cloves
½ tsp. fresh ground pepper
1 tsp. baking soda
½ cup milk
3 eggs
1 cup brandy

Preheat oven to 350°
Place the flour and sugar in a bowl. Add the currants, raisins, almonds, peel, cinnamon, ginger, cloves, pepper, and baking soda. Mix well.
Beat eggs until frothy. Add milk and brandy. Pour over fruit and flour mixture and combine.
Place in pastry. Top with other ½ pastry crimping the edges together. Prick the pastry with a fork in several places.
Bake in oven for 1 hour. Turn oven to 275° and bake for another hour or until top is golden. Cool.
Cover and wrap in plastic wrap at room temperature.
This will keep for at least 10 days or more!

Holidays and Special Occasions

Robert Burns' birthday – haggis, cock-a-leekie, herring, roast beef and trifle
Christmas – haggis, goose or turkey, stuffing, roasted vegetables fruitcakes, mince pies
Hogmanay – New Year's – all night parties with ham, beans, black buns and shortbread

Beverages

Scotch, the nation's most famous drink, comes from the Celtic "uisque-beatha" or "water of life", and was once used for medicinal purposes by the farmers. Distilled from barley, Scotch acquired its distinctive flavor from peat and pure spring water. Whiskies (spelled without the "e") are single malts, made from malted barley in a still, grain – mixed mash of grain in a continuous still to which barley is added, or blended 40% malt, 60% grain. Distilled spirits combined with pure water and peat have been produced since the Middle Ages. They were first taxed by Britain in 1644, after the Battle of Culloden (1754), and in 1823 large stills (over 40 gallons) were banned and taxes reduced. George Smith of Glenlivet took out the first distillery license in 1824, and in 1880 his distillery received the right to be called Glenlivet. The Distillers Company Limited was founded in 1887. In 1907 the Royal Commission proclaimed whisky "a spirit obtained by distillation from a mash of cereal grain, saccharified by the diastase of malt". A 1915 law announced all whisky must be distilled in Scotland and matured for three years in wooden casks. Whisky is made in the Highland, Lowlands, and on the islands.

Scotland also produces Drambuie, a liqueur; Sandeman's Port in Perth; Lochan Ora, a whisky with honey; and Redalevn, a liqueur named after the Manchester United Football Club "The Red Eleven". Beer is also brewed in Scotland as a full-bodied ale or lager. Irn-Bru is a sweet orange colored soft drink.

Did You Know?

Two of the earliest Scottish cookbooks are *A New and Easy Method of Cookery* written in 1759 by Mrs. Elizabeth Cleland and *The Practice of Cookery, Pastry and Confectionery* written in 1791 by a Mrs. Frazer.
The first tearoom for ladies in Glasgow was opened in 1884 by Miss Cranston and the first sandwich shop in 1850 by William Lang.
Dundee Marmalade, made from oranges brought from Seville, Spain, was first produced by James Keiller in the 18th c when a ship loaded with oranges was stranded in the harbor. Dundee made its fortune through trade with Calcutta importing jute and indigo. Later whaling vessels and polar explorers left from the city.
Long ago a bride's pie of mutton or hen was made for weddings in which a ring was included. Whoever found it was the next bride! Shortbread was thrown over the bride's head, pieces taken home by young maidens to sleep on and have sweet dreams.

Senegal

Senegal is located in the western part of Africa, with Mauritania to the north and east, Mali to the east, Guinea and Guinea-Bissau to the south, the Atlantic Ocean to the west, and The Gambia in the middle. Senegal's kingdoms date back to at least the 4th c AD. Islam was introduced in the 10th c. The Portuguese began trading with the country in the 15th c, followed by the French, English and Dutch. The slave trade brought several million slaves to the Americas (abolished in 1848), during which time peanuts became a staple crop. France took over much of the region, which gained independence in 1960, and as a democracy in 1981. Dakar is the capital. French is the official language, with Wolof, Fula (Peulh), Serer, Jola (Diola), and thirty other languages spoken.

Sauteed Chicken with Tropical Fruits

2 tsp. olive oil
3 lbs. bone-in chicken pieces, skinned and trimmed of fat
Salt and fresh ground pepper
2/3 cup chicken stock or water, divided
1½ cups mixed dried mango and pineapple

2tbls. fresh lemon juice
1 tsp. finely minced fresh ginger
1 tsp. fresh thyme, finely chopped
2 lemons, thinly sliced and seeded
Couscous

In a large non-stick skillet, heat oil over medium heat. Add chicken and cook for about 6 minutes per side, or until the chicken is browned. Remove chicken, season with salt and pepper to taste. Set aside.
Add 1/3 cup chicken stock or water to the skillet, and stir to loosen and dissolve any brown bits stuck to the pan. Stir in the dried fruit, lemon juice, ginger, and thyme.
Return the chicken to the pan, placing over the fruit, and baste with the sauce.
Arrange the lemon slices over the chicken. Cover and cook over medium-low heat for 30 minutes, or until chicken is no longer pink inside, and fruit is tender. Watch carefully to avoid burning the fruit.
Remove the lemon slices and place them around the edge of a serving platter. With a slotted spoon, transfer the chicken and fruit to the platter.
Add remaining 1/3 cup chicken stock or water to the skillet and boil for 1 minute. Taste and correct for seasoning. Pour over chicken and fruit.
Serve with couscous.
Recipe courtesy of Hawa Berete, AAFEX, Dakar-Fann, Senegal

Dining Etiquette

Family important, and often extended families live together. There is great respect for the elderly. Please shake hands greeting and departing. Women will kiss on alternate cheeks three times. In more rural areas men may only shake hands, and not always with women. Bring gifts of fruit, or if children involved something for them. Gifts are presented and received with the right hand or both hands. Hands will be washed on entering the dining area with the use of a communal towel. Drinks will be served. In some homes women and children may eat separately. Food in one large bowl will be placed on a mat on the floor, or a low table. People will eat communally with fingers, or spoons, eating from the part of the bowl in front of you. Use only the right hand.

Cuisine

There are many different ethnic groups; the largest tribe the Wolof; and about 90% of the people are Muslim. The main crops are peanuts, millet, cassava, cotton, rice, poultry and vegetables. Rice fields are located in the south. Along the coast are fish – mackerel, mullet, snapper, and sole. Pirogues are the brightly colored fishing boats. Meals consist of rice, millet, or corn and sauce with vegetables, meat, poultry, fish, beans, milk or sugar. Desserts might be fruit or yogurt. Mayonnaise is served with almost every meal (from French influence).

Specialties

Thieboudienne – (the national dish) fish, carrot and tomato stew served with rice, often eaten at lunch

Chicken au Yassa – rice and chicken with onion and spicy sauces

Mbaxal-u-Saloum – rice with sauce of ground peanuts, dried fish, meat, tomatoes, and spices

Avocet au crevettes – avocado with shrimp

Maffe – meat in peanut sauce

Dem a la St. Louis – stuffed mullet

Bissap –sweetened hibiscus blossom tea

Chep bu jen – fish and rice

Holidays and Special Occasions

Tabaski – the head of a household sacrifices a lamb, in honor of Abraham's willingness to sacrifice his son.

Ramadan – fasting from sunrise to sunset

Korite – end of Ramadan – three day feast

For baptisms, circumcisions, marriages, funerals and other special occasions elaborate feasts are held.

Beverages

Senegal is mainly a Muslim country. Among the drinks served are toufam (yogurt with sugar water; mint tea; and bissap (hibiscus fruit juice) and bouye (baobab fruit juice). Ataya is tea served three times. The first cup is slightly bitter, the second slightly sweetened, and the third sweet. Café touba is the national drink – roasted coffee with cloves. Palm wine is also produced.

Serbia

Serbia borders Hungary to the north; Romania and Bulgaria to the east; the Republic of Macedonia to the south; and Croatia, Bosnia and Herzegovina, and Montenegro to the west. The Starcevo and Vinca cultures date back to the 6th millennium BC. The Greeks arrived in the southern part in the 4th c BC, and the Romans the 1st c BC. In the 7th c AD White Serbians settled in the region. The Byzantine and Frankish Empires occupied lands here. By the 16th c Ottomans and Hapsburg followed. After World War I Serbia became part of Yugoslavia, winning its independence in 2003. Belgrade, the capital, located at the confluence of the Sava and Danube Rivers, dates back to the Vinca culture. The official language is Serbian.

Dining Etiquette

Please be prompt when invited for a meal. Please bring a gift – an uneven number of flowers (not chrysanthemums as they are for funerals), chocolates, wine, or a gift for the home. Shake hands greeting and departing, and look the other person in the eye. Close friends will hug and kiss on each cheek. Women will be introduced first. Please wait until a lady extends her hand to shake it. Please use Mr., Mrs., Miss and the last name. Use first names only after you have been asked. Guests will be welcomed with bread and salt. Beverages will be served. The hostess will seat you at the table. Eat continental style, fork in the left hand, knife in the right. Please leave your napkin unfolded in your lap. Do not begin eating until the host does. Salad is served with the main course. Refuse seconds unless the hostess insists. Do leave a small amount of food on your plate. Place your knife and fork together when finished.

Cuisine

The cuisine has been influenced by the diverse cultures that have occupied Serbia including the Byzantine, Greek, Mediterranean, Ottoman, and Austro-Hungarians. Few spices are used in cooking. Bread is a mainstay of the diet, as are meat, vegetables, dough, and dairy products. In villages the kitchen was called "kuća" (house), and the center part the hearth. Family life is centered around this. Breads include Đevrek, ring-shaped bread; langus, a fried bread; and pogacha, farmer's bread.

Ćevapčići (grilled ground meat)

Ćevapčići - the national dish - rolled ground meat, usually lamb and beef are grilled and served on pita, with chopped onions, sour cream, kajmak, ajvar, feta cheese, minced red pepper and salt.

1½ lbs. ground pork
1 lb. ground beef
½ lb. ground lamb
1 egg white
4 garlic cloves, minced
1 tsp. salt

1 tsp. baking soda
2 tsp. ground black pepper
1 tsp. cayenne pepper
½ tsp. paprika
1 onion, finely chopped
Pita bread

In a bowl, combine the ground pork, ground beef, ground lamb and egg white. Add the garlic, salt, baking soda, black pepper, cayenne pepper and paprika. Form into sausages about 3/4 inch thick. Place in a covered dish and refrigerate at least 1 hour.
Grill on a BBQ until desired pinkness.

Serbian Specialties

Pljeskavica – ground pork or beef
Mczc – small appetizers
Kacamak – polenta
Proja – cornbread
Pecenje – roasted meat
Gulas – goulash
Raznjici – veal and pork cooked on skewers
Djuvec – meat and vegetable casserole
Gyros – lamb with pita
Muckalica – barbecued pork
Burek – phyllo pies with meat or cheese
Srpska kobasica - sausage
Paprikas – pork and pepper stew
Prosciutto – thin dried ham
Podvarku – roasted turkey
Sarma – minced meat rolls wrapped in sauerkraut
Riblja corba – fish soup
Jagnjeca corba – lamb soup
Paradajz corba – tomato soup
Ljuta krompir corba – potato soup
Skembe corba – tripe soup
Shopska – tomatoes, cucumbers, peppers, onion, sunflower oil, vinegar and cheese salad
Duvec or sataras – stewed vegetables

Sarma – stuffed sauerkraut leaves
Rezancis makom – noodles with poppy seeds
Punjena paprika – stuffed peppers; punjene tikvice – stuffed zucchini
Valjusci or flekice - dumplings
Seli kupus – sauerkraut
Prebranac – bean stew
Tursija – pickled vegetables
Zito – wheat, walnut and raisin dessert
Vasina torte –
Gibanica – layered pastry cheese pie made from kajmak
Krofne – filled donuts
Slatko – fruit cooked in a thick syrup
Sutlijas – rice pudding with cinnamon
Baklava – phyllo pastry with honey and nuts
Yoghurt, Zlater – white cheese, cream cheese, kackavalj – sheep milk cheese, pule cheese donkey milk cheese
Pita is the word for pie; strudla for strudels.
Pita od visanja – phyllo with sour cherries and walnuts
Kajmak – boiled milk from which the cream is removed, slightly fermented and served as a condiment

Holidays and Special Occasions

Lent – pogacha bread is served. Meat, dairy products and eggs are not consumed during the fast which lasts for 46 days

At Easter eggs are colored, usually red. The meal begins with aviar (eggplant spread), chicken noodle or lamb soup, sausages, lamb, sarma, salads, vegetables, breads, and ending with sweets.

On Christmas Eve a feast is held. The table is strewn with straw and a white tablecloth. At the meal a round unleavened loaf of bread called badnjački kolač (Christmas bread) which has a Christogram impressed on the top, salt fish, beans, sauerkraut, noodles with ground walnuts, honey, and wine will usually be served. After dinner the children go to neighbors' homes and sing receiving gifts of candies, money; fruit, nuts or cakes.

Christmas falls on January 7 because of the use of the Julian calendar. On Christmas a young girl or woman will go to a well or stream, place an ear of corn and basil next to it, and take some home. All will wash faces and babies bathed in it, and then drunk. This is called "strong water". A pig or sheep may be roasted on Christmas Eve or Christmas Day. Česnica is a round Christmas bread in which a silver or gold coin has been placed. The bread is held by all present and rotated three times counter clockwise. The bread is then divided, some for those not present, a piece for a guest who might appear, and the rest for themselves. Ratarica, also a round loaf is prepared for the men and boys. For women and girls pletenica, a braided bread is served. Roast pork is the entrée. The head of house will propose a toast to his family with wine. Christmas is celebrated for twelve days.

Slava celebrates a family's patron saint when a feast is prepared with Slavski Kolac (Slava cake which is made of boiled wheat, without eggs, butter and milk and has a cross, dove, or family symbol on it), kolijivo, and zito.

Beverages

The national drink in Serbia is Sljivovica, plum brandy. Other alcoholic beverages include Lozovaca, grape brandy; viljamovka, pear brandy, Jabukovaca, applejack and Pelinkovak, wormwood liqueur. Fruit brandies are known as rakija, and often are produced at home. Serbia has fourteen breweries producing beer. Wine has been made in Serbia for over a thousand years. Prokupac and Tamjanika are the oldest known wines. The wine producing regions are Negotinska krajina; Vrsac; Fruska Gora; Sumadija; and Zupa. Serbia produces many fruit drinks and mineral waters. Kvas is made from corn. Serbian coffee is quite strong, similar to Turkish coffee.

Did You Know?

Spasenija Pata Marković published the first cookbook in Serbia in 1907 "Pata's Cookbook" (*Patin kuvar*).

Seychelles

The Republic of Seychelles is an archipelago in the Indian Ocean. The 115-island country lies 1,500 kilometres east of mainland East Africa. Other nearby island countries and territories include Comoros, Mayotte (region of France), Madagascar, Réunion (region of France) and Mauritius to the south. Austronesian seafarers and later Maldivian and Arab traders were the first to visit the uninhabited Seychelles. The earliest recorded sighting by Europeans took place in 1502 by the Portuguese Admiral Vasco da Gama, who passed through the Amirantes and named them after himself (islands of the Admiral). The earliest recorded landing was in January 1609, by the crew of the "Ascension" under Captain Alexander Sharpeigh during the fourth voyage of the British East India Company. The islands were on trade routes between Africa and Asia. The islands were named after Jean Moreau de Séchelles, Louis XV's Minister of Finance. The British controlled the islands between 1794 and 1810. Britain eventually assumed full control upon the surrender of Mauritius in 1810, formalized in 1814 at the Treaty of Paris. Seychelles became a crown colony separate from Mauritius in 1903. Independence was granted in 1976 as a republic within the Commonwealth. The capital is Victoria. The official languages are English, French and Sychellois Creole.

Dining Etiquette

Please arrive on time when invited for a meal. However sometimes that means "island time", and though it is made up of islands do dress appropriately. Men should wear trousers and women skirts, dresses, or slacks. Please bring a gift from your country. Shake hands meeting and departing. Drinks will be served. The hostess will seat the guests. Food is eaten continental style with the fork in the left hand and knife in the right. Please place them together when finished. This is still a matriarchal society.

Cuisine

The cuisine has been influenced by African, Chinese, Indian, French, English, and Indian. Staple dishes are served with rice, and may be garnished with herbs or fresh flowers. Common spices and herbs are ginger, chilies, garlic, lemongrass, saffron, and cinnamon. Spices are often blended. Fruit include papaya, golden apple, breadfruit, mango, bananas, cantaloupe, starfruit, watermelon, pineapple, pawpaw, jamlac, and limes. Some are made into jam or dessert, or served raw. Coconut milk is used in many dishes. Rice can be plain, spicy, or with saffron. Palm hearts may be used in place of rice or cassava. Vegetables used in dishes are pumpkin, aubergines, cabbage, tomatoes, and onions. The Seychelles being islands have an abundance of fish – octopus, tuna, kingfish, lobster, crab, grouper, red snapper, squid, parrot fish, barracuda, tec tec, Seychelles beef – turtle, and bourzwa. The fish is served fried, raw, steamed, baked, salted, smoked or grilled; butter or spicy curry or wrapped in banana leaves. Cari (kari) are green or red curries. Meats are chicken, pork, lamb, beef fruit bat, and tern.

Fish Curry

Serve 4

2 tbls. oil
2 onions, peeled and chopped
½ tsp. coriander
½ tsp. cumin
½ ground cardamom
½ tsp. cloves
½ tsp. turmeric

½ tsp. nutmeg
2 tbls. fresh grated ginger
1 green chile, seeded and minced
2 cups coconut milk
2 lbs. red snapper, cut into bite size pieces
2 tbls. lime juice
Cooked rice

Heat the oil in a skillet and add the onions, cooking until just translucent. Stir in the spices, green chili and coconut milk. Simmer for 5 minutes.
Add the fish and cook 10 minutes until fish is tender. Sprinkle with lime juice.
Serve with rice.
For a spicier dish add more chilies, or other spices.

Specialties

Chatini - chutneys made from fruit or vegetables
Chatini Seychellois - chutney made from chillies, ginger and garlic, served with fried fish
Chatini requin - mashed boiled shark with fried onion, spices and lime juice
Kari koko zourit – octopus curry with coconut milk
Salad zourit – boiled octopus with peppers, tomatoes, onions, and limes
Curries – chicken or fish made with coconut milk
Soupe de tectec - clams cooked in tomatoes, garlic and ginger
Bouillon bréde - spinach broth
Cari bernique - curried limpet

Papaya salad - green papayas, onion, chili and seasonings
Rousettes - fruit bat
Pulao - rice cooked with fish, meat or vegetables
Ladob can be savoury or sweet as a dessert made of sweet potato and plantain cooked with coconut milk, nutmeg, sugar, cinnamon, and vanilla. It may also include cassava, breadfruit or corossol. The savoury dish would include salted fish, and salt is used instead of sugar.
Kat-kat banana - banana cooked in coconut milk.
Carotte banana - bananas wrapped in banana leaves with honey and vanilla, which looks like a carrot

Holidays and Festivals

Seychelles International Carnival of Victoria on Mahe
Semaine de la Francophone – French songs, dance and food
Holy Week and Easter – street fests, fishing tournaments, processions
La Dique Festival in August – bicycle tours, competitions including coconut peeling
Creole Fest in October- Creole food and dance
Christmas – people attend midnight mass Christmas Eve and may return on Christmas morning.
Because of the climate Christmas is celebrated with BBQs, picnics, roasts, pork ribs and pig roasts, jams, curries and black pudding
Weddings and other celebrations – kari koko zourit (octopus curry)

Beverages

Calou, fermented coconut wine, is produced on the islands. Seybrew is a Bavarian-style lager; Ekyu, a local beer; Coco D'Amour, a tropical liqueur made with coconut extract; Bacca, a sugarcane liquor; and Dark Takamaka rum. Tropical fruits drinks are popular.

Did You Know?

The Indian Ocean Tuna Company is one of the world's largest tuna canning facilities.

Sierra Leone

Sierra Leone is a country in West Africa, bordered by Guinea to the north and east, Liberia to the southeast, and the Atlantic Ocean to the west and southwest. Sierra Leone has been inhabited for over 2500 years. During the 9th c AD iron implements were used, and by 1000 AD agricultural crops were grown. Portuguese explorers arrived in 1492, and a fort built at Freetown Harbor in 1495. The British arrived in 1562. Many former slaves were brought from Britain, Canada, Jamaica, and the United States, and became known as Krio, or Creole. In 1924 Sierra Leone was divided into a colony and protectorate, and in 1961 became an independent nation. The capital is Freetown. English is the official language, but Krio is widely spoken, as are Mende in the north and Temne in the south.

Dining Etiquette

Whether invited to visit, or just stopping by, the Sierra Leoneans will invite you to eat. Men shake hands with other men, but a woman must extend her hand for a man to shake it. When shaking hands with an older or more senior person, please support your right elbow with your left hand. Men and boys, women and girls will usually dine separately. Hands are washed before eating. People gather in a circle around a large pot or dish on which the food has been placed. You eat from the part of the dish that is placed in front of you. Reaching for any other part is considered rude. Only the right hand is used for eating. Rice is eaten by rolling it into a ball in the hand, and then dipping it in the sauce. While eating people do not usually talk which is disrespectful of the food. Water is drunk after the meal is finished. The eldest males get the most choice food, followed by the boys. The women and girls get what is left. Hands are washed when finished.

Cuisine

There are fourteen ethnic groups each with their own language and customs. The Muslims are more prevalent in the north. Sierra Leone produces rice, cocoa, coconut palms, manioc and fruits. Dishes will include cassava, yams, beans, red peppers, plantains, red palm oil, peanuts (ground nuts), and coconut oil. Rice is eaten at least twice a day with sauces made from potato or cassava leaves, peanuts, beans, okra, fish, chicken, onions, tomatoes and eggplant. Seafood - fish, oysters, barracuda, lobster, shrimp, and crab found along the coast; chicken, goat or pork may be part of the diet, though Muslims do not consume pork. Common fruits are papaya (paw paw), oranges, bananas, lemons, avocado, guava, breadfruit, watermelon, mango, and pineapples. Fruit is eaten as a snack. Stews and sauces accompany rice. The Sherbro people use tender shredded or pounded cassava leaves with palm oil, onions, pepper, fish or meat to make a stew. The food is prepared by only women and girls. The food is cooked in pots on a three stone stove. Kola nuts have a bitter taste, are high in caffeine so can be used as a stimulant, in clothing dye, or medicines, and acts as an anti-depressant. They are chewed, but not swallowed. The nut is a symbol of peace, hospitality, friendship and in some places is considered sacred. The extract is used to flavor Coca Cola! Ginger beer is made out of ginger and sugar, often brewed right at home. The national brewer Sierra Leone Breweries Limited produces Star beer. Palm wine (poyo in Krio), made from the tops of palm trees, is also drunk.

Groundnut Stew (the national dish)

Serves 6

2-3 lb. chicken, cut up
1 lb. stewing beef, cut into cubes
3medium onions, peeled and chopped
2 hot chilies, chopped
1 lb. fresh spinach

¾ cup peanut butter
4 cloves garlic
Salt and pepper to taste
¾ cup oil
¾ cup water

In a skillet with ¼ cup oil sauté the chicken and beef until browned. Put on plate. Add more oil to skillet and sauté the onions and chilies. Add chicken and beef. Let simmer for 10-15 minutes. In a bowl combine the peanut butter and water until smooth. Sprinkle the spinach over the chicken, beef and onion mixture. Add peanut butter mixture, garlic, salt and pepper to taste.
Cover and cook slowly for 1 hour. Add more water if too thick.

Sierra Leonean Specialties

Foo-foo – cassava paste pounded with flour and eaten with a palaver sauce or plassas
Cassava bread
Njeh – goat meat
Gumbondoh – okra dish. The name given for American style gumbo
Plassas or palaver sauces – made from leafy greens
Crain Crain soup – onions, chili, stock

Sawa sawa soup – sour leaf vegetable soup
Jollof rice – chicken, vegetables, garlic and cabbage
Akara - fritters
Koeksisters – deep fried pastries
Kolombyntjes – cake with currants and lemon juice

Holidays and Special Occasions

Because of the diversity of religions Muslim, Christian and other holidays are observed. The public holidays include Eid al Adha, Prophet's birthday, Good Friday, Easter, Easter Monday, Independence Day and Eid al Fitr. During the holidays, chicken stew is served with rice, root vegetables, fruit and desserts.
The Krios have their own customs. The awujoh feast is held for newborns and newlyweds. At the time of one's death the mourning period lasts for one year. Awujoh feast are held on the third, seventh, and fortieth day after the death. The Mende Muslims at a burial will serve lehweh, a ball of rice with water and sugar and a kola nut.
Weddings are very elaborate occasions when money is stuffed into clothing, they last for weeks, all members of village attend. At weddings, funerals, and other occasions large platters of rice are served. Some may be reserved to honor ancestors.
When a chief is crowned there are many festivities, food and beverages.

Singapore

Singapore lies off the southern end of the Malay Peninsula, composed of one large island and 58 smaller ones. A ¾ mile causeway across the Strait of Johore connects Singapore to the Peninsula. Known as the "Garden Isle" much of the island is reclaimed swamp and sea land, or swamp and jungle with a central plateau. Singapore's first settlers were Malay fisherman (7th c), with later settlers coming from China and India. During the 13th c a prince from Palembang, Sumatra landed here, and seeing a strange animal, perhaps a lion or tiger, proclaimed himself king and named the island Singa Pura, Sanskrit for "Lion City". Later Singa Pura became a vassal state of the Thais, then of the Malacca Sultanate. The Portuguese arrived in 1511, followed by the Dutch, and the British in 1786. In 1822 Sir Stamford Raffles came to the island and in 1824 it was ceded to the British. In 1942 the Japanese seized Singapore, and was freed by the Allied forces in 1945.

Dining Etiquette

Family and business connections are still very important. Elders are treated with great respect. When invited for a meal please be punctual. Please bring a gift of food, a cake, a gift basket, flowers, or candy. Gifts are not opened in front of the presenter. Shake hands greeting and departing. The highest ranking or oldest will be introduced first. When seated please keep both feet on the floor. (In some homes you may remove your shoes before entering). Cocktails will be served unless it is a Muslim home. Food is served from the center of the table. The Chinese eat with chopsticks; the Malay and Indian the right hand, or fork and spoon, and wash their hands before and after the meal; the Indonesian and Thai fork and spoon; or continental style with the fork in the left hand, knife in the right. It is impolite to put too much food on your plate. Rice is served at most meals. When finished, place your chopsticks on the table or holder, fork and knife together on the plate.

The toast is "Yam Seng" "To your continuing success". The toast is made holding the glass with both hands, and looking the other person(s) in the eye. The guest of honor should reciprocate a meal.

Cuisine

Singapore is a melting pot of Malay, Chinese, Indonesian, Thai, Vietnamese, Korean, Japanese, Indian, and European. Spices, coconut, fish, chicken, fresh fruits and vegetables are used. Hawkers on the street sell fish, or you can indulge in Chinese dim sum, Indian samosas, Thai curries, or Indonesian satay. Please remember the Hindus and Buddhists do not eat beef, and the Muslims pork.

Chicken Porridge

2 cups uncooked rice
2 tsp. sesame oil
2 tsp. light soy sauce
12 cups + 2 cups water

4 chicken stock cubes
1 lb. ground chicken
Pinch of white pepper
½ lb. carrots, diced

Rinse rice in several changes of cold water until the runs clear. Drain in mesh strainer and place in a large pot. Stir in 1 tsp. sesame oil and 1 tsp. soy sauce. Set aside for 20 minutes.
In a bowl combine the chicken with 1 tsp. sesame oil, 1 tsp. soy sauce and pinch of pepper. Set aside for 30 minutes.
Stir 12 cups of water and 4 cubes of chicken stock into the rice. Bring to a boil over high heat. Add chicken and carrots. After 2 minutes reduce heat to medium-low. Cover and simmer for 1½ hours. Stir frequently and add more water if needed. Lower heat to low and keep warm.
Serve warm.
Recipe courtesy of Ms. Geraldyn Chen, Embassy of Republic of Singapore, Washington, DC

Vegetarian Bee Hoon (Vermicelli noodles)

1 lb. dried vermicelli
1/5 lb. dried shitake mushrooms
1/5 lb. French beans, julienned

2/5 lb. carrots, julienned
½ lb. cabbage, julienned

Soak vermicelli in cold water for about 15 minutes, till soft. Drain and set aside.
Heat oil in a wok over high heat. Add carrots, mushrooms, and fry till fragrant. Add cabbage, French beans, and vegetable stock. Stir evenly, then braise over low heat for 5 minutes.
Add softened vermicelli. Stir continuously to coat all noodles and incorporate all ingredients. Cook at medium-high heat till water is absorbed.
Use tongs or pair of chopsticks to toss the vermicelli as not to risk breaking it.
Serve hot with shredded egg omelet.

Vegetable Stock

1000 ml water (comes from water to soak mushrooms)
2 tbls. vegetarian oyster sauce
2 rounded tsp. vegetable stock mix

3 tsp. soy sauce
1 ½ tbls. sugar
2 tbls. dark soy sauce

Combine the ingredients in a bowl.
Recipe courtesy of Ms. Geraldyn Chen, Embassy of the Republic of Singapore, Washington, DC

Singapore Specialties

Chili crab – crab stir-fried with garlic, sugar, tomato sauce, and soy sauce
Drunken prawns – prawns with Chinese rice wine
Belacan – dried shrimp paste
Hakka – bean curd
Fruits – pineapples, durian, starfruit, bananas, rambutan, and mangoes
Indonesian – sambals, satay, chilies, peanuts, and garlic
Indian – curries, biriyani, tandoori, pratha
Malay – satay, nasi padang, chilies, coconut
Nonya or Straits Chinese- uses lard rather than oils
Cantonese – dim sum, stir-fried, balance between ying and yang (hot and cold), shark's fin soup, wonton
Peking- Peking duck
Szechuan – peppers, garlic, chilies
Hokkien – Hokkien char mee (egg noodles, pork, seafood, and vegetables in a sauce)

Holidays and Special Occasions

Chinese New Year – mandarin oranges, symbolizing gold are given in even numbers for good luck. Yu Sheng, a salad of raw fish and vegetables is tossed by all present and served for good luck.
Moon Festival – moon cakes are made from red bean paste, lotus seeds, and egg yolks. Lantern making contests are held.
Hari Raya Pusa – rice dishes, rice cakes, and ketupat (rice steamed in fronds)
Dragon Boat Races – 38 foot boats are used and rice dumplings thrown into the water to commemorate Qu Yuan, a poet who drowned while trying to drive away corruption in Singapore many centuries ago.
Weddings are very elaborate with huge banquets.

Drinks

All liquor, wine and beer must be imported. The Singapore Sling, a drink of gin, brandy, lemon juice, and soda was concocted in 1915 in the Long Bar of the Raffles Hotel by Ngian Tong Boon.

Did You Know?

Raffles Hotel, one of Singapore's most famous landmarks, was once the home of a sea captain, and then built in 1899 as a hotel by the Sarkie brothers, Armenians. During the two World Wars it housed prisoners of war.

Slovak Republic

The Slovak Republic is a landlocked central European country bordered by the Czech Republic and Austria on the west, Poland to the north, the Ukraine east, and Hungary south. The area was settled by the Slavs during the 5th c AD. In the 9th c the Maygars invaded and remained under Hungarian rule for about 1000 years, and under the Austrian Habsburg dynasty until 1918. After World War I it was part of the Czecho-Slovak state, and was allied with Germany during World War II. The Communists seized control in 1948, and in 1968 the Soviet Union. The Czech and Slovak Republic followed with The Slovak Republic declaring independence in 1993.

Dining Etiquette

Please be punctual when invited for a meal. Please bring flowers in an uneven number, except for red roses which have romantic implications, a bottle of wine, or a gift for the home. Shake hands greeting and departing. Ladies extend hands first. You will be offered drinks – coffee, tea or a regional wine. Before eating a host will say "Dobru chut" similar to "Bon Appetit" and please respond. Eating is continental style with the fork in the left hand, knife in the right. Both hands are kept above the table during the meal, and no elbows on the table. Napkins are used on the table, not in the lap. Sometimes the hostess will not join the guests at a meal, but will serve it instead. Beer or wine is often served with the meal. An empty glass will be refilled. Strong (Turkish) coffee with the grounds in the bottom will be served after the meal.
The toast is "Na zdravie" "To your health".

Cuisine

The staple foods are wheat, breads, potatoes, dairy products, pork, sauerkraut and cabbage, onions, cow and sheep cheese, sour cream fruit – apples, plums, grapes, rice, pasta, dumplings, carrots, pork, sausages, smoked bacon, beef, poultry, lamb, goat, duck, turkey and venison. Meats are usually breaded and fried or served with a sauce, or in stews or goulash. The main meal is eaten at lunch - soup, meat, dumplings, rice or potatoes, bread and vegetables

(Medové Rezy (Honey Slices)

Dough

600g (5 cups) flour
150 g powdered sugar
2 tbls. cocoa
3 tbls. honey

50g (half stick) butter
3 eggs
2 tsp. baking soda

Combine flour, powdered sugar, cocoa, honey, butter and eggs in a bowl. Keep working it until it is like play dough. Form into a cylinder and slice into 4 equal sections. On a floured board roll out each section into a plate slightly larger than the bottom of your baking pan. Place wax paper over the plate. Flip the board over to remove the dough. Place it into a baking pan upside down. Use a knife to cut off the dough sticking over the edges. Also use a fork to poke the dough in several places. This is done to keep it from puffing up. Bake each slice for 8 minutes at 350°.

Custard Filling

0.5 l (2.1 cups) milk
5 tbls. corn starch
250 g powdered sugar
250 g (2 ½ sticks) butter

1 shot of rum
Vanilla extract
1 jar of jam

In a pan combine the milk and cornstarch. Bring to a boil. If not thick enough add more cornstarch. Stir in powdered sugar, a little bit of vanilla, a shot of rum and butter. Use a hand held blender to whip the custard. Fill the layers: to assemble everything together, take one layer and spread the custard on it. Add another wafer and top this one with jam (raspberry or red currant if you can find it). Cover with the third layer and spread on the remaining custard. Then cover with the last wafer. At least that's how it is supposed to be done. I instead made WCJWJJWCJW (wafer/custard/jam/wafer and so on). Weigh the slices down with something like a sack of flour and let sit for several hours in a cool place. Initially, the wafers will be quite hard and crunchy, but will soften and taste like soft Graham Crackers.

Topping

200 g dark chocolate

50 g butter

After the wafers have softened (such as the following day), top them with a chocolate layer. Use a double boiler (one pot sitting in another one containing boiling water) to melt 4 squares of dark chocolate with an half a stick of butter. I used 100/ chocolate. Since this was too bitter, I added about 2 teaspoons worth of hot chocolate mix. The original recipe said to turn the cake over so you end up coating the layer that was on the bottom. I have no idea why you should do this, besides perhaps aesthetics. I ended up coating the top layer because it was more uniform. Place in a refrigerator (or freezer) to allow the chocolate to set. Serve by cutting out individual slices about inch wide and 3 inches long. You'll end up with about 50 of these.
Recipe courtesy of Maria Vidova, www.slovakcooking.com

Slovak Specialties

Halusky –soft dumpling
Bryndzove halusky – the national dish - sheep cheese halusky
Segedin goulash – pork goulash
Rezen – pork schnitzel
Rezen - breaded steak
Jaternice – blood sausage
Slanina – smoked bacon
Svieckova – beef with cream sauce
Lokse – potato dough pancakes
Zemiakove placky – fried potato pancakes
Parene Buchty – jam dumplings
Knedle – dumplings
Vepro-knedle zelo – pork with dumplings and cabbage
Parene buchty – steamed buns
Kolac – nut or poppy seed rolls
Langos – deep fried bread cake

Fazufova – bean soup
Kapustnica- sauerkraut soup
Rezancova – chicken noodle soup
Tekvicovy privarok – pumpkin soup
Zemfovka – bread pudding
Ryzovy nakyp – rice pudding
Laskonky - dough with walnuts and cream
Trotle – tarts with chocolate
Torte – cakes
Zemfovka – apple and bread pudding
Babovka – pound cake
Trdelnik – cake baked on a spit over an open fire
Zincica – sour milk
Ostiepok – sheep cheese
Perenica – semi-soft sheep cheese shaped into a twisted ribbon, and often made into

Holidays

Easter – Paska is the traditional Easter cake baked on Holy Saturday or Easter morning. Paska, eggs, ham, sausages, and cheese are taken to the church to be blessed. On Easter Paska, cirak (traditional cheese), baked ham and beet horseradish are served.
Christmas Eve - vilija (Christmas Eve dinner) - mushroom soup, fish, peas, prunes
Christmas - roast goose. Fried fish and potato salad
Kapustnica - *cabbage soup* is prepared at the end of the year for Christmas and New Year's Eve.

Drinks

Wine is produced in the southern part of Slovakia, which is divided into 6 wine producing regions. Wines are produced in Bratislava, especially around Pressburg which means "place or town of the wine press". Wines were known to have been made there since the 13th c, mainly white wine. Slivovica - plum brandy, Borovicka – juniper brandy, and Karpatske Brandy Special which is made from select wines are also produced.

Slovak beer has been brewed for over a thousand years. The better known brands are Golden Pheasant (Zlaty Bazant), a Pilsner and Corgon, a lager beer. Fruit syrups are made with water or seltzer. Mineral water is very popular. Kofola is a carbonated soft drink produced in the Czech Republic and Slovakia.

Slovenia

Slovenia borders Austria to the north, Italy west, Hungary east and Croatia south. It lies at the juncture of the Alps, Pannonian Plain, Dinaric Mountain Range, and the Mediterranean. Present-day Slovenia has been inhabited since prehistoric times. There is evidence of human habitation from around 250,000 years ago. The area that is present-day Slovenia was in Roman times shared between Venetia et Histria and the provinces Pannonia and Noricum. In the 5th and 6th centuries the Huns and Germanic tribes invaded into Italy. Other parts of present-day Slovenia were again ruled by Avars before Charlemagne's victory over them in 803. By the 11th century, the Germanization of what is now Lower Austria, effectively isolated the Slovene-inhabited territory from the other western Slavs, speeding up the development of the Slavs of Carantania and of Carniola into an independent Carantanian/Carniolans/Slovene ethnic group. By the late Middle Ages, the historic provinces of Carniola, Styria, Carinthia, Gorizia, Trieste, and Istria developed from the border regions and were incorporated into the medieval German state. In the 14th century, most of the territory was taken over by the Habsburgs. The Republic of Venice was dissolved by France and Venetian Slovenia was passed to the Austrian Empire in 1797. The Slovene Lands were part of the French-administered Illyrian provinces established by Napoleon, the Austrian Empire and Austria-Hungary. Slovenes inhabited most of Carniola, the southern part of the duchies of Carinthia and Styria, the northern and eastern areas of the Austrian Littoral, as well as Prekmurje in the Kingdom of Hungary. Between 1880 and 1910 there was extensive emigration, and around 300,000 Slovenes emigrated to other countries. The capital Ljubljana was settled in Neolithic times, followed by the Illyrian camp Emen, the Roman encampment Emona (c15AD). It was first mentioned in 1144 and declared a city in 1220. Slovenia was part of Yugoslavia under Josip Broz Tito and became independent on June 25, 1991.

Dining Etiquette

Please be punctual when invited for a meal. If shoes are left outside the door, please leave yours also. When visiting a home take flowers (wrapped and in an odd number, not 13), whiskey, chocolates, and if there are children, presents for them. Gifts may be opened before the presenter. Please shake hands greeting and departing, shaking a woman's hand first. Good friends and family may kiss twice on the cheek. Refreshments may be served. The host(ess) will seat the guests. Food is eaten continental style with the fork in the left and knife in the right hand. Keep your hands at table level, not in your lap when not eating. When finished place your knife and fork together.

Cuisine

Slovene food is a combination of Austrian and Italian influences. It uses fresh fruit – plums, grapes, cherries, apples, apricots; vegetables – corn, wheat, sugar beets, potatoes, dandelion greens for salad, mushrooms; plum preserves and drinks; honey; a variety of cheese and breads; and meats. Mushrooms are served in salad, soups, as a main dish, or stuffing. The different regions of Slovenia are influenced by the types of vegetables, fruits and meats available. The Maribor (Marburg an der Drau under Habsburgs) region in the northeast uses cream, horseradish, mushrooms, rye and corn breads, stews, chicken, veal, salads with green pumpkin oil. Desserts include *prleska gibanica*, a poppy seed cake. On St. Martin's Day (November 11) sweet grape juice which is just fermenting is served with roast goose. Along the Adriatic coast olives are grown, and at Secovlje the salt pans are over 700 years old. The Karst is known for Karst prosciutto and wine. During the 18th c farming of corn and potatoes was introduced. Tea, especially herbal, has been cultivated for centuries, especially at the monasteries.

Walnut Potica

600 g flour	50 g butter
40 g yeast	50 g sugar
2 tbls. warm milk	200-300 ml milk
2 tbls. flour	Zest of 1 lemon
1 tsp. sugar	Salt
2 egg yolks, reserve whites	

Place the flour in a bowl and put in warm spot.
Combine the yeast with the warm milk. Add flour and sugar. Allow to rise in a warm place.
In a bowl beat the egg yolks, butter and sugar.
Warm the 200-300 milk, then add salt, zest, and butter mixture. Combine the yeast mixture, butter mixture, warm flour, adding only enough milk to form a dough. Knead until it no longer sticks to the bowl. Cover and place in warm area to rise, doubling in size. Roll out. Spread filling over it. Roll up like a jelly roll. Place in greased baking pan. Let rise until doubled again. Brush with 1 beaten egg. Preheat oven to 350°. Bake ½ hour.

Filling

300-400 g walnuts	2 tbls. rum
200 ml milk	100 g sugar
40 g butter	100 g honey
Zest of 1 lemon	2 egg whites
1 tsp. cinnamon	

In a pan bring the milk, butter, and 50 g sugar to a boil. Scald the walnuts. Warm the honey and add to walnut mixture. Stir in lemon zest, cinnamon and rum. Cool. Beat the egg whites and sugar until stiff, and fold into mixture.
Recipe courtesy of the Embassy of the Republic of Slovenia, Washington, DC

Slovenian Specialties

Vinska Pogaca, a wine cake made with red wine, apples, cinnamon and other spices, served with whipped cream

Flancati is also a sweet dough with white wine and rum, braided, then fried.

Kmecka Pojedina is composed of various sausages, pork, cabbage, potatoes and dumplings.

Gibanica – layers of apple, curd cheese, poppy seeds and pastry

Belokranjsko Cvrtje is a meat pie

Cevapcici – meat eaten with lepinje - pita bread

Brodet is a fish stew, made with fish, olive oil, herbs and tomatoes.

Krofi is a type of donut served at Carnival.

Buhteljni is an apricot sweet dough.

Struklji is another filled dough, served with meat or game, or as a meal or dessert, depending on the filling.

Holidays and Special Occasions

During Lent people fast.

On Palm Sunday spring greens are blessed. Plaiting bundles dates back to the 9th c.

Fasting is still adhered to on Good Friday.

On Holy Saturday afternoon Easter foods are blessed.

Typical Easter foods are ham, bread, horseradish, potica – a wheat flour cake made with special fillings of walnuts, hazelnuts, honey, peppermint, cottage cheese, sour cream, bacon, dried fruit, or other ingredients; and pisanica – colored eggs using wax.

On Easter Monday people celebrate, hike, visit family and friends, and change their wardrobes.

Christmas is commemorated on December 25th. Families gather on Christmas Eve, may decorate their Christmas tree, and attend mass at midnight. In olden days trees were decorated upside down from the ceiling with seeds, beans, nuts, apples and other fruit in thanksgiving for abundant crops. Today trees are decorated with bulbs and lights, most likely well before Christmas. Presents are exchanged. Another mass in the morning is called the shepherd mass, which may be followed by another larger mass.

Christmas dinner will start with soup, poultry with side dishes of sauerkraut, potatoes, pastas, and salads, finished off with dessert – the potica, now made with a walnut filling. Family is very important at this time of year.

For Orthodox families gifts are given on name dates (saint's days).

Beverages

Wine has been produced here since Roman times. The country lies in an ideal wine making region at the southern base of the Alps with a variety of soils and microclimates producing some very good wines. Many of the vineyards are planted with old vines, i.e. more than twenty years old, and cultivated on small plots. Most of the wine is produced for personal or local consumption on small vineyards, though a rising number of bottles are being exported. The country is divided into three wine regions – the eastern with good Rieslings, the central dry roses, and western with more Mediterranean style wines. Like France's Beaujolais Nouveau, Slovenia produces *Predstavitev* "Premiere" or young wine, bottled in November and to be drunk immediately. The Ljubljana Wine Festival is held annually in September. Plum brandy *Sljivovica i*s both homemade and produced in the wineries, and is the national drink. Beer *Pivo* is also brewed in Slovenia.

Solomon Islands

Solomon Islands is a sovereign state consisting of six major islands and over 900 smaller islands in Oceania lying to the east of Papua New Guinea and northwest of Vanuatu. Papuan-speaking settlers began to arrive around 30,000 BC. Austronesian speakers arrived c. 4000 BC also bringing cultural elements such as the outrigger canoe. Between 1200 and 800 BC the ancestors of the Polynesians, the Lapita people, arrived from the Bismarck Archipelago with their own ceramics. The first European to visit the islands was the Spanish navigator Álvaro de Mendaña de Neira, coming from Peru in 1568. The United Kingdom declared a protectorate over the southern Solomons in June 1893. In the early 20th century several British and Australian firms began large-scale coconut planting. During World War II most planters and traders were evacuated to Australia and most cultivation ceased. Following the independence of neighboring Papua New Guinea from Australia in 1975, the Solomon Islands gained self-government in 1976 and independence was granted in 1978. The country's capital, Honiara, is located on the island of Guadalcanal. 63-70 different dialects and languages, pidgin English and English are spoken.

Dining Etiquette

When invited to a home arrive on time or slightly late. Please bring a gift from your country. Please shake hands greeting and departing. The host will show you your seat. When seated at the table eat continental style with the fork in the left hand and the knife in the right. In some homes you may be seated on the ground and eat with your hands. Guests are offered the best food and dine first. Try everything that is served to you. They are very hospitable people. If you are dining with Chinese you may be given chopsticks. Leave a small amount on your plate when finished. Respect of elders is still very important.

Cuisine

Few plants or animals are native to the islands, most having been brought from other parts of the Pacific such as New Guinea, Asia, or Europe, but the land is very fertile. Among these were coconuts which is a staple food for its milk and flesh. The early animals brought here were pigs, rats, and dogs; and plants- rice, yams, taro, bananas, sugarcane and lemons. The early settlers learned to cook in underground earthen ovens. Later the Europeans introduced cattle, chickens, pigs, wheat, potatoes, pineapples, rice, cocoa, and spices. However there was an abundance of sea animals – crabs, turtles, fish, snails, eels, and water birds. Today the basic diet consists of yams, pork, chicken, kau kau (sweet potatoes), avocado, fish, taro root, breadfruit, rice, coconuts, and fruit – bananas, paw paw, mango, and papaya. Sago palm is a starch to make puddings and bread. Solomon Taiyo (canned tuna) is canned on the islands by the Marubeni fishing Company. Breakfast is usually a small meal and until recently lunch was the largest meal eaten with the family at home, and often spread over several hours. It this is the case then dinner is usually leftovers from lunch. The land is controlled by the local clans and their members.

Tapioca Pudding

Serves 6

1 cup large pearl tapioca
1 cup water
6 eggs, separated

4 cups coconut milk
1 cup sugar
1 tsp. vanilla

Soak the tapioca in a pan with the water for 1 hour. Then bring to a boil and cook until the tapioca is transparent.
Preheat oven to 325°
Beat the egg yolks and milk in a sauce pan and add sugar. Heat while stirring until mixture thickens. Stir in the vanilla.
In a bowl beat the egg whites until stiffened. Gently fold the egg whites into the tapioca. Serve warm or chilled. Grated coconut can be added.

Holidays and Special Occasions

For ceremonial celebrations poi, tapioca, cassava, roast pig, fish, and perhaps green coconut are served. Poi is made from taro root.
At Kastom feasts guests are given betel nuts to chew.

Beverages

The islands must import all alcoholic and most other beverages. Solomon Breweries does produce a local beer. Some fruit juices are produced here. Kava is made from the kava plant roots which releases a liquid to which water is added. It is a relaxing stimulant.

Somalia

Somalia is located on the Horn of Africa, and is bordered by Djibouti to the northwest, Kenya to the southwest, the Gulf of Aden with Yemen to the north, the Indian Ocean to the east, and Ethiopia to the west. Somalia has been inhabited since the Paleolithic period. It was located on ancient trading routes with the Egyptians, Phoenicians, Mycenaeans, and Babylonians. The Somali supplied frankincense, myrrh, spices and short-horn cattle. They domesticated the camel c3-2 millennium. Indian merchants provided the Somali with cinnamon from Sri Lanka and Indonesia. Islam came to the country very early, and today Somalia is almost 1005 Sunni Muslim. During the Middle Ages several Somali empires existed. In 1920 the regions became a British protectorate, and in 1960 the Somali Republic was formed. Mogadishu, the capital, has been a port on the Indian Ocean for centuries. The official languages are Somali and Arabic.

Dining Etiquette

Please remove your shoes before entering a building. Men shake hands. Women will hug and kiss if they know each other well. A female will offer her hand to a male if she wants to shake hands. But most commonly women only greet very close friends or relatives. You will be offered a milk tea and incense. Hands are washed before and after eating. Women will serve food to the men, and then feed themselves and the children. Food is scooped from a bowl using the first three fingers of the right hand or with a spoon. Rolled banana leaves may also be used instead of utensils Food may be served communally on a platter with rice, meat and vegetables. Please eat the portion that is set before you. Only eat with your right hand. Please wait for the host to start eating. Pork and alcoholic beverages are not served. Please thank the host for the meal. After the meal frankincense or incense are burned.

Skuda Kuriss (Rice Pilau)

Serves 4-6

½ lb. boneless beef or lamb, cubed	1 clove garlic
2 large onions, peeled and chopped	¼ cup oil
4 oz. tomato paste	2 cups rice
10 cloves	Salt
10 cardamom seeds	3 cups boiling water

In a skillet heat some of the oil. Saute the onions until just translucent. Remove. In same skillet brown the meat. Stir in the onions, and the remaining ingredients. Bring to a boil. Cook covered for 25 minutes. Add more water if too dry.

Cuisine

The cuisine is a blend of Somali, Ethiopian, Yemeni, Persian, Turkish, Indian and Italian. The food will vary in the different regions of the country. Staples include lentils, rice (bariis), fruit - bananas, mango, guava and grapefruit; spices – cumin, cardamom, cloves, and sage. Dinner is often served late, often at 9. During Ramadan it will often follow the Tarawih prayers, perhaps as late as 11.

Somali Specialties

Polenta – maize porridge is served with butter and sugar

Canjeero – bread that is served at breakfast with gee and sugar, or sesame oil

Hilib ari – goat meat

Jerky – dried meat

Barris iyo digaag sugar – rice, chicken and vegetables

Maraq – stew

Kaluun – fish

Busteeki – beef

Cambuuul – azuki beans with butter and sugar

Soor – cornmeal with milk, butter and sugar

Sabaayad – bread

Baasto – pasta served with a stew and banana Lahooh or injera bread is made in the north and is circular.

Rooti (baked in wood-fired oven) and muufo (made from sorghum or cornmeal) are other types of bread.

Rooti iyo xalwo – bread and jelly

Malawax – flour, egg, milk and water bread served with sugar

Sambuusa – samosa (snack)

Shah – tea

Gashaato – coconut, oil, sugar and spice sweet

Holidays and Special Occasions

At the time of births, circumcision, weddings, and holidays animals are slaughtered, bread made, and plenty of food served. Xalwo or halva is a sweet made from cornstarch, cardamom, nutmeg and ghee, and perhaps peanuts and is served at Eid celebrations or weddings.

Beverages

Since this is a Muslim country no alcoholic beverages are served. Fruit drinks made from grapefruit, tamarind, lemons, mango, apple, and guava are the most popular. Milk with cardamom, coffee and tea are also served.

South Africa

South Africa at the southernmost tip of Africa is a large plateau bordered by mountains, velds – fields, desert areas, and an extensive coastline bordered by the Atlantic and Indian Oceans,. To the north are Namibia, Botswana and Zimbabwe; to the east Mozambique and Swaziland. Lesotho is surrounded by South African territory. South Africa was home to the earliest humans, later the San and about 2000 years ago the Khoikhoi. Bantu-speaking peoples, who used iron implements for agriculture, and had herds settled near the northern border with Botswana and Zimbabwe by the fourth or fifth century CE. They The Portuguese were the first Europeans to explore southern Africa in an attempt to find a route to the East Indies. The arrival of Jan van Riebeeck, a Dutchman, in 1652 forever changed the history of the country. Sent by the Dutch East India Company to provision ships rounding the Cape of Good Hope, he built magnificent gardens and buildings. These provided fruits, vegetables, and meat for the sailors, helped cure several diseases including scurvy. South Africa was the uniting of four British colonies into the Union of South Africa in 1910. South Africa has three capital cities: Cape Town, the seat of Parliament, is the legislative capital; Pretoria, the seat of the President and Cabinet, is the administrative capital; and Bloemfontein, the seat of the Supreme Court of Appeal, is the judicial capital. South Africa has eleven official languages English, Ndebele, Northern Sotho, Sotho, Swazi, Tswana, Tsonga, Venda, Xhosa, and Zulu

Dining Etiquette

Please be prompt when invited for a meal. Please send or bring flowers with you. Always shake hands greeting and departing. Cocktails are served before dinner- hard liquor and lots of beer. Wine is usually served with the meal. Meals are served at a table with the guest of honor seated to the right of the host or hostess. The table is set with cutlery for each course. Food is eaten continental style. Please wait for your hostess to start. In some rural areas spoons and/or fingers are still used for eating. South Africa has no national toast. Toasting is done one to another at any time and by anyone. Obviously for very formal occasions there is protocol. Thank you notes are handwritten and informal.

Cuisine

The Dutch, French, British, German, Malay, Indian, Chinese and native Hottentot influences abound. Dishes use available foodstuffs such as mutton and fish, mealie (corn) and maize, fruits, and spices brought back from the East Indies. Every part of an animal was used, and methods developed to keep it for long periods of time. Even today, with refrigerators, many of the same recipes are applied. Jellies, marmalades, and chutneys are widely used. Wild sorrel makes a good brass cleaner. In the olden days fruit was often stored and dried in coffins!

The temperate climate of South Africa contributes to the people's love of the outdoors and braaivleis- barbeques are a favorite way of entertaining. Much home entertaining is done which allows for a very informal lifestyle. However, if asked for a meal, do find out about dress. South Africans often entertain formally, and you might want to bring a dinner jacket. Lunch is usually about 1PM, dinner 7:30-8.

ZULU ZESTY RIBS

4 Racks of Baby Back Ribs

Sauce:

1 cup red wine	8 garlic cloves, minced
½ cup brown sugar	3/4 cup Zulu Sauce

Cut ribs individually and place in baking pan lined up tightly next to each other. Combine all ingredients for the sauce in a bowl then pour over the ribs and place in oven at 250° for the 1st hour. After the 1st hour turn up the oven to 350° for the 2nd hour. Finally turn up the oven to 375° for the 3rd and final hour.
Garnish: Toasted Coconut shaving work well on top as well as extra Zulu sauce to spice it up a little.
Recipe courtesy of Nigel Wood, Ukuva iAfrica Wine & Food Collection, Cape Town, South Africa, supporter of "Help the Helpless Program in Africa"

Buchu Tomato Soup

1 Cape Moondance teabag, or 1 regular teabag	3 tsp. fruit chutney
100 ml boiling water	1 tsp. dried mixed herbs or fresh herbs, such as basil
1 x 410g tin of tomato and onion relish	1 ml cayenne pepper
1 clove garlic, chopped	Ground mixed black pepper
2 tsp. Worcester or fish sauce	Salt to taste

Soak the teabag in boiling water in boiling water for 5 minutes. Remove the bag. Add all the ingredients in a food processor and blend until smooth.
Serve with croutons and fresh herbs. The soup can be served warm or chilled.
Recipe courtesy of Ronel Terblanche, Cape Moondance, Stellenbosch, South Africa

South African Specialties

Samp – corn and bean porridge

Snoek – a type of fish, member of the barracuda family

Smoorsnoek – salted fish with onion and potato

Bredie – dish made with mutton, vegetables, and waterblommetjies (waterlily blooms)

Bobotie – spiced minced meat or lamb with egg custard

Melktert – custard tart

Soetkoekies – spiced biscuits mixed with wine

Blatjang – condiment served at most meals

Bookem – dried sardine

Oblietjies – rolled wafers

Sosaties – mutton or lamb on skewers

Koeksisters – spiced and fried doughnuts

Malva – steamed pudding

Boerewors – not Boer War, but a type of sausage

Biltong – dried meat

Denning vieis – stewed lamb with tamarind

Potjiekos – stews

Braaivleis – barbeque

Mealie pap – cornmeal porridge

Samosas – fried dough with different fillings

Gestoofde – stew – can be meat, vegetables, chicken or others

Biryani – mixed rice

Sambals – hot sauces

Akhni – rice curry

Melk porring – baked milk pudding

Rooibos – red bush tea with dried and sweetened condensed milk

Gemmer – ginger beer

Mageu – similar to yogurt drink, given to guests

Mopane – dried caterpillars

Roasted Quinces with Fynbos Vinegar and Sherry

4 quinces
¼ cup superfine, or castor sugar
2 tbls. butter

3 tbls. Rozendal Fynbos Vinegar
¼ cup semi-sweet sherry

Preheat the oven to 180°C (350°F).

Peel the quinces and quarter them vertically. Cut around and remove the core. Be careful as it tends to be very hard.

Place all the quince quarters on a roasting tray, core-side up and sprinkle with the sugar. Divide the butter into little nuggets and place one nugget on each piece of quince. Roast for about one-and-a-quarter hours or until deep orange, turning once.

Add the sherry and vinegar to the hot pan. Toss to combine and return to the oven for another ten minutes.

Divide into serving dishes and spoon over the golden pan juices. Serve drenched in fresh cream.

Recipe courtesy of Rozendal Farm, Jonkershoek ValleyJonkershoek Valley, South Africa

Holidays and Special Occasions

For weddings, christenings, birthdays, and funerals food is served in abundance.
Easter – dyed eggs; hot cross buns; lamb; malva pudding; or Simnel cake with marzipan
Christmas – crayfish, mussels, or other seafood; gammon – glazed ham; roast turkey, duck, or lamb; vegetables; mince pie, puddings, and trifle. Many people follow British traditions with these foods.

Beverages

South Africa produces fine wines that are exported worldwide. The southwest region is ideal with a mild climate, and long, dry summers. A good mix of wines, sherry, ports, brandies, and method champenoise are produced from vines, some dating back to the original settlers. The earliest wine recorded was in Jan van Riebeeck's diary in 1659. By 1700 Constantia was known throughout Europe. The Constantia estate was planted by colonial governor van der Stel and produced sweet wines. Cultivar is a word unique to South Africa and specifies the variety or species of grape. The pinotage grape, a cross between Pinot Noir and hermitage was developed in 1925 and is native to South Africa. The wine is suitable for a warm climate and drinkable within ten years. Among the popular white varietals grown are Steen (chenin blanc), Chardonnay, Colombard, Sauvginon Blanc, Crouchon, Riesling, and Gewurztraminer. Reds include Cinsaut, Cabernet Sauvignon, Merlot, Syrah, Pinot Noir, Gamay, Pontac, and Pinotage. The Ko-operatiewe Winjbowers Verenging (KWV) (Co-operative Winegrowers Association) was established in 1918.

Wijnberg (wine town) is only 8 miles from Cape Town. Besides Constantia, the Stellenbosch region on the east side of Table Mountain, the Paarl district, The Tulbagh, the Worcester, Montagu and Robertson regions also produce wine.

Beer is brewed by SABMillers which was established in 1895 as Castle Breweries and later South African Breweries (SAB). The company is the second largest brewery in the world, brewing over 6 billion gallons.

South Korea

South Korea is bounded to the east by the Sea of Japan and to the north North Korea. The history of Korea dates back 600,000 years when the peninsula was first settled. In 2333 BC Tankun founded Ko-Chosen "Land of Morning Calm at P'yongyang. Successive kingdoms followed. The Mongols invaded in the 13th c, the Japanese in the 16th c., and the Chinese the 17th c. The Yi Dynasty in order to protect the country from invasion adopted an isolationist attitude and the country became known as the "Hermit Kingdom". Japan annexed Korea in 1910, attempting to replace the culture and language with Japanese influences. Near the end of World War II the Soviet Union and the United States agreed that Japanese forces would surrender to the U.S. the land south of the 38th parallel. The Republic of Korea was established on August 15, 1948. 1994 marked the 600th birthday of Seoul, the capital, whose name comes from Koryo "High and Clear". The official language is Korean.

Dining Etiquette

Please be punctual when invited for a meal. The Koreans love to entertain at home or in a restaurant, for which it is an honor to be invited. Please remove your shoes before entering a home. If bringing a gift present it with both hands. Please shake hands greeting and departing. Bow, with a slight nod of the head, and more deeply to elders or superiors. Women offer their hand first. Speak softly and have little eye contact. The most common names are Kim (Gold), Lee (Plum), and Park (White). Women keep and often use their maiden name. Rice wine or beer are served before the meal with panch'an (appetizers). You will probably be seated on cushions around low tables. The men sit crossed legged, the women side saddle. Do not step on these cushions. Before the meal "mulsugun", a moist warm clothe, is handed to each guest to wipe one's hands. Food is always served together, not in courses. On the table will be bowls for serving the rice and accompanying dishes. Do not lift the bowl to your mouth, or even pick up. Please do not use your fingers. Chopsticks and flat spoons are used. Rice and soup are eaten with the spoon, while the chopsticks are used to take the food from the various serving dishes and are left with them. When finished lay them together on the table. Do not leave the chopsticks in the bowl. If something is to be passed, do so with your right hand only.

If dining in a private home, the hostess will often prepare and serve the food, not seated with the guests. A usual meal is meat, rice or noodles, soup, side dishes and tea. Tea is often served after the meal. Meals are considered solemn occasions, and not much talk transpires. Desserts, if served, are sweets, cakes, or fresh fruit such as strawberries, persimmons, plums, or apples. Shikye is a sweet rice drink served following the meal.

For business entertaining a Korean banquet is appropriate. The guest of honor should reciprocate in his/her own country, paying all bills. While in Korea the hosts will take care of the entertaining.

A Korean banquet is similar to a Chinese with many courses served, and toasts drunk. The toast is "Gun Bai" or "Bottoms up". If someone toasts you and drains the glass, you must reciprocate. The glasses will be refilled immediately. The host must start the toasting either standing or sitting down. Enkai are after work drinking parties. Workers pour drinks for their superiors.

Shitake Shrimp and Pork Dumplings

8 oz. dried shitake mushrooms
4 oz. diced yellow onion
4 oz. diced zucchini
4 oz. mung bean sprouts
6 oz. tofu
1 egg

1 oz. minced garlic
4 oz. minced pork
4 oz. minced shrimp
Salt and pepper
50 dumpling wrappers (circle) or wonton wrappers

Soak the dried shitake mushrooms for 30 minutes in warm water. Julienne shitake and sauté. Set aside to cool.
Saute onion. Set aside to cool.
Saute zucchini. Set aside to cool.
Blanch mung bean sprouts in boiling water. Set aside to cool.
Once all vegetables are cool, mix together with remaining ingredients.
Cook a small portion of the mixture to test the seasoning. Adjust salt and pepper if necessary.
Using one wrapper at a time, lightly wet half of it. Spoon 1 tbls. of filling and form into dumpling.
Set completed dumplings on a baking sheet and freeze.

Dried Shitake Mushroom Broth

10 oz. dried shitake mushrooms
3 lb.s whole button mushrooms
1 oz. ginger, peeled

1 lemongrass stalk
4 garlic cloves, peeled

Combine button mushrooms, ginger, lemongrass, and garlic in a large foodsaver bag. Compress until all air is removed.
Place mushroom bag in boiling water, and let simmer for at least an hour.
Remove bag from water, open carefully and strain through cheesecloth.
Add dried shitake mushrooms to broth. Let steep at a low simmer for 30 minutes.
Remove shitake mushrooms and season broth with soy sauce and salt.
To serve: Bring the mushroom broth to a boil. Add dumplings and simmer until the dumplings are cooked. Spoon the dumplings into a bowl, cover with broth and serve.
Recipe courtesy of the Korea Agro-Fisheries & Food Trade Corp.

Yaki Mon Do (cabbage and beef in wonton wrappers)

1½ - 2 heads of cabbage
1 carrot, chopped
¼ onion, chopped
2-3 green onions, chopped

½ lb. ground beef
Salt and pepper
Won – ton wrappers, 1 pkg.
Soy sauce

Cook ground beef. Be sure it is in small pieces.
Cook cabbage crisp till tender. Chop very fine. Wrap in cloth and squeeze out all the water. Place in bowl.
Add carrot, onion, green onions, and ground beef. Season with salt and pepper.
Put 1 tsp. of meat mixture in wonton wrapper. Fold into triangle and seal edges.
Fry in electric frying pan at 350°.
Serve with soy sauce.
Recipe courtesy of Dorthea Turek, and sister-in-law Yon Cha Turek of Leavenworth, Kansas

Bul-go-gi (Korean Barbeque Beef)

2 ½ lb. rib-eye beef, thinly sliced
3 tbls. cooking wine (or Japanese Mirin: sweet cooking wine)
1/3 cup sesame oil
2 ½ tbls. brown sugar

½ tsp. black pepper
½ each medium onion, grated or minced
1/3 cup soy sauce
1 tbls. garlic, minced
4 oz. apple sauce

In a big bowl combine all the ingredients, except beef. Mix with beef gently and marinate for an hour or longer.
Cook on high on ungreased skillet (grill or broil on high) until browned and cooked on each side.
Recipe courtesy of Seyoung Thomas, Falls Church, Virginia

Cuisine

Hansik (Korean cuisine) uses native vegetables, rice, fruits, fish and meat. Cooking combines the five tastes – bitter, salty, sour, sweet, and hot; and the five colors – red, green, yellow, white, and black. Rice is the mainstay of each meal, eaten with side dishes such as kimchi; grilled beef or fish; and vegetables. Food is chopped into small pieces, and each dish must compliment the others – hot and fiery with rice for example. Most meat is cooked in "hot pots" or grilled. Some is cooked right at the table. Pork is basically for the poor; beef for the well-to-do. The Koreans make use of sesame seeds, soybean paste, ginger root, green onions, mung beans, dried chili peppers, and garlic. Seafood includes sea cucumbers, sea urchins, octopus, squid, Pollock, herring, mackerel, tuna, bass, sole, halibut, cod, croaker, and skate. Breakfast is a hearty meal; lunch light; and dinner filling. Southern Korean food is hotter, spicier, and uses more salt than the north.

Korean Specialties

Kimchi – the national dish, Cabbage is seasoned with red pepper powder, garlic, ginger, and anchovies, then put in earthenware jars and allowed to ferment. Each region has its own version.

Hanjeongsik – feast with small plates that might include smoked fish, beef, noodles, and soup

Samgyeopsal – grilled pork belly

Mandu – stuffed dumplings

Hobakjon – summer squash pancakes

Bibimpap – rice with vegetables and beef

Sinsullo – sliced beef served in a brass pot with vegetables, nuts and hot broth

Haemultang – sea food stew

Galbijjim – braised short ribs

Pajon – is a favorite snack –spring onion pancakes

Nanuls – salads or freshly steamed vegetables

Kalbi – barbecued beef ribs

Chigae – a thick stew

Bibimbap – mixed vegetables with rice

Jon – batter fried fish and vegetables

Pokkum – stir-fried dishes

Dak-bokkeum-tang – spicy chicken stew

Han-gwa – sweets, often made of puffed rice.

Hodu kwaja – walnut shaped cake with bean paste

Topokki – stir-fried rice cake

Fruits represent different things – oranges, happiness; pomegranate, fertility; apples, peace; and pears, prosperity.

Gamja-sujebi – soup with dough flakes and vegetables

Holidays and Special Occasions

New Year's – dishes prepared for the family and ancestors – duck kook (duck soup), rice cake soup, kimchi, rice, tteok (rice cakes), fruit, benne (sesame) or ginger candy

First full moon of the year – it is traditional to drink wine to prevent deafness. People visit 12 homes and are feed a great deal of food. A traditional dish consists of plain and glutinous rice, millet, corn, and red beans.

Spring – kimchi is made with white radishes, no garlic or chilies.

Summer - Koreans eat noodles for strength, as they are a symbol of longevity, and are cut with scissors.

Fall- kimchi is made at this time to get families through the long winters.

Chusock (Thanksgiving) – people visit family tombs and bring ancestors food.

Longest night of the year – red bean curd is served

Birth of a son – red peppers are hung on a doorway

100 days after a birth – a feast and rice cakes are prepared for family and friends, and if shared with 100 people the belief is the child will have a long life.

Birthdays – the 1st and 61st are most important. A 70th birthday (kohi) means "old and rare" is celebrated with a large party.

Rice cakes are served for a first birthday, New Year's and weddings

1st and 2nd anniversary of a death – serve five kinds of soup; 5 types of meat, fish or vegetables with wine, rice, noodles, rice cakes, and pickles

Beverages

Tea is a very important part of the meal. Kwangju is noted for its tea plantations. Other types of tea are Bori cha (barley tea); Mogwa cha (quince tea); Hodo cha (walnut tea); and Insam cha (ginseng tea).Kopi is coffee. A tabang shop serves tea and coffee, no food.

Rice wine and rice liquor (makkoli) have been produced for hundreds of years.Makkoli is often served from tubs. A makkoli-jip is a beverage hall. Chungchong is rice wine, served hot.Nong ju (farmer's rice wine) and Insam ju (ginseng wine) are two other types. The finest rice wine, Pobju, comes from Kyongju. European wines are also produced including Ma-ju-ang, a Riesling. Koreans love to drink and sing. When asked to drink, decline several times, then join the fun. Never pour your own drink. Instead hold your glass with two hands in front of you while the host pours. It is improper to drink alone, and most women do not drink. In fact not too long ago only men were permitted to drink alcoholic beverages. Special rice wines are served at weddings, funerals, and for a 61st birthday. One drinking ritual provides that every glass must be passed to be sipped by everyone.

Korea also produces several beers OB and Crown the best known. Pyong-maekju is bottled beer, Saeng-maekju draft beer. One of the unusual drinks is Paem-sool, a tonic liquor made with a snake. Poricha is a drink produced from roasted barley and hot water; soju a clear liquor from rye or sweet potatoes with an alcoholic content of 20-25%.

Did You Know?

Celadon, introduced by the Japanese, has been produced since the Koryo Dynasty (927-1392).
The first known public bar existed in Kaesong c 1102 AD.
A favorite dish of royalty was Kujolpan "nine treasure dish" with nine compartments. These would include crepes in the center surrounded by eight dishes – shredded egg, cucumbers, onions, mushrooms, beef, carrots, cabbage, and shrimp.
Haejangguk or "Hangover soup" is made from poached ox blood.
Garlic dates from prehistoric times. Chilies were brought from the Americas in the 15th and 16th centuries.
A jang terrace is used for storage of large earthenware pots, usually for kimchi.
The tea ceremony was brought to Korea by Buddhist monks during the Yi Dynasty c 14th c. When drinking green tea hold the cup with both hands and sip only a small amount at a time.
Ganjang sauce is a type of soy sauce that dates back at least 450 years, and is a recipe kept in a family of the oldest son and then passed down through the generations. During the fermenting of the soy sauce the wife would add jongja-jang, a new sauce, unique to each family.
Koreans buy and give red ginseng as a gift in May "Harmony Month" and consider it very healthy for the body in preventing cancer, lowering cholesterol levels, and helping with fatigue.
Kimchi is very high in fiber, low-fat, full of vitamins, and not surprisingly, probably contributes to the longevity and beautiful skin of the Koreans.

South Sudan

South Sudan is a landlocked country in East-Central Africa, bordered by Sudan to the north, Ethiopia to the east, Kenya to the southeast, Uganda to the south, the Democratic Republic of the Congo to the southwest, and the Central African Republic to the west. It includes the vast swamp region of the Sudd, formed by the White Nile and known locally as the *Bahr al Jabal*. The Nilotic people of South Sudan—the Acholi, Anyuak, Bari, Dinka, Nuer, Shilluk, Kaligi (Arabic Feroghe), and others—first entered South Sudan sometime before the 10th century. During the period from the 15th to the 19th centuries, tribal migrations, largely from the area of Bahr el Ghazal, brought the Anyuak Dinka, Nuer and Shilluk to their modern locations of both Bahr El Ghazal and Upper Nile Regions, while the Acholi and Bari settled in Equatoria. The Azande, Mundu, Avukaya and Baka, who entered South Sudan in the 16th century, established the region's largest state of Equatoria Region. In the 18th century, the Avungara sib rose to power over the rest of Azande society and this domination continued into the 20th century. South Sudan gained its independence from the Republic of the Sudan in 2011. Juba, the capital, is also the largest city. English is the official language with over 60 indigenous languages spoken.

Dining Etiquette

It is an honor to be invited to a home. The Sudanese are very hospitable. The family is very important and very patriarchal. Several generations may live in the same house. Dinner may be quite late, 9 or 9:30. Please take a small gift, never alcohol. Men shake hands greeting and departing, and may tap each other on the shoulder. A woman must extend her hand first to a man. Women may hug and rub each other's cheek. The host will offer a guest a glass of orange or grapefruit juice, coffee or tea and perhaps something to eat. Always accept food and drink when offered. Men and women will often be separated when eating. The women do the cooking. If a guest is a very important person a sheep may be killed, and dishes made from it. Hands are washed before and after dining. Large cloths are used to cover one's knees, in place of napkins. Guests usually sit on the floor, or cushions with a low table, during a meal. Hands are washed before and after the meal. Soup will be served first, brought in bowls on a tray. The bowl is held in the left hand while eating. When finished the tray and bowls are removed, and a tray with five or six dishes is presented. Food is eaten only with the fingers on the right hand. Never accept or pass things with your left hand. Spoons may be provided. Bread is used to sop up the food. Salad and shata, a hot sauce, then dessert will be served. The Sudanese enjoy crème caramela and fruit. No beverage is served with the meal. Coffee, or tea with cloves or cinnamon may be served, followed by the burning of sandalwood incense.

Ful Medames (mashed fava beans)

Serves 4

1 lb. dried fava beans	Salt and pepper
1 large onion, chopped	½ tsp. cumin
2 large tomatoes, chopped	Coriander
Rocket or other green leaves	

Soak the beans in water for at least 6 hours. Drain.
In a pan heat the beans covered with water, and cook for at least 2 hours until beans are very tender. Drain and save some of liquid. Mash beans and liquid.
Add the other ingredients.
Serve with pita bread for breakfast.

Cuisine

The Sudanese cuisine has been influenced by the East African, Egyptians, Ethiopians, Arabs and the Turks. In the north are the Muslims, and Christians and animists in the south. The Misseriya, a nomadic tribe, still graze cattle. The Nubians may have been the very first to cultivate wheat. Their main dish, gourrassa, is made from wheat and baked in a round shape. In the east, the most popular dish is moukhbaza, which is made of banana paste. This part is greatly influenced by the Ethiopian taste and cuisine. In the west, each tribal group has adopted different forms of food that are basically very simple. Milk and dairy products are a fundamental component to the majority of the people since most of them are cattle breeders. A distinct cereal by which the west is well-known is dukhun. It is used in preparing a thick porridge called aseeda dukhun, to that is added a stew called sharmout abiyad which is cooked with dry meat. Another form of stew is kawal, which is made from a mixture of plant roots that are left to leaven and dried afterwards. As for the south, the abundance of rivers, lakes and swamps have made the people in these regions dependent on fish for their food. Kajaik is a stew of dried fish. It is added to the porridge, which is common throughout Sudan and aseeda made of sorghum. Sometimes natural margarine is added to the mixture. In Equatoria, aseeda is made of Bafra ehich is a plant of the same family of potatoes. To the aseeda is added a green vegetable called mouloukhiya) with peanut butter. Fassikh is one of the most popular dishes in Central Sudan. It is made from a fish which is leavened for some time and after that cooked with onions, spices and tomato sauce. It is most probably of Nubian origin same as Eltarkeen, which could not be found anywhere except northern Sudan.

Common grains are millet, sorghum, wheat, and barley. Cotton, peanuts, beans, rice, okra, and sesame are the main agricultural products. Sudan is the largest supplier of gum Arabic. Beef, cattle, and chicken are raised. Red pepper, garlic and spices were brought by Syrian and Arabic traders. Stews are made with meat, onions, potatoes, or eggplant, spices, peanut butter, Ni'aimya and dried okra, milk or yogurt. They are served with asseda, a porridge made with wheat or corn flour.

Specialties

Bamia - okra soup

Chapati – flat unleavened bread cooked on a griddle

Medeeda Hilba – porridge made with fried fenugreek seed, then boiled in water, milk, sugar and athrun (rock salt)

Basico – ground sesame seeds, greens and smoked fish or meat

Kofta – meatballs in tomato sauce

Shaiyah – fried meat

Elmaraara and umfitit – sheep innards, onions, peanut butter and salt, eaten raw

Miris – sheep fat, onion, and dried okra stew

Mullah – lamb and yogurt stew

Bussaara, Waika, and Sabaroag are stew made of dried okra, dried meat, dried onions, spices and peanut butter, depending on what is available

Sharmout abiyad – dried meat stew

Kawari – animal hoof and vegetable soup

Mahshi – zucchini and bell peppers stuffed with meat in tomato sauce

Gibna bayda – white cheese

Anise kahk – sugar coated cookies

Kabis – Christmas cookies

Ni'aimiya - Sudanese spice mix

Holidays and Special Occasions

Muslims observes Ramadan when a person fasts from sunrise to sunset; Eid –Ul-Fitr (End of Ramadan); and Eid-Al-Adha.

Coptic Christians observe Easter and Christmas

Special occasion foods are Shaiyah made with beef, goat or lamb that has been slaughter for the event. Mahshi are stuffed zucchini and bell peppers in a tomato use. The stuffing is minced meat and rice.

Beverages

Sweet hot tea is consumed at any time of the day, for breakfast, after a meal in the afternoon, and always offered to guests. Tamarind juice is a popular drink. Tamarind comes from the Arabic "Tomur Hindi" which means Indian dates. Sharia law prevails in South Sudan, and there is no alcohol consumption. However Araqi, gin made from dates, is produced illegally.

Did You Know?

Fava beans, sometimes called horse beans, have been around since 6000 BC.

Spain

Spain occupies the Iberian Peninsula with Portugal, and was named by the Romans "Hispania" in approximately 200 BC. The word is a derivative of the Phoenician Shepham "coast or island of rabbits". The country lies on a large plateau with mountains to the north and coastal areas to the south and east. Spain's history goes back thousands of years with a constant mixing of Greeks, Romans, Celts, Phoenicians, Carthaginians, and finally Muslims from northern Africa. The Celts arrived in the 6th c BC, followed by the Romans in the 2nd c AD, and the Arabs in the 8th c. Each of these peoples left an imprint on architecture, language, religion, the legislative system, and the cuisine. Madrid became the capital in 1561. Spanish is the official language.

Dining Etiquette

Please be prompt when entertained. Shake hands greeting and departing. If you know someone well a kiss or embrace is acceptable. A person's middle name is the surname. The last name is the mother's. Please send or bring flowers in an odd number as a thank-you. Dinner starts with drinks, usually sherry, gin and tonic, or whiskey. Do not bring your drink to the table. The guest of honor will be seated to the right of the host or hostess who are seated at opposite ends of the table. Food is eaten continental style with the fork in the left hand, knife in the right. Please do not start until hostess takes up her fork. Wrist should be kept at table level. For the first course two plates will be on the table, the top for the first course. Salad is served first, and usually only at lunch. There may not be a butter plate. The spoon and fork, or knife and fork at the top of the plate are for dessert and/or fruit. Never use your fingers or food to push, only the knife. When finished place the knife and fork together. If placed across from each other it signals you wish more, or have not finished your meal. Remember meals are to be savored and eaten slowly. Coffee is served after dessert. Toasting can be done at almost any time, though mostly at a formal dinner. The host stands, says a few words, raises his glass "Salud", and everyone stands. Glasses will be refilled when empty. Ladies do not usually make toasts.

Cuisine

The cuisine of Spain has been influenced by the Romans, Jews, Arab (the Moors), and later by specialties from the New World. The Moors brought almonds, pomegranates, figs, oranges, saffron, sugar cane and rice.

Spain's abundance of agricultural products make dining a rich and wonderful experience. Whether one is in Valencia savoring paella or Madrid sampling game, fresh vegetables, ambiance, and excellent wines are part of the scenario. Breakfast is a light meal, lunch around 2, and dinner may not start until 9 or 10. Spanish food is not hot and spicy, and heavier dishes such as paella are served at lunch. Much use is made of garlic olive oil, olives, fish and preserved fish – especially albacore tuna from the Bay of Biscay, cheese, Iberico ham, fresh vegetables, piquillo peppers, grapes and wine, tomatoes, and citrus fruits – oranges, lemons, mandarins, limes, and grapefruit. Spain is famous for tapas bars serving light, tasty, hot and cold appetizers. Tapa is a word meaning "lid" and comes from using a piece of bread to cover a wine glass to keep the flies out. Tortillas are omelets made mostly from eggs, potatoes, and onions, and served as a light evening meal. Gazpacho that lovely light summer soup, comes from the Arabic "soaked bread". Paella is made with sofrito (tomato, garlic, onion base) and in Valencia is made with chicken, rabbit, and garrafon, a white bean. Other paellas include mussels, snails, lobster, and different seafood. The paella pan should be thin bottomed and made of cast iron so that the rice will heat evenly.

Paella (Seafood and rice cooked in a paella pan)

Serves 6

¼ cup olive oil
1 medium onion, chopped
2 cloves garlic, minced
1 large tomato chopped
1 red pepper, chopped
6 large shrimp, cooled, shelled and deveined
12 clams in shells and scrubbed
24 mussels in shells and scrubbed

2 lb. lobster, cut into pieces
½ lb. chorizo sausage, cut into pieces
1 lb. boneless chicken, cut in small pieces
1 cup fresh peas
¼ tsp. saffron
2 cups chicken stock
1 cup raw rice

Heat 2 tbls. olive oil in a paella pan or large skillet. Saute the onions and pepper. Add the garlic and tomatoes.
Remove from pan. Add 2 tbls. olive oil to pan. Saute chicken until just browned. Stir in chorizo. Add vegetables, chicken broth, and rice. Cook for 15 minutes. Add mussels, clams and lobster. Cover and cook 5-10 minutes, or until clams and mussels open. Add more stock to keep from sticking. Add peas and saffron.
Serve with salad and crusty bread.

Spanish Specialties

Langostinos con rosa salsa – prawns in a spicy sauce
Morcilla – black pudding
Sopa de pescado y marisco – fish soup
Gazpacho – cold tomato soup
Aoili – garlic, salt and olive oil paste
Saladitos – olive oil crackers
Jambon iberico – cured meats
Cordoero asado – roast lamb, mainly served at Christmas

Mojama – tuna in sea salt and hung to dry in the sun
Autor – cheese made from raw goat's milk
Empanadas – meat; or tuna, tomatoes, and peppers; spinach or kale
Aioli – egg, vinegar, olive oil, and garlic sauce served with a variety of dishes
Chorizo – spicy sausage
Churros – deep fried sweet pastries
Frittata - egg, potato and onion dish

511

Sofrito – sauce made of cilantro, parsley, garlic, onions, peppers and cooked for a long time

Fabada – white bean and black pudding stew

Esparragos blancos – white asparagus that is considered a delicacy

Romesco – tomato, garlic, roasted red pepper, and nut sauce

Ensalada mixed – mixed greens salad

Patatas fritas – home fried potatoes

Patatas picantes- spicy potatoes

Tortillas – Spanish omelets

Pimento – type of Spanish paprika

Turron – almond candy

Polvorones – almond cookies

Mantecados – cakes

Fig cakes

Marcona - almond nougat

Regional Food

Basque – grilled meat, Iberian ham and fish, stews, cod, squid, beans, tapas, paprika, sparkling wine, cider; olives, tomatoes and peppers are used to make many of the dishes. Tapas here are known as pintxos.

Valencia (Mediterranean) - paella and rice dishes. In the 8th c the Arabs introduced rice to the region and paella was concocted. It is noted also for oranges; horchata, creamy drink made from tiger nuts

Galicia (Northwest) - shellfish, fish, beef

Asturias (Northwest) -"fabada" bean stew

Andalusia (South) - gazpacho, fried fish, Bellota ham (jamon iberico de bellota); the Catholic convents are noted for the sweets they make. The recipes came with the Moors (Arabs) in the 8th c. These delicious recipes used sugar and many eggs. Sugar back then was prized as a cure for many ailments, or eaten in a sweet as an aid to digestion. Roses and violets were used to scent sugar, loaf and candy sugar eaten plain, or boiled into syrups or made into preserves. Pumpkin jam was used to cure heart and liver maladies; while quince paste was thought to be soothing.

South – famous for sherry; trout; oranges; sheep and goat; olive groves; figs; wild sage; wild garlic

Central plateau - lamb

Cataluña (NE Mediterranean) - fish, shellfish, and "butifarra"

Sausage, beans; escudella – meat stew

Catalonia – was occupied by the Romans for 700 years who introduced grapes and olives. Later the Moors brought eggplants, oranges, spices, nuts. Later in the 16 and 17th c merchants from Naples and Sicily introduced short pasta.

Holidays and Special Occasions

Epiphany – January 6th – gifts are exchanged, on this date right after Christmas

Easter – godfathers present their godchildren with cake known a as 'La Mona'. These are generally traditional pan shape found in various shapes from simple round or oval to Disney characters, toys and anything else. Torrijas, slices of warm bread soaked in milk, sugar and egg, then fried in olive oil are served, served along with wine, syrup, honey, sugar or cinnamon, and hot cross buns

May - Corpus Christi Day – religious processions

Christmas Eve, "La Noche Buena," "The Good Night" is celebrated with a large family feast late at night. Families attend midnight mass before or after the feast

Christmas – several courses are served beginning with tapas, a first course or fish soup, main course – beef, lamb, poultry or game with rice or potatoes, dessert, good and sparkling wines, and many toasts

Beverages

Spain has many varieties of wines and sherry. For thousands of years these have been a part of Spain's cultural history, including the Moorish period, when people were not permitted to drink alcoholic beverages, but promoted its trade. The finest sherry are exported from Jerez. In England they are called Sack from the Spanish "Sacar" "to export". Sherries are fino – pale and usually drunk with soup or an aperitif, has 15% alcohol, and is best served chilled. The other is oloroso – dark, heavy, sweetened with 18% alcohol, for after dinner. After the grapes are picked and placed in casks, the wines are allowed to ferment for three months, after which it is determined if the sherry is fino or oloroso. The lesser quality becomes brandy. Sherry has no vintage years. Instead under the solara system, sherry are constantly blended and the casks replenished. It is then fined (egg whites added) and the oloroso is sweetened with wine. Sherries are drunk before or after dinner, or with soup. Wine (vino) is served with the meal. Champagne is served during or after dinner with dessert. Spain also produces cider (sidra), much of it made in Asturias; and beer (cerveza). Sidra or cider is from the Hebrew "Shekhar" meaning "strong drink". Beer is served in small glasses that often begin an evening. The Spanish produce a "Champagne cider", made by a secondary fermentation, adding pure sugar cane, and is sweet. Better known are the reds from Rioja (northern Spain near the Pyrenees) and Ribera del Duero, reds and whites from Penedés, whites from Rueda, and a sparkling wine known as cava. Agua de Valencia is cava, orange juice, vodka, gin and sugar. After meals strong coffees, brandies or liqueurs are served.

Did You Know?

Southern Spain is famous for animal husbandry and agriculture. An early book from the 12th c is Kitab al-Filaha (Book of Agriculture) by Ibn al-Awwam
The five hundred year old canadas "cattle trail" was set up by King Ferdinand and Queen Isabella to move cattle and sheep to pastures or markets.
Did you know that when Lord Nelson died he was shipped back to England in a sherry cask?
Olive trees in Jaen, Aragon, and Catalonia are over 2 thousand years old and still produce olives. Almost 6 million acres of olive groves produce olives and olive oil. Olives which not too long ago might sit for days to be pressed when ripened, are now done so in minutes.
Iberico ham is produced from pigs fed with holm oak or cork-oak acorns. It was not permitted to be exported until the mid 1990s.
Spain produces one-third of the world's cork.
The Mercado Central in Valencia is Europe's largest indoor market.

Sri Lanka (Ceylon)

Sri Lanka is an island nation in the Indian Ocean with India to the northwest and the Maldives to the southwest. Human settlements date back over 125,000 years. Remnants found in caves show that even around 12000 years ago the people engaged in agriculture and may have domesticated dogs. An early reference to the island is in the Indian epic "Ramayana". Buddhism was brought from India in 250 BC. Following that there were many invasions from South Asian countries. However the country was led by ruling dynasties. Queen Anula, who reigned from 47-42 BC was the first Asian female ruler. The rock fortress at Sigiriya was built between 477-459 AD and has been declared by UNESCO as one of the seven World Heritage Sites. The Portuguese arrived in 1505 led by Lourenco de Almeida, and in 1638 a treaty was signed with the Dutch East India Company. In 1815 the island became part of Great Britain. It received independence from Great Britain in 1948 and became the republic of Sri Lanka in 1972. Sri Jayawardenepura Kotte is the administrative capital and Colombo the commercial capital. The official languages are Sinhala and Tamil, with English also recognized.

Dining Etiquette

Please be punctual when invited for a meal. Please shake hands greeting and departing, or with folded hands (Namaste). Women do not usually shake hands, and men may not offer hands to a woman. When greeting a superior or to show respect, a slight bow can be used. Drinks will be offered, probably beer and whisky along with a snack, or in some homes where tea is served. You may be seated at a table for the meal, or on cushions where you will cross-legged. In some cases men and women may be separated. Never enter a kitchen. Meals will be served with all courses on the table, or separately on silver or brass trays. Always wash your hands before eating. The hostess will serve the food to the guests and men first, followed by the women. Food is eaten with the right hand. A fork, fingers, or bread can also be utilized. Watch how the hostess eats. Food is passed with the right hand. Men may share food from their own plate.

Raita (yogurt and tomato served with curries)

2 large tomatoes, cut into small pieces	1 tsp. sugar
1 tbls. roasted peanuts, crushed	2 green chili peppers
1 cup yogurt	¼ cup coriander
	Salt

Combine the ingredients in a bowl. Serve with curries.

Cuisine

The cuisine has been influenced by Indian dishes, but also use of native ingredients. The food may be spicy or very mild. Rice is the staple food. Rice, curries, vegetables, coconut milk, lentils, bitter melon, caramelized onion, palm sugar for desserts, samosas, dhal, meat – chicken, beef, mutton; game; fish – dried, crab, cuttlefish, prawns, crayfish, balaya, kelwalla; pickled fruits and fish; chutneys, sambals. chili peppers; fruit – papaya, pineapple, woodapple, durian, rambula, mango, bananas, and lime juice are part of the diet. Karawalla is salt dried fish. Spices such as cardamom, cloves, nutmeg, pepper, saffron, and cinnamon are used. Sri Lanka was once the leading exporter of cinnamon in the ancient world. Irrigation has been very important to the survival of the people. Sri Lanka's irrigation system was extensively expanded during the reign of Parākramabāhu the Great (AD 1153–1186) who built 1470 reservoirs.

Kiri Bath (rice and coconut milk)

Serves 4

1½ cups basmati or jasmine rice	Salt
2½ -3 cups water	1½ cups coconut milk

In a sauce pan place the water, rice and salt. Bring to a boil. Simmer for 15-20 minutes or until all the water is absorbed and rice is tender. Fluff with a fork.
Stir in the coconut milk.
Pour into a pie plate. Cut into diamond or triangle shapes.
This is often served with curries or condiments.

Specialties

Thosai – lentil batter with shallots, curry leaves, fenugreek, and cumin cooked as a pancake, and eaten at breakfast served with coconut, and chili sambal

Koththu – stir-fried roti with vegetables, eggs, or meat, and spices

Coconut roti – wheat, rice, or brown millet with oil and coconut fried as a flat cake

Appa - Hoppers- steamed or pan-fried fermented batter with rice flour, coconut milk, and spices. Can also include egg or honey

String hoppers- rice or wheat flour dough made into circles and steamed

Malu Ambul thiyal – fish in a sour curry sauce

Ala Hodi - Potato Curry

Lunu miris   red onions and spices

Lamprais – rice boiled in stock, meat curry, blanchan, aubergine, curry, and seeni sambol wrapped in a banana leaf and baked

Kool – seafood broth with fish, long beans, jak seeds, manioc, spinach and tamarind

Pittu – steamed rice with coconut

Roti – flatbread

Thengappu –roti with coconut

Uraippu – roti with onions and green chilies

Kevum – deep-fried cake with rice flour and treacle

Moong kevum – mung beans used in cake

Kokis – pastry made from rice flour and coconut milk

Aluwa- rice flour pastries

Aggala – rice balls with treacle

Watalappam – coconut milk, egg and jiggery steamed pudding

Kiri bath – coconut milk and rice
Short eats" - snacks sold by the dozen mainly for breakfast or during the evening. They include pastries, and Chinese rolls, mainly of mutton.

Holidays and Special Occasions

January
Thai Pongol - Hindu festival honors Surya (sun god), Indra (rain god), and the cow. Food is cooked in the temples with milk and foods from the new harvest
April
New Year – new clothes, horoscopes read; presents exchanged; kiribath (rice cooked in coconut milk) eaten
Easter, school holidays
May
Vesak Poya – commemorates birth, enlightenment, and death of Buddha, and marks third of his visits to Sri Lanka. Pageants, pandels (Buddhist scenes), lanterns hung, and food handed out – Vesak sweetmeats, rice, curry to pilgrims
June
Poson Poya – commemorates Buddhism first introduced in 3rd c BC
July/August
Esala Perehera – festival in Kandy to celebrate Buddha's first sermon and arrival of Tooth Relic with processions and elephants. Also many other festivals take place.
Nikini Poya – fasting and retreat for monks
October
Deepavali – Hindu Festival of Light – wear new clothes
December
Christmas and New Year's celebrated

During festivals, auspicious occasions such as Sinhala and the Tamal New Year, and other special events sweet dishes are served. Among them are kiri bath (coconut milk and rice); Peni walalu (deep fried Urad dal and rice flour soaked in sugar syrup; Aluwa (rice, coconut, and cashews); Kokis (rice flour, sugar, coconut milk and fried); Saw Dodol (Welithalpa) (rice flour, coconut milk, coconut treacle, and salt which is boiled and cut into different shapes); and Mun Keum. Kiri bath symbolizes prosperity and abundance and is served when a child is born, to newlyweds, and for the new year. It used to be cooked in earthenware pots.

Beverages

Fruit juices are very popular, especially passionfruit. Faluda is a cold drink of syrup, ice cream, jelly and basil seeds. Toddy is an alcoholic drink made from pine tree sap, and arack from coconut. Tea and coffee are widely drunk as there coffee and tea plantations. Coffee was the primary export during the early 1800s. A devastating leaf disease, *Hemileia vastatrix*, struck the coffee plantations in 1869, destroying all the trees. The British began cultivating tea and rubber instead.

St. Kitts and Nevis

The islands of St. Kitts and Nevis lie in the Leeward Islands in the Eastern Caribbean. The islands were originally settled by Arawak Indians, probably from Venezuela c 500 BC. C 50 AD. St. Kitts was called Liamuiga "Fertile Isle". Christopher Columbus spotted the island on his second voyage in 1493 naming the island "Nuestro Senora del las Nieves" "Our lady of the Snows", reminding him of the Pyrenees. The British and French settled here. They are now part of the British Commonwealth. The capital, Basseterre on St. Kitts, was founded by the French, but became the British capital in 1727. Charlestown is the capital of Nevis.

Dining Etiquette

Please be punctual when invited for a meal. Please bring a bottle of wine, flowers, or a gift for the home. Shake hands greeting and departing. Cocktails are served before dinner. The hostess will escort the guests into the dining room. The host and hostess will sit at opposite ends of the table, with the guest of honor to the right of the hostess. Dishes will be passed, or it might be a buffet. Please wait for the hostess to begin. Do try some of each dish. Dessert and coffee will finish off the meal. Often conversation will continue at the table, or in another room. Please call or write a thank-you to the hostess.

Cuisine

The cuisine is a mix of British, international and West Indian, using fresh vegetables and fruit, chicken, mutton, and fish. The islands produce their own dairy products and vegetables – yellow squash, avocados, cassava, calabash, spring onions, peas, potatoes, onions, cabbage, tomatoes, pumpkins, sweet potatoes, carrots, cucumbers, sweet peppers, asparagus; and fruits – lemons, limes, grapefruit, bananas, mangos, melons, pineapples, and papayas. Large, sweet pineapple were imported to the islands. Favorite foods are roast suckling pig; turtle steak or stews; fish – spiny lobster, crab, bonito, snapper, grouper, king fish, and parrot fish; curries; conch – salad, soused, curried or chowder; rice and peas; mutton stew; christophine; vegetable soups; Creole red bean soup; boiled saltfish stew; The food is slightly spicy. Many types of vegetables and salads are eaten. Meats are highly seasoned with adobo, salt, onion, garlic and pepper. Rice with beans is served with most meals.

Conch Fritters

6 large conch
1 large lime for juice
1 medium onion, chopped
1 medium tomato, peeled and seeded
1 medium pepper, seeded and sliced
2 cloves garlic, minced

1 celery stalk with leaves
1 tsp. hot sauce
2 large eggs, beaten
1 cup flour
1tsp. baking powder
¼ cup parsley

Place the conch and lime juice in a food processor, until it is thoroughly ground. Remove and place in a large bowl.
Using the food processor chop the onion, green pepper, tomato and celery.
Add to the conch and add garlic, hot sauce, and eggs. Stir in flour, baking powder, and parsley.
Heat a skillet with some oil. Drop batter by the spoonful and fry until golden brown.

Specialties

Stewed saltfish - St Kitts and Nevis national dish - served with spicy plantains, coconut dumplings and seasoned breadfruit
Sousc – pork stew
Curries – chicken, fish, potato, shrimp, goat, duck, beef, fruit such as mango
Droppers – dumplings in tomato stock

Sofrito – condiment made of onions, green bell peppers, red bell peppers, cilantro, recao, and garlic
IIot Johnny cakes
Conkies – cornmeal with sweet potato, pumpkin and coconut
Rum cakes

Holidays and Special Occasions

Carnival is held around Christmas and has English and Caribbean traditions with dancing, plays, music, and many events. Christmas Sports start on Boxing Day, especially horseracing the beginning of January. On December 26th in Basse Terre is J'ouvert with calypso music, lots of dancing, and drinking rum! "Last lap" is the end of carnival.
Traditional holiday foods are sweet sorrel, rice, pigeon rice, roasted pork, pastels, sweet coconut bread, rum cake, goat stew, jam cake, mango chutney and conkies.

Beverages

With the cultivation of sugar cane, distilled drinks have been produced on the islands for years. French Baron Edmond de Rothschild produced a cane spirit, Baron's CSR, distilled from fresh cane that is clear, drunk neat, on the rocks, or with a fruit mixer. Other drinks are maubi, made from tree bark; Ting, a grapefruit soda; and Carib, the local beer.

Did You Know?

One of the oldest Jewish settlements in the Americas, prior to 1650, was on Nevis. These people fled the Inquisition or were from Brazil, and introduced sugar processing to the islands.

St. Lucia

Saint Lucia is an island in the West Indies in the eastern Caribbean Sea on the boundary with the Atlantic Ocean. Part of the Lesser Antilles, it is located north/northeast of the island of Saint Vincent, northwest of Barbados and south of Martinique. The earliest inhabitants were Island Caribs and Arawaks. Juan de la Cosa noted the island on his map of 1500, calling it El Falcon, and another island to the south Las Agujas. A Spanish Cedula from 1511 mentions the island within the Spanish domain, and a globe in the Vatican made in 1520, shows the island as Sancta Lucia. The French were the European settlers beginning in 1660, followed by the English from 1663-67. Over a period of time the French and English held the island until the English gained control in 1814. From 1958 to 1962, the island was a member of the West Indies Federation. In 1979 Saint Lucia became an independent state and a member of the Commonwealth of Nations. Its capital is Castries.

Dining Etiquette

Please be punctual when invited for a meal. Please bring a bottle of wine, flowers, or a gift for the home. Shake hands greeting and departing. Cocktails are served before dinner. The hostess will escort the guests into the dining room. The host and hostess will sit at opposite ends of the table, with the guest of honor to the right of the hostess. Dishes will be passed, or it might be a buffet. Please wait for the hostess to begin. Do try some of each dish. Dessert and coffee will finish off the meal. Often conversation will continue at the table, or in another room. Please call or write a thank-you to the hostess. The toast is "Cheers".

Bouyon (Bean, Meat and Vegetable Soup)

Serves 4

2-3 large ham hocks
4 cups water
2 bay leaf
2 red potatoes, cut into cubes
2 carrots, peeled and sliced
1 onion, chopped

1 cup dried red beans
2 garlic cloves, minced
¼ cup vegetable oil
2 plantains
½ lb. yucca, cut into cubes
1 cup fresh spinach or kale

Place the ham hock, water and bay leaves in a large pot. Bring to a boil. Lower heat and simmer 1 hour. Remove the bay leaves and ham hock. Cut meat of hock. Add the beans to the stock. Bring to a boil. Lower heat and cook 30 minutes. Add ham meat and rest of ingredients. Bring to a boil. Lower heat and cook till all vegetables are tender, about 30 minutes. Season with pepper, salt, and hot sauce.

Cuisine

The cuisine is a combination of Carib, Arawak, French, East Indian and British dishes. Vegetables – callaloo (dasheen), cassava, yams, beans, scallions, christophene (cho cho), ackee, carrots, onions, pumpkin (pumpkin); and fruit – mangoes, coconuts, oranges, grapefruit, tangerine, avocado, bananas, and breadfruit grow on the island. Spices and herbs such as thyme, garlic, ginger, cinnamon, nutmeg, cocoa, parsley, cloves, and allspice are used for seasoning. Corn was introduced but is mainly used as cornmeal.

Specialties

Green figs and saltfish – green bananas and saltfish, the national dish
Callaloo soup – made from callaloo, stock, and coconut milk
Green fig salad

Bakes – cornmeal cakes
Breadfruit and saltfish
Accra – bean or root tuber, flour and egg which is fried

Holidays and Special Occasions

Lent – fasting, perhaps no meat, eggs, dairy and chocolate
Holy week – penepis/penny-a-piece – ginger wafers
Good Friday and Holy Saturday – fish and ginger beer
Easter – lamb
Easter Monday – picnics and kite flying
Mid December – Festival of Lights as the island is named for St. Lucy (Saint of Lights)
Christmas – roast lamb, pork, or turkey, yams, plantains, sorrel drink, Christmas pudding, and St. Lucian black cake

Cocoa Tea

Cocoa tea is not made from tea, but rather cocoa grown on the island and is served at breakfast.

Makes 3 cups

2 cups water
4oz. grated cocoa
½ tsp. cinnamon
½ tsp. vanilla

1 cup milk
2 tbls. sugar

Place the water, cocoa, cinnamon and vanilla in a pan and bring to a boil. Add milk and sugar. More sugar can be added for sweetness. Serve in cups.

Beverages

Fruit juices are made from golden apples, mangoes, starfruit, tamarind and limes (lime squash). Rum is produced by St. Lucia Distillers Group of Companies.

Saint Vincent and the Grenadines

Saint Vincent and the Grenadines is a country in the Lesser Antilles island arc, in the southern portion of the Windward Islands, which lies in the West Indies at the southern end of the eastern border of the Caribbean Sea. It consists of the main island of Saint Vincent and the northern two-thirds of the Grenadines, 32 islands and cays. To the north of Saint Vincent lies Saint Lucia and to the east is Barbados. The island now known as Saint Vincent was originally named *Youloumain* by the native Island Caribs who called themselves Kalina/Carina ("l" and "r" being pronounced the same in their language). The Caribs aggressively prevented European settlement on Saint Vincent until 1719. Prior to this, formerly enslaved Africans, who had either been shipwrecked or who had escaped from Barbados, Saint Lucia and Grenada and sought refuge in mainland Saint Vincent, intermarried with the Caribs and became known as Black Caribs or Garifuna. The islands were constantly fought over by the French and British with the British finally gaining control. The islands received their independence in 1979. Kingstown is the capital and main port.

Dining Etiquette

Please be punctual when invited for a meal. Please bring a bottle of wine, flowers, or a gift for the home. Shake hands greeting and departing. Cocktails are served before dinner. The hostess will escort the guests into the dining room. The host and hostess will sit at opposite ends of the table, with the guest of honor to the right of the hostess. Dishes will be passed, or it might be a buffet. Please wait for the hostess to begin. Do try some of each dish. Dessert and coffee will finish off the meal. Often conversation will continue at the table, or in another room. Please call or write a thank-you to the hostess. The toast is "Cheers".

Cuisine

The cuisine has been influenced by the Caribs, French, English, and later immigrants from Madeira. The French cultivated coffee, tobacco, indigo, corn and sugar on plantations. Later the British also grew these crops and added cocoa and cotton. Fish, vegetable – yams, dasheen, tania, carrots, onions, hot and sweet peppers, tomatoes, eddoes, cabbage, eggplant; and fruit – bananas, plantains, breadfruit, christophene, and coconut are in abundance, and some spices are grown here. Among the more common fish are mahi mahi; snapper; kingfish; bonito; black fish; lobster; squid; octopus; queen conch; and jackfish. Vegetables and fruit can be mashed, fried, roasted, or baked. The seafood is fried or baked, and sometimes can be quite spicy. Breadfruit was brought from Tahiti in 1793. It is roasted whole over an open fire and then scooped out from the shell. Arrowroot grows in northeast St. Vincent. The underground tuber is a starch that is dried and ground into gluten-free flour. The soil is volcanic and fertile.

Fried Jackfish and Roasted Breadfruit

This is the national dish.

Serves 4

Roasted breadfruit equal to 2 cups, sliced
2lbs. jackfish, cleaned
¼ cup fresh lime or lemon juice
1onion, chopped

2cloves garlic, minced
1tsp. salt
¼ cup flour
2 tbls. vegetable oil

The breadfruit can be roasted on an open fire or roasted in an oven until soft. Make sure you prick it before cooking.
Place the fish in a bowl and cover with the lime or lemon juice. Let marinate for at least ½ hour. Remove fish.
Combine the onion, garlic and salt. Rub over the fish.
Place the flour on a plate. Coat both sides of the fish with the flour.
Heat oil in a skillet. Brown fish on both sides, about five minutes each side.
Place on a platter and serve with the breadfruit.
A tomato sauce or hot sauce can be served with the fish.

Breadfruit Cheese Pie

1 breadfruit
1 ½ cups milk
½ stick butter
¼ cup flour
1½ cups grated "medium" cheddar
1 small onion, finely diced
1 tbls. mustard

½ scotch bonnet pepper diced fine
pinch of nutmeg
¼ teaspoon black pepper
2 tbls. parsley, chopped
½ cup breadcrumbs
½ cup additional grated cheddar cheese

Preheat oven to 350°
To prepare the breadfruit cut off stem, cut breadfruit into thin slices, peel, and remove soft spots. In a pan with water bring to a boil, and cook until tender. Remove from water and place in a bowl. Drain water.
Melt the butter in the pan. Stir in flour, and then slowly stir in milk until slightly thickened. Add cheese, onion, mustard, scotch bonnet, nutmeg, pepper and parsley.
In a greased pan place ½ breadfruit, top with ½ cheese mixture. Repeat. Sprinkle breadcrumbs and extra on top.
Bake ½ hour, or until slightly browned and sizzling.

Specialties

Billjau – salted fish, tomato, onion, coconut oil and hot pepper stew

Madongo dumplings - are made with arrowroot flour, nutmeg and coconut, and are baked or fried

Curried goat

Lambi – queen conch

Banana fritters – bananas fried in coconut oil

Holidays and Special Occasions

During Lent and Good Friday people fast or give up certain foods. On Good Friday fish is always eaten.

Easter - Easter eggs, hot cross buns, ham, kite flying, and Easter bonnets!

The Easter Regatta in Bequia attracts sailors from all over the world. Children build boats out of coconuts.

Breadfruit Festival – August – music, dancing and breadfruit made into puffs, cheese pies, pizza, candy and various drinks

Nine Mornings Festival – nine days leading up to Christmas people bathe in the sea and dance to steel bands

Christmas – ham, eggnog, sorrel drink, callaloo, breadfruit cheese pie, black cake, fruit cake

Beverages

St. Vincent and the Grenadines once had numerous sugar plantations, some eventually becoming banana plantations. The sugar cane was processed into molasses to make rum. Among the rums made are St. Vincent Golden and Red and Sunset Captain Bligh. They can be drunk straight or fruit juices added. The islands also brew Hairoun beer.

Did You Know?

In 1903, La Soufrière volcano erupted, killing 5,000 people and much of the farmland was damaged. In April 1979, La Soufrière volcano erupted again. Although no one was killed, thousands were evacuated and again there was extensive agricultural damage. In 1980 and 1987, hurricanes damaged many banana and coconut plantations. Hurricane seasons were also very active in 1998 and 1999, with Hurricane Lenny in 1999 causing extensive damage to the west coast of the island. The islands were spared from hurricanes Irma and Maria in 2017.

Sudan

Sudan is bordered by Egypt to the north, the Red Sea to the northeast, Eritrea and Ethiopia to the east, South Sudan to the south, the Central African Republic to the southwest, Chad to the west and Libya to the northwest. The world's longest river, the Nile, flows through the country. Nubia, in the eastern part of Sudan, has been inhabited for over 70,000 years. C 8000 BC the population was known to hunt, fish, forage for grains, and raise cattle and sheep. The region was named the Kush by the Egyptians. During the 8th c BC it became part of a kingdom ruled from Napata. By the 6th c AD the Nobatae and Nubians were connected by various treaties through the Arab commander in Egypt which was maintained for 678 years. Two important tribes emerged in Nubia – the Jaali and Juhayna. In the south the Funj arrived and established the Sultanate of Sennar. In 1820 Egypt invaded northern Sudan, and by the 1890s the British, French and Belgians were laying claims to Sudan. The British ran the country as two territories - the north (Muslim) and the south (Christian) from 1924 until 1956 when it received its independence. Khartoum, the capital, is located at the confluence of the White and Blue Nile Rivers, and was founded in 1821 by Ibrahim Pasha, ruler of Egypt. Sudan has 597 tribes that speak over 400 different languages and dialects. The official languages are Arabic and English.

Dining Etiquette

It is an honor to be invited to a home. The Sudanese are very hospitable. The family is very important and very patriarchal. Several generations may live in the same house. Dinner may be quite late, 9 or 9:30. Please take a small gift, never alcohol. Men shake hands greeting and departing, and may tap each other on the shoulder. A woman must extend her hand first to a man. Women may hug and rub each other's cheek. The host will offer a guest a glass of orange or grapefruit juice, coffee or tea and perhaps something to eat. Always accept food and drink when offered. Men and women will often be separated when eating. The women do the cooking. If a guest is a very important person a sheep may be killed, and dishes made from it. Hands are washed before and after dining. Large cloths are used to cover one's knees, in place of napkins. Guests usually sit on the floor, or cushions with a low table, during a meal. Soup will be served first, brought in bowls on a tray. Spoons will be used and the bowl is held in the left hand while eating. When finished the tray and bowls are removed, and a tray with five or six dishes. Food is eaten only with the fingers on the right hand. Never accept or pass things with your left hand. Spoons may be provided. Bread is used to sop up the food. Salad and shata, a hot sauce, then dessert will be served. The Sudanese enjoy crème caramela and fruit. No beverage is served with the meal. Coffee, or tea with cloves or cinnamon may be served, followed by the burning of sandalwood incense.

Kajaik (Dried Fish Stew)

Serves 4-6

2 lbs. dried fish
2 medium potatoes, peeled and diced
2 medium onions, sliced
2 tomatoes, chopped
1 small chili, seeded and chopped

2 tbls. butter
½ cup milk
1 lemon, sliced
Parsley

Soak the fish in cold water for 4-6 hours.
Pour off water and cook in fresh water until tender. Pour off water. Remove any skin or bones, and flake fish.
Place the fish, potatoes, onions, chili, tomatoes, butter, and milk in a skillet and simmer until tender.
Serve garnished with lemon wedges and parsley.

Cuisine

The Sudanese cuisine has been influenced by the Egyptians, Ethiopians, Arabs and the Turks. In the north are the Muslims, and Christians and animists in the south. The Misseriya, a nomadic tribe, still graze cattle. The Nubians may have been the very first to cultivate wheat. Their main dish, gourrassa, is made from wheat and baked in a round shape.   In the east, the most popular dish is moukhbaza, which is made of banana paste. This part is greatly influenced by the Ethiopian taste and cuisine. In the west, each tribal group has adopted different forms of food that are basically very simple. Milk and dairy products are a fundamental component to the majority of the people since most of them are cattle breeders. A distinct cereal by which the west is well- known is dukhun. It is used in preparing a thick porridge called aseeda dukhun, to that is added a stew called sharmout abiyad which is cooked with dry meat. Another form of stew is kawal, which is made from a mixture of plant roots that are left to leaven and dried afterwards. As for the south, the abundance of rivers, lakes and swamps have made the people in these regions dependent on fish for their food. Kajaik is a stew of dried fish. It is added to the porridge, which is common throughout Sudan and aseeda made of sorghum. Sometimes natural margarine is added to the mixture. In Equatoria, aseeda is made of Bafra ehich is a plant of the same family of potatoes. To the aseeda is added a green vegetable called mouloukhiya) with peanut butter. Fassikh is one of the most popular dishes in Central Sudan. It is made from a fish which is leavened for some time and after that cooked with onions, spices and tomato sauce. It is most probably of Nubian origin same as Eltarkeen, which could not be found anywhere except northern Sudan.

Common grains are millet, sorghum, wheat, and barley. Cotton, peanuts, beans, rice, okra, and sesame are the main agricultural products. Sudan is the largest supplier of gum Arabic. Beef, cattle, and chicken are raised. Red pepper, garlic and spices were brought by Syrian and Arabic traders. Stews are made with meat, onions, potatoes, or eggplant, spices, peanut butter, Ni'aimya and dried okra, milk or yogurt. They are served with asseda, a porridge made with wheat or corn flour.

Sudanese Specialties

Breads – khubz and kissra made from durra or corn

Kissra – sorghum pancake made by the Ngok Dinka in the south

Bamia – okra and lamb stew

Shorba – lamb soup

Kawari' – soup made with sheep or cattle hoofs, vegetables and spices

Elmussalammiya – soup made with liver, flour, dates, and spices

Miris - stew that is made from sheep's fat, onions and dried okra.

Maschi – tomato stuffed with chopped beef

Salatima jibna – salad with cheese

Shorbet adas – lentil soup

Ful medames – broad beans

Tamaya – falafel

Mulaah bamyah – okra stew

Koftah –meatballs

Shata – hot spice

Crème caramela – custard

Ful-sudani – peanuts (are a favorite snack)

Holidays and Special Occasions

Muslim and Christian holidays are followed depending on the part of the country you are in. The Muslims celebrate Ramadan (30 days of fasting from sunrise to sunset), Eid al-fitr, Eid-al Adha, Moulid Al Nabi (the Prophet's birthday), and Sham Al Nassim (spring holiday). Sah'ur is a meal taken late at night during Ramadan. Eid-al Adha takes place during the Hajj and families sacrifice a sheep. At the time of the Prophet's birthday sweets and special refreshments are served. For the spring holiday picnics take place. During Ramadan Hilumur, a drink is made from corn flour and spices, Aabrai Abiyad and Nashaa, which are also made of corn flour are drunk.

Christians celebrate Easter and Christmas.

Weddings may last for days with bridal dancing ending the festivities.

Beverages

Sudan grows several fruits or grains that are made into drinks - tabaldi, aradaib, karkadai and duddaim. A brewery produces White Bull in Juba.

Coffee (guhwah) is made by frying coffee beans in a special pot over an open fire. It is then ground with cloves, ginger, cinnamon, or other spices with hot water poured over it. The coffee is served from a special pot with a long spout and is called a jebena. Coffee is served in small cups or glasses. Teas are made from fruit or herbs, or hibiscus (kakaday).

Did You Know?

The Dinka tie strings around their stomachs to cure stomach aches. They put tea leaves in their ears when infections occur.

Suriname

The Republic of Suriname is a country on the northeastern Atlantic coast of South America bordered by French Guiana to the east, Guyana to the west and Brazil to the south. Indigenous settlement of Suriname dates back to 3,000 BC. The largest tribes were the Arawak, a nomadic coastal tribe that lived from hunting and fishing. The Carib also settled in the area and conquered the Arawak by using their sailing ships. They settled in Galibi (*Kupali Yumï,* meaning "tree of the forefathers") at the mouth of the Marowijne River. While the larger Arawak and Carib tribes lived along the coast and savannah, smaller groups of indigenous peoples lived in the inland rainforest, such as the Akurio, Trió, Warrau, and Wayana. Beginning in the 16th century, French, Spanish, and English explorers visited the area. A century later, Dutch and English settlers established plantation colonies along the many rivers in the fertile Guiana plains. The earliest documented colony in Guiana was an English settlement named Marshall's Creek along the Suriname River. The planters of the colony relied heavily on African slaves to cultivate, harvest and process the commodity crops of coffee, cocoa, sugar cane and cotton plantations along the rivers. The capital and largest city, is Paramaribo. In 1954, the country became one of the constituent countries of the Kingdom of the Netherlands and its independence in 1975. Dutch is the official language of government, business, media, and education, Sranantongo, an English-based creole language, is widely used.

Dining Etiquette

When invited please arrive promptly or up to fifteen minutes late, and remove your shoes. Shake hands meeting and departing. Good friends are greeted with a brasa (hug). Children show respect for elders and speak to them with a formal address. Please bring a gift from your country, wine, chocolates, or pastries. The people are very hospitable and enjoy entertaining. Drinks will be served and the hostess will seat the guests. Please wait to start eating after the hostess. Food is eaten continental style with the fork in the left hand and knife in the right. When finished place them together with the tines down. Elbows should be kept at table level, but not on the table. Do try everything offered to you, and compliment the hostess. If you are offered more food turn it down, and then accept if the hostess insists. You may be offered dessert and drink. Please thank the host and hostess when departing.

Cuisine

The Surinamese cuisine has been influenced by the native Amerindian, East Indian, African, Indonesian, Chinese, Dutch, Jewish, Portuguese, British, Caribbean, and Creole cultures. The rich land produces many types of fruit and vegetables which have been eaten since early times, and then later items were brought by settlers. Foods brought from Latin and South America included tomatoes, peppers, corn, potatoes, peanuts, melons, squash, papaya, chocolate, vanilla, and avocado. The Europeans brought cattle, chickens, sheep, goat, pigs, wheat, rice, fruits, and other produce. Many Indians settled in Suriname and introduced black pepper, cumin, turmeric, and cinnamon. Other groups of people introduced cilantro, limes, garlic, vegetables – broccoli, cucumbers, carrots, and lettuce, and fruit – olives, grapes, bananas, apples, and oranges. Dense forests inhabit the interior and most people live along the coast. Basic foods include rice, roti, sweet potatoes, tayer, cassava, edos, guava, mango, passionfruit, kiwi, bananas, malengo, chicken, yardlong beans, okra, eggplant, napi – root vegetable, Madame Jeannette peppers, salted meat, shrimp, and fish – catfish, gilbaka, hassa, and crabs.

Kippenpastei (Chicken Pie)

Serves 4

Pastry

2 cups flour
1 stick butter

1 egg, beaten
Cold water to mix

Combine the ingredients in a food processor, adding only enough water to make a dough. Roll out on a floured board.
Line a pie plate with 2/3 dough.

Filling

½ stick butter
1 lb. cooked chicken
4 hardboiled eggs, sliced
1 onion, chopped
1 diced pickle
½ lb. peas

1 carrot, sliced
1 stalk celery, chopped
Worcestershire Sauce to taste
Salt and pepper to taste
1 egg, beaten

Preheat oven to 375°
Melt butter in a pan. Fry onion, celery and chicken until just browned. Add peas, carrots, pickle, Worcestershire sauce, salt and pepper. Spoon into the pie plate. Cover with sliced eggs.
Top with remaining pie crust. Seal by pressing upper crust down all around the edges. Brush crust with beaten egg.
Bake for 30 minutes or until just browned.

Yardlong Beans

Serves 2-4

1lb. yardlong beans, cut into 2 inch pieces
1 tbls. oil
2 cloves garlic, minced

1 small onion, chopped
½ cup chicken or beef stock
1 Scotch bonnet pepper, chopped

Heat the oil in a pan. Saute the onions and add the garlic, beans, stock, and pepper. Cook until beans are just tender, about 4-5 minutes.

Specialties

Moksi-alesi - meat or seafood with rice and vegetables
Chicken masala – curry chicken
Rice dishes – masusa, nasi goreng, masala

Soups – saoto, cassava, napi, okra, and peanut
Kouseband – yardlong beans with chicken

Holidays and Special Occasions

The main religion is Hindu, followed by Muslims, and Christians, all of whom celebrate their own holidays. For Muslims Id al-Fitr, the end of Ramadan during which they fast during the day. Christians celebrate Easter and Christmas. The Hindus Holi Phagwa "New Year".
For weddings, birthdays and 50th birthdays huge feasts are held
The Javans celebrate Slametans for birth, circumcision, marriage and death.
July 1 – Keti Keti – Emancipation Day

Beverages

Tea and coffee are drunk along with tropical fruit drinks and punches. Mauby is made from the bark of a local tree, sweetened, boiled and strained. Borgoe and Black Cat Rum are produced, as well as Parbo-Beer, ginger beer, and dawel, a coconut milk drink.

Swaziland

Swaziland is a landlocked country in southern Africa located between Mozambique and South Africa. The region has been inhabited for over 200,000 years. Prehistoric paintings date from 25,000 BC. The early people were Khoisan hunter-gatherers. Later Bantu settled here. Agriculture and iron date to c 4th c. Swazi settlers arrived in the 1700s along the Pongola River. In 1894 Swaziland became a protectorate of South Africa, in 1903 a British protectorate, and independent since 1968. There are 3 main clan groups – the Nguni, Sotho, and Tsonga. The legislative capital is Lobamba and the administrative capital Mbabane. The official languages are Swazi and English.

Dining Etiquette

Please arrive promptly when invited for a meal, and bring a gift from your country. Please shake hands greeting and departing with eye contact and a smile, and place your left hand facing upwards under your right forearm. Women may nod their head, or if a hand is offered please shake hands. A man may kiss a woman whom he knows well. Women should cover their knees, and shorts not worn. Married women may wear headdresses, while unmarried women may have bare heads. Dining may be seated on a floor, or at a table. Please thank your host when finished.

Cuisine and Beverages

The cuisine of Swaziland is influenced by the seasons and also the different regions within the country have their own dishes. There is a Portuguese influence from Mozambique and prawns may be brought into the country. Being a landlocked country freshwater fish is available .Other common ingredients are maize, millet, sorghum, beans, rice, pumpkin, goat, chicken, leaf vegetables, root vegetables – yams, sweet potatoes, fruit – mango, paw-paw, guava, banana, avocado, and marula. All parts of the animals are used including offal, tripe, hooves, trotter, hearts, lungs, and gizzards. Main crops are sugar cane, tobacco, corn, rice, peanuts, and beef. Cattle are slaughtered for special occasions and rituals. Stews are made with hot chilies, groundnuts, vegetables, and chicken or meat.

The marula season is February till May when a harvest festival is held. When the fruit falls women and children gather the fruit and store it until it turns yellow. The marulas are put in a water and sugar mixture allowed to ferment and distill to make beer, or made into jam. This potent alcoholic mixture is called buganu, or marula beer. The king and queen mother visit the different regions of country during the marula season. The king and queen mother receive marula from each family. Only after they have drunk the beer can others drink it! The marula is considered good for fertility, is very high in vitamin C, anti-oxidants, proteins, and minerals. The marula fruit is also used to make a creamy, fruity liquor. Wine is imported from South Africa, and other beers are locally produced. Home brewed mealie beer is known as tjwala. Emahewu is a fermented porridge drink. Emasi (sour milk) is often sweetened with sugar. Soured milk is served to children.

Marula Jelly

Use as many marula as you would like. Wash, and pierce the skins. Place the marula in a large pot. Cover with water. Bring to a boil. Cook 15-20 minutes, until soft but still whole.
Strain while still warm through a muslin cloth. Save the juice. Wash out the pot. Measuring the juice pour the juice back into the pot. Add an equal quantity of sugar (i.e. 1 cup sugar=1 cup juice). Heat and cook to jelly stage to melt sugar. Lemon juice can be added for flavor.
Pour into sterilized jars. Allow to cool and store in the refrigerator.

Malva Pudding (Apricot Pudding)

¾ cup sugar	½ tsp. salt
2 large eggs	1 tbls. butter, softened
1 tbls. apricot jam	1 tsp. vinegar
½ cup flour	1/3 cup milk
1 tsp. baking soda	

Preheat oven to 350°
In a bowl combine the sugar and eggs until thickened. Add jam. Stir in the flour, baking soda, and salt. In another beat together the salt, butter, vinegar, and milk. Pour the flour and milk mixtures into the eggs and combine well. Grease a baking dish and pour batter into dish.
Cover and bake for 45 minutes, or until browned. Cool. Slice and serve with the sauce.

Sauce

½ cup butter	2 tsp. vanilla
½ cup sugar	1 cup cream

Melt the butter in a pan and add the sugar. Stir until it becomes slightly brown in color. Stir in vanilla and cream. Cook until mixture carmelizes.

Holidays and Special Occasions

The Incwala "First Fruits" ceremony is held in December or January and is an all male harvest festival.
The Umhlanga "Reed Dance" is celebrated in August or September. Young females come from all over the country so the king can chose a new whom he will wed in the next year. The girls wear beaded skirts with fringe and buttons, anklets, bracelets, necklaces, and sashes. The upper body is not covered, but beaded jewelry is worn. They dance for the king.

Sweden

Sweden shares the Scandinavian Peninsula with Norway and is separated from Europe by the Baltic Straits and bordered by Finland to the northeast. The earliest settlements date to the Allerod oscillation around 12000 BC with reindeer hunting camps. Tacitus mentions the Suiones in 98AD as a powerful tribe with ships. The Svea were early settlers, followed by the Vikings called Rus (8th-11Th c). Trade was very important in the Baltic region and shipbuilding thrived. From 1100-1400 Swedish kings expanded into Finland. In 1319 Sweden and Norway were united, and in 1397 Queen Margaret I of Denmark formed the Kalmar Union with Sweden, Norway and Denmark. In 1523 Gustav Vasa became king of Sweden. With the formation of the Hanseatic League Stockholm became a leading trading city importing textiles and salt and exporting iron and copper. Sweden flourished as it did not have a feudal class system and people were free. It also began seizing territories from Russia and Poland-Lithuania which led to the Thirty Years' War when Sweden conquered almost half of the Holy Roman states. At the end of the 17th c famine killed off almost 1/10 of Sweden's population. During both World Wars, Sweden remained neutral. Stockholm, the capital founded in 1248 by Birger Jarl, lies on Lake Malar and is made up of 14 islands.

Dining Etiquette

Please be punctual when invited to a home. Please take flowers unwrapped (lilies are for funerals), liquor, wine, chocolates, fruits, or something from your own country. Shake hands greeting and departing. Men hold doors for ladies and stand when introduced to them. Cocktails will be served. The hostess will announce the meal and seats the guests with the male guest of honor to her left. If a smorgasbord, guests will serve themselves, otherwise dishes will be passed. Please wait for the hostess to start. Salad is eaten with the entrée. Do eat everything on your plate, and when finished place your knife and fork together. If they are crossed it means you would like some more. Coffee and aperitifs will be served. The guest of honor is the first person to leave. Do not stay too late. Please try to reciprocate, and call or write a thank-you note afterwards.

A toast is made by the oldest or most senior ranking person, or the host. A glass is brought to eye level, look the other person in the eye, say "Skoal" and drink, wave the glass towards the other person, bow your head, look at the person again, and then place the glass on the table. The guest of honor (to the hostesses left) proposes a toast by tapping his knife on a glass and responds for all present, thanking her for the evening. "Skoal" or "Skal" is from Old Norse meaning "bowl", the bowl originally passed with mead, and the toasting comes from old military precedent.

Jansson's Temptation (anchovy casserole)

5 medium potatoes, peeled and cut into thin strips
2 medium onions, peeled and thinly sliced

14-16 anchovy filets, if using canned save juice
1 cup heavy cream
4 tbls. butter

Preheat oven to 400°
Melt the 2 tbls. butter in a skillet and sauté onion until browned.
Butter a large baking dish. Place ½ of the potatoes in the dish. Sprinkle the anchovies and onions on the potatoes. Top with remaining potatoes. Pour the anchovy juice on top. Bake 10 minutes in oven.
Put the rest of the butter and ½ cup cream on the dish. Cover with foil.
Bake for 30 minutes. Add rest of cream, and cook until golden, about 20 more minutes.

Cuisine

Sweden is renowned for its smorgasbord "bread and butter table", a tradition started in the 19th c and served at lunch, but which has been around since the 16th c when all food was placed on the table. The smorgasbord is formally laid-out with each series of dishes as part of a course. Cold items such as herring, cold meats and fish, boiled potatoes are first, followed by salads, then meat, vegetables, cheese, breads, dessert and fruit, each served on separate plates, and in order of cold to hot. Never take too much, especially starting the smorgasbord, as there is always more. Try a small amount of each, as these meals are to be savored, with little though to time, yet a gracious way to share. Salmon, herring, crayfish, hard breads – Wasa, cheeses and berries, especially hjortron (cloudberries) and lingonberries are some favorites.

The cuisine features dairy products, breads, berries, fruit, potatoes, beef, chicken, pork, and fish. Potatoes are almost always boiled. Fish is an important part of the diet and over the years has been salted, pickled, fermented, or cured. The breads are made from rye, wheat, oat, or grains some sweetened with syrup, and flatbread or crisp breads. Ligonberry jam is served with meats. Fruit soups such as blueberry, rose hip   or are served cold or hot. Cabbage was preserved as sauerkraut. Root vegetables are used as the winters are long. Among them are turnips, rutabaga, and of course potatoes. Mushrooms are used in many dishes with the chanterelle favored. Peas are mainly used in soup. In the far north reindeer are still eaten.

Husmanskost is the word used to describe traditional local Swedish cuisine. The word comes from *husman* "house owner" who would use pork, root vegetables, cabbage, onions, apples, fish, cereals and dairy products in their cooking.

Swedish Specialties

Sill – salted herring
Inlagd sill – pickled herring
Surstromming – fermented Baltic herring
Gravlax – salmon cured with salt and dill

Potkas – pot cheese
Bruna bonor och flask – pork with brown beans, sausage
Nyponsoppa – rosehip soup served cold with almonds and whipped cream

Artsoppa – dried yellow pea soup served with pancakes, usually on Thursdays
Rotmos med flask – pork with carrots, potatoes, and rutabaga
Fiskbullar – fish balls
Kalops – simmered beef with allspice and bay
Kottbollar – mcatballs and herbs
Blodpudding – "blood pudding" that is eaten with ligonberry jam
Rarakor – potato, salt, pepper and chives mixture that is fried
Kaldomar – cabbage rolls, a dish brought back by Charles XII from the Ottoman Empire

Plattar – Swedish pancakes
Raggmunk – potato pancake
Plattar – thin pancakes
Palt – dumplings of unboiled potatoes, filled with pork
Pytt I panna - hash
Lutfisk – lye fish made of stockfish
Spettekaka – "cake made on a spit" – a cake made of many eggs and sugar
Oskaka - cheesecake accompanied by a cherry compote or strawberry jam
Knackebrod – hard, flat bread
Kaffebrod and bakelser are pastries, cakes cookies, or buns served with coffee

Holidays and Special Occasions

New Year's Day – Nyarsdagen – smorgasbord with lutfisk (dried cod), potatoes, ham, and rice pudding
Lent – semlor – wheat flour bun with almond paste and whipped cream
Shrove Tuesday – hot cross buns
Easter – decorated eggs, lamb
Walpurgis Night – gravlax (salmon)
Midsummer's Day – boiled new potatoes, herring, strawberries, fermented milk
Krafishiva (crayfish party) is observed in August – crayfish season with crayfish feasts. Crayfish are boiled in water, salt, and dill, and served cold. After eating the claw a person "skoals" with a shot or "nubbe" of Aquavit. The crayfish is served with toast (Knackebord), butter and cheese, and pickled herring.
St. Martin's Eve –November 10 – goose with apples and prunes
Fall – eels – "time of the eel darkness"
Feast of St. Lucia – December 13 – the oldest daughter in a family wears a crown of candles and wears white. Coffee and Lucia buns are served
Christmas Eve – ham or pork, boiled cabbage, pickled herring, lutefisk (cod), gravlax (salmon), vegetable salads, and Julgrot (rice porridge which contains almonds. The first person to find an almond will be the first to be married in the New Year). Ginger cookies and cakes are baked. Glogg (a drink made from wine, schnapps, spices, raisins and almonds) and mumma (beer and Madeira) are offered.
Christmas – at breakfast julhog (Yule pile) – layered breads, cookies, and fruit. For dinner - blood sausage and pork; potato sausage; Christmas cookies; lutfisk with a white sauce, melted butter, green peas, boiled potatoes and mustard; ris a l'amande (rice and almond pudding). Goose may also be served. Julmust is a beverage drunk at Christmas that is a mix of porter, or a dark beer, light beer, port wine, and something sweet with cardamom usually added. Glogg is a mulled wine usually served at Christmas.
Dopperdan "dipping day" – dunk pieces of rye bread into a meat broth

Glogg (Hot Mulled Wine)

1 bottle red wine
1 cup raisins
6 cardamom seeds
5 cloves
1 piece fresh ginger

Peeling slices from 1 orange
1 stick cinnamon
½ cup sugar
½ cup blanched almonds

Place all the ingredients, except ½ cup raisins and almonds in a pan. Heat almost to a boil.
Remove from heat and stir in almonds and remaining raisins.
Serve in mugs with spoon.
For a stronger flavor. Let sit overnight and then heat before serving.

Beverages

The national drink Aquavit "Water of Life" made from grain or potatoes with caraway, anise or fennel seeds is served straight up in small glasses. During the 17th c the clergy pressed for a ban on coffee drinking and only they were permitted to produce Aquavit. King Gustavus III made producing Aquavit a state monopoly, though many home stills thrived.

Vodka has been produced in Sweden for over four hundred years. Beer has been brewed since the 12th c when King Magnus set up beer laws. During the 17th c there was a Brewers' Trade Guild. In the 18th c a Mr. Carnegie, a Scotsman, opened the brewery in Gothenburg, which later merged with Pripps and Lyckholm Breweries, and in the 19th century Fredrik Rosenquist of Åkershult.

Pils was introduced in the 1870s. In 1905 there were approximately 240 breweries, but because of very strict regulation by the Swedish Brewers Association that number had dwindled to about 25 in the 1960s. Today some restrictions have been lifted and about 40 breweries are in operation.

Glogg is a mulled wine; and there are also wines made from berries such as blueberries, juniper; and ligonberries. Punsch is a traditional liqueur. Beer is also brewed, mainly lager.

Switzerland

Switzerland, centrally located in Europe is landlocked by Germany, France, Austria, Italy and Liechtenstein. Much of the country is composed of the Alps, Jura Mountains, a plateau, glaciers and valleys. Mountain passes made Switzerland a major north-south trading route even prior to Roman times. Swiss history dates back to the Helvetians whose ancient capital Avenches, later became a Roman city. Excavations around Lake Constance date back to about 3000 BC. The Romans appeared in 107 BC, with Julius Caesar taking command in 58 BC. In 1032 it became part of the Holy Roman Empire. The French invaded in 1798 and in 1815 it became independent with 22 cantons. The capital, Berne, was founded in 1191 by Berchtold V, the 7th Duke of Zahringen of the Alemanni tribe. The official languages are German, French, Italian and Romansh.

Dining Etiquette

Please be punctual when invited out. Send or bring flowers, unwrapped and in an uneven number. Shake hands greeting and departing. Women extend hands first. Please hold doors and chairs for them. Drinks are served before the meal. When seated the male guest of honor is to the right of the hostess. Please wait for the hostess to start. Courses are served. Eating is continental style, fork in the left hand, knife in the right. Foods such as salad, potatoes, and other soft foods are cut with a fork. Hands should be kept at table level, not in your lap. When finished place the knife and fork together. Dessert, followed by coffee, will be served. The host proposes the toast with everyone looking him in the eye and saying "Prosit" – German, "A Votre Sante" – French, or "Salute" – Italian, then all may drink.

Cuisine

Swiss food is a combination of German – sausages, roasts, potatoes; French - raclette and fondue; Italian – pastas; Graubunden Bunderfleisch - air dried beef; ham; cheese; mushrooms; fish; pastries; and chocolates.

The production of cheese dates back to Roman times with Emmentaler and Shrinz being two of the oldest produced. During the winter people lived in the mountain valleys and moved to higher mountain huts (sennhuetten) during the summer, taking their cows with them. (Think of the delightful children's classic *Heidi)*. Most cheeses are made from cow's milk and in large wheels. Some of the better known cheeses are Alpkase (cheese made in the Alps); Appenzeller (Alpine cell, which is cured with wine, cider, and spices); Bellelay (Monk's Head); Gruyere; Royalp; Saanen; Saint Otho; Sapsago; Schabzieger; and Vacherin Fribourgeois. About 60% of the cheese is exported.

Rosti (potato cake)

Serves 6

6 medium sized baking potatoes, peeled   ¼ cup vegetable oil
½ tsp. salt   2 tbls. butter

In a pan bring the potatoes to a boil. Cook for 10 minutes. Drain. Cool.
Grate the potatoes lengthwise. Place in a bowl and sprinkle with the salt.
In a skillet heat the oil and butter. Put the potatoes evenly in the pan. Cook uncovered for about 8-10 minutes until browned. Place an ovenproof plate over the pan and invert the potato cake. Slide browned side up back into the skillet Fry 6-8 minutes more. More butter or oil can be added. Do not let stick or burn.
Serve on a warm platter.
Sauteed onions and/or cooked crumbled bacon can be added, or served on top.

Swiss Specialties

Tarts and quiches- cheese, apple, onion
Zuri Geschnetzetles – veal with mushrooms in a cream sauce, served with rosti
Cervelat, Luganighe, luganighetta, bratwurst, schublig – various sausages
Papet Vaudois – leeks with sausage or potatoes
Saucisse au foie – smoked liver
Fondue – melted cheese. Eaten by dipping potatoes or bread in the sauce
Fondue Bourguigonnne - beef cooked in a chafing dish with various sauces on side

Zopf – bread
Alplermagronen – macaroni, potatoes, onions, bacon, melted cheese, served with applesauce
Tirggel – flour and honey sweet biscuits from Zurich, and served at Christmas
Polenta – cornmeal
Chur – meat pie from Graubunden, which is also famous for its barley soup
Pizokel – meat dough with vegetables
Bärner Züpfe - a braided egg bread
Bundner Nusstorte – nut cake

Holidays

Easter - decorated eggs, chocolate bunnies, Osterfladen (Easter cake)
Chaesteilet – annual event in the Justistal region above Lake Thun when the farmers divide the cheese made during the summer according to the number of cows they own
December 6 – St. Nicholas' Day when he visits children bringing nuts, fruit, and other treats
Christmas Eve – families dine early - potatoes, ham, walnut cake, gingerbread cookies, attend midnight church services, and then decorate their Christmas tree
Christmas - Christmas markets; Gluhwein - mulled wine; fondue

Raclette (melted cheese with potatoes)

Raclette means "to scrape" in French. Raclette or other cheeses were taken by shepherds out into the mountains following their sheep. To keep warm they would boil potatoes and heat the cheese over the fire and eat it over the potatoes. Raclette is a semi-hard cheese.

Serves 4

½ lb. raclette cheese
4 -8 new potatoes
8 or more gherkin pickles

Preheat oven to 400°
In a pan boil the potatoes until tender.
Set a table for 4. At each place put a small fork and knife, and a warm plate. On other plates or bowls have the potatoes, pickles, onions, and bread.

8 pickled onions
Bread baguette, sliced thin

Place the cheese in a cast iron skillet in the oven. Cook until the cheese is melted, about 5 minutes.
Place the skillet on a trivet on the table.
Enjoy!
Gruyere can be used in place of raclette.

Beverages

Since the 1st c BC wines have been produced in the south. Vincyards line the north side of Lake Leman (The Vaud), east of Lake Geneva (Valais), the hills above Lake Geneva (Lavaux), and Lake Neufchatel. Most of the wine produced is white made from the Chasselas grape, drunk young, and not for export. Most of the wine from the Rhine section are red, and from the Rhone white, except for Cortaillod. Brandies include Marc (made from the remains of crushed grapes); Himbeergeist (raspberries); Quetsch (plums); Dettling (pears); Kirschwasser (cherries); Pastis (anise); Blanc Cassis Cynar (artichokes); and chocolate liqueurs. Serve fruit brandies in tulip shaped glasses, slightly chilled.

Beers are mainly from the German speaking areas of Zurich and St. Gallen. They have longer lager periods – 2-3 months, are unpasteurized, and pale in color. The strongest beer in the world is made by the Hurlimann Brewery in Zurich.

Did You Know?

In 1992 Emmental cheese producers were stymied by larger than normal holes in their cheese, formed by fermentation.
The Count of Gruyere nearing the end of his life levied taxes on wheels of cheese and from these built the Abbey of Rougemont. Gruyere cheese is still made in Switzerland.
The Swiss invented baby food and condensed milk.
During the 18th c many Swiss families settled in Pennsylvania, including the Hirshi (Hershey).
If one loses bread while eating fondue, a man must buy a bottle of wine, and a woman must kiss a man, or the person to the left!
Birchermuesli (muesli – a breakfast cereal of oats, fruit, and nuts) was invented by Dr. Maxmillian Oskar Bircher-Benner.

Syria

Syria, the Syrian Arab Republic, located in western Asia, is bounded by Lebanon and the Mediterranean Sea to the West, Turkey to the north, Iraq to the east, Jordan to the south, and Israel to the southwest. The country dates back thousands of years. Ebla and Ugarit (once a trading city with Mycenae and Troy and home to the Ugarite script tablet, the earliest known alphabet) date to the third and second millennium. Beginning in the 2nd millennium BC the region was occupied by the Canaanites, Phoenicians, Arameans, Egyptians, Sumerians, Assyrians, Babylonians, Hittites, Persians, and Ancient Macedonia. Alexander the Great conquered Syria, followed by the Seleucid Empire. Pompey the Great captured Antioch in 64 BC when it became part of the Roman Empire. Later the Byzantines brought Islam to the country. From the 16th to 20th Syria was part of the Ottoman Empire. In 1920, an independent Arab Kingdom of Syria was established, but after a short time, was put under French mandate. Independence was gained in 1946. The capital, Damascus, was settled about 2500 B.C and, is one of the oldest continuously inhabited cities in the world. The official language is Arabic. Soccer is the most important sport.

Dining Etiquette

The Syrians are very hospitable people. Please be punctual when invited for a meal. Dining may be late at night. Men shake hands greeting and departing, and may embrace if they know each other well. Female acquaintances will kiss on each cheek. Placing the right hand on the heart when meeting is a sign of affection. Men and women may socialize separately. People will stand close together when talking and gesture with their hands. Many dishes may be served at a meal. Please eat only with your right hand, and pass with your right hand, or both hands. Food and drink are usually offered three times, and accept on the third. The Syrian Muslims do not eat pork or drink alcohol.

Families are very close knit and the father the head of the household. Please do not show the bottom of your shoes, or cross your ankle on the knee of the other leg. Do not point at other people or direct with your hand.

Cuisine

The Syrian cuisine is a wonderful blend of the cultures that have inhabited the country over the centuries. Syria was located on important trade routes so that spices and exotic fruits and vegetables were brought to the country. Wheat, fruit – dates, figs, plums, watermelon, lemons, vegetables, dairy products, lamb, chicken, spices, herbs, onion, garlic, chickpeas, fava beans, rice, yogurt are used in cooking. Meats are roasted or grilled. Aleppo is famous for hot peppers, pistachio nuts, pomegranates, sheep, olives and orchards.

Kibbeh (lamb patties)

Kibbeh, the national dish, is ground lamb patties.

Serves 4

1½ cups burghal
2 cups water
1 lb. ground lamb
¼ tsp. ground allspice
¼ tsp. nutmeg

¼ tsp. cayenne
Salt and pepper
¼ cup olive oil
Pita bread
Hummus

Place the burghal in a bowl with the water. Let sit 10 minutes. Place in colander with cheese cloth and let drain.
In a bowl combine the burghal, lamb, and spices. Add salt and pepper to taste. Make into 8 small balls or 4 large ones.
In a skillet heat the oil. Cook the lamb until just browned on all sides.
Serve with pita bread and hummus.

Syrian Specialties

Mezze – appetizers
Za'atar – dried thyme and sumac
Manaeesh – small pizza
Falafel – fried ground chickpeas
Fuul – brown bean and lentil dish
Hummus – chickpea and garlic puree
Tabbouleh- crushed wheat, tomato, mint, and parsley salad
Fattoush – salad with pita, cucumbers, tomatoes, chickweed and mint
Labneh – yogurt with olive oil and salt or mint
Shawarma – skewered lamb or chicken
Shish taouk – skewered chicken
Shish kebab (mishwie) – lamb or beef skewered and cooked with vegetables
Muhammara –red pepper dip
Vabra – stuffed grape leaves
Kousa mahshi – stuffed squash
Makdous – stuffed eggplant

Halabi – string cheese
Pastirma – dried meat
Sujuk – spicy sausage
Kafta – ground meat with spices and onions
Batlawa – phyllo pastry with chopped nuts and soaked in honey
Swar es – sett- round pastry with with nuts
Znood Es-sett – phyllo pastry with filling
Halawet al-jeben – cheese pastry with atar syrup
Halva – semolina candy
Kenafeh – pastry with cheese, nuts, and syrup
Franjea – farina custard with cinnamon
Ma'amoul – date and nut cookies
Baba ghanouj – charbroiled eggplant dip
Pita and flat breads
Jibbneh mashallale – curd cheese
Baharat mshakale – spice mixture

Baba Ghannouj (Eggplant Dip)

1 medium sized eggplant
¼ cup fresh lemon juice
2 tbls. tahini paste

1 large garlic clove, peeled and finely chopped
1 tbls. olive oil
¼ cup parsley, chopped

Preheat oven to Broil
Prick the eggplant several times with a fork.
Place on a cookie sheet and broil until the skin is blackened, turning several times and not too close to broiler, and the eggplant tender. Cool and peel skin off.
Mash the eggplant until smooth. Add the lemon juice, tahini paste, garlic, and olive oil.
Serve it in a bowl garnished with the parsley. Serve with pita bread.

Holidays and Special Occasions

Food and drink are not consumed from sunrise to sunset during Ramadan. Meals (iftar) are served in the evening.
Aid al-Adha – feast day
Eid-al-Fitr – three day feast at the end of Ramadan with many sweets
For an engagement, marriage contract, and wedding many feasts may ensue. Weddings may last up to a week. It was once customary when the bride entered her new home for wheat dough to be available for her to break off a piece. If it stuck to the door, the marriage was certain to last!

Beverages

Coffee in Syria is quite strong and is served for breakfast and after a meal. Tea is offered before meals. Ayran is a drink made with yogurt, water, garlic, and salt. Arak, an alcoholic aniseed beverage is served on special occasions. Winemaking in Syria dates back to c 3000 BC in Jericho. Glassmaking became an important industry to make wine glasses. Today wine is produced at Bargylus. Mount Bargylus (today Jebel Al-Ansarlye) is located in the fertile Orontes Valley near the ancient city of Antioch. Even during the Greco-Roman era wines vines were grown here.

Did You Know?

In the early 1990s a miniature clay horse figurine was found at Tell es-Sweyhat, once a trading city, along the Euphrates River that dates back more than 4300 years. Through this statue archeologists discovered that domesticated horses had played a major role in the Middle East dating further back than previously known.
The prophet Abraham supposedly stopped at Aleppo to milk his cows on Citadel Hill, in Arabic Halab "milk".

Taiwan

The Republic of China is a group of islands made up of Taiwan, the Penghu Islands, and about 20 smaller ones approximately 100 miles off the coast of China. The history of Taiwan dates back to prehistoric times when it was thought to have been part of mainland China. In 239 AD the islands were conquered by the kingdom of Wu. C 1000 AD the Hakka "strangers" arrived to become farmers. In the 16th c the Portuguese named the island Ihla Formosa or "Beautiful Island". Until 1858 the Chinese closed all ports to trade, but with the Treaty of Tientsin they reopened them and they flourished with the export of opium, sugar, rice, tea, camphor, timber, and coal. Taipei became the capital in 1949. The Han Chinese make up the largest ethnic group.

Dining Etiquette

Please be punctual when invited for a meal. Bring a gift of fruit, wine, liquor, food, chocolates, or something for the home, and present with both hands. Shake hands greeting and departing. Elders are introduced first. Rank is very important, as are respect, humility and patience. A guest is always honored in a home and will be asked "Chir-fan le may-yo" "Have you eaten yet", and offered food. Drinks will be served. Chopsticks and a spoon are at each place. Each person has a bowl of rice. Food is served from the center of the table. Pass an item to someone else with both hands. The guest of honor is expected to start the meal first. Some rice should be left in the bottom of the bowl or it will be refilled. When finished place the chopsticks on the table or in the chopstick holder, never on top of or in the bowl, which signifies bad luck or death. At the end of dinner the guest of honor leaves first.

Loss of "face" can bring shame to a person or family. People may not always say what they mean in order not to lose "face". People show much respect for each other, keeping their distance, being very polite and courteous, not displaying public affection or speaking in a loud tone, holding onto Confucian ideals. Never lose your temper or criticize. The people want to live in harmony.

Cuisine

Taiwan produces many agricultural products including tea and rice. Food consumption is based on Chinese medicine and Confucian ideals of yin and yang. Many dictates span over 2000 years from the Imperial Medicine College (620-630 AD), the National Medical Service (206 BC-24 AD), books and food that date back to the 2nd c BC. Roots, herbs, the yin and yang, balance of the seasonings, color, aromas, textures, and blending of many ingredients contribute to their diet. Even today food is bought fresh or dried for preservation such as seaweed, mushrooms, beef and fish. Ginger has always been used during the winter for its warming effect, especially if boiled in sugar as a broth. Tea provides spiritual harmony and is considered one of life's necessities.

542

Dishes make use of ginger, red chilies, rice wine, coriander and other herbs, tofu, bean curd, and cabbage. Star anise is used to marinate and braise meats. Rice is served at almost every meal, and can be boiled, steamed, fried, used in a dish, on its own, or powdered. Congee is thick rice eaten with other dishes. Being an island, seafood is in abundance – grass fish, carp, tuna, shrimp, squid, eels, clams, turtles, and others. Favorite desserts are Lung Hsu candy "Dragon Whisker Candy" made of confectioners' sugar coated with a filling of peanuts, black sesame, and dates; Ts Ao Chun candy "Kitchen God Candy" malt and white sugars melted and pulled into strands and then broken; Chuang yuan cake, a cake with rice, peanut or black sesame filling; and steamed date buns and shredded radish cakes. Fruits are also in abundance – pineapples, dates, papaya, mangoes, plums, and kiwi. Some special dishes are Tantzu noodles, noodles, broth, pork, leeks, and bean sprouts; red fish; squid balls; dumplings; xiao long bao dumplings with meat and vegetables; and Dim Sum.

Szechuan is hot and spicy, with the use of ginger, onions, chilies, pork, poultry, beans and eggplant Hunan is spicy, similar to Szechuan. Hot peppers, garlic, oils made from tea, and bean curd. Tastes range from sweet and sour to salty. Fukien food is quite mild using seafood and herbs. Mongolian food has barbeques and hot pots, using wine, soy sauce, sesame oil, with meats and vegetables. Rice is used in many ways – jelly, popped, glutinous rice cakes, wine and candy.

Niu Rou (Beef Noodle Soup)

Niu Rou is the national dish of Taiwan.

Serves 6

2 lbs. beef, cut into bite sized pieces	2 hot chilies
3 tbls. oil	¼ cup bean sauce or chili paste
3 cloves garlic, minced	¼ cup rice wine
2 tbls. fresh ginger	¼ cup soy sauce
4 scallions, sliced lengthwise	2 tbls. rock sugar
1 tsp. Chinese five spice powder	4-6 cups water
4 star anise	1 lb. bok choy, cut into pieces
2 tsp. Sichuan peppercorns	1 lb. Chinese noodles

Heat the oil in a large skillet and brown the beef.
Add the rest of the ingredients, except noodles. Bring to a boil. Cover and simmer until beef is tender. Add more water if necessary.
Cook the noodles according to the directions.
Place the noodles in soup bowls and top with soup.
Using beef with the bone in will add more flavor to the soup. Cook the beef as a piece and then cut into smaller pieces when it is done.
More spices can be added for a spicier soup.

Niangao (Sticky Rice New Year's Cakes)

2 cups glutinous rice flour
1 cup water

1-2 cups dark brown sugar, depending on how dark and sweet you want it

Heat the water and sugar in a sauce pan until the sugar is completely dissolved. Cool
Stir in the rice flour.
Pour into a dish that can be covered and steamed for at least 3 hours until very dark and firm.
Refrigerate at least 3 days. Slice and serve.

Holidays and Special Occasions

New Year's – Nien Kao – rice paste; rice cakes – sticky rice with red beans and sugar
Tuan Wu Chie (Dragon Boat Festival) – sticky rice, meat, mushrooms, tsungtzu (rice dumplings), and chestnuts wrapped in bamboo leaves. Realgar (arsenic wine) is drunk to ward off evil spirits, snakes, and insects. Children wear sachets with herbs to cleanse and protect them, and bodies are cleansed with boiled herbs.
Ghost Month – pineapples, whole chickens, lichees and drinks are served for the departed.
Moon Festival – moon cakes which are round pastries with red bean paste and egg yolks, symbolizing harmony and perfection.
Family shrines – food is offered twice a month to ancestors
Weddings – when the groom arrives at the bride's home with fresh flowers, a wedding gown, hungpao (red envelope with money), he is served egg tea – two boiled eggs dipped in tea sugar, while the bride dresses. After leaving the bride, after getting out of her car, is presented a tray by the groom's brother on which are two oranges symbolizing good luck Wedding banquets are usually costly affairs for a family! The bride and groom finish by eating a pig's heart boiled in black sugar in hopes that their hearts will feel and think the same way.

Beverages

Wine has been produced on Taiwan for thousands of years, first from cereals and later fermented rice. Grapes, plums and other fruits are used to make wine. Until recently The Taiwan Tobacco and Wine Monopoly Bureau did not permit competition, but a number of wineries have opened. Kaoliang, a distilled spirit (150%) made from sorghum is produced on Kinmen Island and placed in pottery bottles. Beer is also brewed on the islands. Bubble tea is a sweet drink with tapioca.

Tajikistan

Tajikistan is a mountainous country in Central Asia, bordered by Afghanistan to the south, Uzbekistan to the west, Kyrgyzstan to the north, and the People's Republic of China to the east. The area known as Tajikistan has been inhabited since c 4000BC. From the 4th century BCE until the 2nd century BCE, it was part of the Bactrian Empire, then the Scythian Tukharas and later became part of Tukharistan. By the 2nd c BCE the Chinese had explored Bactria. In the 7th c AD the Arabs brought Islam, followed by the Samanid Empire and then the Mongols. By the 19th c the Russian Empire expanded into most of the Central Asian countries with the Bolsheviks appearing after the Russian Imperial overthrow in 1917. In 1924, the Tajik Autonomous Soviet Socialist Republic was created as a part of Uzbekistan but in 1929 was made a separate constituent republic. Tajikistan became an independent country in 1991. Dushanbe, the capital, is located in the Gissar Valley. The official language is Tajik, but each of the valleys has its own language.

Dining Etiquette

The Tajiks have a great respect for hospitality for guests. When invited for a meal, be prompt. Please bring a small gift for the home, fruit, or a sweet. Shake hands greeting and departing. Hands may be washed before dining. Meals are eaten sitting on a sufa around a low table called a dastarkhan. The meal begins with tea drunk from pialas (small cups without handles) served on trays. Always drink the tea. The eldest person is served first. This is followed by another tray with sweets, fruit, and, flat bread, or cake. Soup with rice (shavlya) or with peas (shurbo) and meat on round dishes are then brought in. Salads are served on plates. The Tajiks have much respect when non (flatbread) is served. The bread can never be dropped to the ground, or put on the dastarkhan with the bottom side up. Also only another non can be placed on top of it. Bread should never be cut with a knife, only pieces broken off. Most of the conversation will be after the meal is completed. Toasts are made, but always maintain eye contact.

The mountainous Tajiks are very hospitable people and will take travelers in, offering shirchoy, a tea with goat's milk, salt, butter or oil. Here the main dish will be kaurdak made of partridge or quail.

Oshi Plov (lamb with rice)

Oshi plov is the national dish.

Serves 4

2 lbs. lamb, cut in pieces	2 quince, diced
2 cups rice	1 cup peas
3 cups water	2 tbls. raisins
3 tbls. melted butter	½ cup pomegranate
6 carrots, peeled and sliced	2 eggs, hardboiled, peeled and quartered
2 onions, peeled and sliced	Salt and pepper to taste
3 cloves garlic, minced	Oil

In a skillet heat 2 tbls. oil. Brown meat. Remove meat.
Add a little more oil and sauté the onions until just tender. Stir in the meat, carrots, garlic, peas, and quince. Cook until tender.
In a pan cook the rice and water until all the water is evaporated. Fluff rice
Add the raisins and pomegranate to the meat mixture. Season with salt and pepper, if desired.
Place the rice on a warmed platter and top with the lamb and the eggs.

Cuisine

The cuisine derives from the semi- nomadic early cultures and is similar to Central Asian cooking. Dairy products used during meals are chaka (sour milk), yoghurt, kaymak (clotted cream. Tajikistan grows grapes, melons, apricots (over 300 varieties), plums, persimmons and figs, and pomegranates. Mutton is the main meat. Grains include rye, wheat and barley. Alliums, onions, beans, and peas are also grown. Tajikistan's high altitude and short growing season have made it into a research center for food diversity. Researchers come here from all over the world to study its plants and seeds. At harvest time ripe ears of rye are bundled and put in homes to insure that the next year's crop will be bountiful.

Tajik Specialties

Manty – steamed meat dumplings
Belyash – fried dough with meat
Shurbo – vegetable soup
Piti- mutton and vegetable soup
Kabob – chopped marinated meat fried on skewers
Plov – rice with turnip or carrot and meat, and fried. This is eaten from a large communal dish placed at the center of the table.
Morkovcha – carrot, garlic, vinegar, and cumin dish
Sheklet – cabbage stuffed with meat

Samsa – meat pies
Shashlyk – mutton grilled on skewers
Kurutob – kurot (hardened balls of salty yogurt) which are placed in water and poured over torn fatir "flatbread" and topped with fried onions, tomatoes, and cucumber (served communally and also considered the national dish)
Lagman – noodle soup
Okroshka – yogurt soup
Mahin mahouri – black bread
Non - flatbread served with meals

Fatir – bread with a lot of butter
Lipioshka - unleavened bread

Kalama – flat bread made from puff pastry, coated with fat, twisted, and fried
Pilita – sweet dough

Pelmeni (pastry with meat and onions)

Dough

4 cups flour
3 eggs

1 cup water
1 tsp. salt

Place the ingredients in a food processor, or knead by hand, until firm. By hand knead into a ball. Refrigerate 1 hour.
On a floured board roll out the dough until about 1/8 inch thick. Cut into squares or circles.

Filling

2 tbls. butter or oil
1 onion, finely chopped
½ lb. ground lamb or beef

¼ cup water
Salt and pepper

Heat the butter in a skillet and add onions. Stir until transparent. Place in a bowl.
Place the meat, salt, pepper, and water in a skillet. Brown. Add onions.
Place a spoonful of meat on ½ a dough square. Fold over and seal with the fork tines.
Bring 2 quarts water to a boil in a pan. Drop in dumplings and cook 8-10 under low heat. You will probably need to repeat this several times. Remove with a slotted spoon.
Serve with melted butter or sour cream.

Holidays and Special Occasions

Navurz – (New Year's Day in the Muslim lunar calendar) - Sumalyak, made of wheat juice, oil and flour, is served to celebrate spring
Ramazan – (Ramadan) fasting from sunrise to sunset for 30 days. The fast ends with Aid-al-Fitr when an animal is sacrificed and given to relatives and the poor.

Beverages

Tea is served for every meal and given as a sign of hospitality. A choykhona is a teahouse.
Kefir, a yoghurt drink, is served for breakfast.

Did You Know?

Apricot oil taken with warm milk is a cure for high blood pressure.

Tanzania

Tanzania, located in central East Africa, is bordered by Kenya and Uganda to the north, Rwanda, Burundi and the Democratic Republic of the Congo to the west, and Zambia, Malawi and Mozambique to the south. The country's eastern border lies on the Indian Ocean with the islands of Mafia, Pemba, and Zanzibar. The country is one of the world's oldest inhabited regions with remains dating back two million years. Hunter-gatherers lived in communities, and may have been the Cushitic and Khoison speaking peoples. Approximately 2000 years ago the Bantu came from western Africa, followed by the Nilotic. Merchants from the Persian Gulf and India followed with Islam introduced. The coast was claimed by Sultan Seyyid Said of Oman who moved the capital to Zanzibar City in 1840. In the late 1800' Germany conquered Tanzania (Tanganyika), Rwanda, and Burundi, to form German East Africa. After World War I the League of Nations charter designated the area a British Mandate, although part of the northwest region later became Rwanda and Burundi. Independence was achieved in 1961. In 1964 Zanzibar and Tanganyika merged as Tanzania. Dodoma is the national capital, Dar es Salaam the commercial capital. Swahili and English are the official languages. There are more than 130 ethnic groups.

Dining Etiquette

When invited for a meal, do not arrive early, but on time or up to thirty minutes late. Please bring a gift – sweets, candies, or something for the home, not flowers. Please shake hands greeting and departing. Women do not usually shake hands with men, unless the woman extends her hand first. You may be seated on a mat or carpet, or around a low table for the meal. Children may be invited to eat with the adults, though in some cases women may not eat with the men. Women do all the cooking. Do not expose the sole of your foot. A bowl of water and a towel may be passed to wash your hands. Please eat with your right hand. Do not use knives or forks, if offered, to eat chapati or ugali. The right hand or both hands are used to pass something. You may leave a small amount of food on the plate fruit or sweets will be offered at the end of the meal. Most socializing is done after the meal. Please thank your host for the meal.

Cuisine

The earliest inhabitants of Tanzania were hunter-gatherers. Bantu-speaking Zaramu, Zigua, Doe and Kwere tribes lived in the region. Later vegetables, millet, sorghum, fruit, coconut oil, and fish became part of the diet. C 800 AD Arabs introduced citrus fruit and cotton. The staples of the diet today are grains millet, sorghum, beans, fruits – plantains, bananas, pawpaw; vegetables – eggplant, tomatoes, okra, spinach, peas; cassava, spinach, maize, chicken, goat and lamb. Cattle, sheep and goats are considered status symbols, and their milk is used. The coastal regions spicy foods, fish and coconut oil are used. Elsewhere, rice, chapati, ugali, grilled or marinated meats, and vegetables are used in cooking. Peppercorn, vanilla-vines, ylang-ylang, cinnamon, clove and nutmeg are grown on Zanzibar. Tanzania also exports coffee, cotton, sisal, cashew nuts, meat, tea, cloves, sugar, coconuts, and tobacco. Trade along the coast has always been important with countries as far away as China and later with the Portuguese and Germans who also influenced the cuisine.

Chapati (Fried Bread)

2 cups whole wheat flour   ½ cup -1 cup warm water
3 tbls. ghee

In a bowl combine the flour and ghee to a coarse meal. Make a well in the center. Pour in ¼ cup water. With your fingers or a spoon blend into a dough. Add enough water to make a solid ball. On a floured board knead the dough folding it from the ends for about 8 minutes until it becomes elastic. Make it into a ball. Place in a bowl and cover with a dampened cloth. Let rest 30 minutes. Shape the dough into 5 inch rounds.
Heat a cast iron skillet. Add one of the rounds for 1 minute or until just browned, moving it around. Turn it over and cook on other side. Cook remaining balls.

Tanzanian Specialties

Ugali – the national dish – dough made of cassava flour, cornmeal, millet or sorghum that is served with a sauce of meat, fish, beans, or vegetables communally in a bowl.
Wali – rice
Samaki - fish cooked in coconut
Kitumbura – fried bread
Chapatti – fried flat bread
Mlkate wa kumimina – rice bread
Vitumbua – rice cakes, usually served with tea in the morning
Pilau – rice with spices and hot peppers
Mshikaki – marinated meat
Biryani – spiced rice with chicken, lamb, beef, or seafood

Nyama choma – roasted meats
Ndayu – roasted goat
Ndizi kaanga – fried bananas
Maandazi – deep fried cakes
Visheti- similar to a donut
Kashata – snack made from coconut or groundnuts
Samosa – deep fried pastries with meat or vegetables
Bagia – dough made chickpea flour, spices and fried

Holidays and Special Occasions

Cattle are slaughtered for the birth of a baby or a wedding.
About one-third of the population is Muslim who celebrate the one month fast during Ramadan where people do not eat or drink from sunrise to sunset. Eid al-Fitr breaks the fast. Children visit neighboring homes and are given cakes and lemongrass tea. The feast will include plantains, fish, dates, ugali, and many dishes.

Farmers and Peasants Day is celebrated to thank the farmers for keeping agricultural products plentiful.

Christians celebrate Easter, Good Friday and Easter Monday. Christmas dinner might include pilau, chai, chicken or red meat, or seafood, depending on the part of country they reside in.

December 9 – Independence Day – ugali with beans cooked in coconut milk

Coconut Fish

Serves 4

2 lbs. red snapper or striped bass fillets	1 small onion, peeled and finely chopped
Salt and pepper	1 hot pepper, seeded and minced
1cup coconut milk	2 tomatoes, chopped
1 tbls. tomato paste	Lemon slices
2 tbls. lemon juice	Cooked rice
3 cloves garlic, minced	
1 tbls. fresh grated ginger	

Preheat oven to 350º

Place the fish in a baking dish and sprinkle with salt, pepper, and 1 tbls. lemon juice. Bake for 20 minutes, or until fish is cooked.

In a sauce pan combine 1 tbls. lemon juice, garlic, ginger, hot pepper, and onion. Add coconut milk, tomato paste, and tomatoes. Stir until thickened.

Place the fish on a serving platter, and pour tomato sauce over it. Garnish with lemon slices and serve with rice.

Beverages

Chai (tea) is served in the morning and at supper, or while socializing. Coffee is drunk in the evening. Fresh fruit drinks are made from pineapples, oranges or sugar cane. Mbege is a banana beer brewed in northeast Tanzania. Tanzania is known for its large coffee plantations. Wine and brandy are produced in the highlands of Dodoma.

Did You Know?

The Mercato in Addis Ababa is the largest outdoor market in Africa.

Thailand

Thailand "Land of the Free" occupies an area in Southeast Asia bordered by Myanmar (Burma) to the north and west, Cambodia to the east, Laos to the north, Malaysia to the south, and the Gulf of Thailand and Andaman Sea. Much of the kingdom is made up of jungles, mountains in the north, plains, plateau, and along the east coast fishing villages. Thai history dates back thousands of years. Ban Chiang in the northeast cultivated rice c 4000 BC. The earliest known settlers came from China c 1st c AD. Bangkok (the City of Angels), the capital, was constructed starting in 1782. Originally the Thai kingdom was known as Siam. The Thais are predominately Theravada Buddhists. The official language is Thai. There are over forty different ethnic groups each with their own language.

Dining Etiquette

Family, education and business ties, plus respect for elders are very important. Please be punctual when invited for a meal. It is considered an honor to be invited to a home. Please remove your shoes before entering a home, wat, or building with an image of Buddha. On greeting a person, the Thai wave or bow. Place your palms together and bring your hands close to body between the head and the chin, and bow slightly. The higher the hands and the deeper the bow, the more respect you show for that person. Do this slowly and with grace. A junior or less senior person initiates the wai. This is usually only between Thais. Wai has several meanings – "Hello", "Thank-you", or "I'm sorry". Some Thais may extend their hands to shake. The first name is used prefaced by "Khun" which stands for Mr./Mrs./Miss. If you are seated next to someone else do not put your arm around that person as it is considered offensive. Please keep both your feet on the floor when seated, and never point a toe at someone else. The Thais enjoy tranquility and peace of mind. Confrontation is not part of their society, and thus their desire to remain a neutral nation.

Tables are set with forks and spoons. These utensils were introduced by King Mongkut Rama IV after the right hand only had been used to eat. The fork is held in the left hand and to push, the spoon to eat with. Noodles are eaten with chopsticks, noodle soups with a ceramic spoon and chopsticks. Sticky rice is rolled into a ball with the right hand. All dishes are set on the table at the same time. Rice is the main staple and around it are arranged smaller bowls with soup, fish, meat, vegetables, and sauces. A plate is given to each person. Rice is put in the center with other condiments placed on or around it. Take a small amount of each. When finished place the fork and spoon together with the ends pointing toward the bottom of the place on the right. Leave some food on the plate, which shows the generosity of the host. Otherwise more will be served. Food is often made more festive with carved decorations of fruits and vegetables. Fruit is usually served for dessert.

Tom Kha Kai (chicken in coconut milk)

½ kg. chicken breast	7 phrik khi nu (small Thai chili), crushed
1 can of coconut milk	½ tsp. sugar
1 cup of water	½ tsp. salt
5 sliced pieces of galangal	3 – 4 tbls. fish sauce
2 stalks of lemongrass	1 tsp tamarind sauce
5 lobes of garlic	1 stalk of coriander
3 bulbs of red shallots, crushed	½ lb white mushroom
2 lemons	5 kaffir lime leaves

Scald the chicken breast.
Turn on the stove. In a pot, mix water and coconut milk until it blends together. Add the galangal, lemongrass, shallots, coriander root and garlic. When it boils, add kaffir lime leaves and mushrooms. Add the seasonings (sugar, salt, fish sauce, tamarind sauce) then add the scalded chicken breast. When the chicken breast is cooked, add lemons and phrik khi nu. Season according to preferences. Sprinkle coriander leaves on top before serving.
Recipe courtesy of the Royal Thai Embassy, Washington, DC

Cuisine

The four regions of Thailand (northeastern or Isan; Northern, Central and Southern) have their own cuisines, which may have been influenced by neighboring countries – Burma, Yunnan province in China, Laos, Cambodia and Malaysia. Chinese dishes came from the Teochew who introduced the wok and stir-frying. The Royal Thai cuisine dates back to the Ayutthava kingdom (1351-1767). In the south curries contain coconut milk and turmeric. In the northeast the dishes use lime juice, mint, and spicy minced meat. In the north are foothills of the Himalaya Mountains, a plateau in the northeast, a river basin in the center, and rain forests and islands in the south. Northern dishes include sticky rice, fried frog legs, and sausage with garlic. Along the Gulf of Thailand and the Indian Ocean there is an abundance of seafood.

Thailand still has many hill tribes, each with its own customs, dress, languages, and religious beliefs. Nan Province is the most undeveloped, but grows sticky rice, beans, corn, tobacco, vegetables, very dark colored oranges, and other fruit, and hot chilies. Central Thailand is the bread basket region growing most of the country's rice. Sugar cane, cassava, and pineapples are also harvested. The Mae Salong province in the north was settled by Yunnan Chinese in the 1960s. They have been encouraged to raise tea, coffee, corn, fruit, and producing fruit wines and liquors, corn whisky, and herbal liquors. Some of their favorite dishes use goose, duck, spring rolls, fresh water prawns, squash, soy milk, and sticky rice. Si Chiangmai is noted for making spring roll wrappers from rice paper. The south is closer to Malaysia and more Muslim. Tin, rubber, coconuts, cacao, pineapples, fish, cashews are produced. Trang has been a trading center since the 1st c.

Meals include rice (khao) and side dishes and sauces (nam chim) and condiments that are served at the same time to be shared by all. Sticky rice (khao niao) is used for eating by shaping it into a ball to dip into side dishes in northern and northeastern Thailand near the Lao border. Jasmine rice is indigenous to Thailand and grown in the central plains. Noodles are also served, made from rice, wheat, or mung bean flour. Rice and tapioca flour are used for desserts and as thickeners.

From the Chinese the Thais learned the blending of the five flavors – salty, sweet, sour, bitter, and hot. The food is a blend of these with amazing colors, tastes, texture, and temperature.

The food uses fresh herbs such as cilantro, lemon grass, basil, mint; five spice powder, curry powder, ginger, garlic, tamarind, turmeric; soy beans, shallots, dried peppercorns, kaffir lime, chilies, banana leaves, and nam pla, fish that has been fermented with salt to make a sauce. Pla ra is also a fermented fish sauce, but is clear in color. Nam phrik are pastes with chilies. Most Nam phrik and nam kaeng (curry) contain crushed chilies, garlic, and shrimp paste. Nam phrik is mainly served with vegetables. There are five main types of chilies used in cooking – phrik khi nu suan (the hottest), phrik khi nu, phrik chi fa (red or green), phrik yuak, and phrik haeng (dried chilies). Eggplant, khana, cabbage, yardlong beans, bean sprouts, bamboo shoots, tomatoes, cucumbers, sweet potatoes, squash, corn, mushrooms are frequently used vegetables. . Fruit is usually served after a meal and includes rambutan, langsat, longan, lychees, papaya, jackfruit, mango, mangosteen, pomelo, pineapples, rose apples, and durian. Tamarind is used for a tart flavor, date and coconut palm for sweetness.

Thai Specialties

Kaeng – curries and soups
Phad – stir-fried
Phed – very hot
Nam pla – fermented fish sauce
Mee krob – fried noodles with shrimp sauce
Prik kee nu - green chilies
Chok – rice porridge eaten for breakfast
Kuai tiao – rice noodles
Khanom chin – noodles made from fermented rice
Khanom chin nam ngiao – noodles with a fish sauce and vegetables
Khao phat- stir-fried rice with chicken, beef, shrimp, crab or vegetables
Khao khluk kapi – stir-fried rice with shrimp paste, pork and vegetables
Khao phat naem – fried rice with fermented sausage
Kuai-tiao nam – rice noodle soup
Khao man kai – rice with chicken and garlic
Chuchi pla – fish in red curry
Khao rat kaeng – curries or stir-fries served over rice as one dish

Kaeng khiao wan (green curry and very spicy) – coconut curry with fresh chilies, basil, chicken or fish
Phak bung fai daeng – stir-fried morning glories and yellow bean paste
Kaeng phanaeng – coconut curry with beef
Kaeng chud woon sen – noodle and vegetable soup
Kaeng tom yam kung – shrimp and lemon soup
Kaeng lueang – yellow curry with fish and vegetables
Kaeng phat (spicy or red curry) – coconut curry with dried red chilies
Kapi – shrimp paste
Phrik kaeng – curry pastes
Nam phrik num – green chili, shallot, garlic and coriander paste
Nam phrik phao – sweet roasted chili paste used in fried meat or seafood dishes
Nam phrik kung – made from dried prawns
Si-io dam – dark soy sauce; si-io khao – light soy sauce
Namman hoi – oyster sauce
Thot man pla krai with fried basil

Yam – sour salad
Kao yam – rice salad
Som tam – papaya salad
Tang kwah ah jad – cucumber condiment
Lap – salad with meat, onions, chilies, roasted rice powder and mint

Khanom bua loi – taro root and flour balls in coconut milk
Khanom mo kaeng – coconut milk, egg, palm sugar and flour pudding sprinkled with fried onions
Khao niao mamuang – sticky rice with coconut milk and mango

Holidays and Special Occasions

Babies – One month after the birth of a child the baby's head is shaved, except for a small amount of hair. An offering of food is made to the guardian spirits.

Weddings – astrology is used to set the date and hour for the wedding. There are elaborate rituals before and during the ceremony. The morning of the wedding the bride and groom give monks gifts and food in return for the blessing of their new home. Much feasting and drinking is done at the time of the wedding.

Songkran (mid-April) is the beginning on the Buddhist New Year. Water is sprinkled on the Buddha and other people. Birds and fish are released. Food is offered to the monks. Families visit and there much eating and dancing. Gifts are given to elders, and water poured on their palms.

Ginger Drink

3 ripe gingers
4½ liters of water

½ tsp. salt
1 tsp. sugar

Peel off the outer skin of the ginger, clean it thoroughly then smash it until it splits. Boil the gingers in the water. When the water turns brown, add salt and sugar, stirring until it dissolves. May add more sugar if sweetness is preferred.
Recipe courtesy of the Royal Thai Embassy, Washington, DC

Beverages

Thailand produces beer "bia" with Singha the largest brewery and Chang, and many local producers. Singha is made from Thai barley and German hops. Rice whisky is produced and is 35% alcohol. Rum is made from sugar cane and is 40% alcohol. Lao Khao "white liquor" is made from sticky rice and is 35% alcohol. Satho is a rice wine from the Isan region. Oliang is a popular drink, iced coffee with sugar! Cha yen is iced tea.

Did You Know?

Chilies were known for years to lower blood pressure.
Tumnak Thai Restaurant in Bangkok made the Guinness Book of World Records for being the largest restaurant in the world, seating over three thousand.
Red Bull got its origin from Krating Daeng, an energy drink.

Tibet

Tibet is a region on the Tibetan Plateau in Asia and the highest region on Earth! Humans inhabited the Tibetan Plateau at least 21,000 years ago. This population was largely replaced by Neolithic immigrants from northern China. The Tibetan empire was formed in the 7th c, and then divided into territories, sometimes under Chinese or Mongolian control. In the 8th c the Tibetan Empire ruled a territory stretching from modern day Afghanistan, Bangladesh, Bhutan, Burma, China, India, Nepal, Pakistan, Kazakhstan, Kyrgyzstan, Tajikistan. Qing dynasty rule in Tibet began with their 1720 expedition to the country when they expelled the invading Dzungars. Amdo came under Qing control in 1724, and eastern Kham was incorporated into neighboring Chinese provinces in 1728. The current borders of Tibet were generally established in the 18th century. The region subsequently declared its independence in 1913. Later Lhasa took control of the western part of Xikang, China. The region maintained its autonomy until 1951 when, following the Battle of Chamdo, Tibet became incorporated into the People's Republic of China, and the previous Tibetan government was abolished in 1959 after a failed uprising. Today, China governs western and central Tibet as the Tibet Autonomous Region while the eastern areas are now mostly ethnic autonomous prefectures within Sichuan, Qinghai and other neighboring provinces. Lhasa is the administrative capital. Buddhism is the main religion.

Dining Etiquette

The Tibetans are known for their warmth, hospitality and the personification of Tibetan Buddhism and believe in Karma. When a guest arrives he will receive a Khata, a white silk scarf, symbolizing the joy of having a guest. The guest will be asked if he/she would like tea, and he politely declines "Lamee" "No thanks". However the hostess will pour tea and presents it to the guest with both hands. Just take a small amount of tea. The hostess will pour more in. She will repeat this two more times. You do not have to finish the tea. After this Chang (barley beer) may be offered. Meals are served at a table where everyone sits cross-legged. Food is eaten with bamboo chopsticks using small bowls.

Cuisine

Tibetan cuisine has been influenced by what could be grown in this mountainous country that does have a plateau, but also neighboring Nepal and India. Noodles, goat, yak, mutton, dumplings, cheese, butter, and yogurt (often from yak or goat milk), and soups, grains –barley, wheat, buckwheat; and rye; potatoes, rice, vegetables and some fruit – mangoes, durian, pineapple, oranges, bananas, and lemons are part of the diet. Flour is milled from roasted barley and made into the staple food "tsampa". Meat is often dried or cooked in a stew with potatoes and spices. Mustard seeds are cultivated in Tibet. Sheep, camels, cattle, dzo, goats, yaks, and horses are raised.

The meat is either dried or made into spicy stews with potatoes. Barley has been grown here since the 5th c.

The monasteries are very important. The monks do their own cooking and raise money for their maintenance by praying for the people. Cooking in the kitchen is done in very large pots. The monks study, pray and are feed soup and tea.

Bulug (New Year Pastry)

"Please be very careful when cooking khapse. The hot oil is extremely dangerous and you don't want to splash it on you. Make sure any utensils you put into the oil are free of water, as the water will pop in the hot oil". Lhasa folk say *kar sum, ngar sum* in reference to the bulug batter, meaning "three milk, three sugar". Bulug is a type of khapse often cooked for Losar, the Tibetan New Year.

2 cups all-purpose flour	2 cups milk
¼ cup sugar dissolved in 1 cup of warm water (more sugar if you like sweeter pastries).	1 quart of sunflower oil for deep frying.

Combine the flour, sugar, and milk in a bowl. Stir the batter in a single direction for about 20 minutes with long handled wooden spoon or chopstick. The consistency of the mixture should be like pancake batter, with no big lumps.

Pour the oil into a large deep pan. Better to do this outside on a campfire than inside. Heat the oil until it smokes a bit.

Pour your batter into a pastry bag.

When the oil is ready, squeeze a steady stream of bather into the oil, working to make first the outline of a large circle and then to fill into the circle. Keep in a circular shape. Once you have a fairly stable circle shape, you will squiggle on more batter to more or less fill the circle with dough. Cook the bulug on high heat for a few minutes, until golden brown. After a minute or two, turn it over very gently, with a long-handled utensil. Turn it only once or twice.

Remove the bulug from the oil with a slotted spoon or large straining utensil, letting the oil drain over the pan. We place the bulug on paper towels to absorb as much as possible of the oil.

It's common to sprinkle some powdered sugar on the bulug after they have cooled a bit, but usually we eat them just as they are, with sweet tea or Tibetan tea.

Most Tibetans arrange the bulug as part of their stacks of khapse on their Losar shrine. If you have extra, store them in an airtight container and you can keep them quite a while, though they do of course get hard over time.

During Losar we often eat khapse in a dish called *changkol or koenden*, which is khapse together with chang and a few other ingredients. Broken up pieces of bulug are very tasty in the *changkol.*
Recipe and comments courtesy of Lobsang Wangdu and Yolanda O'Bannon of Yowangdu Tibetan Culture at https://www.yowangdu.com

Tibetan Specialties

Momo – steamed dumplings
Chura loenpa – cottage cheese from buttermilk
Chura kampo – hard cheese
Chhurpi – hard cheese made from yogurt
Sha phaley – meat and cabbage in bread which is fried
Shab tra – meat with vegetables and green chilis
Balep – bread eaten at breakfast
Thukpa – vegetables, meat and noodles in broth
De-thuk – yak or sheep soup with rice, cheese and droma
Sepen –Tibetan hot sauce

Balep korkun - flatbread cooked in a skillet
Tingmo – steamed buns
Thenthuk – soup with noodles and vegetables
Gyurma – sausage made from yak or sheep blood and roasted barley flour
Sokham bexe – fried dough with butter and meat
Tu – pastry with yak butter, brown sugar, and water
Papza mogu – dough with butter, brown sugar, and curd cheese
Samkham papleg – fried dough with yak butter

Holidays and Special Occasions

Losar – the Tibetan New Year - Dre-si – rice sweet cooked in butter with raisins, dorma, dates and nuts; Khapse – deep fried biscuits made into different shapes; and Guthuk – barley noodle soup. Losar is celebrated with offerings at family shrines and painted doors with religious symbols.
Monlam Prayer Festival – dancing, sports, and picnics which dates back to 1049 founded by Tsong Khapa, founder of the Dalai Lama.

Beverages

Yak Butter tea is drunk daily. Other tea are jasmine, black, and spice. Teacups are carried in the folds of the chuba, the traditional dress. Teacups can be made of different woods and the dzabija is the most treasured. White jade is also used. Sometimes the teacups are lined in silver. The teacups do not have handles. Teapots are made from clay, wood, brass, copper or other metals. Butter tea is made in a dongmo, tea mixing cylinder made of wood with brass. Brick tea is made by boiling water, adding the tea, and later salt. Sugar is not used. Dara is butter milk.

Alcoholic beverages are produced in Tibet and include beer – made from barley, mais, rice, wheat, oats, and millet; chang – barley beer; pijobo – rice wine; and ara – fermented grain alcohol.

Democratic Republic of Timor Leste

Timor Leste is a country in Southeast Asia comprised of the eastern half of the island of Timor; the nearby islands of Atauro and Jaco; and Oecusse, an exclave on the northwestern side of the island surrounded by Indonesian West Timor. Humans first settled in East Timor 42,000 years ago. Timor was part of the Chinese and Indian trading networks, and in the 14th century was an exporter of sandalwood, slaves, honey, and wax. The Portuguese established outposts in Timor and Maluku In 1769 the city of Dili was founded and the colony of Portuguese Timor declared. A border between the Dutch-colonized western half of the island and the Portuguese-colonized eastern half of the island was established by the Permanent Court of Arbitration of 1914, and it remains the international boundary between the successor states East Timor and Indonesia. During World War II, the Japanese occupied Dili until Portuguese control was reinstated at the end of the War. Indonesia declared East Timor its 27th province in 1976. In 2002 East Timor became independent and was named Timor-Leste.

Dining Etiquette

Please be punctual when invited for a meal. Being invited to a home is a privilege. Please check on entering to see if shoes should be left at the door. Please greet everyone with elders first. Please bring something from your country, flowers or a cake to be served later. The small bowl of water on the table is to wash your hands before eating. Food may be served family style. Please accept all food that is served. The host will begin first. Knives are not usually on a table, and the Timorese use forks and spoons with the spoon in the right hand and the fork used to push food. Use only your right hand to eat or pass something. When finished leave a little food on your plate. Place your fork and spoon downward on the plate with the spoon crossed over the fork. You may be offered a beverage after the meal as drinks are not served before or during the meal. If offered a drink accept with both hands.

Cuisine and Beverages

The cuisine has been influenced by Southeast Asian, Indian, Chinese and Portuguese cooking. The Chinese introduced soy sauce, the Indians spices and curries, and the Spanish chorizo, corn, potatoes, peppers, and peppers. The Portuguese brought breads, pastries, cheese and dairy products. Among the ingredients are pork, chickens, goat, duck, boar, water buffalo, basil, tropical fruits - bananas, oranges, breadfruit, mango, melons; sugar, tamarind, rice, root vegetables – sweet potatoes and carrots, cassava, taro and sago; vegetables – corn, cowpeas, onions, spinach, cabbage; grains – wheat; garlic and shallots, akar – dried palm bark beaten into a powder and mixed with water to form a jelly and cooked. Fish are in abundance and include prawns, mackerel, tuna, red snapper, anchovy, and crab. Fish is usually fried. Rice is grown on the islands.

Coffee is a major crop for the islands and is exported. During the Portuguese colonization coffee plantations flourished, but during the Indonesian times many of these were abandoned. However today they have been revitalized and employ many people on the islands. Fruit juices and coconut milk are produced on the island.

Batar da'an (Pumpkin, Corn and Mung Beans)

Batar Daan means "boiled corn.

Serves 4-6

8 ears corn, shucked	1 large onion, chopped
½ lb. dried mung beans	4 cloves garlic, minced
2 lb. squash or pumpkin	2 tbls. olive oil
4 cups water	Salt and pepper

Soak the mung beans overnight in water. Drain. In a large pot of water boil the beans for 10 -15 minutes. Drain.
Heat the olive oil in a large skillet and sauté the onions until just tender. Add the garlic, water, squash, beans and corn. Bring to a boil. Reduce heat and cook until the squash is tender. Add salt and pepper to taste.

Specialties

Ikan sabuko – mackerel in tamarind sauce with basil and capiscum
Katupa – rice with coconut milk
Tapai – fermented alcoholic rice
Caril – chicken curry with roasted capsicum and coconut paste
Feijoada – pork, bean and chorizo dish

Mee goring and nasi goring – dish with fried noodles or rice with vegetables
Pastel de nata - egg tart
Budu – tomato, mint, lime and onion sauce
Bibinka – grilled coconut cake
Pudim de coco – coconut pudding

Holidays and Special Occasions

East Timor has been mainly a Catholic country since the 15th c and those holidays are observed.
Carnival de Timor – parades and bands
From Ash Wednesday and during Lent fasting occurs. Holy Thursday and Good Friday are observed as holy day. On Easter families celebrate the Risen Lord.
Independence Day - May 20th – sporting competitions, parades, mass at churches
All Saints' Day and All Souls' Day – religious services, visiting cemeteries
Santa Cruz Cemetery Massacre Anniversary – November 12 – to remember those killed by the Indonesian military in 1991
Christmas is a time for forgiveness, new clothes, cleaning of home. On Christmas Eve and Christmas Day families attend Mass. They cook many different foods which will probably include meat, rice with coconut, fish cooked in leaves in a pit, and cakes.

Togo

Togo, the Togolese Republic, is a country in West Africa bordered by Ghana to the west, Benin to the east and Burkina Faso to the north. It extends south to the Gulf of Guinea, where its capital Lomé is located. The name Togo comes from the language meaning "land where lagoons lie". Archeological digs show that ancient tribes produced pottery and used iron tools. From the 11th to the 16th century, various tribes entered the region. From the 16th century to the 18th century, the coastal region was a major slave trading center for Europeans, earning Togo and the surrounding region the name "The Slave Coast". In 1884, Germany declared Togoland a protectorate. In 1916 Togo was divided into British and French zones. After World War I, rule over Togo was transferred to France. Togo gained its independence from France in 1960.

Dining Etiquette

When invited for a meal please arrive promptly. It is a privilege to be invited to a home. Please bring a gift from your country. Men will shake hands, and shake hands with a woman if she offers her hands. Water is served on arrival. Women take great pride in preparing the meals. Food is offered to guests coming into a home. Food is eaten with the right hand, unless flatware is on the table. Fufu is served with different sauces and meats. Food will probably be served communally with a large platter or bowl on the table. Take some of the fufu in your right hand, roll it into a ball, and use it for eating. A small burp at the end of the meal shows your appreciation for it. Elders are treated with respect. Interpersonal relationships are important.

Cuisine

The Togolese cuisine has been influenced by West African, French and German foods. Bread baguettes were introduced by the French. Cassava, maize, manioc, rice, millet, yams, spinach, eggplant, groundnuts (peanuts), plantains, beans, hot chili peppers, okra, mango, pineapple, palm oil and peanut paste, fish, beef, chicken, and goat are part of the Togolese diet. Bush meat helps provide protein. The cuisine makes us of sauces and pates made of eggplant, tomato, spinach and fish. After Togo became a German colony in 1905 coffee, cocoa, and cotton became major crops produced using modern technology for harvest taught by the Germans. There are 37 different ethnic tribal groups which influence the food, culture and holidays.

"Do not roast all your corn in the winter", an ancient Togolese proverb

Groundnut Stew

Serves 4-6

¼ cup peanut oil
3 lb. chicken, cut into pieces
1 large onion, chopped
3 cloves garlic, crushed
1 chili pepper, seeded and chopped
2 tbls. fresh ginger

3 cups chicken stock
3 large tomatoes
½ lb. okra
2 large sweet potatoes, peeled and cubed
Salt and pepper to taste
1 cup peanut butter

Heat the peanut oil in a large pot. Saute the onions until just translucent. Add the garlic, chili, ginger, and chicken. Cook until chicken is just browned.
Add the chicken stock and sweet potatoes. Bring to a boil. Reduce heat and cook for 15 minutes, or until potatoes are tender. Stir in the okra, tomatoes, and peanut butter. Cook another 20 minutes, stirring occasionally.
Serve with fufu, rice or flatbread.

Specialties

Akume – ground maize dish served with different sauces
Ayimolu – haricots with rice
Fufu – peeled and boiled yams that pounded into a doughlike consistency. This is served with sauces
Palm nut soup
Okra soup
Pepper soup
Ablo – maize bread served with soups, stews, vegetable and meat
Agouti "grasscutters" – bush rat
Koklo meme – grilled chicken with chili sauce

Colico – roasted potatoes
Kokonte – cassava pate
Pate – cornmeal cake
Dokume – fermented pate
Dienkoume – tomato and cornmeal cakes
Ghomo desi – beef and spinach stew
Ghotemi spice – spice blend
Akpono – sweet bread eaten at breakfast
Atsieke – coarse cassava powder mixed with water and served with fried fish and hot pepper sauce
Jolloff rice – rice with chicken or meat and vegetables

Holidays and Special Occasions

Gadao – celebrated in March in Sokode. The first day is used to thank ancestors for the harvest.
Gbagba – in August to celebrate the harvest, and rest
Voodoo Festival – held in Glidji village where a stone predicts what will happen in the coming year – blue –good harvests; red – war; black – famine and floods; white – good luck

Beverages

Palm and bamboo wines are produced here, mainly at home.

Tonga

The Kingdom of Tonga, is an archipelago comprising 169 islands of which 36 are inhabited in the southern Pacific Ocean. Most people reside on the main island of Tongatapu. An Austronesian-speaking group known as the Lapita cultural complex reached and inhabited Tonga around 1500–1000 BC. The first settlers came to the oldest town, Nukuleka, about 826 BC. By the 12th century Tu'i Tonga Empire was thought to exist. Dutch explorers began arriving in 1616, followed by English missionaries in the 18th c. In 1845 Tāufa'āhau united Tonga into a kingdom and in 1875 declared Tonga a constitutional monarchy. Tonga became a protected state under a Treaty of Friendship with Britain in 1900 with this status ending in 1970, and is now self-governing. Tonga means "south". The capital is Nuku'alofa. Tongan and English are the official languages.

Dining Etiquette

Please be prompt when invited for a meal. Shake hands greeting and departing. Please bring a gift from your country. Never bring food for a meal as it means the host has not provided enough food. The host will seat you with guests at the middle of the table. The may be utensils, although some Tongans eat with their hands. Do try all dishes offered. Do not take seconds. The guest of honor starts eating first, and the others follow. When finished the other guests will also stop eating. If there is leftover food you may be offered to take some home, or to finish what is on your plate. The man is considered head of the household. Women cover their knees and elbows. Men wear pants or Tupenu (cloth wrap skirt). Men also do not show their knees. Eyebrows rather than conversation. There is a great respect for religion and for royalty. On Sundays you cannot swim, play loud music, or engage in business.

Cuisine

Because most of the islands are volcanic and very fertile, better for growing crops, or coral reefs where there are few native plants or animals. Coconuts are used for their flesh and milk, and is the staple in the diet. Fish include crab, octopus, turtles, tuna, shark, lobster, clams, sea snail, mussels, seaweed, sea urchins, and many other kinds. Local birds are terns and noddies. As people populated the islands they brought with them pigs, rats, and dogs; taro, rice, sugar cane, yams, ulu (breadfruit), lemons, and bananas probably before the 13th c. Throughout Polynesia there are many similarities in cooking and ingredients used. One of these is cooking with wood and hot rocks placed in an umu (underground oven) and the food wrapped in banana or other leaves, covered in dirt and steamed. Though the Dutch arrived in the 1600s they did not seem to influence the cuisine. However the British introduced cattle, chickens, wheat, potatoes, cassava, watermelons, tomatoes, pineapples, papayas, oranges, mangoes, and onions. Copra, grapefruit, mandarin, guava, passion fruit, Indian apples, yucca, pele (spinach), squash, pumpkin, and avocado are also grown on the islands. Later with the introduction of canned goods, tuna and corned beef were introduced. Fish is eaten raw or cooked in coconut milk. 'Ota ika - raw fish or seafood marinated in citrus juice and coconut milk is served with uncooked vegetables Today taro root, yams, and coconuts are prevalent in many of the dishes. Taro root is prepared as poi, using it boiled or steamed, and mashed.

Breakfast is a small meal, followed by a large lunch in some places so that the people could rest during the heat of the day. Dinner is the main meal, and food may be prepared so there is enough food for breakfast or lunch the next day.

Lū Pulu (corned beef and coconut milk wrapped in taro leaves)

Serves 4

12 taro leaves	1 large tomato, chopped
1 can corned beef	1 large banana leaf
1 cup coconut milk	Salt and pepper
1 medium onion, chopped	Tin foil

Preheat oven to 350°.
Spread out the taro leaves on a large piece of tin foil. Place the corned beef, coconut milk, onion, tomato and some salt and pepper in the center. Wrap into a bundle and seal with the banana leaf. Seal inside the tin foil. Bake at least 1-2 hours until meat is very tender.
Serve warm.
Spinach leaves can be substituted for the taro leaves.

Holidays and Special Occasions

For special ceremonies, weddings and funerals spit-roasted pigs, lu, topai served with syrup and coconut milk, ota ika, fish, chicken, sheep ribs cooked in taro leaves with coconut milk, octopus, clams in coconut milk, lobster, salads, yams and fruit are served. Feasts can include thirty or more dishes and are served on a pola, a large tray made from plaited coconut fronds. Funerals always have a huge amount of food present. The Heilala festival has singing, dancing, and feasting.

Beverages

Kava is a drink produced from the roots of Piper methysticum. Kava comes from the Polynesian word "awa" which means "bitter". Kava is made from ground kava roots which have liquid to which water is added In Tonga only men are allowed to drink kava. In some places kava is taken to reduce anxiety, stress, and sleeping problems. In a social setting it is served in rounds, first stirred in the kumete, poured into ipu (coconut cups), and then passed around hand to hand. When the cups are empty they are passed around hand to hand. The men are seated cross-legged. They will talk, sing, and then the next round begins! Kava may be drunk every night, or on some islands Wednesday and Satuday nights. Kava is drunk at weddings, funerals, and when the new king takes the throne. Kava is served by a tou's, young unmarried female. 'Otai is made from ambarella or fekika juice and coconut, and then chilled. Beer is imported but also brewed locally known as hopi. Other popular beverages are fruit drinks.

Trinidad and Tobago

Trinidad and Tobago is an archipelago in the southern Caribbean, lying just off the coast of northeastern Venezuela, and south of Grenada in the Lesser Antilles. Trinidad and Tobago were settled by Amerindians – Arawak and Carib from South America. Trinidad is believed to have had one of the oldest settlements dating back over 7000 years. Christopher Columbus discovered the island in 1498. Antonio de Sedeno was the first Spaniard to settle here in the 1530's. During the 1700s Trinidad was part of the Viceroyalty of New Spain. In 1797 Trinidad became a British colony. Cacao became a leading crop. The Dutch and Courlanders settled Tobago in the 16 and 17th c, raising cotton and tobacco. The colony of Trinidad and Tobago occurred in 1889. They received their independence in 1962, and in 1976 became a republic within the British Commonwealth. The capital, Port of Spain, is located on Trinidad. English is the official language.

Dining Etiquette

Please be prompt when invited for a meal. Bring a gift of wine, or something for the home. Shake hands greeting and departing. Beverages will be served. The hostess will seat you at the table with the male guest of honor to her right. Meals may be served or buffet style. Please eat continental style with your fork in the left hand and knife in the right. When finished place your knife and fork together. The toast is "Cheers".

Cuisine and Beverages

The cuisine is a blend of Indian, Amerindian, European – Spanish, French, British, African, Creole, Chinese and Lebanese. Curries were brought by Indian laborers in the 19th c. Callaloo came from Africa and is made with dasheen leaves, okra, crab, thyme, coconut milk, and cilantro. Pelau is also an Indian dish made with rice. The dishes are often made with coconut milk, and are stews, curries, or barbecued, and one-pot dishes. Soups include oxtail, beef, cowheel, and seafood. Wild animals on the islands are hunted, and include agouti, iguana, opossum, wild hogs, and armadillo. A variety of fish is available – flying fish, king fish, carite, sapatay, red fish, bonito, lobster, conch, crab, tilapia, and cascadura. Hot pepper sauces are made from bird peppers, habaneros, or Scotch Bonnets.

Drinks are made from sorrel, ginger (beer), various fruits, soursop and coconut, such as coconut water. Mauby, made from the bark of the mauby tree and spices, is served cold. Carib and Stag Beers are produced locally. Rum is produced from local sugar cane. There is a story that is 1943 Britain traded 22 U.S. warships for naval bases in the Caribbean. One of these was located on Trinidad. Supposedly the troops stationed here mixed Coca Cola with the good local rum, and Rum and Coke was born. However, Bacardi claims to have made the first one, and not on Trinidad! But it may also have been during the Spanish-American War in 1898! Rum is used in mixed drinks, with fruit and punches. Puncheon Rum is a stronger type of Rum (not less than 75% alcohol)!

Callaloo (Crab and Greens Soup)

Serves 6

½ lb. callaloo greens
3 tbls. butter
1 onion, peeled and finely chopped
2 cloves garlic, minced
3 cups chicken stock

½ cup coconut milk
1 tsp. salt
Fresh ground pepper
½ lb. crab meat
Dash of Tabasco Sauce

Wash the greens and tear into small pieces.
In a skillet melt the butter. Add the onions until transparent. Stir in garlic. Add greens until limp.
Stir in stock, coconut milk, salt and ground pepper. Bring to a boil. Reduce heat and simmer for 10 minutes.
Add crab and Tabasco, just to heat crab.

Trinidad and Tobago Specialties

Curried chicken, crab, shrimp and duck
Souse - pig trotters or chicken feet with lime, pepper, cucumber and onion
Pepper pot – chicken and pork stew
Sancocho – beef and vegetable stew
Dasheen pork – spicy dasheen and pork dish
Jerk meats
Bake and shark – deep fried shark in a fried dough
Chip-chip – shellfish, usually curried
Cascadura – freshwater fish, usually curried
Fruit chows – fruit mixed with lime juice, herbs and pepper
Aloo – fried potato pies
Chokas – roasted vegetables
Roti - flatbread stuffed with chickpea curry, meat, or vegetables

Buss up shut – roti torn into small pieces and eaten with curried goat, shrimp, sauces, or vegetables
Macaroni pie
Guava cheese
Ox-tails
Sada – similar to pita
Dalpuri - bread made with yellow lentils
Aloopourie – potato bread
Phoulourie –fried split pea balls with chutney
Doubles – a breakfast food made of flour and split pea patties with chickpeas and relish
Bakes – fried biscuits
Barfi – coconut and condensed milk sweet
Goolab jamoom - milk balls in syrup
Cassava pone
Tamarind or bene balls

Holidays

Good Friday – fish served
Easter – hams, baked pork, chicken, hot cross buns
Goat racing in Tobago on Easter Tuesday is a tradition dating back to 1925.
Christmas – pastelles, garlic pork, curried goat, ham, turkey, pigeon peas; cakes with fruit and soaked in rum; black cake, rum; breads; ginger beer; eggnog with rum; ginger beer, poncho crema (cream punch), sorrel (drink made from sorrel flowers)
Divali - barfi and prasad (pudding with raisins, nuts, and coconut); vegetarian meal
Eid ul-Fitr – sawain (vermicelli)

Tunisia

Tunisia, located in northern Africa, is bordered by Algeria to the west, Libya to the southeast, and the Mediterranean Sea to the north and east. Tunisia was settled by the Berbers and later by Phoenicians in the 10th c BC. Carthage was founded in the 9th c BC by people from Tyre, now part of Lebanon. Carthage invaded Rome, but became part of the Roman Empire in the 2nd c BC, was known as the "bread basket" of the Empire. Later, Tunisia was occupied by Vandals during the 5th century AD, Byzantines in the 6th century, and Arabs in the 8th century. Under the Ottoman Empire Tunisia was known as "Regency of Tunis". In 1881 it became a French protectorate. Tunisia became an independent country in 1956 "Kingdom of Tunisia. Tunis, the capital, dates back to the Berbers. Arabic is the official language

Dining Etiquette

Please be prompt when invited for a Tunisian meal. Men should wear a business suit, women should cover their shoulders and knees. Please bring a small present – pastries, a cake, candies, nuts, fruit, or something for the home. Remove your shoes before entering a home. Men shake hands with men. Only shake hands with a lady if she offers her hand. The meal is usually served at a round table, but in more modern homes a dining room table is used. Male and female guests may be fed in separate rooms. The guest of honor will be seated to the right of the host. Before a meal a basin will be used to wash one's hands. The host will bless the food before eating. Food is served from a communal bowl. Please chose food from this side, not reaching for other morsels. Food is eaten with the right hand, while the left hand is left in the lap. A spoon is used for eating couscous. Please finish everything. The basin will be passed at the end of the meal to wash your hands.

Meals are to be enjoyed and may last for quite a while. They may begin with a lamb soup, a salad, entrees with lamb, veal or fish, vegetables, followed by cheese, fruit, pastries or other desserts, coffee or tea. Pastries are given as a gift for the holidays.

Cuisine

Farming goes back thousands of years in the fertile valleys of Tunisia, though most of the south is part of the Sahara Desert. From earliest times vineyards, olives, wheat, dates, corn and fruit were cultivated. In the 1st c a tax on corn was even imposed. The cuisine is a blend of Mediterranean, coming from the different cultural groups which have inhabited Tunisia – the Phoenicians, Romans, Arabs, Turks, French and Berbers. Olive oil, spices, honey, tomatoes, seafood, lamb, tuna, eggs, olive, pastas, cereals, herbs, and fruit – oranges, figs, grapes, dates, apricots and quince. are the basic ingredients. In the Atlas Mountains one finds game; along the coast, seafood; and on the island of Djerba, kosher food. All parts of an animal are consumed. The food is spicy. Harissa, served with most meals, is a hot pepper sauce made up of red chili peppers, garlic, coriander, cumin, olive oil, perhaps tomatoes, mint or caraway. Harissa comes from the Arabic word "break into pieces". The spices most commonly used are garlic, anise, saffron, cinnamon, caraway, cumin, fennel, fenugreek, ginger, pepper, red peppers, and cloves. Common vegetables include onions, peppers, squash, carrots, tomatoes, capers, celery, turnips, potatoes, cucumbers and eggplant. Fish is baked, grilled, fried, and served with lemon. Fish include red mullet, squid, shrimp, sardines, and tuna. Couscous is the national dish. It is served in a mound topped with vegetables, then meat, a sauce, and basil, mint, or parsley. Most of the almonds are grown in Sfax.

Chakcouka (pepper and tomato dish)

Serves 4

2 tbls. olive oil
1 large onion, sliced
4 cloves garlic, minced
1 red pepper, sliced
1 green pepper, sliced
1 yellow pepper, sliced

4 tomatoes, chopped
¼ cup parsley, chopped
1 tbls. lemon juice
4 eggs
Fresh ground pepper

Preheat the oven to 350°
Heat 2 tbls oil in a skillet. Stir in the onion until transparent, about 5 minutes. Stir in the garlic. Add the peppers and cook until peppers are softened, about 10 minutes. Add the chopped tomatoes, 2 tbls. parsley and lemon juice.
Divide the mixture into four ovenproof dishes. Make a well in each dish and break egg into each one. Sprinkle with a little pepper.
Bake for 15 minutes or until the egg has set.
Garnish with remaining parsley.

Tunisian Specialties

Shorba frik is a lamb soup with tomato paste, coriander, parsley, wheat grains and seasonings
Mechouia – salad with grilled peppers, tomatoes and onions
Tajine – made with eggs, grated cheese, meat and vegetable filling
Tabil – mix of garlic, cayenne pepper, caraway seeds, and coriander which is pounded and allowed to dry
Brik – fried dough with tuna and egg
Koucha – young lamb baked in a slow oven
Shorba – soups
Slata – salad
Bouza – sorghum puree

Brik – egg wrapped in pastry and deep fried
Chakcouka – chickpeas, tomatoes, peppers, garlic and onions served with an egg
Chorba – broth served with pasta, meat
Marqa – stews
Guenaola – lamb or beef stew
Mechoul – lamb chops grilled on a spit over an open fire
Merguez – small spicy sausages made of mutton or beef
Mirmiz – mutton stewed with beans and tomatoes
Mosli – stew
Objabilmergais – hard spiced sausages in potato soup with tomato puree and garlic

Mloukhla – beef or lamb stew with bay leaves

Zitounia – veal simmered with tomatoes, olives, and onions

Houria – cooked carrot salad

Kifka – ground meat

Gnawiya – gombos

Shakshouka - ratatouille

Samsa – pastry

Kaak – pastry

Poisson complet – whole fish fried, grilled or sauteed served with chips, tomato and onion, an egg, and parsley

Kerkennaise – caper, olive oil, tomato, scallion, coriander, cumin, parsley, garlic, vinegar and paprika sauce

Masfouf is a sweet couscous

Mloukhia – green sauce served with lamb or beef

Baklawa – pastry with ground pine nuts, almonds, hazelnuts, pistachios, butter and honey

Bambaloni – fried sweet with sugar

Makroudh – semolina pastry stuffed with dates and soaked in honey

Mhalbiya – rice, nut and geranium water cake

Samsa – pastry with ground almonds, sesame seeds baked in lemon and rose water syrup

Yo-yo - deep fried donuts with orange juice and dipped in honey

Khobz tabouna – bread

Holidays and Special Occasions

Mouled – zgougou, a pudding made with ground pine nuts with vanilla cream is served; acida – boiled semolina with oil and honey

Aid El Fitr – families visit. Baklawa, makroudh and other pastries are served

Aid El Kebir – lamb dishes

Ras El Am - mloukhia

Christenings, weddings, holidays – many sweets

Beverages

Tunisia produces grapes, wheat, barley and fruit for wines and beers. Scented waters are made from rose and geranium petals. Wine has been produced at least from the time of the Phoenicians, grown now on over 25,000 hectares. The wine regions include Khanguet, south of Tunis which produces red and rose wines; Grombalia-Takslsa on the Mediterranean; Kelibia on the coast producing dry Muscat wines; Sidi Thabet-Mornag near Tunis produces full-bodied reds and roses; Tebourtha; Bizerta; and Beja-Jendouba. Mint tea is served with mint leaves or pine nuts. Boukha is a fig brandy; Laghmi, a date brandy.

Did You Know?

Olive oil has played a prominent role in Tunisia since the 8th c BC. The Greek historian Herodotus described the olive groves blanketing Cyranius, now Kerkennah in the 5th c BC. Olive oil blended with rush honey, wine and herbs was made into perfume for the Romans and Carthaginians.

Date flowers are considered an aphrodisiac.

Souks in the countryside are usually only a weekly market, carrying foodstuffs, spices, crockery and cutlery, clothing and other items. Part of the market is set aside for livestock to be bought and sold.

Turkey

Turkey is bordered to the west by Bulgaria and Greece; north the Black Sea; east Georgia, Armenia, Azerbaijan, and Iran; south Iraq, Syria, and the Mediterranean Sea. The western part is known as Thrace and the east Anatolia or Asia Minor. Turkey's history dates back to c 9000 BC when the earliest peoples settled Catal Hoyuk in Anatolia. By 2000 BC Assyrian trading colonies sprang up. The Great Phrygian migration took place in 1200 BC and the Trojan War 1230-20 BC. Cyrus the Great, King Alexander of Macedonia, the Romans, the Byzantine era, the Arabs, the Persians, and the Ottoman Empire all followed. The Republic of Turkey was founded in 1923. Ankara, founded by the Hittites in the 2nd millennium BC, was made the capital by General Musafa Kemal, later Ataturk "Founder of the Turks". Istanbul had been the capital for almost 1600 years.

Dining Etiquette

Turks are bound to honor their guests "misafir" with food and drink even if they are not known to each other. Family ties are very important, and the father is always number one and in charge. There is respect "saygi" for age, wealth, position and family. To show disrespect is "ayip". Men enter through a door first.

Please arrive about fifteen minutes late when invited out. Please bring flowers – roses or carnations, candy, pastries, and the family drinks alcohol, a good wine, whiskey, or liqueur. You will be welcomed by the host who says "Hos Geldiniz" (Welcome) and "Nasilsiniz" (How are you?) and you will reply "Iyiyim tesekkur ederim" (I am very well, thank you). Do take off your shoes and put on slippers, if they are given to you. Do not show the soles of your feet.

Shake hands greeting and departing. A younger person may kiss an older person's hand or press it to the forehead. Men and women must be formally introduced before speaking to each other. People may stand close when speaking, do not back away. Eye contact is important. Please keep your hands out of your pockets and do not cross your arms while speaking. Drinks will be served. The hostess will seat the guests with the male guest of honor to her right. Please wait for the hostess to begin. When seated at the table, please eat with your right hand. Forks are held in the left hand, knife in the right. Meals are served in courses with soup (corba) or appetizers (meze), tomatoes, onions, and flatbread. This is followed by meat or fish, salad and vegetables, desserts, fruit and coffee. When asking for coffee sade is black, sekerli with sugar. When finished place your knife and fork together. A separate knife and fork are used for fish and fruit. Meals are to be enjoyed and people take their time, often chatting for hours on end. The guests always say "Good-bye" first. The toast is "Serefinize" and means "To your honor".

Breakfast (kahvalti) will include bread, feta cheese, black olives, and tea. Women often get together with friends for afternoon tea and pastries.

Hünkar Beğendi (Sultan's Delight)

Hünkar Beğendi, literally means 'the Sultan liked (or chose) it'. It is said that when Empress Eugenie, the wife of Napoleon III, was in Istanbul as the guest of the Ottoman Emperor Sultan Abdulaziz in 1869, she fell in love with the eggplant puree, which was a specialty of the Topkapi Palace. She asked her host if he would allow his chef to teach her how to cook it. The Sultan obliged. The next day, the French chef requested an audience with the Empress and begged to be excused from this impossible task. "I took my book and scales to the Turkish chef" he said, and "he threw them out". "The Imperial chef told me that he cooks with his feelings, his eyes, his nose." The Empress returned to France without the recipe for her favorite dish, but the traditional eggplant puree of the Imperial Topkapi cuisine was named "Sultan's Delight", and to this day in Turkey, it is known as Hünkar Beğendi.

Courtesy of the Turkish Embassy, Washington, DC

3 ½ cups boneless lamb, cut into 1 inch cubes	¼ cup flour
2 large onions, finely chopped	2 Tbls. butter or margarine
2 medium tomatoes, diced	2 cups milk
1 ½ tsp. salt	¾ cup shredded hard cheese
½ tsp. black pepper	1 tsp. salt
¾ cup + 1 ½ Tbls. water	¼ tsp. pepper
6 medium eggplant	¼ tsp. mace

In a sauce pan braise the lamb and onions for 40-45 minutes. Drain.

Add tomatoes. Stir. Season with salt and pepper. Simmer for 5 minutes, or until the tomatoes are tender. Add water. Stir. Cover and simmer until the meat is tender. Drain. Set aside, but keep warm.

Barbecue unpared eggplant over high heat in a covered heavy skillet. Turn around occasionally until all sides are tender (Eggplant may be broiled in hot oven or barbecued over charcoal). Remove from heat; cool. Peel outer skin and chop finely or mince. Brown flour lightly in margarine for 2-3 minutes, stirring occasionally in a saucepan. Stir in minced eggplant and milk, blending thoroughly. Add shredded cheese. Season with salt and spices, mixing well. Place saucepan in a large pan filled with hot water 2 ½ cm (1-1 ½ inch) high. Cook over low heat for 7-8 minutes stirring constantly. Remove from water bath. Spoon into ring in a serving dish. Place meat into center of ring. Serve hot.

Recipe courtesy of "Samples from Turkish Cuisine", Publication of Turkish Ministry of Culture

Cuisine

Turkey's cuisine is a mix of exotic spices, fresh fruits and vegetables, fish, chicken, and lamb. The very earliest grains were thought to have been grown by Neolithic peoples. Cows were domesticated about 6000 BC. From the 8th c AD on the Mongols, Chinese, and Persians all had their influence. *Diwan Lughai al –Turk*, an 11th c dictionary by Mahmud al-Kashghari, mentions cooking terminology and lists cheese and yogurt as staples of the diet. The word "yogurt" is from the Turks, and was a way of preserving milk by the nomads. Pilaf was from the Persians. During the 13th c the Anatolians and the Saljuks doted on their cuisine. The Ottoman Empire outdid all other periods, and more gourmet meals were consumed than any other place in the world. The Topkapi Palace had one of the largest kitchens ever built. Lists of purchases and employees still are preserved. During the 17th c the kitchen was known to employ over 1300 people and as many as 10,000 people were fed per day! Almost anyone involved in cooking or provision of ingredients was a member of a guild.

The coastal areas are low and grow major agricultural products – cotton, tea, and tobacco. Meat and fish are grilled or roasted. Seasonings include garlic, saffron, fresh sweet peppers, mint, dill, cinnamon, cloves, lemon and yogurt. Native foods are pistachios, olives, tea, fava beans, bananas, oranges, honey, pine nuts (pignoli), currants, rose jam, apricots, and paprika. Turkey produces such cheese as Tulum, Beyaz, Mihalic, and Kasar. The different regions of the country have their own distinctive styles of cooking. They are Marmara, the Aegean, the Black Sea, the Mediterranean, and Anatolia (known as the breadbasket of the world). In the eastern part of the country are snow-capped mountains where livestock are raised, butter, yogurt, cheese, honey, meat and cereals prevail. Yogurt soup and meatballs are specialties. In the center of the country is a steppe with wheat fields, and ancient trade routes came through here. Tandir (clay oven) kebabs, boreks, meat, vegetables, and helva dishes date back to the feasts given by Sultan Alaaddin Keykubad in 1237 AD. In the west are valleys, mountainsides, and the Aegean Sea with seafood. The Black Sea in the north with the Caucasian Mountains produces hazelnuts, corn, tea and a variety of fish including hamsi, similar to an anchovy. The southeast is hot with kebabs, spicy foods, and sweets as specialties. The Marmara region includes Istanbul, is very fertile, and specializes in fruit, vegetables, lamb, and fish. As a Muslim country pork is not eaten.
Muhallebici, pudding shops, offer many varieties of milk puddings.

Turkish dishes include grains (rice and wheat), grilled meats, vegetables, seafood, fruit, desserts, and beverages. In cooking herbs and spices are only used with certain dishes such as mint or dill with zucchini and parsley with eggplant. Food is sold in the weekly neighborhood markets or pazars. One of the oldest is the Spice Market in Istanbul. Vegetables are cooked in olive oil and include eggplant, peppers, zucchini, beans, artichokes, and celery root which are eaten with tomato or yogurt sauces.

Turkey is the world's largest producer (75%) of findik (hazelnuts or filbert). The tree is a member of the birch family and originally came from China. Most of the nuts are grown in northeastern Turkey, and are harvested from August through September by hand. The fruit grows in a shell inside a green husk. The nuts are dried in the sun until the husks turn brown, and the nuts are then separated from the husks. The nuts will be eaten as nuts, ground into flour, or used in pastries. The oil is used for high temperature frying and the husks for animal beds. Pistachios are also grown in Turkey, and used in baklava. Baklava was first made in the Middle Ages by Turkish nomads as a layered bread. Turkish baklava's filling is known as kaymak. Baklava was served on special occasions. Gaziantep in the southeast is one of the most famous places for making baklava, although it became well-known at the Topkapi Palace.

Turkish Specialties

Meze – small dishes to start the meal and will include melon, cheese, fish, greens, cold vegetables

Fish include bonito, mackerel, hamsi, mussels, octopus, and squid which will be grilled, fried, or poached

Babaganush - aubergine (eggplant)

Hummus – chickpea puree

Dolmas – stuffed vegetables with meat and/or rice

Borek – filled pastries with meat or cheese, and then fried or baked

Manti – meat dumplings served with garlic yogurt and melted butter with paprika

Kokorec – sweetbreads in lamb intestines cooked over a grill

Tarhana - dried yogurt

Cerkaz tavuk – chicken and walnuts

Kofte - meatballs

Cacik – yogurt dip

Plaki – white beans

Pide – flat bread

Ekmet – white bread

Simit – sesame seed rings (similar to a bagel)

Pilav(f) – rice

Baklava – pastry with honey and nuts

Keskul – almond custard

Kadin Gobegi "lady's naval" – fritters

Sutlac – rice pudding

Dilber Dudagi "lips of beauty" – pastry with syrup and nuts

Kaymac – rich cream used in desserts

Lokma – fried dough and dipped in a syrup

Helva – semolina, pine nuts, butter, sugar, milk or water to form a candy

Asure "Noah's pudding" – a dessert that uses almost 20 ingredients and may have been eaten at Arafat.

Ezme Sebze Corbasi (Cream of Vegetable Soup)

Serves 10

2 carrots, peeled and chopped
2 potatoes, peeled and chopped
2 onions, peeled and sliced
2 celery roots, chopped
3 tbls. butter

3 tbls. flour
Salt and pepper
3 liters meat stock
Croutons

Melt the butter in a pan and add the vegetables. Cook for 5 minutes. Stir in flour, salt and pepper, and stock. Cook for ½ hour.
Serve in bowls with the croutons.
Recipe courtesy of the Turkish Embassy, Washington, DC

Iman Bayildi (Iman fainted) (stuffed eggplant)

Serves 4

4 eggplant	¼ cup parsley, chopped
Salt	½ tsp. cinnamon
4 onions, peeled and thinly sliced	2 tomatoes, sliced
4 tomatoes, chopped	Salt and pepper
¼ cup olive oil	2 tbls. sugar
4 cloves garlic, finely chopped	Cilantro and parsley, chopped

Cut the stems off the eggplant and cut eggplant in half. Reserve some of the flesh. In each half make 4 incisions lengthwise. Do not cut through skin. Sprinkle salt on each half and let rest for 20 minutes. Rinse eggplant and with paper towel dry.
Heat 2 tbls. of the olive oil in a large skillet and saute eggplant until soft. Set aside and reserve oil. In another skillet heat the remaining olive oil and cook onions until translucent. Add garlic, parsley, cinnamon, tomatoes, and eggplant flesh. Saute until just tender.
Preheat oven to 350º
Place the eggplant in a greased baking dish, cut side up. Spoon the mixture into the eggplant. Top with sliced tomatoes, salt and pepper, sugar, and remaining oil. Add a little water in bottom of pan. Cook 1 hour.
Serve with cilantro and parsley.

Holidays and Special Occasions

Ramadan –For Muslims there is no eating between sunrise and sunet. Sahur is the meal before morning prayers; the Iftar, the fast; and the breaking of the fast with sucak – sausages, pastirma, dried beef, simit (sesame rings), followed by prayers
Seker Bayrami – sugar festival, during which sweets are eaten to end the fast of Ramadan
Kurban Bayrami – festival of sacrifice, when sheep are sacrificed and given to the poor
At the agreement to a marriage – sherbet, coffee, lokum (Turkish delight squares with powdered sugar
Wedding – meat, pilaf, vegetables, Tepsi boregi (spinach pie)
Wedding night – desserts are sent by the groom's family to the bride's
Circumcision of a male child – crown with golden threads on velvet is set on the child and zerde, a rice dish is served
Funeral – for three days the bereaved family is sent food on trays. There are no desserts or sweets, which are only served on festive occasions. After the funeral the women prepare helva (semolina candy) and lokum
Helva is also eaten at the birth of a child, buying a new home or business, or return from a trip or recovery from illness.

Beverages

Turkish coffee is very thick and the grounds are not to be swallowed. Tea is brewed with boiling water and served in clear glasses. Boza is a fermented drink of wheatberries and served with cinnamon and roasted chickpeas. Sahlep is served hot made with milk, sahlep powder, and served with cinnamon.

Turkey is thought to have produced wines for almost 10,000 years, the earliest known at Catal Hoyuk. Wines are mentioned in The Bible at Ararat by Noah. The Hittites made wines in Anatolia from at least 2000 BC, and had a code of laws concerning both vineyards and grapes. Ornate silver and gold chalices exist from this period. Wine is still made at Elazig. The Tigris and Euphrates River valleys also made a red wine – Buzbag. The Goreme is known as the Valley of vineyards. Wine festivals are held in September. Most wines are produced for local consumption. The national drink is raki, made from grapes and aniseed which is mixed with water or ice and drunk as an aperitif, or with a meal. Raki means "Lion's milk", the color it receives when water is added.

Beers are brewed by Efes Pilsen and Tuborg, by license. TEKEL, the state monopoly is now defunct. Turkey also produces vodka (votka), gin (cin), and cognac (konyak). Boza is made from fermented millet and drunk during the winter; Kimiz, a fermented mare's milk drunk in the spring; and Ayran, a yogurt drink. Kaymak is made from buffalo milk.

Did You Know?

Coffee was first introduced in Europe during the reign of Suleyman the Magnificent. The Arabic name "kahveh" means "queller of appetites".
Coffee houses were introduced in the 16th c, the earliest one in Istanbul in 1555.
A 1573 prohibited women from pastry shops which were thought to be trysting places!
The Egyptian Spice Bazaar in Istanbul was founded in the 17th c by Turhan Sultan, wife of Sultan Ibrahim.
During the 17th c foods were under the auspices of different guilds with prophet patronage and sponsoring parades. Today, parts of Istanbul are still divided this way, with different areas for shopping.
Altan Sekerleme in Istanbul has been selling candy since 1865, including akide (hard candy) and locum (Turkish Delights).
The dish "Hunkar Begendi", made with beef or lamb and pureed eggplant was named in honor of Empress Eugenie's visit and means "Her name was pleased".
The first printed cookbook was *Melce' ut-Tabbahaim* in 1844.
Brick ovens used to bake bread are still seen in many villages.
Turkey produces about 70% of the world's hazelnuts.
"Overturning the cauldron" comes from the Ottoman military elite known as Janissaries, who when they wanted a change in the Sultan's cabinet or the head of the grand vizier, would overturn their pilaf cauldron.
The "Spice Road" was under the control of the Turkish sultan.
Adam, after his expulsion from the Garden of Eden in The Bible, supposedly learned to make bread from the angel Gabriel, and is the Patron of Bakers.

Turkmenistan

Turkmenistan is bordered by Afghanistan to the southeast, Iran to the south and southwest, Uzbekistan to the east and northeast, Kazakhstan to the north and northwest and the Caspian Sea to the west. The region was once part of the Achaemenid Empire of ancient Persia and was divided between the satrapies of Margiana, Kharezm and Parthia. Alexander the Great conquered the area in the 4th c BC. The Parthia Kingdom made Nisa its capital in the 2nd c BC. Arabs arrived in the 7th c AD, introducing Islam, and calling the region Greater Khorasan. By the 11th c the Seljuk Empire ruled followed by Genghis Khan in the 12th c. The Turkmen people lived under various rulers until 1894 when it became part of the Russian empire. Turkmenistan gained independence in 1991. Ashgabat, the capital, is near ancient Nisa, and was built on the Silk Route city of Konjikala. The official language is Turkmen. 89% of the people are Muslim.

Dining Etiquette

When invited for a meal, please be prompt. Please remove your shoes when entering a home. The Turkmen are very hospitable. Bread and salt are served as a sign of hospitality. Guests are seated in a place of honor usually opposite the entrance to the room. Tea will be served. For dining a cloth is laid out on the floor or a carpet. Never step on or over the tablecloth. This dates back to the time when the Turkmen were mainly nomadic and set a meal wherever they happened to be. The foods they served were made with foods of the region. They raised livestock – sheep, camels, goats, so soups were prepared with meat stock; stews; rice; and dairy products. The rugged land was not conducive to growing crops. Before eating God is praised. Women and men may eat separately.

In Turkmenistan family and honor are very important, as is respect for elders. Elders are seated away from the entrance, but are served first. Men sit cross-legged, women with their legs under them or to the side. Women should not make eye contact with men. Bread is considered almost sacred and should never be turned upside down.

Cuisine

The cuisine relies on using local ingredients and spices – red and black pepper; herbs – mint, parsley, dill, azghon, buzghun, saffron and garlic. Meals include breads, soup, meat – camel, goat, sheep, cattle, or pork. Meat is boiled or fried in dough. Fish come from the Caspian Sea. Dairy products and yogurt are part of the diet. Fruit is fresh such as melons or can be dried. Common vegetables are radishes, tomatoes, pumpkins, and carrots. Soup is served with meat and noodles, and is eaten at breakfast. Bread is served at every meal. Most of the cooking is done with cottonseed oil.

Manty (Meat Dumplings)

Dough

3 cups flour	1½ cups water

In a bowl make a well in the flour and pour in the water. Combine until a ball forms. This can also be done in a food processor until a ball forms.
Roll out on a cutting board. With a large cookie cutter cut circles.
Place a small amount of filling in the center of each circle. Top each circle with 1 tsp. butter.
Fold the sides together to form like an onion with a stem. Seal with a little water.
Pour 1 inch water into a pan. Bring to a boil. Place a colander in the pan with the manty. Cover. Steam for 15 minutes.
Serve in a bowl garnished with the mint or dill and serve with a bowl of yogurt.

Filling

1½ lbs. ground lamb	Butter
1 large onion, chopped	Fresh mint, parsley, or dill
1 tsp. fresh ground pepper	Yogurt

Combine the lamb, onion, and pepper in a bowl.

Shashlik (meat or fish grilled on skewers, garnished with sliced raw onions and often served with a vinegar based sauce)

Serves 4

2 lbs. boned lamb, cubed	1 large onion, cut into small chunks
2 tbls. olive oil	1 red or green pepper, cut into pieces
2 tbls. fresh lemon juice	2 tomatoes, cut into chunks
2 cloves garlic, grated	Skewers

In a bowl marinate the lamb with the olive oil, garlic, and lemon juice for 2 hours, or overnight.
Remove the lamb from the marinade, and alternating with the onion, pepper, and tomato string the lamb on the skewers.
Grill the lamb on a bbq or under the broiler until desired pinkness, about 10-15 minutes.
Serve with a vinegar sauce, and/pilav, or scallions, lemon slices and additional sliced tomatoes.

Turkmen Specialties

Regional specialties include fish from the Caspian Sea, often cooked with pomegranate juice. The Tekke stuff sheep's stomachs with ground meat and fat (garyn), which is buried in the sand and then dried. The Yomut dry camel and mountain goat.

Pilav – rice with onions, carrots, garlic, mutton or fish, dried or fresh fruit, and almonds.

Shurpa – mutton soup with potatoes and tomatoes

Corek – (national bread) - flat bread made in a tamdyr (dome-shaped clay oven outside of the home)

Etli corek – bread baked with meat inside
Yagly corek – flat bread made with butter
Manty – dumplings with ground meat, onions or pumpkin served with yogurt
Somsas – meat stuffed flatbread
Gutap – dumpling with spinach
Ishlykly – similar to pizza with meat, but has dough on top also

Holidays and Special Occasions

There are several dishes that are served for holidays and special occasions. These include:

Pilav – mutton is cut into small pieces and fried, then onions and carrots are added. Salt hot water are poured over these and allowed to cook. Rice is spread over the top and cooked until all the water is gone. The rice is placed on a plate then covered with the meat and vegetables. The meal is usually eaten with your hands.

Kazanlama – lamb chunks marinated in salt, paprika, and garlic, soaked, and then cooked on coals covered with a large pot until the meat is golden.

Dzhazhyly bukche – sheep kidneys, liver, lungs and heart are washed, cut in strips, and fried in tail fat, then salted in a cauldron. Later eggplant, onions, radishes, tomatoes, pepper and potatoes are added with garlic and cayenne. A fermented dough is then made and cut into circles. The meat and vegetable mixture are spread on the dough which is folded and sealed, and then placed in the cauldron with oil and fried.

Dograma – chorek without yeast is baked, while mutton is cooked in a large cauldron. Salt and tomatoes are added. The chorek is then crumbled and onion mixed with it. Mutton pieces are then added to the chorek. This placed in a cup with the mutton broth and sprinkled with black pepper.

Beverages

Hot green tea, black tea, seltzer water, wine, beer, and vodka are drunk. Hot green tea (gok cay) is drunk from cups called käses. The hostess does not completely fill the cup, but will refill it many times to show she is a good hostess. Chai "tea" can meal sitting for a meal or just visiting. Milk may be added to the tea. Gatyk, a thick yogurt is served at breakfast or as a condiment. Chal is fermented camel's milk. Aragan (butter) is made from the cream of the chal. Chal and hot tea are drunk in the summer to cool and winter to warm oneself.

Did You Know?

Konjikala, located on the Silk Road, was first mentioned for growing wine in the 2nd c BC. The city was leveled by an earthquake in the 1st c BC, rebuilt and then destroyed by the Mongols in the 13th c AD.

Tuvalu

Tuvalu, formerly known as the Ellice Islands, is a Polynesian island country located in the Pacific Ocean, situated in Oceania, about midway between Hawaii and Australia. It lies east-northeast of the Santa Cruz Islands (belonging to the Solomons), southeast of Nauru, south of Kiribati, west of Tokelau, northwest of Samoa and Wallis and Futuna and north of Fiji. It comprises three volcanic reef islands and six atolls. The first inhabitants of Tuvalu were Polynesians. The pattern of settlement that is believed to have occurred is that the Polynesians spread out from Samoa and Tonga into the Tuvaluan atolls. In 1568, Spanish navigator Álvaro de Mendaña was the first European to sail through the archipelago, sighting the island of Nui. The island of Funafuti was named Ellice's Island in 1819; the name Ellice was applied to all nine islands and in the 19th c were administered as a British Protectorate. Captain George Barrett of the Nantucket whaler *Independence II* has been identified as the first whaler to hunt the waters around Tuvalu. He bartered for coconuts. It received its independence in 1978. Tuvalu, means "eight standing together" in Tuvaluan which with English are the official languages.

Etiquette and Customs

When invited for a meal please arrive promptly. Shake hands greeting and departing. Please bring a gift from your country. Do not bring food as it may mean the host does not have enough. The host will seat the guests often in the middle of the table so they can talk to others. Flatware is usually available, though some people eat with their hands. A prayer may be said at the beginning of the meal. Try a little bit of everything. Take only how much you will eat, as asking for a second serving is considered rude. If there is food left over from the meal it may be offered to you, though it is better to finish everything on your plate.

The traditional community system still survives to a large extent on Tuvalu. Each family has its own task, or *salanga*, to perform for the community, such as fishing, house building or defense. The skills of a family are passed on from parents to children. Most islands have their own *fusi*, community owned shops similar to convenience stores, where canned foods and bags of rice can be purchased. Another important building is the *falekaupule* or *maneapa* the traditional island meeting hall where important matters are discussed and which is also used for wedding celebrations and community activities such as a *fatele* involving music, singing and dancing. *Falekaupule* is also used as the name of the council of elders – the traditional decision making body on each island. Under the Falekaupule Act, *Falekaupule* means "traditional assembly in each island...composed in accordance with the Aganu of each island". *Aganu* means traditional customs and culture. Tuvalu is a Christian country and observes Lent, Easter, and Christmas. A major sporting event is the "Independence Day Sports Festival" held annually on 1 October. The most important sports event in the country is the yearly Tuvalu Games.

Curried Tuna

Serves 4

2 lbs. tuna, cut into cubes
Juice of 1 lime
2 tbls. oil
1 large onion, chopped
1 tbls. fresh ginger, grated

2 tbls. curry powder
2 tomatoes, chopped
½ cup coconut cream
Cooked rice

Place the tuna in a bowl and marinate in the lime juice for ½ hour.
Heat the oil in pan and stir in onion until tender. Add ginger, curry, and tomatoes, cooking until tender. Add tuna and cook until desired pinkness. Add coconut milk until just warmed.
Serve with rice.

Cuisine and Beverages

The cuisine is based on the staple of coconut and the many species of fish found in the ocean and lagoons of the atolls. Much of the land is not habitable. The early settlers brought pigs, rats, dogs, taro, yams, rice, breadfruit, bananas, lemons and limes, and sugar cane. Food was cooked on hot stones underground. Later the Europeans brought cattle, chickens, wheat, potatoes, cassava, watermelons, pineapples, papaya, oranges, mangos, onions, and tomatoes. Desserts made on the islands include coconut and coconut milk, instead of animal milk. The traditional foods eaten in Tuvalu are pulaka, taro, bananas, breadfruit and coconut. Pulaka (similar to taro but with larger leaves), is grown in large pits of composted soil below the water table. The unprocessed corms are toxic and must always be cooked. Taro leaves are used for soup, au gratin, chips and cakes. Tuvaluans also eat seafood, including coconut crab and fish from the lagoon and ocean. A traditional food source is seabirds (*taketake* or black noddy and *akiaki* or white tern), with pork being eaten mostly at *fateles* (or parties with dancing to celebrate events). Pulaka is the main source for carbohydrates. Seafood, especially flying fish and tuna (and over 300 species of fish), provides protein. Tuna may be served raw or in curries. Bananas and breadfruit are supplemental crops. Coconut is used for its juice, to make other beverages and to improve the taste of some dishes. A 1560-square-metre pond was built in 1996 on Vaitupu to sustain aquaculture in Tuvalu. Fruit juices are popular along with kava made from kava roots to release a liquid to which water is added; pi – coconut milk; and kao – fermented kaleve.

Specialties

Tulolo – coconut cream poured over beaten pulaka
Fekei – grated pulaka wrapped in pulaka leaves and coconut cream and steamed
Palusami or samoa – taro leaves, coconut cream, lime juice, onions, and spices served with taro or breadfruit

Uganda

Uganda, located in East Africa, is bordered on the east by Kenya, the north by Sudan, the west by the Democratic Republic of the Congo, the southwest by Rwanda, and the south by Tanzania. Until approximately 2000 years ago the people were hunter-gatherers. Then the Bantu migrated to the southern part of the country. During the 14 and 15th c the Empire of Kitara was established, followed by the kingdom of Bunvoro-Kitara, the Bugunda and Ankole. The Luo and Ateker peoples came from the north. During the 1800s Arab traders, then British explorers searching for the source of the Nile River appeared. The region was placed under the charter of the British East Africa Company in 1888 and ruled as a protectorate beginning in 1894. Uganda gained independence from Britain in 1962. The capital, Kampala, was once part of the hunting grounds of the king of Bugunda. The official languages are English and Swahili, although other languages are spoken in the country.

Dining Etiquette

Please be prompt when invited for a meal. Bring a gift, preferably something from your country. Please shake hands greeting and departing. Women and children do all the cooking, which is done on an open fire. Breakfast is usually only tea or porridge. The main meals are lunch and supper. Hands will be washed before a meal, which is served with people sitting on floor mats. A prayer is usually said before the meal. Women will serve the food which is generally eaten with the hands. The food is served on a plate and will include a stew (sauce) with beef or fish, vegetables, beans, butter and curry powder. Children speak only when spoken to. Please do not keep the left hand on the table or stretch your legs as this is considered disrespectful. Do not keep up until the meal is over. Water or other beverages are drunk at the end of the meal. Please thank the hostess for the meal.

Cuisine

The cuisine has been influenced by the English, Arabs, Asians and Indians. The main dish is a sauce or stew with meat, groundnuts, or beans. Common vegetables are cassava, yam, sweet potatoes, pumpkins, peas, rice, soybeans, cabbage, onions, corn, tomatoes, and potatoes. Greens are used and stews, and as side dishes. Fresh fruit include oranges, papaya (pawpaw), bananas, lemons and pineapples. Fish, chicken, beef, goat and mutton are used in cooking.

Matooke (Green Plantain Stew)

The matooke leaves and stalks are also used in cooking.

16 green plantain, peeled
2 small tomatoes, chopped
1 medium onion, peeled and chopped
1 tbls. peanut butter

1 tbl. warm water
1 tsp. curry powder

In a pot of water with the bananas, cook until bananas are soft. Drain. Keep bananas in pan. Combine the water and peanut butter in a bowl. Stir in the tomatoes, onions and curry. Stir into the bananas and cook for 10 minutes over low heat.
Serve hot.

Ugandan Specialties

Ugali - maize porridge
Oluwombo – dish made with chicken, goat, pork, or groundnuts, mushrooms,
Kwon – ugali made from millet or cassava flour
Luwombo – stew made of chicken, beef, mushroom, or fish and steamed in banana leaves

Malewa – bamboo dish
Samusa –samosa
Mugati naamaggi – pancake with meat and raw egg
Nsene – grasshopper
Nswaa – white ant

Chapati (flatbread)

2 cups whole wheat flour
½ to 1 cup lukewarm water

2 tbls. ghee

In a bowl combine the flour and ghee. Slowly add the water and mix until the dough is soft, but can be made into a ball.
On a floured board knead the dough using the end of your hand until it is quite smooth.
Let rest for 30 minutes.
Shape the dough into small balls and roll into a 5 inch circle.
Heat a skillet or griddle without oil and add a chapatti one at a time cooking for about 1 minute on each side, or until just browned.
Serve warm on a plate

Beverages

Chai (tea) and coffee are drunk in Uganda. Pombe is a fermented beer produced locally. Tonto is a fermented banana drink. Waragi is a banana gin.

Ukraine

Ukraine is bordered by the Russian Federation to the east and northeast, Belarus to the northwest, Poland, Slovakia and Hungary to the west, Romania and Moldova to the southwest, and the Black Sea and Sea of Azov to the south and southeast. Civilization in Ukraine dates back to at least 4500 BCE. From 700 BC – 200BC Ukraine was part of the Scythian Kingdom. Later Greece, Rome and the Byzantine Empire had colonies here until the 6th c AD. During the 7th c eastern Ukraine was part of Old Great Bulgaria. In the 9th century, much of Ukraine was populated by the Slavic tribes. During the 12th c nomadic tribes invaded. By the 14th c the country was part of Poland and also the Grand Duchy of Lithuania. By 1921 most of the Ukraine had been taken over by the Soviet Union. In 1991 Ukraine became an independent country. The capital, Kiev, the capital, dates back to the 5th c, a Slavic settlement. Ukrainian is the official language.

Dining Etiquette

The Ukrainians love to entertain and are very hospitable people. A plenteous table is expected. They are also very family oriented. Please be punctual. When invited to a home please bring flowers (in odd numbers and no yellow flowers), cakes, liquor, or a gift from your country. Gifts are also exchanged on birthdays and the Orthodox Christmas. Gifts are not usually opened when received. Please shake hands greeting and departing. Close male friends may give a pat on the back and hug. Close female friends kiss each other three times beginning with the left check. Do not shake hands in a doorway which is considered bad luck. You may be given a loaf of bread and salt as a symbol of hospitality and friendship

Beverages and hors d'oeuvres will be served. The hostess will seat the guests. The oldest or honored guest will be served food first. Do try everything. Please do not begin eating until she raises her fork. Eating is continental style fork in the left hand, knife in the right. Please keep your hands above the table, and no elbows on the table. Wine, beer or other beverages may be served. The toast is "za vashe zdorovya", "to your health". The host makes the first toast which is usually vodka. You may clink your glasses after the toast. Guests do not refill glasses. However bottles are finished and not left on the table. Meals center around food, drink and conversation. Expect the meal to last longer than most. Ukrainian customs may differ in the different regions.

Cuisine

The cuisine uses natural ingredients from the county and has been influenced by the Russian, Polish, German and Turkish cultures with over 70% of the land agricultural, 60% black soil. Ukraine is considered the bread basket of this region. The soil is very fertile and many products are grown – vegetables - tomatoes, cucumbers, pepper, lettuce, onions, fruit - apples, berries, grapes, peaches. They are eaten fresh or pickled, made with garlic and dill. Mushrooms, meat, dairy products, sour cream, milk, butter, salo – pork fat, black bread, garlic, salt, herbs, sausages, sugar beets are a main part of the diet. Other products are rye, oats, sunflowers, rapeseeds, grains, and oil, many of which are exported. Fish from the Azov and Black Seas are eaten and exported. Mushroom gathering in the fall (hryby) is celebrated with folk songs, flirting, and knowing which wild mushrooms are edible and how to use them. Mushrooms can be eaten raw, in salads, pickled, dried or frozen.

Ukraine Specialties

Borsch (borshch) – beet soup with cabbage, potatoes, carrots, onions and served with sour cream

Kapusniak – pork, salo, and sauerkraut soup werved with sour cream

Yushka – fish soup, usually carp

Hybivka – mushroom soup.

Olivye – potato salad with dill pickles, hard-boiled eggs, chicken and onion

Vinigret – beet, sauerkraut, potato, onion and carrot salad

Guliash - stew

Kvashena kapusta – sauerkraut

Draniki – potato pancakes

Varenyky - pastries with potatoes, meat, or fruit fillings, served with sour cream, butter, or sugar

Pyrizhky – potato buns cooked in cream and dill

Holubchi – cabbage rolls with meat and rice filling

Blyntsi – filled crepes served with sour cream

Kasha – cereal

Syrniki – cheese pancakes

Pampushky – fried dough, similar to doughnuts.

Torte – flourless cakes using walnuts or almonds

Zhele – jellied fruits

Kutya – wheat porridge

Harbuzova Kasha z Hrybamy (pumpkin porridge with mushrooms)

1 kg. pumpkin
5 tbls. millet or cornmeal
½ cup oil

100 g dried mushroom
Salt
Sugar

Wash and clean the pumpkin, cut in half, remove the seeds and dice. Place in a heatproof dish and pour over some water, such that it barely covers the pumpkin. Place in the oven and bake until tender.

Put the baked pumpkin in a skillet and fry in vegetable oil.

Sift the millet or corn meal into the pumpkin water, add salt and sugar and make the porridge.

Cook the mushrooms in boiling salted water, slice and fry in some oil. Mix the pumpkin, porridge and mushrooms together and stir.

Fold the mixture into a heatproof dish and sit in the oven for ten to fifteen minutes until it turns golden brown. Serve hot, having drizzled with oil or butter.

Recipe courtesy of the Embassy of Ukraine, Washington, DC

Vareniki with Potatoes and Cheese

Vareniki

2/3 cup buttermilk	2 cups warm water
1 tbls. sour cream	1 ½ tsp. salt
2 eggs	7 cups unbleached flour

Place the ingredients in a "Kitchen Aid" using 4 cups flour. Gradually add more flour. When dough no longer sticks to side of bowl (may need to add a little more flour), put on floured board.
Roll out and cut into circles using a cookie cutter or glass

Filling

10 potatoes	¾ Mozzarella cheese, grated
¾ tbls. salt for cooking	3 tbls. butter, melted
4 oz. cream cheese	

Peel and cut potatoes into cubes.
Place in boiling salted water. Bring to a boil. Cook about 10-15 minutes, or potatoes are softened. Drain. Let cool for 5 minutes.
In the pan with the potatoes, add the cream cheese, butter, and cheese.
Place a spoonful of the potato mixture on each vareniki circle. Fold over and seal with finger and a little water.
In a large pot bring water with 1 tsp. salt to a boil. Drop in vareniki, a few at a time. Cook until they float to top. Remove with slotted spoon.
Serve with sour cream, butter, or melted butter with some chopped bacon and onion.
Recipe courtesy of Galina Berzino, Odessa, Ukraine

Varenyky Vyshnyamy (Varenyky with Cherries)

4 cups wheat flour	½ cup sugar
2 eggs	Honey
1 cup water	
5 cups cherries	

Wash the cherries and remove the stones.
Mix the flour, eggs, water, sugar and salt and work into stiff dough. Shape the dough into a tube and cut into slices of equal length. Form a ball of each slice and roll our pastry shapes the size of a cookie. Sprinkle each with sugar, put the cherries, fold the dough over the filling and make a crease in it. Cook in boiling water. Use a slotted spoon to transfer varenyky to a deep bowl. Drizzle with sugar or honey. Serve with sour cream or ryazhanka (fermented baked milk).
Recipe courtesy of the Embassy of Ukraine, Washington, DC

Holidays and Special Occasions

Weddings – a traditional bread, Korovai, is decorated with birds and periwinkles and may be served instead of a wedding cake. This symbolizes good luck.

Easter (Velykden) – in the morning people take hardboiled eggs, sausage, baked cheese, bread, butter, and relishes to be blessed in the church. Easter dinner ham or roast pork, salads, and desserts will be served. Decorated eggs date back thousands of years. The designs were made in beeswax, and the eggs dipped in vegetable dyes. Paska is an Easter bread and Babka, a sweet dough bread with raisins and dried fruit

Christmas Eve - Sviaty Vechir (Holy Evening) – foods served will include kutya, borshch, fish, cabbage rolls, dumplings, peas, sauerkraut, beets, and stewed fruit, usually 12 dishes symbolizing Christ's 12 apostles, Kolach, braided bread served at Christmas and funerals, and Kutia – poppy seeds, wheat, nuts, and honey.

Christmas (Rizdvo Khrystove) – honey bread, cakes, cookies and a feast

Name Days (Imenyny) – children are given the names of saints and celebrate the saint's day. The day is celebrated with family and godparents with gifts and a feast of beverages, wines, fish, veal, chicken, herring, soups, potatoes, cucumber, and desserts.

Beverages

Drinking alcoholic beverages is expected in the country. Vodka and other spirits may include fruit, spices or hot peppers. Beer is brewed with the largest producers – Obolon, Lvivske, Chernihvske, Slavutych, Sarmat and Rogan. Mead, made from honey, water and yeast is a fermented drink. Wine is produced in the Crimea, and was once considered highly prized and drunk by the Russian czars. Other beverages are kompot, made from fresh or dried fruit or berries boiled in water; uzvar, dried fruit drink; kvas, beverage of yeast, sugar, and dried rye bread; kefir, fermented milk; ryazhanka, baked milk; and mineral waters.

Did You Know?

From 1932-33 Ukraine experienced "Holodomor", a devastating famine that killed millions of people. It was caused by the Soviet dictator Joseph Stalin who thought that farm collectivization would provide food not only for Ukraine, but for the rest of the Soviet Union with disastrous results.

United Arab Emirates

United Arab Emirates is located at the southeast end of the Arabian Peninsula on the Persian Gulf, bordering Oman to the east and Saudi Arabia to the south, as well as sharing maritime borders with Qatar to the west and Iran to the north. The country is a federation of seven emirates, and was established on 2 December 1971. The region has been inhabited for over 130,000 years with the discovery of stone tools used for butchering animals. The unification of the peninsula occurred under the Rashidun Caliphate. Because of the harsh weather nomadic tribesmen participated in animal husbandry, agriculture and hunting; and tribal groupings formed. By the 16th c ports along the Persian Gulf came under the influence of the Ottoman Empire. Portuguese, Dutch and English also appeared. The British formed the Trucial Sheikhdoms. Pearling became an important source of income which disappeared in the 20th c with the invention of cultured pearls. Eventually oil was found and became a major export. Abu Dhabi is the capital.

Dining Etiquette

When invited for a meal please arrive promptly. Please bring a gift from your country. Shake hands greeting and departing. Women will extend their hand first. Meals can often be very long elaborate affairs. Please let your host(ess) seat you. In some cases the sexes will not eat together. Unfold your napkin and fold in half placing the folded half towards you. Do not place your elbows on the table. Use your fork and knife to eat, and use the spoon for the soup. Never eat or pass anything with your left hand. If a loaf bread is served, tear pieces from it, do not cut it. When finished place your napkin to the left of your place setting and the knife and fork together on your plate. When finished thank your host. At the close of the meal, it is usual to be served with a red tea infused with mint, which aids the digestion. Other traditions to the meal include a welcome with dates and *gahwah* (Arabic coffee), which are offered on arrival and are kept available through the guests visit. When seated do not place your feet on a foot rest or cross your legs. It is considered rude to show the bottom of your shoes.

Cuisine and Beverages

The cuisine has been influenced by Middle Eastern and Asian foods, and the harsh desert conditions. Camel milk and dates were most commonly eaten. Along the coast fish, dairy products, bread and rice sustained the population. Meat, fish, lamb, grains, dairy, chicken, Houbara bustards, goats, vegetables, dates, and camel milk are part of the diet. Camels are eaten on special occasions. Many of the dishes are prepared in a single pot. Common spices and herbs are saffron, cardamom, turmeric, ghaff, and thyme. Rice and pasta were introduced by traders. This is primarily a Muslim country. Strong coffee, camel's milk, tea, and Ayranser, a yogurt based drink are popular. Cardamom, saffron, or mint are added to teas or coffee. Laban is fermented milk which is churned and the butter removed.

Mehalabeya (rice, nut and dried fruit dessert)

Serves 4

½ cup rice flour
4 cups cold milk
6 tbls. sugar
1 tsp. vanilla

1 tsp. cinnamon
2 tbls. dried currants
¼ cup unsalted shelled pistachios
2 tbls. rose water

Dissolve the flour in 1 cup milk.
In a sauce pan bring 3 cups milk and sugar to boil, stirring to dissolve sugar.
Reduce heat and add rice flour mixture, stirring for about 10 minutes or until thickened. Stir in vanilla.
Pour into 4 dessert bowls. Garnish with cinnamon, currants, pistachio and rose water.
Chill 2 hours.

Specialties

Fareed – meat and vegetable stew served over bread
Dungaw – chick peas cooked with spices and hot peppers
Harees – meat and wheat dish cooked over coals
Machboos – rice dish with meat or fish, turmeric, cumin, cardamom, saffron and Loomy – dried lemon
Saluna – meat, fish, or chicken stew served over rice
Mhammar – spiced fish with carmelized onions and yellow rice
Balaleet – vermicelli noodle, egg, sugar, and spice dish
Maq'louba – meat, rice, and fried vegetable dish
Margooga – vegetable, chicken and bread dish

Ghuzi – whole roasted lamb, served on skewers with vegetables, and hazelnuts over rice
Fattoush – flatbread salad
Raqaq – thin crisp bread
Khameer – bread with dates, cardamom and saffron
Chebab – saffron, cardamom pancake
Luqeymat – deep fried batter rolled in sesame seeds and dibbs - date honey
Khabeesa – breadcrumb dessert with sugar, cardamom, and saffron
Bethitha – semolina dessert with dates, cardamom and clarified butter
Khabees – toasted flour, honey and spice sweet
Esh Asarya – cake made of baked bread and cheese with fresh cream

Holidays and Special Occasions

Harees is served at religious festivities and weddings.
Ramadan – people do not eat from sunrise to sunset. Eid al Fitr – celebrates the end of Ramadan when large feasts are held usually with lamb and other meats.
Eid al Adha – is celebrated when a pilgrim returns from the Haj, a journey each Muslim makes to Mecca. Rice and meat dishes are served.

United States

The United States is situated mostly in central North America, where its forty-eight contiguous states and Washington, D.C., the capital district, lie between the Pacific and Atlantic Oceans, bordered by Canada to the north and Mexico to the south. The state of Alaska is in the northwest of the continent, with Canada to the east and Russia to the west across the Bering Strait. The state of Hawaii is an archipelago in the mid-Pacific. The first inhabitants came to the country c40,000 years ago. The British claimed most of North America, but in 1776 the United States declared its independence and the Revolutionary War followed. In 1789 George Washington became the first President. The capital, Washington, was founded in 1790 and designed by Pierre Charles L'Enfant. English is the official language.

Dining Etiquette

Please be punctual when invited for a meal. Shake hands greeting and departing. Please bring a gift for your hostess – wine, chocolates, or a gift from your country. Drinks and hors d'oeuvres will be offered. The hostess will seat you at the table, with the male guest of honor to her right. Dishes may be passed, or food served buffet style. Please eat continental style with your fork in your left hand and knife in the right. When finished place the knife and fork together at a 5 o'clock angle. People may linger at the table when finished. Please thank you host and hostess, and send them a thank you note. The toast is "Cheers" or "To your health".

New England Clam Chowder

Serves 4

2-3 dozen hard shell clams
1 large onion, chopped
6 slices bacon
Salt and pepper

2 large potatoes, diced
1 quart half and half
½ stick butter

Preheat oven to 350°
Place clams on a baking sheet and bake until clams just open. Reserve the clam liquor and place the clams (minus shells) in a large pot.
Fry the bacon in a skillet until just crisp. Remove and place on a paper towel. Add the onion to the fat and saute until just tender.
In a small pot bring the potatoes to a boil, and cook until tender. Drain.
To the clam pot add the potatoes, onions, half and half, clam liquor, salt and pepper, and the bacon. Simmer until warm, but not boiling. Serve in bowls. Can be garnished with a little fresh dill.

Maryland Crab Cakes

Makes 4 crab cakes

1 lb. lump crab
2 tbls. breadcrumbs
1 egg
1 tsp. Dijon mustard
2 tbls. mayonnaise

Dash of Old Bay Seasoning
2 or more tbls. butter
Tartar sauce
Lemons, sliced

With a fork carefully combine the crab, breadcrumbs, egg, mustard, mayonnaise and Old Bay in a bowl. Make into 4 cakes.
Heat the butter in a skillet. Brown the crab cakes, about 5 minutes on each side.
Serve with tartar sauce and lemon.
Recipe courtesy of the author

Shrimp and Grits

Serves 4

Grits

1 cup grits
4 cups water

½ stick butter
½ cup grated cheddar cheese

Bring the water to a boil in a pan, and stir in the grits. Cook slowly until thickened. Add butter and cheese.

Shrimp

2 lbs. large shrimp, shelled and deveined
2 tbls. olive oil
1 stalk celery, sliced
1 red pepper, chopped
1 onion, chopped

2 cloves garlic, minced
2 large tomatoes, chopped
¼ cup parsley
1 lb. andouille sausage, sliced
Salt and pepper

Heat the olive oil in a skillet. Stir in the celery, pepper and onion, until just tender. Add garlic and tomatoes. Cook 5 minutes. Stir in parsley, sausage, and shrimp. Heat until shrimp are pink. Season with salt and pepper, or a little cayenne for a hotter dish.
Serve over the grits.
Recipe courtesy of the author

Cuisine

The United States is truly the melting pot of the world with cuisines from every country. The Native Americans harvested pumpkins, squash, mushrooms, root vegetables, some fruit and berries, nuts, wild animals and birds, and fish. The early European settlers brought with them cattle, sheep, chickens, pigs, corn, potatoes, beans, spices, grains such as wheat and rye, and herbs. Meats were dried, smoked or salted to preserve them. Because of the different climates each region of the U.S. had its own specialties. The Northeast became known for baked beans, clam chowder, lobsters, mussels, scallop, maple syrup, apples, and cranberries; the Middle Atlantic for crab, oysters, peaches, cantaloupe and fresh vegetables; the Southerners loved their fried chicken, shrimp, grits, gumbo, jambalaya, cornbread, and greens; the Midwest for hearty dishes many inspired by Eastern European and Scandinavians; the West – beef and spicier foods, the influence of Mexico and Spain; and the Northwest – salmon, fruit especially apples and pears. Oranges, lemons, and grapefruit were brought by the early settlers mainly to Florida, and were not native to the U.S. Maple sugaring was an art passed down by the Native Americans to the new settlers. Buckets were strapped to maple trees to collect the "sweet water".

Beverages

The earliest grapes were brought from Europe in the 1600s. Rum was produced from sugar cane from the islands, but when the British blockaded the East Coast Americans took to making cider, beer, and whiskeys. C 1856 Agoston Haraszthy, "Father of California viticulture", brought vine cuttings from Hungary to the Sonoma Valley. Today wine is made in almost all states. Beer, especially craft beers, are brewed in almost all states also. Fruit juices are very popular, as are sodas, and bottled water. Bourbon is an all-American drink produced in Kentucky. It is made from at least 51% corn and aged. The Kentucky Derby is run the first Saturday in May and mint julips are always served. They are made with bourbon, sugar water, mint, and ice. Rye and other whiskeys are also produced in the U.S.

Holidays and Special Occasions

In New Orleans Mardi Gras is celebrated before Lent with red beans and rice, shrimp and chicken Creole, beignettes, jambalaya, parades, Mardi Gras king and Queen, masks, and party beads
Easter – church services, Easter egg hunts, lamb or ham, asparagus, new potatoes, strawberries, Easter eggs and chocolates
Passover – lamb, spring potatoes and greens
Memorial Day (last Monday in May), Fourth of July and Labor Day (first Monday in September) are celebrated with picnics – meat cooked on the grills, potato salad,
Thanksgiving – 4th Thursday in November- turkey, stuffing, gravy, sweet potatoes, creamed onions, green beans, mincemeat pie, pecan pie, pumpkin pie
Hanukah – lighting of the Menorah and celebration of 8 days
Christmas – roast turkey or beef, sweet potatoes, Yorkshire pudding, beans or other green vegetables, and lots of sweets. Most Christians attend church services on Christmas Eve.
New Year's Eve is celebrated with the dropping of the ball in Times Square, New York City, and many parties and concerts

Did You Know?

Many Americans thought the tomato was poisonous until Col. Robert Gibbons of Salem, NJ ate one and didn't die!

The Pilgrims brought on board *the Mayflower* in 1620 Edam cheese from the Netherlands and the first cows to the United States. After so many of the first settlers died, England passed a law that each ship with passengers must have 1 cow per 6 people.

George Washington, the first President, purchased a machine for making ice cream in 1784. The hand - cranked ice cream freezer was patented in 1848. Molds were a popular way of freezing ice cream. However, the early molds were made of lead and should not be used now.

Thomas Jefferson, the third president, enjoyed cheese and a large wheel of cheddar was presented to him on his inauguration in 1801.

Hamburgers (ground beef) probably have many origins, but the one we know today served on a bun dates back to 1885 when the Menches' brothers serving ground pork sandwiches ran out of pork and substituted beef at the Erie County Fair in New York.

The first "dachshund sausage" stand selling "hot dogs" was opened in Coney Island, New York in 1871 by a German butcher. They were first sold at a St. Louis baseball game in 1893 and served on buns at the Chicago World's Fair. Chili dogs were sold at John Patrelli's hotdog stand in Paterson, New Jersey about 1920.Corn dogs, a hotdog in corn batter on a stick, probably came about in the early 1940s

The first cheese factory began in 1851 near Rome, New York by Jesse Williams who produced a cheddar cheese. John Jossi of Dodge County, Wisconsin produced Limburger cheese and invented Brick cheese. Liederkrantz cheese was invented by Emil Frey of Monroe, New York. William E. Lawrence and a man working for the Empire Cheese Company are credited with making "Philadelphia" cream cheese. James L. Kraft is credited for pasteurized processed cheese.

Granola was first baked during the Civil War by James Caleb Jackson.

The boardwalk in Atlantic City, New Jersey was home to the first saltwater taffy in the 1880s.

Ice cream cones were invented at the 1904 St. Louis World's Fair when a Middle Eastern pastry shaped like a waffle was used instead of a dish to serve the ice cream.

Gennaro Lombardi opened the first pizza parlor in 1905 in New York City. Pizzeria Uno invented the first deep dish pizza in Chicago in 1943. Other dishes that are more American than Italian are tomato sauce with pasta, pizza, Turkey alla Tetrazzini, and Spaghetti alla Caruso.

The Oreo cookie got its name because it reminded someone of a mountain in Greece "oreo". The Sunshine Baking Co. began selling Hydrox cookies 1908-10 Oreos were introduced by the National Biscuit Co. (now Nabisco) in 1912. The Girl Scouts first sold cookies in 1936. Kennedy Biscuits, forerunner of Nabisco, named cookies after New England towns – Fig Newton, Beacon Hill and Brighton.

Maitre d' Oscar Tshirky of the Waldorf Hotel in New York City invented the Waldorf Salad, Veal Oscar and Thousand Island Dressing.

Muffuletta, a favorite in New Orleans, was first concocted by Salvatore Lupo in that city in 1906. He put cold cuts, cheeses and olive salad all in a muffuletta so it would be easier to eat.

Meyer lemons were introduced to the United States by Frank Meyer, a plant explorer who found them in China in 1908.

Three famous American companies were founded in 1869, just after the Civil War. They are H.J. Heinz in Sharpsburg, PA; Welch's in Vineland, NJ; and Anderson and Campbell in Camden, NJ.

Abraham Anderson, one of the founders of Campbell Soup, started out as a tinsmith in Newark, NJ, built refrigerators, and eventually founded the cannery in Camden. The Anderson and Campbell partnership was dissolved in the 1870s, and in 1882 Arthur Dorrance became one of the partners. John Dorrance, his nephew, developed condensed canned soups. Some of their products were preserves, jellies and jams, ketchup, fruit butters, mincemeat, and canned fruits and vegetables. Campbell's Beefsteak Tomato soup was introduced in 1895. Today Campbell's is the largest soup maker in the world.

Supposedly iced tea was invented in 1904 at the St. Louis World's Fair, but was probably long before that. The iced tea long spoon came after that.

Observant Jews thought that coffee came from legumes, and would not drink it during Passover. Later Maxwell House coffee found that the beans were a berry, and coffee was drunk by all!

Ramps are a type of onion that grow in the Catskill and Appalachian Mountain region.

Whoopie pies probably, were invented at the Berwick Cake Company in Roxbury, Massachusetts in 1927. The pie is really two small chocolate cakes with vanilla cream in the center.

Fried clams became popular in 1916 when Chubby Woodman of Essex, Massachusetts first fried them in cornmeal batter. Woodman's is still one of the most popular clam shacks in the U.S.

The Washburn Crosby Company received much mail about recipes and in 1921 came up with the idea of "Betty Crocker".

In 1858, Ezra Warner of Waterbury, Connecticut patented the first can opener. The U.S. military used it during the Civil War. In 1866, J. Osterhoudt patented the tin can with a key opener that you can find on sardine cans.

On January 24, 1935, the first canned beer, "Krueger Cream Ale," was sold by the Kruger Brewing Company of Richmond, VA.

The Lady Baltimore cake was probably first made in Charleston, SC and not Baltimore. This delightful cake has three layers with a filling of figs, raisins, and pecans.

J.W. "Bill Marriott" was once a lettuce farmer, sheep rancher, underwear salesman, and Mormon missionary. He moved to Washington, DC from Utah in 1927 and held the A&W Root Beer franchise before founding Hot Shoppes and Marriott Hotels.

Iceberg lettuce received its name from the leaf that was developed to travel when packed in ice.

In 1930 James Dewar, manager of the Continental Bakery in Chicago decided to make small cakes with a banana cream filling in shortcake pans. He named them after the Twinkle Toe shoes he had seen in an advertisement. These later became Hostess "twinkies".

Bob Cobb of The Brown Derby Restaurant, Los Angeles came up with the Cobb salad in 1937.

Old Bay Seasoning, produced at McCormick & Co., Baltimore was concocted by Gustav Brunn at the Baltimore Spice Company in1939, and was originally named Delicious Brand Shrimp and Crab Seasoning. After World War II it was renamed Old Bay.

Plastic milk bottles were introduced in 1967. Until then milk was kept in glass bottles with the cream rising to the top.

Lipton introduced dried onion soup in 1952 and two years later a woman from southern California added it to sour cream to come up with the famous onion soup dip.

The Morton Salt girl first appeared in a Good Housekeeping ad in 1911. Poppin' Fresh, the Pillsbury Doughboy was created in 1965 by the Leo Burnett advertising agency. The Green Giant appeared on the Minnesota Valley Canning Company can in 1925. Tony the tiger first appeared on Kellogg's Frosted Flakes box in 1952. Mr. Peanut dates back to 1916.

Mushrooms have been grown in Chester County, specifically Kennett Square, Pennsylvania since the 1880s. A number of farms remain in the original family hands, and are not open to the public.

Uruguay

The Oriental Republic of Uruguay's only land border is with Rio Grande do Sul, Brazil, to the north. To the west lies the Uruguay River, to the southwest lies the estuary of the Río de la Plata, and the Atlantic Ocean to the east. The earliest inhabitants were the Charrua from Paraguay. The Spanish arrived in 1516. They brought with them cattle, which thrived and brought much wealth to landowners. Montevideo, the capital, founded in the early 18th century, served as stronghold on an excellent harbor. In 1811, José Gervasio Artigas launched a successful revolution against the Spanish, defeating them on May 18 at the Battle of Las Piedras. In 1814 he formed the Liga Federal (Federal League), of which he was declared Protector. In 1820 he was defeated by the Portuguese who occupied neighboring Brazil.   In 1821, the Provincia Oriental del Rio de la Plata, present-day Uruguay, was annexed to Brazil by Portugal. The Provincia declared independence from Brazil in August 25, 1825 but decided to adhere to a regional federation with Argentina. The regional federation defeated Brazil after a 3-year war. The 1828 Treaty of Montevideo, fostered by the United Kingdom, gave birth to Uruguay as an independent state. Sheep were introduced in the late 19th c by immigrants. Cattle and sheep became important products for their meat and wool from the sheep. Spanish is the official language.

Dining Etiquette

Please be prompt when invited for a meal. Uruguayans usually dine between 9 and 10 PM. Shake hands greeting and departing. Please bring a gift for the home, Scotch, or a bottle of wine. Or you may send flowers or candy before the event, Women may kiss each other on the right, and men who know each other well embrace. People will stand close when speaking. Beverages and hors d'oeuvres will be served. The hostess will seat the guests at the table with the male guest of honor to her right. Food will be served or buffet style. Eating is continental style using your fork in the left hand and knife in the right. Please wait for the hostess to begin. Please keep your hands at table level. When finished place your knife and fork side by side on the plate. The toast is "salud y amor y tiempo para disfrutarlo" or just "Salud".

Cuisine

The many immigrants to Uruguay have influenced its cuisine, especially the Italians, Spanish, French and Germans who brought pasta, sausages, and sweet desserts. The Indian influence is seen in the use of pumpkins, squash, corn, onions, peppers and tomatoes. Beef is eaten at many meals. The national dish is *asado* (barbecued meat). The parrillada dish contains beef ribs, kidneys, salivary glands or sweetbreads, the small or large intestine and sweet blood pudding sausage. Barbequed lamb is also served. Breakfast is a light meal, lunch and dinner the main meals during which wine, beer or medio y medio (half wine and half champagne) may be served. Along the

593

coastal areas, such as La Paloma and Maldonado freshwater and saltwater fish dishes are served. Bountiful fish are anchovy, red snapper, sea bass, hake, whiting, shark and tuna. Santiago Vazquez is famous for fish fries. The main agricultural products are fruits, vegetables, rice, grain, alfalfa, corn, tobacco, potatoes, cattle and sheep.

Matambre (flank steak, eggs and vegetables)

Serves 4

2 lbs. thin flank steak
¼ cup red wine vinegar
2 cloves garlic, minced
1 tsp. thyme
½ lb. baby spinach
2 carrots, sliced like match straws lengthwise
4 hard-cooked eggs, sliced

1 medium onion, sliced
¼ cup fresh parsley
1 jalapeno, seeded and chopped
Salt and pepper to taste.
2 cups beef stock
1 cup water

Pound the flank steak until very thin and cut into 2 pieces.
Lay one piece of steak on a cookie sheet. Sprinkle with half of vinegar, garlic and thyme.
Place the other steak on top. Sprinkle with rest of vinegar, garlic and thyme.
Cover and marinate overnight.
Preheat oven to 375°
Lay the steaks out, overlapping and seal middle. Spread the spinach on the steaks, top with carrots, eggs, onions, parsley, jalapeno, salt and pepper.
Roll the steak up carefully. Tie securely with oven string wound around the steaks from one end to other.
Place in a roasting pan. Pour the stock and water over the meat. Cover. Cook 1 hour.
Remove from oven. Let rest. Cut off string.
Serve warm or cooled.

Uruguayan Specialties

Asado – a traditional meal of grilled beef and other meats, or barbeque
Parrillada – beef and sausage platter
Chivito – steak sandwich with ham, cheese, tomato, lettuce, fried egg, pepper, olives and mayonnaise
Bife lomo – sirloin steak
Chivito – beef on top of French fries and salad, then topped with bacon, ham, and cheese and a fried egg
Morcilla dulce – blood sausage cooked with orange, orange peel and walnuts
Milanesa breaded veal cutlet
Olimpicos – club sandwiches

Hungaras – spicy sausage in a roll
Caruso sauce – served with pasta and made with cream, meat, onions, ham and mushrooms
Milhojas – means a thousand sheets or leaves – puff pastry usually with dulce de leche and fruit
Alfajores – shortbread with dulce de leche
Tortas fritas – fried bread
Choripan – grilled chorizo sandwich
Empanada – meat or ham and cheese pastry
Empanada Gallega - fish pie
Pascualina – spinach pie
Pastel de carne – meat pie

594

Faina – similar to a pizza or pancake but made with chick pea flour
Noquis – mashed potato and flour dough, eaten on the 29th day of the month
Pancho – similar to an American hotdog
Bizcochos - flaky pastry
Chaja – meringue, sponge cake, cream and peaches

Flan – custard
Dulce de membrillo – quince paste
Dulce de leche – milk boiled down with sugar and vanilla
Pasteles de membrillo – fried dough with quince jam and dusted in powdered sugar

Holidays and Special Occasions

On Easter and Christmas common foods are dulce de leche, torte de gofio, tarte fritas, and anise bread. Christmas and New Year's Eve are celebrated with family and parties.
The week before Lent is celebrated with gaucho shows.
During Holy Week fish is eaten.
April 19th, the Landing of the 33 Patriots, their independence day, is celebrated with beef and different types of sausage including chorizo.
The Fiesta de la Virgen de la Candlelaria at the Iglesia de Punta del Este celebrates the arrival of the Spaniards in 1516 with a feast.
Fiesta del Mar – the Festival of the Sea takes place during the summer at the beaches where much seafood is served.
Christmas Eve - dinner is the most elaborate meal of the year.
Christmas – Papa Noel visits the children with presents. Christmas dinner might include the asado or a picnic on the beach. Sidra (cider) and pan dulce, a Christmas bread with sweets are served. Budin Ingles or English pudding, is a pudding with fruit and nuts served on Christmas and New Year's.
Birthdays, anniversaries, and other events are celebrated with sumptuous meals or asado.

Beverages

The national drink, Grappamiel, is distilled from grapes and honey. The traditional drink, mate, is drank on any occasion. Mate is made from the dried leaves and branches of the verba mate plant. A gourd is filled with hot water and the mate is sipped through a cane or metal straw called a bombilla. Coffee and tea are drunk with milk.

Uruguay produces most of its wine in the Montevideo, San Jose and Canelones regions. Tannat, the grape mainly used, was brought from Spain in 1870 by Don Pascual Harriague. The blending grape is Merlot. Other drinks are clerico – white wine and fruit juice; medio y medio – sparkling and white wine.

Uzbekistan

Uzbekistan is bordered by Kazakhstan to the west and to the north, Kyrgyzstan and Tajikistan to the east, Afghanistan and Turkmenistan to the south. The earliest settlers were in the Tarim Basin, and mummies have been found dating back to c 1800 BC. Mongoloid and Iranian, and later Turkic peoples settled in the region. During the first millennium the Iranian began an extensive irrigation system. Chinese traders developed the Silk Route and the cities of Bukhoro and Samarqand became very wealthy cities. In 327 BC Alexander the Great conquered some of the region, followed by the Persians and then the Mongols under Genghis Khan. In the 1380s Timur (Tamerlane) ruled over much of Central Asia. By the 19th c Russia began its great expansion. In 1924 the Uzbek Soviet Socialist Republic was created and in 1991 Uzbekistan declared independence. Tashkent, the capital, is an ancient city on the old Silk Route. Its original name, Chach, means City of Stone. Much of the old part of the city was destroyed in an earthquake in 1966. The official language is Uzbek. The majority of the people are Sunni Muslims.

Dining Etiquette

Please arrive promptly when invited for a meal. Men shake hands greeting with the left hand over the heart and a slight bow to show respect. Younger people greet their elders first. If you are not shaking hands the right hand is put over the heart. Men who are close acquaintances or relatives may kiss each other on the cheeks. Women extend their hand first to shake hands. Women may greet each other with hugs, a kiss on alternating cheeks two or three times, and a handshake. Meals are usually served on the floor or on a low table covered with a dusterhon. Guests will be seated on carpets, chairs, or beds. Men sit cross-legged; women with their legs to one side. Respected guests sit away from the entrance. At a banquet cold food items are placed on the table to be served on small plates and will include appetizers, salads, and pastries with fruit in the center. Each guest will give a toast standing with a glass of vodka. Glasses are clinked at the center of the table. One person is designated to pour the drink. For a tea ceremony, tea is served from ceramic pots into pjala bowls, pouring back into the teapot three times, and then half filling the bowls. Tea is served with jam or honey.

Cuisine

The cuisine has been influenced by the local fruit, vegetables, and meat available, accompanies by grains, rice, bread, or noodles. Meals begin with small dishes of nuts and raisins, then soups, salads, meat dishes and ending with palov, which is often cooked by men. Tea, usually green, is drunk throughout the day, accompanied by snacks, and is always offered to guests. Within Uzbekistan is the Autonomous Republic of Karakalpakstan where cattle breeding, fishing and crops such as wheat, rice, sorghum, millet, alfalfa, vegetables and fruit are grown. The

Karakalpaks' national dish is *besbarmak,* boiled mutton, beef, or horse served over broad noodles and a broth. Also within Uzbekistan are Bukharian Jews with their own dishes These include oshi sabo made with rice, meat, vegetables, and fruit; osh palov made with chicken and beef; bakhsh rice with spinach and greens; and many other dishes made with boiled meat, vegetables, and fish, followed with dried or fresh fruit, nuts, halvah, and green tea. Uzbekistan is noted for its flatbreads known as non which are cooked in tandoor ovens. They are made of leavened wheat flour and may have sesame seeds, or made in special designs, but in round shapes. Non is not cut but broken into pieces when served.

Uzbek Palov or Osh

"Palov is a traditional Uzbek main course food. If you ever visit Uzbekistan this is probably the most common dish you will encounter. There are different variations of Palov depending on where you are in Uzbekistan. The most common Palov is Fergana Palov. There is also Samarqand Palov used with yellow carrots so that the rice is still white. In the Burkhorocha method, the rice, meat and vegetables are cooked separately."
His Excellency Ilhomjon Nematov, Embassy of the Republic of Uzbekistan, Washington, DC

4-5 cups grain rice
6 large carrots, peeled and julienne
4 large onions, peeled and cut into ¼ in. half circles
2 lbs. meat, preferably lamb leg or shoulder with some fat on it, cut into 2x2 in. cubes
¼ cup vegetable oil
8 cups boiling water
3 tbls. coarse salt

2 tsp. black pepper
3 tbls. ground coriander
3 tbls. ground cumin
½ tbls. paprika
½ tsp. turmeric or a pinch of saffron for color
½ tbls. tarragon
¼ cup dried barberries
1 large head of garlic, unpeeled

Heat the oil in a large skillet and fry the meat. Add salt, cumin, coriander, paprika and pepper. Fry until browned on all sides. Add the onions. Cook until soft and golden brown.
Add the carrots and brown with other ingredients. Add the water. Push the garlic bulb deep into the pan. Cover. Cook on medium heat for about 20-25 minutes. If using beef, cook for 30 minutes. Remove garlic bulb.
"This is the first major step in preparing Palov called zirvak. You cook the zirvak until the vegetables are well done."
"The second step is the tricky step. This is the rice step". First you must soak the rice in salted water for 30 minutes. (This is very important). After the zirvak is done, place the rice in a flat layer on top. Cover with more water if needed, so that the water is 1 inch above the rice. Do not mix the zirvak into the rice. Bring to a boil, and keep on the heat until all of the water evaporates. Pierce holes in the rice all the way to the bottom with a spoon and lower the heat. Cover the rice with a plate and put the cover on and simmer. "You should hear a "goop goop" sound as the moisture is mixed into the rice. Keep a close eye on it or it will burn. The goal is to get all the fluid whether in the water of the zirvak evaporated and cooked into the rice."
When serving, carefully mix up the rice and the zirvak. Place the pieces of meat on top of the plate.
Recipe courtesy of His Excellency Ilhomjon Nematov, Embassy of Uzbekistan, Washington, DC

Uzbek Specialties

Palov – the national dish made of meat, carrots, onion, and spices
Shurpa – meat soup with fresh vegetables
Shurbo dushpera – dumpling soup
Norin- noodle and meat soup
Monti – steamed dumplings
Chuchvara – dough with meat and onion stuffing
Dholeh- similar to risotto
Lagman – layered dough, then cut into noodles, boiled and served with a meat and vegetable sauce

Shakarap – tomato and onion salad
Oshi toki – stuffed grape leaves
Somsa – meat and onion stuffed pastry
Dimlama – meat and vegetable stew
Kebabs – grilled ground meat
Katyk - liquid yogurt
Suzma – similar to cottage cheese
Non – flat, round bread, which is always torn by hand, never served upside down, and never thrown out
Naryn – dough cut into strips and then boiled, topped with meat (usually horse)

Holidays and Special Occasions

Oshi Nahor or morning palov, is served in the early morning (between 6 and 9 am) to guests as part of a wedding celebration.
Parties and other special occasions end the meal with palov. Vodka, cognac, wine, and beer will be served with elaborate toasts.
Navruz – soup made with milk and seven grains is served.
During Ramadan Muslims observe the fast from sunrise to sunset.
Non (flatbread) is placed beneath the head of newborn baby to insure longer life. It is also placed between the legs of a small child to ensure a good journey through life. At the time of an engagement non is colored in pink or yellow, always served as a pair for good luck. At a wedding two loaves of plain non are served to the bride and groom. They each take a bite, and those loaves are served to them the next day as husband and wife. Two loaves are also held over the bride at the time of the wedding.
Patyr bread is used for festive occasions. It has layers of dough with mutton fat, onion, and herbs.

Beverages

Green tea is the national hot beverage drunk throughout the day. Both black and green teas are served without milk or sugar. Tea is drunk with meals. But is also served to guests as a sign of hospitality. The choyhona (teahouse) is where the local men gather. Ayran is a popular chilled summer drink.

Uzbekistan has fourteen wineries. Khovrenko in Samarkand, is the oldest, and was established in 1927. Vodka and beer are also produced.

Did You Know?

Non (bread) was mentioned in the Epic of Gilgamesh (Sumerian kingdom of Uruk) dating back to 2700 BC. If a crumb or piece of non drops to the ground, it will be put on top of a wall or on a branch for the birds.

Vanuatu

Vanuatu is a volcanic archipelago located in the South Pacific Ocean east of northern Australia, northeast of New Caledonia, east of New Guinea, southeast of the Solomon Islands, and west of Fiji. Vanuatu was first inhabited by people speaking Austronesian languages about 3300 years ago. Pottery fragments dating to 1300-1100 BC have been found. The first Europeans to visit the islands were Spaniards in 1606, and named it *La Austrialia del Espíritu Santo "The Southern Land of the Holy Spirit* and In 1774 Captain Cook named the islands the New Hebrides. During the 19th c cotton was grown, followed by coffee, cocoa, bananas, and coconuts. In the 1880s, France and the United Kingdom claimed parts of the archipelago. The Republic of Vanuatu was founded in 1980. The capital, Port Vila, is located on its third largest island. Bislama, pidgin English is the spoken language, along with English, French and 105 languages. Vanua means "land"

Dining Etiquette

When invited for a meal arrive promptly or a few minutes late. Please shake hands greeting departing. Please bring a gift from your own country. The host will show you your seat. Eat continental style with the fork in the left hand and knife in the right. Some people may eat with their hands. Eat all is served you as the host wants to express his hospitality. Leave your knife and fork together when finished. Elders are respected, especially men. Status is achieved by the exchange of circle-husked pigs and the killing of them. Men and women farm and fish; but men clear areas for gardens and deep-sea fish. When a woman has her menstrual period, women and men sleep separately, and women do not cook during this.

Cuisine

When people first arrived here there were few edible plants and animals. They brought with them dogs, rats, and pigs, along with vegetables such as taro, taro, rice, yams, breadfruit, bananas, lemons, and sugarcane. Later the Europeans brought cattle, chickens, wheat, potatoes, and pineapples. Being volcanic the soil is quite fertile, and many plants now grow on the islands. Swidden "slash and burn" is common for clearing forests. Unfortunately cyclone Pam hit Vanuatu in 2015, and many of the crops were destroyed and water in short supply. Coconut is a staple used for its flesh and milk. Tropical fruit – bananas, pineapples, mango, pawpaw, ulu "breadfruit", and grapefruit, nakatambol, naus, and rose apples whose flowers are used to flavor food; and vegetables such as squash, cacao, coffee, manioc, yams, beans, corn, peppers, taro root, cucumbers, pumpkin, tomatoes, and carrots; and tropical nuts –narli nuts or island chestnuts and nangae are also grown. As an island nation lobster, crab, fish – flying fish; prawns, turtles, and water fowl are consumed. Bread is baked in metal wood-fired ovens or over an open fire. Rice is wrapped in banana leaves, as are many of the cooked dishes, especially with fish. Laplap (banana leaves) is the national dish made with grated manioc, taro roots, or yams and formed into a paste which is wrapped in taro or spinach leaves and coconut cream and baked in a *uma* hot stone oven. Fish, prawns, beef, pork, or poultry may be added. There is little refrigeration. Most families produce what they eat. Tinned fish and meat may be used.

Lap Lap (banana leaves, vegetables, coconut milk and fish or chicken)

Serves 4

At least 2-4 large banana leaves	1 large onion, chopped
2 bananas, peeled and sliced	2 cloves garlic, minced
2 manioc roots, peeled and grated	2 cups coconut milk
2 sweet potatoes, peeled and sliced	2 lbs. filleted fish or 2 lbs. chicken
½ lb. spinach	Salt and pepper

Preheat oven to 350º
Line a baking with the banana leaves draping them over the side. Make a layer of the remaining ingredients. Fold the leaves over the ingredients. Bake for at least one hour.

Holidays and Special Occasions

A feast is prepared for a man making a *nimangki* grade. Pigs are lined up and he kills certain ones and touching others to be killed later. Woven mats are presented, and taro and yams for the feast. At the time of a boy's circumcision the father gives a feast. Villagers dress in native costumes and headdresses and paint their faces and bodies. Dancing may last all night, and many gifts are given to the family.
Feasts are also given for Sunday dinners, births, anniversaries, death, and new houses. Laplap and nalot are served along with pig, fish, or a cow, if available. Food is consumed sitting on the ground and eaten with the fingers. The food is cooked in earthen ovens. Kava is drunk on these occasions. Most people are Christians, but will combine local beliefs, especially ancestral spirits into their practice. There are important places related to this – mountain tops, reef or rock formations. Easter and Bonane – Christmas and New Year's are celebrated.
The first fruit, usually yams call for a celebration.
The *Toka* (or *Nakwiari*) is an exchange of pigs and kava celebrated with two days of dancing.
Other holidays celebrated are Custom Chiefs Day (March 5), Independence Day (July 30), Constitution Day (October 5), Unity Day (November 29), and Family Day (December 26).

Beverages

Most beverages need to be imported. The local beer is known as Tusker. Kava is a native plant whose roots are ground to produce a liquid to which water is added. It is served in a shell which you should drink in one gulp. Kava is drunk at the time of birth, marriage, and death, to welcome visitors, begin conferences among chiefs and to seal alliances. There is a ritual to drinking among men only. First the chief drinks, then honored guests, and other men. As mentioned it is drunk in one gulp, all in silence. Sometimes women are allowed to participate!

Venezuela

Venezuela is the northernmost country of South America bounded to the north by the Caribbean Sea, Guyana to the east, Brazil south, and Colombia to the west. The earliest known inhabitants were Indian tribes, among them the Cumangatos, many of whom were to later settle on the Caribbean islands. Christopher Columbus discovered the country on his third voyage in 1498. Americo Vespucci, an Italian, named the country Venezuela "Little Venice" as the houses on stilts around Lake Maracaibo reminded him of that city. The country declared its independence from Spain in 1810, and then was part of Gran Colombia 1820-30 with Ecuador and Panama. Caracas, the capital was founded in 1567 by Diego Losada and named San Diego de Leon de Caracas. Spanish is the official language.

Dining Etiquette

When invited for a meal please be punctual. Dinner is usually late, often not until 10 PM. Please send wrapped flowers (orchids are the national flower). Men greet friends with an abrazo (embrace) and pat each other on the back. Women greet also with abrazo and a kiss. People stand very close and maintain eye contact. Drinks will be served. Guests may also be served un cafecito, a black thick coffee in a small cup. This is a sign of hospitality. When seated at the table the host and hostess are seated at each end. The male guest of honor will be to the right of the hostess. Several courses will be served. Meals are eaten continental style fork in the left hand, knife in the right. Please place them together when you are finished. Toasting is done on formal occasions, and one does not need to rise. The toast is "a la salud" "to your health". Family and business connections are very important.

Cuisine

Venezuelan food is a mix of European and Amerindian dishes using ingredients native to the that part of the country, especially rice, apio (celery root), caraotas negras (black beans), corn, plantains, coconut, fish and various meats. The national dish Pabellon Criollo is made with shredded beef, rice, black beans, fried plantains and arepas (a mix of corn flour, salt and water to form a dough and then fried). The arepa is sometimes filled with butter, meat or cheese. The name comes from Pabellon "flag" as the design is in the shape of a flag. Meals usually consist of casseroles, meat pies, stews, and pasta dishes.

Hallacas (Steamed banana leaves with chicken and meat filling)

Dough

3 cups dried white corn
6 cups cold water
½ cup lard

1 tsp. annatto seeds
1 tsp. salt

Combine the corn and water in a pan and bring to a boil. Reduce heat and stir for 20 minutes. Drain off any excess liquid.
Put through a food mill.
Melt ¼ cup lard in a skillet with the annatto seeds. Strain the lard and discard seeds. Combine the remaining lard with the corn. Add the salt and knead dough for 10 minutes.

Filling

2 lb. chicken cut into pieces
2 cups water
¼ cup olive oil
1 lb. boneless loin of pork, cut into cubes
1 lb. beef, cut into cubes
2 large onions, finely chopped
2 large tomatoes, coarsely chopped
2 large carrots, sliced
1 large bell pepper, chopped
3 cloves garlic, finely chopped
¼ cup sugar
1 cup raisins
1 bottle small olives, drained
½ cup capers

10 eggs, hardboiled and sliced
1 tsp. cumin seed
Salt and pepper
½ cup fresh parsley, chopped
1 tsp. thyme
1 tsp. sage
Banana leaves, washed and cut into 6-10" squares
White parchment paper, cut just slightly larger than banana leaves
Cilantro leaves
Sour cream

In a pan bring the chicken and water to a boil and cook for 30 minutes. Transfer chicken to plate and reserve stock. Remove skin and bones from the chicken. Cut meat into strips.
In a skillet heat the olive oil and add the pork and beef. Brown on all sides. Transfer to a plate.
Using the same skillet add the onions and peppers, cooking about 5 minutes, or until just soft. Add the tomatoes, carrots, garlic, thyme, sage and parsley. Stir until slightly thickened. Return meat to pan. Add the sugar, cumin, capers, and some salt and pepper. Simmer for about 30 minutes.
Spread some of the dough on the banana leaves. Place a tbls. or more of the meat mixture on the dough. Add a couple of rains, an olive, and egg slice. Fold one corner of the leaf over the filling. Then the opposite corner. Lap the other two ends over. Press seams together.
Put the hallaca on one piece of the parchment. Bring 2 sides together. Make a fold and then bring sides together. Tie with kitchen string.
Bring a pot of salted water to a boil. Place a colander in the pot and add the hallacas seam side down. Steam for at least 1 hour or puffy. Add more water if necessary. Remove with tongs. Unwrap. Serve at once, or reheat if kept longer.
Serve with cilantro and sour cream.

Specialties

Tostones – fried plantains
Pasapalos – finger food
Hervide – soup
Bollos pelones – arepas stuffed with meat and served as a soup with a sauce
Empanadas – pastry with meat and egg filling
Ajiaco - chicken stew with herbs, potatoes, cream, corn and capers

Bandeja paisa - meat with avocado, rice, fried plantain and red beans
Mariscos - seafood.
Punta - trasera – steak
Bien me sabe de coco- cake with muscatel and coconut cream
Arepas – fried masa cakes with cheese

Holidays and Special Occasions

Christmas or "Navidad" starts on December 7th by celebrating the day of "La Virgen de la Inmaculada Concepción" or The Virgin of the Immaculate Conception, also known as "El Día de las Velitas" or the day of the candles. On Christmas Eve the main dish is usually be pork, ham, roasted pig, or grilled meats. Desserts might include Natilla, a custard made with panela (similar to molasses, and made from sugarcane) and served with round deep-fried cheese fritters called buñuelos; hojuelas (a fried dough pastry with sugar and jam); arroz con coco (coconut rice pudding), and postre de natas (a dish with milk and condensed milk cooked with sugar, cinnamon and raisins). Hallacas are served on Christmas Eve or Christmas Day

Beverages

Venezuela makes several rums and beers (Aquila), first brewed in Colonia Tovar. Cahire is a fermented yam drink. Do try ponche crème, a rum punch or batidos, a fruit shake. Miche is a tequila that means "skunk juice". Aguardiente is a hot aniseed-flavored spirit and Canelazo, a rum cocktail. Angostura bitters were named after the city of Angostura, now known as Ciudad Bolivar.

Vietnam

Vietnam, located on the Indochina Peninsula in Southeast Asia, is bordered by the People's Republic of China (PRC) to the north, Laos to the northwest, Cambodia to the southwest, and the South China Sea to the east. The region has been inhabited since Paleolithic times. The Phung Nguyen culture was centered in Vĩnh Phúc Province from about 2000 to 1400 BCE. By about 1200 BCE, people developed wet-rice cultivation and bronze casting in the Ma River and Red River plains. There was also evidence of the customs of betel-nut-chewing and teeth-blackening. The Hong Bang Dynasty in Van Lang lasted until 257 BCE when Thuc Phan merged the Lac Viet and Au Viet tribes. In 111 BCE the Han Dynasty of China ruled Vietnam until 938 CE. From 1859 until 1885 the country was part of French Indochina. The country was then partitioned into North and South Vietnam. In 1976 the north and south were merged to form the Socialist Republic of Vietnam. In 1010 Lý Thái Tổ, the first ruler of the Lý Dynasty, founded Thang Long (now Hanoi) as his capital, but it was moved to other cities over a period of time. When North and South Vietnam were reunited in 1976, it once again became the capital. Vietnamese is the official language.

Dining Etiquette

The family is very important, and still hierarchical. Please be punctual when invited for a meal. Bring a gift of fruit, sweets, flowers no chrysanthemums or yellow flowers), or incense that are wrapped in bright paper. Men shake hands greeting and departing. Please wait for a lady to extend her hand before shaking. Some people may use a two-handed shake by placing the left hand on the right wrist. Please wait to be shown where to sit, with the eldest seated first. Meals are served family style, with dishes passed with both hands. Soup bowls are provided. Utensils are chopsticks and spoons. Spoons are held in the left hand. When finished, rest your chopsticks on top of the rice bowl. Some foods are prepared in banana or coconut leaves. If you are offered a toothpick at the end of the meal, cover your mouth with your hand while using it.

Cuisine

The cuisine has been influenced by the Chinese and French. The cuisines of the different regions of the country vary. Northern Vietnam, closer to China, uses stir-frying, deep frying, chopsticks, and more traditional dishes such as *phở* and *bánh cuốn*. Gingerroot, soy sauce, and noodles are among the common ingredients. In the south the cuisine is a mix of Chinese and French, and has sweeter flavors, is spicier, and uses more herbs. Curries, fish sauce, asparagus, and potatoes are used in the cooking. Central Vietnam serves many side dishes and is spicier. Among the common ingredients are fresh chilies, chili paste, tomato sauce and shrimp sauce. Like the Chinese, yin and yang are applied to selecting the ingredients for the dishes. The dishes also are influenced by the five elements – five spices; spicy; sour; bitter; salty; and sweet; and the five colors – white, green, yellow, red, and black. Rice is the staple food and is served with most meals.

Many dishes use lemon grass, kaffir, peanuts, soy sauce, fish sauce, mint, coriander, basil, and lime. Meat such beef and pork, chicken, seafood, prawns, and duck are commonly used. Food is prepared by being steamed, stir- fried, grilled, stewed, or boiled. From the Mekong Delta come pineapples, mangoes, water spinach, jackfruit, longans, asparagus, papaya, and water apples. Some unusual items found in the cuisine are fertilized duck eggs, dog, snake, paddy mouse, turtle, fetus quail, snail, silk worms, banana flowers, dove, fermented fish and shrimp, and ragworm. Curries are popular in the south made with coconut milk. Raw vegetables are eaten as condiments for their dishes. Desserts are made with sweet beans, tropical fruit and glutinous rice. Fish sauce is an important ingredient in cooking. The highest quality is nuoc mam nhi, and comes from Phu Quoc, a small island off the southwest coast of Vietnam. This is made from ca com "rice fish" or long-jawed anchovies caught off the coast of the island and then placed in vats made of the wood boi loi. Pho is a steaming soup with beef or chicken, rice noodles, fish sauce, cilantro and herbs, spices, onion, ginger, eaten especially at breakfast with bean sprouts and basil served on the side. The spices often used in pho are star anise, cinnamon sticks, cardamom and peppercorns. Bánh mì is a baguette (French bread) with pate, cold meats, pickled daikon, carrot and cucumber, often with cilantro or herbs

Ca kho to (Fish in clay pot)

For 2 to 4 people

Traditionally catfish is used in Vietnam. That is what our family uses. But may be substituted with cod or halibut.

4 or 5 green scallions cut into 1½ " lengths
1 small ginger root (julienned)
Few cloves of garlic (crushed)
¼ cup fish sauce
¼ cup sugar

2 tsp of chili sauce (Vietnamese style/ bottle can be found in any Asian grocery store)
A pinch of pepper
1 tbls. store bought or homemade caramel sauce
1 tbls. oil

Cut fish fillet with skin into serving size. I occasionally find precut catfish in some grocery stores.
Heat I tbls. oil in a pan and fry garlic and ginger. Add green scallions.
Add cut fish pieces and brown all sides.
Add fish sauce, sugar, chili sauce and pepper (taste)
Transfer the mixture to a clay pot, add caramel sauce and let it simmer in very low fire under cover for 15 to 20 minutes.
Delicious served with steamed jasmine rice and steamed spinach or bok choy.
Recipe courtesy of Phi Fostvedt, Washington, DC

Spring Rolls (Not the deep fried kind!)

4 people

4 oz. pork loin	1 cup bean sprouts
8 medium shrimp	Fresh mint leaves
Rice vermicelli (a fistful)	Asian chives
4 lettuce leaves	Bean and peanut dipping sauce

Cook pork in boiling water until done. Drain and slice thinly. (As a short cut, this could be substituted with thin slices of store bought turkey or ham, or thinly sliced pork sausage from Vietnamese grocery stores);
Soak rice vermicelli in water until soft for 15 minutes and drain;
Dip rice paper in lukewarm water, one sheet at a time; lay on a flat surface;
Slice shrimp lengthwise; place sliced shrimp, then pork; then 1 leaf of lettuce and a pinch of mint leaves, and finally the chives;
Fold two ends of the rice paper, then roll tightly the mixture.
Serve with hoisin and peanut dipping sauce.

Dipping Sauce:

½ cup hoisin sauce	1½ cups water
½ cup sugar	2 tbls. peanut butter
1 cup chopped onion and garlic	

Combine all ingredients except peanut butter in a small saucepan. Cook over medium heat until onion and garlic become soft. Stir in peanut butter. Serve cool.
Recipe courtesy of Phi Fostvedt, Washington, DC

Vietnamese Specialties

Mien ga – chicken noodle soup
Mang tay nau cua – crab asparagus soup
Ca ran chuan got – sweet and sour fish
Canh – clear broth with vegetables, seafood or meat
Gỏi - salad
Nuoc cham - fish sauce
Cha ca – fish seasoned with garlic, shallots, and turmeric, and garnished with rice stick noodles, scallions, dill coriander, and basil
Cha cua – deep fried crab rolls
Ngũ vị - five spices
Banh bao – steamed dumpling with onion, mushrooms, or other vegetables

Bánh bột lọc –rice dumplings stuffed with shrimp and gr and wrapped in a banana leaf
Bò 7 món - 7 courses of beef
A less popular version is the Cá 7 Món, seven courses o
Bánh xèo – rice crepe with turmeric, shrimp, pork, o mushrooms, and fried
Thit heo quay – roast pork
Canh chua – sour soup with fish
Bò kho – meat and vegetable soup
Bun bo Hue – beef noodle soup
Banh chung – sticky rice wrapped in banana leaves, stuffed with mung bean paste, pork, black pepper
Dua – to pickle vegetables

Bun mang vit – bamboo shoot and duck noodle soup
Bun rieu – vermicelli soup
Bánh tráng cuốn - rice paper used in making spring roll (aka chả giò), and summer rolls (aka gỏi cuốn)

Bánh tráng nướng (in the South), or bánh đa (in the North) - flat rice crackers often added to vermicelli noodle dishes
Xôi – sticky rice with coconut milk
Chè – bean and sticky rice pudding
Bánh rau câu – gelatin cake with agar, coconut milk, and pandan
Chuoi chien – fried banana with ice cream

Holidays and Special Occasions

Tet - Lunar New Year – Bánh chưng (sticky rice wrapped in banana leaves with mung bean paste, lean pork, and black pepper eaten in north of Vietnam); and Bánh tét (sticky rice wrapped in banana leaves with mung bean and fatty pork eaten in south of Vietnam). Dishes often use all parts of an animal including head, tongue, feet, necks, blood, and tails.
Weddings - Bánh phu thê is served to remind new couples of perfection and harmony
Homes have ancestral altars where food is placed.

Sweet Banana Soup

Serves 4

8 ripe dwarf bananas
10 oz. cassava
1 cup coconut milk
2 oz. roasted peanuts, crushed

10 oz. sugar
2 tsp. salt
¼ cup pearl tapioca

Peel and soak cassava in salt water overnight. Drain well. Cut cassava into large piece. Steam in a steamer for about 20 minutes.
Peel bananas and remove string. Soak in salt water for about 5 minutes. Drain
Soak pearl tapioca in water for about 20 minutes to expand it. Drain
Boil a liter of water. Add bananas and ½ cup coconut milk. Bring to a boil for about 10 minutes. Add sugar and a little salt. Then add cassava and cook for another 10 minutes. Add pearl tapioca and continue cooking for about 5 minutes until the pearl tapioca is clear. Add ½ cup coconut milk. Bring to a boil and remove from heat immediately. Ladle soup out into a boil and sprinkle with peanuts. Sweet potatoes can be used instead of cassava.
Recipe courtesy of Nguyen Thu Huong, Delicious Dishes from Vietnam

Beverages

Sinh tố is a fruit smoothie made with condensed milk, crushed ice, and fruit. Chè, besides being a dessert can be a dessert drink. Dâu Ua is a tart condensed milk drink. Strong coffee is enjoyed with condensed milk. Drinks can be made from local fruit, sugar cane, and even soybeans. Beer is brewed in the country, including Bia hoi, a specialty draft beer.

Wales

Wales, part of the United Kingdom, occupies the western coast of Britain sharing the island with England and Scotland. Known as the "Land of Castles and Song" the country has been inhabited for almost 20,000 years. In about 3000 BC agricultural migrations descended from Europe and c 1800 BC the Beaker people built long cairns, menhirs "long or standing stones", and stone circles. C 400 BC Celts spoke the forerunner of the Welsh language and in 61 AD the Romans invaded. Later invasions included the Norse and English in 1272. Cardiff, the capital, was settled by the Romans c 60-90 AD. Wales (Cymru) means "place of the others" or 'place of the Romanized foreigners".

Dining Etiquette

Please arrive punctually when invited for a meal. Please bring chocolates, wine, or flowers, not white lilies which are for funerals. Shake hands greeting and departing. Drinks will be served before dinner. The guest of honor will be seated at the head of the table, or to the right of the hostess, if a male. Dining is continental style, fork in the left hand, knife in right. Salad is served with the meal. Hands, not elbows, should remain on the table. Courses will be served starting with an appetizer or soup, main course, dessert or fruit, and coffee and tea. A toast is proposed by the host and is "Cheers".

Glamorgan Sausage (Welsh Cheese Croquettes)

Makes 10-12 croquettes

2 tbls. butter	½ tsp. sea salt
1 large leek, finely sliced	Fresh ground pepper
2 cups fresh white bread crumbs	2 eggs, separated
2 tbls. finely chopped parsley	2 tbls. water
1 cup freshly grated Welsh cheddar cheese	¼ cup vegetable oil
1 tsp. English mustard	

Melt the butter in a skillet and gently saute the leeks for about 5 minutes.
In a bowl combine the cheese, 1 cup of the bread crumbs, leeks, parsley, mustard, salt and pepper.
Add the egg yolks and water. Divide the mixture into 10-12 portions. Roll each into a cylinder.
Beat the egg whites. Dip the cylinders into the egg white.
Heat the oil in the skillet. Add the rolls and brown. Be careful not to burn.
Serve hot.

Cuisine

The Welsh cuisine is a blend of local products, but also influenced by immigrants from Italy and the Middle East who came from the mid 18th-19th c. Welsh food makes use of fish – trout, salmon, cockles, lobster, crab, mussels, bass, mullet, ray, turbot, Dover sole, brill and whiting ; cheese – Caerphilly (a white, salty, moist cheese made since the 13th c), Pencarreg (a soft cheese), Panytyllin (a semi-hard cheese); perl wen and perl las, soft brie-like cheeses; Welsh lamb; cream teas; leeks – the national emblem; steak pies; cockle pies; scones; puddings; cider and apple juices; and Glamorgan sausages. Recently the Rudolph potato has been developed on the west coast of Wales which needs no butter or fat added after cooking, and has been nicknamed the "butterless baker".

Breakfast consists of porridge, eggs, bacon, or lighter fare. Lunch is the main meal of the day – meat or fish with vegetables, tea and beer, a snack in the afternoon, followed by a light dinner or "tea".

Welsh Specialties

Cawl – meat and vegetable soup
Faggots – boiled liver and breadcrumb balls
Bara brith – speckled bread – raisin and currant bread

Laverbread
Teisen lap – fruitcake
Welsh rabbit – melted cheese and toast

Holidays

Shrove Tuesday – pancakes
Easter – dyed eggs
Christmas Eve – taffy making; Wassail bowl- fruit, sugar, spices, beer; mulled wine
Christmas – turkey or goose, mincemeat pie or plum pudding

Beverages

Wales produces several types of beer, mainly ales. The Wye Valley produces wines. Can-y-delyn is a whisky and honey liqueur.

Did You Know?

The Welsh are very proud of their heritage and an effort has been made to preserve many traditions, including the men's choirs, regiments, and guards. The heir to the British throne is the Prince of Wales.
Trwyn Du once had a large puffin population which was considered a delicacy.
The oldest inn in Wales and possibly Britain is The Skirrid at Llanvihangel, founded in the 11th c.
The Conwy Estuary has been famous for mussels since Tacitus.
Salami and Chorizo are now produced in Boncath, thanks to pigs being fed with leftover cheese from Caws Cenarth.
During rugby matches "Feed Me Till I want No More" is often sung.

Yemen

Yemen is a country located on the Arabian Peninsula bordered by Saudi Arabia to the north, the Red Sea to the west, the Arabian Sea and Gulf of Aden to the south, and Oman to the east. Ancient civilizations date here from the 12th c BC to the 6th c when the region was part of the Minaean, Sabaean, Hazramavt, Qataban, Ausan and Himyarite kingdoms which controlled the spice trade, and later Ethiopia and Persia. In the 7th c BC the Himyarite king converted to Judaism. By the 7th c AD Islam was brought to the country. During the 11 c Egyptian caliphs ruled, and by the 16th c and in the 19th c Yemen was part of the Ottoman Empire. Yemen gained independence in 1918, and North Yemen became a republic in 1962. North and South Yemen became the Republic of Yemen in 1990. The capital, Sana'a, dates back to the 6th c BC as part of Sabaean. The official language is Arabic.

Dining Etiquette

It is an honor to be invited to a Yemeni home. Please arrive promptly when invited for a meal. Remove your shoes before entering the home. A small gift for the home can be brought, but it is really only after you have made a person's acquaintance a gift is appropriate. Men shake hands lightly greeting and departing. Women will greet other women with a handshake, hug, or kiss on alternate cheeks. Men and women do not touch each other or make eye contact. Elders are always greeted first. Food is served to guests seated on carpets with cushions, or on furniture. Eat with your right hand only. Utensils may or not be used. More food will be offered. Three cups of tea will be served. Men usually eat first and the women and children later. There is little conversation during the meal. When finished, hands are again washed. Coffee is served afterwards to the men in a sitting room. Gat may be chewed and a water pipe shared. Yemeni families are hierarchical with the oldest male the patriarch. Men are expected to take care of business and women the home. Extended families live together. Ancestors are much respected.

Cuisine

The cuisine has been influenced by the Ottomans. Because of the spices brought into the country since early times, food can be hot and spicy. Spices include cumin, saffron, coriander, turmeric, cardamom and fenugreek. Hot chilies, garlic, mint and coriander leaves add flavor to the cooking. Lamb, goat, chicken and fish are broiled or grilled, with stock made from the bones. Fish is prevalent along the coast. Dairy products such as cheese and butter are not common, though buttermilk may be served in the villages, and yogurt in the cities. Vegetable oil and is used in cooking and semn (clarified butter) in pastries. Rice, lentils, beans, fresh fruits – grapes, mangoes, and bananas; rice, wheat, yogurt, garlic, tomatoes, fenugreek seeds, dates, green and red chilies, mint salads, okra, hummus - ground chickpea paste, burghul, lentils, aubergine - eggplant, and sorghum. Along the coast fish with lemon is popular. Eating meat or chicken, dip bread in sauces.

Salta (lamb, fenugreek, and spice dish)

Serves 4

2 tbls. fenugreek (hulba)
1 lb. lamb, cut into small cubes
3 tbls. olive oil
1 large onion, chopped
1 jalapeno, seeded and chopped
2 cloves garlic, minced
1 large potato, peeled and diced

2 tomatoes, chopped finely
Salt and pepper to taste
½ tsp. cumin
½ tsp. cardamom
3 cups beef broth
2 eggs, beaten
¼ cup cilantro, chopped

In a bowl combine about a cup of water and the fenugreek. Set aside for about an hour. Pour out any remaining water from fenugreek.
In a skillet add a small amount of olive oil and brown the lamb. Place the lamb in a baking dish.
Add a little more oil to the skillet and sauté the onion. Add the jalapeno and garlic. Add to lamb.
In a pan stir together the beef broth, potatoes, tomatoes, and salt and pepper. Bring to a boil. Simmer for 20 minutes or until potatoes are tender. Stir in eggs and cilantro. Stir in the cumin, cardamom, and fenugreek.
Serve very hot with bread.
Okra, peppers, or other vegetables can be added. Beef or chicken can be substituted for the lamb.

Yemeni Specialties

Salta – meat or chicken broth with vegetables and fenugreek served in a harthi (heated stone bowl) with flat bread
Fuul - beans, tomato, onion, and chili stew usually served at breakfast
Fried eggplant
Haradha - mincemeat and pepper dish
Hor'i – beef shank
Fatah - beef
Marag lahm - meat soup
Hanid - lamb meat with spices
Kabsa - rice with lamb
Sahawiq (breaking down) – seasoning made with mint, fenugreek, or parsley; also called

Zhug – chilies, pepper, cardamom, caraway, fresh coriander and garlic sauce, used for dipping in bread, on meat, vegetables
Hawayii – spice mix
Malvi - barley bread
Bint al sahn – bread eaten with honey, made of eggs, flour and ghee
Shafout – bread with yogurt mixed with coriander
Fatta – bread with milk, honey and broth
Kedma – traditional bread
Break – bread stuffed with egg and meat
Nashoof – bread with bulghur wheat, milk, yogurt

Holidays and Special Occasions

Mouloud – birth of the Prophet
Eid al-Fitr – peanuts, raisins, pistachios, almonds; women prepare homes, cakes; bint al-sahan (or al-sabaya), which consists of sheets of pastry stuck together and mixed with eggs, butter and natural honey.
Eid al-Adha – Feast of the Sacrifice
Lahuh, round flat bread made from sorghum, is eaten on special occasions
When a groom to be and his father visit the bride's home for the first time, they will be served tea. The betrothal is held on a Thursday or Friday when the groom and friends bring raisins, gat and gifts for the bride's father. The wedding lasts for three days. Raisins are thrown at the wedding and picked up to celebrate the happy future of the couple. After the wedding celebration a huge feast is prepared, usually by many women.

Beverages

Even though coffee beans were known to have come from Ethiopia the first coffee to be recorded as a drink was in Yemen where it was used to keep the devout awake during evening prayers. Red tea, bun (coffee from coffee beans) and qishr or gahwa (drink made from coffee bean shells, cinnamon and ground ginger) are drunk in Yemen. Red tea is served in small glasses. Tea can be served with or without milk. Black tea is made with cloves, cardamom or mint. Other drinks are karkadin, made from dried karkadin flowers, naqe'e al zabib, cold raisin drink, and diba'a, a squash drink.

Alcoholic drinks are forbidden in the country. Seera Beer had been produced by the National Brewing Company in Aden.

Did You Know?

During the 19th c the port of Al Mokha exported over 20 million pounds of coffee a year.
Gat, a leaf that is chewed is an intoxicant.

Zambia

The Republic of Zambia is a landlocked country located in Southern Africa bounded by the Democratic Republic of the Congo to the north, Tanzania to the north-east, Malawi to the east, Mozambique, Zimbabwe, Botswana, Namibia to the south, and Angola to the west. The country was inhabited for thousands of years by Khoisan hunter-gatherers. In the 12th c the Bantu invaded. They included the Tonga (Batonga), the Nkoya from Luba-Lunda (now the Democratic Republic of the Congo and northern Angola). The Nsokolo settled in the Mbala district in the 18th c; and the Ngoni and Sotho in the 19th c. In the 19th c Zambia was occupied by the British as a protectorate of Northern Rhodesia, receiving its independence in 1964. The capital is Lusaka. It has 72 ethnic groups and 18 major indigenous Bantu languages including ChiTonga, SiLozi, ChiNyanja, and ChiBemba. English is the official language.

Dining Etiquette

The Zambians love hospitality and it is an honor to have someone in a home. Even if you are an unannounced visitor you will be invited to partake in a meal. Please bring a gift when you visit if you would like although it is not required or expected. When presenting or receiving a gift extend both hands capped together. The traditional custom of women kneeling when presenting a gift is also practiced and is considered very respectful and courteous. Men shake hands when greeting and may even continue holding hands a moment longer as sign of friendship and warmth. In the Eastern region people will shake hands and place their left hand on the right elbow to show respect. Women have choices of wearing skirts, dresses, trousers in the city or traditional chitenje cloths over their lower waists. Men wear trousers, shirts, or shorts. Men and women do not usually shake hands if they are daughter and father-in-law or have such related customary kinship relationships. Please address people using Mr., Mrs. or Miss. Young people kneeling before elders is also respectful. It is disrespectful for a younger person to look an elder in the eye. Opposite sexes should not stare or look each other in the eye also. It is considered most respectful to glance at and then gaze away when addressing elders.

Tea, soft drinks or beer may be offered. Please wash your hands before eating. The youngest child or host will use a pitcher of clean water to help guests, older adults, father, then mother and children to wash their hands before the meal. After the meal one washes again in the same order. In rural areas men usually eat with sons and male relatives; mothers with daughters and female relatives. When dining you may be seated at a table, but more likely on the floor in a circle around the nshima. Meals are generally partaken with communal dishes. All Zambians use bare hands to eat their nshima staple meals. Utensils are used among non-Zambians, and among patrons in Western hotels and restaurants. The right hand only is used to eat nshima. Nshima and ndiwo are served for lunch and dinner. Nsima is eaten slowly, conversing while doing do. The oldest person is the first to stop eating and will leave some nshima for younger persons or children. Children are expected to listen and learn from their elders while dining.

Nshima (cornmeal dish used for eating)

Serves 4

4 cups water   2 cups cornmeal

Slightly heat the water in a pot. Slowly stir in ¾ cup cornmeal until thickened. Then cover the pot and let simmer for 3-5 minutes. Then stir in the rest of the cornmeal.
Recipe and information courtesy of Dr.Mwizenge Tembo, Bridgewater College, Virginia and the Embassy of the Republic of Zambia, Washington, DC

Cuisine

Nshima, the national dish is made from maize (corn meal or mealie-mealie), and is served at lunch and dinner. It is served hot and should be made from very white meal. A person rolls the nshima into a ball using the palm and fingers. Nshima is served with a vegetable, bean, meat or fish dish, or ndiwo or dende. Meats used are beef, goat, mutton, or wild animals such as mice, hare, antelope, turtle, alligator, or whatever is available. Vegetables include rape, cabbage, pumpkin, or various leaves such as bean or squash leaves, and other green vegetables native to Zambia. Ndiwo or dende may also include peanuts, fish, peanut butter, wild mushrooms, beans and peas. Nshima varies in the different regions of Zambia depending on the type of meal used. In some places it could be sorghum, cassava, or millet. Nshima should always be eaten hot and served fresh only for that meal.

Sorghum, millet, wheat, cassava, sweet potatoes, groundnuts (peanuts), onions, tomatoes; leaves of beans, okra, cow peas, pumpkins and cassava for greens, nshima - corn (maize), bananas, mangoes are grown in Zambia. Traditionally in the villages, the corn for nshima is removed from the husk, women pound it using a pestle and mortar, and then soaked for three days in water, allowing fermentation. The liquid is used to cook a porridge with peanut powder and served at breakfast. The soaked corn is then washed, spread on mats to dry, and then ground into meal. It is then dried again, and stored.

Ndiwo made from meat or fish is boiled in water until soft and then salted. Onions and tomatoes may be added if available. Ndiwos made from mice, caterpillars, or baby doves are roasted and fire dried. In eastern Zambia the chidulo method of burning leaves such as dry banana leaves until ashes are collected and put into a vessel with holes, and cold water poured over them. The liquid is collected underneath. The vegetables will be cooked in the liquid. If peanut powder is added to the vegetables this is known as kutendela. Food is usually cooked over an open fire.

Zambian Specialties

Nshima na nkuku – chicken dish
Kapenta – small fish from rivers and lakes.
Can be dried, fried, or as a relish.
Ndombi –catfish
Mpasa – lake salmon

Ndiyo zotendela or kusashila – raw ground peanut powder and cooked with pumpkin leaves
Nyemba - red bean stew
Nyama ya mbuzi – goat
Nkhuku- chicken
Nsomba – fish

Ndiwo (collard greens and peanut powder)

Serves 4

1 lb. chopped collard greens
1 large tomato, chopped
1 ½ cups raw peanut powder
¼ tsp. salt

2 cups water
½ tsp. baking soda or 2 cups chidulo

Pour 1 cup water into a medium size pot. Add baking soda until thoroughly dissolved.
Add collard greens and tomato, and cook over medium heat for 5-8 minutes.
Add the peanut powder, salt and 1 cup water. Stir and simmer for 15-20 minutes, stirring to keep from burning.
Recipe courtesy of Dr. Tembo, Bridgewater College, Virginia

Holidays and Special Occasions

Among the holidays observed in Zambia are New Year's Day, Easter, Labor Day (May 1), Independence Day (October 24th) and Christmas.
At Christmas or for special holidays a chicken or rooster will be killed and served.

Beverages

Beer is brewed in most villages and includes Mosi Lager, Rhino Lager, Chibuku (Shake-Shake) beer. Umunkoyo is a non-alcoholic drink made from maize, amale, water, sugar, and other ingredients. Kachasu is a very strong spirit and also brewed with maize. Tea, coffee and boiled, filtered water are also available.

Zimbabwe

The Republic of Zimbabwe, formerly known as Southern Rhodesia, the Republic of Rhodesia, and Zimbabwe Rhodesia is a landlocked country in the southern part of Africa. It is bordered by South Africa to the south, Botswana to the southwest, Zambia to the northwest and Mozambique to the east. From the 9th to the 13th c the region was inhabited by people who traded with other south African countries. C 1300 gold was discovered. During the 15th c the Karanga (the forerunners of the Shona) established a trading center at Great Zimbabwe, near present day Masvingo. The Portuguese arrived at the end of the 17th c. In 1830 the Ndebele conquered the Karanga. By the 1890s prospectors from South Africa hoped to find gold in the region. In 1897 Cecil John Rhodes claimed Matabeland (the Ndebele) and Mashonaland (the Shona) as the British crown colony of Rhodesia. Independence was achieved in 1980. The capital, Harare, was founded in 1890 as a fort. The official languages are English, Shona and Ndebele (both Bantu languages). Zimbabwe means "House of Stone", from the ancient stone ruins left by the Shona.

Dining Etiquette

Please arrive promptly when invited for a meal. Bring a small gift for the home. Please shake hands greeting and departing, supporting the right forearm with the left hand. Hands are washed before a meal. You will be seated in a circle on the floor and eat food from a communal bowl. Guests will be served the food. Food is eaten with the right hand. Wooden plates and spoons, or utensils might be provided, but in rural Zimbabwe food is eaten with the right hand. To eat sadza use your right hand to take some from the bowl and roll it into a ball in the palm of your hand. Dip the ball into the relish, eat some, roll into a ball, and continue. If you pass or take something, please do so with the right hand. Please leave a small amount of food on your plate when finished, so that your host will know that you have been provided enough. When someone is handing you something or you want to say "Thank you", please clap twice. Try to avoid direct eye contact with a person. Extended families are still found in rural areas, often living together in one place. Family ties are very important, as is respect for elders.

Beef, goat, chicken, kudo, springbok, ostrich, crocodile tail, warthog, impala, mopane worms, and flying ants are among the animals consumed. Meats are mainly grilled, fried roasted, or used in stews. The Ndebele do not eat corn out of season. Animals that bear a family name are not eaten by that family.

Cuisine

The cuisine of the country varies by the different regions, but has also been influenced by the British who brought sugar, tea, and bread. Archeological digs have found Stone Age tools and implements in Great Zimbabwe, built by cattle herders and a city built with granite walls, once the largest south of the Sahara. The main crops are maize, millet, sorghum, squash, corn, yams, pumpkins, groundnuts (peanuts), papaya, beans, cucumbers, onion, tomato, sunflowers, rice, potatoes, green peppers, and avocados. Bowara (pumpkin leaves) are often used in stews. Since the country has a very dry and then rainy season food and meats are preserved, often by drying.

Sadza (cornmeal porridge)

The national dish!

Serves 6-8

3 cups boiling water	2 ½ cups cornmeal
1 cup cold water	

In a pan add the cold water to the cornmeal to make a paste. Slowly add the hot water, making sure no lumps form. Heat pan and stir until thickened. Be careful it does not burn. Cover and let simmer 15 minutes. Sadza is rolled into balls and dipped in a sauce relish, vegetable stew, gravy, meat, sauces, or soured milk.

Zimbabwe Specialties

Bota – thinner porridge than sadza
Kapenta - dried fish, or small fish cooked in a gravy or a sauce
Mopane worms
Biltong – dried, salted meat
Nyama – beef stew
Muriwo na nyama – greens stew
Nhedzi – mushroom soup

Muboora – pumpkin soup with tomato sauce
Moriwo unedovi – collard greens and peanut sauce
Mapunga unedovi – rice and peanut butter
Roasted groundnuts
Rice with grilled or stewed chicken
Gochi gochi or braaing – grilled beef or pork chops

Holidays and Special Occasions

Christmas – people attend church services, visit with family and friends and feast. Christmas comes at the time of the summer harvest, so fresh vegetables are usually in abundance. Meats such as ox, goat, ostrich, kudu or chicken will be roasted on a spit over an open fire. Rice, muriwo unedovi, bread, jam, tea, sugar, fresh fruit, and desserts are served.
Meat or game are eaten for special occasions.

Beverages

Mazoe is the local orange squash. Rock shandy is a mix of lemonade, soda water, and bitters. Beer is produced in Zimbabwe as lagers or stout beers. Well known beers are Zambezi, Chibuku (milky beer), Lion Lager, Whawha (maize beer), Bohlingers, Scud, and Castle. Makumbi wine is made from the mapfura fruit by the Shona and amaganu by the Ndebele. Many fermented beverages are produced from grains at home and are used for weddings, funerals, and spirit appeasing ceremonies. Maheu is a drink made from maize or sadza.

Conversion Charts

Liquid Ingredients by Volume
(To convert ounces to grams, multiply the number of ounces by 30.)

1/4 tsp	=	1 ml			
1/2 tsp	=	2 ml			
1 tsp	=	5 ml			
3 tsp	=	1 tbl	=	1/2 fl oz	= 15 ml
2 tbls	=	1/8 cup	=	1 fl oz	= 30 ml
4 tbls	=	1/4 cup	=	2 fl oz	= 60 ml
5 1/3 tbls	=	1/3 cup	=	3 fl oz	= 80 ml
8 tbls	=	1/2 cup	=	4 fl oz	= 120 ml
10 2/3	=	2/3 cup	=	5 fl oz	= 160 ml
12 tbls	=	3/4 cup	=	6 fl oz	= 180 ml
16 tbls	=	1 cup	=	8 fl oz	= 240 ml

pt	=	2 cups	=	16 fl oz	=	480 ml	
1 qt	=	4 cups	=	32 fl oz	=	960 ml	
				33 fl oz	=	1000 ml	= 1 1

Cooking/Oven Temperatures

	Fahrenheit	Celsius	Gas Mark
Freeze Water	32° F	0° C	
Room Temp.	68° F	20° C	
Boil Water	212° F	100° C	
Bake	325° F	160° C	3
	350° F	180° C	4
	375° F	190° C	5
	400° F	200° C	6
	425° F	220° C	7
	450° F	230° C	8
Broil			Grill

Index

620

Curried Tuna 579
 Mas Huni (tuna and coconut milk breakfast dish) 344

U
Udang Sambal Serai Bersantan (prawns with coconut milk) 82
Uzbek Palov or Osh (rice with meat, vegetables and herbs) 597

V
Vareniki with Potatoes and Cheese 584
Varenyky Vyshnyamy (Varenyky with Cherries) 584
Vary Amin'ny Voanio (Rice) 336
Veal
 Gjellë me Arra të Ellit (Elli's Veal or Chicken with Walnuts) 6
  Meatballs in a Curry Sauce 150
  Wiener Schnitzel (Breaded Veal) 31
Vegetables
 Cachupa Rica (typical Cape Verdean dish) 90
 Chakakala (Vegetable Stew) 318
 Gado-Gado (Vegetables with Peanut and Coconut Sauce) 253

 Vegetable Samosas 48
Vegetarian Bee Hoon (Vermicelli noodles) 486
Venison Korma (Venison curry) 247
Verwurrelt Gedanken (A Special Pastry served during Carnival) 332
Vindaloo (chicken with spices) 355

W
Walnut Potica (Walnut Roll) 492
Wiener Schnitzel (Breaded Veal) 31
Wonton Soup 109

Y
Yaki Mon Do (cabbage and beef in wonton wrappers) 504
Yam Fufu 212
Yam Puffs 157
Yardlong Beans 529
Yucca
 Carimanola (yucca with meat and/or cheese) 428

Z
Zulu Zesty Ribs 499
Zupa Wisniowa (cherry soup) 444

Order Form for Conduit Press

Please send me_____ copies of The Enchanting World of Food @ $34.95

Please send me _____copies of Chesapeake's Bounty @ $16.95

Please send me _____copies of Chesapeake's Bounty II @ $17.95

Please send me___ copies of God's Bounty @ $18.95

Please send me_____ copies of New England's Bounty @ $17.95

Please send me ___copies of Nantucket's Bounty @ $17.95

Postage is extra. Postage in the United States is $5.00 for first book, $2.00 each additional book. Please make check payable to Conduit Press. Credit cards are accepted.

Please autograph the book to _____
Mail to:

Conduit Press
307 Goldsborough Street
Easton, MD 21601

Ship or deliver the cookbooks to:

Name_____

Address_____

_____

Telephone_____

Phone: 410-820-9915   website: www.conduitpressmd.com

Email: kamoose@goeaston.net